'No one writes the history of the British presence in China like Robert Bickers. In *China Bound* he tells the remarkable story, spread across two tumultuous centuries, of a family-owned company from Liverpool that made itself part of Asia. This is a tale of family, of empire, and of networks.'

John M. Carroll, Professor of History, The University of Hong Kong, and author of Edge of Empires: Chinese Elites and British Colonials in Hong Kong

'This is the story of one of the major British companies in Asia. But it is so much more than that – it is a sweeping tale of how empire was formed, operated at its height, and then had to reinvent itself. Robert Bickers uses a wide range of materials, many of them never before seen by scholars, to tell a story of how Swire created new trade routes and connections in Asia, and how Asia in turn was shaped by the commerce of empire, before having to deal with war and the impact of the Chinese Communist revolution in 1949. Told with the style and verve that would suit the most buccaneering Taipan, this is a powerful and important history that will make its mark at a time when Britain's relationship with Asia is taking new and unpredictable turns.'

Rana Mitter, author of China's War with Japan, 1937–1945: The Struggle for Survival

'How does a Western family business – and a family of businesses – survive and thrive for over two centuries in Asia? How does a pioneering private enterprise navigate the wars, revolutions, and re-openings of modern China? This is the story of John Swire & Sons, narrated so brilliantly by Robert Bickers. This book is many things: It is a magisterial business history that reads like a novel. It is a drama of empires in conflict and competition. It is the story of how commerce created our modern world and its institutions. And it is a captivating history of China and Hong Kong, seen through the lens of business. This is a book for all who study modern China and its foreign relations – and for anyone doing business in China today. This past has many lessons for our present.'

William C. Kirby, T. M. Chang Professor of China Studies, Harvard University

'With unprecedented access to Swire's archives, Robert Bickers has crafted a riveting story of the firm's survival through two tumultuous centuries of modern Chinese history. Nations rise and empires fall, and through the storms sail the ships of John Swire & Sons. This is a brilliant work by the leading historian of Britain and China.'

Stephen R. Platt, Professor of History, University of Massachusetts Amherst, and author of Imperial Twilight

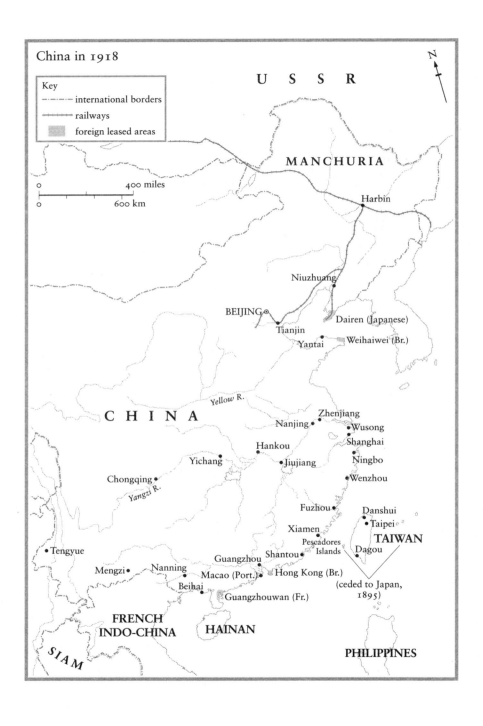

China in 1918

Key
-·-·-·- international borders
┼┼┼┼┼ railways
▨▨▨ foreign leased areas

0 ——————— 400 miles
0 ——————— 600 km

U S S R

MANCHURIA

Harbin

Niuzhuang

BEIJING ◎
Tianjin

Dairen (Japanese)

Yantai   Weihaiwei (Br.)

Yellow R.

C H I N A

Zhenjiang
Nanjing   Wusong
                 Shanghai
Hankou
Yichang   Jiujiang   Ningbo

Chongqing   Wenzhou

Yangzi R.

                 Fuzhou   Danshui
                                   Taipei
              Xiamen   TAIWAN
              Pescadores
Tengyue   Shantou Islands Dagou

Mengzi Nanning Guangzhou
                 Macao (Port.) Hong Kong (Br.)
              Beihai
                 Guangzhouwan (Fr.)   (ceded to Japan,
                                              1895)

FRENCH
INDO-CHINA   HAINAN

SIAM   PHILIPPINES

China Bound

John Swire & Sons and Its World, 1816–1980

Robert Bickers

BLOOMSBURY BUSINESS

LONDON • OXFORD • NEW YORK • NEW DELHI • SYDNEY

For Bob and Joan

BLOOMSBURY
Bloomsbury Publishing Plc
50 Bedford Square, London, WC1B 3DP, UK

BLOOMSBURY, BLOOMSBURY BUSINESS and the Diana logo are trademarks
of Bloomsbury Publishing Plc

First published in Great Britain 2020

A catalogue record for this book is available from the British Library

Library of Congress Cataloguing-in-Publication data has been applied for

ISBN: 978-1-4729-4994-3; eBook: 978-1-4729-4995-0

2 4 6 8 10 9 7 5 3 1

Typeset by Deanta Global Publishing Services, Chennai, India
Printed and bound in Great Britain by CPI Group (UK) Ltd, Croydon CR0 4YY

To find out more about our authors and books visit www.bloomsbury.com
and sign up for our newsletters

Contents

List of Abbreviations

BAL	Bahamas Airways Limited
BAT	British American Tobacco
BOAC	British Overseas Airways Corporation
B&S	Butterfield & Swire
BASIL	Butterfield & Swire Industries Ltd
CAT	Civil Air Transport
CMSNCo	China Merchants Steam Navigation Company
CNCo	China Navigation Company
CIM	Chinese Inland Mission
COSA	China Ocean Shipping Agency
CPA	Cathay Pacific Airways
DOCA	Department of Chinese Affairs
EIC	East India Company
FESA	Far Eastern Shipping Agencies
HSB	Hongkong & Shanghai Bank
HUD	Hongkong United Dockyards

JS&S   John Swire & Sons Ltd

OCL   Overseas Containers Limited

OPCo   Orient Paint & Varnish Company

OSSC   Ocean Steam Ship Company (also known as Blue Funnel)

P&O   Peninsular & Oriental

SMC   Shanghai Municipal Council

SMP   Shanghai Municipal Police

SSNCo   Shanghai Steam Navigation Company

TKDY   Taikoo Dockyard

TSR   Taikoo Sugar Refinery

Pronunciation guide

In general I have used the international recognised pinyin system of transliteration for Chinese words and names, except where there are standard Cantonese transliterations available for those from Hong Kong, and where individuals are much better known by the contemporary names they used in public life (such as Chiang Kai-shek). I have not changed usage in direct quotations or references, and in some instances it has not yet proved possible to excavate original names from beneath nineteenth-century transliteration. I have provided the contemporary usage on the first occasion a place or name has been referred to. As I have noted elsewhere, despite my use of these conventions, it is nonetheless important to understand that foreign residents in the Chinese treaty ports lived in 'Amoy', 'Tientsin' or 'Swatow', not (as these cities are rendered in standard Putonghua, or Mandarin) 'Xiamen', 'Tianjin' or 'Shantou', and they used a rough and ready pidgin English when speaking to Chinese, or relied on interpreters. This is not simply a historical note, but a pointer to the ways they understood the world in which they lived and worked.

'Butterfield & Swire' was always simply 太古 in written Chinese (*sans* Butterfield and *sans* Swire), *Taigu* in Mandarin, Taikoo in the transliteration adopted and still in use today by various group companies (and derived from Cantonese reading of the Chinese characters). The origin of the name remains a little unclear (see Chapter 3, note 34).

I

Taikoo

All history begins in the present. A dispute, a find, a hunch, invitation, journey or query, all these might prompt new study. This one starts like this. You fly to Hong Kong, say from London. As you travel you brief yourself, for you are also later flying on to Shanghai, perhaps a first visit to Asia. It might be pleasure, it might be business that takes you, for many people either has increasingly become routine. Once such a journey took weeks, now it takes 12 hours. As you fly, you read a history of China in the nineteenth and twentieth centuries, and you chat with your neighbour, a Hong Kong-born student heading home to her parents' apartment on a large estate on the island. As you come across the outer islands to land at Chek Lap Kok, Hong Kong's international airport, you gaze down at the ships standing out against the blue sea in the bright stark daylight of south China. After landing and collecting your luggage you travel by car or train to the city, the route taking you across Tsing Yi island, passing as it does a dockyard and then on the Kowloon peninsula racks of shipping containers awaiting collection. Arriving downtown you transfer to a hotel, perhaps one of four built above a luxury shopping mall in Admiralty just east of the central district. You might refresh yourself on arrival with a soft carbonated drink; you might put sugar in a cup of tea.

One company, based in London, where you began this journey, housed in the heart of that European capital, far away in space, but not now in time, owns or has owned, or managed, sold or was involved to a greater or a lesser extent in the development of nearly everything you have seen, travelled in, consumed: the airline, parts of the airport, some of those ships, the student's home, the dockyard, container terminal, the mall, the hotels, the drink, the sugar (elsewhere the tea, the car). The student has friends or family who work for it – 41,000 people do in Hong Kong alone – or whose forebears did so across its over 150-year presence in Asia. In the history you read it would be unusual not to find the company mentioned even if only in a list of the largest British interests that were once present in this Asian city, or that one, or its archives used, and even if one or the other episodes in which it came to public view was not recounted, you can rest assured that it was nonetheless an actor in that history, as it is a presence in Hong Kong today and further afield. Why? How did this come about?

This is a history of that company, John Swire & Sons, Taikoo (*Taigu*, 'Great and Ancient'), from 1816, the year of the earliest record of it that we can find, roughly through to 1980, and the pivot period in modern China's history which saw its reopening to foreign trade and investment after two decades of insularity when it was largely closed to business, whether to the Western or the Soviet blocs. My aim is to understand how it came about that a British company with an indisputably British address today – Buckingham Gate, if you please – one among scores of small shipping agents and merchant houses scrambling for a living in early nineteenth-century Liverpool, now holds such a firm place in Hong Kong, and not only there. It is embedded in cities across the Asia-Pacific. Its logo, discreetly affixed today to aircraft fuselages, ship hulls, information booths in malls, and less demurely shines bright and clear at night from high-rise blocks in Chinese cities, foregrounds a 'House Flag' that flew from steamships that first ploughed their way along the Yangzi in 1873. This is a story of Britain in Asia (Britain broadly conceived).

And Asia in Britain (Asia, too, broadly conceived). Conversely, but less obviously, its traces are also to be found all over the British Isles. Once you start searching for an answer to those questions, you find that in retirement one of the company's managers lived in a house near your home. An earnest lay member of the Church in the same city in the 1900s once ran its branch in Wuhan. A *cha-see* – a tea taster – who lived for more than 40 years in Fuzhou, visited nearby whenever on leave. Looking further afield you will find that woollen goods from a mill at Haworth that operated under the disapproving eye of the Brontë family were sold by the firm in Shanghai and in Yokohama. A bottling factory in Liverpool prepared stout that that was 'good for you' which it sold to slake thirsts in Australia. Chinese seamen recruited by the firm in Hong Kong lived between voyages in boarding houses in the same city on the Mersey. Shipyards on the Clyde, the Tyne and in Belfast built scores of vessels that it ran along the Yangzi River, the Chinese coast and on routes linking Asia and Australia. The careers of thousands of British mariners included a stint on these vessels or others it served. Clydeside newspapers printed reports of the doings of the 'colony' of local families transplanted to Hong Kong to work for the company's sugar refinery. Clerks and shipmasters alike retired to homes they might rename 'Cathay' or 'Taikoo' – after the firm's Anglicised Chinese name – and decorated with their Chinese knick-knacks. Chinese antiquities bought by company managers can be found in museums. An elderly woman, taken to China as a child by her father, widow of one of the firm's clerks, living in a small Surrey village talked of her 60 years of life in China to a novelist whose book can be found second-hand. A nature writer living in Devon (better known, though indirectly, as the inspiration for his sister's most famous literary creation) peppered his accounts of the life of the wasp, the ant, the spider and the snake with episodes from his years of sugar tramping in China for Taikoo.

I began with a speculative exercise, a conceit through which to sketch out by way of introduction how much of this one firm might be visible in Hong Kong in 2020, should you be minded to note it (and I might have chosen other cities). The point, however, is not the nosing out of these Asian facets of the contemporary operations of an entirely British-owned multinational conglomerate and its associate companies, but to raise the obvious questions that shape this book. What follows is not a business history in any technical sense, although it charts the development of that firm and its operations, and I am interested in the initiatives it took, and withdrew from, and the simple complex question of endurance. This is instead a history which foregrounds a business, its people and its world, and their lives, explored to see what light this single enterprise and its development and experience sheds on the story of nineteenth- and twentieth-century Asia, and the interconnected modern world. We gain thereby, I think, a better sense of the roots of the geographies of modern life, and the causes and consequences of this juxtaposition of Britain and Asia, from Buckingham Gate through Chek Lap Kok to Admiralty.

In different ways and for different purposes the John Swire & Sons story has been told in part before, as the focus, for example, of a studious 'analysis of Far Eastern business, shipping, and trading relationships' that covered the British side of the history to around 1898; and as a scrappy tale of the 'personal triumphs and tragedies' of the firm's foreign employees in a book that drew the story to a close in 1926. It has formed a case study for Chinese economic historians of a foreign enterprise that engaged in 'economic aggression' against China (that picture of foreign aggression being still central to China's modern nationalism), yet at the same time, 'objectively' viewed, contributed much to the country's development, notably in shipping, up to the establishment of the People's Republic of China in 1945.[1] It has been the subject, too, as we shall see, of work by scholars interested in the history of British merchant houses overseas, of the nineteenth- and twentieth-century maritime history, of the rich and often contentious political and economic history of sugar, and the story of the rise and fall of British imperialism, of global finance and of nationalist triumph.

Here I present a wider history of the firm, integrating into an account of its origins and growth from 1816 onwards the core activities of this single enterprise, the diverse contexts in which these developed, endured and in places declined. This book builds on my own previous studies of the history of the foreign presence in China across the nineteenth and twentieth centuries and its legacies (in which Taikoo certainly had its place), on the British in the Chinese cities opened to foreign trade and residence, commonly known as the treaty ports, and on the life and experiences of individual Britons who entered that world. It does also depart from that work, in scope and focus, for the subject of the long history of John Swire & Sons has demanded that I think about the fuller history of the global hinterland of the British enterprise in China – one that in this case drew in New Orleans and Melbourne – and understand more fully its British Isles origins and place. I will present a picture of the relationship between colonial Hong Kong, the treaty ports and the wider landscape of British power in Asia-Pacific that is more integrated and fluid than might be assumed. The company's enterprises were firmly embedded in all kinds of wider global networks – of peripatetic mariners, globe-encompassing shipping networks, commodity trades, the movement of people, technology and capital. The account of the development of an enterprise like this offers a focused and extended case study in the history of the processes we call globalisation (that now takes many, so routinely, from China to London, or London to Hong Kong).

The book draws heavily on the archives of John Swire & Sons, which are patchy in places and scattered, but nonetheless extensive. The uneven survival of the company archive is partly a result of the bombing of wartime London, the Japanese occupation of Hong Kong in 1941 and the surrender of records in China when John Swire & Sons withdrew from the country in 1955. But records have also failed to survive the lesser violence of office relocation, closures and the simple challenges their own bulk provided. So to flesh the story out further, and to bring other perspectives to bear, I draw also on records of associates and competitors, on personal papers and on state archives from Britain, China and Hong Kong, Australia and the United States. Newspapers have often provided the only substantial record of particular events or personalities. It says something telling about the firm's imprint on modern history that the records are so diverse and dispersed internationally, and that the act of preparing this book meant bringing together from so many different sites the traces that survive.

Perhaps, then, an act of drawing together things, people and places might well be the appropriate one with which to commence to tell what might seem on the surface to be simply a Taikoo tale, but which will turn out in fact to hold within it far, far more than that.

2

Liverpool's World

Let me begin this story of people, goods and connections between cities and across oceans, with a ship, its cargo and a port. Late in the morning of 1 November 1834, a mild day for the time of year, a 400-ton barque, *Georgiana*, entered the mouth of the River Mersey and made its way to Liverpool's newly opened and freshly named Waterloo Dock. *Georgiana* had left England just over two years earlier carrying more than 180 men sentenced to penal servitude in Van Diemen's Land. Having disgorged them at Hobart its captain, John Skelton Thompson, busied himself for most of the year 1833 shipping a motley set of cargoes between Batavia (Jakarta), Singapore and Canton. Then, on 24 April 1834, *Georgiana* had weighed anchor and left the waters at Lintin in the Pearl River estuary south of Canton for a six-month journey back around the Cape. This was one of the first British ships ever to make the journey directly from China to Britain. As *Georgiana* tied up at the Liverpool dockside it added its three masts and its spars to a forest of pines formed from those of vessels fresh in from Barbados, Halifax, Quebec, and from Newfoundland, from New York, Belize, Salvador, Buenos Aires and Valparaiso. The *Ceylon* was in port loading, ready to sail to Charleston, *Salus* would sail soon to Trieste, *Dorothea* to Danzig and *Mauney* to Lisbon. *Columbia*, *Ann*, *Two Brothers* and *Gondolier* were preparing cargoes for Bombay, Calcutta, Manila and Mauritius.[1] The ports of all the world were tied with thick ropes to Liverpool's docksides: now came China.

Waterloo Dock's name looked back to the triumph over Napoleon of 1815, but the impressive structure itself looked forward to the steadily expanding trade of the second city of British imperial and economic power, if not, some thought, the first; and even as the first ships arranged themselves along the walls of its three basins, the 'Merchants, Brokers, and Ship owners of Liverpool' were already petitioning for another, for a new 'steam dock' to accommodate the yet-increasing business, 'especially the China trade', with its 'ships of large burthen'.[2] Waterloo was also a symbol of a wider triumph than the defeat of Napoleon, for the victory had marked the opening of the long century of Britain's global ascendancy. With the great French challenger defeated, British energies were directed to consolidating and expanding the country's trade networks and securing markets overseas for its manufactures. This was an economic necessity, it was claimed, but unshackling restraints on that enterprise was also a moral imperative, for free trade was 'the common birth-right of all his Majesty's subjects'.[3] The era, whose opening the victory at Waterloo marked, was one for Britain of growing imperial power, global trade supremacy and an aggressive belief in the profound virtues of free trade.

Georgiana was itself emblematic of that developing empire of commerce and of rule. Built in Quebec in 1826, and owned by its captain, a native of Maryport in Cumberland, it had already made two doleful journeys to Australia with convicts before it sailed again in the autumn of 1832. From the Waterloo Dock Thompson would next sail his ship to Charleston in South Carolina, and then the following year can be glimpsed at Portsmouth on the way to Calcutta from Newcastle. He died in the Caribbean.[4] In his East Indies voyaging in 1833 Thompson had brought cassia wood from China to Singapore, carried beer to Batavia and taken rice to Canton. He had thought to take tea back to New South Wales. Almost a quarter of ships leaving Sydney before 1838 made their way to Canton before sailing to Europe. When *Georgiana* sailed from China in April 1834 it carried over 5,000 chests of various teas, a thousand marble slabs and 50 bundles of mats for delivery to local traders, as well as ceramic flower pots and smaller items of chinoiserie and exotica on Thompson's own account: there were cases of lacquerware, bamboo and ivory goods, some Chinese books and paintings, window blinds and two cases of insects.[5] Such was the stuff of a revolution in Britain's trade, and Liverpool's within it, for *Georgiana*'s arrival marked the onset of a new era. Thompson's father had sailed the China seas himself, but this was the first ship to sail from

China to Liverpool, and it had left that country the day after the East India Company's monopoly on the China trade lapsed.

Since 1600, British trade in the East Indies – the world of the Indian Ocean and by extension the rest of Asia including China – had been reserved by government charter to the East India Company (EIC). This joint stock corporation had become the dominant political and military power on the Indian subcontinent and governed Britain's growing empire in Asia.[6] 'John Company' grew high and mighty, rich and complex in its structure, with an army, a navy and a civil service, and it grew irredeemably corrupt, and corrupting. Its privileges had been under attack and slowly but steadily degraded from 1784 onwards, and Liverpool merchants had been active in the successful campaign to overthrow the monopoly in 1813. Although its commercial operations in India ended, the Company's control over the tea trade with China, which had commenced in the late seventeenth century, remained in place for it was thought vital for its finances. Liverpool had embraced the end of the Company privileges, and its sailings to India rose from a single pioneering vessel in 1814 to 33 of them in 1818, while Liverpool firms had established branches in India and set up new firms there as well. By the mid-1830s more than 80 ships a year arrived from India, and around 100 sailed there from the Mersey.

So they should have, for Liverpool merchants then lobbied hard to destroy the last vestiges of the East India Company's monopoly. In 1829, as renewal of the charter in 1833 came up for discussion, its leading merchants reanimated their East India Association, the strongest and nationally most influential of a number of such provincial lobbies.[7] 'There is no class, and no individual,' they claimed, 'whose interests would not be promoted by the opening of trade to India and China.'[8] The price of tea would be halved, and exports to India and to China would increase in volume dramatically. Pragmatic considerations aside, they always argued too for their rights, not only as 'merchants of Liverpool, but for the benefit of the kingdom at large'.[9]

The Company lost its monopoly, and ships were then readied in Britain to sail east as soon as the new legislation would allow, and new vessels were built for the trade.[10] The British in China readied themselves, too. *Georgiana* was one of three ships despatched – 'with much spirit' – from Canton on 24 April 1834 with cargoes of tea for England. The *Camden Francis* sailed to Glasgow, and the *Charlotte* to Hull. These were three of seven provincial ports now allowed to import tea, for London's monopoly on imports was broken with the East India Company's. Behind all three, and other ships that sailed that spring, was a successful and growing firm run by two Scotsmen in Canton, William Jardine and James Matheson, that had recently taken their names, and that had an extensive list of correspondents and associates across Britain. Not only was tea now being sent directly closer to the markets outside the country's capital city, and more swiftly so, but, as Jardine put it himself, 'old ladies will drink good tea' and cheaply, for Jardine Matheson & Co. shipped stocks that the East India Company had routinely held back until its annual late autumn sailings. 'Teas of a sounder quality, or more judiciously selected to please the *goût* of the consumers, were never before imported,' crowed Matheson's newspaper, the *Canton Register*, part commercial venture, part propaganda sheet, and the first English-language newspaper published in China. *Georgiana*'s teas were sold at auction in the public sale room at Liverpool's Exchange, with 'numerous' of the most influential dealers in Liverpool, Manchester and the neighbouring towns flocking to the historic sale. London tea brokers tried to talk down the quality of the goods the free traders shipped east, the local press reported, but 'We hope our Liverpool brokers will show them that they are as good judges of tea as the Cockneys'. And the 'Cockneys' admitted their defeat and came north, too, for, their hold now broken, the capital's traders felt compelled to attend the sale on the Mersey.[11]

Liverpool's thirst for the tea trade was relatively new. The city's wealth stemmed from its prime role in the transatlantic slave trade before its abolition in 1807, and in the transatlantic trade in slave produce thereafter. Slavery remained, as one visitor noted, its 'peculiar disgrace'; it stained the port and the products it handled.[12] It provided capital, and its impact physically reshaped Liverpool (and it is marked there still on the pediments of some of its civic buildings). The port accounted for 80 per cent of imports of raw cotton from the slave-worked plantations in the United States, and in its hinterland these were fashioned into the exports of cloths its ships took back overseas. Cotton was king, but tea, the free trade lobbyists thought, might also have a Liverpudlian future. Ever since Samuel Pepys had recorded his first taste of a cup of the drink in 1660, the British thirst for tea had increased steadily and dramatically. It was 'an article of necessity for the entire population of the United Kingdom', the Committee of the London East India and China Association would later argue. The British exchequer itself had become reliant on import duties placed on the leaf, which by the 1780s provided a significant part of its revenue. China, the sole known home of the plant, had sucked in British, continental European and North American traders, whose presence in the empire of the Great Qing had after 1757 been corralled into one port, Canton, and that for only part of the year, during the trading season. At other times they lodged uncomfortably – in political terms – in tiny Portuguese-held Macao.[13] They chafed at such demeaning restriction, and at living on terms set by others, when theirs was a country of mastery.

Tea duties helped fill the coffers of Britain's Treasury, but paying for it proved a significant drag on the resources of the East India Company, for nothing that it traded to China brought it enough in return to pay for Chinese teas. Its notorious solution to its balance of payments problem also delivered huge revenues in India: opium. The conquest of Bengal in 1757 brought the Company fertile poppy-growing regions, and while it punctiliously observed the letter of the Qing empire's 1729 prohibition on imports of opium, it used its monopoly to sell the drug to what were known as 'Country' traders – to men like Jardine and Matheson – who shipped it to China. There it was in turn taken off their hands, as they saw it, by smugglers (for Mr Jardine and Mr Matheson were never smugglers themselves, they reasoned, for they were formally licensed to take part in the China trade by the Honourable Company). Opium earned them revenues that they negotiated into bills on the EIC, which bought its tea with the money.[14] In 1823 opium supplanted cotton as the principal good the British imported into China. It solved the East India Company's revenue difficulties, but it generated immense social, economic and political problems for the Qing, and steadily and increasingly for Sino-foreign trade.

The Qing empire had been established by the Manchus who had conquered Ming China in 1644 from their homeland in what we now call Manchuria, and held sway also over China's neighbours in Mongolia and Tibet. In the eighteenth century they had conquered the Central Asian lands that were then designated as the province of Xinjiang, the New Frontier. The triumphant and all-powerful Manchus had no reason to think themselves equal in any way with any other realm. The 15-acre site of the factories at Canton where Thompson had found his chinoiseries, and whence had come his instructions from William Jardine, was a tiny portion of the Qing empire, yet still it cast a very long shadow. It was never as peripheral a commerce for China as even the city's southern location might suggest. Customs revenues secured from the port went directly to the Imperial Household in the capital, Beijing, and Canton was the formal site of relations between the Qing and the Western maritime nations. This needs qualifying, for the Qing could not conceive of these nations as states. While it received occasional embassies – Britain's Lord Macartney in 1793, and Lord Amherst in 1817 – they left empty-handed (and in Amherst's case indecently rapidly after a dispute over protocol). Attempts to structure a formal diplomatic relationship that accorded with European notions of state-to-state relations proved fruitless. So East India Company officers at Canton talked to a committee of Chinese merchants – known as the Cohong – who alone could talk to the Viceroy, as the foreigners knew him, the Qing administrator of the provinces of Guangdong and Guangxi. This refusal to recognise any representatives of their state – the state that had triumphed in 1815 – further infuriated the British.

Canton was a lively, bustling and highly efficient trading centre nonetheless. For all that they moaned about the constraints they faced, foreign merchants would testify to the ease and predictability with which their transactions and difficulties were handled by Qing officials and by the Cohong. A sophisticated infrastructure to support international commerce had evolved in the Pearl River delta, with officially licensed linguists and pilots, customs stations and clearly set out procedures and fees. In addition, the needs of ships, and the needs of men of all classes, needs physical, spiritual and commercial and even posthumous – for there was a Protestant cemetery in Macao – could all be fulfilled with ease. Canton was in addition a site of an extensive cultural exchange. Artists and artisans catered for men like Thompson, whose purchases of Chinese *objets d'art* might decorate houses back in Maryport (such as his own childhood home); Chinese goods flowed out, and plants and seeds as well. James Matheson's newspaper provided commercial information and helped build up knowledge about China, at the same time lobbying hard and relentlessly for the free trade agenda.[15]

The Chinese port was a key centre in a growing global network of commerce and business involving multinational combinations of traders. The transnational nature of the enterprises that developed saw

Parsi merchants at Bombay collaborating with Scotsmen, and Chinese merchants at Canton becoming intimately linked with American firms which shipped in opium from the Ottoman empire and sea otter pelts from the Pacific Northwest. Dutch, Danish and Swedish East companies traded there. Interests in *Georgiana*'s cargo in 1834 were allocated politically by William Jardine, with symbolic shares allowed to the firm's business associates at Canton both 'European and Chinese'. The darker side of the Canton story – of its potential for violence – was also manifest in the involvement in Thompson's cargo of James Innes, another Scot, long resident in Canton and notorious for his belligerence and violence.[16] Free trade was certainly fostered, supported and defended by British armed might, but even so, as we shall see, the two centuries of trade that follow were characterised also by a cosmopolitan entangling of interests and nationalities, languages and cultures.

William Jardine had been impatient to ship the cargoes. News of the formal repeal of the Company monopoly by the British Parliament in July 1833 only arrived in Canton in late January the following year, and another month lapsed before clarity was received about due process and procedure. Even so, there were no British officials in Canton who could yet formally approve the shipments being prepared, so they sailed with manifests unsigned. 'We would much rather have seen the British flag flying in Canton, and the free trade commenced under its shadow,' noted the *Canton Register*. But, ever pragmatic, the firm despatched the ships regardless.[17] The setting 'free' of British trade with China meant in practice its formal regulation and oversight by British government agents, not by East India Company officers. While *Georgiana* sailed west those newly appointed officers were sailing east – they might possibly have spotted each other's ships on the way, and they certainly heard news of each other.

An episode of great importance had unfolded in Canton as Thompson sailed north from the Cape of Good Hope towards Liverpool. Britain's first Chief Superintendent of Trade, William John, 9th Lord Napier, had arrived in Macao in July. Not content with simply signing off manifests – hardly the role of a gentleman, perhaps – Napier, whose well of confidence was as full as his reservoir of tact and common sense was empty, had quickly set out to force the Chinese to recognise his official status. In this Napier incontinently exceeded instructions, not least that he should proceed with 'moderation'. He went to Canton, without securing permission, attempted to deliver his credentials to officials, without securing any audience, and plastered the walls of the public square in front of the factories with bombastic notices and proclamations. Goaded by this bumptious intruder, the Chinese effectively placed him under house arrest and eventually forced him to retreat to Macao, where tragedy followed on from humiliation, and the beaten man died swiftly of a fever contracted in Canton.[18] Free trade would grow steadily thereafter, but it grew under the shadow of Napier's failure and death, and of a growing belief among many of the Britons involved in the China trade that only violence could properly lead to its establishment on a proper footing, not just Innes's violence, for on occasion the Scot used his boot and fist, but the armed might of British state power.

The developing complexity and reach of the regional and global connections of Canton was signalled even by the *Georgiana*'s ambulatory travels in 1833 that linked this Quebec-built ship most immediately to Britain's growing important entrepôt at Singapore, but also to Batavia and to Hobart, to Portsmouth and then to Liverpool. So the *Georgiana* set off from one global centre in 1834, and sailed into another half a year later. The flooding of the Waterloo Dock with the Mersey's waters in September that year was another necessary stage in Liverpool's ongoing physical reconstruction, for the total volume of shipping had almost quadrupled in the previous 30 years. Alongside docks and warehouses to handle them, landmark civic buildings were unveiled, elegant residential squares designed and new suburbs were developing. Everything he had seen when he visited, the poet Robert Southey wrote in 1807, was new. There seemed to be nothing of any 'antiquity' in Liverpool: all that he saw was 'the work of late years'. It was not even a city, formally, but a rapidly growing town, its rise founded on the opening in 1715 of England's first commercial wet dock. Southey noted the cultured civic-mindedness of its traders, whose efforts, wealth and ambition funded a botanic garden, the Athenaeum, the Lyceum and other neoclassical buildings. The infrastructure that underpinned this prosperity was equally as impressive. He was, he reported, struck in wonder 'by the height of some of the warehouses'. A later visitor, the American Ralph Waldo Emerson, also noted the 'colossal masonry of the docks & of all the public buildings'. They were 'on a scale of size &

wealth out of all proportion to ours,' continued Emerson.[19] He was also impressed by the self-sufficiency and self-regard of the English, who stood up for their rights – as they saw them – on the smaller things in life, but also on the larger ones, among them the right – he might well have noted – to trade directly with China.

Liverpool's population had rapidly grown in the eighteenth century, and it more than doubled again between 1801 and 1831. Much of this was accounted for by the immigrant labouring poor (who lived in a different city, as Southey noted, for they mostly dwelled 'in cellars, underground'), but this booming town attracted, too, merchants and shippers, hungry for a share of this booming trade, and among this influx was a family of traders from Halifax in West Yorkshire, the Swires. Richard Swire, his younger cousin John Swire, and, later, John's father Samuel. John Swire (1793–1847) can first be firmly placed in Liverpool in 1816 when a trade directory lists his address as 9 Cooper's Row, close by the Customs House in the heart of the town, and his occupation as merchant. In May that same year he is recorded as consignee of a shipment of bark from Philadelphia. This is the earliest point at which we have firm evidence for the existence of the firm that would take his name.[20]

John Swire, the oldest of 10 children, had been born in Halifax in 1793. His father was hardly a consistent success as a merchant, being bankrupted in 1808 (as his own father had been in 1795). The family origins lay in Cononley, in the North Riding of Yorkshire, where the Swires had been the most prominent of local families since the mid-eighteenth century, and where the senior branch still owned the Hall and estate.[21] The junior branch had a rougher time. John Swire seems to have arrived in Liverpool after his father's insolvency to work for his cousin Richard who had been active in the town since at least 1800, but who was also declared bankrupt in 1810. Such financial problems were not unusual, for these were challenging times for British traders. The French wars, and the attendant commercial and then military conflict with the United States in 1812–15, made for an uncertain environment. But they were no less traumatic for that, and the 'stings' of suddenly straitened circumstance would be a sore and guiding memory for John Swire decades later.

Fairly soon after a press report of John Swire's first import from the United States in 1816, records of his trades start to outnumber those of his cousin's. Some 34 references in the *Liverpool Mercury* between then and 1834 show him dealing in a diverse range of products: Swire imported cotton, barrels of apples, flour and turpentine from America; coffee, timber and rum from Jamaica; indigo from Calcutta; ashes from Canada; and hides and timber from Guyana. From the early 1820s onwards the greater part of his imports are from North America, with available records showing him importing goods on his own account, while other sources show him exporting woollens to America.[22] Starting in 1822 Swire also began a 15-year association with a Lancaster-based shipping firm, Burrow and Nottage, acting as agent for their regular runs out to Tortola and St Thomas in the British and Danish Virgin Islands respectively, where they also owned slave-worked plantations. In 1828, for example, two of the company's vessels each made two journeys, taking out a variety of cargoes including lime, an ingredient in sugar refining, and sailing back loaded with sugar to Lancaster. This was a trading route long past its profitable peak in the early nineteenth century, and it marks Swire out as a man content with a steady but unspectacular market niche. In the 1830s and 1840s most of Swire's business as an agent was for ships sailing to Port-au-Prince in Haiti. These early records show a modest but steady pattern of business, with the firm rarely working on more than a single ship at a time.[23]

In August 1822 Swire married Mary Louisa Roose, daughter of Jonathan Roose, a shipowner and merchant from Anglesey. This suggests some financial stability, and the public appearance – at least – of reasonable prospects. There were to be five children, four of whom survived into adulthood, and two of whom, John Samuel Swire (b. 1825), and William Hudson Swire (b. 1830), would continue the firm their father had established. In the 1830s John Swire is recorded in the local press in ways that suggest a reasonably well-established merchant: he was eligible to vote and was listed as a 'House Visitor' to the Liverpool Infirmary and then joined its board, where he sat alongside the powerful figure of John Gladstone, father of the future prime minister. Swire can be found subscribing to public relief funds and was a member of the American Chamber of Commerce (his cousin had been a founder member of it in 1801). In 1834, as the *Georgiana* was readied at Canton, John Swire's focus lay very firmly with the American trade. His name was appended to a petition of Liverpool's American Merchants Association early that year, appealing impositions on exports of wool, and the case of his own substantial trades was described within that document.²⁴ Among the thicket of ships' masts surrounding *Georgiana* in the Liverpool docks on 1 November 1834 there was likely to be one part-engaged with John Swire's American business.

Swire diversified his business in the later 1830s, with records showing imports from the Mediterranean and from Portugal of wine, paste and lastings. He remained a trader and did not diversify as many others would (but he did make a substantial investment in Great Western Railway shares). As far as can be discerned, while his father-in-law had owning interests in at least 11 ships during his lifetime, John Swire seems only to have invested in one. This was not a happy experience and may have encouraged caution towards such a risky business. In July 1840 Swire took a minority subscribing interest in a vessel built at Glasgow, a 200-ton brig, *Christiana*. It sailed for the Caribbean that year, but was recorded as lost at Haiti at the end of January 1841.²⁵

John Swire died on 12 August 1847, after a long decline, leaving an estate valued at around £12,000 (over £1 million at 2019 prices), as well as the business. In his last months the firm had been styled John Swire & Son, John Samuel, now 21, clearly playing a substantive role in its activities. With 'one word of advice to my dear children', his will (drawn up in March 1843) offers the only direct glimpse of John Swire's character that has survived:

> Be steady, careful and truly religious, moderate in your expenditure; for if once you lose, what I have worked hard to leave you, you may then perhaps know, like many others have done, the stings of poverty.²⁶

In a further note he added:

> So far in the life of my dear son J. S. Swire I have formed the most favourable opinion of his steady, upright and religious character and may God Almighty bless him and make him worthy of the trust I thus place in him jointly with his dear mother.

John Samuel Swire later stated that 'from the time that my father commenced business ... we have never been under a monetary obligation to anyone', and also that 'my father had to go into business thro' losses of his father'.[27] The bankruptcies that pepper the record of the Swire family and of his wife's (for Jonathan Roose, although a prosperous 'gentleman' in time – listed as such in an 1849 directory – had also been through bankruptcy) clearly left a mark.

We know little in detail otherwise about the private life of the Swire family. William went to school across the Mersey. In 1841 he was listed in the census at the Revd Edward Bowman's small Rosehill School 'for the Education of Gentlemen's Sons'. There is little reason to doubt that his brother was either schooled there, or at a similar establishment, with similar pretensions: Bowman suggested that references might be sought from 'His Grace the Duke of Dorset', prominent local clergy and 'gentlemen of the greatest respectability whose sons' he had taught, taking either a classical or commercial education. The family regularly holidayed just outside Bangor, a spot popular with the respectable merchant class, and accessible easily by regular steamer from Liverpool or by rail.

Caution and moderation had built the business and built a respectable and comfortable position for the incomer from Halifax. By the time of his death, the family occupied a pleasant house in Liverpool's Hope Street. Their neighbours included fellow merchants, shipowners, a stockbroker, an attorney, the librarian of the Liverpool Medical Institution and some 'boarding houses kept by ladies for gentlemen'.[28] We know that his eldest son, John Samuel Swire, joined the militia (as much a social as a military exercise), and rode to hounds, an activity that, even if he foreswore the expense of a subscription to an elite local hunt such as the Cheshire as a young man, involved a considerable expense in a horse, stabling and accoutrements (as Friedrich Engels later discovered, and he would pay his Cheshire membership dues with alacrity). But there is little reason to assume that the younger John Swire settled for second best and later comments point to his hunting with the Cheshire.[29]

The 30 years of John Swire's business activity in Liverpool saw the city continue to grow. He was a beneficiary of this development, as much as he was also one of those contributing to it. Liverpool's population nearly doubled in size again between 1831 and 1851. By 1847 it had added seven new docks since the opening of the Waterloo Dock in 1834, with five more under construction. These included the revolutionary Albert Dock built on the dock-warehouse system which allowed loading and unloading direct from ship to store, and which became the city's primary centre for the Far Eastern trade. Its scale 'surpasses the pyramids of Cheops' in size', remarked one observer, even if it was 'a hideous pile of naked brickwork to the eye'.[30] Such construction projects helped stoke Liverpool's wider economy, even if they did little for its dignity and appearance.

Into them sailed the ships, and increasingly in they steamed as well, and they came from further and further afield. By 1855 nearly half of Liverpool's tonnage was coming from outside the United States, and a small but growing proportion (some 6.5 per cent in total) was coming from Asia. Tellingly, half of that was coming in Liverpool-registered ships.[31] A later visitor noted the city's 'docks, quays and immense warehouses, piled and encumbered with hides, cotton, tallow, corn, oilcake, wood and wine, oranges and other fruit'; the huge dray horses ('more like elephants') pulling their loads, and there were tales of streets 'blocked by the enormous business and the mountains of merchandise'. At the Exchange, desks and screens were

> covered with the latest telegrams, notices of London stock and share lists, cargoes, freights, sales, outward and homeward bound ships, times of sailing, states of wind and weather, barometer readings.

It was a city of goods and information, and of 'enormous wealth and squalid poverty, wildernesses of offices and palatial counting houses and warehouses, bustling pushing vulgar men'.[32] The retort of Liverpool's elite to such charges was the ostentatious splendour of the neoclassical St George's Hall, an Athenian landmark in all but its location, which was unveiled in 1854. This was, London's *Morning Chronicle* declared, 'an epitome of the times – large, sumptuous, full of architectural faults and anomalies, but striking, stately, and practical'. And on the pediment could be seen 'Mercury, representing commerce', presenting to Britannia, 'Europe, Asia, and America'.[33] And when ship messengers from across the sea arrived in port, a gun was fired that could be heard across the city, heralding the arrival of cargoes, passengers and the mail and the turning of the city's wheel of commerce.

Liverpool interests had marked their entry into the China trade by naming a new ship after the trade's great advocate at Canton. The 690-ton *William Jardine* was built at Liverpool by the slave trader and slave owner Sir John Tobin (who had lobbied for an end to the EIC monopoly since 1812), from where this 'splendid new ship', financed by slave capital, set out in June 1836 on its maiden voyage.[34] It sailed, of course, to Canton (and it took Jardine a gift of a Cheshire cheese). Direct trade was not enough, however. The city's merchants petitioned for 'effectual remonstrance' in February 1836 after Napier's death.[35] In this they were prompted by a visit from James Matheson, who toured Britain in 1835/6 talking to chambers of commerce and urging them to petition the government to act. Tensions at Canton eventually provided enough of an excuse for action for the British government in 1839, even if it did not satisfy a great many in public life, for what ensued was quickly and disparagingly labelled an 'Opium War'. In 1839, exasperated by the poisonous impact of opium trade corruption, and of addiction and demoralisation, the Qing court appointed a special commissioner, Lin Zexu, to suppress the trade. Lin eventually demanded the surrender of all stocks of the drug and held the British at Canton hostage until he had it. Napier's successor as Chief Superintendent of Trade added his person (and so his office, and so the British state itself) to the Chinese haul, and London had its reason for war: its official representative had been seized by the Chinese.

To make sure the decision for war stuck, William Jardine hurried home with others to lobby and suggest a military strategy. For its part Liverpool was enthusiastic for the conflict. Over the next three years a fitful British campaign brought Qing officials to the realisation that they needed to find some compromise with their opponents. On 29 August 1842, on a British warship moored on the Yangzi at Nanjing, a treaty was signed that opened five Chinese ports to British trade and residence, ceded to the British Crown in perpetuity the island of Hong Kong – occupied by the British the previous year – and imposed a heavy indemnity and a fixed tariff. 'No words can magnify the importance of the event,' commented the *Liverpool Mercury* on receiving the news. 'It is difficult to say what may be the limits to the extension of commerce.' 'We have conquered, sword in hand, access to a market of 300,000,000 people.'[36] So free trade, as it ever did, came now to China through the power of the gun, and it came about through the power of a new technology, for the Royal Navy deployed a steam ship in action for the first time. This was the aptly named *Nemesis*, and, of course, it was built on the Mersey. Liverpool brawn and brain helped deliver the blow in the shape of this 'very beautiful iron steamer' that ranged at will the waterways of the Pearl River delta unpicking the fabric of power that held the Qing empire together.[37]

The mid-nineteenth-century world more widely was being remade as a result of new technologies: weapons, steamers, the telegraph, the railway; new scientific developments and the generation and circulation of knowledge newly developed and knowledge newly organised, knowledge of climates, diseases, geography, meteorology and the oceans. It was reshaped as a result of innovations in the organisation of armies and navies, civil services and business enterprises. These gave the Europeans a seemingly invincible advantage, and gave them, too, a strong sense of cultural, civilisational and 'racial' superiority. They would develop beliefs in destiny and in mission, some in a vulgar sense, while others fashioned these into new ideologies of rule, domination and 'stewardship' over peoples they saw – because they held different beliefs, and were militarily weaker than them – as 'primitive'. They roamed, conquered and built. They built new towns, cities and new states, yoking them together physically with railways and steamships lines, and also quite as tangibly through legal codes operating across empires, and through language, culture and belief. They carved the earth to suit their ambitions, building the Suez Canal that from 1869 joined together the Mediterranean and the Arabian Sea and so built a highway to Asia. All of this involved great disruption and destruction, too, of indigenous societies and polities, of landscapes and environments, and of wildlife. They met resistance, but for the moment they triumphed.

This was an era of science, technology and rationality – and also of religious doubt – but the years were punctuated, too, by speculations, manias, delusions and fevered excitements. In California in 1849, and Australia in 1851, mineral discoveries sparked 'gold rushes' that saw hundreds of thousands of people cross oceans and continents to dig to try to find a fortune. These finds served to reorientate societies and economies. The press of people clamouring to grab their share, and the need for material to support them once they arrived, gave a whole new life and function to Hong Kong, for example, turning it inside out, from serving as the headquarters of the newly established British-China enterprise into a city that looked to San Francisco, turning the Pacific from a barrier into a maritime highway along which flowed ships laden with Chinese labourers and supplies, not least fresh beer for the parched throats of California.[38] Between 1847 and 1852 San Francisco's population grew from 460 to 36,000 people.[39] Australian developments would also suck in diggers from China and from Britain and the United States to the Victorian goldfields, and would encourage British merchants and shipowners to broaden their horizons and to look beyond their established routes to knit together these sites of opportunity and activity.

The Swire brothers, working within the restless and richly connected centre of trade at Liverpool, were intensely attuned to these changes. In the 20 years after their father's death we see them involved in individual and commercial initiatives that took each of them to the United States, and John Samuel Swire to Australia. The elder brother may actually have been in America when his father died, but he is also recorded as arriving in New York in 1848, and sailing to Boston in 1849. He later mused on spending five months in 'the wild west', travelling 'further alone amongst the Indians than any other man not a trapper'.[40] It was probably no coincidence that this was the era of the California gold rush. That 'steady, careful' caution his father had hoped for looks as if it was fraying. He may have spent some years on the North American continent, while his brother William oversaw operations in Liverpool. The firm became 'John Swire & Sons' in the late summer of 1849, when William formally entered the partnership that was named in their father's lasting honour, and continued to trade in a diverse range of goods and produce with the Caribbean, initially, North America increasingly, and the European continent.[41]

The diaries of Mary Martin, daughter of a successful Liverpool merchant and insurance broker, Samuel Martin, give us the only intimate picture of the Swire brothers. Miss Martin met them in late 1851 at the home of Adam Fairrie, a well-established and well-known owner of a sugar-refining business. Her father seems to have taken to John Samuel Swire, and to have advised him in business, but he had less confidence in William. The younger Swire was gauche, constitutionally weak and vain. He was the epitome of the smart, modishly whiskered young man about Liverpool town – swapping his drag to become proud owner of a smart new Whitechapel carriage (for which all the young men had a 'mania'), and a card-playing stroller of fashionable Bold Street, where the beaux went to be seen in the afternoons. He joined the swanky Palatine Club, attended concerts at St George's Hall with his brother, as the Martins did, and holidayed in France and Italy with Barbados-born John Moore, son of a merchant and sometime slave owner, a friendship that endured also with John Samuel. While he clearly worked assiduously, John

Samuel Swire was evidently the more effective and accomplished of the pair. Mary Martin tells us less about the elder brother, who was more reserved, perhaps more thoughtful, certainly less flashy than his brother and undoubtedly the leading partner of the pair.

Their social world was a business one, too. We know that the brothers formed a partnership in New Orleans with Liverpool-born cotton broker and shipowner Thomas Rogers Jr, a prominent figure in the British mercantile community in the delta city, who had been there since at least 1846. While the New Orleans partnership was styled under his name, Rogers was admitted a partner into John Swire & Sons in Liverpool, and the key business of the partnership was shipping cotton from New Orleans. The partnership was at the very least nurtured by William Hudson Swire's visit to the city (with which he was 'delighted') in early 1854, in the midst of a boom in the cotton business there, and had been active since at least a year earlier. We only know for certain that it was dissolved in October 1857, when the two firms also agreed to act as each other's agents in their respective port cities. New Orleans was a significant site of British investment, and a bewilderingly diverse boom town, polyglot, legally complex (as the French legal code still operated), ethnically diverse, and with a reputation for lawlessness.[42] Since its acquisition by the United States in 1811, its population had grown rapidly, and it had facilitated and benefited from a significant shift in the geography of cotton production to the neighbouring states in the American Southwest. New Orleans was 'the Liverpool of the United States' declared one British visitor, the Jamaican missionary James Phillippo, whose eye for injustice and moral laxity was also well satisfied.[43] And cotton relied on slavery, and slavery was all too apparent in the streets and business of the city, not least in the two dozen trading depots that sold an average of 7,500 enslaved people every year in the 1850s.

The Swire brothers made another long-lasting connection around this point with a more established businessman, Joshua Dixon, who had lived and worked in New York and then New Orleans as a banker and commission merchant, before setting up in Liverpool in 1852. The older Dixon seems to have been an important figure among those advising the young men in the 1850s and within their social circle in Liverpool (and he and John Samuel Swire shared a passion for the hunt).[44] The brothers also acted as agents, for example, for Butterfield Brothers, a Bradford-based textiles firm that sent shipments to New Orleans and to New York.[45] Unlike their father, they also invested successively in a number of ships including, through the partnership with Rogers, the *Evangeline*, a 950-ton iron clipper, which first sailed to New Orleans in 1853 and, reported the *Times-Picayune*, 'a finer craft never floated in our waters'. At a dinner on board after her arrival, Rogers announced a purse for the captain of the vessel which made the fastest passage from New Orleans to Liverpool over the following 12 months. From the same platform, the purse was handed to *Evangeline*'s captain in October 1854; the third of its four journeys in a year, carrying salt from Liverpool and shipping cotton bales north-east, had taken 26 days and 10 hours, a day and a half quicker than its closest competitor.[46]

We see early on, then, what becomes a familiar Swire pattern: a boom town, a rush of merchants and capital, a single commodity at the heart of the frenzy, competition to ship quickly and pride in speed. The world in which the Swire brothers were trying to establish themselves was unstable, and new arenas for exploitation were repeatedly opened. Liverpool alone was a solid platform from which to launch out into these new markets, but success still required capital, and it required brio. William Hudson Swire first visited the United States himself in 1854 to further develop the company's presence, visiting Kentucky and New York as well, but there were nearly 600 mercantile firms in New Orleans in 1854, and 36 operating in the shipping centre. The city was crowded. In later life John Samuel Swire set out part of his philosophy to his then partners: 'You must look ahead, it is far safer to occupy ground, than to attempt displacing others who have got the start.'[47] In that spirit, in September 1854, not long after his brother's return home from America, and after some delays – as even the business of getting a passage was tricky, as capacity for the Australia run was so restricted and the gold fever still running high – John Samuel Swire set off in quite a different direction, and sailed for Australia.

This move would make the firm, for prospects for the Swire brothers did not look too promising in the mid-1850s. They had inherited a steady concern, but not an exceptional one. The United States had not helped their fortunes. So uncertain did things look that Samuel Martin, whose daughter Mary and William Hudson Swire were becoming increasingly close (they married in 1857), was 'seriously disturbed' by her suitor's financial prospects.[48] What hope, then, might Australia bring? Many asked this question, but more headed there convinced it would bring them plenty. This was – for Europeans – a new world.

Melbourne did not even exist when *Georgiana* had sailed from Canton. It was only formally established as a settlement in 1837, and had grown steadily as the capital of what became in 1851 the new colony of Victoria, dominated by a pastoralist elite, whose thousand runs held some six million sheep and four and a half million head of cattle. The gold finds changed everything. The news from New South Wales, of the Snowy Mountains forming 'one vast field of gold', and of 'truly wonderful mines around Melbourne', started to arrive in detail in Britain in early April 1852. The ships that brought it also carried the first proof: £150,000 worth of gold.[49]

Newspapers in Liverpool, as across the country, relayed reports of Melbourne demented and almost abandoned as seamen, servants, butchers, bakers and labourers – any man with legs to carry him out – flocked to the fields, while back came many 'with their pockets well filled'. In London, Liverpool, and in towns and villages across the British Isles, some barely seem to have finished reading. Ships were straight away advertised as sailing from Liverpool to 'Australia and the Gold regions'. In May 1852, the *Emigrant* sailed from Liverpool with 50 packed into its cabin and 400 passengers crammed into steerage, the first of many. As Charles Dickens wrote that summer, 'everybody appears to be going "off to the Diggings"':

> Legions of bankers' clerks, merchants' lads, embryo secretaries, and incipient cashiers; all going with the rush, and all possessing but faint and confused ideas of where they are going, or what they are going to do.[50]

The dash to the Antipodes was no less traumatic for being undertaken by so many. Her youthful melodramatics aside, Mary Martin's journal hints in her account of John Samuel Swire's departure at the seeming finality of a decision to take passage to Melbourne, a melancholy sense of uncertainty, separation and distant exile. Clearly, also, this was a commercial gamble for the brothers, undertaken with support of some kind, advice at least, introductions perhaps; and a gamble that was seen as a necessity.[51]

Tens – hundreds – of thousands chanced their luck. Between 1850 and 1855 the population of the colony of Victoria grew from 76,000 to 364,000; Melbourne's population quadrupled. Off the ships they poured, 'pale faced clerks from London and Liverpool', farmers from China's Guangdong province shipping out from Hong Kong; large numbers came on from California, and from far and wide, Melbourne's wharves barely coping with the traffic of people and goods. When they struggled ashore they faced yards piled high with timber and building materials, not a room to be had, perhaps space for a tent in canvas town. They joined the crowd of hopefuls of which 'no country on earth', one observer claimed, 'could match for its heterogeneity'. The prospect of gold attracted, but the goldfields denuded Melbourne of labour, ships of their crews, shops of their assistants and the sheep farms of their hands. So Victoria needed men, supplies and tea, and it needed firms and brokers to procure these, and ships and new services to run them in. After all, as London's *Punch* magazine noted, gold had one singular drawback, perhaps one only: it 'cannot be eaten'.[52]

'New Gold Mountain', as the Chinese nicknamed Melbourne, needed feeding. John Samuel Swire sailed on a fine new 800-ton clipper, the Albion Line's *Spray of the Ocean*, 'one of the most perfect and handsome vessels every constructed', its owners claimed, which was making its maiden voyage and which would shortly set a record for the journey to the Antipodes. It was one of 10 ships that sailed for Melbourne from Liverpool in September 1854, and carried 50 passengers and among its load tons of 'first rate' potatoes and onions, and cartwheels 'made purposefully by a practical Colonist'. John Samuel Swire's Australian venture, shaped entirely by the exuberance and seemingly unbounded possibilities of the times, and prompted by the uncertain prospects of the firm, at first looks to be a further diversion from the moral direction set by his father. Swire himself spoke of 'either returning unsuccessfully in two years, or else not before ten years having been fortunate'. How 'practical' a colonist he still was, however, might be seen from the fact that after an initial foray to the diggings he settled more purposefully to doing what he had far more experience of, and established business as Swire Brothers, shipping in the supplies that the booming city needed and shipping out what the colony produced.[53]

Swire Brothers exported wool, wheat, tallow and leather to Britain, and imported a range of goods including, most singularly, Guinness, later rebottled under licence in Liverpool as Dagger Stout. A January 1856 notice offers for sale Irish Oatmeal, split peas, Cumberland and Westphalia Hams, Old Whiskey, Case Brandy, Ale and Porter, Blasting

Powder, and Cotton Rugs: the stuff of work on a dig, and refreshment thereafter, or else solace. Scraping the mud of the gold diggings comprehensively from his feet, Swire was elected to the Melbourne Chamber of Commerce in 1855, served as a juror and was recorded as one of the 'early followers' of the Melbourne Hunt Club, established in 1852 with an imported pack of hounds, and he rode competitively in at least one of its annual steeplechases.[54] Australian opportunity had already beckoned others from the Swire family's social circle. Two men he hunted with in Cheshire had both left for Queensland earlier, in 1849 and 1851. Charles James Royds and Edmund Molyneux Royds would spend more than three decades as pastoralists there, both serving in the Legislative Assembly, before returning to England in the late 1880s.[55] Men from Swire's Liverpool networks would later be invited out to manage the firm, as well as promising clerks from the office back home, while Swire's cousin Jonathan Porter O'Brien had been working with him in Australia before being sent back to oversee the British end of the Australian business. William Swire had been pressing his brother to return, offering to take his place, for he was finding it difficult to manage things in Liverpool.[56]

The personal always partly shaped the character and course of the commercial. His brother William Hudson Swire's intermittent ill health left John Samuel Swire increasingly the deciding partner in the firm, and he would eventually buy his brother out. The death of his fiancée in 1846 is likely to have influenced his first departure to the United States. John Samuel Swire's own character contrasts with the caution of his father. The man tramped the American frontier, and camped out under canvas in Australia to dig for gold. Neither actually provided what we might think of as a sustainable model for business development, but both demonstrated a certain pluck and spirit that would resurface in this story. And while the hunt and the steeplechase were certainly the activities of a gentleman, John Samuel Swire's lifelong thirst for them might also help us understand how his own character would shape the firm. In much later life he would claim that he 'had always gone in for *glory*, and not £ & d'. As the following chapters will show, there was more rhetoric in this than strict accuracy (a suitor's rhetoric in fact), but while the '£ & d' were always husbanded, the single-minded dash of the huntsman, pell-mell chasing the prey, and the tenacious optimism of the goldfield digger, were often somewhere in the calculations of the man who would come to be known as the 'Senior'.[57]

In mid-June 1858, John Samuel Swire left Melbourne and returned to Liverpool. His brother had long been pleading with him to return to oversee business at home. On arrival Swire lost little time in organising the departure to Melbourne of Matthew Marwood, the nephew of a wealthy landowner resident in Liverpool, whose son was a prominent shipbroker in the city. Marwood arrived in Melbourne on 7 December 1858 from Liverpool, and was brought into the Swire Brothers partnership in the city on 10 January 1859.[58] Swire had travelled back as far as Suez on the Royal Mail Steamer *Australasian*, a 3,300-ton iron-screw ship that 'rolled like a barrel when it was rough' and vibrated badly. It was a rough passage and the second officer was lost overboard en route. The fragilities of the still developing British network were starkly exposed by the controversial inadequacies of this mail ship, which had arrived late, and which sprang a leak on its return voyage. Given that it had run aground on a trial run in 1857 and blocked the River Clyde, its fortunes looked poor from the outset. The *Australasian*'s owners had actually gone into liquidation even before Swire sailed from Melbourne. Delivery of the mails was unpredictable and haphazard; commercial information was held up; an empire dependent on information and ships of people and goods across great distances had stretched itself perhaps too far.[59] This was even more frustrating for the colonies still in 1858 offered the stuff of fantastical opportunity: the *Australasian* also carried to Suez news of the discovery of the 'Welcome Nugget' at Ballarat, the second largest piece of solid gold ever uncovered. 'Steam Under Sixty Days Eclipsed!' boasted the agents for the 4,000-ton clipper *Ellen Stuart*, that took Marwood out from Liverpool around the Cape. This did not turn out to be accurate, but while steam had started to be decisive in securing the empire, the technology was yet still incapable of efficiently serving it.[60] This would soon change. Liverpool would in fact change it, and Swires helped finance and support that change.

Australia, too, is vital to this story in a number of ways. Firstly, it assured the health and brightened the prospects of the firm after the years of uncertainty. John Samuel Swire did not find gold, but what was routinely thought of as a specialist Australian House between 1855 and 1867 became steadily profitable with some staple trades such as porter. So important was this new market for the firm that he described himself in the 1861 census as an 'American and Australian Merchant'. And the firm 'stand in very good credit', the Bank of England's Liverpool agent declared in 1862. By 1867 John Samuel Swire alone had a substantial personal cash reserve totalling at least 20 times the capital his father had left him in 1847.[61] Swire Brothers in Melbourne was dissolved in 1861 after discussions in Liverpool with James Lorimer, who with Matthew Marwood and a third partner, Robert Rome, thereafter ran the Swire agency in that port, and in Sydney. Lorimer had arrived in Melbourne in 1853 from Liverpool, where he had worked as an articled clerk for the prominent local firm of W. A. and G. Maxwell. He and John Samuel Swire served concurrently on the Melbourne Chamber of Commerce and had become very close friends. Swire was often frustrated by his business methods, but the relationship would last until after Lorimer's death in 1889.[62]

Secondly, the firm moved steadily towards a closer association with shipowners and shipping lines. Lorimer brought the White Star Line agency firmly into the firm's orbit, and Swire Brothers in Melbourne routinely acted as shipping agents for a growing network of correspondents. White Star was a rapidly growing Liverpool-based line of clippers, led by the expansive and reckless shipbroker Henry Threlfall Wilson. The line grew with the gold rush, chartering and commissioning new ships at speed – American clippers for preference – won and lost the Royal Mail contract, and aggressively promoted its ships. They were

> the largest, fastest and handsomest in the world ... famous for their unswerving punctuality, the superior way in which they are officered and appointed, and the celerity of their passages, which rank among the fastest on record.[63]

Wilson swaggered, and would soon overreach himself, but with the government of Victoria emigration contract the White Star agency was a good, steady source of revenue. Before 1859, when the relationship began, Swire Brothers had developed a regular business in Melbourne serving ships heading to and from Calcutta, San Francisco, and to China as well, with ships sailing out from Britain, heading north to China with ballast and dashing back with tea.[64]

The Melbourne episode was important for Swires in another key way. The gold rush itself accelerated the thickening of links between the Australian colonies and China. Melbourne would become the second most important tea trade centre after London.[65] Where once the colonies had looked north to China as a source of supplies and labour to assist their development plans, now Chinese saw the southern lands as places where they might work or dig out a fortune. Australia's orientation was profoundly reshaped by these developments. It still looked resolutely towards Europe, and towards Britain, but now even more so than before its field of vision included the Pacific and Asia, and not just as ships from Sydney had in the past, as a point on the way to Europe, but now as connections important in their own right.

The opening of the new Chinese ports after 1842 had consolidated that network of steadily busier and busier traffic that the *Georgiana's* landmark voyage had symbolised. It was also accompanied slowly but nonetheless inexorably by the type of infrastructural development that Liverpool and Melbourne themselves were going through. Once arrangements had been established for foreign land occupancy, wharves and warehouses and docks were built in the newly opened Chinese ports. Ships' chandlers and coaling depots were established. Merchants built themselves grand residences, boosting their standing by the manner in which they showed themselves living. Churches were established, social clubs would form, horses would be raced and taverns would open. Newspapers would be started (and Matheson's *Canton Register* moved to Hong Kong). British government mail contracts were issued and letters, people and information travelled in greater volumes, at greater speed, and with greater frequency as each year passed. Some progress would be uneven. At Fuzhou the British were effectively obstructed until 1853; at Canton, widespread bitterness over the violent British campaign led officials to impede, as far as they could, implementation of the new regime. The British response was to inflict more violence in order to secure the point. Everywhere the British, and other foreign nationals, whose representatives darted along afterwards to sign treaties with the Qing (and whose gains applied to all under 'Most Favoured Nation' clauses) were corralled into what became new suburbs of the ports that were opened.

This geographical restriction was largely made a virtue, even in time a 'birth-right' for those who set down strong roots there. Committees of land-renters were set up to organise construction of the new roads and waterfront embankments (it was called 'bunding', from an Anglo-Indian term, and so those roads alongside these became known as Bunds). Later they came to employ overseers and watchmen, who would in turn be formed into police forces, and the Committees would call themselves councils, with all the responsibilities that that entailed. Hong Kong's growth took place as a formal British Crown Colony, with a governor, who served concurrently as Chief Superintendent of Trade in China, and a civil, military and religious establishment. A new city, Victoria – to add to the rash of new settlements across the globe named for the Queen – grew on the north side of the island, framing one of the world's most beautiful natural harbours. Infamous initially, and with good reason, for its lawlessness and disease, the colony was steadily developed by a British administration that started to get to grips with piracy and banditry, and implement infrastructure and public health policies that reduced the death toll from what was known as 'Hong Kong fever'. The colony even shipped off Chinese convicts to Van Diemen's Land, Penang, Singapore, Labuan and Sind. By return came free migrants from the Australian colonies, looking for opportunity. Steadily this Chinese Victoria grew, and grew to be embedded more and more deeply in the existing network of British trade and communications.[66]

It should not be assumed that military triumph, treaty rights and the opening up of ports meant that traders found it easy to move in and contract business. They did not. Even those who had the advantage of experience and expertise in the Canton trade found it difficult to establish themselves in the new ports. For those who had no such experience, but who leapt at the opportunities the opening of China to British traders offered, it could be a bewildering, frustrating and even painful business. After all, where did you start? What information was there? What might the Chinese buy? How would payment be made, or received? How would exchange be handled, and by whom? Who could you trust, and how far could you trust them? What processes might there be to arbitrate disputes or secure redress? These questions faced such Liverpool traders as the Rathbones, long established like Swire, in the American trade. Arriving in China in 1844 with a cargo of 'cotton goods, needles, buttons, American cloth, and £300 of "jewellery"', Samuel Rathbone and James Worthington found fellow traders entirely agnostic in their attitude towards them, neither helping much, nor hindering, Chinese merchants seemingly obtuse and wedded to forms of transaction that ill-fitted foreign expectations, and that they hampered themselves in easy exchange business by refusing to touch opium, 'the greatest single means of acquiring dollars'. They persisted, nonetheless, and eventually prospered, but slowly, and their refrain that the old Canton monopoly 'must have been a safe and simple trade' compared to the market that they faced was not an unusual one.[67]

Despite its steady development, frustration began to take hold among leading British figures in the newly established diplomatic establishment in China. Many British traders objected to the constraints under which they operated. It was a familiar litany, and these were improvements by far over those that had proved so objectionable back in the tiny confines of Canton, but men who objected to any 'shackles' on free trade found restriction irksome. In 1856 Harry Parkes, the British consul at Canton, deliberately seized on a dispute with the local authorities over the status of a British-registered ship, the *Arrow*. The vessel had out-of-date papers and was suspected of smuggling, and so the Chinese had seized it, having been entirely within their rights to do so. But Parkes turned the incident into a pretext for a new display of force that escalated rapidly into a violent conflict. The consul's war – the Second Opium or 'Arrow' War – was more destructive by far than the fighting in 1839–42. It culminated in 1860 when an Anglo-French force landed in north China and was on the verge of attacking the capital when the Qing sued for peace. Another war led to another treaty, and new arrangements that saw more ports opened to foreign trade and residence, most importantly at Zhenjiang (Chinkiang), Jiujiang (Kiukiang) and Hankou (Hankow) along the Yangzi River, as well as at Tianjin (Tientsin) and Niuzhuang (Newchwang) in north China. The opening of the great river meant its opening, too, to foreign shipping that could now travel between these ports and Shanghai. A British envoy, with the rank of Minister, was appointed permanently at the capital, and established himself in grand style there in a former ducal palace.

The eruption of the British into China after 1842 and those who followed them had other consequences. The shift of the geographical centre of China's foreign trade from Canton initially towards Hong Kong and then slowly but steadily towards Shanghai in the north, caused significant disruption to south China's economy and society. Protestant missionaries were now more easily able to establish themselves in the opened ports and disseminate evangelical literature. These trends intersected with ongoing tensions in Guangxi province between local communities and relative newcomers, and exploded spectacularly, if for foreign observers bewilderingly so, in a massive Christian uprising in 1850, led by the self-proclaimed younger brother of Jesus Christ, a man called Hong Xiuquan. Hong's 'Heavenly Kingdom of Great Peace' (*Taiping tianguo*) swept all before it. In 1853 his Bible-chanting soldiers seized Nanjing and established it as their capital. Too strong easily to be defeated by the Qing, but not quite strong enough to overthrow the Manchus, the Taiping civil war would last 14 years and devastate central China with a catastrophic impact on its people. Tens of millions died in the violence or from war-induced famine.

This era of flux and expansion was also one of violent shocks. British troops sailing to the second China war were diverted to help counter the great Indian nationalist uprising in 1857 that the British came to know as the Indian Mutiny. An unprecedented challenge was met with equally unprecedented violence, but in the aftermath the government of British India was finally fully taken over by the Crown. The scale of the revolt also made others think less ambitiously about subduing China. The United States was sliding steadily towards the insurgency of the Southern slave states that in 1861 declared themselves an independent Confederacy. The four-year civil war that followed had a global impact. Exports of cotton from the plantations of the South dried up almost immediately. Large stocks in England and a rush to expand production in Egypt and India would eventually restore the mills in Lancashire and Cheshire to full production.

The war changed the world of cotton dramatically, even though, as a John Swire & Sons circular from 1866 reported, exports of cotton goods to the United States rose dramatically as it drew to a close.[68] But British firms had started looking for new markets to help traverse the choppy course of the conflict. Butterfield Brothers, for example, the Bradford textile manufacturers who had long retained Swires as agents in Liverpool for their American exports, began exploring the China market in the summer of 1864, sending out samples to the American firm Augustine Heard in Hong Kong, Shanghai and later Yokohama.[69] This long-standing connection, as well as a newer one with an innovative and ambitious Liverpool shipbuilder Alfred Holt, would serve to prompt a new direction for John Swire & Sons in the mid-1860s that also parlayed their Australian establishment into a new area of business.

We have little firm detail of the activities of John Swire & Sons after John Samuel Swire returned to Liverpool in 1858. The brothers surface in press reports of mayoral soirées and charitable subscriptions for hospitals and schools, the Liverpool Shipwreck and Humane Society and a 'Fund for the Relief of Distress of the Cotton Districts of Lancashire and Cheshire' in 1862. In 1859 John Samuel Swire married Helen Abigail Fairrie, daughter of the sugar refiner at whose house he and his brother had first met Mary Martin, whose family was intertwined through marriage with his friend John Moore's. Tragedy followed the birth in 1861 of their son John – always known as Jack – when Helen died overseas the following year while travelling in a bid to restore her health. Jack would live with William Hudson Swire and Mary for most of the 1860s.

The lives of mid-Victorian British companies were generally short. One rough estimate suggests that barely one-fifth of firms trading in Liverpool in 1870 had been active in 1855.[70] Even after taking into account changes in partnership arrangements and so changes of name, it is clear that John Swire & Sons was already an unusual survivor. Its business now grew more diverse, but now from that much stronger position supported by the success of the Australian move. There was a new scale of ambition evident as well. The most audacious move was the attempt that was made to parlay the White Star agency into that of a new Australian and Eastern Navigation Company in 1864. This 'purely Australian venture' was designed to amalgamate the new steam navigation activities of the White Star, Black Ball and Eagle lines, which were 'all three fighting together' over the market, as Black Ball's director Tyndall Baines later remarked. Swires would hold the Melbourne agency for the three steamers that would initially run under the company's banner, including that icon of steam modernity, SS *Great Britain*. But the route was overcrowded, and only some sort of co-ordination or combination might protect the substantial investments already made by those involved. John Samuel Swire and Richard Shackleton Butterfield were among those listed as directors in the new enterprise, Butterfield presumably through his Swire relationship. The previous autumn Swire had been named as one of the directors on the initial prospectus for the National Steam Navigation Company, which would in time develop a profitable Atlantic passenger business, but seems to have withdrawn to focus on this new venture.[71]

The scheme rapidly collapsed, however, amid controversy and accusations of market-rigging which were said to have 'shocked the share dealing community'. Perhaps, though, some thought, that shock, and the decision of the Stock Exchange Committee to annul settlement, were prompted by personal losses rather than ethics.[72] Swire himself was one of five directors who took hasty but decisive action to maintain the value of the shares and to counter what they termed 'an opposition unusually violent' that had taken 'a direct set' against the scheme. Although reformulated in May that year as a 'Liverpool, Melbourne, and Oriental Navigation Company' the new initiative then failed entirely and was laid to rest.[73] Henry Threlfall Wilson had finally overstretched himself, and in 1866/7 the White Star Line collapsed, the goodwill and flag alone surviving in a new company that sustained the name. Although the Australian and Eastern Navigation Company episode has secured a place in histories as an apparently classic example of market-rigging, it seems an unlikely course of action for a man of Swire's character and ambition, and we might instead take the defence the directors offered at face value.[74]

Steam and its developing capacity might obscure the view, but these decades were ones in which sail held sway, and in fact grew in cost-effectiveness in the journeys across the oceans. The clippers were faster and their freight cheaper to carry than the steamers, which were still reliant on massive amounts of coal, and lurched from depot to depot to refuel. But the promise of steam focused minds on the technical challenges, and in late 1864, as the Swires, Wilson, Baines and their collaborators licked their wounds, having failed in their bid to create a company that would dominate the Melbourne run, Alfred Holt was busy taking apart his only ship, *Cleator*, and installing a new type of engine that offered a different solution to the problems they faced. Trialled in December 1864 the experiment 'left nothing to be desired,' Holt later recalled. Early in 1865 the Swire brothers invested the first part of what would become a substantial holding in a new Ocean Steam Ship Company (OSSC), designed to build on Holt's success, and his decision, after having been beaten and bought out of an earlier West Indies shipping venture, to have 'a fling at the China trade'.[75]

3

Orientation

Some fling. War corrodes and destroys, but it also creates opportunities. From early 1862 onwards Shanghai boomed as a result of the second China conflict and the Taiping war. The opening of the Yangzi River, and the new treaty ports, the voracious demands of the foreign armies and war fleets, and the need of the Qing for materiel to pursue its slowly stronger and stronger campaign against the Taiping, all sucked in capital and expertise, as well as adventurers and opportunists. From the spring of 1860 onwards, the rebels launched a series of strikes from their capital at Nanjing into the Yangzi delta towards Shanghai, reaching its suburbs in August. Their campaigns caused many in the great cities of the region to flee, including merchants from Suzhou, Yangzhou and Hangzhou with strong links to foreign traders. The British and French stationed forces to protect the settlements, and to start to harry Taiping forces, who they felt had become a nuisance. Over the following months, behind these defences, speculators ran up street after street of housing for refugees, began newspapers for Chinese merchants, rapidly built new dockyards and warehouses, pulled together fleets of lighters and sought new ships wherever they could find them. The Taiping campaigns transformed Shanghai from a foreign settlement often portrayed as sleepy and provincial into a populous site of multinational collaboration and exchange, innovation and experimentation, a city hot-housing China's future.

At the same time, foreign traders bought up all the land they could in the newly opened treaty ports, hoping to secure prime positions by the planned new Bunds at Zhenjiang or Jiujiang, Tianjin or Niuzhuang, and so pole position to benefit from the new trading opportunities. Then, in 1862/3, Lancashire's demand for raw cotton drove prices up dramatically in Shanghai. What fortunes might be made from all this. The China excitement rippled out from the Huangpu: opportunity's name now was Shanghai. An editorial in *The Times* in 1864 joked that the city was 'the present El Dorado of commercial men', language shared with some who made their way there – it was an 'Eldorado of wealth of hope and fortune' scribbled one young Briton as he neared the city – and the dash to Shanghai had all the fever of a gold rush. Twenty or 30 'young hopefuls' arrived in one week alone in early 1865.[1] So opportunity beckoned brightly in the east as the American civil war dragged on, and the North Atlantic trade remained uncertain.

But this perfect storm of opportunity passed. The Qing recaptured Nanjing in 1864 and the destruction of the Taiping Heavenly Kingdom this heralded brought a spectacular crash, its intensity then exacerbated by the surrender of the Confederacy in the US in 1865. Cotton exports simply ceased, and peace ruined dreams of plenty. The difficulties of many foreign firms were compounded by the May 1866 financial crisis in London caused by the failure of its leading discount bank. Many of the refugees crowded into Shanghai packed up and went home, forming a 'vast exodus' that saw land and property values plummet, and leaving an estimated half a million pounds of foreign investments locked uselessly in idle infrastructure. 'So complete a reversal of prosperity as that witnessed between the fall of 1863 and the Spring of 1865,' mused the British consul, 'was hardly before witnessed.' And in its heyday the Shanghai fever had seen extravagance rivalled only by that reported from 'the early days of the Australian gold diggings'.[2] Firms had grossly overstretched themselves. Men, too. A 'fast living' high-rolling culture had engulfed foreign traders, the racecourse and betting often at the heart of it. A bankrupt whose stable, when auctioned, held nine ponies and horses, and a carriage, in a city with fairly limited opportunities for riding, was a man who had spent for status; another, who had bought £3,000 worth of furniture in three years (£283,000 at 2019 prices) was clearly furnishing his social standing, not his home (and doing so with money not his own, in this case: he was later jailed). Clerks at one firm had £1,500 each allowed for food and drink a year; another firm spent £2,000 a year per head on staff, excluding rent, wine and salaries. Both firms crashed. By January 1867, one trader, still nursing the failure of his own dreams of a swift fortune and retirement home, claimed that Jardine Matheson alone was free of any public suspicion about its financial soundness.[3]

Despite all this, the fundamentals of the new era heralded by the treaties remained firm. The Second Opium War had reinforced and extended these. There were still opportunities to pursue in a China more open to foreign traders, foreign ideas, foreign goods and foreign ships than ever before. Shanghai's Chinese population shrank, but great numbers still remained for they saw opportunity and security in the settlements. And hopefuls still headed east from English ports. So, in the mid-afternoon of a cold day in late November 1866, John Samuel Swire stepped ashore at Shanghai. The ground was hard; autumn had been unusually dry and the city had just experienced a sharp frost.[4] He arrived on board the *Aden*, a P&O steamer, which had left Hong Kong five days earlier and made the journey along the coast against strong northerly gales and through a heavy sea.

Swire had travelled as fast as the P&O connections allowed, catching its Alexandria-bound steamer at Marseilles on 28 September, rattling south from there by train to Cairo – passing en route the workings of the canal that was under construction – and then Suez, before arriving at Bombay four weeks after embarking in France. He travelled with a purpose, with a freshly signed partnership agreement representing a new direction for his firm, and with a young clerk, William Lang, son of a long-established South America merchant, who after his father's bankruptcy in 1865 had need to strike out elsewhere. From Bombay the men shipped on to Singapore and then spent just 90 minutes in Hong Kong's harbour before sailing north.

The *Aden* entered the Yangzi estuary, which was almost 70 miles at its widest point, navigated through shifting sandbanks following an almost imperceptible channel towards the mouth of the Huangpu River on the southern bank, 40 miles from the sea. It probably anchored overnight and came in on the morning tide, past a 'rudimentary lightship', and steaming towards the inlet which was framed by low grassy banks, with here and there a ruined fort. The river itself was a 'Dirty looking yellow,' recalled a later arrival, Charles Dyce, who remembered the landscape as 'squalid and miserable', with low banks, 'some dismal trees' looking 'melancholy in the extreme'.[5] At Wusong, a little upriver from the confluence with the Yangzi, ships encountered a customs station and the anchorage outside the harbour limits used by receiving ships – floating opium warehouses. After this they would start to see more of the waterborne life of the river, and then coming into view houses and other buildings in the distance, then wharves, the square tower of an American church and soon the Bund and its array of buildings.

John Samuel Swire most likely stepped into a sampan for the last leg from ship to shore, and landed in the new heart of the city, in what was originally 'English ground' laid out in 1842, just one-fifth of a square mile in extent, fronting the Huangpu from the Wusong River in the north (known to foreigners as the Soochow Creek) to the Yangjingbang, a creek that marked off the boundary with the French concession. On the Bund were ranged the premises of various foreign companies, the Shanghai club, the Customs House – the only Chinese-style building on the waterfront – a newly finished Masonic Hall, and the extensive compound of the British consulate. Reaching from the embankment into the river were jetties and storage hulks. North of the Soochow Creek an American concession had been laid out but was largely neglected, save that it was built up for a mile along the northern bank of the Creek and the Huangpu. The British and American districts had been amalgamated in 1863 under one administration, the Municipal Council of what would come to be called the International Settlement which controlled almost three square miles of the growing city. The French concession girdled the east and northern sides of the roughly oval-shaped walled city of Shanghai, and, like the settlement, reached west a mile from the Bund. Across the river in the east could be seen a thin band of shipyards and warehouses, in among them a cemetery, that fronted the flat miles of Pudong across which on a clear day from a church tower ships could be seen heading up the coast towards the mouth of the Yangzi.

A walk inland along the main east–west thoroughfare, Nanking Road, which led to Park Lane, would take you to the racecourse and its grandstand. Beyond that, outside the settlement and three miles from the Bund, was 'Bubbling Well', a rustic destination for walkers and riders. Within the company compounds on or behind the Bund were offices and warehouses, with accommodation for foreign staff and their Chinese servants. Flower gardens and fruit trees were laid out with plants from home in many of them, a rustic haven in a busy port, but a company 'hong' could still seem a 'small town in itself', for the chief

Chinese agents of foreign firms – known as compradors – would have extensive staffs, and there was no shortage of servants. The walls of the Russell & Co. compound on the Bund enveloped two tea sheds, three godowns, the company offices, two houses for foreign staff and one for the comprador, accommodation for servants and 'coolies', a billiards block and a bowling alley, a well, a garden and a greenhouse.[6]

An English-language newspaper, the *North China Daily News*, provides a good picture of the state of things that met Swire on his first morning's awakening in Shanghai. On 28 November – the 22nd day of the 10th moon in the Chinese calendar, which was also noted below its masthead and is testament to the bicultural foundations of China trading – the harbour was crowded. There were 54 sailing ships, 23 steamers and 14 British and French naval vessels moored in the Huangpu or at Wusong. The merchantmen had come from Japan, the British Isles, the east and west coasts of North America, New South Wales, the China coast treaty ports and the Russian Pacific coast. The steamers were plying the coast, the Yangzi River or running to and from Japan. Their business was consigned to British, American, German, French and Indian firms. Indeed, the bustle of trade and exchange recorded in these shipping lists and notices had prompted the start of daily publication of the paper, which until the previous year had been a more leisurely weekly, as well as new publications for Chinese merchants. Life in Shanghai was speeding up.

The shake-up of the foreign trading establishment after the crash of 1865 was much in evidence in the property notices: bankruptcies had hit Dow & Co. whose premises on the Szechuen Road were available for immediate possession, and the mighty Lindsay & Co., one of the big three British companies in the 1840s, whose large Quong-Loong Hung property by the church was being parcelled out into smaller lots. The Bank of India and the Commercial Banking Corporation had both failed, as had another four banks out of 11 operating in the port; the extensive site of the only just constructed Shanghai Wharf Company was up for sale. Creditors for Jarvie, Thorburn & Co. were meeting at eleven o'clock that morning; and advance notice was given of Robert Mackenzie's bankruptcy hearing at the newly established British Supreme Court for China and Japan. But Augustine Heard & Co. advertised their new branch in Yokohama; recently arrived commission agents and tea inspectors gave notice of their availability to take on business; and Messrs Forbes advertised their agency for a new Keelung-based firm, J. B. Field & Co., that held 'a large supply of BEST KEELUNG STEAM COALS' in its spacious yard.

This was a business world in transition, then, shedding some of those who had first moved in and winnowing out the speculators of the 1862–4 boom. The great Dent & Co., another of the big three, would fail within months and had already shaken the local trading community with a strong retrenchment in 1865. It had felt wild and unstable, but it was also now a lively and sophisticated port city, another of the new Britains across the seas that were being planted in hectic measure in the mid-century.

Shanghai now boasted printers, banks, insurance companies and a new humorous periodical, *The Bund*, was even being launched (it did not last long). The *North China Daily News* abounds with evidence of sociability and indulgence and the enthusiasms of home. The paper hunt was to meet at the Race Course Grand Stand that very afternoon for the first run of the season – 30 turned up, for a 'good field and plenty of fun'. The rifle company of the Shanghai Volunteer Corps was to meet the following day at four, march out and shoot (and the afternoon finished 'with the usual friendly dinner'). Men who had paraded together in Liverpool or Manchester now did so in Shanghai. The first 'Hot Tom and Jerry' of the season with 'Hot drinks of every description' was offered by the Bank Exchange Billiard Room. 'Yankee energy' had seen a grand new theatre built in just nine weeks, and an Amateur Dramatic Society was being formed, no passive members required. Flautist Jean Rémusat announced a 'Grand Vocal and Instrumental Concert' at the Shanghai Club for Tuesday.

A characteristic feature of overseas British life came in the shape of the invitation of the St Andrew's Society to Scotsmen and 'others connected with Scotland' to its second 'annual dinner in honour of the Patron Saint'. Although domiciled in China, recalled Dyce, a Londoner who had never met a 'real' Scot or an American before he arrived, in Shanghai 'their feet so to speak, were on their native hearth', and he remembered the society's members 'ramming the kingdom of Scotland down our throats on every possible occasion'. On this evening 70 attended and sang and drank 'far into the morning'. The Empire Brewery's 'Bright and Sparkling Ales' brewed locally with imported English malt and hops would have supplied some of the lubricant, along with the clarets, champagnes (first class), sherries (superior) and brandy, offered by Maclean Thomas and Co. or Lane, Crawford and Co., and McEwan's Pale Ale and Schweppes tonic from Overweg's. More dryly there were three Protestant services to choose from on the coming Sunday, and Holy Mass at the Roman Catholic chapel near the French Consulate. Maria Jane Coutts had just given birth to a son, Edward; while a 29-year old Londoner, Robert Page Hodgson, had died the same night. A tidewaiter in the Imperial Maritime Customs, Hodgson had just been buried in Shantung Road Cemetery in the heart of the settlement.[7] Sobriety and insobriety, learning and philistinism, high culture and low, with birth, marriage and death, could all be encountered in the bustling settlement.

Where would John Samuel Swire find space in this hard, crowded ground? One of the last songs the Shanghai Scots sang on St Andrew's Day began with a then popular refrain, a parlour song resonant with a bad year's trade:

Let us pause in life's pleasures and count its many tears,
While we all sup sorrow with the poor;
There's a song that will linger forever in our ears;
Oh! Hard times come again no more.

They rued the absence of their fellows now bankrupt and hoped for 'unlimited sales of shirtings, and high prices in tea and silk'. And while the 'factitious growth of Shanghai has thus been brought to a sudden and ruinous termination' noted the first comprehensive guide to the new treaty ports of China, surely its location yet 'promises it a glorious future'.[8] The general collapse had left in its wake a sophisticated infrastructure for trade, and the problems of the wild years had led to the establishment not only of the Municipal Council, but also the creation of the British Supreme Court for China. The macadamised streets were even now lit with gas lamps. There was a firmer basis on which to build.

Even so, we lack any clear evidence as to why exactly the Swire brothers took the decision to open offices in China and Japan. The latest official trade report from British consuls, published in February 1866 and covering the year 1864, hardly painted a picture of opportunity. Nobody reading them would have enthused for China. The overall value of trade was down on 1863, but more to the point it was now barely any better than it been in 1857. The 1865 reports published in July had been a little better, but the die was already then long cast for Swires. The China trade, moreover, was still for some tinged with a 'slight shadow of suspicion and discredit' because of the opium trade, but now also because of the bursting of the bubble.[9] More than tinged, some thought. 'The term "merchant",' essayed Consul Walter Henry Medhurst, 'has become in English almost a synonym for "adventurer," and even "smuggler", and often complemented with "rapacious" and "aggressive".'[10] Defaults and dishonesty, highlighted by the consular reports, added to the picture. But perhaps it was precisely at this moment 'when everybody connected with China is in bad odour', as one Hong Kong trader put it, that a new move might best be made.[11] And, as we shall see, John Swire & Sons had already been drawn to China through two separate partners, R. S. Butterfield, who was sending out woollen goods to Yokohama, and Alfred Holt. As others fell aside – those commercial wrecks listed in the pages of the *North China Daily News* whose staff once lived well, but were now bankrupt – and as new opportunities came into view, it was a time for others untainted by the boom years to start things up again.

Plaintive song was of little use. There were two lines of attack for Swire: commission work and shipping agency business. Over the next six months before he set off back to London in June 1867, Swire laid the foundations on which a new China business would grow, and he got down to business within a day of his arrival, despatching letters to Yokohama terminating existing arrangements with Heards, and settling on premises in Shanghai for the new firm. Within a week, a small notice in the *North China Daily News* announced the establishment of a new company, Butterfield & Swire, Merchants, housed for the moment in the premises of Fletcher & Co., one of the recent wave of failures. The long-established relationship with Richard Shackleton Butterfield now took this firmer shape as a formal partnership with the Swire brothers which had been signed on 24 September and which established two further collaborations, as R. S. Butterfield & Co. in Britain, and R. S. Butterfield in America.[12] News of the proposed China development had come east in the spring with an agent for the new partnership, Thomas Topham Steele, a cotton broker's clerk, who had arrived in Shanghai by early April 1866 with details of the plans, and orders from the new principals. Steele was the youngest brother of a close business associate of both Alfred Holt and the Swires. He was accompanied by Richard Norman Newby, son of a Bradford wool-stapler. Newby was Butterfield's agent, and Steele was Swire's.[13] But Steele, aged 26, was occupying a plot in Shantung Road Cemetery near Holy Trinity Church before the summer was out, his name just one on a 'list of deaths from pure heat and exhaustion' that sobered up the community that year. Writing of another summer death, banker David McLean noted that a young trader 'took ill @ 12 & died @ 5 pm' from cholera. Shanghai careers could be abruptly terminated from one day to the next.[14]

Up to this point Swire and Butterfield had been consigning their shipments of textiles to Preston Breuell, a firm established in summer 1864 by a Liverpool partnership with Bombay interests, Smith, Preston and Killick. William George Killick was based in the Indian city (where he had worked for his brother's firm Killick, Nixon & Co.), while George Frederick Preston, son of a prosperous Liverpool wine broker, and Samuel Breuell, a shipbroker, were appointed as the Shanghai partners. Breuell arrived in China in March 1864 (where he devoted much energy to the Shanghai Volunteer Corps), while Preston had been working in Shanghai since 1857. Shipping records show them acting as agents for ships from Liverpool that carried Butterfield goods, for example.

As we have seen, this had not been a good moment to set up in China, and in addition Preston Breuell were compromised by Zheng Fen (Ah-fun), their Chinese comprador, who had persuaded them to enter the local opium trade, then took purchase orders in their name, without their knowledge and without any opium being available. 'I did not understand the business,' admitted the then Shanghai partner, Preston's brother-in-law William Digby Smith, a successful Liverpool Australia merchant, whose brother held the post of government of Victoria agent in their home city. Smith thought it was 'too risky' and their other business 'sufficiently extended'. A week before Swire arrived their position had turned farcical. Zheng absconded, the firm placed a letter in the *Daily News* denying that they had obstructed the police from apprehending him, and the Council published a formal response from the police denying that they were looking for him. If he cared to, Swire had the opportunity to monitor the Shanghai Supreme Court hearing in mid-December that found them liable for the comprador's frauds, for they had not publicly broadcast their withdrawal from the opium business, however risky Smith believed it to be. By January 1867 the firm at home was declared bankrupt and the partnership was dissolved; and probably not before time.[15]

As he had twice before now, John Samuel Swire had travelled himself to establish a new venture. This time it was far less a speculative move. His Bombay diversion on his journey to China was possibly connected with assessing Preston Breuell's standing in the eyes of Killick, Nixon (with whom the Swire company registers show a steady financial relationship). He was rightly frustrated at the performance of those managing the firm, into much of whose operations, barring the opium trade, he promptly moved his new enterprise. Samuel Breuell had already shipped himself back to Liverpool. Smith followed him in 1867, while Preston would remain in Shanghai as a tea broker. One side of Butterfield & Swire continued to focus on the usual staple exports of Lancashire and Yorkshire textiles. But the new company was also designed to capture and grow a slice of the Australian tea trade. Glimpses of Swire in the Augustine Heard archives in 1867 show him corresponding with their Fuzhou office to commission a consignment of tea for London, and a larger one for Lorimer, Marwood and Rome in Australia, as well as introducing a Melbourne merchant, George Rolfe Jr, to them, with the aim of securing his business for themselves: 'Serve B&S,' he urged Heards.[16] This Asian move was an ambitious but carefully logical extension of the firm's existing network of contacts and operations from Liverpool, Melbourne and the United States.

This new arrival perplexed the American company. Heards had agreed to allow the new partnership of Butterfield & Swire to renew an existing arrangement that they had with Butterfield Brothers whereby they acted as the firm's agents in Yokohama. As things stood a substantial loss on shipments from Yorkshire was inevitable, but for Heards the longer-term prospects looked good and they needed a reliable British source of woollens. However, it became apparent quite quickly that Swire intended to bypass them and set up a branch of Butterfield & Swire. Heards' Shanghai partner suspected a swindle, thought they would be left with the losses, and believed that they were being pushed into financing the operation through not closing on the debt. For his part, Swire later claimed to have been wary of the financial standing of the American company. He sailed down to Hong Kong and talked around Albert F. Heard, the senior partner, proposing an arrangement for Butterfield & Swire to work off the debt, and sweetening the deal with the request for Heards to organise tea shipments from Fuzhou to Australia. Swire was quite unstoppable. Heard thought him 'a clever man, as sharp as a needle and as cold'.[17] Swire got what he wanted. From time to time until they were declared bankrupt in 1876, Heards would quite wonder what they had agreed to, and why. It was their 'sword of Damocles', the Shanghai partner wrote in 1873.[18]

The new venture built also on the shipping agency business, and the investment in Holt's Ocean Steamship Company. As Swire had sped his way from Marseilles, Alfred Holt's *Achilles*, third of a trio of new steamers built after his experiments with the *Cleator*, had been launched on its maiden voyage from Liverpool. It arrived in Shanghai on 24 December carrying, among other cargo, 600 bales of Manchester goods for Butterfield & Swire. Preston Breuell had handled its predecessors *Agamemnon* and *Ajax* earlier in the year, but now Swire stepped in. *Achilles* stands out in the *North China Daily News* lists of shipping in January 1867; for here was a steamer heading to Liverpool, when all other steamships in the harbour served only local or coastal routes. It gave notice, too, of its ambition to make a 'speedy arrival in London'.[19] Holt's trials had confirmed his thesis that the new compound engine that he had designed would take a steamship the long journey to China, the economics of which had been thought instead to favour sail for the foreseeable future. For Holt this was a challenge, not a given. So he designed the engine, had the ships built at Greenock on the Clyde – 'the great venture of our lives' he termed this move – and sent them to China. 'A marvellous success they proved,' Holt thought.[20] And there John Samuel Swire found cargoes for what he routinely called 'our steamers'.

They certainly caused a stir. *Agamemnon* 'took everyone by surprise,' wrote clipper captain Robert Thomson of her arrival in Hong Kong in June 1866. 'No one would believe that they would ever do it,' he continued, and this included Holt's agents in the colony. Of *Ajax*'s arrival two months later he noted that 'she will be home again before me although when I left home she was not all built'. 'She is likely to become a greater favourite than *Agamemnon*,' they thought in Shanghai, for she was even faster. The size of the vessels was an opportunity, but also a challenge, for getting cargo enough was difficult. 'She won't

be here again,' they said at Singapore. It defeated Preston Breuell at
Shanghai, who served as agents after Steele's death. *Ajax* left 'with very
little cargo and poor prospects' and filled up with anything it could find
on the run home, finally diverting to Port Elizabeth and securing a full
load of wool.[21]

Shanghai shippers were cautious about these marvels nonetheless.
A sarcastic correspondent, 'Pekoe flavor', noted in the *North China Daily
News* in December 1866 that *Ajax*, which had sailed in October from
Shanghai, had taken on at Singapore a cargo of Gutta Percha, Tortoise
Shells, Coffee, the plant extract Gambier, Dragons Blood (a resin), and
cigars. Barely ten packages (half-chests) of such articles might taint
an entire shipment of tea complained another writer. Swire himself
responded quickly in print. There was little tea on board, he reported,
and anyway such was the robustness of the division of compartments
that this would not have been a problem even if there had been. Swire
offered Holt's ships as modern in design, modern in their speed and
efficiency, and he had greater ambitions for them yet. (But Holt was
more cautious, instructing his captains not to take any cargo on board
'that smells strongly'.)[22] Swire was also quick to defend reputation,
perhaps pugnaciously so. It was a bold and confident man who took
to the public press so swiftly after arriving in this new environment.
But Swire had a further reason to defend the steamers, for while in
Shanghai he was also investigating the possibilities for the new firm in
the China shipping business. There were opportunities on the Yangzi
River and along the coast, and his discussions even included potential
marine staff. For the present this had to lapse; Holt, for his part, was
not convinced.[23]

There were offices to establish and staff to appoint. In April 1867
Swire travelled to Yokohama. The Japanese port was still recovering from
a devastating fire in November the previous year which had affected
Heards' offices and destroyed a sizeable consignment of the Butterfield
goods stored there.[24] Newby was now moved to Japan to establish the
second branch of the new firm.[25] After Swire left to return to Britain in
June, William Lang was left in charge of the Shanghai office, assisted by
20-year-old James Henry Scott, who had shipped out on the *Achilles*,
and whose father was chairman of the shipyard at Greenock on the
Clyde where Alfred Holt's steamers had been built. This was a strategic
appointment, but would also turn out to be an immensely productive

one and the relationship with the Scotts would prove long-lasting. A Portuguese clerk, F. S. [T.] Dos Remedios, was also appointed, possibly found through the type of advertisement placed in the *North China Daily News* on 3 January 1867 for 'a Portuguese who writes a good hand and is conversant with accounts'. Dos Remedios was in fact most likely to be Macanese, a Luso-Chinese Eurasian whose family had originated in the Portuguese colony at Macao. Men, and later women, from the communities that developed in Hong Kong and Shanghai would find a niche across the Chinese treaty port world in such clerical positions.

What the earliest records fail to note is the Chinese staff of the firm, and most notably its comprador. Preston Breuell's, if he could be found, was hardly likely to have been retained, but the new office (which otherwise took over Preston Breuell's household and office furniture and moved it to new premises) will have needed the expertise and contacts a comprador could bring. With the exception of Dos Remedios, none of the men who now staffed the Shanghai and the Yokohama offices of the firm had any first-hand experience of the world of business in China or Japan. They knew none of the languages, knew little of its culture or business practices and had no direct means of accessing or keeping up with market or other intelligence. Butterfield & Swire had been heavily reliant on Augustine Heard for its entry into the new trading world – they were its 'godfathers', as Swire put it in 1869 – but they needed their own Chinese eyes, tongues and ears to mediate their business and embed themselves.[26]

All firms did. The intermediary figures who were vital to the world of foreign trade were known in English as 'compradors' (in Mandarin Chinese as *maiban*, literally 'purchasing agent').[27] Such indigenous collaborators were certainly not unique to China, but they were a prominent feature in the structure of Sino-foreign trade as it functioned, and as it has been remembered. The old Canton trade system had developed an elaborate infrastructure of licensed translators ('linguists'), provision merchants and pilots. Trade there was undertaken with a state-appointed monopoly group of Chinese merchants, the activities of many of whom became tightly enmeshed with the foreign traders, so much so at times that much of the enterprise was quite clearly transnational and collaborative.[28] The new trade regime inaugurated by the 1842 Nanjing Treaty saw an increased need for Chinese assistance, as the foreign merchants who set up in the newly opened ports had no local contacts and the roles of those involved in the Canton system evolved – and from this emerged the compradors. The term had various meanings, and was applied to men who might in English be designated as a ship's purser or a provision agent or a Chinese staff manager. But the most important of those to whom it was applied were the key Chinese agents of foreign firms.

A firm's comprador handled all business with Chinese traders. As practice evolved, his bona fides were formally backed by financial sureties secured from other Chinese merchants or already established compradors, by deposit of real estate deeds or cash. Preston Breuell's was backed by two of his fellow countrymen from Xiangshan in Guangdong province, whence came a very great number of these men (and they may also have been his relatives).[29] A comprador had further realms of activity. Firstly, he was usually responsible for recruitment and supervision of all Chinese staff of a firm. A Chinese merchant interacting with a foreign company might never in fact have any dealing with anybody but the comprador and his office staff. They were the firm, as far as its interlocutors were concerned. Secondly, a comprador was a merchant or investor in his own right. There were usually understandings about the division of activities (although such lines of division could be blurred). Compradors traded, invested in real estate, or ships, or in the new enterprises set up by foreign merchants. Their capital was as welcome as their knowledge and contacts were necessary. Their finance was also in fact often vital to enterprises that were technically foreign in name, but actually blended capital from a range of sources, and which had often been initiated at their suggestion.

The figure of the comprador has a place in the modern Chinese political demonology. He has been portrayed as a semi-foreignised hireling, a 'running dog', cringingly subservient to foreign imperialists. The term has expanded to encompass, for example, the entirety of the Sino-foreign world of Shanghai, during the era of the treaty ports, deemed a 'comprador city' by its critics. Contemporaries could be equally as hostile, seeing compradors as risible figures, greedy nouveaux riches, traitors, too, demeaning themselves and their country by aping foreign practices and customs, associating with foreigners and studying foreign languages. The established Confucian disdain for merchants (socially, and morally, beneath all other sectors of society) was reinforced by their association with foreign power. Yet the same figure also occupies a place today in the pantheon devoted to China's economic and cultural modernisers. Compradors, or men from the comprador social world, were at the heart of new commercial initiatives, urban development, or social, cultural or philanthropic ventures. They launched newspapers, established hospitals and schools and parlayed their knowledge and experience into initiatives to improve social conditions, or to help strengthen China to deal with foreign aggression. Few of the prominent Chinese business figures of the twentieth century lacked comprador origins. Many had served as compradors temporarily, working with a foreign firm or two before leaving to grow their own independent businesses, although a significant number were associated across generations with individual foreign firms including, as we shall see, Swire.

Reliance on compradors was early on seen as a problem by foreign observers. There were two facets to this: firstly, the character and behaviour of some of those involved, and, secondly, the impact this had on the practices of foreign traders. They were 'men destitute of character and property and wholly given over to commercial gambling of the worst description', complained the Shanghai British consul in 1867. The new system was still evolving, and legal practice lagged far behind and left firms with inadequate sureties and a boom-time demand for Chinese assistance that probably saw men enter the trade who should not have. Preston Breuell were not alone in the problems they faced in 1866, as a number of cases of comprador fraud came before the courts. Zheng Fen's default and disappearance echoed long in the memory of foreign firms.[30] But the courts were kept busy by the frauds and failures of British merchants, too. The second problem would be rehearsed for decades to come. 'We should constantly be working towards gaining independence of our Chinese staffs,' wrote George Dixwell, Augustine Heard's Shanghai partner, in 1868, but he could not 'think it would be desirable to sweep them out – alas'. Heards would gain in commissions, but would lose 'forever' the 'guarantees and safety' which the system brought. What was lost, however, was also the incentive to themselves learn the languages of China and understand better the culture and environment in which they were based. Heards had actually hired two Americans to train them up as Chinese language students, possibly a first for any foreign trading firm, but having got them trained, could not thereafter find them work to do.[31] Compradors and their staff would instead be retained for decades to come. So foreign firms sacrificed efficiency and a steady percentage of earnings for the ease of having a Chinese buffer, and as a result after decades in China they might remain complete outsiders.[32]

In 1867 John Samuel Swire was certainly an outsider. He relied on his Liverpool network, and on the good offices of the nonetheless wary Augustine Heard, as well as on William Lang, James Henry Scott and Richard Norman Newby, and on the reputation of his firm, but there will undoubtedly have been a comprador in Shanghai from the very start. By 1877 a merchant known to Shanghai foreigners as Hop Kee or Chee Woo or Chewoh (in Chinese Zhuo Zihe) appears in press reports as Butterfield & Swire's comprador, a position he would hold until 1892, but the evidence is quite fragmentary.[33] The firm did have a Chinese name, though, and so a Chinese identity. This was 太古, *Taigu* in Mandarin, Tai-koo, or 'Taikoo' as it became in the firm's own English parlance, and as it remained thereafter. The origins of the choice of the name, which means 'Great and Ancient', are obscure. The firm's first advertisements gave its address as Tai-Koo Yuen Hong, mostly likely a transliteration of 太古洋行, situated at the former premises of Fletcher & Co. (also known as 老吠礼喳 Lao Fulicha, 'Lauo Felecha' or 'Olo Feleecha': Old (or former) Fletcher).[34] The hong name offered ambition, even if it did not quite truly reflect the company's freshness on the China scene. Having established his two branches, deployed his staff and met, dined and talked with officials and merchants in Hong Kong, Yokohama and Shanghai, and having probably ridden over the countryside around Shanghai with the paper hunt, Swire departed. Leaving only his shipping plans undeveloped, he sailed back to Britain on 23 June, arriving in the company's office in Liverpool by 15 August 1867, when he initialled the cash ledger for a £5 withdrawal.[35]

Things now seemed established for the new venture, but the Shanghai move would lead, within a year of Swire's return, to a parting from Butterfield after at least a decade and a half of business association. Butterfield probably helped encourage opening up the path to China after meetings he had with Augustine Heard Jr in London in 1864 but was now withdrawing. Richard Shackleton Butterfield was the oldest of five brothers who had taken over the successful firm established by their father, Isaac. Butterfield had followed his firm's exports overseas, basing himself in the United States for a while in the 1840s leaving his brother

Frederick to run operations in New York. After returning, he lived in Haworth, north of Bradford, where in 1848 he bought and significantly extended a mill, and where he was a neighbour of the Brontë family. Butterfield became prominent as a magistrate and an 'earnest Wesleyan Methodist', but his local reputation as an employer and ratepayer was not so positive. 'I cannot help enjoying Mr Butterfield's defeat,' remarked Charlotte Brontë, after sharp management practices at the Haworth mill were exposed in 1852; and he had led those in Haworth who opposed her father Patrick's attempts to bring piped water and a sewerage system to the village, whose population had been scythed by waterborne disease. John Samuel Swire would remember Butterfield as 'grasping'. 'He bothered me,' he continued in a letter written ten years later. In another he remarked that his partner, like his brothers, was cautious by nature.[36]

On 1 August 1868, the men formally dissolved their partnership, the Swire brothers withdrawing from the British and American firms and Butterfield from the Asian house. At the latter's request this was never publicly notified, and the Bradford partner's 'slipping out so quietly' alarmed close observers like Heard's veteran Shanghai partner, George Basil Dixwell. Butterfield was dead within a year, however, but a dispute over fulfilment of the terms of his withdrawal would last into the 1880s, although Swire would continue to collaborate with his brothers. Butterfield's name would remain with the firm for another century while his likeness, dressed in Tudor garb, was later set in stained-glass windows at the ostentatiously grand family home at Cliffe Castle in Keighley, north of Haworth. It was an odd set of memorials, and for business associates certainly a confusing one: 'I don't know who are the partners,' complained Dixwell in the spring of 1869.[37]

But the partners were now John Samuel and William Hudson Swire alone, although to all intents and purposes it was the elder of the brothers who led, setting the strategic direction and tone of the enterprise, and we find very little of his brother in the archive. John Samuel Swire could not run this growing enterprise on his own.[38] The Butterfield relationship had turned sour, although the Butterfield interests were taken over by his former clerks and, styled as Redman and Holt, continued to supply Swire with worsted goods for China and Japan.[39] The breakdown with Butterfield was a matter of personality, and of trust. Working with the right people was vital. Swire operated within a dense and overlapping world of Liverpool connections. Shanghai had its groupings of merchants from Guangdong, from Shantou or Fuzhou. It had this Liverpool nexus, too – or as Alfred Holt put it, a 'knot of friends and relations'. This was true of the collaborators the firm worked with – Lorimer, Rome, Killick, Marwood, Preston, Breuell – as well as within the firm itself. These ties were professional, and familial. If you dig into the background of these men and their families you will find a dense tangle of interests and associations with firms in different sectors, and in India, Australia, the Americas and then across the British Isles and continental Europe. They knew each other as, or through, neighbours, church or business associates. They socialised together in clubs (the Palatine in Liverpool, for the Swire brothers, as well as the Athenaeum), Masonic lodges, in the militia or the hunting field. They married each other's sisters and cousins and employed sons, brothers and in-laws. This way they were able to build a Liverpool world that was rooted around the Mersey, but also grafted on to Bombay, Melbourne and Shanghai, the Americas and Europe. They were many of them, too, conscious as well that it was a Liverpool world, and they were proud of that.[40]

This pattern was partly opportunistic, for using familiar social and business networks meant finding men whose credentials might more easily be established and it partly consolidated business connections through the employment of relations of Swire contacts, and those of their associates. When in 1869 John Samuel Swire wished to sound out the possibility of Baring Brothers providing a formal introduction for the firm to the government of Hong Kong he asked William Lang to approach his brother-in-law in Liverpool, who had been a partner in the firm since 1867, for 'we would rather you sounded Mr Moir as a relative'.[41] Swire was unlikely to have feared rebuff by going straight to the senior partners, but he was characteristically keen to go in strong. This practice of building, and building on, relationships signalled, too, the vital importance of trust. There was no equivalent of the practice by which foreign firms, including in its turn Swire, secured financial guarantees from their compradors. Knowing a man, and the standing of his firm, was vital if credit was to be extended to him, or goods consigned.[42] And if John Samuel Swire was to entrust a significant investment in the future of his firm's operations to young men stationed beyond the reach of the telegraph (which would not be connected to

Shanghai until 1871), and weeks away by sea, then he needed to be able to trust them.

The firm's first agents were, however, a mixed group. Newby did not last long. In the summer of 1869 he resigned, perhaps knowing his patron had left the firm. On his way home in July 1869 Newby vented his frustrations to Augustine Heard's George Dixwell in Shanghai. I advised them 'not to open at Yokohama', he apparently told Dixwell. Sound advice, he reported Swire telling him, but then he ignored it, opened the branch anyway, and sent Newby to manage it, meanwhile appointing 'a young man named Lang very much my junior'. So Newby faced the prospect of further years at Yokohama, he complained, 'without being any better off'. This indiscreet outburst – 'I had as much as I could do to maintain a perfect stolidity and indifference of face,' reported Dixwell – offers us two insights, aside from confirming his unsuitability for the post. Firstly, there was the fact that Newby calculated that Butterfield & Swire had £40,000 worth of goods in store in Yokohama (£3.4 million in 2019 prices), with much more having been invested, and was facing, he thought, a significant likely loss. Richard Shackleton Butterfield might well have had cause to worry. But more striking is the fact that Newby essentially considered himself to be self-employed and not an employee. To an extent this was routine. There was a 'rotten & mischievous' system embedded in the culture of British firms. Their clerks and assistants expected to operate freely on their own account, as well as attending to their employer's business. This meant that they were effectively competing against those employers and driving up prices. There is a tone to Newby's plaint that suggests he was rather more focused on this, and less on selling the company goods in his care. His resentment had been nurtured by a written guarantee from Butterfield, who had promised that he 'should always be in charge at the port where he resided'. Swire honoured the agreement, and at Yokohama it was thought he could do least damage, although that calculation looked fanciful by the time he resigned.[43] Newby would go on to work in a firm in London, then moved to Melbourne and later New Zealand, where his own company eventually went bankrupt. He had begun as he went on.

The first new recruit to arrive after James Henry Scott was James Keith Angus, son of Aberdeen's town clerk, whose brother also headed to China, working as a tea taster on his own account, and later for Jardine

Matheson, in Fuzhou, before relocating to Melbourne. Angus sailed out on the *Agamemnon* in January 1868 for Yokohama via Hong Kong. He was, Scott remembered, a 'protégé of Alex. Collie', a Manchester cotton merchant who had made a considerable fortune running the Federal blockade to trade with the Confederacy, lost it with the end of the war, and who would later flee Britain while on trial for fraud.[44] So this was in retrospect a mixed recommendation, but at the time Swire and Collie exported cotton goods together to Shanghai.[45] More a writer by temperament than a cotton goods man, and lacking, it was later felt – and as he was bluntly told – much by way of application or interest in the job, Angus would draw on his experience in Yokohama in some published essays, but had more of an appetite for literature and drama. Transferred to Hong Kong in 1871, he was released to pursue a career in journalism in 1874.[46] His successor in Yokohama, Canadian John Russell Turner, had been recruited in Shanghai, but was buried in a plot in Yokohama's foreign cemetery in the spring of 1872 barely two months after arriving. Thomas Merry, who succeeded him, came from a family of silk merchants, had joined Reiss & Co. in Shanghai as a clerk and moved to Yokohama as a silk inspector in 1867. Merry had survived a dramatic shipwreck outside Hakodate harbour shortly after arriving in Japan, but declined in health shortly after starting to work for Butterfield & Swire, was invalided and died on the way home in July 1873.[47] Death was expensive. It cost £95 to send Angus out to Japan in 1868, equivalent to a third of his annual salary on arrival, or the wages of an experienced junior clerk in Liverpool. So if recruiting staff and retaining them was one challenge, fate, circumstance and poor public health in these still maturing settlements presented others. They would start in the 1860s to develop all the paraphernalia of British-style municipal administrations, moves driven by recurrent epidemics, and by post-Taiping war lawlessness in the Yangzi delta region, but in the meantime the cemeteries filled steadily with the bodies and the hopes of those who had sailed east to better themselves.[48]

The earliest piece of correspondence in the Swire archives surveys the strengths of the firm's operations in late 1869, and the opportunities it faced, or, as Swire put it, 'our dreams ... as to the future of Butterfield & Swire'. John Samuel Swire was no dreamer, of course, and this letter, sent out to William Lang as he was being made a partner in the firm, provides a hard-nosed assessment of the progress of the Asia house.[49]

It was composed at the point when Swire had decided that the firm should open an office in Hong Kong, and a subsidiary in Fuzhou, and that this should become the headquarters in the east. This last decision was made because it would very shortly be the point at which the new telegraph cables from London would reach China directly, and because Holts had requested that Swire take over as their agents in the colony – those disbelieving agents were being replaced. If Lang could stand the climate, Swire asked, would he please relocate south.

Holts' line was 'only in its infancy,' wrote Swire, and is 'nothing to what it will be'. In addition, he sought to build on the historic relationship with White Star on the Australia route. The newly reconstituted company – after it had gone into bankruptcy in 1867 the name had been purchased by Liverpool shipowner Thomas Henry Ismay – had six steamers under construction for which Swire saw opportunity. If, from Australia, they brought coal to Hong Kong, after that took Chinese emigrants to San Francisco or Panama, and finally picked up wheat there for Liverpool, then all this could be consigned through Swire agencies or partners. (In fact, they were run on the New York line.) As for 'goods for the east', the export trade was now 'second to none and will improve'. Sending tea to America was to be explored, although shipping it to England was not an exciting prospect, but Lorimer, Marwood and Rome would still be placing orders for exports to the South. Swire proposed holding on to Yokohama, at least until that c. £40,000 of stock had sold. Trade was so 'wretchedly bad' it seemed pointless to abandon the port, especially as the company did not rely on it, and as it would likely grow more productive especially when Blue Funnel (the OSSC) moved into the coastal trade, and ran to and from Yokohama, as Swire intended that they should.

Then there was the question of opium. Ask your brother, continued Swire in his state of the business letter of September 1869, if Barings 'do anything in opium to China' from Bombay. All business opportunities in the market needed to be looked at. There is no evidence that the Swire firms ever traded in opium, nor should it be assumed, as it routinely is, that foreign firms operating in China all engaged in the opium trade. They did not. Their reasons for this might be ethical; they might be pragmatic; they might simply have had a different specialist focus of operations and expertise. Attitudes revealed in correspondence can seem contradictory. It was a 'pernicious drug,' wrote one trader,

yet tea and opium were his 'staple lean-upons': he sold about 20 to
30 chests a month in 1862 at £200 a chest. 'The advantage of China
is that one does things in a large way,' he noted. However, even those
strongly opposed to the trade, such as Rathbones, could find themselves
involved in a small way out of sheer necessity, for it was widely needed
as currency in business transactions.[50] In particular, Chinese produce
traders often refused to take any alternative. The Preston Breuell debacle
certainly highlighted the potential perils of involvement more deeply
with opium. The partners, as they later put it, had allowed themselves
to be persuaded into the trade by their comprador, who largely handled
this side of the business for them himself. As well as taking orders from
Chinese dealers, they bought opium at Hong Kong, had it shipped
north and stored it in Augustine Heard's receiving ship, *Emily Jane*, at
Wusong, outside the harbour limits. They made sales to local traders,
and also shipped it to other treaty ports. After Smith arrived in Shanghai
in April 1866, Preston Breuell ceased trading on its own account in
opium, but the boundaries between their own business and that of their
comprador had become unclear, and they did nothing to publicise the
cessation of this line of their business. This undid them.

Greed undid them, too. Returns on investments in opium had been
very high in the early to mid-1860s, but the business was in transition.
In the face of advances across the whole supply chain from Indian firms
such as David Sassoon & Sons, who by the end of the decade held most
of the stocks, and who kept costs extremely low, even firms like Jardine
Matheson found themselves losing ground in the market. After late
1872 Jardines ceased all opium transactions. This marked the end of an
era in one sense, as the prime mover in the entire growth of the trade
stepped away from it, although British-protected firms – and British
colonial administrations – remained involved for decades to come. And
Jardines continued to ship, store and insure the drug.[51] Butterfield &
Swire would also certainly allow it to be shipped on the steamers that
they would shortly introduce on the Yangzi River and coastal trades, and
took its security needs into account when those ships were designed. It
was a commodity among others that needed to have freight rates set,
and as a substitute for specie was treated as such, but while it would be
foolhardy for a trader in China in the 1860s not to look across all the
potential activities a new firm might move into, it was a foolish firm
which actually entered the trade, and a fatally foolish one that did so

with the inattentiveness of Preston Breuell (perhaps, said Smith, in his defence, 'I did sign something relevant, but as I do not read Chinese how would I be able to know'). Not only were they held liable for the claims entered by those who had placed orders with the comprador in good faith, they failed also to recoup the costs of his frauds from his guarantors, for the guarantees were shown to refer only to his work for his foreign principals as their comprador, not for his independent trades. The lessons to be learned from this were several, and 'getting the best of Compradors' was a key one.[52]

For its proposed expansion, Butterfield & Swire needed a freight clerk for Hong Kong, an experienced *cha-see* – a tea taster – for Fuzhou and a silk inspector for Yokohama. It required premises in Hong Kong that should be central, geographically and metaphorically. Butterfield & Swire needed to 'have a position that cannot be challenged', and to stand well with officials. We need a 'special introduction' to the governor, Swire told Lang, so would you ask your brother-in-law to facilitate one? Premises were found and by the end of 1870 the Hong Kong office was up and running. The man appointed as comprador, Ng Ahip (Wu Ye), was backed by Heards' comprador Mok Sze Yeung (Mo Shiyang). Mok was 'rich and one of the oldest compradors' in Hong Kong, so his reputation was as firm as the financial guarantee he provided for Ng Ahip. Ng had worked as assistant comprador at Heards for four years, and before that at the British consulate in Macao. Like Mok, he was a native of Xiangshan county, which bordered Macao, and he maintained a close relationship with his patron, with opium smoking smoothing their business connections. Opium had long been an important feature of elite life in China, and while foreign traders dined each other, and met 'at home' and at more formal events or in their club, their Chinese associates drank tea or smoked together in their homes, or at restaurants or tea houses.[53]

The colony of Hong Kong will become in time more central to this story than was ever imagined, and we will need to understand its topography and its character. It was, and at the same time was not, a Chinese treaty port. As a British Crown Colony it had an entirely singular legal status for the foreign presence in China, and because of that an entirely different administrative establishment was installed locally, and was overseen from London by a different department of the British state: the Colonial Office. 'Overseen' is a relative concept, for colonial governments were largely left to run themselves and there were actually very few officials in London to effect any oversight. While it was embedded in the currents of commerce and communications now established across the opened ports of China, and internationally, it was also formally entwined in the global network of British colonial possessions. True, it was something of a geographical outlier, and often described as such, but its governors came from other colonies, and went on to different ones after serving their term; they came from Vancouver and went to Queensland, or from St Kitts and to Ceylon. A man who learned his gubernatorial trade in Barbados could develop it further in Hong Kong and then move on to Mauritius for, up to a point, all colonies were the same. And so, while the British commercial establishment was more rooted across the foreign presence in China and Hong Kong, it was ruled over in the British colony by men with quite different, and often loftier, views of their responsibilities and indeed their status.

The island of Hong Kong itself was tiny, stretching nine miles from east to west at its widest, four miles north to south at its greatest breadth, and it was dominated by six peaks, the highest of which, Victoria – of course – rising nearly 2,000 feet. It was quite simply stunning. 'Few who visit Hongkong for the first time ...' reported one guide, 'are unimpressed with a sense of the beauty of the scene.'[54] Clinging to the northern fringe of the island at its closest point to the Kowloon peninsula on the mainland (two miles of which had more recently come under British control) was the city of Victoria, strung out along the waterfront abutting the Praya, as the Bund there was known, the name reflecting the history in Portuguese Macao of the first British settlers. The British had steadily raised up on their new possession the essential buildings of a colony: governor's house, government offices, barracks and parade ground, law courts and prison, Anglican cathedral and post office. There was a club. The largest area of flat land, where once villagers cultivated rice, was declared malarial, filled in and then served as a racecourse. This was Happy Valley, and the races were overlooked, in a manner of speaking, by the permanent residents of the colonial cemetery, sited in 'unseemly proximity' to the track, but providing a memento mori for racegoers.

Hong Kong bustled. The harbour was hectic. Clippers, junks, sampans and fast gigs, American river steamers which sailed to Canton twice daily, and the P&O's ocean-going steamers came and went, served by a vast array of small harbour craft. Regular sailings along the coast were fed also by Blue Funnel arrivals from Liverpool, the P&O from Southampton, Messageries Maritimes from Marseilles, and the Pacific Mail's steamers from America. Once on shore new arrivals found that the streets were alive. Some 125,000 people lived ashore or afloat according to the most recent census (a fifth of those on boats) and 1,500 people a day came or left. There were 2,000 'Europeans and Americans', just over 1,600 described as 'Goa, Macau, India and others of mixed blood', and 122,000 Chinese. These latter largely lived out at the western end of the city in Taipingshan. Theirs was an ethnically and socially diverse and complex community, for the British colonial enterprise needed its compradors, merchants and provision merchants, as well as day-labourers and boatmen. Most of the residents, Chinese or otherwise, were immigrants to the island, and more accurately they were sojourners: they did not much intend to stay. But a sojourn could last decades, and Happy Valley called many to stay for good. Hong Kong was, in its early years, a ferociously unhealthy spot, with a 'Hong Kong fever' taking a deadly toll, and for many years after that also still had something of a frontier feel at its margins, for piracy, banditry and street crime were huge problems. The colonial government's response was harsh.[55]

Butterfield & Swire in Hong Kong was opened in May 1870 by Edward Mackintosh, 30-year-old son of a bankrupt West India merchant.[56] Mackintosh had first clerked in that trade, but then learned the shipping business at Swire's Liverpool office (where the harbour connections he built up also brought him his marriage) before setting up its London office in 1868.[57] He worked first in Hong Kong at a desk in Augustine Heard's office, then a lease was taken on two houses with godowns on Queen's Road, backing on to the Praya. 'Far "too glorious",' Swire would later conclude, and too convenient for long lunches 'to the detriment of office work, and the destruction of livers', but they were central, and prominent: Butterfield & Swire were established in the heart of the city and at the heart of its business.[58] Lang did head to Hong Kong to run the Butterfield & Swire China enterprise from the colony, but lasted six months in the stewing humidity of the south before returning to Shanghai, and sending down Scott in his stead. Another office at the coastal centre of the tea trade, Fuzhou, was opened in May

1872 by a *cha-see* recruited from London, Henry Robert Smith, son of a Nottinghamshire parish priest. By that year there were nine Britons and Portuguese on the staff at Shanghai, seven at Hong Kong and three at Yokohama. There was also a 'large' Chinese staff at Hong Kong. This was a fairly rapid expansion for any firm newly setting up in China, yet much more was to come, and was to come very quickly. Butterfield & Swire was now firmly established in China. It was still a minnow compared to the giants that dominated the scene, firms like Russell & Co., Jardine Matheson and Heards, with their diverse operations covering agency work, shipping, insurance, some manufacturing concerns and other ventures. But even so, B&S was settled and it had ambitions yet.

4

Strange Revolution

The river beckoned. John Samuel Swire had long contemplated entering the shipping business in China and, as we have seen, investigated possibilities for it during his first visit. His 1869 survey showed him slowly building an infrastructure for it, and hinted at his working on the Holt brothers to join him. John Swire & Sons could not launch a shipping enterprise in China alone. Such a venture required capital, an experienced and well-connected Chinese intermediary and an experienced and reliable shipping manager; it would need properties and land, and, of course, ships. It would also quickly need to take a viable share of the existing market. This would be a challenge, but by 1873 Swire had all of this, and more, for of course he had cheek, and that cheek was made manifest in the China Navigation Company whose first ships sailed out of Shanghai for 'Hankow and Ports' in April that year.

The story of the opening of the Yangzi River to foreign companies is one involving intense competition in the 1860s that left the long-established American firm Russell & Co. in a dominant position.[1] By 1872 its 'Shanghai Steam Navigation Company' (SSNCo) had nine steamers on the river, two serving the Shanghai–Ningbo route and another six sailing the coast to Tianjin. The Yangzi service was the prize, however. The 1858 Tianjin Treaty allowed for three Yangzi cities to be opened to foreign trade and residence: Zhenjiang (Chinkiang), Jiujiang (Kiukiang) and Wuhan (Hankow), 600 miles west along the river. Not until the Convention of Peking in 1860 ratified this would the opportunity presented start to be realised, at which point, furthermore, the intensifying calamity of the Taiping civil war meant that foreign steamers had a further immediate advantage. As well as serving the new ports, once those were actually formally opened, they could command very high rates for doing so, for they would not be at the mercy of the rebels, unlike slow-sailing Chinese craft. 'The amount of business is almost incalculable,' mused Russell's Shanghai partner, Edward Cunningham, in 1861.[2]

Russell & Co., a commission house operating in China since 1824, was, like Jardines, changing its range of activities. Cunningham argued that it should invest in the river, and should so do quickly. The Yangzi was formally opened to shipping from June 1861. Chinese investors, all associates of the firm, provided most of the capital alongside other Shanghai-based business interests, and in July 1861 Russell had its first ship, the *Surprise*. Two more arrived by the end of the year, and a prime site was secured at Shanghai close to the walled city. In April 1862, the SSNCo began operations. There were the initial teething problems of the type that beset any such enterprise. The ships had sailed from North America and had had a hard passage across the Pacific; and the foreign crews available in Chinese waters were not first-class men. There were others, too: Chinese rumour pointed out that the facilities at Shanghai had been built on the ruined site of the city's once important Tianhou Temple, dedicated to the empress of the sea, so what else might be expected but a series of accidents and mechanical failures. Nevertheless, the SSNCo rallied and ran a regular twice-weekly service along the river, held good sites at the ports it served, charged competitive rates and went all out to attract Chinese customers with cash rebates, free storage on goods and even finance from Russell & Co. Attracted by the high freight rates of the early 1860s, British competitors entered the fray, throwing any ship they could find into the business, but they were forced to combine with the American house in a freight rate agreement in December 1864, while the great shakeout of the mid-1860s removed competing vessels owned by Fletcher & Co., Lindsays and Olyphants. Jardines later withdrew to focus on the coastal trade and Russells 'took in the slack as their rivals eased up', as former senior partner R. B. Forbes later put it.[3] The empress of the sea had clearly been placated.

The river had been conquered by the Americans, whose luxurious steamers bewildered Europeans used to more spartan accommodation. The 'last thing this vessel resembles is a ship,' reported a British passenger on one of these steamers, it was a 'gaudy palace of pleasure', a 'mountain of glass', 'arranged with a view to personal comfort' with 'large and handsome staterooms' housing, for some, four-poster beds.[4] The comforts of travel were one thing that even an Englishman might get used to, but this dominance discomforted others. In January 1867, while John Samuel Swire was busying himself at Shanghai with establishing his new firm, representatives of Dents, Jardine Matheson and Russells met in Hong Kong and concluded a 10-year agreement under which the Shanghai Steam Navigation Company would have the Yangzi trade, while they would stick to the coast. Russells now ran the river; they tolerated various other businesses for form's sake, or as Forbes put it in May 1868 because 'public opinion in Shanghai required an opposition', but they feared none of them.[5] Provocatively, they said so in public, too, in a circular to shareholders taken up and published in the press in 1868, which prompted caustic responses. 'This hasty blazoning of their triumph' reminded one correspondent of 'the nursery story of the foolish hen who could never keep an egg, because she would cackle so whenever she had laid one'.[6] This arrogance would cost Russells dear.

In late September 1871 Swire wrote to his eastern managers announcing coyly that he had 'half a mind to assist Russell in developing the navigation of the Yangtze'. It would involve a 'jolly fight with the SSNCo', but 'still I think that we could make them shake hands'. After asking for as much information as they could discreetly secure on a new steamer Russells had ordered from Glasgow, Swire signed off with the rider that 'we may abandon the idea' – but at present I like it'. He had long liked it. Russells should be 'grateful' he thought, that our faith in the trade and our 'earnest entreaties' had not then won over those he had discussed them with – Holts, it might be presumed – otherwise SSNCo would have struggled. Cackling Russell & Co. did not appreciate the offer of 'assistance', but within 18 months, despite initially dismissing the entire enterprise, for Swire they thought had 'waited too long', and he was hardly the man for the task – 'a blatherskite bagman', Forbes wrote – they sued for peace, and they did so in person.[7]

Keep this 'dark', Swire had urged his managers in 1869, but rumour quickly circulated about the proposed move by 'Holts' – as Shanghai tattle had it in the club and the Chamber of Commerce, and as men strolled along the Bund after tiffin. Would-be agents for Holt wrote from

Hankou to Liverpool correspondents seeking introductions. London buzzed, too. Linked now by cable directly to London, commercial gossip, as well as fact and instruction, flew swiftly to China, finding its way into a *North China Daily News* editorial in January 1872.[8] What a whirl of speculation there was – 'a rumor a day,' wrote Russells shipping manager Frank Forbes: Holts were going to take on the SSNCo; they were building 15 river steamers on the Clyde; no, just a single ship for a China–Japan route; actually, six steamers were under construction for the river, and a tug to pull them quickly through the Suez Canal; no, it was something less ambitious, a single new steamer but Holts would also buy out an existing enterprise, and there would be a rate war. So ran the talk, this way and that. This will not end well, thought the editor, it will only enrich Chinese shippers. The last of these rumours was in fact part of the strategy pressed earnestly on Swire by William Lang, but throughout 1872 rumour ran free and wild.

On Sunday 28 December 1873, John Samuel Swire arrived back in Shanghai. The world of travel to China had changed. The world of travel within China had also changed. He journeyed out on the Ocean Steam Ship Company's *Deucalion* which sailed directly from Liverpool on 2 November, navigating the Suez Canal, which had been opened in 1869. Over the course of the following weeks Swire roved across the estate Butterfield & Swire now occupied in China and Japan, sailing up to Hankou, visiting Hong Kong and assessing the situation in Yokohama. He then returned to Britain via the United States, crossing the Pacific (with, among others, 626 Chinese labourers) on a British-owned steamer that made the journey from Yokohama in 17 days, then a record time.[9] Whereas in 1867 the new firm's operations had a makeshift feel to it, lodged as it was in just-vacated offices and using someone else's just-abandoned furniture, now it was more firmly embedded in the landscape of the Chinese treaty ports. Not only did Swire sail to and from Hankou and to Hong Kong on ships he owned, but he visited ports that were starting to be physically reshaped by the operations of the new shipping line, the China Navigation Company (CNCo).[10] Butterfield & Swire was still a modest enterprise but was operating on a scale far more extensive than anything the Swire brothers had tried before in Britain, the United States or in Australia.

As well as the firm's offices in Hong Kong, Shanghai, Fuzhou and Yokohama, Butterfield & Swire had acquired the infrastructure it needed for steamship operations. At Hankou, the China Navigation Company owned premises and godowns, had acquired rights to berth two ships on the riverfront and was paying for bunding work to be completed. It had a large hulk moored there, as well as a smaller one and two pontoons. There were hulks, cargo boats and pontoons at Jiujiang and at Zhenjiang. At Shanghai, the base of operations was a large installation in the French concession just to the south of the Yangjingbang Creek that separated the International Settlement and French town. Work was going on to expand this.[11] Two steamers had commenced sailing under the house flag in April 1873 and, as they arrived in China, ships commissioned by Swire from A. and J. Inglis in Glasgow were set to work. Swire sailed on one of these, at least, the *Pekin*, when he sailed on the Yangzi in January 1874. This was a growing portfolio of land, property, equipment and people, and it brought the company into contact with a growing range of regulatory authorities and local administrations: British and French municipal councils, the International Settlement administration at Shanghai, staff of the Imperial Maritime Customs and British consuls.

It had all come about swiftly. In mid-1872, William Lang, mindful of how a telegraph office might leak information, had posted to Singapore the text of a telegram he wanted to be readied for transmission to London should he be given the go-ahead. Lang was in negotiation with one of the directors of the Union Steam Navigation Company who, it was reported, wanted 'the satisfaction of seeing a powerful English company on the river'.[12] This was most likely Samuel Brown, an insurance broker with some Liverpool connections, and one obvious spur was the preening confidence of the dominant firm. An 'English feeling of opposition' to the American firm, had long been noted among the Shanghai merchants. Lang's objective was to secure purchase outright of the company's ships and shore assets.[13] This was largely the estate that Swire looked over 18 months later, and which was bought for 199,000 Taels (c. £60,000) and formally transferred from 1 April 1873. It was paid for in cash, using silver dollars shipped out to China. These were expensively bought, for they were Spanish dollars minted before 1840, not more recent Mexican ones, and so carried a substantial exchange premium in Shanghai.[14] The Union Steam Navigation Company, which was established in 1867, and which 'keeps its head above water by our forbearance', as Russells' F. B. Forbes had put it, ran two ships on the Yangzi by 1872. Its shareholders were British, Chinese and American (as indeed were SSNCo's), and it was managed by Olyphants. The directors proved keen to withdraw from the river and move their activities to the coastal trade.[15] The rumours of an 'opposition' saw its share prices fall, for it was clearly vulnerable.

The proposed deal 'ensures success at the outset,' explained Lang, 'and places us in such a secure position that the opposition would see at once that it would be useless to oppose us'.[16] With this move young Lang proved his worth (and buffered himself against some costly later investments in a Japanese coal mine and in rifles). Despite securing this 'strong position', however, Russells did oppose the new line, using a substantial cash reserve that they had built up to halve their freight rates the day CNCo began operations. To their astonishment, however, Butterfield & Swire went even lower. Observers saw rates fall 'to a mere nominal figure'.[17] Russells had planned to drive off the interlopers, and buy them out, perhaps offering a 15 per cent premium on the price of three steamers being built in Glasgow. Alternately it might allow them steamers enough to run on the river, but not the number needed to run a comprehensive regular service. John Samuel Swire was more determined than the Americans ever imagined. 'You seem to have ceded nothing,' complained their negotiator, Paul S. Forbes, and in addition, Swire had more cash than they had calculated. 'Fly your own flag on the CNCo steamers,' Swire had cheerfully instructed Lang in March 1873, and fly they did.[18]

Swire had staked a great deal on the Yangzi move, the single biggest investment the firm had yet made, and its most public move to date. Both firms believed the other's 'pride' was at stake, and said so; both also knew that the rate war unsettled business quite dramatically, diverting shipments of Anhui's tea to Jiujiang, for example, which usually headed towards Ningbo for despatch, and throwing into inactivity the greater number of foreign-flagged lorchas that were usually far cheaper than the steamships. Both knew, too, that a long-term conflict would only weaken both to the advantage of any future opposition. The public press reminded them of this as well. It was 'sheer imbecility' was the reported view of 'Chinese traders,' claimed the *North China Herald*. Well, mused the Chinese newspaper *Shenbao*, it was all very good for business, though hardly so for the steamer companies.[19] And that opposition was taking shape even as CNCo launched, in the form of the first Chinese-owned shipping enterprise, the China Merchants Steam Navigation Company. Low freight rates generally also had the effect of accelerating the transformation of the Sino-foreign trading environment. The foreign traders who had leapt into the new concessions had aimed to sell goods sent on from Shanghai, acting either as branch offices of firms long based in the settlement, or as new enterprises, but instead, Chinese traders themselves came down on the steamers and bought their goods in Shanghai. Jiujiang and Zhenjiang, in particular, were hit by this, and Hankou struggled to grow as a site for foreign trade as a result.[20] The cheap rates of the Russells/Swire struggle in 1873 simply diverted their cash reserves into the pockets of shippers.

Agreement on a modus vivendi was reached in May 1873, and pledged Swire not to increase tonnage on the river to Hankou for two years, beyond the five ships now owned, excepting any tributary services that might be started, or the river beyond Hankou to Yichang if that was to open (as was widely expected). It barred CNCo from the busy Shanghai–Ningbo route, but excluded any coastal services. Success had required meticulous planning. The capital for the firm was readily secured from the network of Liverpool associates, including Holts, Ismay, William Swire's father-in-law Samuel Martin, Joshua Dixon, the Melly family and shipowner William Cliff among others.[21] Ships were ordered from A. and J. Inglis on the Clyde, who had just finished a new vessel for Russells, and likely office and marine staff were identified. Men were poached from Russells, and taken on from the Union line, but Swire was determined not simply to make do, but to find the best, and did so in close collaboration with Alfred Holt. To invade the trade the new company needed to be able to start strong, but it would be a year at least before the new steamers would reach China. The China Navigation Company's successful launch and operations depended on much more than John Samuel Swire's impassive negotiating style. Key to the firm's growth were two appointments that highlighted the new enterprise's position between the old but evolving landscape of the China trade, and the steadily developing new world of Chinese entrepreneurs.

Lang had secured a very good comprador indeed for the new enterprise. This was Zheng Guanying (1842–1923), known also by his soubriquet Taochai, and referred to in contemporary documents as Cheng Kuan Ying, Cheng Tao (or Tou) Chai or Tôchai. Zheng, like

Ng Ahip, came from Guangdong province's Xiangshan county, whence came many of the compradors who worked in Shanghai, including his own father, his uncle and his elder brother. Just as John Swire & Sons operated in a world of familial and Liverpool connections, so Zheng came from a dense network of Cantonese, and, in his case, Xiangshan fellow countrymen.[22] He had come to Shanghai aged 17 after failing the imperial examinations. His uncle was then working there for the British firm Overweg & Co. (and had stood guarantor for Preston Breuell's troublesome comprador Zheng Fen), while his brother worked with Dents and then with Russells. Zheng himself worked for Dents under the patronage of his influential and later immensely wealthy fellow Xiangshan man, Xu Run. Having studied English at a night school established by the missionary John Fryer, Zheng worked for a tea company for six years as an interpreter before coming to Swire. Zheng had also invested in the Union Steam Navigation Company. His examination failure was no indication of his talents or future career as a keen observer of, and commentator on, current events – he was already starting to publish as he came to work for Swire – and Zheng learned much more than English and the business of the foreign houses he worked for.[23] He would become a vocal and influential advocate for China's need to wage 'commercial warfare' (*shangzhan*) against the foreign powers. His later book, *Wise Warnings to a Prosperous Age*, was one of the earliest works of political polemic that the future Communist leader Mao Zedong read.

If in Zheng we see one facet of the transition from the old trading world to the newer one, in Henry Bridges Endicott (c. 1843–95) we see another.[24] Endicott was the company's first shipping manager, having been poached by Lang from Augustine Heard – they doubled his salary – where he had had 'entire charge of their coast steamers'. He came from the same milieu as Zheng and was born not far away, in Macao, but on a distinctly different side of the Canton trade. The Endicott family were prominent in New England history, prominent in the China trade and so, therefore, prominent in the opium trade, and they were long associated with Heards. His great-uncle was buried in Macao's Protestant cemetery; his uncle William Endicott was latterly captain of one of Heards' opium hulks at Wusong; his father James Bridges Endicott, now buried in Hong Kong, had captained a receiving ship at Whampoa (Huangpu) off Macao, then became co-owner of a chandlery based in Hong Kong with a branch in Shanghai, and eventually had a large share of the Hongkong, Canton & Macao Steamboat Company. H. B. Endicott's mother was Ng Akew, a Tanka boatwoman, 'protected' by Endicott for about 10 years until his marriage in 1852 to a British woman, at which point he settled on her properties in Hong Kong and secured a husband. Ng was an opium trader in her own right, and not afraid to confront pirates when they took her goods.[25] Although Endicott was separated from his mother as a child, and sent to Kentucky for his schooling, this was, even so, quite a pedigree. Endicott returned to China in 1863, and first worked for his father's chandlery in Shanghai, and then as a clerk for Heards. His managers had noted his talents early on. With 'young Endicott' as a shipping clerk they relocated their own coastal shipping agency to Shanghai from Hong Kong. Despite his roughly 15 years in America, Endicott was fluent in Chinese, clearly had a strong understanding of Chinese social and cultural norms and was 'well acquainted with native shippers'.[26] After leaving Heards, he worked in this role for CNCo until his death in 1895.

Zheng Guanying later explained the rapid success of CNCo – it carried half the Yangzi's tonnage in 1873 – as resulting from effective use of his networks as well as a range of inducements to shippers and canvassers. He also reproduced a series of 'Ten principles of Steamship Company Management' that he attributed to Endicott, including fastidious attention to detail, intimate knowledge of personnel, ships and market details, planning and canvassing freights well ahead of time, and keeping the fleet efficient and modern. Zheng saw rational management principles and astute personnel hiring as the foundations of their success. But Endicott was also a pragmatist, and helped give shippers what they wanted, including long credit and discretion.[27] And Russells' Frank Forbes saw 'an undignified style of action' as the British firm held 'a big chin-chin [a banquet] to all the freight brokers, at which the foreign clerks assisted. Respectable Chinese laugh, as they ought to at this,' he concluded.[28] Pique aside, there is a clear racist slant to Forbes's comment. In his eyes, Europeans were demeaning themselves, publicly, to secure Chinese custom. Viewed more objectively, the new firm was announcing itself and directly introducing its staff to those whose custom they solicited. Racism, and the tensions between notions of dignity and status, and the simple realities of conducting a business for Chinese, in China, would long plague the foreign trading world.

Such attentiveness was vital, for, as the British consul in Zhenjiang put it in 1866, there had been a 'strange revolution' in the nature of Chinese-foreign commercial relations. The foreign merchant, he observed, was 'simply the carrier' of Chinese property. The comment was echoed by a colleague at Yantai (Chefoo). Chinese traders used the foreign ships now available to enter trades previously barred to them

> and settled at the ports opened to them through the intervention of Europeans, and by their industry and special knowledge of the country they have become the greatest competitors that the foreign merchants have to contend with in business.

The foreign trader was becoming a facilitator. Our ships are reliable and strong, ran the China Navigation Company's first advertisement in the *Shenbao* (itself part of that strange revolution – for this Chinese newspaper was owned by two Englishmen, the Major brothers from Southampton) – our captains and crews are experienced and know the Yangzi. 'You will be courteously received' at our offices.[29]

From Shanghai Zheng Guanying established a set of 'canvassing hongs', agencies in each of the Yangzi treaty ports, and later on the coast, to whom drumming up Chinese freight and the sale of passenger tickets was delegated on a commission basis. Some of these were agencies of the company itself (designated as such with the name Taikoo: Taikoo Zheng, Taikoo Chang, Taikoo Hui), some were his own. To encourage involvement, and to secure orders, Zheng also offered inducements – the right to nominate shipboard compradors for individual ships, for example, or rebates.[30] George Yuill, who joined the Hong Kong office in 1876 and acted as shipping clerk, later described his office's approach to securing Chinese freight: 'We have Chinese clerks who go round the town to visit the different hongs, and bring merchants to our office.' He also worked through agents, providing them with tickets for sale and paying them a commission. Such relationships were greased with credit and social interaction.[31] Ng Ahip 'went often' to visit shippers, building up knowledge of the business they did and their connections. Where he 'did not trust them on their own responsibility' he sought formal guarantees from those he did trust.

The new enterprise raised all sorts of puzzling questions for Swire, not least in designing ships for Chinese passengers. Nothing in the experience of John Swire & Sons had ever prepared them for this. Should London send out 'eatables and drinkables' for passengers? (No.) Would Chinese passengers need cabins? (Only for women, and only a few was the reply.) Foreign and Chinese passengers travelled in separate accommodation with separate kitchens. What about a purser? ('We suppose that you will employ a Celestial in that capacity.') Instead of a purser each steamer carried its own comprador whose duty it was to

> tally cargo on board and be responsible for its safe delivery at destinations. He also has to look after the native passengers providing them with chow chow, and be answerable to the ship for their passage money.

In effect the management of Chinese passengers and cargo was subcontracted to the comprador, who brought on his own staff and worked from an office on board.[32]

From the Union SNCo Swire took over the *Tunsin*, a 10-year-old ship built in London to run the Union blockade of the South, but which had come straight to China at the height of the boom in 1864, and the *Glengyle*, originally owned by Jardine Matheson. The three steamers contracted from Glasgow were shallow-draught side-wheel paddle steamers. Each was allotted the name of a Chinese city. The *Pekin* and *Shanghai* arrived in July and September 1873 respectively, and *Ichang* in April 1874. Another, *Hankow*, followed in 1874. The Yangzi route now offered the 'best means of river travelling civilization can afford', reported one Customs Service Commissioner. And, in an echo of Forbes's comment on Swire chin-chinning: 'Chinese travellers infinitely more cared for than the first class passengers on board those disgraceful little channel boats at home.' There seemed to such observers to be something discordant, if not distasteful in this. At the moment when the echoes of the post-Second Opium War triumphalism still reverberated, when Hankou consul Walter Henry Medhurst crowed that 'Foreigners are everything', the foreigner was using his power to provide fast and comfortable accommodation for Chinese merchants.[33] There were still things to learn, though. Why, asked London, are you waking Chinese through-passengers up in order to check their tickets when ships stop at night at intermediate ports. They have 'grumbled greatly' about this.[34]

This theme – the proper focus of the activities of foreign business – will recur. But in the meantime the situation on the river remained unstable. In February 1874, as the arrangements reached the previous summer had been fraying, a new agreement was reached. Although each company suspected the other was operating contrary to the understanding that Swire and Forbes had reached, it was in fact probably the energy with which Zheng and Endicott had developed the new company's business that was undermining the SSNCo's position, as well as the lacklustre performance of Russells' ageing comprador. Swire proposed a quite different arrangement, however: each company would run the same number of services, charge the same rates, pool the receipts and take half the total. Neither Swire nor Russells were in fact much interested in allowing competition.[35] What Russells said in public, Swire voiced in private. They both intended to bar the river from any meaningful competition for as long as possible. The new pooling agreement – which was a tightly kept secret – worked smoothly (and it ran largely to the benefit of Russells), but it gave CNCo space in which to grow, averted a possible return to a rates war and allowed them to pull back on the generous inducements offered in 1873.[36]

This general pattern of subcontracting the operational business of CNCo would later prove costly, but it was an established norm in foreign business operations in China, and there was strong pressure to maintain it. In shipping, long credit was extended to freight shippers. Settlement in some was being made only once annually, at Chinese new year, when debts were customarily paid off. This cannot but have helped attract custom. At CNCo it became a habit to leave the supervision and collection of these to the comprador, who was also 'by custom' the firm's 'native banker'. This would persist until 1884. As the comprador stood security for shippers, and was backed by other guarantees, this encouraged a culture of loose supervision, despite the dangers that were showcased frequently in court proceedings taken out by foreign firms trying to recoup debts.[37]

Such practices were reinforced by the need to keep customers sweet, for new competition could not be prevented from arriving. The most substantial started services in October 1873, and it was Chinese.

In fact, the Chinese opposition took two quite different forms, one indirect and the other with all the power of the Chinese state behind it. Firstly, Jardine Matheson, with a great deal of Chinese finance, set up the China Coast Steam Navigation Company in late 1872. The news of the emerging opposition to Russells on the Yangzi galvanised the company to consolidate its existing operations and create a new joint stock company. At least 20 per cent of the shares were owned by Chinese interests, and all the capital was raised in the treaty ports. Crucial to this was another Xiangshan merchant, Tang Jingxing (known as Tong King-sing), Jardines' comprador. For the moment Jardines stuck to the coast. In 1873, Tang resigned altogether to direct a new enterprise, known in English as the China Merchants Steam Navigation Company. This was a hybrid entity, established by government officials, backed by state loans, but also heavily financed by share issues and managed by merchants like Tang. It secured a hefty annual subsidy through award of the contract to ship Yangzi delta tribute rice from Shanghai to the Tianjin for the capital, and it was a powerful competitor on the river and on the coast. It employed foreign crews and foreign-built steamers. Nobody seriously believed that a Chinese steamer company would be a success, but, still, 'sometimes', John Samuel Swire wrote in 1874, 'I feel that we have got into a hornet's nest'.[38]

Hornets: while the business of a shipping operation brought with it the business of running warehouses, negotiating for land and access, managing more and more people, these abstractions brought risks and bother with them. Warehouses might be robbed; shippers disputed charges or claimed compensation for damaged or missing goods, or they had to be dunned for payments. More and more often the company found itself in the settlement courts, prosecuting or defending itself, sometimes prosecuting its staff or agents. And the treaty port newspapers are rich in detail of the unexpected problems people created. Snapshots from 1874 include the murder in September of a gangmaster overseeing the loading and unloading of CNCo ships at Hankou, and a boycott by the Cantonese Guild at Zhenjiang in July. The foreman had caught a labourer pilfering and punished him by forcing the man – who later confessed he had only signed up for the work for the opportunity it presented for theft – by making him stand in the sun. This it was alleged was done with the assent of the CNCo agents, Drysdale Ringer & Co. Afterwards the man told his persecutor not to rely on the Westerners' backing, because anyone could be 'meat on somebody's chopping block one day'. He later ambushed the gangmaster, slit his throat, and, satisfied, promptly handed himself in for punishment. At Zhenjiang a group of CNCo and SSNCo seamen had gone to a Cantonese opera house and refused to buy tickets, the resulting quarrel became a fight and two of the men were detained in the theatre. The CNCo agents, J. M. Canny, sent a group led by a foreigner – 'a black man' *Shenbao* pointedly noted – to rescue the men. These were, it was claimed, armed. The situation was defused but the Cantonese Guild demanded that Canny's man be dismissed, that the authorities investigate the incident, and also bundled in claims for compensation for missing and damaged goods. None of these claims being met, they ordered a boycott, and even Cantonese in Shanghai refused to load on CNCo for Zhenjiang.[39] However exceptional such an event might be, all had the capacity to injure a company's reputation, or spark a political controversy. Zhenjiang in particular would prove an awkward, crotchety place.

The question of how these Chinese lines fed international routes was always present. For Swire, the Ocean Steam Ship Company agency remained vital. It was 'the parent establishment,' Swire told Scott. Once the line was bedded in, Holts' long ships, with their distinctive tall blue funnels, proved a highly profitable venture. Holt started ordering new ships even before the *Ajax* had set sail back from Shanghai on its first voyage in January 1867. By 1875 he had 14 ships, and that year contracted three more for the China route. Each new batch benefited from design improvements that gave the company a strong technological advantage over its rivals into the late 1870s. As Holt put it in September 1866, 'the "mechanical" part of the problem' had been solved, 'the commercial one remaining'.[40] The opening of the Suez Canal cut 3,000 miles from the China trip, and 10–12 days from journeys that brought tea, tin and tobacco from Asia in ships that had carried out cotton and woollen goods. Holt sent a trusted captain to witness the opening and sent the first Blue Funnel ship through in March 1870, long before its chief rival, P&O.[41] Despite his spirited move into his 'China scheme', John Samuel Swire continued to think his partner overcautious as he himself looked for opportunities to expand.

Swire remained keen to expand the agency business. He had been in Hong Kong on 1 February 1867 when the Pacific Mail Steam

Navigation Company's *Colorado* arrived on the line's maiden run from San Francisco to the colony via Yokohama. There it was met by a 21-gun salute from an American warship in the harbour, answered by the shore batteries, twin salutes that heralded a new era in the history of the ocean highway from Asia to North America. As the reverberations faded and smoke drifted across the harbour, there will have been a moment to ponder. Having sailed across the Pacific himself in April 1874, he met Pacific Mail's president in New York, and after returning home unsuccessfully submitted a formal tender for the line's China and Japan agencies. Swire would continue to muse on the potential of opening a Pacific operation, even a Pacific line, on developing a 'great steam house', but the takeover of the American company by the powerful railroad interests seemed to put an end to any venture that might be launched. They could not be run against.[42]

We have few glimpses from this period of the Blue Funnel agency business as it was conducted at the Chinese ports, although the newspapers report the arrival and despatch of the liners. However, the Heard archive includes rich documentary evidence from its agents handling the business of the *Achilles* at Fuzhou in 1870/71.[43] From Shanghai the steamer decanted packages of Chinese medicine, rattan baskets, fungus, ginseng, cotton goods, iron and other merchandise, all consigned through Butterfield & Swire. Shippers at Fuzhou pitched for space across a hectic couple of days the ship was in port. '100 tons' please at £2 10s. a ton, and first refusal on another 100? Thirteen tons if we send them down today? Do you have room for 256 chests? The master worries that shippers are not sending down what they bid for. Phipps, Hickling & Co. deliver 768 half-chests of tea for London. 'Long Tom', the stevedore, needs paying for loading and unloading. Captain Russell sends a farewell note at 12.45 p.m. 'abreast of Sharp Peak': 'my time for the voyage Home commences now.' Don't take any bets on our passage, he adds (the ship set a record 52 days in 1869), though he is 'sanguine on making a good voyage'. 'I hope to have the pleasure of meeting you next year,' he signs off. He was back before the end of 1870 in fact. The journey to London took 55 days – twice as fast as any clipper that year – even though it lost 24 hours grounded on a mudbank at Port Said.

The Chinese operations loom large in the record of the activities of John Swire & Sons in the 1860s and 1870s, but it retained the strong Australian business and opened branches in America and in Manchester. Swire Brothers in New York was established in 1873 and for 10 years, working mostly at a loss, oversaw imports of tea from the Yokohama branch of Butterfield & Swire. The issue of what to do with these two offices was addressed inconclusively time and time again, but they remained open in the hope of future development.

We would have shut up shop 'years ago', Swire told his Yokohama manager, Edinburgh-born James Dodds, in 1875, if it was not for an expectation of Pacific steamers. That dream now faded, Swire put Dodds on a new footing and harassed the New York agent James Gibbes with instructions to get out and sell. But Gibbes 'has a retail mind', Swire would say, and this was no compliment. Self-confessed pride played a large part in the survival of the two operations. 'It goes against my grain,' Swire announced in 1876, 'to confess failure and retire from a trade.' Dodds, son of a parliamentary agent, largely surfaces in Yokohama's press as an able cricketer, prominent race club member, rower and club man. He would remain in charge at the port until 1904, 'too good living' taking over from the athletics. 'If he had to earn a living one day a week by running a Jinricksha & feeding upon the earnings,' mused Swire in 1879, 'he would be alright.'[44]

The Australian connection was slowly changing. The partnership of Lorimer, Marwood & Rome – which parted with Matthew Marwood in 1876 – continued to hold the White Star agency, and also energetically marketed the new shipments of tea 'carefully selected' and 'shipped expressly' by Butterfield & Swire's new *cha-see* at Fuzhou. The notices of wholesale auctions of 'CONGOUS, TRUE KAISOW, RIPE PEKOE, RICH PEKOE SOUCHONG, CHOICE PAKLING' have their own sweet poetry, but this was a prosaic and it was an evolving business. The Fuzhou *cha-see*, Henry Robert Smith, twice visited Melbourne and Sydney by way of securing a 'colonial education' – to find out what the traders there wanted. But although John Samuel Swire would declare in 1876 that the tea trade was 'not a millinery business', that 'Congou will retain its hold on public favour when "Devonshire hats" are obsolete' he was proved quite wrong.[45] In the 1870s, Chinese green teas began to lose their place in teapots overseas to Indian and Ceylon black leaves. Tastes changed, and this was hastened by aggressive marketing campaigns impugning the safety of Chinese green leaves, dyed such, it was insinuated, with poisonous chemicals.

The John Swire & Sons network grew. In 1870 the firm officially relocated its headquarters to London, where an office had formally been opened in Billiter Street in the City in July 1870.[46] It was probably not a coincidence that the move came at roughly the same time as the opening of the firm in Hong Kong. The Liverpool office was now a branch left under the management of one of the firm's cashiers, Thomas Woodward. Attached to it, Swire family cousin J. Porter O'Brien focused quite profitably on the business of bottling Dagger Stout for the Australian market, a business line whose continuing success John Samuel Swire thought simply a 'fluke'. But even the Blue Funnel agency was handled from Billiter Street from November 1870 onwards.[47] In 1870 John Samuel Swire sold off his stable of hunters, ridden with the Cheshire in the previous winter's season, and by the time of the 1871 census was living in modest style in a very modern apartment block in Victoria Street in London.

The expansion of operations brought with it an increase in the number of staff, and a dilution of the Liverpool flavour of the business. The move to London did see Swire bring to the capital a core of long-established clerical staff from the former head office, which suggests something about the still intimate world of the firm in this period. But the backgrounds of the 34 or so men who joined in the 1870s with a view to being sent out to work in Asia as mercantile assistants show a significant swing towards recruitment from London.[48] Most of these were recruited in the first half of the decade. The occupations of their fathers give an indication of their origins: merchant, insurance underwriter, accountant, cotton dealer, barrister, surgeon, clergyman, stockbroker. They seem rarely to have had an existing overseas connection. Edwin Mackintosh, and a clerk, A. E. Turner, hired in 1872, who had been born in Ceylon where his father was a sugar planter, were early exceptions. Although the firm was 'anxious to promote our own people if possible' – that is, from the London office of John Swire & Sons – this does seem to have been an exception rather than a rule at first. One of these was William Drought Harrison, Liverpool-born son of a teacher, who sailed out in 1868 after at least two years in the office in Liverpool. Some clearly had experience with other firms before they signed contracts with Swire: J. C. Bois was a banker's clerk, John Amos Blogg a cotton broker's, Arthur Burrows clerked for a shipbroker. Two men joined with substantial China experience. Silk trader Frederick

Gamwell had worked in Shanghai from 1860 to 1874, would rapidly become John Samuel Swire's chief collaborator in London and was quickly admitted into the partnership. Herbert Smith had worked for Jardine Matheson for at least five years before joining Swires. Tea tasters demanded a premium in pay. One or two experienced men were appointed out in Asia by the partners in Shanghai and Hong Kong.

We know much more overall about the men who sailed east, but we might pause to think a little more about those who pushed pens and minded the accounts in Liverpool and London. 'No dramatic interest attaches to the obscure clerk,' B. G. Orchard, the first chronicler of their kind in Liverpool, claimed in 1871, but these were the men who staffed John Swire & Sons. There were clerks and there were clerks. Orchard essayed that there were clerks 'among the scented dandies who patrol Broad Street about three p.m.', and 'the rakish swells who drink bitter beers and play billiards round the Exchange', yet also a large proportion among 'the meanly dressed, anxious-faced, half-fed mortals who dine in Wapping at the four-penny hall'. Orchard calculated that there were 17,000 clerks employed in Liverpool in 1870, and that the average firm employed four of them. The Temple, the building on Liverpool's Dale Street to which John Swire & Sons moved in 1865, housed 49 firms and 224 clerks, and six of these were Swire men, two of them juniors, and another seven men were also on the books.[49] Their salaries ranged from £12 a month to barely a quarter of that. They formed part of a steadily changing world of employment in Britain in which the proportion of the urban workforce engaged in office administration increased in size. Into their office came news from the east, in letters, in the weekly edition of the *London & China Telegraph*, in the shape of arrivals on the Blue Funnel steamers, or gift boxes of tea requested by the Senior. They booked passages for those travelling to Asia, shipped out clocks and stationery for the company offices there, despatched telegrams and perhaps learned a little of the China-side lingo that China returnees such as the Blue Funnel captains spoke: *cha-sees*, pidgin, chin-chin. The permeation of Liverpool's commercial world with overseas trade hardly made this unusual. But the greater bulk of the port's traffic still came from North America – some 30 per cent of it – South America and the European continent. Just six in a hundred ships arriving in 1870 came from the 'Far East'.[50] What the firm's senior clerks like John Ball or Thomas Salisbury made of the directions taken by the operations of their principals we cannot know, but there in the Temple they had these glimpses of another world.

By 1882 there were 15 staff in the London office, overseen in the first instance by John Ball, who had worked for the firm since 1858. We get some traces of the texture of life in the offices from the archives. A man receives the text of a pledge he is expected to sign to curb his gambling habit. Salisbury is ticked off for lackadaisical attendance and for taking overlong visits when he does come to the office to a 'neighbouring establishment', perhaps to drink 'bitter beers'. A clerk, 20 years in the firm, is advanced money to help meet debts raised by his wife's illness, and a gratuity to help his son's schooling. Ball is reprimanded for lax supervision of petty cash which allowed a junior to pilfer small sums. A man is fast-tracked to China to effect a separation for an unhappily married couple. Swire's copyist is sent off to Port Said for his health, the firm paying (but not, it was made clear, covering his wine bill). It did 'poor Young' no good, however: he seems to have died before the voyage was over.[51] The clerks expect gratuities, and some with 'visions of China' clamour for a chance to sail east. But 'really', wrote Swire in 1879, 'I cannot make good the dreams of all in our employ'.[52] Most of those recruited into the general staff of the London office will be disappointed. The clerks start at a salary of about £70 a year in London, roughly average for the era, though John Samuel Swire thought his staff were paid 'considerably higher' than the prevailing rates for such work. Those who went to China were paid £300 in the first year, rising over a five-year engagement to £450, board and lodging provided in addition, and the cost of the passage out. The odd man leaves to take another post that will get him out more swiftly, or goes to work for associated firms, such as Mansfield's, Blue Funnel's agents in Singapore. Minor controversy or incident generates records, of course, when routine leaves little trace, and this skews the picture we have, for in the main we know very little otherwise about what went on in Dale Street or Billiter Street. But we do know that John Samuel Swire himself was involved in many of these arrangements, the company still small enough for its senior partner to be involved in managing the men who staff the firm. He kept staff records in small notebooks and paid close attention to even the minor detail of office expenses.

Benjamin Guinness Orchard claimed that 'half the partnership firms in Liverpool twenty years old contain a partner who was once a clerk'. There was a period when this was the pattern at John Swire & Sons.[53] The term 'clerk' is unhelpfully general, and John Samuel Swire would himself distinguish between partners, managers, clerks and ordinary clerks, but some of the men appointed early on as the agents of Butterfield & Swire in China were later brought into the firm as partners: William Lang in 1869, W. D. Harrison and J. H. Scott in 1874, Gamwell in 1875 and Edwin Mackintosh in 1876, and William Hudson Swire retired from the partnership that year. Both brothers nurtured the growth of the capital of the younger partners – who had little to bring to the partnership at first – wiping off their losses in 1876, for example. Harrison's elevation would prove a mistake and William Lang would always remain of erratic value. But the other partners proved useful. With his brother in poor health, John Samuel Swire needed to bring men on to share the responsibilities of running the growing firm. But he remained the senior partner, as he made clear more than once, and expected his 'orders' to be obeyed. This was framed as a shared adherence to the agreed partnership articles, but this was never a partnership of equals.[54]

We know much more about John Samuel Swire's energetic networking in the capital in the 1870s than about the routine business of the firm, and well might he network. Swire had ruffled many feathers. The Butterfield withdrawal in 1868 caused 'malicious' rumours to circulate that the firm was in serious trouble. 'Butterfield is said to have died from chagrin at his loss'; it was said it was 'doomed'. It was tarred by association with Alexander Collie and his 'irregular finance'. 'We are informed on good authority that Butterfield and Swire have had to obtain assistance', the London partner in a Yokohama firm wrote in August 1873. Others disagreed: 'they are A1 people,' wrote the Hongkong & Shanghai Bank manager in Shanghai in July 1870. But these tales were persistent. Swire gave short shrift to such talk, and did not forget or forgive those who acted on it, but took measures nonetheless to demonstrate the firm's soundness.[55] When he felt Alfred Holt needed to stand up for his line's safety record, Swire presented the text of a letter to *The Times* for him to complete and send, and it duly appeared under Holt's name.[56] The aggressive entry of Butterfield & Swire into the shipping trades seemed hurried and ungentlemanly. Ham-fisted attempts to browbeat an agency out of the Hongkong, Canton & Macao Steamboat Company in 1875 went awry. 'They demanded the agency,' wrote the firm's marine superintendent in astonishment. 'Gentlemen, ... we beg to tender our services as General Agents,' wrote Harrison in June 1875. 'Failing our appointment we shall be compelled to enter into active competition.' It was, responded the company's chairman, 'almost like saying "Your money or your life"'. (In fact it was Harrison's life; he died a few days later.) There was 'a strength of will and a description of character' which British officials might learn from, thought one Singapore newspaper. But it was a 'far from modest' note from a 'young and ambitious firm'.[57]

Reputation was also a matter of style and confident performance, and, after all, as Swire started to muse, 'we ought to be the greatest house in China'. Although keeping costs low was a pillar of John Samuel Swire's business strategy (along with selling immediately on receipt), James Henry Scott at Hong Kong was too spendthrift for his liking.[58] The hong needed to be 'respectably and liberally conducted,' he wrote in 1876. It needed an appropriate social prominence to complement its physical presence. Likewise Lorimer was involved in helping ship to William Lang in Shanghai Australian horses for his stable. He was furious to learn that Scott's predecessor Harrison was hastened to his end by 'drink and stupidly offensive morality', which had brought to Swire's ears 'reflections on his character from a community neither over-moral – nor over righteous' and had threatened 'disgrace' to the firm. The community had, nonetheless, marked Harrison's death with flags at half-mast across the harbour at Hong Kong, being rather less averse to turning a blind eye than perhaps Swire assumed.[59] Still, reputation mattered. Swire could win over Albert Heard in Hong Kong with an hour or two's discussion, but he was, of course, mostly working in London. Others ran the firm in China.

They were running it at a moment of change, too. The 'strange revolution' was not quite as odd as it seemed. It was the logical consequence of a pragmatic approach to the opportunities offered by the status of foreign subjects and foreign enterprises by the treaties. Chinese and foreigners alike made rational use of the distortions these introduced. At its most outrageous the new arrangements invited the passing off as foreign-owned goods or property that belonged to Chinese. 'Lie hongs', as they were known to consuls, were firms that claimed foreign status as they were ostensibly owned by a foreign national, a British subject for example, but which were simply working under a flag of convenience. All this required a consideration: commissions, fees, a bribe, a bottle even: the lowliest beachcomber drinking his way along the China coast had at least his nationality to rent out this way. Officials did their best to root out what they termed 'abuses'. But the entire structure of foreign commercial enterprise in China worked under the protection of the treaties, was based in ports opened and protected by treaty (and by foreign armed force) and offered services to Chinese customers and investors through those same privileges and for decades worked in markets that would have been closed to it without those agreements.

What John Swire & Sons was steadily undertaking was a partial transformation of itself into an enterprise that was integrated into this new melded world of trade in China. Once an Australian House, and with little otherwise to distinguish it from the other 50 or so shipping firms in Liverpool or that city's 350 merchants, John Swire & Sons now owned hulks on the Yangzi, properties in prime locations in Shanghai and in Hong Kong, and worried about the peaceful slumbers of Chinese passengers on its steamers. This was entwined into a network that included the Yokohama and New York offices, and the work for Blue Funnel and White Star that yoked it together. It continued its adventures in tea, but started to find the silk trade too difficult, and still shipped out east cottons from Manchester, woollen goods from Yorkshire, and to Australia, among many other goods: stout, rum, iron gates, boiler plates, fencing wire, slates, candles, currants – most profitably of all these, it turned out – raisins, nuts, caustic soda, herrings and sardines. But the Swire enterprise was steadily embedding itself into the Asian scene, transforming itself from an agency business into a different kind of company, and a company that remained tightly controlled from London even as it changed. It also began to plan the building in Hong Kong, a long way from Liverpool, of what would eventually become a small town. This was because John Samuel Swire, ever restless, took a shine to the notion that what the company now needed was a sugar refinery.

Sweet Smell of Hong Kong

'Of course I am aware that he hates me like poison.'[1] It is odd to find that a landmark enterprise had its roots in such rancour, but the Taikoo Sugar Refinery – a venture that saw John Swire & Sons build the largest such installation in Asia, and the second largest in the world, start up what became a small company town in Hong Kong and foster development of a 'colony' there of men from Scotland's sugar town Greenock – owed much of its impetus to bitter rivalry with Jardine Matheson & Co. This is not to say that it was not also a level-headed and robust initiative which aimed, as John Samuel Swire told prospective shareholders, to 'comfort our declining years', but 'nothing has pleased me more than beating Keswick', he had written in 1879 when rivalry between the principals of the two firms was intense. It was at this point that he began exploring the possibilities of sugar, and beating Jardine Matheson was part of the objective.

Jardines, the 'Princely Hong', whose then Hong Kong partner, William Keswick, hosted a private dinner for Prince Alfred, the Duke of Edinburgh, on his first night in Hong Kong when visiting in 1869, was a power in the colony and across the treaty ports where, by 1879, the firm had the greater part of its almost two dozen offices and agencies. With the collapse in 1875 of their old Canton trade rivals Dent & Co. – 'English nabobs' thought Swire – Jardines was the longest surviving British company in China, and had continued to diversify its range of operations away from the core business of opium, which had made the firm during the partnership of Keswick's great-uncle William Jardine and James Matheson, and which had undone the Canton trade system. Keswick sat on the Hong Kong governor's Legislative Council, was chairman of the Chamber of Commerce, the City Hall Committee and of the Hong Kong Club. The extensive company complex at East Point with a modestly sized, but nonetheless grand, No. 1 house (with separate summer residence on the Peak) was a real centre of power in the colony. They were the 'all powerful Dictators of the Far East' noted one Hong Kong editorial in 1882, into whose hands seemed to fall one enterprise after another. We have 'interfered with and upset "divine rights",' noted John Samuel Swire to Alfred Holt in December 1879 (not the last time he put it like that). 'I should have been popular with the China merchants had I not entered the China trade, or having entered it, had I kept a back seat, and wished for promotion through death.'[2]

Such was not his style. Swire actually disclaimed being on 'unamiable' terms with anybody 'save J. M. & Co.', but that exception at times disrupted the smooth running of operations in China. 'JM&Co phobia' was shared by other partners, too, and while sometimes suspicion as to the intentions and role of the older house was unfounded, it generally was an active competitor, and sometimes simply played an obstructive role, driving up land prices purely to harass Swires, or using its presence on other company boards or municipal councils to oppose the firm.[3] But it, too, had to adapt to changing markets, the evolution of China's commercial culture and a bumpy political environment, and both companies were always ready to look into new initiatives.

Personalities aside – although difficult in fact to keep aside – the original source of the problem was the river, and it was firstly the new Chinese opposition that appeared in 1873 – the China Merchants SNCo. Swire had underestimated the tenacity and strength of his new opponents. If he and others had been aware of the nationalistic debates crystallised by Zheng Guanying's writings, they might have been readier for the degree of opposition that the Chinese firm provided. It was ably managed by the former Jardine Matheson comprador Tang Jingxing, who spoke fluent English, and even if it was not actively heeding Zheng's call for commercial warfare to save China, its managers had no intention of respecting the assumed divine rights on the river of the British – any of them.

The Yangzi challenge was next intertwined with a Canton problem. This was a new sphere of operations for Butterfield & Swire who now managed from Hong Kong a new shipping business on the coast and wanted a share of the business between the colony and the Chinese provincial capital. In late 1874, John Samuel Swire had bought three new ships on the cheap for coastal services. This venture was largely a partnership with John Scott, James Henry Scott's shipbuilder brother, and Henry Isaac Butterfield, one of his late partner's brothers, as Swire used his personal network to bring new allies and their capital into the collaboration with Holts.[4] The vessels had been commissioned for trade with Spain, but political strife there rendered them unusable. Once again, political events elsewhere in the world prompted an initiative in China. The new services were set up as a separate company, the Coast Boats Ownery, which carved out a successful charter operation shipping soya beans for Chinese merchants from Niuzhuang in the north to Shantou (Swatow), where they were milled and processed into fertiliser.[5] With Blue Funnel steamers stopping in Hong Kong on their journey to and from Yokohama and Shanghai, a Canton operation also seemed a logical feeder route, and Holt himself pushed for it.

There was an obstacle, in the shape of the successful business of the Hongkong, Canton & Macao Steamboat Company (the 'Boat Company' as it was known), that had been running steamers on the route since 1865. In the first instance it seemed logical to try to secure the agency for the existing line. The opportunity appeared to be opening, as the current agents, the old-established firm Augustine Heard, were now clearly heading for a crash. As they did so Butterfield & Swire misguidedly tried out themselves a tactic that had so notably failed Russells in April 1873. Then, late on the evening of the day before the formal transfer of the Union Steamship Company assets to Swire, Russells had had an ultimatum delivered to William Lang demanding that he sell up or face the rates war that, in fact, Swires had prepared for. As we have seen, the result was a failure. In June 1875, Butterfield & Swire's then manager in Hong Kong, William Drought Harrison, presented a démarche to the Boat Company's board. This was so ill-judged – 'discourteous in the extreme,' said the chairman to applause at a shareholder meeting, printing the correspondence for good measure – that John Samuel Swire sent out to Hong Kong a letter of apology to forward on to the directors.[6] It was, of course, no way to secure the desired agency, which went to Russells instead. But the problem was compounded by the fact that the *Ichang*, the steamer that was thereafter run by Swires in opposition on the route, was old and inefficient, and thereby too costly to win the struggle, and the protracted four-year-long conflict proved more widely unsettling because the chairman of the Boat Company was, naturally, William Keswick.[7]

In the north significant changes had also rapidly unfolded. In December 1876 Russells opened discussions to sell up, and their 16 steamers and well-sited shore properties were bought by China Merchants.[8] Sheer numbers of ships alone suggested that they might well now be an even stronger opposition. Foreign prejudice, however, was such that few believed a Chinese-managed enterprise stood much chance, or concluded that any progress it did make was due to foreign involvement or advice or 'extravagant official support'.[9] For it was, after all, a government-owned enterprise, with that significant annual state subsidy in the shape of the northern grain shipment contract. But China Merchants was run by a particularly astute and capable team, which had learned much in the past from working for and collaborating with foreign traders and competing against them, and they proved resolute. John Samuel Swire had assumed that the pool agreement reached with Russells which had delivered the 50:50 split, and a generally steady level of good profits for the China Navigation Company, could be continued now that the Russells fleet was running for China Merchants. But the Chinese had 10 steamers on the Yangzi, while CNCo had three. Tang Jingxing suggested that his firm should have two-thirds of the pool, Swires declined, and in response a costly rate war was fought for most of 1877.

The political context more widely was poisonous. In August 1874, Augustus Raymond Margary, a young British consul well known in Shanghai, had been despatched up the Yangzi River on an SSNCo steamer to then travel overland to meet a British expedition testing the route from newly occupied Burma into China's south-western Yunnan province. British diplomats had been tight-lipped about the actual objectives of the mission when they had secured permission for it in the Chinese capital, and they took little note of the fact that Yunnan had only recently emerged from a long-running Muslim rebellion which left local officials wary of outsiders. In addition, a Japanese military incursion in Taiwan rightly concerned the Qing. This was ostensibly a mission to exact revenge, to 'punish' Paiwan indigenes who had attacked shipwreck survivors, but it was clearly a probe that might presage conquest. As Margary travelled upriver on his way to Yunnan on a Russells steamer, one of their 'American river palaces' he called it, Qing troops travelled down.[10]

In a period of heightened tensions, it seems almost inevitable that Margary would meet with fatal mishap. He was killed by local levies in obscure circumstances close by the border the following February. But there was nothing obscure about the fact that his head was placed on public view afterwards, and the British were outraged. Out of this wretched incident Sir Thomas Wade, the British Minister, fashioned a serious diplomatic crisis. Some thought it all threatened a new war and he did little to disabuse Qing officials of this notion, and this was used to extract a series of new concessions from them in the 1876 Chefoo Convention.[11] In addition, although the killing was wholly unplanned and accidental, Britons in China firmly believed that it must have been ordered at the highest levels of the Qing state. This quixotic and unusual faith in the efficiency and capacity of the Qing to order a killing 1,400 miles from Beijing fuelled a wider belief that the status quo established by the Second Opium War was under threat, and that the Qing was pushing back against the foreigners. In shipping, this took the shape of a firm belief that the state was working to support China Merchants to fight the foreigners. 'It becomes difficult … to make out what is left of the plain and simple stipulations of the Treaty of Tientsin,' sighed the *North China Herald*, when the SSNCo sale was unveiled and the largest foreign company on the river vanished overnight.[12] Talk in Shanghai had it that the sale was all part of this grand plan to drive the foreigner out of China.

Another facet of this assault, for Swire, seemed more pointed and direct. This grew out of an 1876 request by the Imperial Maritime Customs that CNCo temporarily abandon its use of its receiving hulk at Zhenjiang, the *Cadiz*, while investigations were made into the cause of a whirlpool that had appeared shortly after it was first moored in February 1874.[13] The company refused. This seemingly obscure hydrographical mystery dragged on for over four years, saw Britons serving different states disputing the nature of the current of a Chinese river at this exact point 150 miles from the sea, experimenting with bottles and floats, drawing up charts, plans and cross-sections, the British Minister, Wade – still in bellicose mood – screaming at Robert

Hart the Customs Inspector-General in Beijing that 'he'd never been so outraged in his life', that 'by the living god he'd be damned if he'd stand it', all resulting in lengthy reports, three pamphlets, much newspaper comment and protests that worked their way up through British and Chinese state bureaucracies, with John Samuel Swire signing a formal letter of protest to the British Secretary of State for Foreign Affairs.[14]

This is the first time in the Swire archive that a clear and sustained resort to diplomatic support can be found, and it is also almost the first occasion on which politics – Chinese or otherwise – is mentioned at all in the company's archives. It is a sign of the discomfort involved that the letter seems awkwardly set out and self-consciously formal. This was not how John Samuel Swire had liked to operate. But the partners in China and their agents were more accustomed to calling on their consuls (and used the possessive routinely). They lived side by side with the diplomats in the hothouse world of the treaty ports. Their families intermarried (William Keswick's younger brother James Johnstone Keswick married Marion Parkes, daughter of British Minister to China, Harry Parkes). They had frequent opportunity to talk with them, were required to register with them as individuals, to register their property with them and thought little of calling on them to support sometimes even trifling claims for compensation. They discussed consuls' individual merits (and more commonly their perceived shortcomings) and their collective incompetence (in their eyes): for consuls were never strong enough, assertive enough or quick enough for the British trading community, ever ill served as they saw it in return for their taxes (which, being China-based, very few of them paid). Despite these tensions, British consuls were embedded in the commercial landscape in a way that was quite removed from the trading world in Britain.[15]

The problem at Zhenjiang was that the placing of the hulk, through which CNCo cargoes were transhipped, and where they were inspected by customs staff stationed on board for the purpose, had created a tidal effect that from December 1874 onwards carved out an enormous gash on the Bund. At one stage this collapsed to a point where the 40-foot-wide road was narrowed to just over 12 and cracks appeared in buildings fronting the road. What began as a routine request from the customs and local officials to help resolve the problem rapidly escalated into a diplomatic controversy. The company refused to move the ship to allow tests to take place, arguing that it was unnecessary, for their own consulting engineer had investigated and cleared the hulk – as well he might – and that it would interrupt business at a point when that business was still being established. Naval surveyors were invited to look as well as their ships passed by the port, and they too confirmed the company's own findings. The result was stalemate.

In May 1876, after a succession of warnings, the Commissioner of Customs ordered the removal of customs staff from the hulk, meaning that all CNCo cargoes had to be taken to the customs jetty and could not use *Cadiz*. For 11 months, rather than impair its business this way, the firm simply suspended cargo business at the port, and when it did resume it demanded a precise figure of £11,075 5s. 7d. compensation for lost business. For Qing administrators this was simply a matter of China's sovereignty, and the authority of its staff over the river. This was entirely in accord with the treaties, as they understood them. But the company's agent (who had already blithely ignored its agreement with the Municipal Council at Zhenjiang on the siting and size of the bridge connecting the hulk to the shore) was disinclined to co-operate, and was backed in this by British officials. The dispute was fuelled by the obstreperous Shanghai consul, Walter Henry Medhurst, who claimed that customs staff had overreached themselves and that the real aim was to dislodge British rights, not a British hulk. 'If they can deprive one house of their business,' wrote Lang from Shanghai, in a request to the Secretary of State for support, 'is there any limit to the restrictions they can impose' and thereby make 'the Chinese government arbiters what foreigners shall conduct business in their country'. And for John Samuel Swire this was all about China Merchants, not simply the 'arbitrary action of the Chinese officials'. The company 'starts with the avowed intention of crushing foreign steam interests', by fair means or foul, such as this one.[16]

The diplomats and many others lost sight of the *Cadiz*, a 1,000-ton former P&O steamer bought by China Navigation after a busy life on the coast.[17] Wade and his staff held the Chinese responsible for maintaining the river frontage of the British concession, and at the same time held that they had no right to 'arbitrarily' order British subjects as to their business. The company's agent in Zhenjiang, John Macnamara Canny, was steadily heading towards bankruptcy, and might well have been acting bullishly to demonstrate his usefulness to his principals in Shanghai. He huffed and puffed and fashioned himself as a 'Civis Britannicus', signing letters to the public press with that moniker, drawing on former British Foreign Secretary Lord Palmerston's infamous assertion in 1850 that the reach of British power would extend to British subjects wherever they might reside, as a Roman might have claimed his rights as a citizen anywhere within the empire with the phrase *civis romanus sum* (I am a Roman citizen). British power, then, would recognise no borders if its subjects needed defending. Customs staff were largely bewildered, initially, at this loftily principled response to their attempts to serve foreign trade by protecting a stretch of river bank from collapsing. And the busy steam life of the Yangzi caused other problems of which this was but one. The correspondence from Zhenjiang alone at this time touches on such accidents as steamers (including one of CNCo's) running down slower moving salt junks and other small craft at night; there were disputes over Royal Navy surveying on the river; and Zhenjiang itself was in rapid decline as a treaty port. Its British land-renters were lobbying to be permitted to rent property to Chinese – then forbidden under the Land Regulations – while several, including Canny's keeper on board the *Cadiz*, ran profitable sidelines fronting Chinese companies in return for a fee (and thereby masking Chinese goods as British).[18]

Throughout most of the period of the dispute China Navigation was in hot competition with China Merchants. Despite its now seemingly overwhelming strength in numbers of ships and its government subsidy, the Chinese firm was not faring well against the British. For a start, a consular report from Shanghai noted, they had got 'an exceedingly bad bargain' paying too much, too readily, when the American fleet was offered to them. Throughout 1877 CNCo's steamers came downriver from Hankou full and China Merchants' struggled for cargoes, and the line was much 'more economically worked', he reported. China Navigation was able to run 'boat for boat' against China Merchants despite having fewer ships, through rapid unloading and loading 'by a perfectly organised system of coolie gangs' within 24 hours, even at busy Shanghai. CNCo's Chinese passengers showed a 'marked preference' for the line and Chinese shippers 'met with more consideration and courtesy' from its agents and staff – as its first publicity had promised. They also enjoyed much less 'prying' from roving Chinese tax officials into the nature, quantity and destination of their freight (on which transit taxes might well be due). The departure of China Merchants' ships might unexpectedly be held up to allow Qing officials travelling on business to join them. The hybrid nature of the company gained from official subsidies, but lost from such official interference. Zheng Guanying and H. B. Endicott's management of the line, its passengers and shippers and staff seemed to be proving its worth. But still, for all its inefficiencies and the 'worn out' boilers and hulls of some of its fleet, the 32 ships run by China Merchants offered a substantial opposition, and freight rates from Shanghai had gone into free fall, each company reportedly taking what it could get.[19]

It was against this fractious background that the Zhenjiang hulk dispute was conducted. But, after hundreds of letters were exchanged, tempers lost, expertise and integrity impugned, the British government's law officers in London concluded that the Chinese actually had a perfect right – as they knew they had – both to request, and to order, the removal of *Cadiz*. Sir Thomas Wade had brought his case back to London in person in the summer of 1877 'in anything but a good humour' it was reported.[20] Guo Songtao, the Chinese Minister in the British capital – itself an innovation, for he was the first – had pressed the case adeptly and the legal finding was that under international law the Chinese administered their river, not Civis Britannicus. This statement of the seeming obvious was nonetheless one more signal that the wilder days of table-thumping, bullying Qing officials, vowing to 'smash' the customs, and shipping a small fleet up the Yangzi to press British points with the threat of violence might be starting to pass. Robert Hart also thought the dispute finally showed the Qing the independence of the customs from the British and demonstrated its subordination to its Chinese paymasters.[21] So the Earl of Derby wrote to John Swire & Sons in February 1878 regretting that Her Majesty's Government would no longer press the case, and that it would not support that detailed claim for compensation.[22] The *Cadiz*, throughout all this, had actually stayed where it had been moored, but after this decision it was finally, temporarily moved. The Bund was shored up, but the waterfront would continue to degenerate, steadily, inexorably, and Zhenjiang rather sank as a site of foreign trade.

For John Samuel Swire the black hands behind China Merchants were actually Jardines'. Jardines were encouraging the Boat Company in their fight, 'to frighten us from going on the Tientsin line', and were 'doubtless telling Tang Jingxing that if he makes peace on the River he wld have opposition to Tientsin'; they were fighting a proxy 'battle' – the language used was all combative – 'at the expense of others', which they had denied to his face. 'Thro' fear of the future', felt Swire, Jardines were incapable of dealing 'in an honest manner with us'. His letters to Shanghai and to Hong Kong at the time are full of such comments.[23]

The reality was, nonetheless, that it was the China Merchants and China Navigation who were competing on the Yangzi, and across the year CNCo continued to lower its rates in order to do so. This got neither of them anywhere, and William Lang, the partner in Shanghai, was an obtuse and passive man who failed to make any attempt at finding a resolution locally. So, in October 1877, Swire set out once more for China, sailing from Liverpool on a Blue Funnel steamer with Philip Holt and leaving a two-page list of telegraph ciphers covering every possible combination of agreement on 'amicable arrangements' that might be made on the disputed routes, or of the sale of CNCo or the Ownery to its rivals. The result, mediated by a British barrister (for neither company would visit the other's offices), was wired back as 'Tenotomy': oddly representing 'a favourable arrangement' for a joint purse operation on the Yangzi with China Merchants which would run three services a week to CNCo's two, but with the Chinese taking 55 per cent of the earnings and the British 45 per cent.[24] Swire's tactic was to persuade Tang that he had simply been playing Jardine Matheson's game for them, that opposition was 'worse than useless' and an alliance offered additional benefits, for Swires and Holts would be at CMCo's service in London and Liverpool. Coincidentally he was advocating the type of policy that Robert Hart and others pursued, articulating a position based on what they claimed was – and indeed they believed to be – a perfect alignment of British and Chinese interests. 'Working in amity with the British flag,' Swire argued, would actually serve to allow CMCo to achieve its own objectives, fostering China's trade and making them both 'lots of money'. Tang, who was no fool, and no dupe, was certainly capable of making his own decisions about the utility or otherwise of working with CNCo, and he chose to do so. The new agreements worked 'beautifully', Swire reported. A period of calm ensued.[25] Swire next inspected the firm's river and coastal branches and agencies, nosed around the Upper Yangzi as far as Yichang, and went to Yokohama and then on to Australia to talk stout and tea with

James Lorimer, spending the best part of a year away from London (and experiencing the dangerous discomfort of a shipwreck on the way).

This mission of peace to talk with Tang Jingxing proved successful on that score, but at the same time, John Samuel Swire 'rubbed [Jardines] up the wrong way' during his visit. He was, he wrote gleefully, quite pleased that he did: 'we've cut them down completely.' The company's then Shanghai partner, Francis Bulkeley Johnson was 'awfully sore', and felt that the two firms were 'trying to squeeze' Jardines out.[26] Wounded *amour propre*, 'hurt' occasioned by his 'plain manner of speaking' – which on the evidence of his letters could be very plain indeed – made it difficult to come in any speedy fashion to the inevitable resolution of the problems that flared between the rival British companies.[27] Their senior partners were conscious of their dignity, and public reputation and character. None of them trusted each other. We might see this as a drearily timeless clash of ego between successful men, but it was a product also of the specific social world in which they lived, born as they were in the 1820s and 1830s, another country in time where reputation and character mattered: dignity was the currency of their lives and their businesses. The 1860s had even seen intense public debate in Britain about honour and even the necessity or otherwise of a recourse to duelling.[28] Swire, Keswick and Johnson were hardly likely to resort to physical violence, but they were gentlemen, their language was martial and their notions of honour hugely affected the ways they acted and allowed themselves to be seen. Notions of 'face' and dignity may have shaped the negotiations between Tang Jingxing and Swire in December 1877, but they shaped, too, always, the way in which the British themselves interacted.

And the Jardine Matheson challenge was really only just starting to evolve. The company was venturing into new businesses, most strikingly making loans to the Qing court and covertly building a passenger railway from Wusong at the mouth of the Huangpu River to Shanghai.[29] This way they hoped to bounce the Chinese into a programme of railway development. But after some controversy and dispute, Qing officials bought the line, shut it down and shunted the equipment off to rust away on a beach in Taiwan. Foreign observers decried what they assumed was the ignorance and backwardness of the Chinese, for whom in fact the matter was again simply one of sovereignty, as it had been in the *Cadiz* case, for they perfectly understood the utility of railways. Steamships were proving a more reliable and profitable prospect for

Jardines, however. News of the launch of CNCo had prompted them to build up their own shipping operation, the China Coast Steam Navigation Company, mostly funded by capital raised in China. This ran services from Shanghai to Fuzhou, and more frequently to Tianjin. China Merchants also ran on this northern route, and after the joint purse compromise on the Yangzi with Swires, they came to a similar arrangement with Jardines. In 1877, however, on the expiration of the 10-year agreement they had signed with Russells in Hong Kong, Jardines began to look closely at the possibilities offered by shipping. In 1879 they ordered two steamers from a Shanghai shipyard to run on the Yangzi. When John Samuel Swire heard this he was outraged. Johnson, he believed, had promised to give 'due notice' of any such initiative.[30] Swire had been punctilious in not threatening Jardine interests, tearing H. B. Endicott off a strip for a 'trifling' transgression of CNCo's commitment not to run passengers or freight to the north, and now here they were, threatening China Navigation's hard-won 'rights' on the Yangzi.[31] He began planning a bold response.

A temporary rapprochement was mediated by the chairman of the Glen Line of steamers, James McGregor, and in September 1880 Swire and Johnson met in London. Keswick and Johnson were adamant that they did not realise that Swire had understood from any previous exchanges that they had made any commitment to give 'due notice', nor did they themselves believe that they ever had. Johnson remarked that it was in both their interests to 'work amicably', that China Merchants was a 'moribund concern' and that together the British firms could 'control' 'River, Coastal Ocean business'. He was shortly heading to China again for his last stint in Shanghai, was 'as anxious as any man to make dollars' and not lose them through unnecessary competition for 'I don't want to be a slave all my life'.[32] A three-way pooling agreement was eventually reached in 1882 after lengthy discussions, more tensions over dignity and self-respect, and delays perhaps designed to weaken rivals ahead of talks. China Merchants, Jardines' Indo-China Steam Navigation Company – which had been founded in 1881 and which took over the Coast Boats and Yangzi fleets – and China Navigation – which from 1 January 1883 would itself be amalgamated with the Coast Boats operation – agreed a joint purse arrangement for the Yangzi and Tianjin routes. Each line agreed to leave various routes to the others. 'One of our greatest gains,' mused Swire, 'is having broken down a barrier of pride, and having been placed on equal terms in the negotiations.'[33] His own pride, however, still left him pursuing his 'sweet contemplation', that tool with which to beat Keswick, a Taikoo sugar refinery.

Few commodities had a greater impact than sugar on the history of the nineteenth century.[34] Its production, processing, distribution and consumption shaped agriculture, commerce, international shipping networks, politics, diet and health. It was the focus of intense technological research and development. Steam power and steel became crucial to its development in the early nineteenth century; but blood, sweat and bondage remained intertwined with it. The world of sugar was intimately connected with the enslavement of Africans and their descendants, and others, and remained at the heart of post-slavery economies and new forms of organised transportation of labour to work plantations, not least from China. The Swire brothers had grown up in a world of Caribbean sugar wealth and sugar economy trading – the heart of their father's business and once a feature of their own. Sugar was adaptable and widely diffused as a crop in the tropics, but uniquely, European technological developments also allowed sugar to be extracted from beet grown in temperate climates. Sugar took a huge range of forms, depending on the processes used to extract it, and on the tastes, habits and wealth of those who consumed it. Those tastes could change, and change dramatically and rapidly. Across the century per capita consumption rose, production grew and prices fell. An item of elite conspicuous consumption became a major dietary staple. And it was also, perhaps more than any other foodstuff, always much more than a foodstuff.

Individuals, societies and economies, and states, became enthralled to a sweet tyranny. As cotton production had been dispersed globally during the American civil war, so sugar production was sensitive to global market changes. The 1870s saw a crisis in beet production in Europe – the crop failed in France in 1876 and 1877 – and the resulting European demand sucked in imports from Asia, Shantou, Java and India. In response to this, Jardines took over a sugar refinery that began operating in Hong Kong in 1868 with Chinese capital as Wahee, Smith & Co. (later the China Sugar Refinery), and in 1881 Chinese businessmen built a second plant, the Lee Yuen Sugar Refinery.[35] These installations processed raw sugar shipped mainly from Shantou, east along the coast, where the cane fields were fertilised with beancake brought down from north China (on Swire steamers, among others). Two refineries might seem sufficient for a place like Hong Kong – in fact three were at one point running but, under-capitalised, the third fell into the hands of Jardines. But, as an Australian observer remarked in 1885, it was 'its "thrust ourselves in" policy for which the Swire house is now so famous' and had made them, a Hong Kong newspaper editorial remarked, 'the natural rivals of the East Point magnates in nearly all branches of business on the coast of China'. So thrust in Swire did.[36]

The planning, financing and operation of the new sugar refinery provides a good case study of the way in which John Swire & Sons was now able to operate, and the changing nature of the British enterprise in China, and the evolving global economy. Plans were developed on and off over the best part of two years after 1879 when Swire asked his partner in Hong Kong, Edwin Mackintosh, to look into the opportunities for a new initiative in sugar or insurance. 'If we have, as seems likely, a row with JM&Co,' he then wrote, 'we must oppose them at all points.'[37] In cooler moments he acknowledged that the 'old standing, social & personal influence' of the rival firm meant likely as not that they could only grow in strength and add agencies to their portfolio. But 'we should be able to play a respectable second fiddle', nonetheless – placing quiet emphasis on that word 'respectable' – and after exploring and discounting such options as establishing a cotton mill or a dockyard in Hong Kong, he decided on developing the sugar refinery. Entering this business would require land, water, an efficient installation, experienced staff, the capital to fund all this and working capital to secure raw material once production commenced, a managing agency and access to markets. This would prove a complex, costly and at times frustrating development.

In June 1881 John Samuel Swire wrote personally to a circle of his correspondents – China Navigation Company shareholders most prominently – enclosing a prospectus for the new enterprise and inviting them to invest. 'We could get English capital for any concern that provided satisfactory results', he had claimed earlier in the year, and the China Navigation Company's earnings and dividends were sound evidence that those with 'spare cash' could have 'faith' in him, and receive a 10 per cent return to 'comfort' their 'declining years'.[38] Those he wrote to included Holt and Butterfield Brothers, his own brother's father-in-law Samuel Martin, and other old Liverpool connections such as Joshua Dixon, Robert Topham Steele (whose brother's career in Shanghai as Swire's agent had been so swiftly cut short in 1866), the Scotts, insurance broker Robert Dale, Thomas Ismay and William Imrie. Among these were men who Swire regularly approached to invest in tea shipments, in individual ships, or in CNCo's expansion. Business historians have made much of the Swire–Holt–Scott network, and its involvement across the operations of John Swire & Sons, but the network was far more extensive than that and connections which long pre-dated the Holt and Scott relationships remained just as vital to the firm.[39]

The files are rich in the Senior's letters inviting his friends and associates to invest in a variety of enterprises, sometimes demanding it, as they would be fools to refuse, he would say, reporting on the results, extolling or defending the nose, taste and judgement of his *cha-sees* and managers in China, and otherwise cajoling or reassuring them. One of the wealthiest, H. I. Butterfield, was particularly cautious. This was a family trait, thought Swire – the ghost of Richard Shackleton Butterfield always with him – but who nonetheless in one letter assured him that, yes, his ship might be wrecked; yes, that was a risk; yes, it might well be stolen by its captain, but then this was called piracy and there were safeguards in place, internationally; or perhaps, yes, 'if your steamer killed a Bishop or other swell' in an accident and 'being at fault' Butterfield might personally be sued for damages, but in general liability was not a problem for the owner in this way.[40] Maintaining the firm's reputation, and his own, after the collapse of Alexander Collie in 1875, and the shock this had caused the business, and in 1878/9 when the business outlook was poor, was vital if Swire's access to capital from this network was to remain unhindered.

Capital for the refinery was forthcoming and it was entirely metropolitan in origin.[41] The new firm was formally established in June 1881. But still, Swire and his partners knew nothing about sugar. He had been investing in shipping or acting as agent for others for over 20 years when CNCo was founded. Cotton goods had been a staple since he had entered business in the 1840s. He had worked up a reasonable enough knowledge of the drinks market in Australia to advise on new brands of porter in correspondence with Lorimer, and sugar had long been one of the staples the firm had imported, but a sugar refinery

itself was going to be a different enterprise. Here again Swire called
on his network of associates and relatives. Adam J. Fairrie, brother of
his first wife Helen, ran that family's long-established sugar refinery
in Liverpool. Swire's shipping partner Thomas Ismay introduced him
to James Barrow, a Liverpool refiner and a national figure in the sugar
industry.[42] Swire called on Barrow to look over the plans and proposed
specifications, to interview his proposed manager and the firm that was
chosen to build the plant. Barrow subsequently also became involved
in the new enterprise.

They hired an experienced manager, Scotsman John McIntyre,
who had worked in Japan, in Hong Kong, firstly for Wahee, Smith,
and then in Manila, but had been dislodged from his post there by
a destructive earthquake in 1880 that had damaged the plant. Plans
of the most recently constructed and up-to-date refinery were pored
over, and Blake, Barclay & Co., which had supplied the equipment for
this – Richardson's Roxburgh Refinery at Greenock – were invited to
prepare plans for a refinery 'unsurpassed by any at present constructed,
or in the course of construction'. Suitable land was bought at Quarry
Bay, five miles east of the city of Victoria in Hong Kong, despite a
last-minute spoiling operation orchestrated by Jardines that drove up
the price significantly.[43] This was a rural district, linked to the city by a
single road that passed the China Sugar Refinery at East Point and led
on to barracks at the harbour's eastern approaches. It felt quite remote,
and was the furthest point reached by Victoria's residents when it had
earlier been fashionable to take the air in carriages in the afternoon.[44]

The land needed to be filled in and levelled, slopes strengthened and
the harbour side bunded. Photographs show the development of the
site, a jetty built, foundations laid, a nine-storey boiler house rising up –
which was the tallest building in the colony by some measure – and
the extensive equipment shipped out from Greenock being installed.
'A splendid structure,' wrote Swire, 'no waste of money on ornament –
plain and substantial.' He was in Fuzhou when the refinery started
operating on 17 March 1884, but F. B. Johnson was in the colony and
just about to leave China after 33 years. It must surely have marred his
departure to see press reports carrying extensive details of valedictory
addresses and laudatory editorials accompanied on the same page by
news that the Taikoo Sugar Refinery had started production, 'a surprise to
everyone,' crowed Swire, 'Johnson gave 6 years as time of completion'.[45]

Within three months Johnson himself might have been laughing, and loudly. The world sugar price collapsed just as the refinery began operating. Swire began deeply to regret the move. His triumph, and no small measure of relief at the opening of what was surpassed in size and capacity internationally only by Havemeyers & Elder's enormous plant in Brooklyn, built coincidentally at the same time, was overshadowed by a number of significant problems that were faced in the first two years of production. As well as the unparalleled slump in prices caused by European and Asian over-production, the firm met obstacles in finding markets, maintaining production quality, protecting the welfare of staff and securing finance.[46] For a start, McIntyre was quickly dismissed. He was 'experienced', but the training and experience of this 55 year old was now years out of date in a business in which technological development was rapid. His first recorded position was as an assistant in a Hong Kong department store. He was 'ignorant and illiterate', a 'rule of thumb' man who could judge, roughly, production of one grade of sugar, but had little other experience. Two of his department heads quickly followed him, drink not much helping their judgement, but then to the rescue came Dr Ferdinand Heinrich Korn, a young German chemist. Here was talent, but, more than that, this was a wholly different way of thinking about production. 'Science must take the lead,' wrote Mackintosh, and Heinrich Korn brought science to Quarry Bay.

Dr Korn became chief superintendent of the refinery and started to improve and stabilise quality, which was also tested and contested in court when inconsistent quality was the subject of a contractual dispute in 1886. The Chinese consumers who were to become crucial to the refinery scheme began to 'trust the chop'. 'We started,' Mackintosh later wrote, 'without accurate knowledge … of where in fact we were to find ready outlets for our production.' The challenge was that Chinese consumers were used to types of sugar largely originating from Chinese producers in Shantou. As Swire himself had written in 1884, 'we have now to educate the Chinese into preferring clean to dirty sugar, a work of time I fear'.[47] In fact, Chinese consumers were as ready to embrace 'modern' sugar, as they had been to travel on steamers, ride the Wusong railway, use the telegraph and accept other foreign imports. Theirs was an open culture. Sugar had that additional resonance with modernity that would come to be a distinctive element of early twentieth-century Chinese consumer culture.[48] A sweet tooth was a modern tooth.

The 1884 slump had, for producers, a long-term, very positive impact on consumption, for it brought industrially manufactured sugar to a wider public that could now afford it.[49] But Chinese consumers were also increasingly weaned away from non-industrial coloured sugars by forms of cheap 'factory white' products, which had been bleached rather than refined. These in time became passable substitutes for refined sugar. And when prices of industrially produced white sugar became lower, consumers were ready to switch: the cheap prices of the past two years had 'caused the products of the refineries to get into markets that before were closed to them,' reported Mackintosh, and this 'injuriously affected sugars that formerly were used'. Changes in consumption were driven, too, increasingly, by that association of the new products of the new refineries with modernity, and with health. White sugar was 'clean', produced through a hygienic industrial process that became increasingly automated and reliable. And for that to be sustained, 'We must work under and with the chemist,' wrote Mackintosh.[50]

The Taikoo Sugar Refinery was fully integrated into the Swire shipping interests. China Navigation Company ships alone had the right to carry the refined sugar from the refinery and much of the raw produce was brought to Quarry Bay on its vessels. Demand for beancake to fertilise the Java plantations that fed the Hong Kong refinery also meant increased CNCo business. Sugar went north from Hong Kong on Swire vessels that brought beancake south. As agents, Butterfield & Swire distributed Taikoo products through its branches in China and in Japan – it was the reason that the Yokohama office was kept open. Butterfield & Swire at Hong Kong were the managing agents of the refinery itself. John Swire & Sons were significant shareholders. Despite the daunting problems of financing the operation, which forced the firm to look for levels of capital unprecedented in its previous experience, and despite market volatility and competition from the Jardines plant, the Taikoo Sugar Refinery delivered substantial and steady profits and dividends totalling over £1 million between 1884 and 1900.[51]

These were novel predicaments for the firm. So, too, were those raised during the construction of the plant and after by its Chinese labour force. For, at a stroke, John Swire & Sons found itself employing more Chinese staff than Britons, or those of any other nationality. The Liverpool network starts to lose its visibility in the story of the firm, which was already more and more embedded in London. Shipping, and now sugar, brought many Scots into its employ. There were Portuguese and Indian watchmen, Portuguese clerks and book-keepers, and, of course, there was Dr Korn, and he was only the first of a number of Germans recruited for Taikoo Sugar. But the construction of the refinery led the company into this further new situation, employing, directly, large numbers of Chinese and this was creating an arena for new types of interaction, not all of which proved welcome. For a start, the original contractor had underestimated the scale of the operation, and when Edwin Mackintosh had tried to substitute him with another, the company was boycotted by his peers. 'Guilds tabooed us', as Swire put it, 'for the first time in the history of China for any work of magnitude.'[52] He meant in the history of British businesses in China. The company's response was to hire labour directly – although a court case in July 1883, when large numbers of workmen downed tools – suggests that this did not entirely ease things. But 'the building was erected in half the time,' wrote Swire, and the men were better paid, he claimed, as they were directly hired and lost nothing on commissions that might be due contractors.

Labour now became an intermittent source of tensions. In 1886, 170 men were brought in from Shantou to work in the refinery. There may have been an element here of assuming that they had some familiarity with sugar production, given its role in the region's economy, but this generated new problems. The 1880s saw new phenomena appear in Sino-foreign interactions, not least nationalistic actions by workmen and others arising from the 1884/5 war between France and the Qing, and the tensions preceding it over the French seizure of Tonkin. At Hong Kong in September and October 1884 dockworkers and boatmen had boycotted French warships that had put into the harbour. Magistrates fined workmen at the behest of their employers for breach of contract, prompting demonstrations and violent incidents involving workers from across different sectors of Hong Kong's Chinese population.[53] Sino-foreign conflict before 1884 always had been accompanied by elements of Chinese popular mobilisation, although equally as many subjects of the Qing had worked for or supplied foreign forces. But as companies like Butterfield & Swire established manufacturing enterprises as their portfolio of businesses evolved and expanded, these became new sites of conflict, and we enter the era of the boycott and the strike.

We also now enter the era of ostensibly non-political industrial unrest. Keeping the workforce contented would start to prove a recurring feature of company activity. The construction boycott at the refinery is still obscure – there is little detail in any of the records so far found – but in February 1886 'rather heavy fighting' broke out at the refinery between some of those workers brought in to the plant from Shantou and those already working there. Armed Indian watchmen had to restore order and the police were called. All these new recruits were then dismissed, but as they embarked to return to Shantou further violence threatened.[54] Managing what was often derided as labour factionalism, seeing to the safety and the health of the workforce – there was deep anxiety in September 1885 at 'great amount of sickness amongst the Native workers' – and incipient nationalism were new undertakings for the firm. Butterfield & Swire learned a great deal from directly managing the building of the refinery, and it boosted their prestige significantly. But now they had to learn to manage a Chinese workforce.[55]

Politics had also battered the company in September 1883, when a watchman on board the CNCo steamer *Hankow* had sparked a destructive riot in Canton. Early one morning, as a crowd of passengers jostled to board the ship, Luo Fen, a young boarding-house servant tasked with securing good berths on board for customers, was assaulted by the watchman, Faustino Caetano Diaz. Luo fell into the river and drowned. Anger swiftly mounted among the crowd and the steamer pulled away from the wharf, which was owned by Russells, but was now shared by the Boat Company and CNCo as part of the agreement between the companies. With the ship out of reach, the crowd set fire to the wharf, and then left to attack the Russell offices on the island of Shameen, home to a small British concession and its French neighbour. Before the day was out and Qing troops had restored order, 15 buildings there had been burned and looted, three demonstrators shot dead and foreign residents had either been evacuated or had mounted a trigger-happy picket. The protests were fuelled also by anger at the drunken killing on 11 August of a Chinese boy, Pak Wa Kung, by a British tidewaiter in the customs, J. H. Logan.[56] Neither of these incidents arose from the actions of the China Navigation Company, but with Butterfield & Swire more and more entrenched in China the actions of its staff, private or official, or the actions of others in what was seen as a homogeneous foreign establishment, dragged it into a brittle and sometimes bloodily tense world. This time the setting was Canton, on the Russell wharf, but wherever the company operated it was vulnerable.

The conflict between France and the Qing in northern Vietnam was already moving towards all-out war, and the heated response in Canton in the late summer of 1883 to these purely localised incidents of foreign thuggery was directly inflamed by rising tensions with the French. It also distorted attempts by the diplomats and consuls to resolve the affairs afterwards, which were not helped by the fact that the belligerent former Canton consul Sir Harry Parkes was appointed British Minister to China late in September. Parkes thought nothing of thumping tables and shouting at officials during meetings in Peking. As Robert Hart put it, 'a man with port experience [that is, a consul] does not quite do at Peking in some respects: knowing how to handle Provincial Taotais and even Footais does not necessarily mean ability to deal with Metropolitan Presidents and vice-Presidents'.[57] On Sunday 24 February 1884, taking a different tack, John Samuel Swire went and called on a Chinese Viceroy.

Swire met Zhang Shusheng, governor-general (Zongdu) of Guangdong, Guangxi and Hainan. This was a powerful and important position within the Qing state, although Zhang was an unexceptional administrator. Swire went to Canton to try to salvage something useful from the burned remnants of the wharf, and the violence of Faustino Diaz, and indeed to improve on the opportunity that the debacle actually presented for the firm. This meeting was originally mediated through contacts provided by the company's Hong Kong comprador.[58] As a result, a proposal emerged whereby the cost of the compensation demanded by foreign diplomats was largely covered by Swires in a complex and somewhat surreptitious arrangement John Samuel Swire negotiated directly with Zhang. In what the British consul thought a 'curious' and 'very extraordinary proposition', the company arranged a loan to the provincial authorities from the Chartered Bank in Hong Kong, covered by a bond issue and augmented by a passenger tax. In this way, the Canton authorities secured, free, the resource needed to settle the claims that were duly made, which, it was reported, the firm would endeavour to get reduced, and would be left with a useful surplus. Butterfield & Swire would secure goodwill, permission to extend the wharf after 'years' of failing to secure their own site and a promise to 'refuse water rights' to opposition companies. The Luo family was to receive compensation, and in return for some of the extra privileges, so were Pak's family.[59] Swire had bypassed the British consul, who only heard of the proposal from his American counterpart.

This is still an obscure episode. A shady local financier, John Pitman, who had first come to China in the Royal Navy during the Second Opium War was also involved in facilitating the discussions. After some years in Japan, Pitman was now based in Canton, perplexing the consul when he accompanied local officials to meetings as an adviser. Pitman himself visited some of the compensation claimants, offering them immediate settlement, at 80 per cent of their claims.[60] These Canton discussions were heavily shaped by the course of the war with France. The governor-general was superseded in August 1884 by Zhang Zhidong, a much more powerful and influential figure. Zhang was tasked with supporting the war effort in Vietnam, and the defence of his provinces, potentially at the mercy of the French navy after the Qing's southern fleet had been sunk in a matter of minutes in Fuzhou on 22 August. For this he needed money and arms. Through Pitman, Butterfield & Swire was able to offload a large consignment of rifles bought by William Lang in Shanghai against the expectation of a quick sale during the 1877 Satsuma Rebellion in Japan, but which had been left on his hands when it drew too swiftly to a close. Pitman also surfaced as an agent for British arms manufacturer William Armstrong, and negotiating possible reconstruction by Swires of an arsenal at Whampoa on the Pearl River, building on Swire's 'power to put thro' a big work', evidenced by the refinery.[61]

This was a period when, as one scholar put it, 'loan fever was rampant'.[62] Qing officials like Zhang Zhidong were intent on strengthening the country to face this new wave of foreign threats from Japan and from France. They explored the development of railways, arsenals and shipyards, and they needed ready cash to fight the war. In the 1870s John Samuel Swire had firmly opposed following Jardines into the business of government loans, for there was great reputational risk, he thought, and some of those involved in this business were men of poor reputation, Pitman certainly not excepted.[63] But at this point he seems actively to have considered it as a tactic, not an end in itself, to purchase goodwill to smooth the passage of the core business of the firm. It is not exactly clear how this episode concluded. Zhang Zhidong was a much more bullish man when it came to dealing with foreigners, official or otherwise, than his predecessor. The Hongkong & Shanghai Bank provided one substantial loan to the provincial authorities, but so, too, did the Chartered Bank, that business brought to it by Swires, and the family of Logan's victim apparently received compensation that came from Swire.[64] The wharf was rebuilt, and the *Hankow* resumed docking at it without opposition. This was only the first time, however, that contingent events, the simple accidents of human stupidity or negligence, would rock the general calm of company operations in China.

Aside from its ongoing ventures in tea – although this was starting to go markedly into decline as Indian tea came to hold greater and greater sway in foreign markets – and its steady shipments of Manchester cottons and Yorkshire woollens, one other major activity dominates the firm's records in the 1870s and 1880s: the business of Blue Funnel and ocean shipping. John Samuel Swire still hankered after a Pacific agency, but none was forthcoming even when T. H. Ismay's White Star Line established a presence on the Hong Kong to San Francisco route when its ships were chartered by American interests. The new contacts could not be brought to any greater advantage, although meetings were held, and Swire refrained from launching a line himself so as not to harm Ismay's business.[65] But the OSSC kept him busy enough. Philip Holt's journey to Asia with John Samuel Swire in 1877/8 helped deepen further the commitment of the Holt brothers in their Asian venture. Philip Holt returned announcing, his brother Alfred reported, that he 'wishes we had entered the trade 20 years earlier'. For his part Swire thought Holt's trip a 'very paying one to the future of B&S, for he has completely identified himself with the firm'. Several weeks cocooned with the relentlessly chipper, and probably continually hectoring Swire, on the *Orestes*, on its journey from Liverpool to Shanghai, was hardly likely to have produced any other result.[66] But the trip galvanised Philip Holt into initiating new services in Southeast Asia that further entrenched it in the region.[67] The early technological advantage Blue Funnel had once enjoyed had by now been lost, and newer firms – the Glen and Castle lines among others – were proving strong competitors. Alfred Holt had generally proved resistant to change, despite the barrage of letters and memoranda that flew his way from John Samuel Swire as OSSC agent in London and, through Butterfield & Swire, in China, and as shareholder and as a friend of the Holt brothers. But Alfred Holt was more amenable to the most significant development that Swire proposed: a China and Japan shipping conference. For after all, what had brought some commercial sanity and stability to the Yangzi might well do the same for the ocean lines.

Such cartel arrangements, the first of which was initiated in September 1879, are now illegal, but when tested in the English courts in a complex case in 1887–91 their then legality was affirmed, and this would last until well into the late twentieth century.[68] The spur, for Swire, was the weakening comparative position of the OSSC, over-production of new shipping in the 1870s in the first flush of optimism after the opening of the Suez Canal and the great seasonal variations in the trade. Freight rates declined markedly in the 1870s. From 1875 a conference had operated among firms sailing to Calcutta, but the China and Japan conference would prove the most influential. It came to work on the following lines: members – most prominently Blue Funnel, the Castle, Glen and Shire lines, the French firm Messageries Maritimes and P&O – came together to agree standard rates and a share of tonnage among the firms, ports to be operated from, and by whom, and they agreed sanctions against transgressors, and sweeteners for freight shippers to tie them to using what were termed 'conference ships' (these took the form of rebates, deferred to ensure longer term loyalty). The conference was fluid in its composition and its specific arrangements, which were complex and fine-grained. It constantly evolved, expanding and contracting, and covering new services or closing them down (in conference terms). Nurturing and managing the conference – of which he was founding chairman from 1879 to 1882 – clearly took an immense amount of John Samuel Swire's energy and patience, not least with the Holts who, once involved, proved sullen and unpredictable members, despite benefiting immensely from it.

The China Conference – and its various successors – brought some measure of stability to a volatile trade, ending 'the old chaos' in Swire eyes, for shippers as well as shipowners.[69] It had many opponents, and produced a great deal of controversy, and it had the additional unintended effect, as it evolved and strengthened, of supporting what became a vital British strategic artery, along which – as a later handbook, *Imperial Military Geography*, put it – raw materials flowed to the 'heart'. 'Stoppage' of such an artery could mean 'death'. Although upheld by the

High Court in London, and endorsed by a Royal Commission report in 1909, opposition remained strong, and in Singapore in 1910/11 local interests persuaded the Crown Colony's government to outlaw the practice. But these imperial defence considerations meant that the Colonial Office in London declined to support the administration, and the veto was dropped.[70] The transition to steam and the opening of the Suez Canal brought a greater predictability and regularity to communications, so the conference brought more predictable costs to shippers and earnings for members. Rates rose markedly. Holts and their competitors within the conference secured higher profits and most, but not OSSC – even though it was 'a gold mine to that company' – took the opportunity to steadily invest in modernising their fleets.[71] Shippers seem to have gained, too, as rebates, predictable and stable freight rates, and more frequent sailings, reduced their costs, and overall, the volume of trade increased.[72] It was with the shipping conference system that John Samuel Swire became most widely known.

A long-running debate among historians of modern Britain assessed what was termed 'declinism': the loss of a competitive economic edge after about 1870, crudely demonstrated by its shrinking relative share of the world economy.[73] Much attention was paid in this to the social and cultural world of the British mercantile elite. For a while an accepted explanation was seen to lie in a recurring pattern whereby merchants, having made their fortune, swiftly thereafter bought landed estates – a sterile investment – and, aping the aristocracy, even marrying into it, abandoned trade – 'slavery', as Johnson had put it – for unproductive leisure. 'Trade' nonetheless remained a socially problematic category, although the changing status of the families in the Swire network can certainly be seen. This explanation is now largely discredited, but it serves usefully to alert us to the importance of understanding the social world of merchants like the Swire brothers. Doing so with John Samuel Swire would hardly have supported the thesis. Certainly he hunted, but he had always hunted; certainly he took a place in the country, although only after remarrying in 1881, but, no, he did not retire from the front line of the firm's business. Quite the opposite. As the conflict with Jardine Matheson unfolded he was, thought his brother, 'thinking and talking business morning, noon & night'.[74] We can see also from correspondence that the Senior was still intimately familiar with the daily business of the London office, as he comments on would-be passengers who have come to buy tickets for China. And when in Shanghai in 1877 he 'sold ... all the goods that he could', acting in person on the maxim that litters the pages of his letters to New York, Melbourne, Yokohama, and to his partners in China: sell, sell everything, and sell it at market prices as soon as it arrives.[75]

This single-mindedness does go some way to explain the tenacity with which the firm pursued some objectives that were in themselves never anything but rational, but which were undertaken for reasons that had more to do with pride, to the Senior's penchant for 'glory & not for £ & d' (as he put it to his fiancée Mary Warren in 1881), and for contesting the 'divine rights' of Jardines in the 1870s as he had those of Gibbs, Bright & Co. in the Australian trade in the 1850s and 1860s.[76] This is certainly partly a reflection of the man. But Edwin Mackintosh was also clearly equally attentive to the daily business of the firm, although William Lang in Shanghai took his partnership responsibilities rather less diligently, ambling off out of the office daily for his whist club and not bothering himself much with detail.[77] Still, while Swire quite astonished Alfred Holt with his thirst for 'theatres and operas by night, excursions by day' and racing, too, when he visited from Liverpool, his metropolitan friend would also make Holt, a diligent but not doctrinaire Unitarian, work on Easter Sunday if he needed his collaborator's attention.[78]

Our view of the firm's character may be distorted by the records that actually survive. For the earliest decades of the firm's years in China are documented largely by what seem to be John Samuel Swire's personal letter books and records as senior partner. We have almost nothing from William Hudson Swire at all. We can only assume that before he retired and left the partnership in 1876 he was wholly in accord with the strategy his brother pursued.[79] We have no branch archives either. What survives in the records certainly includes what we might term 'official' letters of John Swire & Sons, but these are interspersed with notes to Swire's groom, calculations about household expenditure and directions to wine merchants. The correspondence with Mackintosh and with Lang includes references to parallel 'officials', and when Swire went on his travels to China the paper trail is largely broken, or incomplete. But even taking this into account, John Samuel Swire remains a driven man. News of his imminent arrival at any of the firm's offices must have clouded the day.

There is a final point to draw out of the *Cadiz* episode, the Canton riot and the Taikoo labour problems. This is that John Swire & Sons was now quite literally embedded, physically emplaced, in China. The land, the river banks, the jetties and hulks, its steamers and installations, these were all now potential sites for conflict, not least as many of them were placed at the intersection of the brittle sovereignty of the Qing with the assumed rights of the British and other foreign powers. As with sites, so with its staff, their working lives and private transgressions or experiences in China. The unthinking, lazy violence of a man like Faustino Diaz could have profound – and expensive – consequences for the firm. The response of the company to this new situation took two forms. The first looked to the British government and its agents for support, although in the *Cadiz* case this hardly worked. As Swire bluntly put it in 1877, in his letter to the Earl of Derby, 'Our existence as a company depends on our receiving that protection from injustice and arbitrary dealing for which our Treaties provide.'[80] It had always been the case that the operation of the company in China was reliant on the framework provided by the treaties, but in this letter something more engaged was being demanded. We can see the second in the proposed resolution of the Canton riot claims and the dispute with China Merchants. John Samuel Swire travelled in person to meet Tang Jingxing and Viceroy Zhang. Swires needed now to try to establish, and to nurture, contact with Chinese powerholders. The business of the British firm was changing yet again. For now they were no longer simply in China: they were of China.

At Work

Robert Hart, Inspector General of the Imperial Maritime Customs, hosted a dinner at his home in Peking on Friday 11 April 1884. Among the eclectic assortment of guests were Elizabeth Pirkis, a composer of popular songs, whose husband was British Legation accountant, Clare Hillier, whose husband Walter was Chinese Secretary in the British Legation, Dr Stephen Bushell, Legation doctor, already launched on his parallel career as a connoisseur of Chinese ceramics, and Alfred Hippisley, Chinese Secretary in the Customs Inspectorate. For the observer of the long course of China's relations with the Western world nearly everything involved in this seems quite surreal. But such was the steady pace of change that a gathering like this was now routine in the heart of the empire of the Qing. It was a hastily arranged affair, organised in honour of John Samuel Swire and his wife Mary, who had just arrived in the capital.[1] Getting there took three days in a small boat traversing the Hai River from Tianjin to Dongzhou, and then a 13-mile cart or horse ride, or involved hiring a pony and riding overland, staying in a Chinese inn on the way. Travellers were advised to take their own provisions for the journey, and to hire a servant in Tianjin, for southerners would not be understood in the Mandarin-speaking north. Travel in China away from the small network of treaty port steamer lines was to remain challenging for decades to come, but there might be found at the end of it, even in Peking, *Potage printemps*, *Poulet à l'Anglais* and *Meringues à la crème* served at a well-set table in a pleasant dining room.[2]

Visitors were a rare treat in Peking, especially visiting foreign women. Ordinarily Hart might have invited the British Minister, Sir Harry

Parkes, but Parkes had just left the capital on a mission to Korea. He and Swire would have had something to say, but perhaps other Legation staff relayed the Minister's profound unhappiness at the moves the firm were taking to expedite unofficially a resolution to the Canton mess. For his part, Hart had been very impressed when he met Swire the previous day: 'The firm has now 53 steamers or is building them: one steamer every week from S'hai to Europe – that is something for a private firm to do!' he noted in his diary. In nature the men were not too far removed: both were supremely confident in their judgement of events and character, and both combined a capacity for patience and long-term planning, with restless but focused urgency when the time came to act. Hart, however, understood China, or at least the world of Qing officials he moved smoothly within. He spoke the language and more importantly knew how to communicate and knew the values that the dynasty's administrators most prized. Swire did not, but nor did his enterprises seem yet to need a deeper knowledge than a good comprador could provide. In Peking, the two men did not talk of Canton, but of wharves that might be built by Butterfield & Swire and Jardines in Xiamen and Shantou. Hart thought Swire shrewd looking, and told two of his staff to accompany them around the sights of the capital which ought to have impressed the visitors, for there was 'lovely spring weather', and almost none of the city's infamous clouds of dust which blew down from the Mongolian plains.

For all its impressive beauty, the capital was actually in turmoil. As Swire arrived in Peking there had been what Hart and others described as 'almost a coup d'état': Yixin, Prince Gong, who had had charge of state policy, and most importantly foreign relations, since 1861, had been dismissed, along with others blamed for the defeat the previous month of Qing troops by French forces at Bắc Ninh in northern Vietnam. Attempts to broker a truce in the unfolding conflict over the French advance into Indo-China were being undertaken through negotiations in Tianjin, but others were less sanguine of the chances of peace: 'war party now in' wrote another resident in the capital, Customs Service language student J. O. P. Bland. A truce was reached, but would fail, and China and France went to war later in the year. Hart wondered if the fall of Prince Gong now meant a wider 'anti-foreign policy', but Bland was more complacent: 'Everything in a state of change and uncertainty – an uneasy sort of feeling, which I suppose is an ingredient of life in China.'[3]

This Peking episode provides an opportunity to turn to explore 'life in China' as it had developed and its ingredients for those employed by the firm, its changes and uncertainties, its routines and opportunities. The tiny world of foreign life in Peking was perhaps an outlier, though an important one, given the importance of the diplomatic relationships that had been established with senior Qing administrators, but by the mid-1880s the days of makeshift seemed to have passed. The foreign presence in China beyond the old ghetto on Canton's riverfront was now in its fifth decade. Local savants had already started to publish short histories of the earlier years. Hong Kong in 1891 and the Shanghai International Settlement in 1893 would celebrate their golden jubilees with processions, parades and more surveys of their histories and achievements.[4] The treaty ports and the British colony would continue to grow steadily in size and in the complexity and diversity of the societies they housed. Between 1870 and Swire's visit, the foreign population at Shanghai more than doubled in size, with the greatest proportionate increases coming in the number of women and children, which both increased fivefold. The small makeshift bachelor settlements of mercantile assistants and merchants had evolved into something slightly better resembling those in the towns and cities left behind, at least in the texture of the foreign community itself. The 1885 census at Shanghai recorded an actor, confectioners, curio dealers, drapers, grooms, hairdressers, journalists and photographers, five 'music professors', five solicitors, eleven foreign tailors and six watchmakers. The numbers of residents would continue steadily to increase (although one or two of the smaller treaty ports would start to decline), but the turnover remained high, especially among the traders who made up a quarter of those whose occupations were listed.[5] Between one census and the next, a large proportion of the foreign residents of Hong Kong or of Shanghai would move on. As these populations expanded, though, the Swire companies directly and indirectly contributed to this growth with mercantile assistants and clerks, ships' officers and engineers, hulk captains and godown men, sugar boilers and accountants, chemists, their families, and their servants, including foreign servants.

Between 1866 and 1900 about 100 men sailed to Asia to work for the Butterfield & Swire branches while others were recruited in China and Japan. More went out to work for Taikoo Sugar, which had 22 foreign employees by 1888, and double that number by 1900, and well over 700 served for a time on the still growing China Navigation Company fleet, which employed just over a hundred foreign officers alone in 1884, and 260 in 1900. By the end of the century there were 18 branches and 41 ships in the fleet, 32 vessels having been added to the 15 operating the year Swire visited Robert Hart (the number of Swire ships conflated with Blue Funnel's in their discussion). Eleven steamers were lost in accidents by 1900 and others passed out of service, sold, broken up or refashioned as hulks or pontoons. This growth was also one of geographical reach. By 1900 there were eight branches along the Yangzi, including the existing agency arrangements which had been superseded by offices run by Swire staff, outposts at Tianjin, Yantai and Niuzhuang in the north joining Shanghai, while Canton, Xiamen and Ningbo had joined Shantou and Fuzhou along the coast from Hong Kong. Kobe had been opened in Japan. Six offices alone were opened in the four years after Swire sailed home in 1884.

The pace of expansion left records in some disarray, and in the early 1890s the London office found itself reconstructing details of historic terms of engagement of its staff in Asia or even trying accurately to record their names. Originally John Samuel Swire himself kept the sketchiest of details in a series of pocket notebooks: surname, initials, sometimes the full name added later, salary per year during the five-year agreement. When a man left the firm he simply ripped out the pages and crossed them off a list at the start of the book. The details slowly become a little fuller: 'Left in 1879'; 'Died 1883'; 'To China May 1881'. But much seems to have remained unwritten. Occasionally the destinations of former employees began to be noted. These records are hardly systematic, and the men were clearly contracted functionaries: there is very little sense yet of anything resembling what would come to be thought of as a 'house staff'. Letter books show that some, marked out as especially able and potentially future managers, were certainly indulged. Might shipbuilder John Scott in Greenock take John Bois, home on leave, out on his yacht? Bois would become Shanghai manager. Sir James Lorimer helped despatch two ponies on Swire's behalf to Shanghai for partner William Lang ('are they the best in China?' he asked, 'How do they compare ... with a Swell London Pair'?)[6]

We know little about the actual process of recruitment, but it is worth asking how a man came to present himself at Billiter Street for an interview, and then, once he had cleared a medical inspection by Dr Patrick Manson, the 'father of tropical medicine', who had worked for many years in Fuzhou and in Hong Kong, set out on a Blue Funnel steamer to China. Some men simply answered newspaper advertisements. In 1891 one such notice in *The Economist* announced: 'Wanted, for the East. First class book-keeper' with 'good commercial experience', age 'about 30' ... 'exceptional references required as to Capacity and Character'. A very high salary of £700 was offered, and £450 was also offered for a 'good book-keeper'.[7] This was not the first advertisement, men who had joined having responded to such notes in 1889 and 1890. Hugh Matheson Brown was one of those who applied, prompted not least by the fact that a friend had just joined. Brown had extensive experience, and came with a strong recommendation – though, as it was from a Jardine Matheson associate, this rather worried Edwin Mackintosh in Hong Kong, who feared a Jardines protégé holding a confidential position in the firm. Despite better relations between the firms, old suspicions died hard. Jim Scott in London dismissed this: there was nothing to worry about, but he also added an unpleasant rider of his own. Brown had no connection either to 'the chi-chi family at Penang'.[8] Race mattered. Personal introductions still carried weight, family ties, too. James Cummings's application letter noted that his brother worked for the company, and that he wished to 'better my position' by joining John Swire & Sons.[9] This was the routine language of the application letter, as set out in the guides that men like Cummings will have studied. Cummings quite explicitly did not propose himself for service 'in the East', which would have seemed a little too eager, and there might be other men in the London office who had a prior claim to be considered.

But why apply at all? Working for Butterfield & Swire would involve long years of separation from family and friends, work in a climate that many found trying and a good chance of damaging one's health. In the early 1860s, Charles Dyce recalled that his relations and friends thought his appointment to a China house meant his 'fortune was as good as made'. There seemed also, he thought, 'a prospect of adventure in going to China', and like many mid-Victorian boys he was 'inspired by reading lives of Clive and Warren Hastings'.[10] P. G. Wodehouse, recalling his own days as a Hongkong & Shanghai Bank recruit, had a character put it more chirpily in his thinly veiled account of work at the bank in *Psmith in the City*: 'you get your orders, and go to the East, where you're the dickens of a big pot straight away, with a big screw and a dozen native Johnnies under you'. Glory would be as hard to find in the account books of the Taikoo Sugar Refinery, as it proved in Dyce's long career as a silk merchant; that 'big screw', too, for most, but a comfortable income and if not a 'dozen' 'Johnnies' then at least a world of servants in general much more within ready grasp. 'We may state for your guidance,' wrote Jim Scott to Stephen Forsyth in 1891, in a covering letter accompanying a draft agreement, 'that after a man of your standing has been with us for three years he may count, if he fulfils his duties satisfactorily, on obtaining a decided increase in salary.' And by this point they wanted to find men who intended staying for longer than three years. Some balked: 'we presume you knew where Hong Kong was situated,' wrote Swire in a strong reprimand to an applicant who had withdrawn after interview and the medical.[11] But the firm generally found the men it needed. The mercantile world remained a mobile one, and young men were often eager, certainly ready, to take up opportunities overseas, for the world of routine employment openings for Britons extended across the footprint of formal empire and out further into areas of British commercial dominance.

And when the company sought recruits, what did it look for? Forsyth had been awarded his MA by the University of Aberdeen in 1884, and he was possibly the first graduate John Swire & Sons ever recruited.[12] But this would remain unusual for some years to come, although John Samuel Swire's own son John ('Jack') had been sent to University College, Oxford, and was groomed to join the company.[13] For the clerks and assistants some business experience was certainly an asset, and in some cases specific expertise was sought: Forsyth was a chartered accountant. But there were obstacles in the way of hiring such men. Applicants with extensive experience were likely already to have married, and might not wish to relocate, even if the firm was minded to accommodate married staff, which it was not. But, equally, the men who first responded to the *Economist* advertisement and who best fitted it, were then, after agreeing in principle, promptly offered equally good terms by their current employers, and so declined the offers. Well, Swire wrote, 'We want "Swans"', but we will have to make do with '"eggs"', and invest in potential, and train men up. This had its advantages, for eggs were decidedly cheaper: Brown – who was not one of those first selected – was paid a lot less than £700.[14] The 'China trade', as Swire remarked in 1876, was 'no longer a Swell one', and expenses needed to be kept low, so that, aside from heads of department, 'common clerks' would suffice, and such 'ordinary clerks' could be found cheaply in China or Hong Kong.[15] So there was no need to recruit a man from London who would cost the firm £700 a year in total, but whose routine work would have brought him but £60 a year in London. Even so, 'manners' remained important. The firm needed 'men who have been brought up as gentlemen', not those who were 'simply the better educated of the lower classes'.[16] The public world of business in the Asian treaty ports remained steeped in the niceties of social distinction, as did, of course, Britain itself. In China and especially in Hong Kong, the importance of position and background was greatly accentuated. 'The necessity of having companionable gentlemen', as Swire put it in 1876, might already have started to decrease, but it remained impossible for them to do without gentlemen, at least of a sort.

It should not surprise us that neither an interest in China itself nor any facility with any of its languages was expected. Interpreting, where it was required, was provided by Chinese staff, or it was simply dispensed with in most ordinary interaction where men instead used pidgin English, easy enough for Chinese and Britons alike to learn (and heaven forfend that the servant might understand the talk at dinner table through having studied English). As in most foreign firms, the idea of learning Chinese or Japanese would simply not have occurred to them. Guidebooks provided handy selections of the pidgin that would get most people by. William Robinson's declaration in 1891 that he was learning Japanese is possibly the first evidence of an employee of Butterfield & Swire learning an Asian language. He was, he wrote, 'confirmed' in his belief that 'future possibilities of business in Japan lay in the cultivation of the natives'.[17] In some areas – the refinery, godowns, wharves and ships – a sizeable Chinese staff was employed, and some experience of working with them would have been valued. But they were usually supervised most immediately by Chinese or Japanese contractors, who relayed instructions. And in many cases a familiarity with working with any 'natives' would have sufficed. Certainly, well into the twentieth century British men who had supervised indigenous staff would see their experience as self-evidently portable: a native was simply a native, the east was simply the east.[18]

Cheap clerks were hired out in China, as London directed. The Hong Kong office recruited a number of office juniors in the 1880s and 1890s who had either been born in the colony or largely raised there. The Grimble brothers were two of the sons of a military storekeeper. William Armstrong's father had arrived in Hong Kong in 1849, working as an auctioneer. Another auctioneer, George Reinhold Lammert, found billets with B&S for two of his eight Hong Kong-born sons, which must have been a relief to him. Hugh Arthur was the locally born son of the headmaster of the Diocesan Boys' School. The three Shepherd brothers had been brought to the colony as youngsters by their father, who held a series of posts in the Supreme Court administration and who in 1893 published Hong Kong's first guidebook. There is some evidence that the local men were set apart socially from the home-recruited assistants (and they were much, much lower paid). This was not simply a function of their probably having grown up knowing each other in Hong Kong's small British world. They were not automatically considered for advancement within Butterfield & Swire. Their knowing Hong Kong might have been an asset, but might equally also have been seen as a hindrance to them. Men were also taken on at the outports, sometimes inherited from the agencies which had previously served the firm. They were certainly not expected to move very far from those. And they might have what were considered to be profound disadvantages. Louis Grunauer at Shantou was 'a tip top man at his work', but Edwin Mackintosh 'would not trust him as head even tho' he could run the agency alone, he is a half-caste'. This would repeatedly be noted of Grunauer, who served the firm in the port for at least 14 years before his death there in 1896.[19]

The terms of service that were offered for those recruited in London remained attractive. Men were given a five-year contract, calculated in sterling, a passage out (but not home, unless invalided), and free board, lodging and washing. They were housed communally in the Taikoo 'mess'. Salaries rose over the course of the five years, at which point engagements might be renewed or terminated. Locally recruited staff who moved from being cheap clerks to positions as assistants would have had cause to resent, as it seems some did, the higher salaries and benefits of younger, unexperienced men who arrived in the offices in China.[20] There was originally no provision for leave to be taken back in Britain, and at one point the rule was that men should resign if they wanted leave, with no guarantee that they might be reappointed.[21] The terms changed slightly in the mid-1870s: newer recruits lost their free laundry, a penny-pinching oddity, and it was specified that the cost of their personal servant was to fall to them, while from the mid-1880s salaries were valued in local currency. By 1893 the 'custom' regarding leave was that a man needed to have put in at least seven years' service: Mackintosh worked for eight, as did Bois; Poate served nine years.[22] A stint with Butterfield & Swire involved a lengthy exile.

The 'mess' was common across all sectors of the foreign presence in China. While the men each hired a Chinese personal servant – their 'boy', in local parlance, who was rarely a boy – the 'very best and foremost' of China's 'natural productions' as one visitor put it, the mess employed a cook, probably a porter, and would have been overseen by a major-domo, answering to one of the foreign residents who was charged with the task. A 'knowledge of housekeeping' was one skill young mercantile assistants had not expected to have to learn, but one most acquired.[23] All the Chinese employees would have been 'guaranteed' by the company's comprador. From the mid-1880s contracts indicate that staff had the option to rent their own accommodation. As an institution, the mess had its advantages for the firm (in terms of costs, and especially in supervising young men) but it had its drawbacks, too. As one journalist noted, 'enforced association in the same mess of men of uncongenial natures and widely different resources ... proved an undoubted evil'.[24]

We have little by way of records of the texture of mess lives, congenial or otherwise. But men can be spotted outside in local press reports as they rowed, played cricket, joined the Jockey Club or Hong Kong Club, or shot in Volunteer Corps rifle competitions. Volunteering in Hong Kong or in Shanghai, or in small contingents raised in other cities, involved regular parades and annual camps. Volunteer Corps were important parts of local defence schemes; they were also seen as a source of diversion and healthy exercise for young men with much time on their hands outside office hours, and the sports field was thereby also a hectic site of activity. Men went to meetings of Masonic lodges; they sang; they acted. Company employees appear as victims of petty crime, witnesses in court cases, or sometimes serving on juries: letters are stolen from the Taikoo office in Hong Kong; a civil action is launched for debt; the Taipan Edwin Mackintosh has 'very important business to attend to' and fails to appear for jury service: fine $50 for contempt of court. This latter case delighted the editor of the *Hongkong Telegraph*, Robert Fraser Smith, who pursued a steady vendetta against 'Tosh of Taikoo' (which he did not mean as a term of endearment; he felt that Tosh spoke tosh), and against the firm: the 'Scavengers of the East' Smith labelled them.[25]

The combination of youth, money and a largely male social environment could undo even the best intentioned and well-brought-up new arrival. 'The fault in the East with the large houses', Swire once complained, with characteristic facetiousness, 'is that all the clerks who have lived in the Hong think themselves entitled to injure their health with pleasure and then to claim leave of absence to recuperate.' He cited the example of W. J. Robinson who got fever 'standing in a swamp after a snipe', recuperated in Japan but then 'kept it up at Shanghai races. Got invalided again then had to come home' where he nurtured his poor health 'with seeing friends and late hours'.[26] Robinson would pull through and survive the Senior's caustic comments as well.

It would take more than a swamp fever to keep men away from shooting, riding or simply messing about in houseboats on east China's waterways. J. Keith Angus provides glimpses of the houseboat life for a Swire clerk in the 1870s in pieces he later wrote about a picnic west of Shanghai, and snipe shooting from Yokohama. Shanghai's summer Sundays were 'far too hot – uncomfortably and unpleasantly hot to sit in Church, notwithstanding the adornment of white clothes and the help given by the air-stirring punkah', and there was really 'no Sunday east of the Cape'. Men might have their own houseboat and crew, or firms provided one. They travelled with as much of home as their bearers could carry including, he recalled, cans of Moir's Mulligatawny soup from Aberdeen, and bottles of Bass (the empties much prized by country people). They took bread and butter. They shot snipe, duck or goose, or they simply lounged, smoked or read magazines sent out from England. Jim Scott had London subscribe him to the *Pall Mall Gazette*, *The World* ('an amusing chronicle of current history') and *The Field*.[27]

Others will not have skipped Church. After leaving the firm, Arthur Warrick, who joined after working for seven years as a tea taster for Russells, became a leading figure in Bristol's Missionary Society, supporting the work of the Congregationalist London Missionary Society. On the whole, the foreign business community, while paying lip service to a generally positive view of Christian evangelisation, steered well clear of the missionary world in China. Most, like foreign diplomats, rather thought missionaries needlessly complicated relations with the Chinese. They sparked controversies that could turn violent, and affected the wider foreign presence, and they were, in addition, socially often rather less well placed than the gentlemen merchants. But for Arthur Warrick it was impossible to travel through China, he told a meeting in Bristol in 1889, 'without feeling there was a power at work influencing men's minds, the result of missions and that alone'. He 'knew of villages in the far West' – he had worked for many years in Wuhan – 'where the people flocked to chapel at the sound of the bell, and they imagined it was Sunday at home'.[28] For some, the flavour of home was best conveyed by pale ale and tinned soup even on a canal somewhere near Suzhou, or through reading 'The Country Gentleman's Newspaper' in Hong Kong; for others it was the sound of church bells.

'Home' it remained, though, as an idea, as a part of speech – for the mails to Europe went 'homeward', and the newspaper that best captured the names of those travelling was the *Homeward Mail from India, China and the East*, while men wrote of 'taking a run home', meaning going on leave. The greater part of those appointed found their way home again before too long. If we set aside those who became in time directors or partners, the average length of service is not much longer than a single five-year engagement. There were exceptions. James Hall worked for 27 years in Shanghai, retiring as head book-keeper in 1900. Frederick Aubert spent 18 years with the firm there, and when he left Butterfield & Swire in 1887 he stayed on working for Wheelock & Co., exhibited his Scottish Terriers at the Shanghai dog show and died in Shanghai in 1895. Walter Poate spent 25 years, mostly in Hong Kong; James Denison Danby 33 years, returning to the company fold after trying another in 1920, and after retiring went into partnership with a former Butterfield & Swire colleague. Tea man Henry Baker spent 42 years with B&S, mostly as Fuzhou manager. W. J. Robinson had completed 50 years of service when he retired in 1923, his unhealthy life notwithstanding, 33 of them in Kobe, where he amassed and then sold a notable collection of Japanese *objets d'art*, grew intensely interested in Buddhism and co-founded Japan's first golf club.[29]

The occasional man sank: 'turned out badly', a 'thoroughly bad lot' are two terse verdicts accompanying dismissals. In the former case the man stayed on in China, in the latter he can next be spotted in Salford. Another man is described as indolent and intemperate: 'I don't think he drank, drunk, but he drank, stupid' was the verdict.[30] Stupidity, in this case, was the bigger potential problem. He was dismissed and went off to work in Japan. More often, men were released as not being up to the job: 'let the duffers take care of themselves.' The occasional bad apple bobs up in the records. Frederick Shepherd embezzled over $1,300 in Yokohama, before being caught and dismissed in May 1893.[31] After 10 months in the London office, one young man arrived in Hong Kong in 1904 to work on the Taikoo Sugar Refinery books, fell in with a 'bad crowd', ran up debts amounting to his annual salary and started to steal from the firm. All was revealed when an 'American demi-mondaine' arrived at the office to ask his manager, sweetly, how she might be repaid. Tolerant to the extent that he was clearly beyond his depth (and disinclined to have such details in the public press), the firm quietly fired him, but granted a passage to North America where, eventually, he made a new life under a new name.[32] More routine was the man who was a 'hopeless muddler', or one 'good in his place', but 'not the Typan class', while another 'will not have enough ballast for years to come'.[33] Poate, the Hong Kong Taipan reported in 1899, was a 'very first class no. 1' but that was 'his limitation'.[34] Arthur Franks's limitations, reached after 12 years with the company – 'he is not a genius and ... would not be worth more to us than ordinary clerical labour is valued at' – moved the firm to conclude he was superfluous, even if 'honourable' and 'careful', and to dismiss him in January 1893. Distraught, for 'I dread more than I can say the idea of being at home without a billet ... it means ruin', Franks was found a clerical position with the firm's Melbourne agency and eased out that way. Sir James Lorimer had died in 1889. His sons took over the business, but had mismanaged it into bankruptcy in 1893. Swires set up a new agency for their Australian business under the supervision of their former *cha-see* George Martin with whom Franks next worked as his number 2.[35]

Most of the company's British employees, at any one time, were fairly young men who had to make a new home in the east. But a home assumes a residence, and for many it assumes family. 'Wives, and sisters, and female friends are undoubtedly essential to the full enjoyment of social life', as Hugh Lang put it in an 1875 lecture on Shanghai foreign life. But the settlement lacked for most of its first five decades even enough family houses for its foreign residents, whatever their resources (he divided local family society into: 'artizans, ships' officers, and mercantile assistants').[36] Some men had relatives in Asia: two of Poate's brothers worked in Hong Kong and Shanghai respectively, a third was a missionary in Japan and a sister had been living in Hong Kong when she died in 1875. Warrick's brother worked for an insurance company in Shanghai, James Cummings's brother in Hong Kong. Montague Beart's brother had been secretary of the Hong Kong Club for a decade when he arrived. Henry Shadgett had been born in Hong Kong. Orphaned and destitute in Shanghai when his hotel-keeper father died in 1882, a Masonic fund had sent the boy to board at a school in Chefoo until he came of age. Joining the firm after working in the Municipal Post Office at Shanghai, Shadgett would eventually become chief shipping manager in Shanghai. James Danby had also been born in Hong Kong, where his father worked as a civil engineer. After schooling in England – he would become a stalwart in the colony's Society of Yorkshiremen – he joined Butterfield & Swire there after briefly working for his father.[37] Bois's brother also briefly worked for the firm in Hong Kong, but stayed out in China thereafter, and his sister came out to Shanghai and married Joseph Welch, who would become the company's tea purchasing agent. Herbert Baggally's cousin came out to Asia three years after he joined the firm: men followed relations, and they were in turn followed themselves. But most knew no one when they got off the Blue Funnel steamers that brought them through the Suez Canal to Asia.

They were single, and the firm did not relish the prospect of its staff marrying, or, to be more precise, of employing married junior staff in Asia, for it brought them additional expense. Some were lucky: on pointing out the financial burden of marriage to one man, Lang was assured that 'he had an income independent of his salary and felt quite certain of being able to get on comfortably without running into debt'.[38] It was this potential to incur debt that was the key objection – though being unmarried was quite obviously no guarantee against it – and the related concern that men might end up in court being sued, or would press the firm for help, or would help themselves (which seems to have been embezzler Frederick Shepherd's approach).[39] None of these were attractive prospects, and the paternalistic regulation of staff marriage entitlement would last well into the twentieth century. In 1905 James Allport Knox was dismissed within six months of arriving in Shanghai for 'marrying without leave'. His wife was perfectly respectable, but he had wed her before sailing and kept this secret from the firm. 'We felt ... we could place no further confidence in a man whose first act after signing [his agreement] was to deliberately deceive the Firm', the Hong Kong Taipan wrote. Knox's dismissal 'will have a salutary effect' on other staff, and no man earning less than £500 a year was to be given permission to marry.[40] In this Butterfield & Swire operated as most other British firms of similar standing did, and missionary societies and treaty port administrations did likewise.

But even if men had the resource, and seniority, the chances of finding a marriage partner brought challenges of their own. For where, in communities in which sex ratios were heavily unbalanced, was a man to meet a woman, and more difficult yet, a woman of the appropriate social background? Some were clearly already committed when they sailed east, for they married women from their hometowns. Bois took a run home in 1880 to marry, and to fetch back his bride, Margaret Philips. For his part, Walter Poate looked to the firm, or, rather, his first wife Lilian was one of the four daughters of China Navigation Company master mariner John Whittle. (And Whittle's stepsons both worked for Butterfield & Swire.) Whittle's daughters had a far greater chance of social advancement in China's foreign communities than back in their former Liverpool home. Conversely, at least one man went out specifically to effect a separation from his wife.[41] Other men's wills show what the financial arrangements suggest were settled relationships with Chinese or Japanese 'housekeepers', a common euphemism for an unmarried Asian partner.[42] Although not exceptional, William Robinson's two marriages to Japanese women, the name of the first of whom is – characteristically – lost to us, and then some years after her death, to Sayoko Sakakibara, were unusual for the time, and his background.

Life in China had its own challenges for British women married into the company, especially outside Hong Kong and Shanghai. Mary Dodds, Swire complained, 'growls about the social disadvantages of residence in Japan' (though in marrying Dodds she had married her second Yokohama merchant: she clearly knew the score).[43] For others it was precisely the small size of such communities – there were 2,800 foreign residents in Yokohama in 1891 – that allowed them to shine more brightly than might ever have been possible at home.[44] Names are hard to spot, but we can reasonably assume that the social round, and the threadbare but certainly active cultural life of Hong Kong or

Shanghai, augmented lives that were also charged with running the household and raising children. 'Mrs P. ... is very careful,' wrote the Hong Kong manager of his locum's handling of the hong expenses while he was on leave.[45] As in many sites of British residence overseas, hygiene and housekeeping were reputed to require some careful vigilance and so fell to the 'missee', the mistress of the house. The better off – Scott and Bois, for example – hired foreign governesses instead of Chinese nurses, but the amah and the ayi were fixtures in the foreign household. In hot weather women took the children north to Yantai, husbands managing a break north when business allowed. Still, the picture is often a mournful one. Cemeteries in Hong Kong, Shanghai or Kobe accommodated the wives and children of Swire employees, as well as more of the men themselves. Lilian Poate was buried in Happy Valley in 1887, dying shortly after giving birth; Jim Scott's wife Emily Yuill was laid to rest in Yantai in 1883, three years after their marriage. Beart's wife Rachel would join her there 20 years later. Bois would lose his sister, and one of her children. Fanny Matchitt, widowed at 32, left her husband buried in Shantou's Kakchieh Foreign Cemetery when she sailed back to England on the *Patroclus* in 1891. The same cemetery took Ernest Shepherd, his death widowing his bride of but six months, Alice Macgowan. Finding it impossible to 'shake off the fever that has been hanging about him', Edwin Mackintosh and his wife sailed to Japan for a month in April 1882, leaving their infant son in Hong Kong in the care of their English nurse. The boy died of a sudden illness while they were away. His gravestone stands today in Happy Valley.[46]

The greater risks to health for Europeans living and working in Asia than staying at home were diminishing steadily across the second half of the nineteenth century, but still seem high. Eleven of the hundred or so men engaged between 1870 and 1900 died in the company's service. The average age at death was 36. All things being equal, and given their social background, and the fact that the medical check-up in London will have winnowed some recruits out, most of these men would have lived longer if they had not left Britain for Asia. Typhoid and cholera took the greater toll. And the letters abound with comments about this man's 'general seediness' or that one's 'very feeble' looks. Aubert 'is not strong and I'm afraid he will have to give up China before long' runs one report, while 'Georgehan has hardly yet recovered from a severe attack of cholera'. Herbert Baggally resigned because of the climate in

Japan, and complaints about climate echo through the records.[47] Asia was a gamble, and a significant number lost their all.

The foreign position in China had been established through war and was maintained by treaty and the threat of force. It did not go uncontested. Hong Kong and Shanghai were, on the whole, stable. But business at the smaller ports had its challenges in an era of change in China. In 1889 the Zhenjiang hulk *Cadiz* came back into the news, when an altercation on the Bund there spiralled out of control. The recruitment of six Sikh policemen by the British Municipal Council was the underlying source of tension. Very swiftly a row became a riot. The police station and the British consulate were set alight as were other foreign homes, and the five dozen foreign residents rushed to the hulk for safety. A frenzy of angry violence left 'Not a lamp ... standing, the roads were torn up in places, the railings and trees along the Bund pulled down'. Some of the refugees were taken away by a China Merchants steamer, and the rest boarded CNCo's SS *Ngankin*: 'arms and ammunition were served out, while hose connected with the boilers was laid, so that should the rioters attempt to board, they would meet with a warm reception.' This fever quickly expended itself. The experiment with Sikh police was discontinued. CNCo, like other foreign interests, submitted a claim (conceded and paid) for damage to property and delays to its steamers. Consulate flags were raised again in May (the British one replacing the standard that was spotted having been recycled into clothing), and although residents reported continuing hostility, and jaunty ballads were sold in the streets commemorating the incendiarism, the port resumed its general calm. It was a 'local boil' wrote Sir Robert Hart, and had 'no political meaning': 'such a thing might break out anywhere, and just as unexpectedly, in China.' One retort to this came in a verse that circulated later: foreigners 'may hoodwink Guangxu [the emperor] and all the Princes / But they can't hoodwink us', it claimed.[48]

Hart was wrong. The war with France heralded a new era of tensions in China. While the military struggle was perhaps ultimately inconclusive – despite the rapid destruction of an entire Chinese fleet in Fuzhou's harbour by the French – the diplomatic result was a heavy defeat. For increasing numbers of its subjects, Qing failures came to be seen as essentially just that. Ethnically Han Chinese increasingly came to see themselves as such, in contrast to their Manchu rulers, whose predecessors had overthrown the last Chinese dynasty, the Ming, in 1644. In the late 1880s and 1890s we enter a period of slowly developing opposition to Qing rule, and contestation of the foreign position in China, those Sikh policemen at Zhenjiang, for example. The CNCo hulk at Wuhu also served as a vital redoubt in May 1891, when, in one of a number of attacks in Yangzi cities on missionaries and other foreigners co-ordinated by secret society gangsters, a crowd, inflamed by rumours of missionaries killing children to use their eyes in medicine, attacked and burned foreign compounds. Missionaries and others flocked on board, while the customs station's force of volunteers charged the mob – 'in first class style', it was reported – and subdued it until reinforcements arrived to end the affair.[49]

In 1892 Thomas Weatherston, CNCo hulk-keeper at Wuhu in 1891, who had worked for the company there and before that at Wuhan since 1874, moved downriver to establish a formal branch of Butterfield & Swire at Zhenjiang. CNCo's interests had previously been managed by an agent, Farquhar Carnie, a man remembered for his skill in the 'science' of pig shooting, which seems to have helped wipe out the animal in the local area.[50] For the first few years, Weatherston, a former mariner and son of a colonial chaplain, lived on the *Cadiz* with his wife and daughters.[51] It is quite likely that this was as well-equipped as its neighbour, the hulk *Orissa*, described as having 'a beautifully furnished, large, quiet, brightly-lighted dining room … a real proper, luxurious drawing-room, … sofas, lounges, small tables … all the et-cæteras of an English … sitting room … a large, grandly-furnished bedroom'.[52] Hulk life was comfortable: it was after all a former P&O packet. But, still, as Weatherston explained when successfully requesting a house allowance, 'the deck is crowded all day with coolies loading the coasters who are in a dirty half-naked state', the noise was constant, and steamers pumped out their tanks when moored alongside which raised an 'almost unbearable' smell, while small boats surrounded the hulk, the habits of their occupants not a fit sight for the Weatherston family. It may also explain why Weatherston was frequently ill for long periods with 'typhoid', his wife having to keep Shanghai informed in the meantime. There were tensions with the Customs Commissioner, W. T. Lay, whose 'discretionary power' was open to abuse: Lay found official ways to object to personal discomforts such as the chatter and work songs of labourers outside his house, or the CNCo steamer whistles, and flew into a rage when Weatherston refused to discount a passenger fare for him. The small stage on which men like Lay strutted at Zhenjiang was often the site of hysterical, operatic display precisely because of its size. And the still shifting river bank continued to bedevil trade. In October 1895 came reports to Shanghai of an incident during the loading of the steamer *Kweilin*: a 'coolie' was caught stealing some rice, the 'Cantonese' beat him, were checked by the concession police and turned on the constables, an incident that threatened a boycott of CNCo ships. Weatherston, then council chairman, sacked two policemen and calm was restored and loading continued. The man was too calm, however, and after his 'most straightforward and honest' comprador Yuan Zhizhen threw himself into the Yangzi in June 1900 and was fished out alive, it emerged that the man was in debt, being ruined, he said, by the extravagance of his sons. To help extricate himself, Yuan, once recovered, promptly, and secretly, sold $10,000 of Taikoo sugar from company stocks.

The firm eventually covered the losses from Yuan's guarantors, but not without trouble. Weatherston left China the following year. Zhenjiang had long disappointed the great hopes held of it in the early 1860s. Fuzhou's story was one of a slower but still steady decline. There a succession of managers oversaw the fading of the annual tea crop frenzy, but not before a clearly distressed W. J. Robinson requested a transfer in 1888: 'a man has only a certain amount of combativeness in him', and he had expended his, was 'thoroughly broken down', had 'lost heart' and requested a post in Japan. His successor George Martin left 'for good and all I hope' in 1890: 'my wife cannot stand the climate.' Fuzhou business was more complex than Zhenjiang's. There was steamer business to Australia (of which Butterfield's retained the largest share), and the Blue Funnel agency to London as well as inter-port traffic, and shipments to Tianjin of poles that were brought down the Min River. The Fuzhou letters to Shanghai provide intelligence of the likely need for space on upcoming steamer departures, reports on confronting steamer competition and worries about the comprador ('not so sound as he should be'). By 1893 the foreign community was not large enough to field a cricket team to play Xiamen's XI.[53] Baker, who ran the branch after 1890, and by 1899 ran it alone – it was once staffed by three men – was for his part more a man of the turf than the pitch. Despite John Samuel Swire's own life in the saddle, the firm came to look with disfavour on its staff becoming involved in racing, a circular to its Hong Kong assistants in 1899 advising that 'the firm does not approve of their employees being interested in ponies', it would 'certainly prejudice their chances of promotion'.[54]

Tea tasters – *cha-sees* like Baker – were a class apart, the mercantile aristocracy, operating alongside, but rather separately from, the core activities of the branches at Fuzhou, Shanghai and Yokohama. Much hinged – profit certainly, but also reputation – on their judgement. They were paid almost twice as much as other staff, and would have an option to trade on their own account. They might also get holiday pay and a 'run home'. Tea men needed sweeteners. Getting a good one was always tricky. He needed experience – seven or eight years with a London tea firm in Mincing Lane preferably – and would then need to gain some familiarity with the needs of buyers in New York or Australia. Training men up to the job proved difficult. 'Get rid of Wyatt,' ordered Swire in 1878 as one man's term of service came to an end. He had once been spoken of very highly as 'a judge of both blacks and greens' but had turned out 'indifferent', 'not a Merchant – no head'. 'I am sorry for the poor fellow,' wrote Swire, but he needed to go and, no, he would not be allowed to use the Butterfield & Swire tea room if he set up on his own out in China.[55] Swire routinely lamented that good tea men were generally poor salesmen.

The work was seasonal, and intense, if not needing a robust 'combativeness' (as Robinson put in 1888). At first the firm's *cha-sees* in Shanghai journeyed up to Wuhan ahead of the opening of the season. As the tea arrived a hectic period of tasting and bargaining ensued. A man might taste 150 samples a morning, judging also the smell, the look and the feel of the samples. Was it free of dust, were there traces of blossom (confirming it had been picked early)? Instructions from London set out the value of purchases authorised. These were very large sums. Swire worried that the febrile atmosphere at Hankow, as the steamers impatiently waited to carry the cargo swiftly to London, would cause men who were far from the hong and their colleagues to be rushed to poor decisions. He tried, fruitlessly, to persuade other firms to boycott the port, and draw the site of the purchasing downriver to Shanghai.[56] Increasingly, contracts issued to the *cha-sees* stipulated that they should also be active as directed in the general business of Butterfield & Swire branches. Between 1868 and 1880 the company generally made losses on tea – after its own charges had been deducted – barring an exceptional profit in 1879 that cancelled all previous debits. As well as its commissions, Blue Funnel had cargoes to carry as well, so that overall the group covered its expenses, and profited modestly, but the continued decline of consumer demand for Chinese teas meant that after 1893 the company left the trade altogether.[57]

For John Samuel Swire, despite his voracious appetite for data and news, and attention to minute detail, much hinged on his partners and managers in Asia. They were the public face of the firm, and needed to play their role in chambers of commerce, and other such bodies, although the Swire companies remained cautious on that score, unlike the Jardines men. William Lang was often more a liability on this score than a reliable asset. The Shanghai partner was never to be 'seen' in society. He never married, and he played little by way of a role in public life, aside from a stint on the French concession council at Shanghai. But this was a one-year role, and both Edwin Mackintosh and Jim Scott would serve, too, there not to serve the concession, but to protect the company's interests: the CNCo wharf on the French Bund. 'Why can't you make personal friends of your business equals,' wrote an exasperated John Swire in 1877, after Lang got tangled up with 'an infernal scoundrel', Henry Smith Bidwell, who had then disclosed that he was working for the firm, a story that had spread to London where John Swire's disbelieving associates stopped by Billiter Street to ask him for confirmation. Bidwell was a jobbing commission agent, then trying to fix loans to the Qing government. Extraterritoriality had nurtured the growth of an arena in which such speculators might work, hustling from one new project to the next, lobbying provincial officials, or seeking entrees to figures in the Chinese capital. 'You have got amongst a wretchedly bad commercial set,' wrote Swire to Lang, who had actually given Bidwell office space at the Shanghai hong. Swire was bewildered, wondered if drink had undone a second head, but was reassured to find out that Lang had simply been 'foolish, nothing more'.[58] He tore off both China partners in a letter in August 1877: 'you are not to compromise the name of our firm by being associated with any China house,' he wrote.[59] The distinction is worth noting. Butterfield & Swire was not to act as if it were part of the opportunistic world of local entrepreneurs like Bidwell, men who squeezed what advantage they could out of the imprecisely defined world of extraterritorial privilege in

China. It was a British firm, not a Shanghai or a Hong Kong company. The difference might be one of degree, rather than absolute, but it was absolutely important to the good standing of Butterfield & Swire.

The rare personal vignettes aside – whist at the Shanghai Club daily at four, shooting trips on houseboats out to the Lake Tai region, a sightseeing holiday in Japan – the first Shanghai partner has left little trace of his personality. Lang raced a China pony in 1876 – those 'Swell' ponies were barred from the Shanghai races – and perhaps he was the owner of a stable sold the previous year whose names were taken from the first three Blue Funnel steamers.[60] In 1884 Swire thought him living 'in the 1860 period, before telegraph, steam and competition … as averse to improvement as a Chinaman and far more obstinate … Just about a century old.'[61] The press seems not to have noted Lang's departure in 1888, which was unusual, and suggests he had continued to cut little of a public figure for himself. When Jim Scott sailed on leave from Hong Kong in 1878 the fact was noted in a laudatory paragraph in the *Hongkong Daily Press*: 'a merchant of the best type', 'a citizen who has ever been foremost in promoting the interests of the places he has lived in, whether in his private or public capacity'. His successor in the colony, Edwin Mackintosh, was also a much more public figure than the Shanghai Taipan. This had its downside, of course, as 'Tosh of Taikoo' found out. More reasoned critique would also be made of company partners and managers in their public roles, but nevertheless the company needed to present this public face. He might be an 'able and outspoken' chairman of the Chamber of Commerce, thought the *China Mail*'s editor in 1891, but Mackintosh was 'a militant ship-owner' whose 'range of vision is narrowed by his zeal'.[62]

By the 1880s, the merchants and clerks in Butterfield & Swire formed a minority among the staff of the firms managed by John Swire & Sons. The refinery and China Navigation employed many more people, and their world needs exploring as well. Taikoo Sugar had its own quite distinctive culture, as a colony in Hong Kong of lower-middle-class Scots from Greenock, largely, managed by a German, who lived in what they felt was a distant isolation from the city for 'there were no trams, few ricshas, no electric lights – nothing but kerosene lamps'. One man recalled, 25 years after the event, that when he arrived there were '100 coolie matsheds, one matshed bungalow in which was housed the little European community, numbering only six solitary individuals', and 'two large holes in the ground receiving foundations'. But there were 'other things that went to make the good old days merry': mainly liquid ones.[63] Greenock's exiles conquered their solitariness and convened annually with their peers at a banquet of the 'Sugar Refining Trade', laying aside the fierce competition the three refineries now operating were engaged in, in favour of haggis, whisky, paeans to the trade, to Scotland and to each other. These were sung, orated and they were probably slurred. The Greenock connection was reinforced as new staff were recruited through notices in the town's papers, but Dr Korn kept away from this gathering (his absence noted). The community at the refinery might have felt distant and self-contained, but they were closely managed from Victoria. Edwin Mackintosh reassured the Senior that the German would never think to assume a 'Dictatorship' over operations at Quarry Bay, or, to draw a comparison closer to home, would never become 'another Endicott', another too autonomous an employee, for such Endicott had rather at times become. Science remained in the lead, but Butterfield & Swire was in control.[64]

Science had also come to the rescue in 1886 when a health crisis traumatised the still infant refinery. An intense rainstorm in July that year had swept some island residents to their death, brought walls and buildings down and damaged the culvert that took a small stream through the works to the harbour. Within two weeks two senior foreign employees, who lived on the site, had died from 'fever', the rest 'in a panic' had moved on to a ship, and then refused to move back into their houses. And, 'with "down" Scotch workmen,' reported Mackintosh, 'it is no use attempting to argue'. Prevailing understandings of malaria (later identified as the cause) had it that it stemmed from a 'miasma' released from disturbed soil. Even so, the sanitary advice rapidly sought led the company to repair the drain and fill in the marshy valley that had accommodated the floodwaters. The staff and their families at Quarry Bay, one of their number later recalled, were 'tied together for their own protection because they never knew who was going to be sick next'.[65]

'Quarry Bay' was socially quite different, and that tied its staff together as well. 'Is it possible to procure a better stamp or class of employee?' asked Mackintosh in 1892 in a letter to London. A new recruit, John Macfarlan, 'no doubt will turn out a good clerk, but as you know a little "breeding" is necessary for the good of the staff & for the employees' own personal comfort'. To compound the faults of his birth – his father was a clerk in Greenock – Macfarlan's brother was a CNCo third engineer, who 'associates here with the employees at Quarry Bay' who were 'all good in their own way but rather below the standard we look for in the office'. Quarry Bay was out of sight – far, far out of sight – from the offices in Queen's Road, but not out of mind.[66]

The growth of this company town continued apace. Some of this was aimed at providing richer leisure opportunities for those marooned out in the east than those liquid 'other things' that continued to bedevil the work. 'I have persuaded Mr Crombie to sign the enclosed pledge,' wrote George Fitzpatrick to Mackintosh in 1891, after a discussion 'anent drinking'. Might you 'reinstate him this once, it might be the means of showing the Europeans of Quarry Bay your magnanimity'.[67] The refinery was later expanded, its capacity thereby doubling and staff increasing. A sports ground was laid out, and a Taikoo Club. The success of the plant depended on retaining its staff, but sickness continued to prove a worry, and Hong Kong was beset by public health crises at the turn of the century, including an outbreak of bubonic plague that first appeared in 1894, which highlighted the delinquent approach to urban sanitation that the colony's administration had up to that point employed. Taikoo was somewhat ahead of the government, having learned the hard way in 1886. In 1891 the company constructed a block of apartments for summer residence on the cooler heights up along the valley from Quarry Bay which also came to serve as a sanatorium. This also involved installing an aerial ropeway – a chair lift – to connect it to the refinery below, one of the more eccentric additions to the portfolio of equipment and properties in the company ledgers. But keeping Quarry Bay happy was important.

Staff discontent led to the departure of Dr Korn, a dictator after all, it transpired, at least as a manager of men. His focus on quality and consistency, once seen, rightly, as vital to the performance of the plant, was by 1900 deemed insensitive. He did not treat staff 'as thinking beings, given responsibility'. 'Individual talent and effort was ignored or squashed', 'he has not a friend in the place'. While Korn was on leave his Scottish replacement showed the power of 'practice v theory'. Hong Kong wired London that the German should not return as general manager of the refinery. The cipher used was 'YEOMANLIKE' which, clearly, he was not thought to be. There may well have been an echo of imperial politics here as well. These were more overt when it came to another of the chemists. British relations with Germany had become steadily more brittle in the 1890s. The 'scramble for concessions' in China after the Sino-Japanese War had seen a notable heightening of fears of German and of Russian designs on the Qing empire, and on Britain's position within it. The Russian seizure of what became the Port Arthur naval base near Dalian, and Germany's establishment of a navy-run colony at Qingdao in Shandong, prompted the British demand for a lease territory centring on Weihaiwei. And what, the army's chief of staff in Hong Kong asked, having popped by the Butterfield & Swire offices in 1900, was a man called Obremski doing up there taking photographs: 'our Intelligence Dept have been on his track for some months past.' He says he works for you. Yes, replied Walter Poate, Dr Marian von Obrembski is one of our chemists, and is a Polish refugee from Russia: he's no spy.[68] The company found itself entangled in imperial as well as Chinese politics, even in the British Crown Colony.

For most of its customers the face of Butterfield & Swire and its companies was Chinese: it was *Taigu*, not Swires. The most prominent and best documented of the Chinese staff of Butterfield & Swire were its compradors, but a survey from the early 1890s gives us a more detailed picture of the company's Chinese employees. The Hong Kong office employed the comprador, two shroffs (cashiers, or accountants), a writer, two shipping and two godownmen, three godown assistants, a watchman, three office boys, three 'office coolies', a watchman for the office and four 'chair coolies' (presumably for the Hong Kong senior staff). Swatow recorded a comprador secured by three 'responsible Swatow hongs', two book-keepers, two shroffs, four cargo brokers and an office boy, a 'native writer' named 'Ding Shao Lin' and a marine insurance clerk. CNCo at Swatow had, like most branches, its own comprador, and 30 staff. Shanghai employed its two compradors, 10 native writers, 'Black watchmen' – Sikhs most likely – and other office, warehouse and docks staff, teaboy and tea-room coolie. The comprador hired and paid the godown staff, receiving a monthly allowance to do this, and being expected to meet any additional costs from his own profits. At Fuzhou, Helbling reported in 1889 that there were three teaboys, the comprador, two office boys, nightwatchman, five chair and chit coolies, launch engineer, helmsman and lookout man. The No. 1 shroff, when released from his post of 17 years in 1898, sought help from the firm to find a place in Shanghai operating as a ship's comprador. The arrangements reported often reflected the strongly parochial nature of the commercial environment in each port, vastly different as many of them were, with their own resilient customary practices and conventions, and, of course, languages and patterns of social relations, but they also show how, as the firm broadened its operations, Chinese employees also moved with it if they could.[69]

At Quarry Bay the company actually housed them. Alongside the refinery it built around 55 mostly three-storey houses alongside the road. The refinery site was at such a remove from the main Chinese suburb on the north-western side of the island that the company needed to house its labourers, and not just the colony from Greenock. As the refinery expanded so this 'Native Village' would also grow, and others would move to service the growing community, helped by the fact that the streetside houses were configured on the ground floor as shops. By 1893 the refinery employed nearly 2,000 Chinese workers.[70] The company housing took the form of the by then standard model of mixed-use building that came to characterise the urban environment of south China and Southeast Asian port cities. A very different style was adopted for the next major building project. In September 1897 fresh new flags flew over Butterfield & Swire in Hong Kong, as the company opened an impressive new headquarters to throngs of local residents. This was the first hong building the firm had commissioned. 'Fire and typhoon' proof, its Amoy red brick fronted the 'New Praya', the waterline of the colony's latest reclamation of the harbour. Up to this point the firm had made do and rented, but now it was able to present its vision of itself in the heart of the colony. Spacious and confident, and much more centrally located than its offices had previously been, the building would serve the firm for over 60 years. And, like the Quarry Bay developments, as well as accommodating some of the foreign staff, this also housed some of the Chinese ones. The comprador was formally installed in the building, although like all Chinese staff he was quartered on the ground-floor mezzanine 'which has the advantage of excluding a large portion of the Chinese employees from the public and business part of the premises', as the firm put it in a handout duly transcribed in the local press. An 1892 plan of the former offices in the Beaconsfield Arcade, part of the former Augustine Heard hong, and quite dilapidated when the firm moved out, does not indicate at all where the comprador was to be found. An album of photographs of the new building's interior and exterior, and its views, shows the offices allowed to the comprador as well as his living quarters.[71] These, in their decor and mix of foreign and Chinese ornament, are closer to the style adopted in the homes of men like Robert Hart.

Compradors were at the heart of the firm's activities, even if hidden out of view like this, and hidden out of view, too, in the firm's archives, for we have far less by way of material about them than we do about the British clerks and assistants. The comprador accommodation in the new building was provided for Ng Ahip's successor. Ng died in October 1889 – fabulously wealthy, thought the press, for 'sugar is evidently a paying business'; moderately so, thought Mackintosh. But he provided in his will for his three wives, children, extended family and his ancestors: an ancestral hall was to be built, rites and ceremonies to be held at their graves. Ng was succeeded by Mok Tso Chun (Mok Koon Yuk), son of his former patron and business partner Mok Sze Yeung. Ng had been secured for $100,000 by guarantors, mostly by a Macao-based member of the Mok clan, Mok Wai. This bond was then transferred to Mok Tso Chun, who had been working with the firm since the 1870s.[72] Through the Heard connection, the Mok family had been associated with Swires since it commenced operating in the colony, and would do so until the 1930s. Like his father, Mok Tso Chun would serve on the board of the most important Chinese organisations in Hong Kong, the Tung Hwa Hospital, effectively the community's representative body, and the anti-trafficking charity, the Po Leung Kuk. Even so, and for all that Ng bestowed an ancestral hall, and Chun Koo Leong and Wong Suen Hing and some of their sons acquired honorary or substantive titles and honours and decorations, these men were moderns. They studied English (and another of the Mok clan not only worked as a CNCo comprador, but published a number of English primers and manuals), worked and studied overseas, grasped new knowledge about telegraphy and electricity, and set up their own firms to collaborate with, and compete with, foreign businesses. They were mobile, moving far from Xiangshan and from the cities they had rooted themselves in. Their wealth and influence, lifestyle and values, served further to displace and disorient the settled hierarchy of the Qing. Quite whether their associates in firms like Swires understood this is another matter. But there was one notable convergence. In a period when the Liverpool character of the firm was fading, and the ties of friendship and family from which staff and capital were drawn were being diluted, the Swire, Holt and Scott family network would remain visible and vital in the company, joined by a new set of Chinese families which had become embedded in the company across its branches in China's port cities.

One of these was the Chun family. Zheng Guanying resigned from CNCo in 1882 to take up a role with China Merchants, a move that aligned with his political writings. His younger brother continued to work for Taikoo, having become the Tianjin comprador in 1886, a post he and his sons would hold until 1931.[73] Zheng was followed as CNCo comprador by Yang Guixuan, who was succeeded in his turn in 1884 by an already well-established businessman, Chun Koo Leong (Chen Keliang). Born in Xiangshan in 1830, Chun had spent half a decade in San Francisco in the 1850s, before returning to work in Shanghai and eventually acting as comprador for Fearon Low & Co., a partnership that emerged from the ruins of Augustine Heard and into which he had been brought by a cousin. Chun brought his own family and relatives into CNCo as well. His third son, Chun Shut Kai, would eventually succeed him, his second son worked with CNCo and his nephew Chun Kwan Yeh served as assistant comprador. Another relative, Chun Ming Hung, was brought in as CNCo shroff, having worked for Heards and then with the patriarch in Fearon Low. In 1892 Chun Koo Leong added the position of Butterfield & Swire comprador to his CNCo responsibilities. Another Xiangshan family entwined with the Swire firms was that of Wong Suen Hing (Wang Xianxing). Wong had worked with CNCo from its inception as a cargo broker. All four of his sons worked with the firm, either at Shanghai, or running agencies or brokerages in Shanghai, Wuhan and Yichang. They were educated variously at Queen's College in Hong Kong, in the United States as one of 120 students sent from China on a government scheme in 1874, in Shanghai and Tianjin. At his retirement in 1897 his fourth son, Wong Kwei Chek, took his father's position.[74]

Kinship networks and affective ties were important, but financial standard was vital, and underpinning that were comprador guarantees and securities. How easily they might be enforced continued to be another matter, however. Shortly after returning to Shanghai from Peking in April 1884, John Samuel Swire set about revising processes for payments on freight which involved, he believed, too much by way of extended credit for shippers. CNCo comprador Yang Guixuan promptly failed. Since succeeding Zheng Guanying, Yang, it now transpired, had systematically and substantially defrauded the company. He had exploited these lax credit arrangements to cover his losses when other ventures he had pursued had failed. Yang took ill and died in the winter of 1884/5 shortly after the case came to court. He owed over 100,000 Taels.[75] One of the guarantors was Zheng – Yang was, of course, a fellow countryman from Xiangshan. The loss itself fell to CNCo and not Butterfield & Swire, but all concerned were confident that most of the money would be covered by the guarantees. Zheng refused to pay. As he travelled through Hong Kong in February 1885 on his way to Xiangshan, Edwin Mackintosh had him arrested and jailed for debt. 'I trust we can squeeze something out of him,' he reported, 'as he is said to be wealthy and influentially connected. Tho' he protests that he himself has not a cent.' Zheng proved obstinate. Mackintosh sought what information he could on the former comprador's assets, and rejected small compromise payments offered by Zheng's associates in Hong Kong. Zheng sat in jail in Hong Kong for 12 months, and was then released, thereby expunging his debt. Or so he thought: six years after his release, however, John Bois still sought to press him for the money. Let it be, London recommended.[76]

In 1892 an extensive fraud, committed by the long-serving Shanghai Butterfield & Swire comprador Zhuo Zihe (Chewoh) became apparent. As was becoming routine at that point, William Lang's delinquent management of the branch was thought to be most at fault – the fraud commenced 'a good many years ago' – but even if this had been the case, since Lang's retirement in 1888 the company had been complacent about regularly checking the securities. Zhuo's guarantors, who had presumably vouched for him over 15 years earlier, were dead, and the securities turned out to be worthless. 'It is an expensive lesson to learn,' concluded Mackintosh. Well, well, responded John Samuel Swire on hearing the news, 'make up your minds that most Chinamen are both impecunious and unprincipled, and that they have greater talents for finance than are possessed by Europeans'. So 'trust your Compradore as little as possible'.[77]

There are two separate issues here, which were routinely conflated: individual dishonesty and the inadequacy of arrangements – securities and guarantors – that it was assumed would place this form of

cross-cultural commercial collaboration on a firm basis. Responses to the
first were heavily influenced by prevailing notions of Chinese honesty
and morality. These were, if anything, growing more extreme: in the
period of Chewoh's frauds English-language newspapers in Shanghai and
Hong Kong were serialising articles on 'Chinese characteristics', under
that title, written by an American missionary, Arthur Smith, threading
through which was the assumption that it was 'literally impossible to be
sure of finding [honesty] anywhere' in China.[78] The racist assumptions
underpinning this can be exposed by a cursory glance at the records
of trials of British merchants at Shanghai's Supreme Court: Chinese
traders had no monopoly on dishonesty. Both the devolved nature of
oversight in foreign firms in China, whereby compradors effectively
ran important areas of activity in a quite autonomous manner, and the
imperfectly regulated commercial environment, provided opportunity
for the dishonest and the desperate, for Zhuo Zihe in Shanghai,
Yuan Zhizhen in Zhenjiang, or, it would emerge in 1900, Ah Fook at
Yokohama, who fraudulently sold 8,000 bags of Taikoo sugar, literally
hollowing out the stockpiles in the warehouse in a way that allowed
him to evade detection, at least for a while. In all of these cases, the
firm did not go to law to exact redress, preferring to work with the
business associates of those concerned to try to secure redress. This had
its limits – Zhuo had already 'bled all his friends severely' – and so
Bois worked on the Canton Guild in Shanghai, aiming to shame it
into preventing the public 'scandal' a prosecution would bring to the
'whole Canton community'.[79] The issue of guarantors and securities
and effective supervision of these was more obviously within the ability
of Butterfield & Swire to manage. Here there was a series of failures by
partners and managers that left the company exposed more than once.

Clearly some better form of security for compradors was needed
than jailing their guarantors to try to force them to pay up, as even
Bois later admitted.[80] But the episode also highlights how commerce
and politics continued to remain inextricably entangled. Whether it
was a hulk, a jetty or a comprador, the politics of foreign business in
treaty port China could be brittle. And the network and infrastructure
created by Swires in China and other companies moved commodities,
but also moved smuggled arms and undoubtedly moved rebels and
their sympathisers as well. That Zheng Guanying was already a keen
and articulate nationalist thinker cannot undermine the fact that being

held in prison for a year at the behest of Butterfield & Swire cannot but further have kindled his zeal. Zheng claimed that the action was pursued out of resentment at his joining competitor China Merchants. 'Truly heartless,' he later wrote, they refused to compromise and ignored 'my service to the firm'.[81] The way to save China, he would argue, was to play them at their own commercial game. Others thought differently. The fate of China seemed to hang in the balance as the century drew to a close. Ideas circulated widely about the threat of 'national extinction', of China's vulnerability to being 'carved up like a melon' by foreign powers. For increasing numbers of their subjects, the Qing ruling house seemed to be failing to protect China's sovereignty, let alone its dignity. Zheng Guanying sought a salvation for China through development and reform, regaining Chinese sovereignty by besting foreigners commercially. Others, smuggling rifles, pistols and bayonets on ships reaching China from Hong Kong, or fomenting the Yangzi valley disturbances, would explore a different way of saving China from destruction. For now, the company flag flew high and confident from the new hong on the Praya at Hong Kong, and British and other flags flew high from buildings and installations scattered across scores of Chinese cities, and on the foreign vessels that plied Chinese waters and the Chinese coast.

7

Shipping People

On a cool, wet winter morning in 1910, if you were to look out westwards across the harbour at Hong Kong from the vantage point offered in the Butterfield & Swire building you would be able to count 12 of a record 22 ships owned by the China Navigation Company that were present in the colony that day. The other 10 were at Quarry Bay. The Shanghai press reprinted a *South China Morning Post* note to this effect, most likely nudged the editor's way by someone at the company who thought it worth recording.[1] We might note it as well, for, to a great extent, John Swire & Sons was its ships, anchored in the colony's harbour or in the dockyards there, traversing China's coastal and river routes, and steaming south to Singapore, Batavia, Manila and Australia. As well as CNCo's flag – two opposing red triangles on a white background, with a blue band down the centre dividing them – Taikoo offices still managed the Blue Funnel agency, and from 1883 a new one, for Scottish & Oriental whose ships ran from Shantou to Bangkok. In 1892 this was extended to Hong Kong. Swire was more a company afloat than ashore.

Those 22 vessels will have carried at least 700 mariners. *Foochow* and *Swatow* were worked by six or seven Europeans, and a Chinese complement of seven firemen, two quartermasters, eight sailors and a carpenter, and cooks, a steward and his staff.[2] The *Hoihow* carried 33 Chinese crewmen. So it is clear that the largest community of staff employed by the Swire companies worked on China Navigation's ships. Even less by way of nineteenth-century staff records survive for these men, so we need to patch together a picture of their world from other sources. Most CNCo vessels carried a complement of at least six foreign staff, nearly always Britons: captain, chief and second officer, chief and second and third engineer. Except on their maiden voyage out from shipyards in Britain, the crewmen otherwise were generally Chinese, recruited through brokers, and not the company itself. To make matters more complex, one chief officer reported his ship carried 'Cantonese stevedores and compradors, Ningpo firemen and sailors, [Tianjin] bo'sun and quartermasters, Ningpo stewards, cooks, boys etc'.[3] 'I am a Canton man,' deposed Ah Chow, *Tunsin*'s comprador, in 1876, 'and the ship steward comes from Ningpo. I can talk to him and make him understand a little, and I understand a little what he says to me.' This splintered world in which different groups – speaking different languages, and with different cuisines and customs – occupied different roles, was entirely routine in China, but it could also foster conflict and more than a little confusion. Filipino quartermasters – helmsmen – were also being employed into the 1880s, and some will have been trained at Manila's nautical school. Then known as Manilamen, they added another layer of linguistic and cultural complexity to ship life.[4]

Where had the new company found these men? Some came direct from Britain. Many of the ships' officers and engineers came out on newly built vessels. John Whittle, for example, brought out the *Tamsui*, sailing for Hong Kong on 30 December 1880 with a crew of 31. The ship's cook got no further than a jail in Antwerp ('through an Quarrel', as he later put it). A dozen men signed off at Hong Kong and took other work from there, and an equal number accepted a gratis passage home. Whittle was 44, and had held a master's certificate for almost two decades. He had been based in Calcutta in the mid-1860s, had captained ships sailing to Hong Kong and had been commanding the P&O steamer *Duke of Lancaster* before taking on the *Tamsui*. As either John Samuel Swire or Frederick Gamwell interviewed all candidate captains personally, Whittle must have impressed despite the fact that he had just emerged from the wrecking of his vessel in the Red Sea after it ran on to an unmarked spit.[5] Fairly recently widowed, Whittle stayed on with CNCo, bringing out the *Changchow* in 1883, arriving in Hong Kong in time to go to the spring race meeting, and captaining it on the coast route and voyages to Australia. He became marine superintendent for the company in 1884, holding the post for six years, and would hold it again before retiring in 1910 after 27 years with the company.

Tamsui's chief officer Robert Mack also stayed on, as did the chief and third engineer.[6]

So, new ships brought fresh staff, but the novice company had also needed people who already knew the Yangzi, who were known to shippers and passengers, and who might potentially bring custom with them when they joined, and certainly bring a degree of local experience. When CNCo launched, Swire had paid particular attention to the quality and reputation of the captains, aiming above all to secure as commodore 'the best – most popular and steadiest man on the river'. This was, they decided, Glaswegian James Hardie, who had been on the river since 1856, latterly with Russells, and was poached away with an enormous salary of £700 a year. Others hired included Robert McQueen, who had been working in China since 1857, and William Deville, who had been coast pilot 'for many years' for Messageries Maritimes before starting with China Navigation.[7] Shetland Islander John Hutchison had been on the coast since at least 1865, and had worked his way from seaman to become mate and then master of the Jardine Matheson ships *Glengyle* and then *Rona*, bought and sailed his own vessel, then came to CNCo. In this way the company was both novel and a familiar enterprise at the same time.

This was a world of highly flexible and transitory employment. At least 750 different foreign nationals, mainly Britons, are recorded sailing on CNCo ships between 1883 and 1900 alone as deck officers or engineers.[8] Men moved from position to position, seeking promotion, higher pay, or better prospects, a more settled billet, or a more active one, a more congenial superior, or a less tedious route (the Wuhan to Yichang river route was thought extremely dull). They might take up with a pilot service, join the Chinese Maritime Customs Marine Department, which had a fleet of revenue cruisers and lights tenders, take a position with another line in China or more further afield. This was the most transient and mobile of the different groups of employees managed by the Swire firms, although it retained some men for decades. And they might easily move to any of CNCo's competitors, helped not least by the fact that the employment of foreign officers and engineers remained the norm even on the ships of the China Merchants SNCo well into the twentieth century.

The routine world of a term's service with CNCo comes from the diaries of Norwegian-born Fritz Lewis, engineer first on a West River steamer, a post he took up in 1904, and then on the coast, sailing back and forth from Shantou via Hong Kong to Saigon. There was very little drama. When off duty the crews hunted for game, watched sports fixtures, drank, yarned or played billiards at the Marine Institute. Lewis was there to make enough money to get married on, and at the end of five years shipped home and did precisely that. China left his life at that point, almost: photographs of him in later years capture him still wearing some Chinese slippers, small relics of half a decade far from Cornwall. Aged 32, Frank Davies had already knocked about most of the world's routes, and signed on with CNCo for a five-year contract in 1904 as a second officer. Gripes about promotion, salaries and benefits pepper the letters he sent to his family, but the company kept the ships 'like yachts', he thought. This, at least, impressed him. Sailing first on coastal and then river steamers, Davies stayed for 10 years with CNCo, then moved successively to the Moller Line, China Merchants and then the Indo-China SNCo. He stayed in China until 1937, bringing up a family in Shanghai.[9] Veteran mariner James Wiltshire had brought a War Office store ship to Singapore in 1886, next took 'anything I could get', including 'various ventures' in Australia, Borneo and Singapore, some 'very prosperous' and some 'the reverse'. Arriving in Hong Kong he took ill with malaria, found some diving work and secured service with CNCo on *Sungkiang* in 1891 from his precarious billet in the colony's Sailor's Home. James Tippin arrived as a quartermaster on *Achilles* in 1888, and spent seven years as a pilot for China Navigation before working for the Mitsubishi line and as a harbour pilot until 1938. Lewis came with a purpose; Davies sought a steadier post; men like Tippin and Wiltshire drifted to Asia on the currents of work, taking what they could get, regardless of where it took them.[10]

Shipmasters were men who were in some ways awkwardly placed: for they were not gentlemen, but they had a strong sense of their own dignity. When in Shanghai Jim Scott thought Blue Funnel captains lacked respect, for they failed routinely to come to the office to see him on arrival in port, as he felt that they ought; China Navigation masters did. 'Whilst I wish you to maintain strict discipline,' wrote John Samuel Swire to CNCo's Shanghai marine superintendent in 1892, 'be as considerate as you can in your manner & speech … older Captains … are touchy.'[11] They had their dignity, personal, but professional, too. Hauteur was part of the culture of shipmastering: the 'Old Man' kept his distance on board, and so retained his authority. Mates managed

the actual business of the vessel. It must also be remembered that ships'
captains – shipmasters – were managers, not mariners alone. In effect,
they were business agents of the company, taking decisions on their
own initiative – to accept a charter from a circus, or a complement of
pilgrims – they managed the staff, although this was delegated through
the chief officer and the comprador; and smoothed those passengers
who warranted smoothing (with chess, or music). They were to all
intents and purposes the manager 'of a branch office of the shipping
company' entrusted with considerable capital: ships and cargoes.[12] The
telegraph was changing their role steadily, for they were increasingly
able swiftly to consult Butterfield & Swire branch managers or shipping
clerks, but they retained considerable autonomy and responsibility still.

It is easy to overlook the sheer dense, busy volume of this business of
shipping. In November 1898, for example, the *Ngankin* marked with
bunting the conclusion of 1,000 voyages since it had entered service
15 years earlier. It would sail on until 1933. John Whittle's logbooks
record near-constant activity – and, after all, a ship not moving is losing
money: Shanghai to Wuhan, trip number 261, departing 19 September
1895, arriving Wuhan 21 September, departing 23 September back to
Shanghai on the 26th, departing on the 28th, arriving back in Wuhan
on 1 October, and on, and on, and on. Trip 541: 6,630 piculs of cargo
(almost 400 tons), 90 passengers; trip 543: 4,905 piculs, 75 passengers;
trip 553, 4,623 piculs, 140 passengers. SS *Tungchow*, trip 277: March
1890, 1,700 piculs in forehold, 40 tons coal in bunkers, 400 passengers.[13]
Although apparently a rough log, it is a carefully precise technical
record, and all the more thereby does it capture the maritime network
developed by China Navigation, which pulsed with movement. We are
left to lift our heads from such records to imagine the noise: foghorns
and ships' whistles and bells, wharfside labourers chanting as they load
and unload, watchmen and passengers shouting, captains yelling at the
ship compradors to hurry the passengers on or off the vessel, and the
throb of the engines; and it was a business marked also by ephemeral
smutty columns of smoke and steam as the ships moved on.

Their cargoes and passengers might be more interesting than a simple
measure of weight or total carried suggests. When Captain Lighton
brought the *Newchwang* out in 1878 he picked up a large contingent of
Straits-bound pilgrims returning from the Hajj. (Blue Funnel, though
never a passenger carrier, transported thousands of hajjis every year.)

Captain Young accepted a charter for the *Changchow* in September 1884 to take Chiarini's Circus and Menagerie – a China coast favourite – from Melbourne to Auckland, where crowds of sightseers watched the 'Wondrous Faust Family & Troupe', 'a Ponderous Den of Royal African Lions, Royal Bengal Tigers, Learned Zebras, Educated Elephants' and other exotics disembark. The bedding in of the Pacific maritime highways meant it became easier and cheaper for such enterprises to ply their peripatetic trade – Chiarini's was San Francisco-based, and the European shipping networks became essential to already existing patterns of pilgrimage, migration or seasonal employment.[14]

The dead moved, too. In April 1885 the Butterfield & Swire office at Shanghai arranged for a deck cabin to be made available on Blue Funnel's *Anchises* for Sir Harry Parkes's coffin, when his body was repatriated to London after the British Minister's sudden death in office. Europeans who died in Asia were in fact generally buried there. But the Chinese were sent home. Transporting the dead, or their bones, was quite routine, though most did not get a cabin. In 1883 the *Hoihow*, on its maiden return voyage from the colonies, having carried south that season's new crop of tea, conveyed north the remains of 286 Chinese sojourners who had died in New Zealand. They were carried in coffins ('some ten feet long') and caskets from Dunedin. The large shipment ran into problems with quarantine officers in Sydney but eventually made its way north. 'A somewhat peculiar cargo,' noted the *China Mail* when the ship arrived in Hong Kong. But it was 'peculiar' only in terms of the number carried. A large part of the activities of Chinese native place associations abroad, as at home, lay in providing for the shipment of remains back to the ancestral homes of the deceased. One of these in Sydney kept a 'supply of coffins ever ready upon each China Mail Boat' for deaths at sea. In Hong Kong the Tungwah Hospital co-ordinated the storage and onward shipment of remains. This was so routine that CNCo freight tariffs listed the prices: from Shanghai to Yantai in 1883 it was $15 to ship a coffin, $10 if empty. In 1901 the Shanghai Siming gongsuo (the Ningbo native place association) contracted with CNCo and China Merchants to ship up to 400 coffins a year. These were, of course, ideal passengers: they took up less space, did not need feeding and were charged significantly more than the living.[15]

They also caused far less trouble than ships' crews might. For all the experience and routine professionalism of deck officers or engineers like

Lewis, Davies or Whittle, ships could be floating cauldrons of personal conflict. On-board disputes often ended up in the courts and the public press. Bad blood between the *Foochow*'s captain John Thomas and chief engineer Hardie led to a muddy assault by the latter on the former on Pudong's mudflats in 1876: 'I am going to whip Captain Thomas if I can', Hardie had announced. In 1898 Chief Engineer John Wardrop sued the company, alleging that it had dismissed him without cause and owed him salary. Wardrop had 15 years of experience when he joined from Scotts of Greenock in 1895, sailing out on the new ship SS *Wuhu* and staying on with the firm. Transferred from ship to ship, each captain complained of his temper and his 'violent language', and his tendency to try to interfere. Wardrop in turn accused the masters of drunkenness, violence or spite. Yes, admitted Captain Thomas Gyles, I certainly did pick up my pistol and threaten to shoot him if he did not go away. Gyles, 14 years certified a master, and 16 years in CNCo's service was, the second mate stated, carefully – and damningly – 'to a certain extent sober' when he separated the two men, 'but four hours before he was not'. 'Entirely without foundation,' retorted Gyles of the charge. CNCo 'cannot carry on their business if they have to suit every engineer to every captain,' deposed an exasperated John Bois. This was, of course, all simply the routine bother that stemmed from employing and managing people. But in the relatively insular public world of the treaty ports and Hong Kong, a crotchety chief engineer and an allegedly drunkard shipmaster were much, much more trouble. The case was then settled out of court. Both Gyles and Wardrop left the company, but the damage was done so far as publicity across eight columns of the *North China Herald* was concerned.[16]

The seafarers clubbed together, when not clubbing each other. They rather had to for 'Shanghai people are for the most part utter snobs,' complained Davies in 1905, 'and affect not to recognise shipping people.' We might not entirely wonder at that, given the squabbles that got to court. 'Some of these clerks make my blood boil', Davies had written earlier from Shanghai: 'In B&S's office the officials and under shippers are most insulting.' 'Hong Kong people are much nicer.'[17] The worlds of John Wardrop and the young men who joined the Butterfield's house staff were generally far, far apart. In Shanghai mariners living ashore largely settled in a different part of the city, mostly in Hongkew (Hongkou), north of the Soochow Creek (Wusong

River). Office men lived south of it. When looking for new premises for their club in Shanghai, the shipmasters rejected one neighbouring the Shanghai Club, not wanting to 'butt up against every bloody Taipan in Shanghai'. The captains and deck officers congregated with harbour and coast pilots in the Mercantile Marine Officers' Association and its Club in Shanghai, founded in 1885 when a more exclusive Ship Masters' Association of 11 years' standing opened its doors more widely.[18] Their below-deck partners had formed a Marine Engineers' Institute in 1876. These were social organisations, but they also represented the interests of their members, or at least attempted to: Jim Scott refused to meet a delegation from the Institute in a dispute about the introduction of new, lower, pay scales in 1885: 'we are not aware that there is any question, between us and the Institute, which requires settlement.'[19]

From surveying the records it is easy to gain the impression that mariners either drank, or else that they were upright temperance men, that they sought 'Square Face', 'Ready-made Lightning' or 'Forty-rod' at Hongkew grog shops, or brandy and beer in their club, or that they drank coffee, sang hymns and listened to earnest addresses at the Temperance Hall. There seemed little ground in between.[20] For one scholar, ships' officers were more likely than not 'bookish teetotalers', but the sorry roll of court appearances suggests otherwise.[21] CNCo certainly had its share of these. The *Foochow*'s first chief engineer died shortly after being hospitalised in Shanghai in July 1875 'suffering from a debauch with incipient symptoms of Delirium Tremens'. In 1890 one former captain, and late steward at the Mercantile Marine Officers' ball, appeared in the police court at Shanghai 'in the most wretched condition', charged with begging on the Nanjing Road and reduced to this state 'through drink'.[22] Shanghai's Marine Temperance Society was founded in 1871, and had gathered a large roll of 'pledged abstainers' by the time its first premises were inaugurated in May 1873, including captains, officers and engineers. In Shanghai and Hong Kong missionaries, mariners and administrators worked to establish facilities for seamen that they hoped would keep them out of the hands of crimpers, and grog-shop owners.[23] The Butterfield & Swire shipping offices also had to watch the Blue Funnel crews as well. They were called on to explain when seamen became a public charge having signed off in port, or otherwise went astray. In June 1879 two firemen from the *Stentor* went missing in Shanghai. One was found in a settlement police

station, having been picked up in the street 'incapably drunk'. It was a
warm and pleasant evening, and the other attempted to swim back to
the ship, singing as he went. But this was not, the inquest into his death
concluded, a good idea.[24]

Grog was dead cheap. But Frank Davies found Shanghai expensive.
Only one or two of his fellow second officers were married, and they
could barely make ends meet, having to take in boarders. The company
refused to reimburse leave passages home, a source of widespread
complaint, as was slow promotion ('that is the worst of having sober
men in the Company,' he joked; nobody got fired and no jobs thereby
became available). But still, Davies enjoyed an '8 course dinner every
night' and sent home menus for the breakfast served on SS *Kinling*:
'Porridge, Fried fish, Hamm egg, Bacon egg, Poach egg, Boiled egg
to Order, Beef steak, Mutton chops, Cold Boiled Ham, Cold Corned
Beef, Cold Game pie, Cold Roast Beef, Cold Sucking Pig, Cold Leg
Mutton, Beef Curry, Jams, Tea and Coffee, Fruit.' Little wonder he put
on weight, rapidly, but still 'the thought of three years seems to take the
gloss from things'.[25] There had been less joy in the steward's fare on the
Poyang in August 1903: in a matter of hours cholera killed the master,
chief officer, chief engineer, second officer, pilot and mess-room boy as
the ship journeyed from Wuhu to Wuhan.[26]

So sustenance was not, usually, a problem. Companionship proved
a challenge, however. When Captain Edward Le Messurier Robinson
of the *Tientsin* married 18-year-old Mary Linklater, daughter of a late
Shantou harbour pilot, in Shanghai's Holy Trinity Cathedral in 1884,
the CNCo steamers in harbour put out their flags. Publicity of a less
welcome kind was offered gratis to 'J._- C _Third _ of S. S. _' 'Trading
for Taikoo Sugar Refinery' in 1892, after he wrote to the *Kobe Herald*
office asking them to help him 'obtain' a 'Japanese girl willing to marry'.
He had not been the only such correspondent, but he was the only one
all but identifiable in a lengthy rejection published in the paper under
the heading 'A Taikoo Man in Search of a Wife' and reprinted in Hong
Kong and Singapore. Most men fell somewhere in between these two.
Many were sojourning, as rooted in Britain as any seafarer was ever
rooted anywhere. Those who stayed longer in China found a sparse
population of women of their class, and those might look to better
themselves socially, as the Whittle daughters did. David Martin, over
30 years with the firm, only married shortly before his death in 1907 to

regularise the status of his daughter with Eurasian Kang Fung Que, also known as Mary Haden. Between 1869 and his death, friends thought he had visited Britain just once. Martin's clearly long-term relationship with Kang was rather common, and more discreet by far than 'J. C.' had managed.[27] 'I wish I could get married and get a snug berth ashore,' lamented Frank Davies.[28]

David Martin's estate was a valuable one, and other wills and inventories show how a successful man could thrive, especially in the treaty port property market or through the stock exchange. But not all did so, and most estates are small in value, and inventories are thin. Mariners more than once lobbied for increased pay. In 1878 in response to disquiet among the employees, John Samuel Swire put all China Navigation Company staff – river and coast – on the same rates, and on par with their competitors. In June 1881 officers lobbied collectively for an increase, but 'caved in' when Lang held firm, believing scales high enough already. 'One of our best men left in consequence,' he reported drolly, but returned when he found no better rates available. At the same time the engineers had forced him to give way on a similar point.[29] A later dispute in Hong Kong developed over Sunday working. It was on this point that Mackintosh, opposing the introduction of any restrictions as chairman of the Chamber of Commerce – Hong Kong was unusual in not having any – was described as a militant shipowner. The issue was first brought up by the chaplain of the Seamen's Church in 1888, was rebuffed, and then renewed by the newly established British Mercantile Marine Officers' Association. The conscience of the religious militated against their working on the Sabbath, the Association contended, but their contracts bound them to work when directed: they were, therefore, slaves. Well, it really does not happen very often, retorted the shipowners, sidestepping the issue of principle. Then-governor William Des Vœux issued a Sunday Cargo-Work Ordinance on the eve of his departure, although a permit system largely eroded the intended effort. 'There is no religion for seafaring men', Davies would write, 'shipowners do not care about their spiritual welfare so long as they get the work done.'[30] The Sunday labour dispute was a harbinger of collective bargaining to come.

About CNCo's Chinese crews in the nineteenth century we again have little information, in fact much less. Court cases offer snippets that suggest that the diverse make-up of the ships' crews could be a source of tensions. William Deville, captain of *Tientsin*, twice took some of his crew to the Police Court in Shanghai in December 1877: the men, egged on, it was said, by their 'headman', had refused to work on Christmas Day, when other lines gave their men a holiday. They were, the judge told them, presumably through an interpreter, bound to obey their captain. Two days later crewmen A-Sung, A-Mee and A-Chee were back before him. All the crew had now left the ship and it needed to sail the next morning. We are ill, they claimed. I don't think so, replied the judge. Deville had previously asked only that the court reinforce his legal authority, not punish the men, apart from the ringleader. Now he wanted them fined, to prevent later problems when they came to be paid. *Tientsin* departed as scheduled the next day. This crew at least was willing, collectively, to argue for what they considered to be fair treatment, and looked across at other companies for a standard by which to judge equity.[31]

Deville will not have been alone in deploying both negotiation and law to run his ship. Chief Mate Paul Holtz tried to use a hatchet, however. He thought his boatswain on the *Wuchang*, a man from Xiamen, with whom he had remonstrated about cleaning the ship's funnel, had ordered his followers – 12 of whom appeared in court to support him – to attack Holtz – 'they were crying out *ta ta*' (hit, hit). Quartermaster Tsu A-chung, who had been recruited by the boatswain six years earlier when the latter had himself joined the ship, contradicted Holtz's account. Captain Vallack had ordered his mate to put the hatchet back, then knocked down the boatswain when he had run at Holtz. The judge told Holtz he had been 'extremely unwise' in picking up the hatchet – perhaps an understatement – said he thought both men had been in the wrong, but fined the boatswain for 'common assault'. Tell him, he ordered the interpreter: 'that he should have known he was on board an English ship and was subject to English law, and if he had thought he was badly treated he could come to the court and have redress.'[32] This was an unexpected extension of British extraterritoriality, for in all other respects Chinese were certainly not subject to the British courts, although they had to use them to prosecute or sue Britons. English maritime law confounded the system. But there were ways around it. At Shantou in October 1891, the Chinese authorities demanded the surrender of the entire Chinese crew of the *Sungkiang*. It was returning south from Tianjin, where the customs had discovered a huge cache of hidden arms, which were, it was assumed, being smuggled to rebels. The master paid off the Chinese and foreign crew alike, then re-signed the Europeans, and a fresh complement of Chinese seamen was brought on board. The original crew were last seen being shipped towards the shore and prison.[33]

Ship compradors surface a little more often in the record. So they should, for in large part they ran affairs on board CNCo ships.[34] A ship's comprador had the Chinese passenger business of the ship devolved to him, and was responsible for receiving cargo on board, and safely delivering it. For these he received a salary, largely designed to contribute to his costs, and a commission. He employed a team of assistants and stevedores. In time compradors would sell in turn the concession to provide other passenger services, notably catering. Chinese passengers came on board without tickets, and there was no limit to the numbers that could be taken on. If the Chinese saloon was full, and if there was space, passengers might be housed in cargo holds. The comprador issued tickets on board. Passengers without the money in hand might pawn their clothes and belongings. As John Whittle's rounded-up passenger totals might suggest, there was always some uncertainty about the numbers of Chinese passengers carried as a result (and it was not unknown for compradors to sell more tickets than they would later admit to, so that second mates might be charged with collecting the tickets to provide a check).[35] Captains retained overall responsibility for the ship, but this subcontracting of oversight for passengers and cargo would lead to problems. Not the least of these was overcrowding, for compradors would take as many passengers as they could, while smuggling would become a problem.

Compradors on ships themselves can be spotted in newspapers, not least as they held rich pickings for thieves. The *Shanghai*'s loses 2,000 Taels, the ship's cook fingers two suspects, who leap into the river to escape arrest. Both drown. The *Kweiyang*'s has his cabin burgled by a cargo handler; the *Hangchow*'s man is accused of failing to pay crew members, and his shroff admits embezzling funds. Butterfield's Tianjin agent reports that *Shengking*'s is 'a good sort of man', but as a southerner, and a 'dignified' one to boot, ill-suited to securing passengers:

the successful passenger men here are the northerners or Ningpo men, Shantung men are the best. They hobnob with the passenger-hong people and go around the hongs and give the people there a rollicking good time.

We have a pen portrait of one ship comprador, Leang Shing Hem (Liang Chengxing), a native of Jiujiang, who started working for the firm around 1882. By 1908 he was comprador on the *Peking*, ran a ship chandlery on Shanghai's Fuzhou Road, held a contract to supply Blue Funnel steamers and had sent his elder son to Britain whence he would return in 1918, a qualified barrister with a degree from Cambridge University. Clearly, this could be a profitable business.[36]

The division of ships into these different spheres of responsibility, which itself overlay the standard divisions of spheres of responsibility of master, mate and chief engineer, was complicated further by another division between the spaces aboard used by Chinese and by foreign passengers. The foreign passengers paid much more for their tickets, and were accommodated in ways that contrasted markedly with the crowded free-for-all of the Chinese saloon. *Ngankin*, reported one consul, 'was most comfortably and luxuriously fitted up'. There was 'a good and thick carpet … lounging chairs … scrupulous cleanliness', and 'a handsome and fine-tuned piano'. The captain was a 'musical genius' and the chief engineer accompanied him on the flute. The pianist was Manxman Charles Lacy Perks, who joined CNCo in 1873 after some seven years with Blue Funnel. Perhaps they were there at the piano, 'discoursing harmoniously', as Percival put it, 'Mendelssohn, Beethoven and Mozart' when the ship 'narrowly escaped running down a lorcha' (doing it considerable damage, nonetheless).[37] The restriction of foreign passengers to the foreign saloon on deck was eased in the case of missionaries, notably those associated with the China Inland Mission. This was largely, on their part, for reasons of economy, but also of belief: they dressed in Chinese clothing – much to the horror, in general, of fellow Europeans and Americans in China – and to the bemusement of Chinese who encountered them and with whom they shared the bunk-filled below-deck saloon. The only difficulty, one Briton reported, aside from the good-natured but persistent curiosity of their fellow passengers, was the smell of opium that some of these smoked. But as another traveller earlier remarked when in a similar predicament, it might have helped them sleep.[38]

Captains organised catering for the foreign passengers, hiring a Chinese steward who in turn hired cook, waiters and others. This might lead to disputes, such as when steward Se Che sought redress in the British court, suing Captain Robert Morgan for the balance of wages he claimed were owed for provisioning Morgan and his officers. Other reports indicate that ships' masters also took their personal servants on board – the 'boy' was as indispensable to shipborne life as on shore – and captains might take their families, too. A British passenger in 1888 travelling from Shanghai to Tianjin reported her disquiet at finding a Chinese steward on board the *Chung King*, for she would have preferred a 'Lady stewardess', and a European instead. But what Alice Hayes was more exercised about was the presence on board of Elizabeth Williamson, wife of the captain, John Hutchison: 'I cannot say I approve of Captain's wives at sea telling the passengers where they may sit, and lording it over the ladies!' A peripatetic riding instructor, on her way to Tianjin to provide lessons for 'ladies' – among whom, we might note, she did not include a shipmaster's wife, in this case a crofter's daughter from Shetland – Alice Hayes was famed for breaking in zebras, and she was not slow to provide opinions on any other subject that exercised her. Her husband, Matthew Horace Hayes, focused his own account of the journey north on the quantity and quality of food that was served ('brandies and sodas all day long ... the best four days I have ever spent on board ship'). But he had also warmly recommended Blue Funnel, that had brought them from Singapore to Hong Kong, for although the ships were slow and small they did not employ Chinese crews.[39]

The Hayes, otherwise, journeyed quite smoothly. But travel was never without risk. The proficiency and experience of masters mattered for the simple reason that these were significant investments and the company could ill afford to lose them, or to lose its reputation. Yet lose ships it did. The Library at the Marine Officers' Club in Shanghai housed a cheerful frieze of photographs of local shipping accidents. China Navigation vessels will have been there, too. *Glengyle* was the first the company lost, en route from Amoy to Shantou in November 1875 with a cargo of wheat and rice. It sank in 10 minutes after the 'negligent and reckless navigation' of Captain Amherst Carnell caused the ship to run on to a reef near Nan'ao (Namoa) island. Several passengers and two of the crew were lost, including Carnell. The *Pakhoi*, with 'one of the firm's oldest and experienced captains', struck a rock as it entered the harbour at Amoy six years later. A customs buoy was 90 yards out of place: crew absolved. There were no casualties, but boatmen and people on shore looted the ship even as it foundered. The *Wuhu* ran aground in February 1883 near the Yangzi River mouth, the court of inquiry evidence highlighting the polyglot environment on the bridge: the four quartermasters were all Malay, and one of them at least seemed to speak no English. The captain was reprimanded. Six months later *Foochow* ran aground in thick fog: 'culpable error of judgment' on the part of the first mate. The *Tientsin* became a total loss in August 1887 on a 'dark night' 'thick with rain' when it ran aground on Rees island north-east of Shantou. Steward Sze A-pau drowned when the crew tried too hastily, and without orders, to launch one of the boats. The captain had earlier failed to come on deck when called. The second mate was on the bridge on 22 February 1888 when the *Swatow* ran on to a reef near Nan'ao island, taking any explanation he might have offered with him when he drowned in what was clearly a dangerous spot for CNCo shipping. Other men clung to the rigging, but several fell, exhausted, and were lost before rescue.[40]

In twelve months in 1890/91 the company lost three ships. Despite crew vigilance and injunctions, a passenger's hidden charcoal cooking stove probably set alight cotton bales in a cargo hold on the *Shanghai* as it steamed upriver away from Zhenjiang. More than 200 of the at least 450 passengers on board perished – one report thought 700 were being carried. Crews of nearby junks simply looted what they could, and robbed the passengers, throwing some back into the river after doing so. Many who made it ashore were also viciously robbed. Comprador Lee Lok-tai reported, 'I shouted till I was hoarse for assistance'. 'I do not know why the boatmen would not help. It is not the usual conduct of Chinamen.' Photographs of the dead were posted up at Zhenjiang for relatives seeking news; coffins were piled up on the shore to await shipment. After being salvaged the ship entered another 45 years of service for China Navigation as its hulk on the Bund at Xiamen, a macabre relic of a grim disaster. The SS *Ichang* 'always steered badly' argued all who had ever commanded her. But its master John Cruikshank Foster was himself deemed at fault when it struck a rock on its way to Ningbo from Shanghai in November 1891. This proved a bad week for the company. 'Good God what are you doing with the ship in here,' exclaimed Captain Peacock of the *Yunnan* three days later, belatedly emerging from his cabin as his ship neared Shantou. He should have been on deck. Well, the chief officer was lying to the court in his account of how the ship came to grief, Peacock claimed, but the inquiry found against him as well. It was a 'quite inexplicable' accident, thought the press. As another steamer, the Chinese-owned *Tongshan*, assisted the evacuation, its propeller became fouled with ropes, and it too was lost, concluding the second act of an expensive Shantou farce.[41]

There were, of course, other serious accidents that did not lead to wrecks. The grounding of the *Kaifong* in 1889 forced a review of the management of the fleet. Its captain had not come up when roused – too heavy a nightcap, hazarded Swire from London – and there seemed to be a lack of standing instructions about navigation and procedures. The then marine superintendent John Whittle was 'too amiable' with his captains, and had not imposed discipline on them, it was concluded. The firm returned him to the fleet and appointed a new man from the Orient Line, who, being married, wanted a 'shore berth'.[42] The job at Shanghai was a busy one: 19 coast and river steamers, seven pontoons at Shanghai and one at Ningbo, 10 harbour cargo boats, hulks upriver and pontoons, too, and bridges to the wharves, and a steady flow of supplies to indent and monitor, costs to keep low, and then the officers and engineers to manage.[43]

For a large and steadily growing line, running an intensive range of services along a coast and waterways that only began to be systematically lit after 1868 – a process its engineers deemed complete only by 1912 – this was hardly an exceptional record of loss. And John Samuel Swire, unlike most shipping line owners, had experienced a wrecking himself, in 1878, on his way to Australia from Hong Kong.[44] 'Gross carelessness', he thought, nonetheless, of the *Ichang* loss. Captain Peacock 'had no right to be in bed so close to shore'. And he was there probably so as to be 'wide awake for enjoyment' when he moored, continued Swire, although Shantou is not often associated with pleasure. Perhaps captains needed a financial incentive to focus their minds, such as being responsible for the first 4,000 Taels of any loss.[45] 'It's very strange,' he remarked less facetiously than it might appear, after receiving news of the loss of the *Yunnan*, 'but drunken captains are often more fortunate than sober-sides': they took more care, knowing their condition. Make it a rule that any captain who loses his ship 'and not his life also, shall be drowned'.[46] A different solution was implemented. By 1891 the company was paying lower than average rates of pay, and instead of raising them the previous year had instituted a Safety Navigation Bonus system for its European crews.[47] This certainly could be withheld. After the *Sungkiang* arms smuggling incident in 1891, the officers were denied theirs, it being reasoned that they were either negligent in allowing the arms to be hidden on board – some were stashed in the quartermaster's cabin – or else had been paid to be so. When Second Officer James Wiltshire objected and tried to resign in protest as the ship was about to leave Hong Kong, he found himself arrested and in the magistrates' court. Wiltshire was jailed for a week, provoking a furious barrage of criticism of Mackintosh and the firm in the local press. The ordinance under which Wiltshire was charged provided no alternative to imprisonment, but the company had declined to drop the charge, persisting with it 'as an example to those employed on ships'.[48] This was hard on Wiltshire, but the Yangzi disturbances were still fresh, and fresher still was the enigmatic case of Charles Mason, a young British customs assistant, and fantasist, who had set in motion a plot to smuggle arms from Hong Kong, real ones, to, he claimed, secret society rebels in Zhenjiang. This scheme was uncovered, and the main consignment of weapons was seized at Shanghai. Mason was arrested, as he later recalled, stepping off a CNCo river steamer on to the deck of the *Cadiz* at Zhenjiang.[49]

The picture overall for CNCo was one of steady growth. Between 1883 and 1900 the company acquired 38 new steamers. One profitable business was the beancake trade: shipping soybean, crushed and shaped into blocks, from Niuzhuang (Yingkou) to Shantou, where it was processed into fertiliser. Six 'beancakers' were ordered in 1897 alone. The Shanghai–Tianjin route and Tianjin–Canton line also grew in importance. The expansion of CNCo was also driven by, and in turn further drove, the Taikoo Sugar Refinery investment: beancake, raw, and refined sugar, were all shuttled along the coast and to and from Southeast Asia.

The long history of Chinese emigration entered a new phase in the 1870s with greater and greater numbers travelling to Australia and the Americas. There was much that was dark about the practices that encouraged, crimped and often impelled Chinese men to travel to work overseas. They harvested guano, worked on plantations or in mines. Reports on scandals and of conditions little different from slavery led the Qing to send missions overseas to investigate, and in fact led to its establishing its first permanent consular offices. By the 1870s a meshwork of Qing and colonial regulations seemed to have curtailed illegal coercion – the trade in 'piglets' – but across the decade demand for Chinese labour increased markedly. The plantations that supplied raw sugar for the Taikoo refinery, for example, needed workers. This was a legitimate business, but it remained one that attracted official suspicion, and it was associated indelibly with illegal practices.

In August 1883, for example, 53 men boarded SS *Woosung* at Shantou for the journey north to Shanghai, there to join *SS Taiwan* for Queensland, where they had been contracted to work. Advances had been made to them by Butterfield & Swire. A very strong typhoon encountered on the voyage delayed the ship's journey and washed away much of their baggage – it must have been a rough passage indeed – and they missed the departure of the *Taiwan*. They were housed in lodgings in the French concession to await the next departure, but their presence became known to the Chinese authorities in Shanghai, who formally objected to their leaving. Consuls and police became involved, and the men were taken by the French police to the Mixed Court. Representations were made by Butterfield & Swire for compensation, but rebuffed by Qing officials, and not much supported by British ones. That it was entirely legal to transport men contracted to labour in Queensland was not doubted, but there was something evasive about shipping men from Shantou north to Shanghai, rather than direct to Hong Kong, at which the *Taiwan* would also call. The ship arrived in Queensland in late September and landed 86 Chinese labourers and 54 Malays, but the contingent held at Shanghai were not able to make the journey. Moreover, where Qing officials expressed concern, their Australian counterparts were wholly alarmed. When the *Taiwan* next docked in Queensland, a law introduced after it had left Hong Kong led to its master being fined £220: £10 a head for each of 22 Chinese passengers carried in excess of a deliberately low limit.[50] The Australian colonies were beginning to pull down the shutters.

Shantou was a prime source of the outflow of Chinese labour, and opposition to it when it involved effective debt-peonage. Butterfield & Swire gained substantial expertise in this business through the Blue Funnel agency, for Holts had been carrying labourers to Singapore on a regular basis from the port since 1875, and their ships carried around half of those who travelled south to seek work and would continue to do so until the end of the century. Working initially through a 'coolie hong' – 'Yueng-Sing-Fu' – run by the Kwok brothers, one of them a comprador to a German firm, Butterfield & Swire provided passages for those who could not afford them on the Holt ships through the hong, against the usual securities, an advance repayable by the labourer once he had secured work through the hong's contacts with labour recruiters at Singapore. It might take him three years of work to pay back advances received. This was a business that could and did get Butterfield & Swire entangled in controversy, notably in 1883 when local officials moved against the Kwoks, one of whom fled on a Blue Funnel to Singapore, and the hong was discovered to have no assets, and to have assigned its securities elsewhere.[51] The money was recovered this time, for it was a profitable business, for those who managed it, if not for the labourers themselves whose experiences could be bitter, and Butterfield & Swire would continue to act as agents for both the Singapore and Bangkok passenger trade and moved more directly into managing it after the problems of 1883. Through its 'Taikoo Nam Kee' passenger or 'coolie' hong, and a network of 'coolie shops' (hostels), it continued to arrange passages (and credit, where needed) for migrants. In late 1914 CNCo entered the trade itself, building on the very strong position B&S had established as agents, running vessels from Shantou, and, after the First World War, from Xiamen. Facilities were 'modest', perhaps 'primitive', recalled one shipmaster of conditions on this route for the passengers, and provisioning 'spartan'. They largely travelled on deck and faced continual importuning from the ship comprador's staff. The scandals of the mid-century, however, lingered long in representations of this traffic.[52]

John Samuel Swire had long mused on how the firm might profitably engage in the business of shipping people across the Pacific, or to Australia. Would such a service secure Chinese passengers, he had asked in 1875, 'or is immigration diminishing'? The firm bid for transpacific agencies in 1891, 1894 and again in 1898, but either without success or without profit.[53] New liners were built in the early 1880s especially for the route from Fuzhou via Hong Kong, Singapore, Batavia to Australia, a significant branching out from the coastal trade. But the Australian venture fell foul of the racist immigration regime that the colonies there began to implement to prevent Chinese arrivals, who certainly were not diminishing in numbers, a development which also had severe consequences for Chinese Australians. Few episodes exemplify the viciousness of the regulations, and the glee with which they were implemented, than the aftermath of the wrecking of the CNCo liner

Changchow on 24 October 1884, 200 miles north of Brisbane. Barely a year old, the 1,100-ton ship, carrying about 70 Chinese passengers to Hong Kong, was too close to the shore of Fraser Island when it ran aground and then sank. Six people were drowned. Having struggled ashore in the dark, boats capsizing in the surf and heavy swell, the survivors were stranded for nearly three days with little to sustain them, while the second officer and some of the men trekked along the deserted coast to a lighthouse and then the port of Maryborough to arrange for them to be picked up. Having arrived at the port, the passengers, with the Chinese crew, were treated like prisoners and 'escorted by the police to the immigration barracks where they were comfortably housed with close gates', as it was euphemistically reported. Each was forcibly searched – 'like a thief', reported the sole woman on board – to see how much cash and valuables they carried. If they wished to escape their confinement temporarily a hefty sum of £10 was demanded: this was the immigration poll tax, imposed in this case on exhausted, traumatised shipwreck survivors who had been trying to leave an increasingly hostile Australia.[54]

That hostility grew and reached a crisis in May 1888 that scuppered Swire plans for the southern route. The SS *Changsha*, one of four liners commissioned for the service that had begun operating in 1886, arrived in Sydney on 28 May from Hong Kong with 144 Chinese passengers, including returning residents. It sailed into the midst of a bitter controversy that had seen four other vessels, including its sister ship, *Tsinan*, held in quarantine to prevent the landing of their Chinese passengers. There was no illness on board, but Australian politics were profoundly choleric. Anti-Chinese immigration rallies had been held in Melbourne and Sydney: 'Out with the Chinaman' demonstrators had cried in Sydney. Their ire, and that of Australian politicians, was also directed at the London government, which had failed, in their eyes, to address the colonists' anxieties. New restrictive regulations were rapidly introduced. *Changsha* had to steam back to Hong Kong with 52 of its passengers who were refused entry, had had to be forcibly restrained on board and who were accompanied north to the ship's last port of call, Newcastle, by a body of armed police. Captain Williams then issued revolvers to the handful of European passengers on board 'to be used without restraint on the slightest sign of an uprising'. It cannot have been a happy voyage, with matters hardly improving at Hong Kong.

The day following the ship's arrival on 3 July, 30 of the passengers trooped to the Butterfield & Swire offices and demanded a refund of their passage money. Edwin Mackintosh quite mishandled the protest, suggesting they petition the Australians instead. The police were called to remove them from the building, and there was a fracas which saw 18 arrested. 'Some of them can speak pidgin English,' stated shipping clerk Montagu Beart, and 'said they did not care a damn for the police or whether they were sent to gaol or not, and that they would stop there although they stopped till they died.' 'We must look upon the Chinese passenger trade to the colonies as done for,' concluded Swire, 'I wish that we had never entered the trade, or built the boats.'[55]

He could afford a mistake, or four, however: the average annual gross profit from 1888 to 1900 was £141,396. It took a dip when the pool agreements lapsed in 1889, and when, to their immense surprise, Swire went back into competition with China Merchants and Jardines over the shares each should have in the pool. He wanted more, told them so, and held out for it. It was almost three years before a new settlement was reached involving only a minor compromise on CNCo's part. Despite the costs incurred in the course of the battle, Swire was quite content with the outcome, telling Mackintosh and John Bois that 'you have now got the upper hand – Keep it'.[56] An important and constant presence in the Shanghai office, and in keeping that hand well in play, was shipping clerk Henry Bridges Endicott. Despite reprimands from John Samuel Swire about his lax handling of shippers' accounts, Endicott rather continued to run an office within an office – and apart from the office, for it was on the Bund and not at the hong – and run it as he saw fit. He wrote directly to Swire with policy proposals, getting things done and keeping clients and others sweet. 'I think there is but very little doubt,' he wrote to Jim Scott in 1893, 'but that a cumshaw of Taels 9,000.00 to the officials will allow us to place passenger hulks at Nanking and Ngankin [Anqing].' It was, he asserted, 'the only way to deal with them'. His seniors demurred. Lang's distance from the routine business of the office was clearly a factor in the free hand Endicott took, but the shipping clerk got results, which was just as well for he became the firm's highest paid employee despite decisions that sometimes left the firm in a 'painful and humiliating position' over its rates agreements with Jardines.[57] Succession planning was tricky for they 'could not reckon upon his imparting to an outsider, that he does not approve or suggest as successor, any of the information he is possessed of'. The Shanghai managers were rather afraid of a man one of them described as 'a curiously constituted individual'.[58] Endicott's health – harmed partly by his weight, and then too rapid a slimming diet – was the subject of much concerned comment, yet it was Endicott to whom it was 'hinted' that hosting a good Chinese New Year feast for Ningbo shippers might solve a problem. Affairs were quite thrown into disarray when Endicott died suddenly aged 51 in 1895.[59] The Hong Kong shipping clerk, Tomlin, was sent north to take over. But CNCo continued to grow, and its profits in 1900 were over £300,000.

For CNCo staff the political was also personal. Endicott had married the Eurasian mother of his seven children sometime before his death. Although the daughter of a British subject, she spoke no English. The fact of Endicott's own Eurasian heritage was suppressed by his American executors, who worked assiduously to send his children to the United States, building a case on the basis of his US citizenship, and his 'integrity and industry'.[60] Under the terms of the 1882 Chinese Exclusion Act and subsequent judgements, Endicott himself was barred from entry to the United States, let alone his children, or his wife, who did succeed in entering the country in 1906, some years after her children. Endicott had friends, including the US consulate's shipping clerk, who worked assiduously to help the family. Most people had no such assistance. The Australian walling-off of Chinese immigration had its melancholy North American counterpart, and employees of the firm itself, like Endicott, were faced with it, no less brutally than the hapless survivors of the *Changchow*, or the men shipped back to Hong Kong on the *Changsha* after being denied entry in 1888. They were also faced, as Louis Grunauer in Shantou was, with social and professional prejudice. Endicott's managers had no idea, it seems, that he was a Eurasian, so he was spared that indignity.

Although in practical terms the Swire companies made comparatively little from the connection, their business remained intertwined with that of the Holt brothers' Ocean Steam Ship Company. In fact, rather than a source of lucrative commissions, Blue Funnel business was instead a continuing source of exasperation and frustration, and it ate up a good deal of the time, not only of John Samuel Swire, but also of Frederick Gamwell. Correspondence about conference politics, in particular, continued to fill up company letter books, crowding out

other topics and, if anything, the two companies grew closer in the
1880s and 1890s, even as Blue Funnel developed its Southeast Asian
business more fully, through its network of agencies there, especially
Mansfield & Co.

In the early 1890s, Butterfield & Swire in Hong Kong even became
involved in supplying Chinese crews for Blue Funnel ships. Captain
Hayes would not have approved. The recently established Sailors' and
Firemen's Union – the forerunner of the British National Union of
Seamen – did not approve in principle, for 'Lascars and Chinese seamen
are not physically constituted to stand the rough weather which vessels
have to contend with in European waters' (a familiar claim) – and while
it reduced costs for the Holts, the replacement by shipping companies
of British by Asian labour would lead to national political controversy
in time.[61] This was part of a series of cost-cutting and other initiatives
that led to the long-awaited revival of the Blue Funnel fleet. In 1891
the company commissioned the first of 23 new ships that came into
service between 1892 and 1900, trebling the line's overall tonnage. These
were much bigger ships as well. In 1895, a new generation of managers
came into the company, including Alfred Holt's son, George Jr, and
more significantly his nephew, Richard Durning Holt. Throughout the
1870s and increasingly in the 1880s, John Samuel Swire had repeatedly
urged the Holt brothers to renew the fleet. In 1882 he even sent them a
résumé of his 12 years' record of frank advice, all of it explicitly requested
by them, he noted.[62] Blue Funnel ships were of the highest possible
standards in design and construction – from 1876 the company self-
insured – and its officers were second to none in the British merchant
marine – but the ships were smaller and slower than the new vessels
introduced by their more virile rivals, the Glen, Shire and Castle lines,
and P&O. Only in 1892 did Blue Funnel acquire vessels over 3,000
tons; P&O had eight of them by then. As a result, the Holt liners had
to offer lower freight rates, and if it had not been for Swire's assiduous,
and pugnacious, working of the conference system, Blue Funnel would
probably not have survived. But survive it did, and from this decade of
renewal grew to take a very strong position internationally.

Blue Funnel's reach, and interconnectedness with the Swire estate,
were experienced first-hand by Richard Durning Holt in the course of
a 57-week circumnavigation of the globe in 1892/93. Holt had been
working in his uncles' company for three years when he made this

voyage, seen off as he left on the *Palamed* by a large gathering of Holts' 'knot' of friends and relations. Such a journey was very much a rite of passage for a rising figure in a firm like Blue Funnel or Swires. His journal, written for family reading, shows the importance for a young manager of gaining personal experience of the world that companies like these were shaping. Holt sailed through the Suez Canal out to Singapore, and from there along the routes of Blue Funnel's feeder lines, sailed north to Hong Kong, then Shantou, Fuzhou and Shanghai, along the Yangzi to Wuhan on China Navigation's *Poyang* with musical Captain Phelps – the men played chess – and then back and over to Japan, and North America. The young man saw 'Blue Funnels' arrive, depart, load and unload – labourers forming he thought an 'ant-hill' – watched the *Palamed* load up with pilgrims, busied himself looking into the operation of agents' offices, journeyed to tobacco, sugar and other plantations, took in Quarry Bay's sugar works, noted down the details of the operations of the coolie trade – men were indelibly inked on their cheek with their destination, were paid $4 a month, were contracted until they had repaid a $25 advance, and sometimes had to be 'forcibly prevented from leaving the ship': 'too near the slave trade to be a very pleasant business', but good business for Blue Funnels.[63] In Beijing, still 'abominably stiff' from the journey he met Sir Robert Hart – freshly raised a Baronet, and distracted by the business of finding a suitable design for a crest. Happy Valley cemetery, Holt reported, was 'most beautiful and would be very convenient for anyone wanting to be buried'. He shot, 'fished' with dynamite, and rode, and then he shot some more. Chinese food was 'beastly' and Japanese little better. He found one of the firm's agencies entirely staffed by Germans, travelled with 'several different crosses and races of the human species', and was introduced to governors, compradors and planters. This was an interlocking world of British, Dutch and German interests in particular, of different Chinese and Southeast Asian networks and brokers.

In China and Japan Holt was entirely in the hands of Butterfield & Swire. The first of the Swires to make such a grand tour himself was the younger John – Jack – who in 1885 sailed out to Australia, meandering back via India, Singapore, the China coast, Japan and San Francisco. Jack had just graduated from Oxford – itself a sign of the changing character of the old once-Liverpool business world, for what use, many might ask – including Jim Scott – was a university education to a businessman?

'I think it is a pity that I did not go into the London office for two or
three months before starting on my trip,' Jack wrote from Japan, 'as I
should then have known what was important from a business point of
view.' His letters to his father are diffident on company matters, but
like Holt he looked and asked, at least when the surname Swire was no
obstacle to an answer (which it was on the Jardines ship he took to Hong
Kong). The sugar enterprise impressed him. Jack tried a little market
research in a small Japanese town, buying seven different grades of sugar
from a shop, asking the shopkeeper which sold best, results of which,
he felt, rather undermined Dr Korn's 'sacrifice' of 'sweet taste for looks'.
Like Richard Durning Holt, Swire looked over and passed judgement
on the ships he sailed in. 'Holt's steamers seem to be great favourites out
here,' he concluded.[64] It was more a pleasure trip, in intent, than Holt's,
but after his return Jack Swire was more and more a presence in the
office in London, formally working there from early 1887. In later life
he reflected that the trip served not only to introduce him to the firm's
activities and its staff, but for those employees to get some measure of
him. When he started work 'the members of the firm in the East had
got to know me, and my father was in a position to form an opinion,
as to the influence I had amongst my contemporaries'.[65] It was a form
of probation.

A stray remark in the letters points to another change, inexorably
looming. A new generation was moving, tentatively, into position. Jack
Swire would enter the company partnership in January 1888. Mary
Warren had given birth to a son, George Warren Swire, in May 1883,
who would enter the firm rather later. The older generation was still
quite active, and as tenacious as ever. Alfred Holt and John Samuel
Swire would still despatch frank notes back and forth about OSSC,
about conference matters and about Holt's unsuccessful bid for the
Australian mail contract in 1896/97. But in 1886 Jack was already
urging his father to let up. Gamwell and others were 'able and willing
to do their fair share of the work', so 'do let them do it!' This the Senior
would find difficult to do, even when he began regularly to take spa
cures in the 1890s. 'I have been very busy here all the time writing
office work,' he wrote from Bath's Grand Pump Room Hotel in 1894,
'China Nav. returns for the year very good'. 'High living', as he called it,
had taken its toll, and he was also beset with the simple complications
of age. At the spas he bumped into men from his past: Captain James

Hardie, the Royds brothers he had ridden with in Cheshire as a youth, a man who had served with him in the militia in 1859. Swire began drafting a memoir of sorts: 'I review the past – commencing from my A B C time', a document that does not survive, but shortly reported it was 'rather stopped thro young medical friend, who has a fund of professional anecdotes'. 'In retrospect have got to A.D. 1843 – becomes exciting,' he noted, but our story's own person from Porlock seems to have cut this off for good.[66]

John Samuel Swire, aged 65, not yet letting up, made his last voyage out east in the summer of 1891, joined later by Mary Warren – with two maids – and a small family party. His visits, noted the *North China Herald*, 'although few and far between, invariably result in the removal of all unnecessary friction connected with the extensive commercial ramifications of his firm'. The original comment from which this was extracted was more in fact a sarcastic *Hongkong Telegraph* knock at Mackintosh, but the visit did lead soon thereafter to the new pooling agreement after three years of costly competition with China Merchants and Jardines.[67] Jim Scott had made an extensive tour around the firm's estate in 1888/9, when he came to sort out a replacement for Lang (who jumped off from Shanghai before Scott landed), inaugurating a practice of regular visits by partners and directors.[68] Two years later John Samuel Swire sailed from Liverpool to New York on White Star's still fresh 9,600-ton *Teutonic* – 'the greyhound of the Atlantic' on what was at that point the year's fastest passage. Its speed and its luxurious fittings and their scale will have impressed him.[69] He entrained to Chicago and then to Victoria in British Columbia, the Canadian Pacific Railroad and its beautiful new 500-foot, white-hulled, creak-funnelled liner *Empress of India* taking him to Yokohama – it was just back from its (record) maiden return voyage there – then speeding its way back across the Pacific in 13 days (no record), yet four days swifter than Swire travelled across the ocean back in 1874; a Messageries Maritimes steamer then took him to Shanghai.

Swire spent his time at Shanghai meeting the heads of Jardine Matheson and China Merchants. He might have read the translation published while he was there in the *Herald* of a poem about the burning of the *Shanghai*: 'The whole family is weeping / We thought you were coming home to see us again, Now only your spirit will return'. The Senior went north to Tianjin on the *Taiwan*, came back with John

Whittle on the *Tungchow* – trip 378, running into and through the centre of a typhoon with 'a very high confused sea' after a three-hour stop at Yantai. Swire travelled on CNCo's new beancaker *Kweilin* – Captain Vardin was a 'very bad caterer' – then south to Hong Kong on another Blue Funnel, *Dardanus* – fine weather to Fuzhou and then eight hours of typhoon by Lamock island – inspected the sugar refinery where work to expand it was behind schedule (it should have been completed for his visit) – took against Hong Kong superintendent engineer John Mitchell's face, and his claims that his high salary was recouped through the signal efficiency of his methods, and generally shook up his staff, as he usually did. (Mackintosh wrote back in favour of Mitchell, though the *Hongkong Telegraph* pilloried him in bad verse as a drunk, which scandal saw him depart after he won the libel suit he brought as a result.) The party travelled back by P&O taking in a pleasure tour in India. This was a typhoon-beset trip. The day after he spent the night in Herbert Baggally's seaside villa near Kobe a typhoon destroyed it: 'it has disappeared!!' After his return Swire wrote to Albert Crompton, who had joined the Holt brothers as a manager in 1882: 'AH & you should go out East, spend one year in the Straits, and another in China and Japan – you would then get a run of the trades as they affect the interests of the O.S.S. Co.'[70] Philip Holt's trip with Swire in 1878 was the only one he ever made. Alfred Holt never travelled further east than Suez.

Storms aside, this was by the 1890s a world of relatively frictionless travel. It took a negligent master mariner, an ill-corrected chart or a rule-breaking passenger, to wreck a ship. Of course a storm might still do so, but new technologies, including better scientific understanding of typhoon systems and weather forecasting, helped significantly. A man with money might leave Liverpool on the fifteenth of the month, land at New York just under six days later, take two trains to the west coast, then head across the Pacific to Yokohama on something resembling 'a large first class hotel' (with Chinese cooks, stewards and waiters). The duration of the journey was now 'practically halved' by Canadian Pacific's new service, it was claimed, which was chock-filled with 'Globe-Trotters' (and also, the North American press dourly noted, increased numbers of Chinese migrants on the return).[71] He might, as Swire did, leave instructions as to when to post on to Hong Kong his next issues of *Punch* and *The Economist*, and the telegraph cables alerted his staff to his progress: they knew when he would arrive even when the weather was bad. He could rely on the scheduling of ships, trains and the mails, to ensure that he would receive his weekly budget of reading, for pleasure and for business, on the other side of the globe. And there he might find in the pages of *Punch* a representatively poor squib about the 'Modern Traveller' in the issue that met him: 'Most travellers now take their Cooks' – their Thomas Cook guides.[72]

This was the world made by White Star, the Eastern Extension Australasia and China Telegraph Company, the Great Northern Telegraph Company, Canadian Pacific, Messageries Maritimes, Blue Funnel, China Navigation and the P&O: rail, steam and cable knitted it together. These interlocking transport networks facilitated the movement of pilgrims, labourers, tourists (with or without their guidebooks), entertainers, businessmen, mariners in search of a berth (on shore or on board), the living – all sorts, all ages – and the dead – all sorts – 'Learned Zebras' and Mrs Hayes, breaker-in of zebras. CNCo formed a vital, and profitable, component of this global infrastructure, tied as it was into the running of the Blue Funnels, and based on its networks of compradors and brokers, with the conference agreements regulating a business that might otherwise, it was argued (and strongly so by government), degrade itself (and the security of the British empire) through competition.[73] As rational and efficient as it seemed, there were people to manage, and the politics of moving people, or of refusing them movement, and of how they were employed or treated. This was an infrastructure that grew through the enterprise and initiative of these combines of businessmen and engineers, and the thousands who took their shilling, but it also relied on the fact and force of empire, and the exercise of colonial power, even though this was so obvious a fact of nineteenth-century life that it is often barely acknowledged in the records. But empire was not unchallenged, not in Australia over London's expectations over immigration polices, and it was certainly not unchallenged in China.

8

New Eras

On the afternoon of 1 December 1898, John Samuel Swire was resting at his London home in Notting Hill's quiet Pembridge Square. Ill health had kept the Senior from the office and confined indoors for most of November, but three weeks short of his seventy-third birthday Swire was cheerful and sharp, and just about to venture out again despite the overcast weather. At about three o'clock that day one of the clerks travelled from Billiter Street to Pembridge Square with some business that needed attention: a proposal sent to Blue Funnel that it should accept cargoes from Japan for onward despatch to the European continent from London. Swire's advice was firm and clear: no, it would be impolitic, the Hamburg America Line would take umbrage: the balance within the conference needed maintaining. The company letter books show that across the autumn of 1898 Swire had been regularly firing off letters on conference matters, especially to Alfred Holt, and had engaged in all the routine business of John Swire & Sons: the company had introduced a new mechanism to help soften the blow to staff salaries in China of a depreciation in the value of silver, and so of the exchange rate with sterling; he had berated two clerks in Hong Kong for their evidently too public, too loose living, threatening them with dismissal if they did not desist (yet he also personally asked John Whittle, stepfather of one of the clerks, to intervene); he had deflected a plea for a billet for a son – the young man should stay in the Hongkong Bank, he replied – instructed Butterfield & Swire to provide free passages in China to Lord Charles Beresford's mission to investigate British trade, and told off John Bois, although obliquely, for the tone of a recent letter.[1] The Senior was in mid-flow, still the force at the heart of the firm in all its concerns, yet at a quarter past five that day he was dead: his own heart gave way as the afternoon turned to evening.

John Samuel Swire has dominated this history so far, and will continue to shape its course as we proceed. Soon after his death his likeness was sent out to hang on company office walls in China and Japan, while his nostrums shaped the way the men who sat beneath this portrait worked, and it was his enterprise that had placed them there in the first place. Ships being built by Scotts which, in the spring and summer of 1898, he had persuaded Holts to invest in would sail in 1899; this was 'the last contract I shall engineer,' he told Mary Swire, four 7,000-tonners, but Holt will 'regret not ordering eight': his legacy shuttled along Blue Funnel routes for decades yet to come.[2] The firm smoothly survived his passing, and his partners were freed to launch initiatives that he had blocked, partly through force of argument, more often through force of personality, but it was an entirely unexpected and unwanted freedom, and something quite singular was lost with his death. Friends were shocked. Letters went straight out from Edwin Mackintosh to Alfred Holt, Thomas Ismay, Thomas Imrie, H. I. Butterfield, and John Scott at Greenock, men who with him, through their enterprise or capital, had shaped the world-girdling infrastructure that he had journeyed along in 1891. Jim Scott, heading out east on another tour of the company, was handed the news as his steamer docked at Singapore, and he travelled straight back home. The Senior was known to have been periodically beneath the weather in late years, regularly travelling off to Aix, to Bath and to Buxton for spa treatment, but despite this he had seemed simply unstoppable.

The letters of condolence have set the tone of most subsequent reflection on the character and achievements of a man who had never held back his thoughts if he believed they were right, which generally he did. We can see from the record that the paeans in these to his integrity, generosity and 'keen sense of justice' were more than mere formulaic politesse. 'He did what he believed to be his duty in the widest and best sense,' wrote Thomas Ismay. 'I don't think I ever met a man with a stronger sense of justice in business – he never claimed for himself what he would not give to others,' wrote Philip Holt, whose brother, Alfred, was quite inarticulate with grief.[3] These men trusted each other. Trust was what allowed Swire to secure investment commitments for

Taikoo Sugar, for him to feel that he had moral standing enough with his network to approach them, and they in him to agree, when there really was precious little to go on. Trust allowed Swire to contract with Scotts for new steamers with a letter that read, in its entirety:

Messrs Scott & Co.

27th September 1894

Dear Sirs,
   We accept your offer to build us two more coasters, duplicates of those now building, at the same price – please put these in hand at once.

Yours truly,
John Swire & Sons

This was trust presented in an extravagantly demonstrative fashion, but it signalled the standing of John Swire & Sons within this network, and so of the firm, and in particular the person, character and record of John Samuel Swire.

Swire made mistakes – the partnership with R. S. Butterfield was a mistake – but then the name stuck after the man left, and stuck for a century. For years before he left, William Lang did not well serve the firm, and had often been wayward, but Swire stood by his first protégé in China (or the first who survived more than a matter of weeks). Sentiment and family loyalty kept men like J. P. O'Brien in the firm's orbit when they should long before have been cut loose. The Senior appointed men who turned out bad (but that is simply the risky business of people); opening in Japan, and so swiftly, was too rapid an extension; the refinery suffered from a huge miscalculation about the levels of working capital it would continually need and this was a source of deep anxiety. Swire stuck by his friends and associates even when they exasperated him beyond measure. But then there were the gambles that paid off – but did so precisely because they were *not* gambles: the China Navigation Company, and the Taikoo Sugar Refinery, and, of course, the alliance with Alfred Holt and the visionary China initiative of a man who otherwise rather lacked vision. Swire was interested in making money and making it fairly. He was generous in providing his capital, his time, his advice – generous whether asked for or not – and generous with opportunities – again, whether asked for or not. He made the careers and fortunes of Jim Scott and Edwin Mackintosh. He rescued Frederick Gamwell: in 1894 he reported an exchange with his London partner and anchor, who had just encountered an old acquaintance from silk trade days in China, 'who was a millionaire and a swell' but was now 'borrowing when able': 'Had it not been for your ability and kindness, I should, in all probability, have been like him. I always feel this.' Swire reports replying that 'We have mutually assisted each other'.[4] The old China trade was often one of chance; Gamwell was a man of business talent in a risky business, and his luck had run out. Mutual assistance is a thread that runs through the tangles of connections that formed the core of the Swire enterprises. That word, assistance, was the one he reached for, we might recall, when he announced to William Lang and Jim Scott that he was setting in motion the creation of a competitor line for Russells on the Yangzi.

It is worth noting that John Samuel Swire was really not interested in China, and he understood very little about it. This conclusion is not to his detriment (and was hardly unusual), and he really knew very little about the other countries in which he spent time living and working. That was not his skill. Understanding China, and how to work there, was for others – his delegates and agents – to develop with the tools he provided. His own letters to Tang Jingxing are culturally tone-deaf. China was a field for enterprise, in association with the interests, enterprise, and capital of his friends – that Liverpool nexus, mostly, with its Greenock arm. He was a businessman from England's north-west, from a city that more than any other held in its hands the traces of empire and Britain's global reach, and so his was an enterprise that naturally looked overseas, to New York, to New Orleans, to Melbourne, and then to China, and Japan. Swire's gifts were persistence, timing, friendship, persuasion, and patience with men and the times. There was audacity, too, in the direction of energy, capital and careful planning into new enterprises. The Senior was also very much that: he dominated the firm and he will have dominated, one way or another – the most appropriate for that moment – any and every meeting and discussion he joined.

The archive loses some sparkle after his death. Swire's style was robust, and clearly often patterned quite closely on his speech. Ideas and points, caveats and clarifications all came tumbling after each other on to the page. Sentences scramble up the margins, the hand gets smaller – there might always be need for yet another line – and then the mails need to go and the letter stops. He could be facetious, and he could be terse. His letters are rarely boring. His correspondence with Mary Warren before and after their marriage in 1881 reveals another side to him, playful, emotional, certainly uxorious. His relations with his older son Jack were not comfortable – 'I want everyone to look through my spectacles,' he wrote in 1881, and Jack 'occasionally ceased to take advice which I am too fond of giving'.[5] That is, Swire was as exacting a father as he was a senior partner, and Jack long struggled against this before the older man's death, in his relations with his stepmother, and latterly his half-brother. It was not helped by the fact that Jack had little natural inclination for business, nor real interest in it. He was by nature a countryman. There is little trace of religion in John Samuel Swire's outlook. Alfred Holt's philosophy of business was shaped by the tight-knit Unitarian community he lived within in Liverpool. Religious belief and practice underpinned the work of other important Victorian men of commerce. For his part, John Samuel Swire was as unreligious a public figure as can be found. (His brother William was more pious in later life, but had been something of a preening dandy in his younger days.) Nothing in the surviving archive shows any religious interest save some local philanthropy in Leighton Buzzard, but this was socially appropriate for a man of his standing in the community. It signalled little otherwise.

Public obituaries were laudatory: he had 'remarkable ability, great energy, and unflinching integrity', he was 'The father of shipping conferences'. Flags flew at half-mast on CNCo ships in the harbour at Melbourne, and of course in Hong Kong, and over the hong there and over Jardine Matheson as well.[6] His passing was not much noted in the Shanghai press, for he was but an infrequent visitor, although there, too, China Navigation ships flew their flags at half-mast and added a blue mourning stripe. And, of course, in *The Field* it was noted that the 'Vale of Aylesbury' mourned the death of 'one of the best sportsmen ... who had visited these pastures for many years', and the *Leighton Buzzard Observer* noted the same, though he had not been able to hunt for a couple of years, and that the town and its inhabitants had lost a local benefactor.[7] When Swire took over Leighton House there he was announced, simply, as 'well known in sporting circles, and as a member of the Rothschild Hunt'. John Samuel Swire was buried in Leighton Buzzard on 6 December 1898 amid a large crowd of mourners, and in a 'heavy storm of rain'.[8]

China was experiencing its own storms when John Samuel Swire died, and these rocked the company's activities. In 1895 the Qing admitted defeat in a war with Japan over the domination of the Kingdom of Korea. In the aftermath, the Japanese sliced off Taiwan as a colony, and secured other new rights. A 'triple alliance' of powers – France, Germany and Russia – pressured the victors to renounce some of the spoils. These events heralded an open season for new demands on China, one of what British Prime Minister Lord Salisbury termed the 'dying nations' whose fate had the potential to upset the European balance of power, among which he also included the empires of Spain, and of the Ottomans. In 1897 Germany found a pretext and seized a place under the Chinese sun, developing a navy-run colony at Jiaozhou (Qingdao) in Shandong. The Russians immediately demanded what they christened Port Arthur on the Liaodong peninsula; the British secured what they thought a counterweight to both with the Weihaiwei-leased territory in Shandong. The French took Guangzhouwan in Guangdong as a leased territory, expanding their 'sphere of influence' in south-west China, and the British the 'New Territories' north of Kowloon. Consolidating these territories involved bloody local conflicts with Qing subjects who resisted their transfer to foreign overlordship, the types of small war it is easy to overlook but which were calamities for those affected. Fearful of what was widely termed 'national extinction', Qing reformers persuaded the Guangxu Emperor to seize power from Cixi, the Empress Dowager, inaugurating the 'One Hundred Days' of reform decrees that spilled out of the capital between June and September 1898. Cixi struck back, imprisoned the emperor, and purged the reformers, some of whom fled with British help overseas. CNCo's SS *Chungking* carried the most prominent, Kang Youwei, to Shanghai, was intercepted by the British at sea, and Kang was transferred to a British warship to await a P&O steamer heading south to Hong Kong.[9] It seemed to many, especially in China, that an end was needed: an end to Qing rule or an end to the foreign presence.

John Swire & Sons, like all British firms, was affected by its aftermath, and the new geography of foreign power in China – and the new opportunities that became available: the Treaty of Shimonoseki that ended the Sino-Japanese War allowed foreign enterprises to establish factories in the treaty ports and the number of those cities opened to foreign trade and residence this way was increased. As the Germans, or the Japanese, for example, took possession of their prizes they favoured and privileged the commercial interests of their own nationals; demanded, for example, that commissioners of customs in these ports should be appointed from the ranks of their own nationals in the service, or more recruited; and destabilised what had seemed to the British, whose predominance overall in China was upset by all this, the balanced open-door trading environment that had evolved since 1842 and from which all benefited, China not least of all, it was claimed, but mostly the British. Most dramatically of all, however, were the events of 1899/1900 that saw a massive popular uprising against foreign religious influence that was co-opted by the desperate Qing state which on 15 June 1900 declared war on the world.

An early indirect reference to these troubles came in a letter from the Tianjin agent Walter Fisher in October 1899, when he noted that the year had seen a 'severe drought'.[10] Drought continued, and it followed terrible flooding the previous year when the banks of the Yellow River in Shandong broke. Hundreds of thousands of farmers in the Shandong/Hebei borderlands of the north China plain south of Tianjin were affected, their land unusable, their days long with despair. Their world disorientated, increasing numbers took solace and power from a new bundle of ideas and practice that offered a way to put things back in order. The idea was that the dislocation of the world was caused by its pollution by foreign ideas and beliefs, and by foreigners – Christian missionaries and, as these rural people saw it, foreignised Chinese: Christian converts. The world could be put right if the land could be cleansed. Spirit possession teachings offered a means to do this, through a form of boxing that, if practised properly, offered invulnerability to foreign bullets. Bands of 'Boxers' grew in number in 1899 and spread across the countryside, their skills easily imparted to others. Confrontations now took place as they encountered Qing troops – whose stuttering rifles rapidly disproved the invulnerability claims, but without denting Boxer confidence – Christian communities, and then mission stations and outposts of the newly laid railways. This millenarian rural uprising erupted out of its heartland in the spring of 1900 and the Boxers marched north.

A Bristol rope-maker's son, Walter Fisher was a 12-year veteran of the firm, first putting in two years in Hong Kong after working for a wine merchant in his hometown and then for a firm of accountants. He had worked at Shanghai on the shipping desk on the French Bund and spent a year in charge at Wuhan before assuming the management of the Tianjin branch in 1893. Fisher had celebrated his arrival there with his marriage to Maud Williams, daughter of a Shanghai pilot. As Philip Holt reported when he passed through, Fisher was very much a sportsman, notably a cricketer, and his bowling prowess helped make him a popular man in Tianjin's British community. He served in other ways, on the British concession's Municipal Council, the Recreation Trust and the Chamber of Commerce. Tianjin's sporting life had improved markedly once the railway to Beijing began operating in 1896. The hard journey by boat, pony or cart was now history, although thousands of boatmen were thrown out of work by this development. The 80-mile journey between cities which once might as well have been 'in Greenland and Peru' could now be done in three hours and 40 minutes, and that meant that 'Pekingites' and 'Tientsinites' could hold 'inter-port' cricket matches (Fisher hitting a 'brilliant' 43 in one of the first). Nothing in his life, however, had quite prepared him for being besieged by China's most thoroughly well-trained and well-equipped army. I 'make but a poor soldier,' he wrote on 3 July 1900, after a day of shelling. It was all a long, long way from Bristol, and from his old firm's annual works outing to Badminton in England's balmy July.[11]

The siege of the foreign concessions at Tianjin, or, from the Qing perspective, the defence of north China from an unprecedented and unprovoked foreign invasion headquartered at Tianjin, lasted for 27 fetidly hot days from 15 June, and was at its most terrifying during the weeks after 17 June when Krupp-made artillery pieces started bombarding the settlements.[12] Only on 16 July were the last of these captured by British troops, although fighting continued afterwards. At the same time, assaults had been made on the settlements by soldiers and by Boxers, and repulsed. 'The whole Northern Army is around us,' Fisher scribbled in a note on 24 June, 'I hope to get through alive, but the immediate future is very uncertain.' On 5 August a hastily assembled force of 16,000 foreign troops – Japanese, British, French, German, Russian and American – attacked and defeated Chinese forces in the walled city and then drove on towards Beijing, where foreign residents and Chinese converts were under siege in the foreign legations and the Roman Catholic cathedral. Boxers had started arriving in Tianjin in March, and by late May had largely taken control of the walled city. But as they moved on the north that spring, Fisher's letters had focused on reporting a record year's results for the branch in 1899, the impact of the new political economy and geography of north China – the laying out of a new German concession and international rivalries over railways. New land needed to be purchased for railway sidings: the Customs Commissioner, German Gustav Detring, a power in the city through his relationship with veteran Qing administrator Li Hongzhang, aimed, it was believed, to divert trade flows into the new German concession and Butterfield & Swire needed to try and prevent this 'rabidly pro-German' – as Fisher characterised him – getting his way.[13]

'We have no fear whatever here in the settlements,' Fisher wrote confidently on 5 June, his first direct reference to the 'local troubles', for 'we can muster 600 or 700 men', but business 'is at a standstill'. Over the course of the next month Fisher was consumed with anxiety about the safety of his family, his southern Chinese staff and their families, and a considerable number of its constituents, the firm's properties and its books. He was assisted by Lionel Howell, recently appointed and the son of the CNCo hulk-keeper at Wuhu, who now served as the company's agent there, although Howell, having been despatched to escort some refugees to Tanggu at the mouth of the Hai River, was stuck there when the siege began, and had to join the relieving forces to get back in. British marines were allowed to occupy an empty godown (which gave 'confidence' to his staff and, Fisher assumed, somewhat naively it turned out, secured the safety of the building), and he allowed the firm's offices on Victoria Road to be used as a British military headquarters (surely, it was thought, why it had attracted shellfire). For the first six days of the siege the chance presence of 1,700 Russian troops alone stood between the settlements and some 20,000 Chinese regulars and great numbers of Boxer fighters. 'Some of the best native soldiers in China were shelling us and at no distant range,' reported the Customs Commissioner drolly.[14]

Stock in the godowns was hauled out for barricades. Artillery shells rained down across the settlement, hitting the Butterfield hong and warehouses 'many times'. All was 'pandemonium'. Things got so bad, it was reported, that on 23 June the bar at the Tientsin Club was ordered to be closed: the attackers, if they were to succeed, were to be met on sober terms. But if being besieged was awful – 'I feel quite done up with the strain and worry,' Fisher reported – being relieved was far, far worse. Foreign soldiers looted what they could, burned what they could not take, or, to hide their tracks, killed Chinese they encountered without reason or mercy, and terrorised the remaining foreign residents. The Russians were worst, but the British were 'as despicable a gang of thieves and villains as any,' concluded Fisher. In mid-July British marines raided the hong claiming that they had been fired on from within. They tied up the company's remaining Chinese staff, holding them 'by the pigtails ready to be hauled off and possibly shot as the authorities are "treachery mad"'. Fisher managed to persuade their commander to release the terrified men. On the following day he got them all off by boat to the coast and safety in the south. The next night the office was ransacked. Meanwhile, Indian troops who had billeted themselves in a sugar warehouse set it alight to hide the evidence of their depredations.[15] In this way foreign civilisation restored order to Tianjin.

A CNCo engineer escorted Fisher's family down the Hai River to Tanggu on 5 July. The company's steamer *Shengking* then took them and another 160 British refugees, 'huddled together like sheep', the steward doing what he could, out across the Dagu Bar where a US navy supply vessel took them on to Nagasaki. Go home, Fisher told them in messages he managed to send out. Meanwhile, of course, as crisis always begets opportunity, Fisher sought to make sure that supplying the allied military administration that took over Tianjin did not simply become a 'Jardine show', and pitched for tenders to bring rice north to the hungry city. He begged Shanghai to send back the comprador, Zheng Yizhi (Yik Kee), not least to chase money owed by the firm's sugar brokers who, despite the seeming odds, were all still alive and buoyant, guaranteeing to meet him personally and escort him up. Nobody trusted the Russians still. It took 'a lot of talk and assurances' but Zheng came back in late August with the No. 1 shroff, and a shipping clerk, and, Shanghai reported, 'we also send 60 stevedores' (as well as shoe polish for Fisher). With, presumably, his boots newly shined, Fisher busied himself preparing as much information as he could for a formal compensation claim – which included a large sum for Zheng's looted possessions, now squirreled away, in all probability, in British marines' packs. He rented out the hong to the American Quartermaster General's team ('we use our own verandah as an office and it suits us' – and it was safer than letting the British at it), pressed the British authorities to contest a Russian grab for land on the east bank of the Hai River that included his newly purchased Butterfield & Swire plot, and then in November he collapsed with the strain of it all. No wonder.[16]

Fisher's experience, and that of Howell, who stuck it out with him, was a singular one, although there was violence – and bubonic plague – in Niuzhuang, and worries at Yantai as well. The 'trouble in the North' was 'crippling trade' and money was scarce, reported Weatherston from Zhenjiang. There was a big 'scare' at Wuhan in August, when it was feared that 'reformers' were to launch an uprising, but some 20 beheadings calmed things. All quiet here, reported Baker from Fuzhou, although there was some unease. Women and children were ordered out down the Yangzi from the river ports, and the No. 1. Chinese clerk at Wuhan took his family down as well.[17] The Boxer crisis was the most traumatic nationalist uprising that would be faced for decades to come, but China's new century was a nationalist century, and the company's agents would experience their share of its travails. Sometimes the company's properties, its claims or the actions of its staff, would themselves spark protests, as well as boycotts, and violent reactions. We have already seen this at Canton, and in responses to the *Shanghai* disaster. Walter Fisher himself would see no more of it. Stung by what he considered the precipitate promotion of men his junior to more senior management-track posts, he took a job with the Kailan Mining Company and then left China altogether to work for the 'Jardine show' in London (soon chairing that firm's Indo-China Steam Navigation Company). But Fisher's handling of events in Tianjin, especially the potential catastrophe in July when the Chinese staff were seized by British Bluejackets, was certainly remembered warmly by those concerned, as his nephew attested long afterwards on himself visiting Tianjin for B&S in 1911: he remembered being 'nearly killed with dinners from eminent Cantonese merchants' when his relationship to their guardian in that summer of heat, fear and death was revealed.[18]

A minor but noteworthy role in the defence of Tianjin was played by the Tientsin Volunteer Corps, British residents, mainly, in summer khaki or winter blue, which was formed in early 1898 at the height of the 'scramble for concessions' – 'it is the unexpected which always

happens', argued one of its advocates, as indeed it did – as well as a
scratch 'home guard' of untrained men. Wuhan's British volunteers
turned out in August when the fear was at its height. Volunteering
remained an important feature of British life in China, as it did back
home. Young British men were encouraged to join up, sometimes
directed to by firms, but many did not need much encouragement.
Such units provided a reserve of strength for defence of concession,
settlement or colony, but volunteering was also seen as a healthy,
character-building activity, and men who were bivouacked under
canvas at, for example, the Hongkong Volunteer Corps' annual camp
on Stonecutters Island, were far removed from the island's vices. But
these were social organisations as well, and opportunities for men to
meet their peers. The Tientsin Corps was 'a welcome addition to our
many societies for the promotion of social harmony, and amusement',
read a report on its second 'Smoking concert' in 1899; it offered
'excellent sport and fine exercise', but it was also a tool for self-defence.
The British consolidation of the New Territories was resisted by its
inhabitants and securing control had needed force. Fear in Hong
Kong had galvanised the rapid expansion of the previously somewhat
moribund volunteers, and their calling out twice to man positions in
1899's short conflict. By 1901 there were 300 men in the Corps, more
than twice as many as there had been in 1898.[19]

In 1900 at least eight Butterfield & Swire staff at Hong Kong were
on the strength of the colony's Volunteer Corps. The following year one
of these, William Armstrong – who took a striking photograph of his
soldiering Taikoo colleagues in 1901 – acted as second-in-command of
a 42-strong 'Coronation Contingent' that sailed across the Pacific on
the *Empress of Japan* to cross Canada for London, there to take part in
the festivities surrounding the enthronement of Edward VII. (Another
TSR man joined the detachment in London.) Helped, and happily
well-lubricated, by all reports, by those they met en route, sometimes
roughing it, unimpressed by a visit to Spithead for a Naval Review –
Hong Kong's harbour, they thought, had spoiled them for maritime
spectacle – they took their turn among units from across the British
empire in providing honour guards and escorts, were inspected by Lord
Kitchener, the hero of Omdurman, the King and Queen, and then
returned to a formal welcome in Hong Kong. The 'Taikoo Detachment'
featured in later Corps orders about weekly training, and the men

paraded on the roof of the company offices on the Praya, or from 1906 used the 'beautiful little' Taikoo Miniature Rifle Range by the colony's recreation ground. One of the 15-pounder artillery pieces used by the Corps in 1904 was kept at the Taikoo Sugar Refinery for convenience. When the colony was 'invaded' by the Emperor of Blue in a large-scale exercise in 1905, Taikoo was one of the three Corps encampments.[20] Some of Coronation Contingent would meet Kitchener again, in a sense. Company men, and others who served in the Corps, would in 1914 parlay their record into volunteering for service with the 'New Army' that Kitchener raised at the onset of the Great War. In the meantime, Taikoo men and other volunteers prepared for all that China's turbulent new era might throw at them.

This has, so far, largely been a masculine story. The dramatis personae have mostly been the men of the firm armed with ideas, capital, pens or rifles. Their relationships and families were part of their lives, of course, and to an extent a feature of the company's business, as we have seen (and play: Maggie Hoskins, daughter of the dockyard's Thomas Hoskins, took first place in the Ladies' Shoot in 1908 on the Taikoo range). 'We have your letter ... informing us of your wish to be married', runs a John Swire & Sons note in January 1899, 'and have written to your father giving assent.' The addressee, Walter Feast, had convinced London that this was a financially viable step for him to take. And so Walter presently wed Edith, Miss Smithers, daughter of an accountant, in Kobe in April.[21] As we have seen, Edith will have been expected to play her role in the social realm in treaty port society, but the formal world of work in the firm was male. That is, it had been until 12 November 1892 when Katie J. Reece began working in the London office as a 'Typewriter' and stenographer. Miss Reece had come from Burney & Wells on Bedford Row – that is, a secretarial agency. She came at a moment when the arrival of the 'white blouse revolution', the entry of women into clerical office work, was gathering pace, marked in 1891 by the appearance of a first journal aimed directly at female typists.[22] Reece worked for 15 years before resigning in 1907, but more than that we do not know, save that she evidently quite impressed Herbert Smith, in charge in Hong Kong in 1900. In January that year Smith wrote to Jim Scott, now the senior partner, to petition for a stenographer, and specifically a woman, 'same stamp as the girl you have in the office' at home. His request is a convoluted mix in which a statement of personnel needs meets chauvinist, if not misogynist, embarrassment and hesitation: 'we don't want anything over young & lovely, but a good, sensible, well-educated, smart woman of say 30 to 35', although 'not so hideous as to choke ideas out of our heads, or stop the clocks'. She would need $150 or so a month and could afford to live at the Peak Hotel on that (for where, indeed, would a single woman live). Firms were starting to appoint women to such posts in Shanghai, Smith reported, and any number could be found in the United States on a three-year contract. Scott said no: 'it would not work.' No reason was given. Instead, he replied, 'use as many native Typewriters as you have use for', but also, do not waste time composing long letters which 'our late Senior discouraged'.[23] (Scott was particularly quick to resort to the presiding spirit of 'our late Senior'.) Miss Reece probably typed up this reply.

The entry of women into the clerical labour market would proceed and gather pace, however difficult Jim Scott thought it, albeit slowly in John Swire & Sons. The 'New Woman' of the late nineteenth century, well-educated, independent, earning her own living, was a phenomenon that unnerved the world of men like Jim Scott, formed in the mid-Victorian era. Two more women were hired in London in 1902, and in 1905 a fourth. This was largely in line with the pattern nationally, and especially in London. Miss Reece was one of some 7,000 female commercial clerks in London in 1891: by 1911 there were 32,000.[24] Only in 1912 did any of the China offices employ a woman. Setting aside Smith's request, there was probably greater resistance, possibly on moral or practical grounds, in the treaty ports: for what sort of place was a treaty port for a single woman (and for some, what discredit might her working do, to the 'prestige' of the body of her peers.) In fact, Shanghai's first appointee was married. This was Beatrice Mary Bland, née Coulson, who had seven years' experience as a stenographer and typist, four in London and three in Shanghai to which she had moved in 1909 (and where she married an SMC sanitary inspector). She lasted all of three months in the post. A year later a Mrs Marshall joined but found her 'services dispensed with' quite swiftly, no explanation given in either case (and we do not know Mrs Marshall's Christian name). It was not until the First World War that the offices in China started to appoint, and retain, women, and not just as typists. By the end of 1916 Shanghai had hired four women as assistants in the book office. It was generally perceived by employers that women were more punctual, efficient and accurate than male clerks. And better educated women could be hired more cheaply than the men they replaced. Men who were initially threatened by their arrival in the clerical labour market found solace in the fact that most women held specific roles that increasingly came to be perceived as feminine, and that held no prospect of any further promotion.[25] The long-persisting marriage bar also facilitated this: single women, on marrying, were usually required to leave a firm's employ. A male clerk might still dream that in future he might make partner, the path, however difficult to navigate, at least remaining open to him.

Hong Kong seems to have had to wait until April 1916, when the records show a Mrs Hidden joining as a stenographer. Twenty-one-year-old Agnes Hidden, née Johnson-Lee, had been born in Venezuela, daughter of a man who had business interests in Trinidad, was educated in Hong Kong and had married an assistant at a local department store. In 1910 she had taken a class in dictation at the Technical Institute, a continuing education initiative located at the colony's Queen's College and founded in 1908 with a government grant to offer courses in engineering, commerce and science. Women were 'admitted to certain classes on application to the director', but pass lists soon start to contain a good proportion of women's names: clearly a demand was growing and it was accelerated as men volunteered for military service and replacing them proved increasingly difficult.[26] This pattern of wartime recruitment was entirely in line with trends in British society as a whole, and while the end of the war would see sharp reverses for women in the labour market more widely, their employment by firms like John Swire & Sons and its companies had become, within those limits, entirely routine by 1918.

There was also much anxiety among male clerks in late nineteenth-century Britain over employment of foreign nationals, Germans in particular. Slowly developing Germanophobia was augmented by perceptions that Germans worked for less, learned British trade secrets and practices as they did so, and then left to use these for German firms. In China the type of tension that Fisher gave voice to over Gustav Detring would co-exist with an entanglement of British and German commercial interests in many ways and social and even personal relations, and many firms in Britain, especially Manchester cotton goods interests, would also come to rely on German agency

The Customs House, Liverpool, 1864:
heart of an empire of trade

The founder: John Swire
of Liverpool, 1793–1847

Strand Street, Liverpool Waterfront, 1857

Bradford 1849:
wool for the world

Evangeline, 'a finer
craft never floated
in our waters'

New Orleans, 1852,
site of the first
overseas partnership

Off to the diggings! Gold hunters, Ararat, Victoria, 1858

Melbourne docks, *c.*1860

John Samuel Swire, *c.*1854

Alfred Holt, 1829–1911

Steam to China: Holt's *Agamemnon*, 1865

Shanghai Bund: a new world of junks, sail and steam

First home in Hong Kong: the Augustine Heard & Co building in 1860

Foreign settlements on the river: the Bund at Hankow, *c*.1870

Encounter on the Yangzi: observing the foreigner, *c.*1871

Hong Kong, 1880

North coast of Hong Kong island, 1845, from West Point to Quarry Bay

CNCo's early steamers: *Glengyle* and *Ichang* at Shanghai, 1874

Taikoo triumphant in the 1880s: the fours team, Shanghai Rowing Club regatta, including J.C. Bois, back left

Yokohama comfort: James Dodds and family, 1878

A hulk and its bund: the *Cadiz* (centre) at Zhenjiang

'Comfort' for investors in their 'declining years': Taikoo Sugar Refinery under construction at Quarry Bay, 24 October 1882

John Samuel Swire, 1886

James Henry Scott (1845–1912)

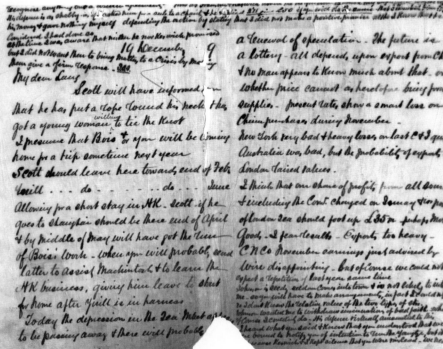

The Senior writing as he thinks until the mails close, 19 December 1879

Yangzi river upstarts: Zheng Guanying (standing, third from left), H.B. Endicott (standing, right); seated: Captains Robert McQueen and David Martin, Shanghai, 1883

Robert McQueen and H.B. Endicott in Shanghai, c.1883

Sikh watchmen on guard, entrance to the Taikoo Sugar Refinery, 1897

Networked businesses: Alfred Holt (third from left), John Samuel Swire (fifth from left), and John Scott (right) at the launch of the *Menelaus*, Scott's yard, Greenock, 5 June 1895

Digging deep for the Taikoo Dockyard, Quarry Bay, 1904

Future foreshadowed: a last portrait of John Samuel Swire, photographed by
G. Warren Swire, 1896

River business: CNCo steamer, lighter, hulk, cargo, dockers at Jiujiang, *c*.1906–07

Moving people: deck passengers on the *Taming*, 1911

Typhoon: one of William Nicholson's photographs of the 1906 storm, taken from the Butterfield & Swire offices on the Praya, Hong Kong

Launching the SS *Tencho Maru* from Taikoo Dockyard, 9 December 1911

Tiffin time in Hong Kong: Butterfield & Swire clerks relaxing in the Praya building, *c.*1897. Left to right: H. Arthur, G. Grimble, E. C. Shepherd, A. Donald, William Armstrong (who took the photograph)

houses to distribute their wares. Firms like Swires, chemists aside, did not employ Germans, but they would come slowly more to hire those 'native Typewriters' and Chinese assistants. They had for a long time past, and still yet to come, made use of Macanese clerks and book-keepers (and most of the names of women on the Technical Institute pass lists are Macanese), among whom in Shanghai and in Hong Kong a distinctly Anglophone community developed that would buffer this development further. Chinese heads of departments at the Taikoo Sugar Refinery had been under discussion almost from the outset, for they would certainly be cheaper than the men imported from Greenock, and probably rather less trouble (and certainly less bibulous).[27] But often there was a concern about the timing being not right, or the right men not yet being available, or, in some enterprises and organisations, European staff contrived ways effectively to bar Chinese from working alongside them.

Miss Reece's employment was not simply a question of replacement. The entire culture of office work was changing. The volume of paperwork was increasing rapidly. For a company like Swires with complex networks of activity, and vast numbers of customers across those networks, the logistical challenge of processing and organising information, and analysing it, of preparing accurate documentation, swiftly, and in multiple copies, meant greater numbers of clerical staff were needed. Before Reece's appointment, the London letter books show typing of documents had already begun, but only recently. From November 1892 onwards, the vast majority of documents in the files are typed. New technologies like the typewriter and new methods of document duplication would also change the way offices were organised and laid out. Some of these new subdivisions of labour were 'feminised' – the telephone joined the typewriter in that regard. Staff records, for example, are one way in which we can see record-keeping evolving. Where John Samuel Swire once kept a pocket notebook with contract details and a file of copies of contracts, an elaborate system of staff record books, noting men's education, leave, posts held and salaries, summary assessments – 'Shapes well', 'very well' – was developed from the 1880s onwards, cross-referenced with sets of 'Staff Letters'. In 1899 London even requested photographs of all staff to be sent to it ('My own is rather a failure,' wrote Fisher from Tianjin, as he sent along his and Howell's, 'so I send you two for you to choose the lesser evil.')[28] This

became more important still as the company introduced a bonus system
for staff in 1900. The company was certainly adding more work, taking
on new insurance agencies, for example, which generated more and
more documentation, but the nature of that work was clearly changing
markedly. Staff duties often became more and more specialised, and
while men were often rotated from desk to desk to build up familiarity
with a range of work, some of it became almost wholly the preserve of
the specialist.

Before the Senior's death, one notable area of potential activity had
never been advanced by the firm, although it would have been a logical
extension of its interests and could have harnessed its network, expertise
and administrative capacity: a dockyard. Swire had resolutely opposed
this. Nevertheless, his presiding spirit might surely have smiled at the
launching of a 6,000-ton Blue Funnel liner, *Autolycus*, at the Taikoo
Dockyard and Engineering Company in Quarry Bay on 27 March
1917.[29] This dockyard had taken in its first vessel nine years previously,
when CNCo's *Sungkiang* had docked on 3 October 1908, but with
Autolycus it came of age – and the keel of a sister ship was immediately
laid down. This was a moment indeed. It was not the first ship the
dockyard had built – that was a CNCo Yangzi steamer, *Shasi*, laid down
in 1909 – but that knot of partners and associates now had this triumph
to mark on the slipway at Quarry Bay.

A dock company had been seriously discussed by the partners as early
as 1881, and to an extent even earlier, back in 1872. But it was the land
purchase at Quarry Bay that seemed to force the issue and Jim Scott
and Edwin Mackintosh were keen. But John Samuel Swire believed that
while it would certainly be possible, there was no room for a second
company in the colony.[30] Patience, it transpired, was a virtue he alone
did not possess: his partners were content to await the opportunity.
Quite shortly after Swire's death, the prospect was being discussed again
eagerly in Hong Kong and Jim Scott began the process of preparing the
new enterprise. This involved, when it was completed, reclaiming 20
acres of land from the harbour, levelling off land in spectacular blasting
operations by contractors that were sometimes invitation events, and
that led to the removal of one and half million cubic yards of granite.
A dry dock large enough to hold the biggest vessels then sailing, nearly
790 feet long and 120 feet wide, was first flooded with water in the
summer of 1907. Three repair slips, a building slip and associated

shops, power plant and other installations covered 52 acres in total.
Scotts were the technical consultants, and with Holts and two other
partners, formally registered the new company in 1908. That same year
the installation was badly hit – 'I could cry when I see it,' wrote the
Taipan – as was the colony more widely, by a devastatingly powerful
typhoon which led to a delay in the start of its general operations.[31]

The prospect of competition in docks quite fluttered Hong Kong
commercial circles when rumour started doing the rounds in early
1900. There was a strong, entrenched interest: the Hongkong and
Whampoa Dock Company, with an extensive installation in Kowloon,
a firm of long standing and little desire to allow another to share its
business.[32] The initial development work at Quarry Bay was amateurish.
An ageing Hong Kong architect, William Danby, was contracted to
prepare a survey and a plan, but proved unreliable and unpredictable
and (it was later discovered) incompetent; moreover, he ran a one-man
show. In his stead, Donald Macdonald, who had been resident engineer
in charge of the construction of dry docks at Blyth and agent in
charge of part of the Admiralty dock works in Dover, was recruited,
joined by other experienced engineers, Albert Griffin and William
Clarke.[33] Construction continued to be plagued by problems, not least
Macdonald's ego, which turned out to be considerable – please do not
send him back, wrote Hong Kong in July 1907, and anyway, 'Mr Griffin is
the brains' behind the construction – cost overruns, persuasive rumours
of corruption within the construction team, a land slip, what proved to
be a defective sea wall, and fluctuations in the labour supply due to fears
of bubonic plague that caused large numbers of Chinese residents to
leave the colony. The local press had sniggered in 1900 that 'it will take
B&S ... a long time to get docks – if ever', and it did take longer than
was hoped.[34] And in the same vein, perhaps, on 31 December 1908, the
shipbuilders in Kowloon held their New Year's Eve dance there, ferrying
300 guests in launches across the harbour, ineffably confident in their
future. Across the harbour at the Peak Hotel the following day, Jim
Scott, on his last visit to Asia (and probably, characteristically, blind to
their New Year's Day constitutions), addressed his assembled staff from
the three enterprises about the history of John Swire & Sons. And that
same day marked the official opening of the Taikoo Dockyard.[35]

As John Samuel Swire had confidently remarked in 1881, the firm
could mobilise capital for any enterprise it cared to develop. It could

also, as the dockyard again proved, secure the technical expertise needed, and deploy its management skills to operate a large-scale project that largely relied on numerous small contractors – Chinese firms – working with equipment brought in from Britain and raw material shipped in from across the Pearl River delta. Construction involved a significant expansion at Quarry Bay: more homes for the European – Scottish, indeed Clydeside – staff of engineers, foremen and superintendents: 36 names are recorded in a 1905 list of staff at the dockyard site, in addition to the three senior engineers, 79 in 1910, with another 24 temporary staff (and a further 43 at the refinery). A Greenock newspaper printed advice for those who might take a post in the colony: take your winter clothes, take as many boots as you can muster – expensive in Hong Kong – and buy a solar topi – a pith helmet. Although the cost of living was high, once you had furnished your house, you would be able to save half your salary, it confidently predicted.[36] Homes were built for the Chinese staff, and a hospital, too, and private speculators built more as well as shops, and the government's sanitary board approved the building of a public market. Census records show the population grow steadily: 2,517 Chinese adults in the entire Shau Kei Wan district in which Quarry Bay sat in 1881, 5,447 in 1891. In 1901 Quarry Bay was first recorded as a separate 'village', with 1,875 Chinese residents, which grew to 3,219 in 1905.[37] The Taikoo installations employed most of these, and more were indirectly feeding from them. Quarry Bay, once the far point of a carriage drive out of the city into the country, and even for the past two decades relatively difficult to get to – most people travelled by launch on a 30-minute journey to or from the 'city' – was now a bustling suburb.[38] By 1904 a tramway operated out to the works, and workmen's specials ran in the mornings and afternoons.

The speed of operations once they commenced impressed observers; large cuttings had already been made by September 1900, four months after work began.[39] But as with the construction of the refinery, the tale of triumph, of 'coolie labour operating under engineering intelligence', as one press report commented in 1906, was also one punctuated by controversy. Antipathy towards the four dozen Indian security guards and talleymen at the site exploded in a riot in December 1902 that left one of them dead. A few days later, possibly in a revenge killing, the body of a Chinese worker, bound hand and foot, was found at the works. One of the Indian watchmen had assaulted a Chinese woman he suspected of stealing wood. Within a short while a crowd estimated at a thousand-strong confronted the guards. Six Chinese workers were eventually jailed for riot. A threatened strike was averted. In 1904 and in 1906, two overseers, one a 23-year-old New Zealander, Thomas Hynes, barely days into the job, and the other an Indian, Harbaj Roi, were charged with the manslaughter of Chinese staff they had 'prodded' or kicked. The verdicts were respectively: not guilty, and guilty (three months' hard labour).[40] The environment in which Chinese labour was employed and overseen was one in which low-level violence was routine: this was a colonial world and this was how labour was treated by those set to the task. The interpersonal politics of difference, of perceptions of 'race' and dignity were one cause. Indians continued to be recruited across East and Southeast Asia by British colonial administrations and private firms, and not just British ones.[41] Notions in particular that Sikhs were a 'martial race' underpinned their use in security and policing roles, regardless of, as we have seen, Chinese opposition to their deployment – itself partly racist in character – and friction and conflict at Zhenjiang, Shanghai or at Quarry Bay. And sheer simple ignorance was a factor, too – for what language might young Hynes otherwise use to speak to Cantonese men, given his prior experience in New Zealand and, most recently, three years' active service, then farming and policing, in South Africa, other than the stark language of physical violence?

Such episodes passed and now lie buried in old newspapers, but they caused ructions as they unfolded. More long-lasting were two challenges the dockyard presented to John Swire & Sons. In the first place, the Hongkong and Whampoa Dock Company fiercely opposed the upstart across the harbour. As with the early refinery operations, Taikoo also had a lot to learn, and, as with the refinery, the dockyard also did not always learn it quickly enough. Getting the right man to manage the new installation, and to do so in harmony with the Butterfield & Swire agent at Quarry Bay, proved difficult. Typhoid also took away early an experienced and able engineering manager who it proved difficult to replace.[42] Butterfield & Swire felt themselves the object of a sustained campaign of malicious rumour, but also quietly acknowledged shortcomings. Rates fell, and for three years there was destructive competition for work. An agreement was thought to be within their grasp in February 1910, but was sabotaged by the newly appointed managing director at Hongkong and Whampoa. Moreover, many of that firm's shareholders, who had rather looked upon their shares – which had markedly lost value – as 'gilt edged securities', were in a position to deny Taikoo work, and deny it they did. In 1913, however, a pooling agreement was reached that finally brought to an end a period of very heavy annual losses for the new company. And there really was, it turned out, work enough for a second dockyard.[43]

The second challenge was labour. At first it faced difficulties in recruiting, training and retaining enough Chinese workers – especially when there were outbreaks of plague. The colony was not felt by its dockyard managers to be 'fully equipped' with trained workmen until 1912. But Butterfield & Swire had also, in developing an installation that employed some 4,000 local workers, positioned itself as a key future site of the political and labour activism that would soon be visited upon the colony in the nationalistic and revolutionary era that was starting to unfold in China. As at Taikoo Sugar, conflict within the labour force, largely shaped by native place identity, would also occur.[44] The company started to provide amenities for the workforce, as it had for its European staff, including a hospital, though not on Mount Parker, the peak above the works, which remained a preserve of its European employees. But in an evolving political environment, a company that employed labour on such a scale would in time find labour organising itself, and allying itself with political movements. By 1909 Butterfield & Swire enterprises across China were estimated to be employing some 10,000 Chinese staff in total.[45]

More immediately, however, the next political challenge John Swire & Sons faced seemed to be an old one, and although it cost the company dear – a sum equal to one-fifth of its investment in the Taikoo Dockyard – the longer-term impact was more positive. On 29 November 1908, as Jim Scott was making his way to Asia, a 40-year-old Chinese man, He Yuting, took passage on the SS *Fatshan* from Hong Kong to Canton. The side-wheeler was carrying over 660 passengers, and was captained by a China coast veteran, Wexford-born Charles Lloyd, who had been around long enough to visit Canton 'prior to the last war', as he put it in 1902. Lloyd was born in 1838, and he meant the Second Opium War. He knew enough to pen a guide published in 1902, *From Hongkong to Canton by the Pearl River*, and recommended there that October or November was the best time of year for the trip:

the *Fatshan* left the wharf, passed through 'the line of junks moored thickly outside' and set out on what he was 'willing to admit ... is the perfection of sea voyages'.[46] But He Yuting died during his voyage. Fellow passengers immediately accused the ship's Macanese watchman, Candido Joaquim Noronha, of having assaulted him and causing his death. Their evidence was detailed and compelling, and those who testified were respectable merchants. Certainly, the man was dead, and Noronha admitted having physically woken him to ask him to pay his fare. However, the watchman, who had worked with Lloyd for 23 years, and had, the captain deposed, a 'very good character', was cleared of any blame at an investigation convened by the British consul in Canton.[47] Lloyd was not alone in arguing that it was clear that He Yuting was already dying when he came on board. 'The proclivity of the Chinese in Hongkong to head for Canton when attacked by grievous illness is well known,' he claimed in a letter to the press. Lloyd, of course, will have felt he 'knew' 'the Chinese'.[48] He did not lack confidence, and had not been afraid either of committing his poetry to the public in his guidebook, in a verse dedicated to the 'G. T.' – globe trotter:

And in your huge sea-palace barbed with steel
Shearing the tumbling surge with driven keel
All things are planned to cater for your ease
Trouble unspared your lightest whim to please.

Local bards in Canton penned different rhymes, barbed verse, after the consular inquiry:

Methinks the Chinese are classed lower than ants
They are sent with a kick to the next world
...
Stir up, brothers! Or we shall be as insignificant as a handful of sand.[49]

While this and similar songs were being sung at rallies and meetings, and 'on all the passenger boats playing the delta', Cantonese merchants and activists made a stand, and initiated a full-scale boycott, first of the *Fatshan*, and then of Butterfield & Swire more widely.[50] This might seem simply a restaging, with minor variations, of the Diaz affair 25 years earlier (and Lloyd had then in fact been an officer on the *Hankow*), but it was shaped by new factors including the raucous political environment in Canton, growing and effective use of boycotts as a political weapon, the greater speed and ease of communications and the development of a sparky Chinese press.

The Qing, despite having to pay a seemingly crippling indemnity to the foreign powers under the terms of the 1901 'Boxer Protocol' (and most of Fisher's compensation claims were allowed, including the bulk of Zheng Yizhi's) had bounced back quite remarkably from the disaster of 1900. From 1902 onwards a series of reforms collectively labelled the 'New Policies' had been instituted which started wholly to reshape the institutions and practices of the state, and stave off its collapse into the hands of its enemies, both internal and external. New government ministries were created, the old examination system and curriculum were abolished and a template for a constitutional monarchy was developed. At the same time, however, those internal opponents grew in number and vigour, and men and now women who were once reformers became or were joined by revolutionaries. Groups such as those led by a Xiangshan-born, Hawaiian-educated and Hong Kong-trained doctor, Sun Yat-sen, plotted a violent end to the dynasty. The New Policies raised expectations and generated intense debate and excitement and this found its forums in public meetings and associations and in the new press.[51]

The renewal of US immigration restrictions against Chinese in 1905 had provoked a strong and effective boycott of American goods. In Guangdong province there had been large-scale protests against the unilateral decision of the British to mount anti-piracy patrols on the Pearl River tributary the Xi Jiang (West River), a newly opened shipping route – after the piracy of a CNCo steamer, the *Sainam* – and especially about the Foreign Ministry's capitulation to the Japanese in a dispute over the seizure of a gun-running Japanese steamer, the *Tatsu Maru*, off Macao. The presence of private Japanese interests in the Pratas shoals led to a renewal of the anti-Japanese movement in the province.[52] This nationalism was no less real a force for also being a safe way indirectly to marshal opinion that could also target the Qing, for who else was truly responsible for the recurrence of what was articulated as 'National Humiliation' (Guochi), a term that came to lie at the heart of China's new nationalism. The death of He Yuting on the lower deck of the *Fatshan* reignited the activities of the city's Canton Merchants'

Self-Government Society (Yueshang Zizhi hui) which organised a hostile demonstration when Lloyd steered the ship back to Canton.

The boycott was lengthy and effective. The existence of networks of Cantonese provincials across China's treaty ports and CNCo's international routes – the men who Fisher, for example, had helped flee Tianjin – eased the spread of organised protest against the company far, far from the wharf at Canton. A Canton problem became a national and international problem for Swires, and a Swire problem became a wider British problem, and in the same way a British problem could become a Swire one. At Jiujiang in 1909, for example, yet another death, of yet another apparently already terminally ill Chinese man, at the hands, feet, truncheon or stick of a British official, in this case John Mears, Kiukiang British concession policeman, sparked a strong boycott that targeted all British interests. British officials and businessmen were alike in believing that the only way to respond to such pressure was to stay their course, and put pressure on the Qing to suppress such activists, arguing that it was in its own interests to do so. Hong Kong Taipan D. R. Law argued that it would lead to revolution if left unchecked. Law was a verbose worrier who – with the boycott and the dockyard, a shipping slump and stiff new competition in the sugar market from the Japanese – had much to worry about. He would eventually resign to save his health. A 24-year veteran of the firm, Law's attitude towards China's new generation was hostile and reactionary, and indicative of a new turn in foreign attitudes towards China, especially from those resident there, one that was hostile, if not combative. But still, in June 1909, the company had had enough, and ordered Comprador Mok Koon Yuk to bring the episode to an end, or to cover its losses himself.[53]

Eventually, in August 1909, the firm's chief shipping clerk, Mok Wing Yu, travelled to Canton to sign an agreement at a public meeting with the victim's brother that effected an end to the boycott. As in 1883/84, the company eventually bypassed British officials and negotiated directly with its opponents. Swires agreed to pay compensation to the dead man's family, transfer Lloyd, dismiss Noronha and pledge itself, with notices to be placed on his ships, to look after its Chinese passengers. A week later Captain Lloyd sailed out of the colony on the *Empress of Japan* and into retirement. British diplomats and Hong Kong's governor, Sir Frederick Lugard, were furious. The firm had humiliated itself, they charged. Yes indeed, responded Law, but you have not backed us. It was 'surrender to blackmail' complained G. E. Morrison, the *Times* China correspondent, which of course it was (and he was not alone in saying so), but Morrison did not have steamers to run, and shippers who refused to let them have cargoes to carry.[54] It has seemed to some observers in retrospect an even more expensive compromise than it looked, for a hefty £40,000 donation had also just been made by John Swire & Sons (including £5,000 each from Taikoo Sugar and Blue Funnel) to an endowment fund for a proposed University of Hong Kong. This gift, eight times the level of pledge that came from the other big companies in Hong Kong, proved crucial to the entire initiative, but it was made prominent in the public resolution of the *Fatshan* impasse.[55] This move was already in train, pushed by Jim Scott within the company, and within the China Association in London of which he was president and at which he had first announced it on 4 May that year. From the colony Law opposed it: 'European sentiment is against it,' he announced, that is, sentiment in Hong Kong, while others thought the university would simply incubate revolutionaries.[56] The Provincial Viceroy drew attention to this amiable act of generosity in a proclamation he issued that instructed the public that the issue should now be considered closed, at least as far as the British were concerned, and pressure should instead be applied to the Portuguese, to try Noronha for murder. However, the now unemployed watchman resolved the issue himself shortly thereafter by dying of consumption.[57] There were, of course, sound reasons to support the new university for a company that had need of a steady supply in future of young trained engineers, even though understandings of the origins of the close relationship between Swire and the University of Hong Kong have become inextricably tangled up with the intertwined fates of He Yuting and Candido Joaquim Noronha.

The deal with the Guangdong authorities may also have helped to heal the damage caused to relations by an earlier controversy in 1904. The continuing involvement of Butterfield & Swire in Chinese labour emigration looked in 1903 as if it might profitably be deployed to meet a pressing new need: the resumption of work on the South African goldfields. In the 1905 edition of the *Directory and Chronicle of China*, Butterfield & Swire branches at Hong Kong, Fuzhou, Xiamen, Shantou and Canton were listed as agents for a 'South African Labour Association'. The 1899–1901 South African War (Second Boer War) had devastated the Transvaal mining operations, dispersed the labour force and wrecked the country's transport infrastructure. Operations to restore the economy, and an influx of speculative capital and speculators large and small – including small fry like Thomas Hynes – made it difficult for mine owners to secure labour, and secure it cheaply. China, happily, ever figured in the Anglophone imagination as an inexhaustible source of labour, now a threat, now an asset. South Africa had need; China had people.

The South African Chamber of Mines developed an organisation to procure labour recruits from China, and Butterfield & Swire at Hong Kong, although initially quite sceptical, secured the agency for recruiting in south China in 1903. At first promising 4,000 men a month, and up to 50,000 a year, the scheme was in fact to prove a costly mistake for the company. The taint of the illegal trade of the mid-nineteenth century and its atrocities still poisoned official Chinese views of labour emigration. The governor-general in Canton resolutely opposed Hong Kong having any role in such a scheme, but Butterfield & Swire had developed an infrastructure in which the colony was vital to its plans. As well as being the port of embarkation for the recruits, the company built an emigrant camp at Lai Chi Kok on the Kowloon peninsula, circulated notices in Guangdong in February 1904 seeking recruits and by mid-May had 1,600 men awaiting medical inspection in 10 large matsheds at the site. 'A Happy House' puffed an article in the local press, it was full of 'strapping fellows, in the pink of perfection' recruited by agents employed by Swires. But only a thousand of those men sailed on 25 May 1904 on a chartered ship, and the entire scheme faced concerted opposition from Chinese already in South Africa, from companies that recruited labour for Southeast Asia, whose supply was being tapped by the new scheme, from political and popular opinion in Britain and in South Africa, that saw 'Chinese slavery' undermining the rights and wages of 'white labour' or simply as morally abhorrent, as well as from the Guangdong authorities. This latter opposition was the rock on which the Swire efforts foundered. And things were made much worse when, operations having been halted by government order, and heavy penalty charges were looming on the next chartered vessel as a result, D. R. Law in 'an act bordering on lawlessless', as the British Canton consul put it, arranged a covert recruitment operation instead, and this was uncovered.[58]

The crucial point with both the *Fatshan* and emigration episodes is that despite the Qing disaster of 1900, when it looked as if foreign interests might pick it all apart, foreign firms started to find themselves in an unfamiliar place. Along with most foreign observers and savants, they had demanded that China modernise, and argued that until it developed modern institutions and practices – by which they meant ones like theirs – the Chinese could not expect fully to be treated as part of the international community. But when the Chinese actually did this, it left them perplexed and defensive. Their reliance on the precise detail of treaties and agreements that provided them, as they interpreted them, with rights and privileges, and which had become routine for many, and even by this point, for Butterfield & Swire, started to become problematic. Qing officials, and new groups of informed Qing subjects – merchants and students especially – began to contest these assumptions. This was, as it were, only the end of the beginning of foreign high-riding across China's sovereignty, but clearly things were starting to change. Butterfield & Swire retreated altogether from the labour scheme, and with them south China lapsed as a recruitment area for the association: of 63,695 men who arrived in South Africa, only 1,689 left from Hong Kong. The wider Chinese labour controversy raged on, and had a strong impact on the 1906 general election in Britain. Swires certainly remained in the business of facilitating labour emigration, of course, and supplying Chinese seamen as well for Blue Funnel ships, and Law actually went to the Transvaal in early 1905 to try to drum up orders for supplies to the Chinese workforce there, but the South African venture as originally conceived was over.[59]

The relationship with Blue Funnel remained close despite the deaths of John Samuel Swire and, in November 1911, Alfred Holt. It was reinforced by the co-investment in the dockyard and, in 1904, in another new company, the Tientsin Lighter Company, which aimed to correct the problems and performance of an existing monopoly enterprise in the port that Walter Fisher had grumbled about before he truly had things to grumble about. In December 1908 the first ship docked at one of two new joint ventures, Holt's Wharf on the south-eastern tip of the Kowloon peninsula, a complex of warehouses and wharves, in a key site next to the new Kowloon Terminus of the railway linking the colony with Canton, which was to start operating in 1910. A similar installation was also being built at Shanghai. Blue Funnel had taken over the China Mutual Company in 1902, and with it its transpacific routes. At Hong Kong, Butterfield & Swire lobbied hard for the line to upgrade its accommodation for what its staff argued – with revenue figures to support them – was a very great demand from Chinese passengers.[60] The benefit to Swires of the close association with Holts remained multi-faceted. The corporate and personal Swire holdings in Ocean Steam Ship formed the largest block after the Holt family. John Swire & Sons charged a fee for their work in London which, it continued to point out, happily, continued to be inadequate, and the branches secured profits on their commissions. The relationship with Scotts grew stronger, too: they were purchasing agents for the dockyard, funnelled pith-helmeted staff out to it, designed many of the CNCo vessels Taikoo built, and remained overall technical advisers. Scotts also continued to build new vessels for China Navigation, with 20 ordered between 1901 and 1905.

John Swire & Sons continued to grow. One hundred and forty-four men sailed east to join Butterfield & Swire alone between 1901 and July 1914, twice as many as in the previous 14 years.[61] One of those, who joined the staff in London in November 1913, and then in March 1914 sailed to take a post in Hong Kong, represented a further generation of the Swire family in the firm: John Kidston Swire (Jock), Jack's older son, one of the four children of his marriage in 1889 to Emily Kidston, daughter of a Glaswegian shipowner. His younger son Glen was also being prepared for a place in the firm after studying at Oxford, which he was preparing to go to in October 1914. Staff records show men who are generally better trained than their predecessors. Many had certificates or diplomas from the London Chamber of Commerce and Society of Arts, and they had more prior experience overall, and more specialist experience, too. The assumption that likely men might learn the ropes on the job, when much of the work was more and more specialised and complicated, was passing. Of course, much about living and working in China would prove quite impossible to teach or certify for some time to come.

Long residence in China was still felt to be dangerous. Men's 'lives are shortened by long residence here', argued Walter Poate, who by 1902 had been in Hong Kong for 28 years, with only three trips home. Later in the year he resigned on health grounds. Law would later resign to save himself from a nervous breakdown. They also needed better provision for retirement, Poate argued. Salaries were fair, but nothing could be saved, and senior men, especially, felt that they had to live as Taipans were expected to live (and were mistakenly thought to be partners) – though the firm itself had a policy of not participating in official public life – so business entertaining meant 'champagne and extras' and in one Taipan's case a household that was staffed by a European nurse, No. 1 Boy, No. 2 Boy, Cook, two house coolies and six chair coolies, market and bathroom coolie, washerwoman, gardener, baby and sewing amah.[62] Such were the problems of Taipan life.

One trend that emerges from the staff notebooks and worth recording is that a handful of the men had studied some Chinese in London before sailing. The China Association, a London-based lobbying group formed in 1889, had established a 'School of Practical Chinese' in 1900 (and John Swire & Sons had contributed a modest £50 to its funds). Anxiety about the threat to Britain's commercial position – which formed a strong stand in public discourse at the turn of the century – encouraged fears that the trading rivals of British firms were being subsidised by their governments, or otherwise assisted by them, operated in underhand ways, adopted unfairly innovative business practices and trained their staff in the languages of their customers. The upshot of Lord Charles Beresford's visit on behalf of the Associated Chambers of Commerce, which was facilitated with free travel by Butterfield & Swire, was a report published as *The Break-Up of China* in 1899, which concluded with a plea for 'teaching the Chinese language to British youths who are to seek employment in that country'.[63] The small minority of Swire recruits who studied Chinese after working hours at King's College will not much have dented the culture of the firm, especially as, structurally, the comprador system remained intact, and also because the sons of compradors spoke English far better than they could likely ever learn Chinese (and they were, increasingly, far better-educated than their British colleagues to boot).

Jim Scott died in October 1912, his son Colin having been admitted to the partnership in 1910: so the tie with Scotts remained familial as well. Jim Scott's role in the growth of the firm had been important. He had, after all, joined in Shanghai as Butterfield & Swire came into existence, and the dockyard was clearly his signal achievement. He lacked the charisma of the Senior, and was also rather less tolerant of human failings, or simply of human nature. Of all the senior staff he had lived longest in Asia and imbibed most deeply its attitudes and prejudices, but at the same time had acquired precious little of the latitude that others showed. It was during his watch as senior partner that the firm instructed its branches that Eurasians were not to be hired, and if any were employed they were to be sacked.[64] Scott was also certainly wrapped up in the firm's history, and was in fact its first historian, turning the notes of his New Year's Day 1909 talk to the Hong Kong staff into a draft short history as he journeyed home from Asia that year, which was completed and published privately after his death. But it remains hard otherwise to trace his personality in the archive. He was by then the last of the old guard still in the firm. Frederick Gamwell died in 1896, and Edwin Mackintosh in 1904. Gamwell had already left the partnership, but complications over Mackintosh's share became the source of a legal dispute between the company and his executors. Lang went last, however, his will causing some press comment, as it provided a considerable 'windfall' for his 32-year-old nurse. He was, to the very last, quite unpredictable.[65] The partnership by the end of 1912 was in the hands of the next generation: Jack Swire, his younger brother G. Warren Swire, who had entered it in 1905, and Colin C. Scott. Colin's younger brother John Swire Scott would join the firm in 1924 after graduating from Cambridge, and became a director in 1931. This team and their managers in China faced the challenges presented by revolution and civil war in China, and the tremendous changes that that unleashed, and they faced the European conflict of 1914–18, which changed Europe, but which also changed China utterly.

9

New China

Two separate company gatherings at Quarry Bay provide contrasting tableaux of the year 1914. In January, George Edkins, the Hong Kong Taipan, watched his wife Winifred catch the prow of a new CNCo steamer with a bottle of champagne as it slid rapidly down the slipway at the dockyard, the descent accompanied by 'much cheering and the explosion of numerous crackers'.[1] This was the *Wuchang*, the second of that name, a fine new vessel for the Shanghai and Yangzi routes and the first in a new class. It was the eleventh ship built at the yard, and the largest so far, at 3,200 tons. Edkins, sometime apprentice draper and Hong Kong manager for two years, gave a bullish speech. The last 12 months had been a record year for Hong Kong shipbuilding, but 1914 would see that record outdone, he claimed, as three more China Navigation steamers were already on the stocks. For the Taikoo Dockyard, and for Hong Kong's economy, prospects looked very bright. This might all seem the stuff of a predictable script for such gatherings, brought out, dusted off, the odd detail changed (the ship's name), but globally shipping had now pulled out of the serious recession that had provided excruciating results for the China Navigation Company between 1906 and 1911: no dividends for three years, and losses for four years in succession. There had been a very rocky meeting of shareholders in 1911 which had even seen the re-emergence on the scene of a real Butterfield: Frederick William Louis d'Hilliers Roosevelt Theodore Butterfield. He was a second cousin of the late American president, a nephew of Richard Shackleton Butterfield and inheritor of his father's significant shareholding in the company. Butterfield charged the managers – John Swire & Son – with abusing their position, for they were certainly not losing out, and they employed, he claimed, 'an army of employees … enjoying fat salaries at our expense'.[2] This assault on the company's management of CNCo was deflected, largely by the intervention at the meeting of Richard Holt, and that year had seen a return to profit and dividends. The network of John Samuel Swire's friends had once provided any amount of capital, but now their heirs provided his successors with any amount of headaches.

At Hong Kong orders were being placed, the pool agreement was working and the fledgling Taikoo yard's problems seemed behind it. But on 3 July 1914 the staff club at Quarry Bay hosted a different gathering: roughly half of the foreign staff of the dockyard and refinery gathered to listen to Hong Kong's governor Sir Henry May give an 'eloquent and stirring speech' 'On the individual responsibility of every man to become a Volunteer'.[3] As a young administrative cadet, May had been learning Cantonese in 1883 in Guangzhou when the *Hankow* affair prompted the riot and destruction on Shameen. A Volunteer force might have prevented that, he claimed. And as in 'these civilised times wars started without much notice', so 'it was important to be ready' and to defend 'this important outpost of the British Empire'. This was not unfamiliar language. His predecessor Frederick Lugard had tried to put volunteering on a compulsory footing in the colony in 1910, which Jim Scott firmly supported, although this had not come to pass. Hong Kong's commander-in-chief, Major General Kelly, followed Sir Henry. It was 'their duty', he told the men of the Taikoo companies, 'to take a share in the protection of such a great heritage'.

While May and Kelly lectured Quarry Bay, the shockwaves of the assassination of Archduke Ferdinand in Sarajevo five days earlier were spreading across Europe. A month later Britain declared war. China would not be immune to the conflict that unfolded. It had already been a tumultuous decade politically. In October 1911 the Chinese revolution that many had long predicted and others had worked for – and which the Swire companies had encountered when conspirators smuggled guns on CNCo ships, or merchants agitated against foreign interests partly as a proxy for attacks on the Qing – broke out quite by accident. Revolutionary bomb-makers blew themselves up in Wuhan's Russian concession – rather demonstrating one extreme hazard of smoking, for it was a discarded cigarette or match that lit China's fuse.

Events unfolded so rapidly that the assault on the Qing this sparked was almost over by the time veteran revolutionary leader Sun Yat-sen had made his way home from a fundraising trip to the United States. It was in some ways an odd revolution, for all sides feared a prolonged period of chaos that might prompt a final foreign assault on China, and they acted accordingly. The Qing abdicated, and a republic was proclaimed. Yuan Shikai, a once-loyal general and administrator, turned against the Manchus, and assumed the position of president in a peace-making deal with Sun who stepped down from the post in his favour. Yuan was no republican. In March 1913, in the aftermath of China's first democratic election, the parliamentary leader of Sun's new party, the Guomindang, was assassinated in Shanghai's railway station by the president's agents. Four months later the Guomindang launched a revolt against the new strongman in Beijing, but its supporters were defeated, helped not least of all by British finance released to Yuan's allies in Shanghai to persuade their forces to remain loyal.

The revolution was in places a bloody affair, but it was largely a contained one, and the intentions of its peacemakers – to thwart any foreign intervention – mostly proved successful. In cities that had foreign concessions or settlements and where power changed hands by force, or the threat of it, Volunteer Corps units were called out, foreign troops or marines landed or gunboats moored off Bunds and in harbours, their machine guns and cannon ostentatious but silent. Banks closed, business paused, foreign residents might restage historically familiar scenes and seek shelter on the ever-welcoming Swire hulks at Zhenjiang or Wuhu. Meanwhile, revolutionaries cut off their queues, the braided long hair that signalled their subservience to the Manchus, or they forcibly sheared off those of men slow to act. The new republic seemed a Western-style republic, and it adopted all manner of forms and processes that consolidated the reforms of the Qing New Policies.[4] Essentially, this was a transfer of political power, in many cases to just those merchant and political activists who had been involved in the boycotts in Guangzhou, or who had long worked with Swires: 'We are all anti-Manchu', a China Merchants director assured Jack Swire in November 1911; 'we do not see why ten Manchus should govern a thousand Chinamen'.[5] Quietly, some significant areas of the empire that had been built by the Qing were lost – its domination of what became the state of Mongolia for good, and of Tibet for some decades – the foreign-led Customs Service arrogated to itself the right to collect tariffs (and to disburse them to government, or to service foreign loans), and legal sovereignty in Shanghai was degraded when the Mixed Courts were taken over by the foreign concession administrations. Overall, the terms on which foreign interests met Chinese sovereignty shifted yet further in favour of the foreign powers. The Chinese might now govern themselves, but they still did not have unfettered hands.

As Yuan Shikai struggled to consolidate a new state – even, in late 1915, having himself proclaimed emperor – the tone of foreign commentary and the character of foreign attitudes grew more and more critical, and in many places disdainful. Once, foreign observers had justified their legal advantages, and the network of treaty ports, as temporary bulwarks that would last only until China 'modernised' and, of course, they looked forward to that era, or at least they would trouble to say so. As China reformed, however, the terms of that necessary 'modernisation' were revised, barriers to its attainment strengthened and the prospect of a surrender of foreign advantages receded further and further. A degraded China best suited most of those foreign interests involved with it, though they would see it as rightful protection of their interests, and of the real interests of the Chinese people, against the warlords, bandits and Babus, the 'foreignized', 'inauthentic', 'unrepresentative' Chinese, who they now saw as populating the land and fattening on it.

The consequence of the end of Qing rule would continue to unfold for many years to come, politically, socially and culturally. In the short term, for the Swire interests, the Great War was a rather more significant episode. That January 1914 buoyancy at the Taikoo Dockyard would be overshadowed by the grimmer call to the flag in July and then on 4 August by the British declaration of war. Of course, it was confidently believed on all sides that the conflict would be over quickly, and this continued to be a factor for the best part of the war's first year, not least in China on what became an economic front. The British state swiftly implemented a set of regulations to govern and restrict 'Trading with the Enemy' with the overall strategic aim of crippling the German economy, and at the same time it moved to protect its own. It quickly introduced state insurance – accepting 80 per cent of losses – to keep the ships moving which kept Britain fed and supplied. Consignees would only secure this protection if they used war risk-insured ships, so there was a double incentive for companies like Swires to fall in with this scheme.

The China Navigation Company had insured 57 vessels by 13 August. After initial turmoil and confusion, British ships sailed again, and despite losses, requisitions and diversions, harbour congestion and transport bottlenecks, such improvised arrangements lasted into 1916.[6] But the strain of a lengthy total war would tell, and the state would move further and further into taking control of the economy, bringing experts from private enterprise into its new agencies and ministries. Creating the new agencies showcased what one analyst thought was some 'organisational virtuosity', and the historically prickly relationship between shipowners and civil servants turned into an effective partnership in Whitehall, although expressions of disdain for the limitations of the official mind can be found peppering the Swire letter books.[7]

In East Asia the key means by which the Allied blockade of Germany was in evidence lay in controls on trading with the enemy but they were untested and often proved impractical. They also simply did not match the reality of the commercial world in China, where different foreign interests were often quite intertwined and many British firms relied on German partners, capital, agents or technicians. This caused 'a lot of worry and trouble' for Butterfield & Swire but was less of a problem for the now 21 branches of the company than for many others. However, for example, the firm's agency in Vladivostok was the large German company Kunst and Albers, and while it aimed to abide by the new regulations, and replace them, finding a Russian-speaking British subject with shipping experience proved very difficult. The German heads of the company, who were naturalised Russians (and who had once already managed to spring themselves from Russian detention), professed themselves 'frankly astonished' at the decision in October to end the arrangement, but the switch was made.[8] Blue Funnel agency business was challenged by the parting of the ways with German firms, for loss of their freight to Europe 'discloses clearly the poor British participation in China's export trade', reported Hong Kong.[9] The war period also saw new efforts on the part of officials to bolster British trade in China. British Chambers of Commerce were established under diplomatic auspices, and commercial attachés posted to consulates. The state and business came closer and closer together in China, too, as the emergency lasted.

The firm that faced this war was legally a quite new entity. On 31 December 1913 the last partnership agreement expired, and on New Year's Day 1914 John Swire & Sons became a limited company. The three partners, half-brothers Jack and Warren Swire (who together held a controlling interest in the company's shares), and Colin Scott, became its directors, swiftly adding a fourth, Henry William Robertson, who had served the company since 1891, and Jack Swire, senior partner since Jim Scott's death, became chairman. This was some years overdue. As Jack Swire explained in 1905, the firm had manifestly outgrown its partnership structure, and had become so vast, so rapidly, that the potential liability of the partners, and the scale of their personal responsibility, was too great.[10]

But there were other reasons as well. The 1893 partnership agreement permitted sons of the partners to enter into the partnership after attaining the age of 21 should they be considered 'eligible' by virtue of aptitude and experience. But Jim Scott and Jack Swire had good reason to have little confidence in Warren Swire's business ability, or, at that stage, character. A man who behaved in an 'aggressively disagreeable manner' to the clerks, who considered the company's managers as his 'employees' was a potential liability. Behave like a gentleman, his brother wrote in one of a number of exasperated notes.[11] Warren was unpredictable and socially maladroit. Although taking an interest in the profits after his father's death in 1898, he was not permitted to take any active role until 1905, and was constrained thereafter for some years by his partners.[12] In addition the family of Edwin Mackintosh, who had died in 1904, aimed initially to keep a place open for his son Edwin (known as Jack), who would turn 21 in 1909, but who in April that year confirmed formally that he would not attempt to exercise his right to enter the partnership. The 'Mackintosh interest' had blocked the first attempt at converting the company in 1905/6, and Mackintosh drew a share of the profits until 1909. In Jim Scott's eyes he had probably disqualified himself from actively joining the partnership through having gone to university, thereby missing years in which he might have gained business experience. This was the route his own son Colin had followed, spending three years at another shipbroker's in London, and then four years with Butterfield & Swire in Hong Kong and Shanghai, moving from division to division, before returning to London in 1909.[13]

The 'Mackintosh problem' took a difficult turn in 1909 when 'very hostile allegations' were received in which the partners were effectively accused of 'manipulating' the accounts to disadvantage Jack Mackintosh in a final settlement. Company finances were complex at this point, because of the huge investment in the Dockyard, most of which initially came from partners' funds, and because of the shipping depression. An audit cleared the firm of the charge, but the legal advisers found they were analysing 'most perplexing partnership articles' and convoluted finances. The dispute took up much time and legal fees over a two-year period, but an agreement was reached in August 1911 and the family, having withdrawn the charges, was bought out of the company on the basis of the position of the partners in April 1909.[14] A tour around the world and of the firm's Asian estate and partners in 1907 seemed to have begun to make a difference to Warren Swire but it would be some years before he was fully trusted and he never lost his sharpness of tongue, and pungency of opinion, freely, liberally and insensitively offered. Warren Swire would, however, begin to gain a skilled understanding of the business of shipping (and from 1912 managed CNCo) but his erratic behaviour reinforced the desire of his fellow partners to convert the company. In 1911 Jack Swire confided to Jim Scott that he feared 'grave trouble with him in future'. The conversion of the firm was announced to the managers and others as being undertaken for 'family reasons', and so indeed it was.[15]

Socially and culturally the firm's character had been transformed as well. There was no longer any tangible Liverpool connection at all save the fact of Jack Swire's birth, and the strong partnership with Blue Funnel. Gone, even, was the long-lingering business of Australian stout.[16] Jack Swire made his home in Essex. His heart lay there, in its hunting – he was Master of the Essex Hounds in 1906–10 and again in 1922–4 – and in horsemanship. He published translations of two French manuals on the topic, and in 1908 published his own guide to *Anglo-French Horsemanship*. This is not to detract at all from any assessment of his sound leadership of the company during this difficult period but, as he reminded his stepmother when there was dispute about Warren Swire's suitability for a role in the firm, he had never been asked by his father whether he actually wanted to join John Swire & Sons. Jack abided nonetheless by a philosophy he also urged Warren to understand: that managing the business required an unselfish attitude towards the significant duty of care represented by the extensive interests that John Swire & Sons now managed, and the thousands of employees who worked for it.[17] He saw it as a legacy and duty, and cheerily announced that he had never personally earned a penny in his life: it was his father's work, and he would not undo it.[18] Although Scott, Mackintosh and Swire sons would school together, and some headed together to university at Oxford – for Jim Scott's strictures on the grim perils of a university education were trumped by the social benefits it might bring the Swire boys – the ties of family and social relationships that once characterised the firm became steadily more and more diffuse.

The complexity of the operations now being managed from London meant that while family sentiment features in the private correspondence between Jack Swire, his brother Warren and Warren's mother Mary – who seems to have been a prickly and vigilant guardian of the position and opportunities of her son within the firm – it could not possibly feature in any operational decisions without endangering the company. The scale of operations across four different businesses – shipping, shipbuilding, insurance and sugar – however interlinked and interdependent they were, the finances needed to service these, the political work in China and Hong Kong that underpinned them, the volume of data that flowed into Billiter Square (to which the firm had moved in 1901) meant that experts, not kith nor kin, were needed. The family motto, 'Esse Quam Videri' – To be, rather than to seem to be – was more than usually apposite.

In this period of the company's history, we can best look at the operational challenges the war posed, not least on shipping, on the opportunities it provided and war work Swire firms undertook, at changes in the culture of the China Navigation Company, and the development of a new sphere of Butterfield & Swire activity, the 'upcountry' sugar-distribution network, known initially within the firm as the 'Manchurian system' for the region in China where it was pioneered from the mid-1900s. The expansion of China Navigation shipping routes saw Swire interests represented in all the Yangzi provinces, and those through which the West River system in south and south-west China ran, as well as along the coast. Experiments were made with new routes along Yangzi tributaries, and the pre-war files are peppered with reconnaissance reports on the potential of this port or that one to sustain a service. But paradoxically it was the refinery in Quarry Bay which spurred the company to spread itself further across China when a new sugar distribution network was developed that saw it entrenched in China's 'interior' far away from the Bunds and the foreign enclaves that surrounded them and in which some simulacrum of a life at 'home' might be lived by the 140 or so British men who worked in Butterfield & Swire offices.

For China Navigation the key challenge of the government's requisitioning of ships or tonnage was maintaining existing services – and pooling shares – and preventing encroachment into established coastal or river routes by Japanese or American firms. Keep 'the essential regular lines ... fully supplied on the present scale, if necessary to the exclusion of all else', wrote London in 1917. And if that proved impossible then it was vital to avoid any carving of routes into separate spheres with different firms monopolising each. China Navigation needed to retain its overall presence across its Chinese and ocean routes.[19] War service for some had begun immediately. On the day after war was declared Chief Officer Frank Davies jokingly headed a letter home 'H. M. Collier Szechuen', for 'we are busy coaling for the British fleet and are sailing with a cargo of Welsh coal with sealed orders'. For two months the *Szechuan* worked under Admiralty charter and sailed in support of Royal Navy China station vessels under the command of Admiral Jerram as they searched for German shipping, and then supported the Japanese campaign to seize the German colony at Qingdao.[20]

After the bad years, the war provided a lengthy period of profitable sunshine. Rates reached record levels and demand was incessant. Although it acquired nine new ships in 1914–18, it still lacked the tonnage increase it needed, as well as the staff. Taxation in London took in turn record amounts of its earnings – carefully detailed in letters sent east (£22,720 in 1915, a projected £511,820 in 1917) – but CNCo had never been so profitable: it averaged an annual profit of £87,000 during the war years. This had a potential downside in the public and political realm: 'Daddy, what did YOU do in the Great War?' ran the caption on the famous British recruiting poster of 1915. For one radical MP the shipowner could only answer his child: 'I did everybody'. Shipowners were widely blamed for food price inflation.[21] And Swire firms, quite regardless of the facts, experienced the same suspicions about their patriotism as others in China. As well as largely running its routine business and, as we shall see, significantly expanding its work in sugar, CNCo and Blue Funnel invested heavily in new and expanded property development at the Holt's Wharf installations in Kowloon and Pudong. Business as usual was at the same time part of Britain's overall strategy, and a target for critics.

All British liner shipping was formally requisitioned in 1917 by the newly established Ministry of Shipping. This was compounded for Butterfield's Blue Funnel operations by the low priority given to allocating space for tonnage to China – 'it means a lean time for B. & S.', wrote Hong Kong to London in June 1917 – which led to a 'considerable' reduction in services. 'We think ourselves very lucky to have any steamers left on the coast, considering the tonnage position', Warren Swire noted in February 1918. Blue Funnel itself saw 78 of its 83-strong fleet actually requisitioned by the end of the year (it would lose 16 ships to enemy action in total, but saw profits jump sixfold). London learned in May 1917 that all CNCo's coastal steamers were to be subject to requisition, though Yangzi and other river routes were exempted. Eight vessels were taken over in March 1917 and despatched to the eastern Mediterranean where the crews found themselves on new beats, transporting grain and fodder from Port Said to Sukarieh, or firewood, goats and potatoes south from Famagusta to Egypt, shipping around all the banal materiel of war. Another two vessels were taken over shortly thereafter. Providing a full complement of British officers and engineers for these proved a challenge given the number of foreign nationals now serving, and men had to be shuffled around the fleet. One young second officer, just six months in service, was transferred to the *Pakhoi* for this work, refused duty and was prosecuted and jailed for two months in Hong Kong, by way of encouragement.[22] In 1918 the company was still running a Hong Kong to Shanghai and Hong Kong to northern ports service, and Shantou to Bangkok, but the shipping notices in the Hong Kong press were dominated by advertisements for Japanese lines.

One familiar task the war brought was servicing the transport of Chinese labourers at least part of their way to service on the Western Front and in the Middle East. In the autumn of 1916, at very short notice, the Admiralty requisitioned space for 30,000 men to travel on Blue Funnel steamers from the British-leased territory at Weihaiwei. As well as the ships, Butterfield & Swire of course had much experience of transporting Chinese labour. Several vessels were refitted at Yokohama under the company's supervision, each to accommodate 1,000 men and their British officers. Butterfield & Swire then also victualled and otherwise supplied each ship, and the company was outraged when the Admiralty decreed that it had no right to any agency commission. The conditions under which the men travelled shocked some of their officers, but that was in part due to the fact that the worlds of Chinese migrant labour and foreign passenger travel remained entirely segregated. Conditions in the labour transports were probably little worse, and possibly conditions overall were a little better, than the Straits Settlement migrant business generally allowed. Company staff serviced this wartime initiative in other ways as well. Taikoo Dockyard's Edward Henry Evans, a 43-year-old army veteran, was one of the many British volunteers from China who saw service with the Chinese Labour Corps in France.[23]

The war wanted such men, and men so often dearly wanted the war. They upped from their desks and dashed off to serve as soon as it came. Seven had gone from the London office within four days of the declaration of war, and 40 per cent of the July staff had left within four weeks. Probably the first into action were two Royal Naval Reservists, CNCo Engineer Robert Blackie and Second Officer Ronald Langton Jones, who were among the mariners in Hong Kong who manned a pre-Dreadnought battleship, HMS *Triumph*, which was in the colony's Naval Dockyard being refitted as a depot ship in July 1914. *Triumph* was instead rapidly overhauled, repainted and commissioned on 5 August, sailing the following day with a scratch crew of merchant seamen and army volunteers. By the end of the month it had taken two German liners, and then – having picked up at Shanghai more crew including China Navigation's Engineering Superintendent Frederick James – provided support – and taken a hit – at the Japanese siege and assault on the German colony at Qingdao. After refitting at Hong Kong, the battleship sailed to take part in the Dardanelles operation, and all three men, and others from Shanghai, were on board when it was sunk by a German submarine on 25 April 1915. All survived.[24] Some men's wars were shorter than others. London office shipping clerk John Bell was back in Britain within just two months, permanently unfit for further military service having been wounded at Messines when serving with the London Scottish. There was much muttering early on among staff that London was too hesitant to release people. But letting four out of 10 go seems instead the opposite, and as Jack Swire wrote in late August, 'as there is a commercial war we must have a fighting minimum' and that commercial struggle, which had been the subject of much public debate in early twentieth-century Britain, would continue after any peace.[25]

At Hong Kong the Volunteers were mobilised across the colony and until late November staff at the Taikoo office worked in khaki in between stints guarding strategic defence positions across the colony and patrolling in case of a surprise attack. John Kidston Swire – 'Jock' – was by then out in Hong Kong taking his turn to learn the company ropes, joined a newly formed mounted volunteer unit, the Hongkong Scouts, and had joint charge of 50 men from the Duke of Cornwall's Light Infantry and the defence of the island's southern coast from Stanley to Aberdeen. He was elated at being liberated from his perch in the stuffy, humid building on the Praya (whose metal ceilings meant it constantly dripped condensation down on to the staff) – 'I am thoroughly enjoying myself and wishing to goodness I had been a soldier,' he wrote home. This turned to frustration as no attack was made, the only German forces in the region were despatched when the Japanese captured Qingdao and the Australian navy sank the commerce raider *Emden* (but not before it had sunk Blue Funnel's *Troilus* and with it a thousand tons of Malaysian tin), and as the names of a great number of his former classmates appeared in the casualty lists. Jock's desire to 'see some fun myself' was stymied by the authorities, who refused to allow him to leave while there seemed a strong threat to the colony. He also grew critical of the seeming absence in Hong Kong of the war and 'the hypocrisy of the East', a cliché, to be sure, but a feeling shared by British diplomats in China who felt that their fellow countrymen were too focused on their local interests at the expense of imperial ones and their 'great heritage'.[26] Many British businessmen in China were at first more than a little cautious about enforcing the provisions of the Trading with the Enemy legislation about commercial contact with German firms.[27] Being horrid to the Hun was all very well in principle, but these were men with whom they sat on company boards, served alongside as stewards at the race clubs, were related to through marriage and had been sharing toasts to Anglo-German amity with for years. Aside from the sentimental and practical difficulties of disentangling such complex relationships, China itself remained neutral until 1917. As Jack Swire put it, they did not want to 'appear to be damaging the trade of a neutral country'. They also feared that Japanese interests would advance to fill any vacuum. On this point they would be proved right.[28]

By the end of 1918 almost 50 men had joined the army from the London staff, roughly 35 from Butterfield & Swire offices – about a third of the men employed in China and Japan in 1914 – and more from the Taikoo companies.[29] Some Chinese staff also found themselves conscripted into the war in 1917 when China Navigation Company ships were requisitioned, at least 11 of whom, including Second Cook

Chong Chui and Fireman Kam Wong and seven other men on the SS *Szechuen*, the steward on the SS *Anhui* and a member of the crew of the SS *Kalgan*, were killed when their ships were torpedoed in 1918. At least 23 Chinese seamen recruited for Blue Funnel through B&S at Hong Kong lost their lives. Enemy action also led to the deaths of 46 Indian crewmen on SS *Yochow*, as well as its veteran CNCo shipmaster, the chief and the second engineer, deaths often overlooked when rolls of honour were compiled at the end of the war, further evidence of the status of mariners in these treaty port communities, and even more obviously the status of Asian seamen.[30] Others, of course, many, many more, were maimed, or deeply scarred for life, physically or mentally. The company rather felt that British interests were stretched too thin in Asia to accommodate much loss of staff to the armed forces, but patriotism and conscience, and the simple excitement of war, meant it had to allow men to leave.

Service in the Hong Kong Volunteers or Corps at Shanghai, Wuhan or Tianjin was parlayed by some into the prior experience they needed to apply for a regular army commission.[31] Frank Richardson was one of those, his work with the Maxim Company of the Shanghai Volunteer Corps helping this 'genial' man gain a position in the London Regiment. Arthur Joseland, a missionary's son born in Xiamen, had joined the firm in Hong Kong as a postal clerk in 1910, although his prominence in Hong Kong's sporting world must have left him little time for stamping letters. Joseland wrote in detail about his service with the Nigerian Regiment in German East Africa. In one letter he reported stumbling across an outpost that reminded him of 'Amoy's recreation ground', but there was less nostalgic cheer when he came under fire: 'It is a weird sound that of bullets going by and over you, a sort of burn and hiss combined, quite devilish and angry it sounds, and I had very little use for it.' Joseland was killed in German East Africa in September 1917. Richardson died at Messines earlier in the year.[32] At least seven Butterfield & Swire men were killed, eight from China Navigation, one from the Dockyard and four at least from the London office staff. These are certainly underestimates. In 1923 a figure of 17 dead was provided for the Hong Kong interests of the firm alone when the cenotaph there was unveiled.[33] Jack Swire's younger son Glen was killed at Ypres; Jock Swire was wounded twice; Colin Scott's brother died on the Somme. Warren Swire, characteristically, jumped off to serve without consulting his fellow directors. Already a volunteer cavalryman, he went to Egypt with the Bucks Hussars, very much an elite territorial regiment, Rothschilds and all. This proved a bad fit for an awkward character. He experienced a little fighting but, as he saw it – and, report has it, told it – witnessed rather more by way of military incompetence and inefficiency, and was released in the summer of 1916, probably to the relief of all concerned, to work in London on the firm's shipping operations.[34] Almost half of Butterfield & Swire staff who joined up, and who survived, did not choose to return, and some of those who rejoined did not last long back at work, unsettled by their experiences at war.

Staffing was an increasing challenge as the war was prolonged. Three men sent out in 1914 were deemed 'poor stuff', and one of these went astray among Shanghai's temptations (as 'some young men do', deposed the firm in court, in mitigation). He then forged payment orders from the comprador, was caught, tried and jailed for six months in June 1915.[35] Replacing men who had joined up, or left, or who, like this man, had otherwise removed themselves from the office, proved difficult. Those who worked were also still expected to serve after hours in Volunteer Corps or reserve police, especially in Hong Kong, where the weekly details of Volunteer duties were full (and 'volunteer' was simply now a euphemism). Branches were short-handed, took on more staff locally and hired more women, and not just as stenographers or typists, both in Billiter Square and in the China offices. In October 1915 London authorised a more radical experiment: 'we think the time has come when we must seriously consider the employment of well-paid, good-class, Chinese in some of the less responsible positions', the principals told Shanghai and Hong Kong. This would prove preferable to employing Macanese: 'get the best class available ... and pay them very well.'[36] There were obvious longer-term strategic reasons for bringing Chinese employees further into the company itself instead of leaving them within the parallel comprador offices. Well, replied Hong Kong, 'we have been experimenting here in this direction for some time', at the direction of Jim Scott, and they identified 16 Chinese clerks, book-keepers and assistants. However, 'these could not in any way be defined as "less responsible positions", as they carry practically no responsibility'.[37]

The introduction of conscription in Hong Kong in the summer of 1918 gives us some unusual detail about the actual extent of these staff changes which were discussed in public at several of the meetings of the tribunal that sat in the colony in July and August. Such exposure went quite against company habit. Unlike many other British interests in China, Butterfield & Swire had rarely opened up publicly about its operations. You will search in vain among the portraits of the men of Jardines or other enterprises for any substantial account of Swire work or staff in published surveys such as *Twentieth Century Impressions of Hongkong, Shanghai, and Other Treaty Ports of China* (1908), a lavishly illustrated volume that served to advertise the history and services of China coast firms, and the institutions and administrations that supported them. The firm was mostly absent, too, from a later enterprise, *Present day Impressions of the Far East* (1917). But in July 1918 the company had to bare all. It deposed that in August 1914 it had 33 European staff and 13 Chinese clerks in the colony, but by July 1918 there were 29 European men, a dozen European women and 22 Chinese. Twelve men had gone to war. Taikoo Sugar employed 45 British subjects in 1914 and 41 in 1918; three men had joined up. The Dockyard had seen five men leave to enlist out of a total of 87. All the firms were working with a bare minimum, the company argued, and it could spare no more. It was dealing, for example, with over 20 per cent of shipping that had arrived in the colony in 1917, serviced a significant set of Admiralty requisitions – all of its coastal fleet – and its operations were a vital part of the colony's economy.

G. M. Young, then No. 2 in the firm locally, faced sharp criticism during the hearing, honed further when the company appealed the tribunal's decision to conscript three men from the hong and Governor May, still hunting men, took the chair. May was now even more the militarist and seemed incapable of understanding how a business functioned, or interested in knowing how. He gave short shrift to the company's arguments. 'Will you excuse me,' the firm's acting chief, Robert Ross Thomson, begged, interrupting one of these harangues, 'I think we don't understand each other about the word "clerical" ... it doesn't mean simply copying figures.' These men, he argued, had sustained practical experience of working complex systems: they could not be replaced. Hire older local residents as substitutes for the duration, retorted the governor, or more women. The former would not work, responded Ross Thomson. The firm had even tried a university graduate living in Hong Kong once, 'either Oxford or Cambridge ... who read Latin and Greek and spoke French almost like a native', but 'from lack of early business training he was quite unsuited', and nobody could improve on our record in employing women. We even recruited one from Canada; we have tried.[38] In July and August 1918 as the tribunal sat, almost 600,000 American soldiers arrived in France. All the time and manpower expended by the tribunal, governor and all, resulted in the 'combing out' from what was deemed non-essential employment in the colony of 37 men who were promptly conscripted, if they had not previously indicated their readiness in principle to serve, or allowed to leave for home to enlist if they had. The conscripts were despatched to India, and then returned the following year having rather done nothing much at all. Hong Kong's effort was a tremendous waste of time and energy, but the publicity attending the tribunal was deemed to have helped in 'clearing the atmosphere'. His work done, Governor May, 'sparing of speech and sparing of smiles', took himself off on leave to Canada, never to return.[39]

A different staffing challenge came from inside the firm, with a resurgence of discontent about pay and benefits by the officers and engineers of the China Navigation Company, a long-running issue which in 1916 culminated in an unprecedented episode of industrial action. In the early years of the Marine Officers' Association and Marine Engineers' Institute, Butterfield & Swire had been able to rebuff attempts by these bodies to be recognised even implicitly as in any way representing the interests of CNCo mariners. The long shipping depression, however, and exchange rate changes, saw terms of service on China coast shipping worsen compared to service at home or in Australian waters. Union pressure in Australia and in Britain exacerbated these differences. The war brought matters to a head, and in May 1916 the company recognised the right to unionise, increased pay, agreed to offer leave passages and holiday pay and to introduce a pension scheme. It had taken a strike, however, to bring this about.

On 8 May 1916 two dozen steamers were laid up, officers and engineers on strike, though many stayed on to protect the vessels, while others bunked down in the Marine Officers' Club for the duration.[40] It was the culmination of a five-year struggle. Discontent among the 370 or so British officers and engineers was evident in spring 1911, with widespread discontent about pay, and especially about leave passages. This was a period of high tension in maritime labour relations more widely. In July 1911, after a successful strike in Britain, the forerunner of the National Union of Seamen had been recognised by shipowners. Ships' officers came together in the Imperial Merchant Service Guild, formed in 1893 (and in rival bodies, but this became the most influential). An Australasian Maritime Service Guild had been established in 1904, and a China Coast Officers' Guild was founded in Shanghai in September 1911. Officers in the P&O fleet threatened to resign unless their salaries were increased in 1913. One notable activist in China, reported John Swire & Sons in a letter to Shanghai and Hong Kong, was 'Davies', initials unknown, apparently called 'the Duke'. He was writing letters to the local mariners' newspaper, *Leading Light*, and canvassing for Guild membership on company ships. This was Frank Davies, who we have heard from already, and who had been active in guild work since returning from leave in 1910. For the company he was an agitator: watch him, wrote London, and try to get him out of China. Davies's family correspondence shows that the concerns that motivated him and his colleagues were genuine and of long standing. The cheapest passage home in 1908 would be overland on the Trans-Siberian Railway, but even that would cost £100 return, half a year's basic salary, and Davies had been complaining about slow promotion from early on in his service with the firm.[41] He did not, he wrote, object to the principle of seniority, but it meant that men were long underpaid in relation to their experience, when promotion was delayed and they remained in the junior ranks. The firm's obduracy on this point and its treatment of the staff was contrasted by more than one of them with its generosity to the University of Hong Kong. We do more for the colony's economy, they argued, why not look after us instead. A petition for a pay increase in 1911 was eventually and very grudgingly met, but not other requests the men made for hospital pay, half-pay on leave and passages, 'but they pay the expenses of the men in the office,' noted Davies.[42]

The most effective strategy the men had was publicity. Through the Liverpool-based Imperial Merchant Service Guild, through circulars and private letters, potential recruits for CNCo were warned off from joining the company. This began to bite, for men were leaving the firm, too. In 1911 28 second officers resigned, against an average of eight a year over the previous half decade. Might we hire Scandinavians, asked Shanghai in the summer of 1912? Yes, do, replied London, but no Germans. 'We have about 20 Scandinavian, Russian and Yankee officers', Davies would later write, 'until one begins to doubt the nationality of the ship.' Pay was increased from 1 January 1913, but nothing more was offered. And then, of course, the Taikoo refinery staff promptly added their voices: what about us?[43]

'We are not satisfied yet,' wrote Davies in a letter home after this first concession. The peace proved only temporary. The China Coast Guild increased its membership further, and opened a branch in Hong Kong in February 1913. At the end of the year CNCo finally offered passages and leave pay, but only after six years of service, instead of five, which fuelled rather than dampened the discontent.[44] By 1916 almost all CNCo captains and officers had joined the Guild. On 12 April 1916 its leadership wrote to the managers of CNCo, Jardine Matheson's Indo-China Steam Navigation Company and China Merchants, with an identical set of demands: recognition, a salary increase, nine-month leaves and a passage home after five years' service, and a pension on retirement at the age of 60. With no response forthcoming, and despite the efforts at mediation of the British consul-general at Shanghai, a strike began on 1 May that would last just shy of two weeks. The men secured all their demands. Frank Davies had not had the patience to wait.[45] Jack Swire had long before recognised that the staff demands were 'not unreasonable', and worried about the quality of the officers the firm was able to recruit, which was thought to have declined markedly in wartime. But he and his fellow directors balked at the cost to the company in challenging times of providing passages and he remained alert to the mood of CNCo's obstreperous shareholders. With no prospect of promotion anytime soon, Davies had resigned in March 1916 and took a captaincy on a smaller China coast line, straightaway earning over 25 per cent more a month than he could expect to start off with when, or if, he secured the same billet in China Navigation.[46]

Mariners routinely contrasted their conditions of service with those of the comfortably desk-bound shipping clerks, who might, like Fisher, face the odd bout of excitement and danger in China, but never routinely had to face the China seas' typhoons or the social alienation of seafaring life. Clerks in turn wrote to the press to say they thought mariners fared rather better than they did (this was, initially, the firm's position), had some legal protections and had little to complain about (and a healthy outdoor life to boot); a clerk's lot in an airless office was much more insecure.[47] Moreover, Butterfield & Swire's assistants could start to respond in this period, let us tell you what is now expected of us, let us tell you about sugar inspecting. In this second decade of the century a wholly new type of activity became a distinctive feature of company life and business. Taikoo went travelling cross-country.

To set the scene, we might look back to Tianjin, and September 1900, when Walter Fisher re-established the firm's business in the aftermath of the siege at Tianjin. Fisher, as we have seen, reported himself bereft of information and powerless to act until comprador Zheng Yizhi had been persuaded to return. His correspondence provides us with a picture of the way in which Taikoo sugar was being distributed at that point. The comprador worked through three sugar brokers. They were based in Tianjin, and in turn each had a network of 'small clients' spread across a 'big area' including the capital, as well as Tongzhou to its south-east and Baoding to the south-west. These were 'respectable and well to do Shansi men', Fisher reported. He did not know their names or locations.[48] This was perfectly routine and an example of the way in which firms like Swire worked through compradors and agents. We can assume that other branches of Butterfield & Swire that handled refinery sales worked in the same way. But in the face of increasingly strong Japanese competition it was not enough. Japanese firms had entered the Chinese market in 1903, and the Japanese government had also established new tariffs to protect this growing industry and these were pushing Taikoo and other foreign importers out of the market there. So there was both a greater need to focus on China, and to adapt to what proved to be significant new competition. The response was known in the firm as the Manchurian system.[49]

'Outport life is a capital education,' wrote D. R. Law in 1904 in a letter outlining his thoughts about a proposal for all junior staff to undertake what he termed 'inspection' duties. Gaining experience at the smaller branches of the firm in the outports – those concessions and cities outside Hong Kong, Shanghai and Tianjin – became a rite of passage for foreign staff, and it took them far from the ports. The Manchurian system, later the 'Upcountry Sales Organisation', involved a shift from Walter Fisher's blind groping for basic information, to a structured network of formally appointed Taikoo Sugar Refinery agents, inspected regularly and directly by Butterfield & Swire foreign staff. The agents were vetted and provided securities. They were forbidden from stocking Japanese or other sugars. Inspectors were to visit them at least three times a year to check stocks, and the standing of the agents, and to visit dealers. Staff were enjoined to 'endeavour to make each Agent feel that the Inspector is not there as a spy but as a friend'. These were friends on a mission, of course. A massive fraud uncovered in Yokohama in 1900 by the Chinese comprador, who sold large amounts of stock but evaded discovery through the simple expedient of hollowing out the stacks of sugar bags in the warehouse so that to the lazy eye everything seemed fine, meant that particular attention was paid to thoroughly checking supplies in hand. A quick look through the godown door at a wall of sugar bags meant nothing. Stocks also had to be kept as low as made sense, allowing for elasticity of demand, with main stocks held at branches, thereby reducing the risk further. Branch offices supplied a number of main agencies, and those in turn sub-agencies. These agents supplied local dealers. Quantity and price were controlled as far as possible, agents received a 3 per cent commission, and marketing material such as branded signboards and posters was provided. The aim was to oversee the smooth running of a system 'to keep sugar from the Refinery to the up country purchaser as directly as possible', cutting out comprador and middleman, working directly with those 'respectable and well to do Shansi men', for example.[50]

The company first needed to get to know the territory, and to do so first-hand. In 1904, William Nicholson, then formally attached to the Dockyard, but with seven years' experience in the sugar department at Hong Kong under his belt, undertook the first of a series of surveys to see how the new railways being built across China could be used by the firm. In mid-January 1905, for example, together with the firm's acting Hankow branch chief, James Fraser and a Chinese shroff, he left Wuhan's French concession railway station on a 'filthily dirty' train travelling north along the Belgian-owned Peking-Hankow railway towards the Yellow River. The line was still under construction, and the men travelled part of the way in a construction truck and then a bullock cart (which rather disagreed with the shroff). At the 'very poor' small cities along the route they quizzed merchants about the volume and content of any import and export trade, and Nicholson in particular assessed the potential sugar market. It would be another 18 months before the line formally opened: this was scouting ahead. It was an uncomfortable expedition, and Nicholson was also battered by it, but it provided an unusual account of Chinese life and business away from the centres of European business. Without such direct knowledge, the firm would be little further on than it had been in 1900.[51]

Circumstance and opportunity dictated that Manchuria would be the region in which this new regime was inaugurated. The Russo-Japanese War of 1904/05, largely fought for, and in, Manchuria, disrupted existing networks. The Russian defeat inaugurated a period of growing dominance in the north-eastern provinces by the victors, which would steadily make it more and more difficult for British and other foreign firms to operate. There was no 'open door' policy in Japanese practice, even if there was one in Japanese diplomatic rhetoric. And the Japanese consular courts would also prove to be difficult places in which to try to secure redress for trademark violations, as British firms like Swires would discover.[52] Opportunity came in the shape of railways: this was also a region of pioneering development, and the new lines would prove important to the emerging system. Nicholson tramped around potential sugar markets again later in 1905 and in 1907. The experiment commenced swiftly. A 1929 survey listed Taikoo Sugar agencies operating in 1924 and the dates they were established: three of those run from Niuzhuang had been established in 1906 (it is possible that others had been discontinued before 1924). These were supplied by and situated along the Japanese-controlled South Manchurian Railroad from Niuzhuang. Costs were shaved further by foregoing the services of transportation agencies: Butterfield & Swire themselves hired goods wagon space, sending 20 tons of sugar at a time, with a company watchman accompanying the deliveries.[53] More centres were established in the north-east and then in 1910 London gave instructions to extend the system to the Peking-Hankow railway districts, with the aim of applying it 'to all parts of the empire'. In 1912 it was extended to Shandong. In 1914 orders were sent that agencies were to be established 'without delay' by branches at Jiujiang, Wuhan and the Upper Yangzi ports, and then Shanghai. The market had also evolved wholly in favour of refined white sugar away from the browns that had once dominated Chinese sales. Consumers wanted the cheapest, whitest sugar, and that is what they were to be sold. In 1915 47 main and 16 sub-agencies were opened and 67 more main ones in the next three years with 34 sub-agencies. Profits rose sharply, and stayed on average very high until the mid-1920s when the political turmoil of civil war and the Nationalist Revolution forced what became a complete overhaul of the system, which was also challenged by new state-supported refineries in southern China.[54]

The Hong Kong office was at the apex of this new organisation, with a foreign chief inspector based in Shanghai, working with up to 14 foreign inspectors and 13 Chinese interpreters and inspectors. The development of this network helps us understand why the prior experience of new recruits recorded in the Butterfield & Swire staff records starts to become much more varied and eclectic, if not at times surreal.[55] Frederick Henry Robinson, for example, who joined in 1914, had been a rancher in Southern Rhodesia, and worked there for two and a half years before moving to British Columbia where he was employed as a surveyor. Robinson might, then, have been accustomed to the discomforts of a bullock cart, or equivalent. Rex Herbert had worked 'upcountry' for the Siam Forest Company. Edmund Burton was a former professional big game hunter, had served for five years in the British South Africa Police and farmed in Canada. The year and a half he had worked for the Bank of England cannot much have subdued him. John Lamburn had left Manchester University for six years in Rhodesia with the British South Africa Police. Overall, this type of recruit was later judged 'not entirely satisfactory'. The men first gained experience of office work, but they needed some experience and strength of character to negotiate with the Chinese agents and officials they had to deal with. Hunting game was not much of a preparation for that.[56]

Gordon Campbell joined later, when, instead of hiring men specifically with the rigours of the job in mind, who might otherwise not prove suited to company life, it became a routine experience for the young recruit (and kept him out of the temptations of the big ports, at least for a while).[57] After two years of shipping work and having taken classes in Mandarin – for the new system required for the first time that foreign staff acquired some proficiency in the language, his was 'fairly good' – Campbell worked as a sugar traveller out of Tianjin for 10 months in 1924/5. This ex-Indian Army officer toured for up to three weeks at a time with an interpreter and a servant, travelled on foot, trains ('from first class down to coal truck') 'Pekin mule cart', wheelbarrow, mule litter, sampan (with sail) and sledge (on frozen rivers). Accommodation ranged from the Wagon Lits Hotel in Beijing, to 'sharing a kang [a raised platform of mud or earth] with local noisy roughnecks in a village inn', as well as with the local wildlife. Lamburn, later a published novelist and naturalist (and the inspiration for his older sister Richmal Crompton's comic creation Just William), left some glimpses of inspecting life in his nature writings. 'I have travelled in filthy steamers in the tropics and China and ... have slept in filthy Chinese inns where – with the rats – cockroaches made night a purgatory.' And this from a man who took every opportunity to observe and record wildlife, and was particularly interested in insects. Most men had no such interest. Even on an SMR Pullman carriage he recounted passing the time swatting fly, after fly, after fly. He remembered scaring buffalo ('on one occasion I suffered the ignominy of being rescued by a naked Chinese urchin'), enduring the musical entertainment at banquets ('the noise was a mixture of pigs being killed and cats serenading at night; chiefly, I think, the latter'), treating Chinese agents and dealers in return to dinner on the company houseboat with gramophone accompaniment which left his guests 'shrieking with laughter' (for in turn 'Ave Maria' sounded to them, evidently, as if it came from cats and pigs), and waking in the morning to find the boat's skylight carpeted thickly with discarded termite wings.[58] It was all a long way from Bund and Praya, let alone from Billiter Square.

Campbell remembered the job as being to check the books, and stocks, and the shape of the local market. His brief memoir touches in particular on water, bread, bandits and sanitation. He had to take the first two along with him, evade the third, and there was rarely any sign of the last, except at the Wagon Lits Hotel. Arthur Dean worked out of Nanjing at the same time. The office had its own sailing houseboat for journeys along the Huai River from Bengbu in Anhui province. The work was, at least in later memory, 'enormous fun', and nothing could be better for improving spoken Chinese. It had its risks. Those feasts with sugar agents were one of those, for banquets also involved toasts and very strong liquor. But there were other dangers. John Arnold Barton, a recruit of two years' standing, failed to evade a 200-strong group of bandits in May 1924, despite police protection. After an uncomfortable wait in which his captors discussed the utility or otherwise of killing both him and his interpreter, Barton was allowed to depart with only minor pillaging.[59]

In this period, too, British American Tobacco (BAT), the American Standard Oil Company of New York and the Asiatic Petroleum Company were all extending closely supervised distribution networks far away from the old existing coastal and river networks.[60] This brought their staff into more frequent contact with local authorities, especially over disputes around the extraterritorial status of goods and agents, and local taxes and impositions that were made despite goods already having 'transit passes' to show that they had paid tariffs due. There was often little that could be done. Butterfield & Swire would file formal protests through the local British consulate, and in most cases nothing came of these. Agents instead paid the taxes and passed on the cost to the consumer. A 1918 report noted phlegmatically that 'Provincial governments have to be financed somehow'.[61] These new networks also exposed men to what became an increasing possibility of danger in a politically fracturing country, in which those who held the guns held power, whether in the national capital or provinces or localities. Arms flooded into the country and banditry unsettled rural life. Discomfort was one thing; lethal violence quite another. The biggest dangers would be experienced, as we shall see, by crews and passengers on China Navigation Company ships, and the company's sugar men were largely spared such episodes as had been visited on John Barton.

As well as a new granularity of detail about sugar sales, the inspection forms men completed as they travelled gathered additional information on postal and telegraph facilities, other local industries, the nature of any foreign business presence, 'general trade conditions', credit facilities and more. Knowing China directly and at this different scale of detail was proving more and more important. Knowledge had never not been important. Consuls and customs commissioners, compradors and agents had long gathered data, published in reports or newspapers or circulated in market reports. But Walter Fisher had largely worked in a fog through which he was led by the comprador, and beyond that only knew really what the comprador told him. By 1929 the refinery staff in Hong Kong had much more by way of precise detail of locations and local markets, agents and sales.[62]

The rapid growth of the new distribution network took place in the midst of the war, and the convulsions that afflicted China in the aftermath of 1911. In March 1917 the Republic of China broke off diplomatic relations with Germany and Austria-Hungary, and on 1 August declared war. Bringing China into the conflict had involved much British and French diplomatic energy, but the republic's leaders entered the conflict to secure their own objectives, including some revision of the existing treaties. By breaking with the Central Powers, China was able to take over their concessions in Wuhan and Tianjin, and other assets across the treaty ports. This would be viewed with concern by its allies for the precedent that it seemed to set. But for China any advantages it secured were also aimed to help it in the unequal struggle it faced with Japan while the ability of the British to restrain their ally was compromised by their desperate need for Japanese military and logistical support. In 1915 Japanese diplomats presented a set of what became known as the 'Twenty-One Demands' to Yuan Shikai's government, which, if accepted in full, would all but have subordinated the state to Japanese interests. Yuan's acquiescence to many of the demands, and his own extraordinary attempt to revive the monarchy in the winter of 1915/16 (after which, conveniently in one sense, he died), fuelled both popular nationalism and hastened the fragmentation of political power in the new republic.

The Japanese had arrived in force after the Treaty of Shimonoseki, which brought to an end the 1894/5 war with China over control of the Korean peninsula. The treaty accorded the Japanese all rights in China already granted other treaty powers, and further extended the possible reach of shipping by opening new treaty ports, ports of call and river routes. It also carved off Taiwan from Qing control. Alongside these new arrivals, French and German shipping firms – like Japanese ones heavily subsidised by their home states – posed a significant new threat to the 'Three Companies' that had apportioned shares of China's shipping routes between them since the 1870s. Competition meant rates wars between the pool companies and those they saw as interlopers, and China Navigation and its allies also had to invest in new services. They also called on the services of the British state more routinely than ever before. When the Japanese firm Nippon Yūsen Kaisha (NYK) acquired the McBain company in 1904 it had gained access to its ships and the firm's Bund-side properties in Wuhan, Jiujiang and Zhenjiang. Surviving Shanghai branch files contain correspondence with the Yangzi offices showing how Butterfield & Swire agents worked with Jardines and other British land-renters in the concessions to lobby British consuls and diplomats to prevent Japanese interests securing these plum properties and moorings. Thus began another battle of hulks and jetties, and yet again where a hulk was placed, and by whom, and who might stop there, became the stuff of letters and meetings, indignation and protest. Flags were waved: 'this concession is a British concession.

We are members of the British Municipal Council appointed to take the executive charge of the concession in General British Interests,' huffed Councillor James Danby (Butterfield's agent) in Zhenjiang in 1906. McBains was now 'nothing more than a cover for the Japanese,' noted Jim Scott to William Keswick.[63] The Britons succeeded, to an extent, at least in inconveniencing their rivals for a while, but the problem of an energetic competition did not recede, and although the French retired altogether, and the Germans were knocked out, the Japanese only grew in strength. British firms had gained time, but not a victory.

The war undid this. The change to the position of the British commercial sector in China as a result of the diversion of capital and shipping, and by wartime requisitioning and shortages, and a rapid growth in demand from all sides for its resources, saw a growth in Chinese commercial interests and in the Japanese presence of the Chinese market. In 1899 Japanese interests accounted for 11.5 per cent of China's total foreign trade, in 1913 that was 21 per cent and in 1918 it had risen to 38.6 per cent (although this would be whittled down as more normal conditions resumed). In the same period its share of all shipping tonnage in China rose from 7 per cent in 1899, to 25 per cent, and then to 31 per cent in 1918.[64] A strong and heavily subsidised and state-supported Japanese interest had become a fact that companies like Swires had to start to negotiate with, and eventually did, before 1914 (accepting the Nisshin Kisen Kaisha, an amalgamation of existing private firms, into the Yangzi pooling agreement as a full member in 1913), but Japanese gains of 1914–18, economic and political, disordered the pre-war status quo among the foreign powers, and an unfolding anti-Japanese nationalism would in time destabilise all foreign interests.[65]

In early November 1919, Blue Funnel's 5,000-ton *Teiresias* sailed out of Liverpool heading to Yokohama and into this changed environment in East Asia. Added to his usual responsibilities, shipmaster James Reipenhausen had on board Richard Durning Holt and family, and Warren and Jock Swire. Holt and fellow director John Hobhouse, with the Japan Butterfield & Swire managers, would hold important meetings in Tokyo with the heads of the high-riding Japanese lines, feeling out directly the changed balance of commercial power. The Swires were sailing east to survey their firm, its estate and their agents. Warren Swire's private letters narrate a sequence of what were by then the usual episodes of the duty tour of inspection, spiced with tourism.[66] Meetings with agents in Penang, Port Swettenham, Singapore and Bangkok were interleaved with visits to a rubber plantation, tin mine and a timber enterprise. From Singapore the Swires travelled on CNCo's *Linan* with 400 labourers returning home to Hainan (they 'will soon start gambling, when they find their legs'). Warren Swire quizzed the ships' officers about their grievances (they proved 'amazingly frank'), and in Hong Kong pulled together for a 'set-to' every CNCo man in port who was available to try to smooth relations (and to defang the Guild). From 1911 onwards London had taken its lead from Marine Superintendent John Whittle, but a superintendent was a master, and ships' masters were by custom and practice simply not approachable men. They kept their distance to maintain their authority. Now directors talked directly to staff.

A new relationship with staff was a feature of the post-war chapter in the firm's history. Two weeks before the pair sailed, London sent east instructions introducing a new set of house staff pay and conditions. These were transformed: leave on full pay, free passages for wives, hospital costs, life insurance for married men, transfer costs to be met by the firm. During the war the company had introduced a profit-sharing scheme and it now introduced a benevolent fund. The standing of women, too, was to be put on a firmer basis.[67] This was largely the work of Jock Swire, and although it was aimed at perceived lack of *esprit de corps* within the firm, it was also entirely in the spirit of the post-war times, of a land 'fit for heroes' and a new social compact that would take the wind out of the Bolshevik threat. The corollary of this new treatment of its staff was that the firm would now more promptly retire men from senior posts at the age of 50 (on good terms). Talent would have its turn, faster, and the days of long, long serving managers blocking promotion, and gently and affably decaying as they did so, would come to an end. The refreshing of terms accompanied a refreshed Butterfield & Swire staff: 21 men were sent east in 1919, and 37 in 1920. It was 'all honey and conciliation' Warren Swire later remarked of this moment, but of course, he continued, 'if they have good conditions of service, they've jolly well got to earn them'.[68]

If the visit, and what became a regular annual tour 'out East' by one of the directors, brought the London Taipans to China and face to face with staff, Warren Swire also brought the Asian establishment to London, at least visually. Swire was an accomplished photographer. On this trip as on earlier ones he took hundreds of photographs, and back in London they were made up into albums which allowed those in Billiter Square to see exactly what they were talking and corresponding about. It is in some ways a potentially dull and dreary *oeuvre* – there are no portraits, and people do not much feature as individuals – but it is striking almost because of that. As a systematic record of the built environment of the treaty ports it is quite unusual if not unique. Here are the hulks, wharves, jetties and godowns, and the Bunds and streets which housed them.[69] There are rivers and harbours, and the ships under steam, at anchor, at the quayside, loading in progress, all the waterborne world of CNCo and its bustling interface with the land; on shore are offices and company houses (and there on an office wall is John Samuel Swire's photograph), the dockyard and the sugar refinery. The photographs are functional, but always well-crafted and also in many cases quite beautiful and evocative. His eye roamed – to houses clinging above the Yangzi River banks at Chongqing, or the 'Bridge of Ten Thousand Ages' at Fuzhou – and he took time to compose effective and memorable views. Warren Swire's view of the world was patrician, impatient, often jaundiced and distasteful. Through his camera lens we do, perhaps, find our way to another view of the man. We encounter, too, a panoramic survey of the company at nearly all the ports in which it operated. It looks firmly established and deep-rooted, a confident feature now of China's landscape, movement and commerce. But it would also prove – and very soon – to be fragile, vulnerable and in pressing need of even greater change yet if it was to survive the angry decades it was entering.

Building Bridges

How British were the Swire interests in China by 1925? In many ways they did not look British at all. They employed thousands of Chinese staff – seamen, engineers, contract day labourers, clerks, agents and compradors and many more across nearly two dozen cities. For the villager buying a small bag of sugar in April 1925 from a dealer in a town in Shandong some distance from the sub-agency at the nearest railway station, or at Zhangzhou, west of Xiamen, to which it was carried by junk, it might have been obvious that the bag held 'Taikoo' sugar, for the shop might have a metal plate announcing this. The name might actually have attracted the specific purchase. But this might not be the case, and would buyers, even if they knew, think of 'Taikoo' sugar as a 'British' or a 'foreign' sugar? This is not clear. And most sugar, refined or otherwise, was probably consumed in candies, or other prepared foods. Consumers supped on Taikoo silently. Or if we take the passenger waiting on the quayside to board the *Poyang*, say, at Wuhan on 18 May to travel downriver, or the *Wusong* at Shanghai on 23 May to journey to Zhenjiang, would they think of it as a British ship? They would see the large characters of its name in Chinese painted on the side, they would probably deal only with Chinese staff in buying the ticket, settling themselves down on board for the passage, or buying refreshments from the ever-garrulous teaboys on board. As the China Merchants line still largely employed foreign officers and engineers, then the foreign ships' officers who might be seen in passing would have been a quite unexceptional sight for any Chinese traveller on a coastal or river journey. Shippers would largely have dealt with the comprador's staff as they arranged the deals. They would be unlikely to have met Knutsford-born and Bristol-educated CNCo shipping manager at Shanghai T. J. Fisher (whose uncle had weathered the Tianjin siege). Refined white sugar and steamships were once quite evidently 'foreign' things, but by the 1920s they were no longer unusual or distinct: they were snugly assimilated into Chinese life and business.

This was not to last. Bringing back into clear focus the foreign character of this company, and others, and their products and services, and doing this to highlight it as a problem, became an active political project in the 1920s. This was in part spontaneous, as students (especially), merchants and others passionately engaged in the politics of a country in crisis, and it was also part of a conscious strategy by China's new revolutionaries, notably the re-energised Guomindang led by Sun Yat-sen until his death in March 1925, which was reorganised, equipped, trained and part-financed by Soviet and Comintern agents. The foreign was recast as 'imperialist', and imperialism was cast as China's key problem, for it underpinned 'warlordism', the other obstacle to China's rejuvenation. Butterfield & Swire, of course, had always remained a British firm: legally, in terms of its actual status – company registration, for example. The companies it managed – TSR, Taikoo Dockyard, the Tientsin Tug & Lighter Company and CNCo – were all incorporated in London. In practical terms, it also continued to draw on British diplomatic support when it encountered problems: managers called on consuls, shipmasters hailed the Royal Navy's gunboat commanders, the directors wrote to the Foreign Office. The impression its archives give is that it did this more and more often after 1900, in large part because it greatly extended its physical reach, but also because once-quiescent disputes were reignited in the new nationalistic era. In addition, Butterfield & Swire held title deeds to properties that were registered at British consulates, and its British staff were increasingly involved in the running of concessions and settlements. Significant events in their private lives were regulated by British consuls and by the British Supreme Court for China: marriages and births were duly registered, divorces administered, deaths and probates registered and processed. The company's very presence in China outside Hong Kong relied ultimately on its formal British status, and on extraterritoriality, and did so in many different ways. This was a strength, but it also became a significant weakness. It protected the firm, but now it began to expose it as well.

So what to that consumer or passenger seemed to be a Chinese face was actually a Chinese mask. After May 1925 this mask was ripped off. Butterfield & Swire, along with all British interests in China, became the target of a sustained and devastatingly effective nationalist anti-imperialist movement. This would at the time cripple British trade, and force a number of significant changes in business practices, and also in the culture of British firms and other institutions and organisations in China. The era of heightened nationalism which followed the shooting dead of a dozen demonstrators by British-led members of the Shanghai International Settlement police on 30 May 1925 was one in which mass boycotts targeted foreign firms and their Chinese partners, associates, employees and customers. Activists aimed to convince that passenger, the ships' crews, that dealer in Taikoo sugar, that their association with a British firm, however tenuous, was itself a political act – even a simple purchase of sugar for sweet-making – and a profoundly unpatriotic, if not a treasonable one. This was accompanied by campaigns to promote 'national products', that is, Chinese-made or Chinese-owned alternatives. This economic nationalism, which was wholly in the spirit of the calls for action that the first CNCo comprador Zheng Guanying had long before made, echoes of which still reverberated in political discourse, went hand in hand with a political nationalism, that seemed (especially to old-timer residents of the treaty ports) to echo the old boycotts in Guangzhou or even a resurgence of 'Boxerism', but which heralded a more profound shift in Chinese society and politics.[1]

Revolution took other forms. The 1920s and 1930s also saw profound changes in China's urban culture especially, but with echoes across the still predominantly agrarian nation. A dynamic new consumer culture was evolving, fuelled most ostentatiously by the establishment in the 1910s of iconic department stores in China's great cities – Sincere, Wing On, Sun Sun – bright neon-decorated temples to consumption, but also extending into smaller cities, towns and villages along steamship lines, railways and bus routes, and the postal networks that carried people, goods and ideas along them.[2] Even the villages were now lit by foreign goods: British and American paraffin fuelling simple new lamps designed expressly for the purpose, and supplied by extensive new networks that paralleled in scale and practice those of the Swire sugar distribution system.[3] This can be seen in its boisterous and multi-faceted print culture, rich with new magazines targeting women, youth, movie fans and many more. A home-grown film industry, radio stations and new forms and sites of entertainment all grew – dancehalls, hotel lounges and coffee shops among them. China's cityscapes had long been written over with shop signs, but now large advertising billboards joined them, broadcasting images of beauty, health, hygiene and success and the keys to each (the cigarette, the toothpaste, the tonic) all crowding out the view along city thoroughfares. New universities and colleges were established and old ones grew, bringing students – spenders and creators – to the major urban centres. More people travelled around the country, and more often, and went to study or work overseas. There was a rage for foreign things (in Chinese a 'fever', *re*), foreign words that peppered the talk of the urban in-crowd, foreign-style clothes (and these à la mode), foreign music (the piano in particular), translations of foreign novels and poetry. A classic novel of 1933 opened with the night-time arrival of a steamer at Shanghai, the city seemingly surtitled with the neon-lit words 'Light Heat Power', in English (advertising the American-owned electricity plant). A great and lasting romantic poem of the era marked the poet's departure from Cambridge, where he had been studying.[4] This was a syncretic not a mimetic culture: it was new, and it was Chinese. The Swire companies operated within this rapidly changing scene. They helped facilitate it – they moved people and sugared their leisure time – but they would also have to accommodate the changing expectations of customers, Chinese staff and associates. This was a matter of company policies, marketing, ship design and political engagement, but it was also a matter for British and other foreign employees who found themselves living in a new world in which some of the old certainties of treaty port life would have to be abandoned. Hong Kong was subject to the same whirlwind urban change, but as a British Crown Colony had its own distinctive politics of colonial difference and domination which became less and less possible in China, even in the concessions and foreign-controlled settlements.

For Butterfield & Swire the political side of this era might be said to have begun in Xiamen, and over one of those installations photographed by Warren Swire on his first visit to China in 1906/07. This was the wooden bridge that connected the company's hulk there, SS *Shanghai* of melancholy fame, with the Butterfield & Swire offices that opened on to a Bund built on reclaimed land fronting the tiny British concession in the port. Reconditioned after the disastrous Yangzi River fire in 1890, the *Shanghai* now served as a bonded warehouse for the unloading and loading of goods; along the bridge stevedores carried goods to and fro, and then on to China Navigation ships on the coastal run. The ship had further survived a ferocious typhoon in 1917 that had driven it ashore (and which ripped off the roof of the company's godown). In late 1921 it became the focus of what became a significant four-month boycott that became increasingly bitter the longer it lasted. After bad weather in summer 1910 the old bridge connecting the *Shanghai* to the shore had become unsafe and was dismantled. Sampans were used thereafter to transfer cargoes and people. This was hardly satisfactory and in 1919 the company secured permission to rebuild it. But what had gone up in one era without demur – initially in 1900 – could not easily be reconstructed in another, even though remnants of the pillars that had held the original could still be seen and rights had been reserved to do this back in 1910. In a new China this was now seen as an act of appropriation and an infringement on sovereignty: on what grounds, nationalists asked, had a British company any right to stake a claim on Chinese soil?

The land itself was also at issue, for the bridge had linked the hulk with a small piece of land that had been reclaimed from the harbour in 1878 after the creation of the original British concession. Its status and use were subject to dispute. In September 1918 the concession's council – a tiny body, for this was the smallest British concession in China, smaller even than tiny, tinpot Zhenjiang – erected walls and gates as a precaution against civil disorder at a moment of military conflict in Fujian, as well as signboards barring access to non-Britons not on business. Walls tend to stay up when raised, signboards, too. Officials moved on, and so did council members, and people forgot or misremembered why the concession had barricaded itself this way and, as in other British concessions, it rather became accepted as the way things had always been done.[5] But the way things had always been done, even, was questioned, protested and resisted by China's new generations of officials, merchants and activists.

A new bridge was deemed necessary to allow CNCo to cope with a surge in traffic on the Xiamen–Niuzhuang and Shanghai–Hong Kong routes, but this became tangled up in what the belligerent local British consul Berthold Tours, a 28-year veteran of the service, and the only recently appointed British Minister to China, Sir Beilby Alston, both decided was a question of 'principle'. In May 1921, although the local Chinese authorities had protested about the plans, based as they were on an understanding that was 11 years and one revolution ago, preparatory work began on preparing the new bridge. This immediately sparked further protests, and local groups called a public meeting that voted to impose a boycott unless work ceased. The firm had hired a Shanghai contractor to carry out the work, and for practical reasons it had to be paused. 'Dignity' demanded it proceed, argued the consul, trained back in the days of the Qing, arriving even before the Sino-Japanese War. Colin Scott, out east, called on Alston in Beijing, and the Minister asked him to have the work resumed. A British naval vessel was sent to Xiamen. A little more rumination might have suggested to Scott that he resist these requests, for taking a stance on issues of principle and dignity rarely end well. This episode proved no exception. Work resumed in November and a boycott was immediately imposed. The bridge and the company became hopelessly entangled in the question of those walls and gates, the signboards, the legal status of the reclaimed land, and even, ever a potent addition to such a mix, a flagpole from which the Union Jack flew over the concession.

So was inaugurated what would prove to be a textbook boycott. Since the 1905 movement in protest against the renewal of the American prohibition on Chinese immigration, the boycott had become a familiar and potent form of political action in China.[6] At Xiamen CNCo ships were prevented from unloading and loading, and passengers were stopped from disembarking (the sampans that carried them to shore were picketed). Student activists were everywhere cajoling, hectoring, declaiming, appealing to the patriotism of their fellow countrymen, and their sense of dignity. Hotels were forbidden from offering accommodation to passengers if they did land, and shippers were enjoined to use other lines (Japanese firms gleefully offered alternative services). The four dozen men from Shanghai hired by the contractor were lobbied to cease work. Telegrams flew out from Xiamen's telegraph office, seeking the support of trade and regional associations in Shantou, Shanghai and Beijing. Back came statements of support, all duly recorded in the local press, for this was the pattern in China's politics, the press the stage on which patriotism was performed and declaimed. The Royal Navy had landed a party of marines, but this did not help the works' foreman, who was assaulted in the street and had his right ear cut off. Two of his men were arrested by Xiamen police on trumped-up charges of opium smoking. Others, by now suborned, engineered the scuttling of two lighters on which the operation's pile-driver was carried, and it sank into the harbour. Shippers across China – all along the coast and Yangzi ports – started to refuse to ship on CNCo vessels to Xiamen. There was a boycott at Manila also, and seamen in Shantou went on strike. This was much more than the company had anticipated or desired. 'Our livelihood … depends on cordial relations with the Chinese', London wrote to Shanghai in mid-November. The point of principle at issue for the diplomats was a 'very doubtful' one. The firm was 'being used as a weapon' by the British Legation.[7]

The Minister, consuls and the company sparred: Butterfield & Swire must stand fast and finish the work, the diplomats argued, but CNCo was 'losing heavily' by February. The managers in China and in London wished to compromise by ceasing work on the bridge until the other points at issue were resolved, and to offer to pay some sort of rent for it regardless. The diplomats called instead on the 'solidarity of the British commercial community' and were intent on not backing down. Consul Tours saw narrow self-interest at the root of the problem: it was driven by the sampan-men, he claimed, who stood to lose their livelihoods if the bridge was built, or it was the fault of Japanese merchants of Taiwan eager to kick the British out. Anyway, the activists were all barely children. He could not see nationalism for what it was, for nothing in his career had prepared him to, and he would not prove alone in this in the half-decade to come. Back down the British eventually did, not least as a new consul concluded, after looking more closely at the archives than his predecessor had ever done, that there was really no legal basis at all for the position taken by Berthold Tours. The signboards were 'quietly' taken down on 2 March 1922 and the walls demolished two weeks later.

It had been a long, costly and wholly fruitless battle. The local administration had demanded acknowledgement of its authority and respect for due process. The activists asserted their claims on specific points in local treaties and agreements, but they also used a new and emotional language of national honour – and the national was personal – and mobilisation, and a faith in mass action, that had become pervasive in China since nationwide protests in 1919 sparked by the handling by the victorious Allies at the Versailles Peace Conference of the issue of Chinese territory in Shandong taken from Germany by Japan during the war. The decision to build 'shows complete disregard of sovereign rights', 'have we no sense of when foreigners jeer at us and compare us to dead men?' asked one handbill: 'Men of Amoy! rise up and make an effort! This matter is as painful to us as if we were being skinned!' 'Rise, men of Amoy, rise!' But this was also about fighting:

> If every Chinese man will dare to die and to risk his life by attacking the British with his hands and fists, his flesh and his blood, big guns and strong warships will avail the British nothing.[8]

But it was foreman Zhu Jinsheng who was actually attacked: for this bullish new nationalism aimed to educate compatriots, as well as fight imperialists, and it taught them such lessons using a blunt grammar of violence.

Butterfield & Swire would argue that it was only incidentally involved even over this diplomatic point of principle – the right of the British concession authorities to administer the reclaimed land, and erect walls and gates – but it was actually wholly a part of that concession. It was the only clearly British company that was based there (although the agent lived on the rather more pleasant island of Gulangyu, across the harbour). One of those controversial walls abutted the Taikoo hong; one of the controversial signs was fixed to its own compound wall; and its bridge would link its hulk to the shore. From Shanghai, manager E. F. Mackay rebuffed Warren Swire's criticism of his handling of the boycott, and pointed out that the firm needed to navigate carefully and to remain in good standing with the diplomats 'to whom we have constantly to appeal in connection with our various interests in China'.[9] If the Amoy boycott proved an episode representative in its language and activities of the new, assertive mass nationalism developing in China, it also tells us something about the hubris of British officials there. And this local issue, this relatively small question of a bridge, became a controversy across China as young activists – often in fact very young, school students and not necessarily college students – networked in person, sent their public telegrams and despatched circulars and newspapers through the mails. There was also a worrying potential for violence. Persuasion might turn physical; 'dare to die' rhetoric might turn literal. And as naval vessels made their presence known, and marines landed, they would prove more likely to inflame than pacify the angry young of Xiamen, or in turn, Wuhan, Shantou, Shanghai, Hong Kong.

This was all prologue. The Amoy mess was followed by a much more powerful challenge in Hong Kong. While not in origin politically focused, the 1922 strike of Chinese seamen in the colony rapidly assumed a political character, especially when the colonial government banned their union, and gave itself emergency powers to close the border with China, and censor the mails. The roots of this protest by some 23,000 seafarers working out of the British port were economic.[10] The cost of living in Hong Kong had risen sharply since the end of the war, while wages remained static. A Chinese Seamen's Union had been formed in early 1921, and in June decided to write to all shipping companies in the colony to request a substantial increase in wages, and to prepare to strike if its demands were not met. These demands were at first not even answered. But in this new China, labour was finding its voice, and needed to be heard.

On 13 January 1922 the strike began. Seamen had struck before – CNCo's firemen, very briefly, in 1913 – but now they had an organisation, had planned for a lengthy dispute, and would secure very wide support.[11] Seamen knew that they were paid far less than foreign seamen – and knew, too, for example, that CNCo's officers and engineers had received an increase because of the high cost of living in 1921 – and they knew of the successes overseas of seamen's unions in a wave of post-war disputes. And increasing numbers, of course, worked for foreign lines far beyond the China coast. The union moved its strike base to Guangzhou, and striking seamen made their way there to receive strike pay and relief from the more than 160 ships which formed 'a great idle flotilla' in the harbour at the peak of the strike.[12] Sun Yat-sen's party, the Guomindang, had established its own government in Guangzhou, and its local military protector provided funds for the strikers.

Shipowners proved reluctant to compromise, and kept some services running by hiring crews instead in Manila (deemed inefficient), and Shanghai (not as bad, but not a patch on the Cantonese). The colonial government handled things badly. On 2 February it outlawed the union, and, as sympathy strikes broke out, called for foreign residents to volunteer to maintain essential services, closed the border to prevent strikers leaving and took other ham-fisted measures. The dispute involved a campaign of intimidation against strike-breakers and those working with or for foreign concerns. This hit hard and close. On 24 February as he was carried along the Praya in a rickshaw for a meeting at the Butterfield & Swire offices, the manager of Taikoo's main stevedoring contractor, portly, affable Leung Yuk-tong, was shot in the back. Leung, who had persuaded Taikoo Sugar Refinery staff not to strike earlier in the month and was supplying provisions for them, died before he reached hospital. This was more fully a Butterfield's affair even, for the man convicted and hanged for the killing had been a cook on CNCo's new ship *Kwangchow* until the strike began. It was hardly surprising, then, that when threatening letters arrived in the hong on 4 March the entire Chinese staff walked out.[13]

It got worse. As a column of striking office clerks, labourers, household servants and shop assistants made their way to the border at Shatin on 3 March police fired on them, leading to three deaths. By this point, around 120,000 people were on strike, the seamen joined by engineers and mechanics, dockers, lightermen, coal haulers, teahouse and restaurant employees, domestic servants, clerks, tram company staff, tailors, carpenters, market stall and restaurant staff: it was a general strike.[14] Despite the violence, British residents pretended to be enjoying themselves, living, servantless, rather as if in a state of siege, making their own beds, cooking their own food and cleaning: 'Please play the game' read a sign at the Repulse Bay Hotel aimed at guests checking in who were asked what domestic chores they were best at.[15] But the escalation after the Shatin killings and the onset of the general strike prompted a rapid climbdown by the shipping companies and the Hong Kong government. The firms conceded a rise in wages was warranted, and agreed to reinstate strikers. Butterfield & Swire were prominent in the discussions, and very much the target of union ire. Accepting back the strikers was a particularly galling concession for CNCo, but back they came. The union's confiscated signboards were reinstalled at its offices in Des Voeux Road in front of a large crowd and to the trumpeting of a school bugle band. And in an odd moment of symbolism, the five-barred flag of the Chinese Republic, the Red Ensign and the Union Jack were raised together on the roof of the building.[16] Warren Swire was enraged at the settlement. This was giving in to force, and the

Hong Kong government had been foolish to threaten harsh measures and then not follow through, or even withdraw them, as it had done so by legalising the union. But the firm had already acknowledged the difficulties its staff faced. In 1921 it had introduced a version of its Staff Provident Scheme for Butterfield & Swire's Chinese office staff and it knew that times were hard for its employees. For all that Edkins in Hong Kong and the directors in London averred that the strike was purely a political episode, they were in large part wrong, at least in terms of its inception. But it became intensely political and its legacy was a politicised labour environment across China.[17]

CNCo offered the same 30 per cent rise in Shanghai to its crews based there, as it had conceded in Hong Kong, and many other shipping lines did the same. This was wise: in July 1922 a Shanghai branch of the Seamen's Union was established and promptly requested salary increases in line with Hong Kong's. A strike was launched among crews on those lines that had not raised wages already. There was much talk in official circles in Hong Kong and Shanghai, and within the Swire correspondence, about the need to increase police capacity, especially intelligence capacity, to deal with a new political threat that was clearly becoming entangled in all this – communism. E. F. Mackay in Shanghai sent back to London a report prepared by the deputy chief of police in the International Settlement which reinforced this analysis, but also argued cogently that the key lesson to be learned from the Hong Kong strike was that in the first instances employers had 'to treat seriously, sympathetically and in a business-like manner any demand of labour, however unreasonable it may appear at first sight to be'. They had themselves to be reasonable when it came to economic disputes and could not simply shout down their employees.[18]

This was sensible, prescient, but it was ignored, even by the author's own police force, which opened fire on demonstrators in Shanghai on 30 May 1925. The protests had grown out of a labour dispute in a Japanese-owned cotton mill. The few seconds of firing by the Shanghai Municipal Police turned this into a nationwide movement aimed at the British, that began with a general strike in Shanghai, then mass protests and boycotts across China. Amid the volatile situation that followed there were further confrontations in the British concession at Wuhan, and most bloodily in Guangzhou, where in the 'Shaji massacre' on 23 June 1926 at least 52 Chinese men and women were shot by British and French marines, as well as the volunteer Shameen Defence Corps, firing from the concessions on Shamian. The resulting 16-month strike and boycott engulfed British trade in Guangzhou and Hong Kong. Public indignation was first conveyed in print, at meetings and through an efflorescence of societies and associations that brought people together from across Chinese society. At the same time, Communist and Guomindang activists became deeply involved in these movements – Communist Party membership rose tenfold in 1925 – aiming to harness this popular anger to support their revolutionary programme. That programme next saw the new Soviet-trained armies of the Guomindang break out of the Guangzhou region in July 1926 on a 'Northern Expedition' to bring the party to national political power.

Anti-imperialism and nationalism were intertwined in the mass activism that paved the way for the victory of the National Revolutionary Army, as it was renamed, which brought the Guomindang to a new national capital that it established at Nanjing in 1927, and which was dominated, after internal factional struggles, by the army's commander, Chiang Kai-shek. The new National Government would never fully control all of China, and was challenged by militarists in the south-east, south-west, north-east and in Xinjiang in the west, but it gained greater and greater credibility and status as the legitimate government of China year by year after 1927. If the victory of the Nationalists – as the Guomindang were often referred to in English – was partial, the victory of nationalism was unquestionable. Until early 1927 the party was formally allied to the recently established Chinese Communist Party, then turned on it, brutally, in a wave of purges that also brought its own left wing to heel. But many foreign residents in China failed to see nationalism as the underlying force driving the new regime, for some years after 1925 thinking of it as a child of Communist or Comintern conspiracy. As a result they would prove stubbornly resistant to change. Shanghai, reported visiting *Manchester Guardian* journalist Arthur Ransome, was the 'Ulster of the East': these were men who would brook no surrender.[19] But the Guomindang aimed to abolish what were now routinely labelled the 'unequal' treaties which supported the foreign presence in China and it would, in the long term, brook no opposition. Navigating these challenges would become a key priority for Swire directors and managers in the later

1920s and 1930s. Historically averse to becoming involved in public affairs in the colony or in the treaty ports, the firm now had actively to play a role, and aimed, formally or informally, to change the way these bodies worked, as well as the wider culture of the British presence in China. The Swire firms also had to change the way they worked themselves and how they identified themselves and managed relations with their staff, with Chinese collaborators and competitors, and with Chinese officials.

By virtue simply of its presence in China, and the scale of its operations, Swire interests were regularly caught up in the unfolding events of the Nationalist Revolution. Mostly this was unexceptional, that is, it was one more British company in the firing line. But two disasters stand out. In the febrile aftermath of 30 May 1925, at Hankou on Wednesday 10 June, a company watchman, a Sikh, reportedly struck and injured a wharf coolie when trying to break up an argument that broke out during unloading of the *Wuchang*. Demonstrations in protest took place the following day, culminating in a march on the British and Japanese concession council buildings. A 'mob' was reported to have attempted to 'rush the British Volunteer Armoury' (for there was, of course, a Volunteer Corps at Hankou). Under instructions from the Royal Navy authorities the Volunteers turned machine guns on the crowd, killing eight people. Replacing the company's Indian security staff and treating workers with respect became key demands of those leading the resulting boycott. This incident would in time seal the fate of the British concession which, public anger still palpable 18 months later, was invaded again by protestors and surrendered to Chinese control. But the outbreak had its roots in the actions of a lowly watchman, that old story of the Swire companies in China, B&S again finding itself at the mercy of the fist, foot or nightstick of one of its staff.[20]

A worse disaster overtook the Upper Yangzi city of Wanxian in September 1926. On 29 August CNCo's SS *Wanliu* was seized en route to the port by provincial troops enraged that her wash had sunk a vessel carrying dozens of their fellow soldiers. More reportedly died when the ship attempted to evade being boarded. Sichuan's powerholders funded their administrations and paid their troops through levying all sorts of charges that foreign firms deemed rightly, at least on technical grounds, illegal. Military units expected to be able to requisition space, gratis, on ships, and the settled life of the river was made more turbulent by the foreign steamers that rocked it. Against this background *Wanliu*'s master attempted to take his vessel to Wanxian and set in motion the events that followed. A contingent of soldiers managed to get on board and escort the ship west, but they were then evicted by an armed Royal Navy contingent when they reached their destination. In response, the provincial commander, General Yang Sen, ordered the seizure of two other CNCo ships in port, the SS *Wantung* and SS *Wanhsien*, as well as three officers on each, holding them as collateral until reparations were negotiated. Some 800 soldiers were stationed across the two ships and shore batteries covered the British gunboat in the harbour. Local British naval commanders were furious. On their own initiative, without consulting the Foreign Office, or even the Admiralty, the naval command launched an operation to release the ships and free the CNCo officers on 5 September. By the end of that day the city was ablaze, 'a raging inferno' lit the sky and could be seen five miles downstream. Hundreds, if not thousands, of the inhabitants perished in the conflagration or bombardment from naval guns ostensibly targeting the artillery on the river banks. With the operation's commander killed in the first volley of defensive fire, British 'firing became very wild', and 'control was difficult'. Hundreds of Yang Sen's men were killed, their bodies, it was reported, piled up in pyramids on the decks of the CNCo vessels, *Wanhsien*'s 'deep in a muck of blood, brains and filth'. Seven British sailors were killed, as well as one mariner.[21] The British attack had been expected, and the response had been deadly, prompting a rapid and devastating escalation.

Treaty port diehards, safe in their clubs downriver, applauded the 'wonderful epic of Wanhsien' – as the *North China Herald* headlined it – for here was a muscular British response at last, the Royal Navy restoring British prestige when the flag had been besmirched at Wanxian. British diplomats were aghast, for they found themselves at the mercy of gung-ho navy commanders who resented the 'humiliation' visited on them by the seizure of the two ships. This proved to be a very dangerous period for British officials, who found lower-level officers in the large British reinforcements sent to China as the Nationalists neared the Yangzi River all fired up to provoke a conflict. Warren Swire was not alone also in blaming the English-language press in China, and

its 'wonderful' verdict on such appalling events, although his language
was as extreme as theirs:

> If anyone would murder Green [editor of the *Herald*] and possibly
> Fraser [the *Times* correspondent) I would gladly pay for his defence
> and the education of his orphans. They are two of the most dangerous
> enemies we have in China.

Less dramatically, Swire managers and directors became involved
in trying to calm the temper of the times – and of *The Times* – by
lobbying newspaper proprietors to rein their wilder journalists in.
A large congregation attended a memorial service for the British dead
in Shanghai's Holy Trinity Cathedral on 3 October, including among
those the *Wantung*'s chief engineer, William Johnston, a 56-year-old
married veteran of the firm, who drowned after jumping from the ship's
deck in a bid to escape.[22] The legacy for Butterfield & Swire was a
boycott that lasted until 1929, but the fires of outrage smouldered in
Sichuan long into the 1930s.

The company became more conspicuously British in this unstable
era. For a start, activists sought out British goods and those providing
services to the British, targeting these in their boycotts. TSR's
up-country agents were in many instances forced to close down during
the crisis of 1925.[23] In some episodes – at Hankou and at Wanxian –
Butterfield & Swire itself was the actual target. But mostly the firm
was swept up in the great run of British interests that were attacked
during the anti-imperialist wave. A handbill from 1927, with the
caption 'Made in England' written in crystal-clear English, showed
four crouching skeletons and a number of skulls, each labelled with
the site of a violent clash with the British. One of these is Wanxian,
and all sit under the Chinese text 'British imperialist foreign trading
company'.[24] But at the same time, British firms found that they had
clearly to label themselves. In such a period of revolution and civil
war, and a widespread breakdown in civil order that drove many rural
people into armed self-protection bands and banditry, extraterritoriality
provided a necessary safety. Union Jacks were painted on the sides of
ships; the flag was raised over offices and installations. On the whole,
this deflected interference, or at least second thoughts, on the part
of those who might have been tempted, for it raised the spectre of

retaliation. Feeling embattled, Britons also closed ranks, and at the moments of greatest tension performed an exaggerated Britishness loudly and clearly, cheering the 10,000 troops who arrived with a 'Shanghai Defence Force' in the winter of 1926/7 – Britain's largest single overseas intervention of the interwar period – and looking after the substantial naval reinforcements deployed to Chinese waters.

There was also another way in which this enhanced and accentuated British character had its advantages. Just as the foreign-controlled concessions and settlements served as safe havens for Chinese refugees in times of conflict, for political actors in disgrace, or for Chinese capital to secure safe returns in a legally stable environment, a foreign-flagged ship offered greater security for Chinese passengers and goods. In the rocky waters of the 1920s and 1930s, this proved an important commercial asset for firms. It was hardly failsafe, for it also attracted piracy, for such bandits did not respect any flag. Between 1923 and 1935 CNCo ships were seized on 10 occasions, the *Sunning* and the *Tungchow* twice each.[25] But in general, and especially during the war with Japan, foreign extraterritoriality proved to be an asset for Chinese, including the Chinese state, as we shall see. This also suggests how far the world of much British business in China had moved away from trade towards service provision, but services of a sort that might not last unchanged in any new era of political stability and central control in China.

That seemed the stuff of dreams. But the long crisis accelerated changes in company practice that were already being contemplated, making an urgent political necessity out of developments proposed for commercial reasons or adaptation to a changing market. In among the thickets of political and policy correspondence that fill the company files that survive for the 1920s and 1930s – unparalleled in the history of the firm for their focus on issues beyond its immediate commercial or operational concerns – two documents catch the eye for the light they shed on the character of China's evolving urban classes. A March 1927 discussion of a possible reorganisation of the 'comprador system' in the firm (as it was being labelled in the documents) provides details of the educational background of 51 Butterfield & Swire Chinese office staff. Most had studied in the colony's English-language schools, 18 of them at Queen's College, others at St Joseph's of the Diocesan Boys' School. Two had been to university overseas, one in London and the

other in Chicago. This was a good cross-section of the new world of
Chinese urbanites.[26] They were not looked on as having any potential
substantive role in the future of Butterfield & Swire, especially in
the Shanghai and Hong Kong branches (more so in the latter): they
were part of the Chinese organisation, not the firm. They sat on a
different floor of the office buildings and were not part of corporate
life. When John Lamburn wrote a thriller set in Hong Kong – in a
firm clearly modelled on his time with B&S – the Chinese clerks
his British protagonist encounters are silent, sullen and distant.[27] Yet
these employees were part of the new social classes that made Taikoo's
business possible, and they formed a pool of experienced employees
from whom a new model of operation could be developed.

Some of them might also have agreed with the type of comment
relayed to the directors by a contact in late 1925, reporting a conversation
with Chinese university students studying in England. These singled out
Taikoo for criticism (as well as the Hongkong & Shanghai Bank and
BAT) because their entrenched positions in their various markets, which
were buttressed by the treaties, and protected in China Navigation's case
by pooling agreements and use of rate-cutting to meet challenges, and
barred access into markets of new Chinese enterprises. These were quite
able, the students believed, to compete effectively – they evidenced the
Nanyang Brothers Cigarette Company – but had little chance to. And
when in addition British firms did not pay taxes in China, the Chinese
state gained little directly from their presence, and neither did these
students nor their families and networks (nor their capital).[28] For these
Chinese commentators, sons, mostly, of the commercial elite, such
foreign firms were privileged parasites. One political response aimed
to degrade and remove that privilege, but for these critics the crucial
point was that they were excluded from collaborating and benefiting,
formally or indirectly, from these markets. Taken together, and placed
in the context of changes in Chinese urban culture and society, and
especially the development of new elites, there are pointers in these
vignettes to one significant change that the Swire companies began to
plan on making in their management and organisation of their Chinese
and foreign staff in China. They could no longer afford to ignore the
potential of these groups, nor their interests and aspirations. They
needed more positively and generously to collaborate with the new
Chinese elites.

There were other aspirations to take account of, too. One of the leading figures on the powerful Boycott Committee that co-ordinated the long campaign in 1925/6 against the British in Hong Kong was a Taikoo Dockyard mechanic, Luo Dengxian, who had started working there in about 1915, aged 11. In 1923, in the aftermath of the 1922 strike, Luo had joined the Chinese Communist Party. The son of a seaman, he became president of the Hong Kong General Union by 1926, and would become a high-ranking member of the Party (and one of its small minority of cadres with genuinely proletarian background).[29] Luo would go on to play a leading role in the Party's apparatus in Shanghai, then led its labour activities before being assigned to efforts to create a Communist-led resistance in Japanese-occupied Manchuria. He was later arrested in Shanghai and executed at the age of 29. This, too, was a career that grew out of working for Taikoo. If the Swire companies could no longer afford to ignore their Chinese office staff and Chinese elites, they certainly could no longer afford to manage their Chinese labour as they had done in the past, and that labour was now organising itself in different ways, and it would have an impact on the national political stage.

Luo and his colleagues had much to complain about. Butterfield & Swire and the companies it managed still ran a devolved system. We might see this simply as the 'comprador model', but it was actually replicated in all its companies and at most different levels of activity. For example, at TSR senior European Foremen (as they were labelled) worked through 25 Chinese 'No. 1s', and had 'practically no control' over relations between these No. 1s and the employees those men controlled. And control them they did. Hands were recruited by the No. 1s who, it was suspected (because it was never investigated) sold access to these positions (and might extract a recurrent tax on post-holders), provided food for them and were responsible for ensuring the right number of men were available for each shift. They also controlled the housing the company provided for its workforce at Quarry Bay, being 'responsible to the Refinery for rent'. There were housing units that could accommodate some 4,000 people unless subdivided, as many of them were. They might limit access to positions only to their own kin networks. Foreign foremen, if satisfied with a recruit, approved him being issued with a staff number. Frequently the man using the number on any given shift was someone else. This was effective for the company, which got the men when it needed them, but it placed recruitment and labour relations and welfare in the hands of a small number of Chinese staff who were themselves difficult to control. Foremen were not generally young men when they joined the company, and were largely ignorant of Cantonese, and so relied on the No. 1s to interpret for them. At the Dockyard 31 Chinese foremen controlled 1,134 of the jobs in 1927, according to one report, and seven contractors a further 1,215.[30]

Similarly, CNCo staff, even those considered trained and experienced enough to join a proposed 'Native Provident Fund', were mostly known only to CNCo shipmasters and engineers: no record was kept of their service or experience, which might stretch across many years and different ships. It was to each ship's chief engineer individually that firemen made representations when they demanded higher wages in 1913. When European staff left the company, they took with them any knowledge, however imperfect, of the service of their Chinese crews. Across all the Swire companies, little detail was kept of staff outside the offices. These labour management practices were quite common in China at this time.[31] Foreign observers usually assumed that taken altogether they paid more attention to labour conditions and relations than Chinese managers, but it is not easy to see proof of this. The devolution of any actual management also proved a challenge when it came to introducing reforms.

Elements of this employment model at Shanghai were under a further layer of control. Ostensibly, dockers ('wharf coolies') were supplied by labour contractors. But there were others who, by 'established customs' or 'former ownership of land', asserted 'various rights' over labour contracting, and with whom the contractors were likely to be entangled. These were 'people who have superimposed themselves' and 'who secure the squeeze', it was noted. They were 'what may be termed vested interests'. They were in fact what may be termed gangsters or secret societies, such as the Red and Green gangs. Three of the company wharves at Shanghai were located on the Pudong side of the Huangpu River, and will have fallen, like other operations there, under the shadow in particular of the Shanghai Green Gang. One of the wharf labour contractors was later described as 'the Firm's tame gangster', but others were less tame. As state power fractured, such societies evolved into complex organised crime networks, and by the 1920s and 1930s the Shanghai Green Gang exercised a powerful influence on labour, among other spheres, including politics. When gang boss Huang Jinrong – 'Pockmarked Huang' – invited Jardines and Taikoo to send representatives to his son's wedding in the mid-1930s, they assembled their gifts (cash), went, and literally bowed to power.[32]

Another challenge was provided by the culture of its foreign staff in China outside Hong Kong who were socialised rapidly on arrival into what was to all intents and purposes a colonial lifestyle, with associated expectations and attitudes, though they were not living in a colony. Familiarity bred contempt, but there was in fact very little genuine familiarity to be found. As a 1927 letter from Hong Kong showed, most interaction with most customers was handled by the firm's Chinese organisation. The attitudes of European office staff – whether Taipans, department heads or mercantile assistants – were moulded by the instinctively conservative atmosphere that pervaded all the treaty ports and the colony at Hong Kong. The fragmentation of state power in China after the death of Yuan Shikai had encouraged a stubborn resistance to contemplating any change or reform, and these were golden years of foreign power and autonomy. There was no functioning national government worth its name, and what there was was entirely hamstrung by the fact that the foreign-managed Customs Service controlled its only reliable source of revenue (for local power-holders kept their revenues to themselves) and this body only released funds to it once foreign loan payments had been serviced. The Inspector-General of Customs, Sir Francis Aglen, injudiciously remarked that he ran a 'practically independent' 'imperium in imperio' – a state within a state – and was all but the paymaster general of the Chinese government in which he rather acted as if he held ministerial rank.[33] Treaty port residents saw no reason to consider surrendering their privileges to those they viewed with contempt, and who as far as they were concerned had no real legitimacy as China's rulers. As banditry seemed to become endemic, and as civil wars large or small seemed to become pervasive, foreign diplomats would pledge to revise treaties and agree to changes, but only when China had put its own house in order, that seemingly fantastical prospect, always in the documents, never getting any closer.

We can see evidence of foreign attitudes in John Lamburn's lazy fictional caricatures of sullen clerks, urbane but vicious warlords and wily, scheming comprador; this was, of course, what the thriller market expected of its Chinese characters, but they might be found also populating the hostile reporting from China of the foreign journalists who controlled the flow of news about the country overseas. We might see it, too, in the attitudes of CNCo officers whose guild circulated a note to them in October 1926 complaining that 'certain capitalists and traders in China' – whose identity was quite obvious – 'were penalising the foreigner to the advantage of the Chinese'. They were 'prostituting our nationality to invite favours'.[34] Less dramatically we can see it in the way that the managers both in Shanghai and in Hong Kong were slow to the point of passive obstruction when it came to merging Chinese staff into their respective offices – 'We were under the impression that this had been done long ago', wrote London in 1926 – or providing the company's first Chinese graduate trainee (as we might now term him) with routine work in Shanghai as they would a new British recruit: they had set him to culling items of interest from the Chinese press.[35] They had not set about training him in office work. This type of resistance to the contemplation or enactment of reform came both at a corporate level, among most foreign enterprises, including such bodies as municipal councils or even the customs, and at the individual level, among men whose livelihoods depended on the structures of foreign privilege and power. Training a young Chen or a Wang meant in time ruling out a job for a young Smith or Jones.

Change was needed, though, and the view from London was more flexible. In the first place, there were new made plans to extend its provident funds to CNCo's Chinese office and then floating staff, TSR and Taikoo Dockyard office and experienced skilled staff, plans largely drafted in outline and explored before the crisis began in 1925. 'Welfare' work among staff began to be pursued more actively.[36] A 'Taikoo Chinese School' opened, for example, at Quarry Bay in 1924 for the children of Dockyard employees. An obstacle to this type of initiative was that the managers in Shanghai and in Hong Kong thought of welfare as a more intangible politics of public gesture, assuming it meant subscribing funds to the Chinese YMCA for good works, further demonstrating their narrow eastern horizons. London saw it as something that involved and benefited its own staff. The directors in London were clearly thinking more widely about 'present ideas' in company management and labour relations that were being discussed in Britain, sending out pamphlets and newspaper clippings as food for thought.[37] London began to work on two important longer-term initiatives: the wholesale reorganisation of the comprador system, and much more active political engagement in China and in Hong Kong. Taken together the objective was to put the company on a new and firmer footing in a China that had markedly changed. It is not at all easy to identify who among the directors was most forward in furthering this new policy. Warren Swire, by virtue of ever having the most strongly put opinions, clearly identifiable intemperate phrasing (and idiosyncratic punctuation), and by dint of involvement in the public conferences and meetings that started to be held, such as at the Institute of Pacific Relations meeting in Kyoto in 1929, was certainly strongly in favour. But there is little evidence of dissent from any of the directors.

To a very large extent, compradoring remained a family business. This was assumed to have reputational and practical value, but it also proved a reputational trap, for the firm proved wary of sacking prominent men and the impact that might have, and the entire system was deemed by 1933 to be 'obsolete, expensive and inefficient'. In Shanghai new generations of the Chun (Chen) family retained the key role, and in Hong Kong the Moks. In 1919 Chun Koo Leong was succeeded by his son Chun Shut Kai (Chen Xuegui). Mok Kon Sang followed his father, Mok Tso-chun, after the latter's death aged 61 in 1917. That had been the occasion for a mile-long funeral procession, watched by large crowds, that took half an hour to pass those watching. The Moks were socially very prominent and Mok Kon Sang grew ostentatiously prosperous, building himself an extravagant mansion – in 'a British royal palace style', his son wrote – on Connaught Road in downtown Victoria. Well might he do so, for in June 1928 an audit by Butterfield & Swire identified a long-running and lucrative fraud that he had committed on the Taikoo Sugar Refinery (overcharging on the bags used). It failed, however, to reveal the true extent of his swindling, for Mok used a front company to buy sugar from TSR when it was cheap, and sold it in Guangdong province when prices rose, competing with Taikoo's legitimate products, whose distribution network in Guangdong and Guangxi he controlled.[38]

As a comprehensive 1934 company report noted, it was this and other 'actual breakdowns' that forced Swires to act. At Hankou, during the time of greatest revolutionary turmoil there over the winter of

1926/7, comprador Wei Xuezhou (H. T. Wei) reported making very large losses (but there was also probable, but unprovable, fraud). A significant portion of this was written off. This propelled Chun Shut Kai to advance his own claims in compelling detail. He had made significant losses in 1924–6, and greater ones in 1927. He, too, was released from a significant part of his debts to the company. This did not really help, and in 1932 Chun went bankrupt. The Nanjing comprador also came forward with claims. Certainly, trade had been very bad, and greatly disrupted by the revolution. TSR also faced unremitting competition from imports of Japanese sugar. Labour was militant, and dockers demanded and got increases in pay that came from comprador accounts, for it was politically too dangerous to refuse them. Butterfield & Swire managers thought that many of the claims their compradors made were reasonable, but they would also point out that any rupture with such men, who were to all intents and purposes the faces of the firm in Chinese circles, would prove damaging reputationally. They also worried about the impact the actions of an 'embittered' man who knew their business might have on his former employers.[39]

But the tangle was made worse because of the lack of any effective control and oversight by Butterfield & Swire managers. And Chun Shut Kai was 'not and never will be a man of initiative', the Moks were 'to all intents and purposes quite useless', a 'necessary evil', and Mok Kon Sang a 'figurehead comprador'. It was at first thought that bringing into comprador offices 'progressive' younger men such as Yang Moi Nan (Yang Meinan) might catalyse change, but the problem was structural (and 'younger' was relative: Yang had been born in 1873).[40] After some precipitate moves in the mid to late 1920s to try and nurture such young Chinese men within the Butterfield & Swire house staff, putting most compradors on different terms and conditions, bringing them on to salary rolls, a more measured new 'Chinese staff organisation' was developed and outlined in a detailed report completed in 1934 by Charles Collingwood Roberts, who had joined in late 1922 straight from Oxford University, and had been detailed to this work in 1932.[41]

Roberts composed a realistic and pragmatic framework for developing and managing a Chinese staff within an integrated company organisation. Much still needed to be learned, and aspects of cultural norms in China needed to be recognised: hiring suitably qualified men introduced by established contacts, for example, finding a form of guarantee. Roberts admitted that Taikoo had a very poor reputation among the pool of potential recruits. Its current pay scales were low, and management of their careers poor – think of Lamburn's portrayal of an office of alienated clerks – and there were other defects. The 'cream', moreover, would never join, for they knew that they could never rise to the top of a foreign-owned company. But with patience and a dedicated team in a specialist new department, it was believed that both a class of well-qualified clerks and a cadre of Chinese managers and senior advisers could be established and nurtured. Roberts was perfectly confident that the firm could develop a Chinese staff that might wholly supersede the foreign employees. And after all, in this new nationalistic era they might need to. Swires were not alone in aiming to build a new structure like this. Japanese firms in China had pioneered the way from the late nineteenth century onwards. The Hongkong & Shanghai Bank was also revising the way it worked with its compradors. The logic of business, and of politics, demanded it.

The company's new Department of Chinese Affairs (DOCA) was up and running from 1 January 1934 with the objective of implementing the Roberts report. It was led by a colourful figure, brought in from outside the firm. George Findlay Andrew was every inch the muscular personality that his 26-year record of service with the China Inland Mission (CIM) might promise.[42] Andrew had been born in China to CIM parents, spoke Chinese fluently and was thoroughly attuned to Chinese social and cultural practices. He had long ago spent three years' apprenticeship in an office in Manchester, but he was not taken on for his commercial potential, but because he saw things 'at a different angle to that of the ordinary B. and S. businessman', as Warren Swire later put it.[43] Andrew had earned a strong reputation and widespread recognition through work in famine and disaster relief agencies. Nobody within the firm had such a range of expertise or contacts although, to be fair, no other foreign firm in China would have been able to bring such a character forward from its own ranks. Still, Tom Lindsay, a promising recent recruit to the office staff, was sent off to Beijing for advanced language training and to be groomed as a deputy. DOCA did need to be of and in the firm.

DOCA's role was threefold. It was partly a political office, tasked with recasting and supporting Taikoo's direct relations with Chinese officials and other leading figures. Secondly, it was the Chinese recruitment arm of the company, and responsible for staff welfare; and thirdly it was charged with handling labour relations. At first met with suspicion by British managers and Chinese staff alike, it steadily began to make a difference to the culture of Chinese employment within Butterfield & Swire. It began by setting about building for the first time a systematic and comprehensive set of detailed records about the Chinese staff. Up to this point, it really knew very little about them. As well as better management of promising men, and of underperforming ones, it allowed the firm to use data to identify where it was getting good clerks from, and to recruit more steadily from those sources. This was elementary hiring practice, but simply had not been used in its recruitment of Chinese staff before. As well as 'revolutionising our entire Chinese relations', as Jock Swire put it in 1935, DOCA worked to revise the public identity of the firm. It advised a change from the usual Chinese rendering of its name, Taigu yang hang ('Taikoo foreign house'), to Taigu gongsi: Taikoo Co.; and it provided correctly prepared Chinese-language letters for the company's correspondence with Chinese officials. DOCA smoothed the blunt British edges of what remained still a British firm, but one better assimilating itself into the Chinese political and public environment.[44]

The fact that Chinese university graduates, including those who had studied in Britain, were now welcome (but not those who had focused on a 'commercial education', which just provided a 'mass of theory'), paralleled a significant change in the recruitment of British staff as well. During his first post-war trip to China Jock Swire had an epiphany. 'Any number of my contemporaries at Univ,' he wrote,

> would have jumped at the prospect of a life out here and there is hardly one graduate from Oxford or Cambridge employed here or in China. B&S must change their recruiting system and I must get in touch with the Oxford Appointments Committee and find out how we can recruit Oxford Graduates and make a practice of replacing the present Board School boys with Graduates. I am sure they would rush to the top but it may be difficult to persuade the present seniors and departmental heads to accept them but we have got to see that they do.[45]

He wrote as a director, but mostly as an ex-officer, and he wrote in the midst of the post-war depression during which ex-officer unemployment had become a subject of concern. There were, of course, many unemployed former 'Board School Boys', too, but Swire was thinking of those he had studied and played with at Oxford, and had fought with in France. The company began recruiting from Oxford in 1920/21, Jock joining the Appointments Committee himself in 1931 (serving on it for 30 years), and bringing men into the firm also from Cambridge, Edinburgh, Glasgow and London. He looked, he later recalled, for evidence of 'leadership', and 'didn't give a damn what they got'. Many of these recruits did not make it east, for health reasons, or they had second thoughts, and a substantial proportion left at the end of their probationary period. Those left were managing the firm's branches from the 1930s onwards, and some moved into directorships.[46]

In the summer of 1926 John Swire & Sons started hiring British university graduates on a substantial and systematic basis. Six joined that year, one in 1927, three in 1929 and four in 1930. In total, 14 of the 24 men recruited in London as probationers for Butterfield & Swire in that period were graduates.[47] DOCA's Tom Lindsay was one of these. Son of an Indian Civil Service administrator, he was inclined to look overseas for work upon graduation, but China was an accidental choice. Set up with some interviews by the University of Cambridge's 'appointments board', he accepted the first offer of employment he received, and that came from John Swire & Sons. Lindsay's induction was short, and he spent it shadowing the work of the experienced older clerk on the Blue Funnel desk in London. After work he studied book-keeping and took lessons in elementary Mandarin at the School of Oriental Studies. There he studied with Sir Reginald Johnston, sometime chief administrator of the British-leased territory at Weihaiwei, and the last emperor's English tutor. Johnston was no language teacher, however, and largely reminisced, so while Lindsay was one of only a handful of Swire employees who formally studied anything about the country before they left for it, the China he learned about from Johnston scarcely survived in the land of the Guomindang.[48]

The complexity of the firm's activities was one reason the company needed to develop a cadre of men who would in time lead the firm, and not simply serve their time out in it. It had long passed the era of sending out clerks, for there were well-educated Chinese ones aplenty to be found. A continuing exception was gendered: British women were still sent out from home to work as stenographers, largely to work with managers and in private offices in order to retain confidentiality. There were at least 14 of them by the end of 1923 (including one university graduate). There was a limit to how far the new Chinese organisation was to be developed within Taikoo. It was not that Chinese staff could not be trusted, although popular British attitudes certainly thought this; it was instead most likely a practice underpinned by the assumption that they might be vulnerable to external pressure (from those untame elements, for example).[49]

The key reason the firm set out to build up its graduate recruits – some 60 per cent of annual recruiting by 1936 – was the profound changes in the culture of Chinese business and politics.[50] New China was run by highly educated, urbane cosmopolitans. There were exceptions, but the greater part of those in positions of influence and authority were men best engaged with by their equals. The old-style B&S man, trained in a 'good' school and technically proficient, often lacked the wider vision and sympathies, and networks, that might be developed by those with more advanced education. Similarly, British diplomats and consuls found themselves negotiating with men who were far their superiors in terms of educational attainment. It made a difference. No other strategy was going to work, certainly not the one seriously discussed in early 1927, with Wanxian still in ruins: making a documentary film. London relayed a proposal it rather liked to Hong Kong and Shanghai. How about commissioning a film, and then arrange showings in cinemas in China? It could highlight the operations of 'the British companies that have their home in China', showing labour conditions, and that 'the British, after all is said and done, are really quite decent people to work with'. BAT had its own studio. TSR liked this idea; it could show the workings of the plant and the 'native village'. Taikoo Dockyard agreed, as it 'would help to dispose of the false statements made by those whose only wish is to cause trouble'. Shanghai concurred, and when 'the present agitation subsides' thought it should be explored further.[51] This was written in the days after armed Communist Party units had just seized control of parts of the city, its leadership arguing for an immediate surrender of the foreign concessions. The plea that if only 'they' better understood 'us' was an old one, but in fact 'they' did understand 'us', and always had, but they did not like what they saw. The idea was dropped.

Butterfield & Swire continued to face one significant challenge over which it had much less control than its own organisation and modes of operation: the fractious politics of the British presence in China. Long rather neglected by diplomats, British residents in Shanghai especially considered themselves politically autonomous by right, and not by the haphazard accident of the development of the International Settlement, and their vehicle was the Shanghai Municipal Council, elected by, and, it was argued only answerable to, its ratepayers. Until 1928 that franchise was restricted to treaty power nationals only: Chinese were excluded. There were other areas of exclusion and structural and racist discrimination in council practice and policies. On top of this, the SMC had responded with little tact or flexibility to the disaster of 30 May 1925. Swires had long kept out of municipal politics, although E. F. Mackay had joined the council in the early 1920s, but now the company engaged directly with it and as a matter of some urgency. Neilage Brown was transferred from Hong Kong in 1929 to take over as Shanghai Taipan, and moved quickly to join the council. He also engaged in a frenetic campaign to 'cultivate' – the favourite word – contacts with Chinese officials and prominent and influential figures in the city, and they became an important part of the Shanghai manager's job. Working with other figures, the British Minister Sir Miles Lampson, and the new Jardine Matheson leadership in China, brothers John and Tony Keswick, among others, firms like B&S aimed to rein in the inflammatory actions and at least smother the angry rhetoric of the more conservative British residents.

Swires was also one of a number of firms that contributed to the costs of the informal diplomatic efforts of Sir Frederick Whyte, former British MP and then active in India, who was sent to China to try and ameliorate the generally poor state of relations between British and Chinese circles. When out in Shanghai in 1929, Warren Swire reported that thanks to Whyte he kept on 'meeting Chinese ministers and commercial and political magnates', to 'lay the foundations for personal relations'. A personal scandal meant that Whyte's mission went awry, but the momentum was maintained. That former British diplomatic negligence was superseded by a strong attention to the detail of solving the 'Shanghai problem' (a coupling of words that headed a thousand articles). Diplomats worked in partnership with big business to bring the 'small treaty port people', and 'Shanghailanders' to order, and to neuter their ability again to cause such havoc as they had in 1925. The firms that came to the fore in this new dispensation were mostly those with wider international interests as well – ICI, the Asiatic Petroleum Company (through its parent, Royal Dutch Shell), and British American Tobacco. Jardines and Swires, along with the Hongkong & Shanghai Bank, were the largest of the China-based firms, and worked within this new partnership to salvage a British future in a nationalist China. The work of men like Whyte and the more fleet of foot British diplomats was critical to this. The need for better relations was soon clearly mutual. Colin Scott found himself in October 1931 invited with other British businessmen to watch the presidential review in Nanjing to mark China's national day. Afterwards he was introduced to Chiang Kai-shek, and then dined with the others, his own table's host Song Ziwen.[52] With Japanese forces at that moment rampaging through Manchuria, the once-hated British were cultivated assiduously by the Guomindang.

Directors and managers directed a great deal of energy into this sort of diplomacy, but of course the business of the Swire companies remained business. As well as their Chinese problems, the global economic environment threw up steep challenges. The effects of the Great Depression that followed the 1929 Wall Street Crash were slower to reach China, but John Swire & Sons was a company working across other markets, and was sensitive to conditions in Britain as well. It fought to cut costs, reducing all salaries by 10 per cent, for example, and cutting down on any expenses it could slimline. It also invested in a new operation, a paint factory in Shanghai that was developed after 1933 (firmly in the tradition of venturing into a new business about which it knew practically nothing), but its focus remained on ships, the dockyard, insurance and sugar. The revolution proved disastrous for sugar.[53] Political opposition, disorder and a very strong new challenge from Japanese competitors, led TSR to overhaul its policies and practices completely in 1928/9. A new refinery complex was completed in late 1926, but spent most of 1927 shuttered (rents were waived on company housing during these periods). In 1928 the managers decided to refocus on producing only high-grade refined sugar. It shut down the upcountry selling organisation altogether, liquidating stock and dispensing with its agents. Despite its undoubted successes, it was too expensive to maintain this network in such an uncertain time. A severe cost-cutting programme in Hong Kong also saw the replacement of 21 foreign-staffed posts with retrained Chinese operatives. Blue Funnels took back to Scotland many 'old servants' of the company who were made redundant. The jobs of these sugar boilers, assistant engineers, storekeepers, housemen and timekeepers were filled by Chinese apprentices who had been trained up to take the roles in a successful move that was then held up as a model more widely across the Swire companies. They were no less efficient, possibly more so, and they were certainly cheaper.[54]

This refocus was economically and politically sensible. As well as prioritising high-grade sugar, Taikoo bought a cubing plant from its rival, the China Sugar Refinery, when that was wound up in May 1928, and in September 1931, having transferred part of it to Shanghai on a CNCo ship, began producing carton sugar there, which proved a 'profitable venture'. Shanghai newspapers carried news of the arrival in stores of stocks of presentation boxes of sugar after production began in Hong Kong in 1929, but there was also energetic marketing far from China, especially to India.[55] Here the company tapped into Hong Kong/Bombay Parsi networks, hiring Burjor Talati, son of the head of a prominent firm in the colony, and a Hong Kong University graduate. Talati, a 'find', began as an interpreter and quickly proved his worth, working in Bombay until his early death in 1933 when he was succeeded by another Parsi, E. D. Damri, who took Jock Swire along to the Calcutta bazaar in 1935 to show him where Taikoo sugar was being sold: new territory for the Swire interests.[56]

By the mid-1930s TSR reported sales in India and Malaya, most other Southeast Asian markets, East and South Africa, and even in Canada and the United States, markets from which the company had long been absent. If in China Taikoo sugar had one identity, and that Chinese, in India it had quite another. There it was 'An Empire Sugar', 'British and Pure', in its marketing, it was 'refined and packed in the British colony of Hong Kong by a British firm', 'untouched by hand'. It was, directed the advertiser's brief, pure, hygienically made, cheap, unadulterated, and British.[57] These themes were highlighted because the name 'Taikoo' suggested, to those unfamiliar with it, that the firm was either Chinese or Japanese. Packaging that used Chinese text, or symbols, did not help.

New designs incorporating Hindi text or English only, with no hint of any chinoiserie, were developed. (In China itself, a new design was introduced that incorporated a laughing Buddha, and used the shade of blue found on the Guomindang's flag and that of the Republic.) The focus in the early 1930s was on building up brand awareness. The preferred vehicle, though expensive, was the British humorous weekly magazine *Punch*. This was the venue for a large campaign that began in late 1932: 'Sugar East of Suez! Something New! Taikoo Sugar' ran the advertisements, positioning Taikoo as an empire product at a time when 'Empire preference' was a topic of much political debate.[58] Before 1931 the company had never advertised in English at all; now Taikoo could be found in among such household names as Player's and Three Castles cigarettes, Lindt Chocolate, Oxo, Listerine and Pepsodent (as well it might).

The new international focus on TSR sales had become even more important in the 1930s. Having established its authority, the Guomindang's National Government secured the return of tariff autonomy in 1929, its first major success in renegotiating the mid-nineteenth-century treaties. It now had a mechanism to build its fiscal resource and set out to use it, and raised tariffs on sugar among other products. This was challenge enough: Taikoo's refinery was now outside China's tariff wall. But the government's hold over its former base of Guangdong province was challenged and rebuffed by a strong provincial regime, and one that had its own economic development policies, and sugar was important to those.[59] The Guangdong authorities introduced a monopoly on the import, distribution and sale of white sugar, and, given the prominence of the Mok interests, it was only to be expected that Mok Ying Kwai would play a leading role in the supervisory body. This move was aimed at stimulating production in Guangdong itself, as well as securing revenue for the regime.

Pragmatism won through. TSR became one of a number of firms from which the monopoly secured refined sugar – through brokers – which it then sold within the province as its own products. This was quietly sanctioned by Taikoo. A 1932 report noted that most sales in Hong Kong went to the 'Mok or other smuggling organisation', and on into China.[60] Discussion rumbled on among the directors about closing down the refinery and establishing a new one in Shanghai, but while the discreet partnership with the Guangdong monopoly provided some respite from the problems facing TSR, which was also succoured by the intense anti-Japanese boycott campaign that followed the invasion of Manchuria, a volatile new environment was engendered along the coast as state and private interests smuggled sugar into Guangdong, and a wave of violence swept maritime southern China.

This was a truly transformative decade in the orientation and character of the company. It had never been static, for neither the ambition of the directors, nor the politics of China or global affairs, allowed it an easy ride. But in the 10-year period that began in blood and anger at the end of May 1925, its operations changed – not always as it would have liked – it adapted a truly radical new way of working and relationships with its Chinese staff and it assumed a leading role in the politics of China-British relations. These had reached one of their lowest points in 1925–7, and Swire interests were caught up in the clashes and confrontations of the period, and sparked at least two of them. But the directors who sailed east in the 1930s found the doors open for discussions with Chinese officials and politicians. When Jock Swire visited in spring 1935 he had two meetings with Song Ziwen, the second at the minister's own request. The principle subject was shipping: the China Merchants Company had been taken over by the National Government, whose long-term ambition was to build an effective Chinese merchant marine, barring from operating on China's coasts and rivers shipping from states that did not reciprocate this surrender of its sovereignty. What, Swire wanted to know, were the prospects for formal 'Anglo-Chinese' co-operation? What if China Navigation opened itself to Chinese capital, or what chance might a new jointly owned company have? (And Taikoo had already invested in joint companies to run on the lakes and Upper Yangzi.) These were significant discussions, but what catches the eye is the report of Jock's closing statement:

> We had been so long in China that we felt that we belonged to the country, and intended to stay in it whatever changes time might bring about. That, if and when the time came when the Chinese government introduced reservation, we would presumably have to move with the times as we have done many times before, and haul down the British flag.[61]

His point was not that they would fold it and leave; they would instead raise another: China's. This statement was more than what sensible diplomacy required. It signalled an acceptance of the need entirely to surrender the privileges of empire that had long supported the Swire interests in China – its profile outside China was, of course, another matter – and a commitment to a transformation that might permit the operation of the company in a post-colonial state. It stands out clearly as a firm acknowledgement that the company was ready to transform itself yet further as China transformed itself. This in time China would do, but first the country faced its severest challenge yet: all-out war with Japan.

Catastrophe

Over three bitingly cold days in early December 1937, scores of dockers carried some 5,000 crates of cargo slung from bamboo poles up gangplanks and on to the CNCo's steamer *Whangpu*. Moored at the dockside at Xiaguan, the port area just outside Nanjing's high city walls, the 320-foot *Whangpu* had been built at Quarry Bay and launched in November 1920. 'She embodies', the Hong Kong Taipan had ventured (as such men were prone to on these occasions), 'the overseas spirit of British enterprise': built by a British firm in a British colony for the British shipping trade on the Yangzi. The ship's career had been largely uneventful before the month that opened with these wet chilly mornings in Nanjing. Now, as the labourers set to haul the crates aboard, they were time and time again interrupted by Japanese air raids that had been hammering the defenceless city for over three months. As warning klaxons were heard, the shipmaster, William McKenzie, a 42-year-old Scot with 17 years' service in the company, ordered the ship to be moved out into the river close to the British gunboats that were moored there. The planes gone, loading resumed. The *Whangpu* had been chartered at the behest of President Chiang Kai-shek's office to carry this cargo upriver to Wuhan. Deputed to arrange matters, the secretary to the British Boxer Indemnity Committee, Han Lih-wu, had begged funds from the Customs Commissioner to pay the dockworkers to move the crates, which otherwise would have remained on the quayside, for the Japanese army was close at hand, and a general panic had set in.[1]

Han watched the crates loading, the dockers having to force their way through a desperate crowd as they carried their loads on to the ship. Meanwhile, *Whangpu*'s sister ship *Wantung* had been chartered by the government China Travel Service to evacuate its staff, and was now carrying the Post Office inspectorate staff and its archives, and *Wuchang* was carrying 'the whole of the Ministry of Health'. Staff, equipment and records of universities and colleges boarded CNCo ships. *Shasi* had taken on board the Central Bank; *Siangtan* also the Post Office; while Butterfield & Swire's Wuhan office had been asked for vessels to carry six shiploads of banknotes west from Changsha to Chongqing. Nationalist China was in flight, moving its personnel, its records and its cash. Civilians fled: 1,500 passengers a ship were being carried out of Shanghai; and industry was being relocated, with machinery from dismantled factories being ferried along the old Grand Canal from the city all the way to Zhenjiang to await transhipment. Refugees rushed ships when any docked at the port, desperate to flee. The *Whangpu* already had on board machinery from a chemical plant, as well as staff and records from one of Nanjing's universities. When it departed, recalled one of the crew, it was 'packed with refugees, many hanging on outside the main cabin rails until, gradually, they could find a foothold on the inside'.[2]

On 7 July at a village near Beijing, Japanese and Chinese troops had engaged in a firefight, and the fragile type of peace that had held since early 1933 was brought to an end.[3] Chiang Kai-shek, who had faced mounting popular pressure to resist continued Japanese encroachments – and had even been held hostage in December 1936 in Xi'an by senior Nationalist commanders in a bid to try to force him to commit to fight – decided at last to take a stand. After the initial skirmish, the Japanese demanded further concessions in the north (after having occupied Manchuria, they had already secured a demilitarised buffer zone south of the Great Wall), then occupied Beijing and Tianjin, which they already largely surrounded. Chiang decided to confront the enemy at Shanghai, where all the world might watch and so be forced to intervene. It certainly watched, and it photographed and filmed, and reporters filed reams of copy; but no one intervened. The politics of Europe were growing fragile; the United States remained isolationist. China's best troops – armies new-trained by German advisers – were thrown into the fray, and there they were destroyed – 30,000 officers were killed or wounded – as the enemy convoyed more forces in across the Sea of Japan. The suburbs outside the settlement and concession at

Shanghai were devastated, but bombs fell inside as well on 14 August, leaving the refugee-packed Nanjing road a charnel house. Images of this horror were very widely circulated. A popular novelist, Vicki Baum, set straight off to turn the tragedy into a bestselling novel. Nobody else did much.

Shanghai secured, the Japanese pushed west, advancing rapidly towards Suzhou and on the north bank of the Yangzi towards Yangzhou, columns of tanks and troops dashing across the rich farmlands of the Yangzi River delta towards the Nationalist capital, eager for the glory of seizing the city. Shattered by the fighting at Shanghai, the Nationalist armies could not hold them back, and Japanese dominance in the air meant that they could attack Chinese formations at will. One estimate indicates that at the very least nine million Chinese eventually made their way west to Sichuan, following the Nationalist capital first to Wuhan, which then fell in late October 1938, and after that on to Chongqing. But there were scores of millions more on the march before the war ended, each seeking a foothold on safety, somewhere, anywhere. Well might they flee. Rumours of atrocities being committed as the Japanese advanced struck terror across Nanjing in the days before it fell to them on 12 December. Rumour proved right; the victors killed tens of thousands of captured soldiers and the civilians still in the city, disregarding a safety zone set up for non-combatants, and despoiling the capital in a foul atrocity quickly labelled the 'Rape of Nanking'. The ill-discipline was sanctioned by their commanders, some of whom would eventually be hanged for this crime.[4] And it was rightly named: women bore the brunt of the assault; large numbers of them were raped and large numbers were slaughtered.

The war would last for eight years, halfway through becoming subsumed within the wider conflicts in Europe and Asia of the Second World War. But for four years it ran its own ghastly course, and no other powers became involved (and even those Germans were withdrawn in 1938). The Japanese, at least nominally, respected the status of foreign-controlled concessions and the international settlements. Hong Kong was largely untouched by the conflict, but its population grew, especially after the fall of Guangzhou to the Japanese in October 1938, and it became a major transportation hub for the refugee republic at Chongqing. Foreign firms continued to operate on both sides of the front line, which was in any case often a quite porous boundary.[5]

Ships continued to sail, at least outside the battlefields. CNCo would maintain services from Shanghai to Japanese-held Tianjin in the north, and to Nationalist-held cities in the south. On the early morning of 3 December, bedecked with Union Jacks painted on each side, on its awnings and sun deck, CNCo's *Whangpu* was one of those ships, carrying west to Wuhan a thousand tons of material that some thought embodied the spirit of China: the treasures of the old palace of the Manchus – the Forbidden City – including paintings, screens, ceramics and other antiquities that formed the collections of the National Palace Museum. There were no guards, only Han Lih-wu, at McKenzie's insistence accompanying this thousand-ton cargo of China's history. Because of the crush of refugees that grew as it got ready to sail, the ship kept a 15-foot distance from the quayside. Han recalled having to leap for a rope and then being hauled on board.[6]

Captain McKenzie spoke to the press about his task shortly after arriving in Shanghai later in December.[7] The antiquities were well known overseas, for in an unprecedented move, aimed precisely at garnering international sympathy for China's plight, the National Government had allowed over a thousand items to be conveyed to London in 1935 where they formed the core of a sensational exhibition at the Royal Academy. Stored in Nanjing after their return, their evacuation further west to safety had been hamstrung until Han Lih-wu secured cash to pay the dockers, and the British embassy asked Butterfield & Swire to assist. The whole episode provided 'recompense, however small, for the burning of the Summer Palace', wrote the *Manchester Guardian*, smugly.[8] Warren Swire, CNCo managing director at this time, pointed to the rescue in his annual report, and his own visits to China had always included lengthy visits to the National Palace Museum. But this episode was largely overshadowed at the time by its immediate sequel. Having offloaded its cargo at Wuhan after its three-day voyage upstream, the *Whangpu* returned to Nanjing. There it was held with a handful of other British vessels, including the *Wantung*, under the eyes of two naval vessels, waiting to be convoyed down the river.[9] On 10 December the British consul ordered an evacuation. *Whangpu* took on board some 25 foreign nationals, including staff of the British and German embassies, and Chinese Customs Service personnel, as well as 350 Chinese women and children, and 800 men. The Butterfield & Swire and CNCo employees and their families, office furniture and records, and even the office car (with its chauffeur and his family) were moved on to a CNCo lighter. The ships moved three miles upriver, away from the fighting that now enveloped the city but there, on 11 December, they were deliberately targeted by Japanese heavy artillery, which fired at the *Whangpu* for over an hour, and then the following day, having moved over 10 miles further west, they were attacked by Japanese fighters and bombers. The British gunboats warded off some of the onslaught with fire from their own guns, but still the bombs fell in among the merchant ships causing widespread but largely superficial damage, and a great deal of terror.

To seek some safety from further attack, the ships were that night moored in line alongside the high banks of the river, and McKenzie ordered his passengers and crew to prepare to seek shelter from early the following morning until dusk in the tall reeds that grew by the banks, and in the villages nearby. Looters rushed on to the deserted ship as soon as people disembarked. Some were rounded up by McKenzie and his officers 'and suitably dealt with', after which the foreign members of the crew stood guard, revolvers drawn, when not flinging themselves into muddy ditches as Japanese aircraft flew by. But contact had been made with the Japanese by then, and the actual attacks ceased. After making some repairs, and under naval protection, most of the passengers having returned, the ships made their way to Shanghai, arriving on 17 December. Some of the crew had deserted. McKenzie asked that they be treated leniently: 'some of them have become temporarily mentally deranged', he concluded. His own report was bitter in tone, as well it might be, written as it was in the immediate aftermath of the harrowing attack. Rex Warren, an Australian journalist who was on the *Whangpu* when it was shelled, retold the episode instead as one of British pluck and Chinese panic, with a soup course left unfinished in the dining saloon, and the air rent with the howling of the ship's dog and the crying of its cat.[10] But still, it had been a terrifying episode. Well, responded the Japanese, it was a battlefield, they could see no flags because of fog and a curtain of black smoke from the steamers, evidently put up deliberately, and anyway they had orders to sink all enemy vessels. The British refuted each and every one of these claims.[11]

There were other attacks. The deliberate strafing and sinking of the American gunboat USS *Panay* with four fatalities on 12 December, the same day as the air attacks on the *Whangpu*, shocked America,

an impact heightened by widely screened newsreel film of the entire
attack taken by Norman Alley, one of several correspondents on board,
as the bombs fell and sailors fired back. The British gunboats HMS
Ladybird and *Bee* were also shelled and machine-gunned, and a medical
orderly was killed. Swire and Jardine shipping at Wuhu was bombed,
repeatedly, and godowns, too, with one receiving a 'direct hit ...
through the Union Jack' painted on the roof. So much for neutrality.
A hulk was burned out. Three Chinese employees were confirmed
killed, eight wounded, and two vanished, 'believed blown to pieces'.[12]
Lighters and tug crews mutinied, but most ships kept moving. Formal
protests were transmitted, compensation claims filed, the costs of
repairs totted up and compassionate grants to families assessed. Tom
Lindsay watched the burning of Shanghai's Chinese suburbs from the
roof of the Butterfield & Swire hong (and took photographs from up
there as well), and then went back downstairs to work on preparing
claims for compensation.[13] The Japanese rolled on into central China
along the river, seized Qingdao in the north and bombed Wuhan and
other cities. The International Settlement at Shanghai was surrounded
by Japanese-controlled territory, and of course the invaders formed part
of the International Settlement administration, as a treaty power, even
if one that was at war with China, though no war was yet declared.
While the victors moved to set up a collaborationist administration in
the areas of the city outside international control, Nationalist guerrillas
commenced a terrorist campaign against them within the settlement,
and Japanese agents responded in kind.

The terrifying chaos of winter 1937 was a new feature for the Swire
firms to deal with, and it would be repeated in the years to come as
other cities fell. But some observers saw it simply as a continuation of
the unsettled conditions that they believed characterised contemporary
China. When, they would ask, had China ever been stable in the decades
since the fall of the Qing? There had been uprisings, and warlord scraps,
and large-scale civil wars, then the Nationalist Revolution, and then
in turn rebellions against the Nationalists. Political power, any power,
seemed to grow out of the barrel of guns imported from overseas, despite
an arms embargo enforced from 1919 to 1929 by the major powers.
Militarists hogged the political stage; bandits and pirates plagued land,
river and coast. 'It's just the natives fighting', the Hongkong & Shanghai
Bank's managing director provocatively told two of the many travellers

sent to cover the war, poet W. H. Auden and novelist Christopher Isherwood.[14] Unlike responses to the war of 1931/2, far fewer Britons in China this time believed that the Japanese had any case, and most instinctively sided with the Chinese – and it was Chinese civilians who could clearly be seen in most photographs and film to be bearing the brunt of the Japanese campaign – while the vocal few foreigners who did support Japan were often well paid to do so.[15] Steadily, too, it also became more and more apparent that the Japanese aimed not just to suborn China, but to drive out other foreign interests as well.

The view that violence and disorder were endemic was a useful one for those who opposed the surrender of extraterritoriality and reform of the treaties, which had been given a stay of execution by the Japanese assault on China after 1931. There was more of a germ of truth in the picture of a nation in which power was fractured and in which there was a sizeable gap between the National Government's calm and persistent assertion of its legitimacy and its authority, and the lawlessness that now seemed to be ingrained. As well as militarist resistance outside the core regions the Nationalists controlled, in central south-east China it had also faced down a self-proclaimed Soviet Republic, the largest of several highland regions held by the scattered but growing forces organised by the battered Chinese Communist Party. There were party activists elsewhere, of course, even, one record shows, a small 'steamship' cell on CNCo's *Woosung* in early 1933. In 1934, throttled by a government blockade, and facing imminent collapse, the Communists had retreated on what they would later recast as a 'long march', the survivors making a new base centred on Yan'an in Shaanxi province. One of those who made his way there was a former CNCo mariner, one of the Ningbo crews, Zhu Baoting. Zhu begun sailing on CNCo ships in about 1893 and had been involved in union activities since 1914, joined the Communist Party in 1922 and held leadership positions in the Communist labour movement.[16] There will have been others who had sailed or worked under the Taikoo flag, and who now fought under a red one. The Yan'an base was saved from extinction by the Japanese invasion, and the Communists would from that point onwards bide their time, husband and grow their forces and let the Nationalists defend China against the invader.

The company that faced this crisis was, of course, in some important ways different from the one that faced the challenges of the mid-1920s.

In July 1927, after serving first as Senior and then as chairman since 1912, Jack Swire stepped down, and was succeeded by his brother Warren. 'For 40 years I have placed the interests of the business before everything', and it was time 'to leave my business interest in the hands of my co-directors'.[17] This probably made little immediate difference to the direction of the firm, although Jack probably continued to provide some restraint on Warren's aggressive temperament, but it marked a historic break with the era of John Samuel Swire, for none remaining had worked with the Senior, and while Warren always wore his father's watch chain, he was not John Samuel Swire, whatever he might have thought. Who ran what within the company board is difficult to say. As well as chairing John Swire & Sons, Warren was clearly focused on CNCo, while his nephew Jock Swire largely saw to staff, for example. (The death in action back in 1915 of Jack Swire's younger son Glen, who had been set for working in the firm alongside Jock, would in time come significantly to affect the character of the management of the firm, for it meant that one potential family counterweight to Warren had been removed.) However, the collective nature of Private Office decision-making, of which there is very little by way of record, makes it difficult to assess the individual contributions of each of the directors, including H. W. Robertson who had been brought in from the staff in China. A later assessment suggests that Jack was probably acting less in any hands-on fashion and more as a non-executive director by the 1920s. Having resigned his position as Master of the Essex Hunt in 1910, due to the press of business, he resumed it in 1922, just as he turned 60, suggesting that by then he was less active at his desk in Billiter Square. At his death in May 1933, the lengthy obituary in the *Essex Chronicle* is testament to Jack Swire's keenest interests as a prominent figure in county society and China got barely a mention. And he had little by way of any profile in China or Hong Kong, which he had rarely visited, but for six months CNCo ships sailed with a blue mourning band added to their hulls.[18]

CNCo provides a good focus for examining the Swire story in these war years and in the years before. Its fate was, of course, both always wrapped up in China's and, because of its role as feeder for Blue Funnel's British and its Pacific services as well as for Butterfield & Swire's other agencies, including the Australia Oriental Line which sailed via Manila to Queensland, Sydney and Melbourne, and shipper for Taikoo Sugar, it was intertwined with the travails of the global economy. The critical international challenge was the Great Depression that set in after 1929, exacerbated in the shipping world by very significant over-capacity globally, a legacy of the First World War and government programmes in the United States and Japan, in particular, but more widely as well. To an extent, China's own economic course was unaffected and the impact of the slump was muted.[19] What hit CNCo hardest was a sharp fall in exchange, which meant that Chinese receipts delivered far less in sterling to John Swire & Sons than formerly. Stores routinely purchased in Britain shot up in price. Salary exchange commitments increased in cost. Significant economies were sought across the operations of all the Swire firms, including an across-the-board 10 per cent cut in salaries in 1931. When this same exercise had been carried out in 1927, China Navigation Company operations largely ground to a halt in the face of a sustained strike by officers and engineers. This time there was no strike.

The economy drive was comprehensive and while, for example, conditions of service and quality of life for foreign staff in China remained better by far than they would have been at home – and unemployment among mariners in Britain was substantial, with some drift of those seeking employment out to Asia – the sweeter aspects of the floating life were reassessed. The groaning table and lengthy bills of fare preserved in Frank Davies's papers, for example, disappeared, although they still seem plentiful. 'Profits are the results of economy quite as much as of increased earnings,' wrote Warren Swire in December 1931, and menus were certainly not exempt. Nor, for example, were the hock, port and liqueur glasses once routinely carried. These were to be dispensed with. Sherry glasses might remain, but must have a measuring line added to them. All such stores were assessed, but Warren Swire's attention to the minutiae of company operations is striking: double-line spacing in correspondence ought to be discontinued, paper would thereby be saved. Blue Funnel also instigated comprehensive cost-cutting programmes in response to the crisis that were in large measure a factor in its own recovery from a significant fall in revenues from 1929. A staunchly patriotic advocate for 'buying British', Warren Swire had to admit to opting for Chinese suppliers for many lines in 1930, although some British firms were able to match prices in China. In his patrician way, Swire blamed the 'proletariat' for its wage demands, and government for high taxation.[20] London's attention to detail was indicative of the continued tight control over all Butterfield & Swire operations exercised from Billiter Square. The firm was 'directed by a set of autocrats in London', complained new recruit Maurice Scott in 1934, or, rather, he added, by one in particular. This was, of course, Warren Swire. 'The ships were his ships, the agents' houses were his houses,' wrote Tom Lindsay; later, 'It was his firm'. This had a deadening effect on individual initiative and the culture of the company, Lindsay reflected, for rare was the employee who wished to get anything wrong or draw attention to himself.[21]

Economy also meant renewal. Until 1935 CNCo continued replacing the older vessels in its fleet, but also reduced it quite dramatically in size. In 1931 the company employed nearly 400 foreign officers and engineers, and some 9,500 Chinese staff, 6,900 of them on the 61 steamers, 2 diesel motor vessels, 11 tugs and 39 lighters it was operating at the end of the year, and 2,600 ashore in its network of wharves, godowns and other installations.[22] Between 1929 and 1940 16 new ships were built, nine of them at the Taikoo Dockyard, and 37 went out of service, a cut that reflected a worldwide trend to reduce tonnage (and cut salary costs: between 1929 and late 1931 the number of foreign marine staff fell by 60). Most vessels that left the firm were sold to ship-breakers, but nine were casualties: *Kanting*, gutted by fire; *Ichang*, damaged beyond repair at Xiamen during a typhoon (two others were lost this way at Hong Kong); while three were stranded beyond recovery on the Yangzi, including the 50-year old *Ngankin*. Only in March 1933, when a sizeable complement of the crew and male passengers on board the seven-year-old steamer *Antung* panicked was there significant loss of life. In heavy seas and very poor visibility, the ship struck rocks on the shore of Hainan island on its way from Shantou to Singapore with 420 passengers, mostly migrant labourers, and 111 crew. After the order to abandon ship was given, two of the lifeboats were rushed and capsized. The captain, R. H. G. Ashby, 19 years in the company's service, was exonerated of all blame, but resigned. His wife and son were only rescued when a Russian guard and the only British passenger dived in and brought them back on board the ship. Some 70 people died.[23] New technology, in the shape of radio, quickly made a difference to the ability of ships to signal distress and secure help. CNCo's *Anhui* had quickly come on the scene, but no technology could truly help a shipmaster always safely to navigate foul and dangerous seas, and human error, frailty and fear inevitably undermined such advances, too.

The principal manifestation of China's unsettled state that faced the Swire operations was coastal piracy, which became a problem in the second half of the 1920s, but labour relations were also rocky, despite a steady extension to staff across its interests of provident schemes. The years before the invasion in 1937 had been turbulent ones, but overall CNCo had been kept profitably busy. While Swire directors out east engaged in the high politics of cohabitation with China's National Government, the firm's managers battled to maintain their allotted share of the pool arrangements that still structured core operations. On the Upper Yangzi the firm admitted defeat, and piloted one form of collaboration by transferring ships to a new Taikoo Chinese Navigation Company in 1930, for: 'we shall never get fair treatment,' claimed Warren Swire, when reporting this move to the firm's annual general meeting, 'until we amalgamate in some way with influential local Chinese.'[24] On this stretch of the river the nationalist politics of the provincial power-holder, Liu Xiang, were too strong to fight. And it was Liu that the Royal Navy had taken on at Wanxian, and the bitter legacy of that shambles continued to haunt CNCo: the boycott was not lifted until 1935. The company also fought and lost two further battles: one aimed at securing complete control of its ships, the other aiming to force the British government to pay the costs of piracy protection.

At the start of the 1930s, control over cargo-handling operations and passenger accommodation remained in the hands of ship compradors, as it always had. But as this model of devolved control and extensive shadow organisations was being reformed elsewhere in the Butterfield & Swire operations, it was logical to attempt to deal with it on the ships as well. The situation there gained greater urgency because Chinese passengers were no longer willing to tolerate the poor treatment that they had received on foreign-owned ships. Historically these had been designed as strictly segregated spaces, arrangements that had been reinforced in the courts in Hong Kong, and that had long been tolerated.[25] While the importance of changes in passenger expectations had started to be recognised, and these were made manifest in the designs of newer vessels in which better arrangements were made for a more mixed Chinese passenger complement, the legacy of outdated cabin accommodation (as well as sanitation and catering) remained a problem. So, one letter ponders, shall we rename the First Class 'Second' (and change fares), then Saloon can become First? Will Chinese passengers be likely to travel Saloon and eat foreign food? Can we make arrangements to serve Chinese and foreign dishes in the same class of travel? No, was the conclusion. If Saloon (which by 1931 was a euphemism for 'foreign') became First, might the old 'Chinese First Class' become Intermediate? And how were standards to be made consistent if each ship comprador was entirely responsible, as indeed they were, for furnishing his vessel's saloon? These discussions are somewhat bewildering to follow, but the key point is that passenger expectations were changing. While better-off Chinese travellers generally took berths on ocean liners when they moved from port to port, and not CNCo's coasters (not least as the cabin accommodation was always better), even the 'lower middle classes', 'superior artisans' and 'coolies' who patronised respectively CNCo's first-, second- and third-class accommodation, expected more. London now directed that the firm take control and 'run it properly'.[26]

Another issue that needed to be dealt with was the on-board activity of the passenger attendants, known in English as teaboys, or cabin boys (these were 'boys' only in the lingua franca of the colonial world, where a male servant was always 'boy'). These men effectively bought their posts from the ship compradors. As these were, as they saw it, their own property, it was not in the gift of any company – and CNCo was not alone in facing this problem – to take it from them. The economics of the teaboy system were more complex yet. Ship compradors appointed (for a fee) a chief steward, who appointed (for a fee) some 'No. 2's, who sold on the teaboy posts for – one police report had it – $20 a round trip. No. 2s would often sell more posts than any ship could reasonably support. The teaboys recouped the expense by selling refreshments, snacks and cigarettes, and by demanding tips – if not extorting them – sums representing a large proportion of the actual fare. Some compradors took a cut from these.[27] There was obviously an urgent imperative for teaboys to recoup their initial outlay and make a profit, and this routinely led to unpleasant interaction with passengers and during the crisis of the war with Japan in 1931/2, when the ships carried large numbers of refugees, to 'unbridled robbery', especially of the poorest. They were also routinely involved in smuggling salt, opium and in fact anything that might profitably and easily be carried, including additional passengers. In the aftermath of the 1931 piracy of the *Hanyang*, 101 passengers were identified as having been on the ship: but only 15 were officially recorded. The others were hidden in the crew rooms.[28] They had all paid for their passage, but CNCo would see nothing of their fare.

Smuggling was often brazen. Contraband (known as 'pidgin') was 'usually rushed on board by a gang of roughs a few moments before the vessels leave the wharf', reported the customs at Wuhan in 1934. It was routinely dropped overboard to waiting craft as ports were entered. It was equally routinely often seized by the customs, and the companies were fined. And when, for example, one consignment of opium being readied for taking on board CNCo's *Whangpu* in this way was seized by the customs, the smugglers fought back, retrieved it and carried in on board. Ship compradors knew better than to contest gangster infiltration, and were not necessarily distant from it, for they were known to intercede for the return of contraband goods when they were seized. As one reportedly put it in 1931, it would be 'great trouble' for him if this was not done. Were masters and mates also taking bribes, asked Warren Swire – more than once – in discussions about this aspect of the problem, for customs fines were cumulatively a costly nuisance. Opinion differs on this, but they were also certainly smart enough not to elicit 'great trouble' for themselves by looking too closely.[29] Those who ultimately ran these smuggling operations were not gentle people. CNCo was not alone in the moves it eventually took against the teaboy 'menace' (as it was routinely labelled). The China Merchants line also acted – one of its ships carried 564 of them, when 170 would have sufficed. 'They do no work in the ship,' reported the chief officer of the Indo-China Steam Navigation Company's *Tuckwo*, in 1931, of the 150 'excess' teaboys on his vessel, 'they are here only for running pidgin cargo'. They were a 'powerful uncontrolled lot of men,' reported Warren Swire.[30]

In December 1932 CNCo took initial action, and decided forcibly to remove 126 teaboys from SS *Woosung* and, when they attempted to rejoin the ship on 10 January 1933, prevented this by calling on armed police who 'somewhat severely handled' them. The men were replaced by a very much smaller complement of salaried attendants, hired by the company. It was a decisive move, and would prove profitable, at least as far as the *Woosung*'s earnings were concerned, but only that far. In striking at the teaboys, the firm was taking on a

much larger challenge. That became clear early on when, in petitions
for redress, the *Woosung*'s displaced teaboys called for the intervention
both of the leading Chinese shipping magnate, Yu Xiaqing, and of
Du Yuesheng, 'prominent Frenchtown resident', as he was routinely
described, a key figure within the Shanghai Green Gang. The world
of teaboy employment, unlike that of the Butterfield & Swire branch
compradors, was wholly embedded in that of the quayside gangsters.
There were networks of family and patronage relationships that could
not easily be broken.[31] There were dangers to taking on the Green
Gang as well, as suborned Shanghai French concession officials who
failed to protect the gang's interests against a reformist new consul-
general found out in March 1932: three died, suddenly, in the course
of a single week.[32] Many noticed the coincidence, as they were probably
meant to.

The most sustained opposition in this case came from the Canton
Branch of the Seamen's Union, for the teaboys were also members of
an affiliated Cabin Boys' Union, which launched a strike and boycott
in May 1933 that was at one stage apparently nurtured by funds raised
by 'Sing-Song' girls in a prominent Guangzhou restaurant and that was
only resolved in November at a substantial cost to CNCo. The central
issue in the strike demands was in fact the use of force by the firm, and
the apparent disappearance and alleged death of one of the teaboys.
Although CNCo had to abandon its plan to remove them from its
current fleet, and had to redeploy the *Woosung*'s teaboys elsewhere, it
did at least move to a policy of only employing paid stewards on new
ones.[33] There were, of course, teaboys on the *Whangpu* in December
1937. Their rapid departure was 'the only blessing of the bombing',
Captain McKenzie reported: 'They were the first to flee, and behaved
like rats during the day of terror,' he wrote, no love being lost between
ships' officers and their unwelcome staff. CNCo operations continued
after 1933 to be shaped by this only ever partial control over what
happened on its own vessels. They were also affected by an external
threat: piracy.

On nine occasions after the events at Wanxian CNCo ships were
pirated. Given that the fleets were operating at near-full capacity for
most of the 1930s, the incidence of piracy per day's sailing was very low,
and the loss of life (three killed in the nine incidents) was also small.
But there was a great international public taste for news of Chinese

banditry, kidnappings and piracies, and the reputational cost was also exacerbated by the costs of retrofitting piracy defences on to ships – which, in segregating with grilles and gates the crew and the bridge from the rest of the ship, hardly helped the company regain control of their on-board operations – and in paying for armed piracy guards.

Two incidents stand out. In March 1933 the *Nanchang* was attacked at the mouth of the Liao River as it waited for a pilot to take it into Niuzhuang. Despite a stout armed defence, five of the British crew were taken away, and while one was released with a ransom demand, the others were held for five uncomfortable months on a junk and then in the delta, while their captors bargained for a sufficient ransom. Eventually Butterfield & Swire stumped up $20,000 to cover the bandits' 'expenses' – and reimbursed the British consulate for the opium it had bought for the pirates themselves (the TSR candy they demanded was easier on the corporate conscience) – and the puppet Manchurian authorities provided another $30,000 or so. The 'worst hardship of all', the men told the press on release, was that 'for five months ... we have drunk nothing but water'. 'The bandits were decent enough to offer us Samshu (a Chinese spirit), but we did not like the look of it.' The diary, scribbled on bits of paper and cigarette packs by Chief Officer Clifford Johnson, and which was published the following year, conveys rather more of the occasional terror of their tedious, long captivity, notably the dangerous period when a second band of pirates seized them from the original crew.[34] 'A little more of this life,' they wrote after four months, 'and we won't be worth rescuing ... Kwai-kwai [quick quick] is the watchword now.'[35] After their release Johnson and Second Engineer Archie Blue spoke on the BBC about their experience, and Johnson's book joined such luridly titled volumes as *Vampires of the China Coast*, *Corsairs of the China Seas* and captivity memoirs like 'Tinko' Pawley's *My Bandit Hosts* in the bookshops. Unsurprisingly, the obituary for Jack Swire reported that his company's 'ships often come into internal prominence by reason of encounters with pirates in Chinese waters'.[36] But most damaging for the company was the seizure of the *Tungchow* as it sailed from Shanghai to Tianjin via Yantai in January 1935. Not only was this the second time the ship was pirated, it was the second ship to be taken in six months, and, to cap it all, it was carrying 73 British children back to their boarding school in Yantai. Losing yet another ship was one thing, losing 73 children quite another.

They all survived, unharmed, but Ivan Tikhomiroff, a Russian guard who had once faced a Bolshevik firing squad did not: wounded in the initial takeover, he was later shot twice more in cold blood. Captain James Smart and his crew wisely decided thereafter to co-operate to protect the passengers. The mother of one brood – four out of her six – might have despaired more than most at the news when it reached Shanghai: her husband was already in captivity, having been seized three months earlier by Communist fighters.[37] Some of the children on board seem rather to have enjoyed the whole experience, for they were given a fine time in Hong Kong after release (and a much more hedonistic one than many missionary children were used to), and their captors had fed them liberally with oranges from the ship's cargo even if they had been robbed of prized watches and pocket money. 'Never has there been a more magnificent school-treat,' ventured one journalist. But 'at the moment Taikoo stinks', Colin Scott reported from Hong Kong in February: 'every mother and father & the navy are after our blood.'[38] The pirates, who were Cantonese – which itself should have been a clue – took the ship as it left Shanghai, turned it south to Daya Bay (Bias Bay), north-east of Hong Kong, repainting the funnel and name to disguise it as a Japanese ship, and that way sailing unchallenged past several vessels, including a British warship that was searching for her which was deceived by the cosmetic changes. To cover their own error, naval officers were vocal in criticising CNCo and, Scott reflected,

> We do on the face of it appear to be open to a good deal of criticism. It was China New Year, they had received a warning that a gang had left for Shanghai, a party of Southerners were travelling North, there were $250,000 in Bank notes on board and 75 [sic] children. The grille doors were not locked.[39]

The gang had even actually travelled north on CNCo's *Yochow*.

Any lapses in security were presumably fairly routine, but could not be said to be a cause of the episode: the gangs were large, well-organised and determined. The company investigated the possibility of pirates being aided by leaks from an informer in the shipping office, or even that there might be a Green Gang-assisted campaign against the company (as was, briefly, the idea of seeking some sort of arrangement with Du Yuesheng to secure immunity for the ships: 'too dangerous to think of seriously,' concluded Scott). But fitting security grilles on such ships was, it was admitted, never going to make them secure. Barring stairwells meant the pirates simply hauled themselves up the side of the ship to the upper deck. The system in place of requiring passengers to furnish guarantees from recognised shops or banks had also failed. Although 18 of the Chinese passengers on board actually embarked without these papers, the 12 pirates had them. They were all, it seemed, honourable men and had papers to prove it. And one of them also boasted that he had been on the ship before, when he took part in its seizure in 1925.[40] The banknotes, at least, were unsigned, and so were unusable. The children wrote essays about their adventure for the *North China Daily News*. 'I was not as scared as I thought I'd be,' wrote one boy, 'for they disappointed me. I thought they'd have knives and be villainous looking, but they only looked nasty and hadn't got knives.' This pantomime vision and the fragrance and colour of the oranges could not remove for some the sight of Ivan Tikhomiroff as he lay murdered on the deck.[41]

Tikhomiroff was one of six guards on board the ship, all of whose salaries were paid by CNCo, and had been working as a piracy guard for a year. The firm paid that salary under protest. Warren Swire seems to have been the prime mover of a sustained attempt to require piracy protection to be funded by the British government. During the crisis of the Nationalist Revolution, Royal Navy personnel had been deployed to some merchant ships sailing in Chinese waters, and in the wild winter of 1926/7 the Hong Kong governor had even ordered a raid on the 'pirate base' at Daya Bay, to the consternation of British diplomats in China, but from 1928 companies like CNCo were warned that they would be expected to continue funding protection themselves in future and from March 1930 this came into effect.[42] Carrying guards created additional problems, whoever paid for them – perhaps the ship compradors, it was ventured at one point, who in 1930 were required to pay a significant contribution to their cost on each round trip. Even bunked six to a room they took up space that would otherwise accommodate paying passengers. And what nationality should they be? Indians? Unreliable, complained the firm. Chinese? But Hong Kong Chinese seconded from the police force found the meals provided by Ningbo cooks unpalatable. British police sergeants objected to sharing the bunk room with subordinates, and expected to eat at the Saloon table. Four

Chinese policemen from the British-leased territory at Weihaiwei were dismissed in 1929: one took bribes from gamblers, one was medically unfit, the third neglected his duty repeatedly and the fourth released a prisoner. In general, it was feared that Chinese might 'join forces' with pirates. Sometimes – on other lines – they did.[43]

'As British subjects', barristers for the company argued in the appeal court in 1932, CNCo was 'entitled to the protection of the Crown against ... piratical acts without payment'. Precedent was sought far back into English history in terms of the duty of the Crown to its loyal subjects. Well, replied Lord Justice Scrutton – himself the son of a shipowner – who dismissed the case on appeal, 'Henry II would, I think, have been surprised to hear that if his tenant went to China the King was bound to follow and protect him'. The Crown had 'no legal duty ... to afford military protection to British subjects in foreign parts'.[44] Warren Swire's characteristically idiosyncratic view was actually that a British subject could not be expected to pay twice for protection, if already paying income tax, but this was not the line of argument pursued in court. The proceedings were expensive, and the company lost. It is worth noting also how the judgement ran entirely counter to the culture of the British presence in China as it had developed after 1842 and which was now unravelling. British residents had grown accustomed to demanding – and securing – the services of their consuls, the despatch of gunboats and the support of the courts in China. They assumed that this was a right; some talked in Shanghai of their position as a 'birth right' that needed to be defended.

Even as it took on the cost of paying for the guards, CNCo continued its profitable course in the 1930s.[45] But the widening of the China conflict after August 1937 presented it with a range of logistical challenges. The most dramatic was the closure of the Yangzi River. On 12 August 1937 the Nationalists banned traffic below Zhenjiang and sank blockships to create a barrage across the river at Jiangyin. One of these was the old CNCo steamer *Hupeh*, built at Greenock in 1901 and sold in 1931. This barrier trapped 12 of the company's ships upriver, leaving five of the river fleet outside. Only the *Whangpu* and *Wantung* made their way out after Jiangyin was captured by the Japanese and a new barrage was established further along the river at Wuhu, 200 miles from the sea. Agility and improvisation were needed to weather these months, for neutrality, to an extent, allowed CNCo to keep running its ships. At first it ran highly profitable services from Shanghai to Haimen on the north bank of the Yangzi, from where passengers and cargoes were ferried in lighters along a hundred miles of delta creeks to meet the trapped steamers. Inside the blockade, ships carried on a 'brisk' trade carrying people and plant further and further west. Japanese advances would end the 'creek trade' but did not lead to any reopening of the river to neutral traffic.⁴⁶ In 1939 the river ships were operating for only one-fifth of the time that they might be employed. When Canton fell, the coastal fleet started to carry goods for unoccupied China to Haiphong in French Indo-China, until this booming trade was hit by Japanese bombing of the railway into China, and then by the obstruction of the French, under Japanese pressure. Even so, high freight rates meant that overall the years of the China–Japan war were extremely profitable for CNCo.

The onset of the war in Europe in September 1939 started to affect the company's operations in China in a number of ways, notably in the requisition of tonnage and ships, and then a growing shortage of British personnel, especially engineers. The management of the company was moved out east, to Hong Kong, in October 1939. There was no disorganised dash from desk or deck to volunteer for the forces, as there had been in 1914, but many CNCo mariners were Royal Navy reservists, and were quickly needed. The first ship requisitioned was the motor vessel *Anshun*. Travelling back from Singapore to Hong Kong in late August 1939, on its usual route, the ship was ordered about, and would initially serve for almost a year as a store ship in Sierra Leone. A hundred of the Chinese crew refused to travel beyond Singapore, and had to be repatriated by CNCo. It was, after all, not their war.⁴⁷ Seamen were easily found in Singapore for the *Anshun*, but CNCo had more difficulty with staffing its senior complements in China. 'Far more Chinese engineers than we like' had to be hired, Warren Swire reported in June 1940 (the company had been slowly introducing Chinese deck officers and engineers at lower grades in the 1930s), and in 1941 'names appear on our lists which we should be very glad to do without'. Britain's precarious position after the fall of France in 1940, and the understandable concern with the European situation, also meant that Japanese pressure on the British on all fronts was intense. An inconsistent British response, sometimes appeasing the Japanese – closing in July 1940 for example, for three months, Chongqing's only land route for supplies, the Burma Road – only served to embolden them and alienate the Nationalist government.[48]

In July 1940 Warren Swire sailed into all this across the Pacific, making the last of the directors' visits 'out east' for six years. 'I've merely left England,' he wrote in a personal letter, 'as an insurance that, if the place is besieged, communications cut off, and everything generally b—d up, one of the family directors may be clear of it and the people in the East not left entirely to their own devices.'[49] On balance it is also quite likely that his unshakable and vociferous antipathy to Prime Minister Winston Churchill ('the Duce' he called him, routinely), and to British persistence in the war – very heavily influenced by his vicious anti-Semitism – made it desirable to keep him out of London. He was never to withdraw from these views. Warren Swire was also unusual in being vocally pro-Chiang Kai-shek, and he met 'the great man' in Chongqing on this visit in 1940, 'pretty well the biggest man in the world today,' he wrote. This was very much a minority view, even within a firm that had been actively engaging with the Nationalist government since the early 1930s. Swire followed a limited version of the usual directorate round – landing in Shanghai, heading down to Hong Kong, flying to Chongqing, then back to Shanghai and Tianjin before arriving back in Britain in December. At Chongqing, he reported, the firm simply had 'two men in the office to keep each other company at this end of the earth', one of the three trapped ships laid up, too big to run in anything but high water, and only (expensive) rape seed oil to run on, one ship making round trips to Wanxian, and another to Suifu, and 'd—d little cargo either way'. Company staff across China were 'stiffened' up, largely to stand up to British consuls (who were, anyway, in his eyes, all 'rabbits'), to try to force them to enforce British rights, but the war little recognised any such rights. Swire had been from early on in the China war 'a most completely last ditcher about the Japs', had been drawing public attention in Britain to the need to push back against the Japanese, and if he learned nothing else on the trip it was confirmation in his mind that the coming of a wider conflict was now only a matter of time.

Swire found London a battered city when he got back, for he returned to the Blitz. Between August and the end of December there were 96 major bombing raids on Britain, 57 on successive nights on London alone. Over 18,000 civilians had been killed in the first three months.

Bad weather had relieved the pace as the year closed, but the campaign was far from over.[50] Although its Blue Funnel operations were much curtailed, John Swire & Sons and its companies were running fairly much as usual in December 1940. The big news for British-China interests was the announcement that same week of a £10 million loan to Chiang Kai-shek's government, half to help stabilise its currency, half for sterling materials purchases. Out in China Shanghailanders held the last race meeting of the season, the paper hunt had a particularly fast-paced outing and a great crowd thronged the British Women's Association fundraising Christmas bazaar. As they did so, rival secret service units and gangsters – often difficult to tell apart – murdered or kidnapped their enemies on the streets of the occupied cities, and high prices and a rapidly rising cost of living added to the anxieties of the foreign administrations in Shanghai. Hong Kong was more relaxed, although there too food prices were a problem, and the government stepped in to impose wholesale price controls on rice. Still, Dodwells was yet able to sell McEwan's red label beer: 'Be British Buy British', ran advertisements targeted at patriotic tipplers. And with a deft absence of any sense of proportion, one columnist on shipping matters argued that 'never a thought is given to the question of recompense for [the] denial of Treaty privileges in inland waters' – the bottling up of British Yangzi River vessels – and the 'very serious financial burdens British shipping companies bore as a result'.[51]

Twelve months on all had changed. The situation for John Swire & Sons was, simply put, that most assets had been lost, most staff had been taken and little at all remained for London to manage. A lone branch operated in Chongqing (almost the only functioning British enterprise anywhere in China), and two ships alone carried the company flag. Letters between the directors, who had been scattered by the war, are striking for their absence of any substantial content: there was very little to discuss or to be decided. At that darkest moment in the war, all John Swire & Sons really seemed to have left was cash, a vast surplus that caused its own anxieties, £4 million sterling in the bank, more coming in, and almost nothing to spend it on.

The first major casualty was actually the offices at Billiter Square, burned out on the bright moonlit Saturday night of 10 May 1941. One of the heaviest raids London had yet faced – 550 planes – caused more than 2,000 fires, one of which consumed the building. That night nearly

2,500 people were killed, and many historic buildings were destroyed or badly damaged, the latter including the Palace of Westminster, the British Museum and Westminster Abbey. 'London was in flames,' reported one journalist. After looking around the vicinity the following day, Jock Swire wrote that he had 'never seen such ruins since Ypres'. That day, while a spring sun bathed the city with its warmth, Jock walked through the smoking 'shambles' looking for replacement office space – contingency plans had been nullified by the destruction of planned alternatives – and Jardine Matheson stepped in to offer room for a few days. Swire also hunted out typewriters, but what was there to write about? 'All our books & records have gone,' he wrote (by hand), but, worse still, 'the duplicates were burnt in Holt's fire last Saturday & the triplicates when Scott's office in Greenock was burned on Monday'.[52] Shipping records stored in a dockside office had been destroyed 10 days earlier when that too had been hit. When strong-room safes had cooled down sufficiently they were opened and a surprising amount proved to have survived, but instructions nonetheless flew east for copies of large amounts of current and historically important material. Send us, London ordered, charts of the Yangzi, a copy of the latest *Who's Who in China*, the *Taikoo Shipping Gazette*, a Post Office map of China, the booklet of CNCo staff service conditions, a *Hong List*, photographs of staff and steamer schedules. Surviving records were shipped into the countryside; some, deemed superfluous, were sold for pulping. Out in Hong Kong and in Shanghai typists clattered out duplicates, tracings of ship and property plans were copied and a project began to use microphotography to copy property records, surveys and drawings.[53] And what began as a task to replace the vacuum in London became a race to send copies of key documents into safe storage outside China and Hong Kong, as tension with Japan mounted. Some material was shipped to London, some to the Hongkong & Shanghai Bank in Singapore and another set to Sydney.

But time ran out. Filed at the end of a folder of documents on the reconstruction of the archives, without comment, is a note dated 23 December 1941 on office paper from the Hong Kong branch of Butterfield & Swire composed by No. 1 Stores Keeper Albert Farrell. It reports to London the shipment of 19 cases of files from Tianjin, Yantai and Shanghai 'which we have brought with us'. Farrell probably wrote this at sea as the *Hanyang*, on which he was travelling, made its way to Fremantle in Western Australia, where it arrived on 3 January 1942, towing the *Anshun*, two of six CNCo ships that arrived in the port at this time. War had come to the Pacific.

The day before the Japanese attack on Pearl Harbor on 7 December, 18 of the company's ships had been ordered out of Hong Kong's harbour, where they had been concentrated with other British shipping, and directed to sail to Singapore. They carried a number of Butterfield & Swire staff and their families, and others who had secured passage. A large group of Taikoo Dockyard men and their families had boarded the *Kiangsu*. The evacuation of shipping had been ordered by the Hong Kong government. When news of the Japanese assault on Honolulu and the simultaneous attacks on Malaya and Hong Kong reached them, the ships decided to make their own way to safety, some continuing to Singapore, the rest to Manila.⁵⁴ While they sailed the entire Butterfield & Swire enterprise in China, barring the marooned ships and under-employed agents at Chongqing, fell into Japanese hands.

The ships that continued to Manila found themselves under bombardment there almost immediately as the Japanese bombed the city. The earliest company casualty of the Pacific war was a 39-year-old Darlington man, James William Bennett, chief officer on the *Anshun*, killed on 10 December when a bomb exploded near the bridge. His son was on board. Another bomb killed a number of passengers. The *Taiyuan* was also hit, without casualties, and the *Yunnan* had a lucky escape as bombs fell either side of it. Six ships left to head to Fremantle. Others went to Sourabaya where the *Taiyuan*, having been requisitioned, was eventually scuttled by orders of the Dutch authorities. Most of the rest made it across the Indian Ocean to Colombo. The *Kiangsu* alone was caught as it fled, and taken to Xiamen. Four vessels were at Singapore when the war broke out, having already been requisitioned. One was eventually scuttled, another was lost to enemy action – *Anking*, on 4 March 1942, as it attempted to get to Fremantle from Batavia, with eight company dead and few survivors out of 250 men on board – and the *Wuchang*, converted into a munitions store, was ordered to flee as the island fell. It survived a bombing, the desertion of its stokers, a well-targeted torpedo that nonetheless passed underneath the ship, and arrived in Colombo with a large complement of refugees.

Eighteen ships were seized by the Japanese, caught at Shanghai, Yichang, Hong Kong and Bangkok and at sea. Some were scuttled but recovered and restored to service by the enemy. James Smart, his ship the *Tungchow* now renamed the *Hsin Peking*, was intercepted in an attempted dash to safety from Tianjin, and tried to beach it beyond use. Ill luck had it that he drove it ashore on a very soft sandbank. In anger his captors kicked his teeth in. The ship was undamaged.[55] Only three of these vessels would survive the war. There were casualties elsewhere among the requisitioned fleet. On 23 December, barely four months after being requisitioned, the *Shuntien* was torpedoed in the eastern Mediterranean. Thirty-one of the crew died, but there were in total nearly 900 men on board, most of them Axis prisoners, and just one in 10 survived, some only to be killed a few hours later when their rescue ship was itself hit. The youngest casualty was a shipboard servant, Liu Shao-wo, aged 15, 'missing presumed drowned', one of the 23 CNCo mariners lost.[56] The company's 1942 report noted that the surviving 28 vessels not in enemy hands were employed in West and in East Africa, in the Persian Gulf, the Mediterranean, and in India, concluding that 'except very indirectly, we hear practically nothing of our ships'.[57]

The first air raid on Hong Kong took place the day after the CNCo fleet set out. It presaged a hard-fought but futile three-week-long defence of the colony. Hong Kong had no air defences; it had no chance of receiving any reinforcements; it had no chance at all. The Japanese broke through the British defence lines in the New Territories almost straight away. Undermined by gangster and fifth columnist-inspired disorder in their rear, the British pulled back through Kowloon and had abandoned the peninsula by 13 December. After their attempts to secure a surrender were twice spurned, the Japanese landed on the island close by the dockyard on 18 December and the British surrendered on Christmas Day. For some days following Japanese troops ran riot. Most company staff killed in the battle were serving in the Hong Kong Volunteers, but others had been working as air raid wardens. There were 22 British casualties, but many more Chinese staff died. Dockyard watchman W. H. Bonner was serving as a baker when he and three dozen other men were killed after they surrendered on 22 December. Stores clerk Francis Jorge escaped the same massacre site but died of wounds that night. Wounded on Christmas Eve, Donald Blackman, an 18-year-old clerk at the yard, was sent with others to receive medical treatment but was killed en route. Harbour Engineer J. J. Jacobs died of wounds after the launch he was in was shelled. Another watchman,

A. J. Headington, was killed in action by machine-gun fire. Long-serving refinery foreman William Sneath, serving in the ARP, was bayoneted to death at Quarry Bay. Among the Volunteers taken prisoner was a Dockyard storekeeper, Henry Kew. He died when the SS *Lisbon Maru*, carrying prisoners of war to Japan, was torpedoed by an American submarine in September 1942 and the Japanese machine-gunned the survivors or left them to drown.[58]

The war brought this terror and pain, but for most it simply brought tedium, battered people's health and rasped the spirit. C. C. Roberts was Taipan when the colony fell. From the civilian internment camp at Stanley he reported in July 1942 that 155 members of staff and their families were in the camp with him (the latter forming only half the total, for many families had been evacuated to Australia at the orders of the government in June 1940). 'All are reasonably well.' Ten men were held as prisoners of war. 'We are keeping fairly well,' reported Dockyard accountant Frederick Elliott, in an inter-camp note to acting chief of the firm Arthur Dean in March 1943, 'but our shadows are not so large.' They did not get any larger before the end of the war. A few members of staff secured passages in 1942 in one of the half-dozen exchanges of Allied and Japanese nationals, but most simply had to sit the war out. Most, but not all. For Jack Conder, a warehouseman in Shanghai, the problem internment presented was personal. Conder was the only member of staff to escape from captivity but, as he wrote in a letter to the Japanese camp commander, his objective in doing so was 'getting away from my wife'. Even being shot in the attempt, he noted, would have helped him achieve this.[59] Camp conditions even in Hong Kong were better by far than those endured in Southeast Asia, but this is all relative. Ill health in bodies weakened by malnourishment and little access to medical help took some lives. The only violent death was that of Aileen Guerin, who worked in the passenger department of Butterfield & Swire. She was killed in Stanley in January 1945 when an American aircraft bombed the camp by mistake.[60]

By contrast, at Shanghai the war brought a weird sort of business as usual. There was almost no violence at all when the Japanese announced they were moving to occupy the International Settlement. A lone British gunboat refused to surrender and was attacked and sunk, naval honour secured at the cost of at least six lives. British councillors were soon to resign, but the Shanghai Municipal Council continued to administer the settlement, and Allied nationals continued to work for it, most of them for another year and a quarter. Aside from the paint plant, and its ships, the company was initially rather left alone, but tight restrictions were put on its access to cash. Over the course of much of the next 10 months staff worked to pay retiring grants to all Chinese employees, eventually paying off 1,100 of them by the end of January, with retainers paid to dozens of men with a view to a return sometime to normality, and formally winding the company up by 15 August 1942 when the offices were taken over by the Japanese shipping line, Toyo Kisen Kaisha (whose manager, Arthur Dean reported hopefully, 'is an old acquaintance of mine'). Insurance interests were taken over by the Tokyo Marine & Fire Insurance Co., and Dai Nippon took over the paint company.[61] Many Chinese and neutral staff continued working for these enterprises, and in the main they had been navigating the daily politics of occupation or semi-occupation in most of these cities for some time already and would continue to do so. The British staff developed a comprehensive list of assets and liabilities in Shanghai, adding to it similar data that was sent in from the other captured branches. As long as he could, Dean sent funds to Roberts in Hong Kong, and was reported writing that 'the whole staff are fitter and better than they have ever been as a result of the open-air life, digging and bicycling ... he goes to the office every day and seems thoroughly fit and happy'. 'Most people appear to be thriving on a reduced diet and lack of strong drink', reported branch manager Edward McLaren from Tianjin in September 1942. The British concession there had also been peacefully occupied. As at other ports, McLaren and staff had burned Private Office files as soon as they realised what was happening, but there was little else that they could do.[62] In August the firm's interests were taken over by the Japanese Okura Trading Company, which offered to keep key British staff on the payroll, not to make use of any of them, but to be able to provide them with some sort of income.[63]

'Hazelwood', the Taipan's house at Shanghai, became a hostel for staff and families largely run by Tom Lindsay. The tennis courts were turned into vegetable plots. Only in February and March 1943 were Allied civilians interned in Shanghai, although in November 1942 men deemed to be a security threat were rounded up and interned at a camp set up in a former US Marines Barracks on Haiphong Road.

Arthur Dean was to join them in February 1943 after an uncomfortable three-month spell in the Bridge House detention centre run by the Kempeitai, the Japanese military police, from which he emerged hungry and filthy (and somewhat perplexed as to why he had been taken). A week after he was taken he was tortured – his assailant's 'zest in these proceedings was unmistakable' he later reported, but aside from one hideous episode he was not otherwise harmed. Company staff at Tianjin were interned in a former missionary compound in Weixian, Shandong province, in March 1943. Some of the Taikoo Dockyard staff caught on the *Kiangsu* later joined the complement at Haiphong Road, welcomed there as men with useful practical skills largely lacking among the Shanghai British. In particular they made themselves popular by making instruments for a camp band. 'The name of Taikoo stood very high there,' Dean later reported.[64]

As Arthur Dean later put it, while the course of the war across the terrifying year after Pearl Harbor and then the steadily better and better turn of events after the victories at El Alamein and at Stalingrad in 1942 were easy enough to follow, even from within the internment camps, the sequestered staff were all 'engrossed in our own day to day problems'. These included: hunger, enforced close-quarters living – 'Taikoo Dockyard hands,' reported one observer, who clearly relished the contrast, queuing with the colony's Attorney-General, Sir Atholl MacGregor, rice bowls in hands – personal and family worries, lack of news, lack of drink. Information found its way to London, accounts of the months after the war's outbreak, details of the winding up of affairs and of the experiences of individuals – who was where, if known, who was not coping well, who a tower of strength. A company newsletter was started in London, relaying what news came in. A comprehensive report on the Shanghai office was smuggled out by a fairly recently appointed clerk, Dawson Kwauk, who made his way to Chongqing via Wuhan and Changsha with the document hidden in a suitcase.[65] The front line remained porous, and the biggest danger was not so much the Japanese or puppet forces, but bandits. The International Red Cross also facilitated some correspondence for individuals and news also filtered back to London that way. Much, then, was known in London, and none of it seemed good.

Less well known was the fact that the Japanese promptly put the Taikoo Dockyard in Hong Kong back to work as soon as they could.

Any demolition plans had been overtaken by the speed of conquest, although the yard was thoroughly looted. Well, said the Japanese, if looted material does not find its way back, and is instead discovered locally, there would be consequences. This had the desired effect. And once department heads had been relocated, the new managers began recruiting staff back to their posts. The installation was placed under the management of Mitsui, and a cadre of Japanese managers and technicians was drafted in. Intelligence reports provide much detail about the work being done, although supplies were never plentiful. Partially completed ships were finished; and new vessels were built, including the *Heikai Maru*, a 4,000-ton, 300-foot standard ship, which was launched at the yard on 21 July 1944.[66] We do not know if the Mitsui-appointed manager extolled the virtue of Japanese wartime enterprise in the east as the ship slid down the slipway; it would not be unreasonable to assume that he did. January 1943 Japanese newsreel footage of a launch at the yard shows somebody doing so as a ship is launched in front of a flag-waving crowd. War-damaged or scuppered ships were restored, and at one point CNCo's *Fatshan*, which ran as in more peaceful times to and from Guangzhou (where its British officers and engineers were interned) was docked in July 1944 for repairs. Many among the 4,500 Chinese staff will have been quite familiar with the ship. Some men made their way to Macao, though. Jock Swire later met seven who had spent the occupation years there and 'had been in a starving condition', without any subventions from Butterfield & Swire.[67]

The British Army Aid Group (BAAG) – an intelligence and rescue organisation, created by Lindsay Ride, Professor of Physiology at the University of Hong Kong and based north of the colony – also tried to exfiltrate skilled dockyard hands from the colony, to deny their talents to the enemy, and to try to get them to British yards in India. This 'mateys scheme' brought about 175 men from Hong Kong's yards out of the colony by September 1942, and many brought with them their families and dependants, providing a logistical challenge for BAAG, for they needed housing and feeding – and their children needed schooling (one of the unlikelier operations of the British military in China).[68] It was not physically difficult to escape, but they could not leave behind their families at this time of crisis and insecurity, which made their support a tall order. In addition, the Japanese then forbade the men from resigning their posts, so any departures would have had to have been precipitate. The simple daily facts of life kept most men in Hong Kong, and most men kept at their work. For their part, the Japanese also tried to recruit from the same pool of labour in spring 1944 for yards in Singapore and Malaya (to counter this, the British revived the mateys scheme). This was a backhanded compliment to the way in which British firms like Taikoo had developed a pool of skilled labour in Hong Kong over the decades since the dockyard and refinery had been established. These men were in demand. American air raids in January 1945 – part of Operation Gratitude, a sweep into the South China Sea – caused 'heavy' loss of life among Chinese staff and workmen at the yard, which was a key target and the docks sustained 'considerable damage'.[69]

Unlike the orderly and legalistic takeovers in China, British firms in Hong Kong were spoils of war, banks aside, where an orderly administration was undertaken, and British bankers kept at work. The Butterfield & Swire offices had been taken over by the Japanese navy as their headquarters. All records were 'swept into the street' 'immediately after the surrender'. Roberts himself, attempting entry shortly thereafter, was unceremoniously ejected.[70] No staff were paid off. The refinery was restarted, however, and continued in production until May 1944. Early on, Roy Philips, the manager, was asked if he and senior staff would resume work there themselves, with a promise that the output would only go to Shanghai or locally, but they declined, seeing this as 'probably a bait to get Chinese employees to return'. By the end of 1944 it was being stripped of all its machinery, including the power plant, as part of a concerted scrap-metal drive that also consumed the bronze First World War memorial from the Butterfield & Swire offices.[71]

CNCo mariners not caught in the Japanese net kept sailing, working now for the Ministry of War Transport. Three of these remaining ships were lost to enemy action (and a fourth was gutted by fire in the accidental Bombay harbour explosion in April 1944). *Sinkiang* was one of 20 ships sunk in two days in early April 1942 in the Bay of Bengal, after they had been ordered to head to India's west coast without escorts. Two Blue Funnels were also lost. The ship was shelled 'at point-blank range', recalled its radio operator, Stanley Salt, who, otherwise powerless, shut the wireless room door and waited to die. Salt survived to watch her go down 'almost perpendicular' as he floated, wounded, in the sea. Only 18 men survived; the dead included CNCo's

three engineers, the mate and third officer, four firemen, a seaman
and a cook. Gordon Campbell, who had just arrived in India, found
himself interpreting for injured Chinese seamen in hospital. SS *Kaying*
was torpedoed off the coast of Libya a year later. The *Hoihow* suffered
the same fate north of Réunion on 2 July 1943. It sank in 90 seconds;
147 died.[72]

Wartime casualties among British merchant seamen were high. Some
50,000 were killed, a greater proportion by some measure than any
of the fighting services. Around a quarter of seamen in British ships
were Asians. They were Indians and Chinese in the main and between
ten and twenty thousand of the latter served during the war. Over one
thousand would die.[73] They were not victims and they were not passive
in their contribution to the Allied war effort. Chinese seafarers actively
worked to protect their interests in a workplace culture of systematic
discrimination and unequal treatment. They did so in Shanghai,
in February and March 1942, when crews from the ships that were
seized by the Japanese started to arrive back in the city and came to
the Taikoo offices for their pay. *Chekiang*'s crew caused 'considerable
trouble', and the French concession police had to be called. The ship
had been intercepted at sea on 8 December, en route from Tianjin to
Shanghai. The dispute was solved with the arrangement of passages for
the men either to Tanggu or to Ningbo. They protected their interests
in Fremantle in January 1942 when men on the *Chungking* got into a
dispute with the master over pay and war-risk benefits – which initially
were not forthcoming for any Chinese seamen in British employ. They
demanded an advance of wages. Mustering them, Captain Naismith
ordered his crew back to work, threatening to cut a day's pay. In the face
of what Naismith thought a mutiny, 300 Australian soldiers boarded
all six of the CNCo vessels in port to remove the men. An altercation
on the *Chungking* led to two deaths at the hands of the soldiers. All the
crewmen were detained, some of them for six weeks (and 62 members
of the recalcitrant crew of the *Chungking* and 288 of the other men
were eventually formed into an army Labour Company, that worked
in northern Australia 'out of sight and sound of the sea'): and no
Chinese crews would work thereafter on the ship while it remained in
Fremantle.[74]

Chinese seamen demanded their rights in Britain. Two hundred
gathered in Liverpool in April 1942 having struck for higher wages

and war-risk payments, for they were being paid at a third of the rate of British seamen. This led to a fracas, one of several on ships and off them, and to an intervention by the Chinese embassy that led to a formal Anglo-Chinese agreement that substantially improved terms, but did not equalise them. Desertions from British ships in American ports had increased markedly as a result, leading to conflicts.[75] Many of these were men who had served with Taikoo, or been recruited through its offices to Blue Funnel ships. Often popularly denounced as unreasonable, violent and prone to panic, and still saddled with a popular press focus on opium use and gambling – as any cursory look through the wartime Liverpool press will show – they faced an uphill struggle to assert even their basic rights as seamen. Kenneth Lo, then a vice-consul at Liverpool, was one of those who tried to recast their image in newspaper articles later collected in a small volume of essays narrating instances of confusion, of heroism, endurance and exhaustion, painting a human face over the grotesque caricature that still too often held sway.[76]

Meanwhile, in London, during the years of conflict, while some of their staff were locked in a theatre of cruelty, a curious script for a theatre of the absurd was improvised by two of the directors. Warren and Jock Swire, uncle and nephew, did not speak to each other. In fact, they barely saw each other. Without much business to attend to, barely a day a week was needed in order to get through the major business of the firm during the conflict, which largely involved administering support for staff and their dependants. But even when seated in the same office, the room was divided by a thick wall of silence. Warren made it very clear that he had no confidence in Jock, unless the latter had 'ballast' – active support from their fellow directors, but these were busy elsewhere: John Swire Scott with the army in south-west England; Colin Scott in Greenock at the Scott shipbuilding yards. Jock himself spent most of his time at London's Dock Labour Board, which he chaired. Both men confided in John Masson, who had early after his arrival in China in 1922 come to fore as a potential director, joining the board in July 1939. Masson spent the war working for the Ministry of War Transport in Bombay, part of a substantial transfer of shipping expertise from firms like Swires into the wartime British state. (It was also, relatively speaking, convenient for Chongqing, and for supervising the company's temporary Bombay office.) 'Relations between our partners do not improve,' wrote John Swire Scott to Masson in late summer 1943, 'and reasonable discussions or any objective discussions are almost impossible.'[77]

Aside from this painful situation at the top, there were two quite different pressing problems facing the firm. First, there was a surfeit of money, and secondly there was a surfeit of uncertainty about the future. This latter was not just uncertainty about the course of the war, for after the end of 1942 this was never considered in doubt. But in January 1943, the British government, its position utterly undermined by the humiliating collapse of its Asian colonies in the face of the Japanese attack, signed a new 'Friendship Treaty' with China. Extraterritoriality was abolished, the British hold on the Customs Service surrendered, the remaining concessions and settlements were retroceded. Among the various measures listed, Annex Clause 2g dealt with inland navigation rights: these were abolished. The river trade was finished. For good measure, on 1 August 1943, the occupied settlements were also returned to China by their administrations – that is they were handed to the collaborationist state. For all its work in the 1930s to embed itself rhetorically and practically in China as it changed, all the companies managed by John Swire & Sons still relied on the fact of the asymmetrical power relationship upheld by the nineteenth-century treaties. Now these had been signed away, and there was nothing put in their place for the future but airy rhetoric and good intentions: once peace came a 'comprehensive modern treaty' was to be signed within six months. 'I don't quite see what this country gets out of it,' wrote John Swire Scott, all but calling it an unequal treaty. 'It might be worse,' thought Warren Swire. He and Jock managed to secure a 30-minute meeting with Song Ziwen in London in August 1943, but the discussion was frustratingly general.[78] All of this made planning a challenge.

But first the cash.[79] There was simply too much of it, half a million pounds' compensation for losses alone, and there was nothing to spend it on. As Jock and Warren sat in an initially windowless set of new offices in Billiter Square, a large photograph of Quarry Bay gracing the wall, they pondered what to do with it. They had equities but these offered a poor return. So John Swire & Sons bought farms, initially mainly in Cheshire, a diversion back to the family's roots where cousins, the descendants of William Hudson Swire, still lived and helped the company orientate itself locally. Eight estates had been bought by October 1942. But this was simply a stop-gap. At one time they considered starting operations of some sort in Abyssinia (there were factories to be managed, reported a correspondent); or perhaps better move into India. But where was 'elbow room' to be found there, with its long-established firms? Well, might they buy another shipping line? But what was there to buy, and would the ships be worth it in the long term? They would not serve the Asian trade. No. They had 'got the bloody powder – millions of it,' scribbled Warren Swire in May 1944, 'and it will be practically worthless outside this country, when it can be spent, & not worth much inside'.

They really did not know how things would turn out, and in this they were not alone. John Keswick, one of the directors of Jardine Matheson, who had been leading an SOE commando training mission in China, and who had effectively been expelled earlier in the year – for the Nationalists were rightly suspicious of the objectives of the British presence in free China, geared as it was to regain Hong Kong and support a re-establishment of British interests generally – shared his own despondency about the future with Jock Swire in July 1942.[80] He floated the idea of a combination between the operations of the two conglomerates, a 'fusion', a new 'China Traders Association' that would corral key British interests into a 'national enterprise' that would be too big to be easily ignored and that might more easily garner official British support. Such an alliance would historically have been quite a radical departure. As Keswick himself later noted, 'owing to some foolish traditions staff of the two firms hardly know each other'. This led to a steady discussion that in time evolved into preparations for an umbrella body uniting Swire and Jardine staff, and those of P&O and other firms as the 'Far Eastern Shipping Agencies', that would take over the management of their requisitioned ships at the end of the war until they were released by the Ministry of War Transport.

If the future was opaque, perhaps it was time to look to the past. And there were good men with little to do who might assist. Frank D. Roberts, acting No. 2 in Hong Kong when he left with the CNCo fleet on 7 December 1941, arrived back in Britain in late 1943 for medical treatment after working in India and Chongqing. 'It seems a pity not to make some use of his enforced leisure,' wrote John Masson to Warren Swire. Why not set him on to the old Private Office letter books, copying important ones for you 'for the pious task which you once promised yourself for your years of leisure' – a history of the firm.[81] Not a bad idea, thought Warren, it 'ought to be written', and he had clearly been looking through the archives himself. Swire himself longed to retreat to his Scottish estate, but that was all shut up, and instead took himself off into reverie: 'when the office door is shut, it is shut, & I walk out into the country or the 18th century to browse in peace.' At this point Warren was actively planning his departure. There was so little to do in 1942 it was 'definitely a one-man job,' reported Jock Swire, and by September 1943 his uncle had 'definitely said that he is clearing out immediately after the war'. There were slow and painstaking, and at times clearly painful discussions about this which would culminate in late 1946 with his replacement as chairman by Jock Swire. Warren Swire fought this, but even though he was 'bored with destruction or mere recovery of value of destroyed stuff' and wanted to build, and even though in late 1944 the company was able at last to start to order new ships and planning for peace stepped up a level, his tenure at the head of the firm was drawing to a close.

Part of the discussion in 1944 revolved around recruiting another director. Jock Swire and John Swire Scott were adamant that the appointee should come from within the firm. 'I think the one real asset we have left,' wrote John Swire Scott, in the face of Warren Swire's opposition to this, 'is the quality of our Eastern Staff … and we must get them back with their tails up. If we take one of them in, it will have a most heartening effect on them all.' Aside from the wider concern with the demoralising effect of occupation and captivity, this was also a concern with the still unfolding impact of the steady recruitment of university graduates into the firm. While Butterfield & Swire managers in Asia complained that they needed shipping clerks but were only sent graduates – how about equal numbers of each, suggested Shanghai in 1936 – London retorted that only 'university men' would now consider going abroad (itself a reflection of the overall increase in standards of living in 1930s Britain, despite the slump).[82] These were also the men who chafed at the 'autocrats' in London, and whose talents might not be retained if they were not given scope in which to use them.[83] For the moment the matter rested, but the next director, Charles Roberts, would come from the Eastern Staff, and in 1944 he was still in Stanley internment camp.

Not, however, for too much longer. The war in Asia concluded in August 1945 as brutally and suddenly as it had begun with the destruction of Hiroshima and Nagasaki. In the days after the Japanese surrender on 15 August and before the arrival of British forces two weeks later, Charles Roberts drafted a letter to send back to London, seizing the opportunity when he could to type it up, battling for a typewriter, for Stanley was suddenly disturbed by the clattering of managers filing reports for their heads in London.[84] He and the refinery and dockyard managers had already made visits out of Stanley to see if they could assess the state of the Quarry Bay installations and to talk to any Taikoo staff they could find. The district itself was 'a scene of desolation – 50% to 75% of the property there is derelict, and the population is not more than one tenth of the pre-war population,' he reported, and 'the greater number of people appear to be destitute'. They could see dismantled machinery littering the refinery and dockyard. At Stanley the 'Chinese have been flocking in'. Contact was re-established with the Mok family, who had fled upcountry. C. P. Wong, who was in charge of sales at TSR, had turned up on the first day, and had been maintaining covert contact since the start of the occupation, having sent his own family to Macao. But the war's toll on the Chinese staff in the colony was high. Bombing aside, malnutrition and starvation had taken many older men, and we might amplify that for the impact on dependants.

A telegram had winged its way east from Billiter Square via Chongqing: 'INSTRUCT ALL RELEASED INTERNEES OCCUPY ALL PROPERTIES MOST URGENT STOP BEST OF LUCK'. And as soon as they could, they did just that. Arthur Dean had been moved from Haiphong Road camp in Shanghai, with most of the other inmates, to Fengtai, south-west of Beijing, in early July. Shortly after the surrender they were moved to the city itself at the insistence of American advance forces that were starting to arrive in Japanese-held China. These were also persuaded to fly 'key men' from their sites of captivity back to the cities. Dean flew to Shanghai, passing through Tianjin where he met Edward McLaren, one of 19 company managers flown from Weixian internment camp back to the city. Long before Dean landed back in Shanghai chief accountant Robert Chaloner had made his way out of Longhua camp – just two days after the surrender – and went straight over to check the offices on the Bund, 'advising' the sitting tenants that they needed to leave, and promptly. Three men went straight from the camp over to the Holt's Wharf installation, their journey arranged by OSK (the Osaka Shosen Kaisha Line office), where they were met by the Japanese managers who 'stressed their urgent wish to transfer the wharf properly at the earliest opportunity'. As general confusion began to set in, and as there was soon little by way of a workable currency, and as Nationalist guerrillas were close by, they clearly had their reasons, but it all proved very orderly. Tom Lindsay slipped quickly back into a DOCA role, and went to talk to local officials, newly appointed to replace the collaborators, as well as partisan commanders, to ask them to provide security.[85]

Chinese staff popped up swiftly all over. At Tianjin it was reported that there would be 'little difficulty or delay in getting together a strong nucleus of our old staff immediately'. Some had done well during the hiatus. 'Young Lo' is 'quite prosperous, having been running a share-broking business, also with an interest (well-paying) in a cinema,' McLaren reported. Khoo Se Deng (Qiu Shiding), Xiamen's Chinese manager – since 1934, before that for 16 years its comprador – had set up a profitable business 'operating junks to free China under permit'. Some had not done so well and even Lo, along with other Tianjin staff, had had a rough time with the Kempeitai at one point, after the firm's Japanese adviser committed suicide, exciting police suspicions which took some time to allay. At Shanghai senior men met Chaloner on 17 August (and Tom Lindsay's 'house-boy' turned up at Pudong camp with 'a bottle of fairly good whiskey').[86] Soon, unwanted tenants began to leave, and while many buildings had been stripped of furniture and fixtures, staff started to move in and began typing up inventories and first assessments of what was missing, what was left, what needed to be done.

At Hong Kong a small staff was quickly moved into the dockyard; and the *Fatshan* was taken back over: it had been 'badly maintained' but it worked and it made its first journey almost immediately, fetching food supplies from Macao and bringing back some of the thousands who had found wartime refuge in the Portuguese colony. But the 12-year-old ship had been active throughout the war, and this strand in company activity was far more readily restarted than any other. There were no records in the hong, and no records at the dockyard. Important files had been taken away on the *Kiangsu*, but then vanished after it was seized. Staff 'are all eager,' Roberts wrote, 'to get fit and play their part in rebuilding that grand institution "Taikoo", and I hope that the rebuilt structure will prove a fitting memorial to those who have gone from it'.[87] These were brave words coming from battered bodies and battered souls. They had had no news, no sense of the real detail of the world's turn for over three and a half years. They had no idea if the firm had a future, or if it did so where that future might lie, or if it did, if they had any future within it. They could only assume that they did, and like Hong Kong's interned Colonial Secretary, Franklin Gimson – who in a remarkable act, for there were as yet no British forces in the colony, declared the resumption of British rule and himself acting governor on 26 August – summon their strength and stride as well as they could back into possession of all that they had lost.

12

Flight

Tom Lindsay spent his first night of freedom between crisp clean sheets in a soft bed in CNCo shipping manager Yang Xiaonan's Shanghai home. But thereafter, it seemed, all was horsehair, sackcloth and ashes, for post-war China was bewildering and frustrating, and their wartime allies seemed to regard the British as enemies, barely better than the Japanese, and treated them and their interests as such. For the Swire firms, in the decade after the defeat of Japan, we might focus on three themes: rehabilitation, which was only partially successful; adaptation, which was cut short by the radical political reordering of East Asia after 1949, when the Chinese Communist Party seized power; and innovation, upon which the company's future came to rest. This is also in the main a story of reorientation, for by 1955 John Swire & Sons and its companies had been forced to withdraw from China, their assets first held hostage and then surrendered in an 'all for all' deal: that is, all assets were set against all liabilities. This was hardly a fair exchange, but it was the best that could be agreed. It was carefully arranged and legally watertight, in the context, that is, of the revolutionary legality practised by the new regime. The origins of the profound redirection of the prime focus of the firm's operations and interests that characterised its history across the 1960s and 1970s lay in the triumph of Chinese nationalism in 1945, the Pyrrhic victory of the Guomindang that year as one of the allied coalition and the destruction of their power on the Chinese mainland by 1950.

The Second World War made nations, many more than it broke. As the conflict drew to a close, colonies began to fight themselves free with armed force or unarmed might and moral power: the Philippines, India, Burma, and then Indonesia, and Indo-China would all soon be free of formal European and American imperial power.[1] The Japanese empire was dismantled. China brought back into the Republic the Manchurian provinces seized in 1931, and it brought into it for the very first time the island of Taiwan. China came into its own in other ways as well; the long search for dignity and recognition that had been a feature of its politics since the humiliation heaped on its negotiators at Versailles in 1919 seemed to have ended in triumph. It was one of the allied Big Four during the war, at least, but most importantly, symbolically and rhetorically, it was a founder signatory of the United Nations, and took a permanent seat on the Security Council; it played a leading role in the establishment of the World Court and UNESCO. There was to be no turning back to the days and decades of extraterritoriality, and the century of partial subjugation and degraded sovereignty. That same nationalism, too, combined with viciously tight discipline and substantial if ambiguous Soviet assistance, fuelled the rapid growth in the north-east of the National Government's nemesis, the Chinese Communist Party and its armed forces, which in October 1949 proclaimed the establishment of a People's Republic of China. And in consequence, really quite unexpectedly, for most thought these Communists would turn out to be as pragmatic and reasonable as the radical Guomindang had turned out to be after 1927, Butterfield & Swire took flight from China.

Across the world, the end of the conflict led first to a great mass movement of people, as refugees returned to their homelands, or sought new ones, or were forced to by the redrawing of borders or the expulsion of ethnic minorities, and armies were demobilised. In the Asia theatre, six and a half million Japanese alone were outside the home islands by August 1945, three million of them civilians. Peace immediately prompted movement. The surrender brought back to Hong Kong on the first vessels that sailed some of the 10,000 refugees who had found a precarious safety in Macao (60 Portuguese bank clerks in one transport alone), and the tens of thousands who had fled north from the colony rapidly began to return.[2] While staff of the Swire companies began to rejoin civilian life – John Masson was back from India by November 1945 – the firm's own refugee diaspora began its return from across the fields of conflict and sites of refuge. Many of its ships were scattered as widely as its people, but they, too, began to be restored – six derequisitioned in Hong Kong in February 1946, for example – or tracked down: a tug located in Korea, stranded outside the eastern port city of Samcheok, was one of the more wayward.[3] More than 300 of the Chinese seamen who had manned the fleet that fled Hong Kong at Pearl Harbor returned on the vessels that started to bring repatriates back from Australia in December 1945. War had also spun out some permanently into new lives, and while the company honoured the obligations it felt it had to its staff, it also sifted out some it no longer wished for various reasons to retain. For a minority of the Chinese mariners who had found temporary refuge in Australia, new lives begun there came under attack from a return to the aggressive immigration regime, wartime solidarity thrown to the wind, that led to the passing of a Wartime Refugees Removal Act of July 1949. Among those targeted by this act included former CNCo crewmen. Space was booked for deportees on CNCo's *Shansi* and jointly owned *Changte*.[4]

In February 1946, Jock Swire arrived in Hong Kong by air, joined later by John Scott, who had been diverted en route to Rangoon, for post-war transport could be wayward. Swire had come to spend four months or so getting the lie of the land, assessing the new political context and challenges, and the state of the firm's properties, equipment and staff. He met the former internees, some just boarding a liner to head home for recuperation leave: Tom Lindsay looked 'older but hard'; this man was 'all right physically but obviously tired mentally'; that man was 'tired but well'. In general, Swire thought Hong Kong 'had got under weigh quicker than any of us had dared to hope', and the 'caretaking stage [was] definitely over' but the dockyard was an 'even worse smashup' than he had thought.[5] The refinery was a husk, its equipment only fit for scrap. Shanghai, however, was a real mess:

> little law and order, no coal and therefore no fires or hot water, municipal services are in a state of decay, the cost of living is fantastic, there is always the risk of the present labour troubles developing into civil commotion and riots.[6]

Despite the overwhelming US military and civil presence in north China, there was some respite in Tianjin and Qingdao, 'like returning to a forgotten world of the past,' he thought.[7] But even though Swire wrote back asking for replacements to be sent out of the 'founder's pictures' that ought to be restored to main branch offices, Jock was not there to dwell on nor to restore the past although it was in his mind, and he and John Scott chatted about the company's past as they travelled north to Tianjin.[8] The firm was trying to reclaim its estate, however, and in that it found itself confronted and confounded by this new, self-confident and inflexible Chinese nationalism.

There was, Jock wrote, exasperated, a difficult atmosphere among the Chinese, 'so swollen headed and full of their own importance as the fourth great power, and all that nonsense'.[9] But China had emerged as one of the victors in the war, an independent Asian state in the front ranks of the institutions of the global order. This was – in modern history – unprecedented, and it was real, not simply rhetorical. In practical terms it meant all had changed for the foreign presence: no extraterritorial rights; no British Supreme Court; no Shanghai Municipal Council – its staff had left the camps and then had mostly left China for uncertain futures, and the foreign presence in the Customs Service was being whittled away. CNCo could not regain its river routes, nor its coastal trade (excepting that which originated in Hong Kong). No 'comprehensive modern' commercial agreement, as promised in the 1943 Friendship Treaty, was yet under negotiation, nor in fact would one ever be signed. First, the discussions were postponed, and then they ran only fitfully into 1948, but were overtaken by events. In the meantime, foreign firms could continue to operate under Chinese law, or try to. These formal manifestations of change aside, there were others. The new authorities in Shanghai had no appetite for restoring the physical symbols of the foreign presence. Only the plinth of the Allied War Memorial on the Bund survived, all its metalwork stripped away – among the names cast on it those of Butterfield & Swire's Great War dead – and no amount of lobbying moved the city government to allow it to be restored. The Shanghai Race Club ground had held meets well into the later stages of the conflict, but had now been taken over by the city and so it was goodbye to all that.

But this did not change the fact of possession, or at least in many cases title to it, nor the fact of the continuing presence: Butterfield & Swire was there, it occupied the river frontages, equipped with pontoons, hulks, piers and godowns, and its staff had the experience and the ships, tugs and lighters, and the staff and customers. It was quite understandable, then, that firms like Butterfield & Swire and Jardine Matheson would try to restore their old roles in shipping through more indirect means, and there was, as all agreed, a great demand for a rehabilitation of the country's transport infrastructure. The China Merchants SNCo had taken over all Japanese shipping assets, but found getting things moving an insuperable challenge, and when it did succeed it seemed that the military requisitioned anything that moved along the Yangzi. The stock of shipping was old and in poor shape. So, if Chinese interests could not get the country moving again, why not allow foreign ones to? The vehicle for China Navigation and for Jardines' Indo-China SNCo's efforts was the China National Relief and Rehabilitation Agency (CNRRA), the Chinese partner of the United Nations Relief and Rehabilitation Agency (UNRRA) (for in a wholly sovereign China, UNRRA was not to be allowed to operate independently).[10] In October 1945, through the Ministry of War Transport and Far Eastern Shipping Agencies (FESA), which was set up – the latter much on the initiative of Jock Swire – to manage requisitioned British ships, CNRRA contracted with CNCo and Indo-China SNCo to carry supplies out of Shanghai to northern and river ports. Much of this was paid for in London in sterling, a significant bonus, for currency controls made getting money out of China very tricky. Excess capacity on these runs was to be made available for commercial cargo and passengers. So CNCo was quickly also moving, and advertising its services to the public. In January 1946 this was confirmed to run a further six months, on the understanding that after the winding up of FESA on 2 March that year, the companies themselves would manage their ships themselves and administer the charters. In mid-March CNRRA's permission to use foreign-flagged vessels was extended for one year to March 1947.[11]

Things looked rosier than they had for some time, for the more deeply the firms became re-embedded in China's shipping infrastructure this way, the more weight, surely, that British arguments about restoring their legal positions in coastal and inland traffic might carry. But these moves prompted sustained and organised public protest, not least from Chinese shipping organisations, and the concession was abruptly withdrawn in July 1946. Butterfield & Swire and Jardine Matheson published a notice in the English- and Chinese-language press arguing that they were simply helping China's recovery: that they had the ships, the infrastructure and the experience with which to do so.

This, Chinese commentators responded, as the dispute rumbled on, was all perfectly true. But the issue in dispute was not China's need, it was China's sovereignty, and it was about nurturing and growing the country's own capacity. That was of far greater importance. Of course, it was an easy and convenient piety for comfortable merchant oligarchs to utter, for all were nationalists when nationalism provided them with commercial opportunity (and Jock was not alone in thinking, rightly, that the Chinese commercial interests managing CNRRA found it a very profitable enterprise), but even if so, sovereignty and independence was what China had fought for, for eight long years and at such horrendous cost. Millions had not died at Japanese hands to restore the Union Jack to the Yangzi. Swire staff were hardly unusual in being slow to develop the new understanding of China's politics that was needed. Some could not take it seriously; many had never given it much thought; many others were simply too busy with the noise of everyday life and work, and always still insulated from the world around them, to notice that things had changed. They might have lost the racecourse at Shanghai, and at Wuhan they had lost the Hankow club, but they had restarted one there in two rooms at the Hongkong & Shanghai Bank, reopened the Race Club with rooms in a private house and laid out a nine-hole golf course. They had improvised the old world, in among its ruins, for Wuhan had been very badly bombed, but they really did not seem to understand how ruined that world now was.[12]

The second strand of the CNCo China strategy was one which harked back to the position on the Upper Yangzi after the Wanxian disaster and to those conversations with Song Ziwen in the mid-1930s and wartime discussions about forming an Anglo-Chinese company. This idea was pursued, but here, too, the company ran into political opposition. The Shanghai Commercial and Savings Bank, which was headed by a friend of the company, financier K. P. Chen (Chen Guangfu), withdrew from discussions about a joint venture; and even long-standing Chinese partners and staff of Butterfield & Swire made it clear that they could not be involved. A plan had been hatched that would involve appointing them as directors, but with the capital coming from Butterfield & Swire until real Chinese shareholders felt comfortable enough with the political environment to participate.[13] This pragmatic sleight of hand was too obvious and carried too much danger for those who would be its most visible Chinese associates.

All CNCo could do then was run charters when it could secure official permission to – so in December 1948, for example, it was formally allowed to carry goods for eight months to a number of designated river and coastal ports for the Economic Cooperation Administration, a new vehicle for US aid to the beleaguered Nationalist regime. The *Tsinan* and *Nanchang* were among the ships that brought emergency shipments of rice to Shanghai from Hong Kong.[14] Meanwhile, the *Fatshan* continued to shuttle from Hong Kong to Canton, attracting as it did so larger and larger fines for smuggled goods discovered by the customs in hides cleverly constructed by members of the crew as China's economy continued steadily to collapse and import bans were put in place to stem hard currency outflows. There was 'no legitimate trade' at Canton, remarked John Masson in February 1947, and Chinese navy gunboats were the chief smugglers. But it was CNCo that was fined: £10,000 worth of these had accrued by 1948.[15] In the face of all these restrictions, and in the atmosphere of fervent nationalism, all CNCo's managers could do was improvise as circumstance allowed; but this was not a sustainable strategy.

The company also found itself saddled with those riverfront properties that it could no longer use, or certainly not use itself profitably. Yes, said the diplomats, your ownership rights are intact; however, under the 1943 treaty your right to use them for river traffic has lapsed.[16] At Nanjing, Wuhan and at Jiujiang (where 'our own coolies' were possibly behind agitation to evict them, for they wanted the work) properties had not been returned. At Xiamen the hong on the once-controversial 'Seaback' reclaimed land was now rented by the city government's Social Bureau which ran a tea shop there. At Tianjin they had two tenants: the US Marine Corps, who paid rent, and the Enemy Property Administration, who certainly did not. At Pudong, vacant lots had been occupied by squatters and now hosted a permanent looking village. And why, asked the authorities, do you station ships off your properties, for you have no right to use them. But these are hulks, responded the firm, they do not move, and they serve as floating warehouses and jetties. But this portfolio of repurposed vessels left the firm vulnerable, for they were, after all, ships, and they were ships on the river, where they should not be. As well as the charters, Butterfield & Swire had also done well from CNRRA's rental of space at Shanghai, Wuhan, Zhenjiang, Wuhu and Changsha, but this was all due to lapse with the end of CNRRA's work. In April 1947, with a view to extracting some return on its network of properties, and to keep it active in the expectation of some return to pre-war shipping rights, and, importantly, too, to protect itself against requisitioning of unused or underused property, the firm hived off CNCo's shore operations into a new wholly owned subsidiary, the Taikoo Wharf and Godown Company. This was to be registered in London and with the Chinese authorities. Formally established on 1 June 1948, a new policy of accepting 'outside' business at CNCo installations had begun as soon as the move had been confirmed.[17] There was no time to lose.

Meanwhile, the Chinese government's Navigation Bureau asked the firm to do something about the *Changsha* (which had struck a mine in 1945) and *Woosung* ('bombed, beached and burnt' in November 1943), or waive its claim to these wrecks which it said imperilled Yangzi shipping. Then there was the 'graveyard' of 'derelict craft' at the firm's Longhua anchorage, up the Huangpu River from Shanghai. Jock Swire visited it in March 1948 finding there, among other smaller vessels, the *Shasi*, 39 years old, the first CNCo steamer built at the Taikoo Dockyard now rusting and ill-suited for any profitable use. All were to be scrapped; 70 years of work and struggle on the Yangzi rotting at Longhua and the river network and the infrastructure at those ports not open to foreign trade stagnating. On 4 April 1946 Jock Swire and John Scott had dined with the Hongkong Bank's manager and the Customs Inspector-General, Lester Little. 'Gloom everywhere; all think we are heading for disaster in China,' recorded Little in his diary. I wonder, Jock wrote the following day, what opportunities there might be in Canada.[18]

But the London directors went to China in 1946 to scout out new possibilities, not admit defeat and retreat to the Rockies. One of these had been the subject of discussion in the constrained period before Pearl Harbor: a return to merchanting. John Swire & Sons had abandoned its trading operations over half a century earlier: tea, cotton and beer had lasted longest but had all been let go. Now it looked instead the best option for adapting the company's infrastructure to the new era in China. 'Almost anything will sell here,' reported Jock from Hong Kong. They knew they lacked the specific expertise required, although in a small way they had recommended such work as agents for Maclaine Watson's raw sugar in the 1930s, but even then the sales department was a 'Cinderella' operation that did not comfortably fit, and in 1941 had toyed with the idea of buying a company already operating in China, such as Dodwells. In 1945 and 1946 other options were discussed and in early 1946 a joint agency, Swire & Maclaine, was formed in partnership with Maclaine, Watson and Co., a company long established in Batavia. This firm had been closely connected with TSR since its creation, acted as Java agents for Blue Funnel and was working with CNCo as it directed energy into the Netherlands East Indies in 1946 as part of its response to the closing of routes in China.[19] The new company was registered in Hong Kong in 1946, and aimed to trade in Hong Kong, China and Japan. An early list of the agencies it held provides surreal reading after decades in which the story of the Swire companies has focused on shipping, sugar, shipbuilding and insurance. Here are synthetic fibres, pharmaceuticals from Boots, Beefeater gin, Winsor & Newton artists' colours, Schweppes cordials, Oxo, tennis rackets and more from T. H. Prosser and Sons, and Swift-brand tinned meat from Argentina. An engineering department was also set up.[20] This move, and this range of agencies, exposed the gulf between Warren Swire and his partners. Jock Swire was not impressed, thought the list 'simply fantastic' – and he did not mean this positively: he thought that it would 'do our reputation much harm', and that the new firm's name was 'vulgar' and inappropriate for China. But the commitment had been made, by 'London' – which meant by Warren Swire – and had to be implemented. Other ideas were thrown about. Perhaps we should set up a biscuit factory on the Quarry Bay site? Perhaps, Jock pondered, the future was bicycle-shaped? Two wheels had been the key mode of urban transport in China and Hong Kong since the onset of the Pacific war. Might we secure an agency? Or might we market a 'Taikoo' brand bicycle?

But instead of bicycles, John Swire & Sons turned to aviation and took to flight. The war had turned people's eyes to the air. It had been a tank war, an infantry war, a war at sea, a war on civilians – all these things – a bombing war and a rocket war, too. But it was also a war in which extensive networks of airborne transportation had been improvised across the globe. Chongqing had relied on these, first from Hong Kong and then from India, for moving supplies, mail and people. The wartime American airlift across the Himalayas was an astonishing achievement, moving three-quarters of a million tons of supplies across the mountains, in close on 200,000 flights. It would change strategic understandings of air power and the possibilities of air transport.[21]

These numbers mask the impact on the individual experience of the reality and the potential of aviation, including that of the firm's directors. In February 1942, for example, John Masson set off for his post at the Ministry of War Transport in India. He flew from Poole to Ireland, then to Lisbon, and on to Banjul, Lagos, Libreville – 'all very Conrad' – Kinshasha, along the Congo River and on to Kampala, and then north, flying low to watch crocodiles and hippos – 'literally thousands of the brutes in a most incredible sight' – to Khartoum, then past the Pyramids ('which did not look as impressive as I'd expected') to Cairo. The next stage took Masson to Basra, Bahrein, then Sharjah and eventually across the Gulf to Karachi and on to Calcutta. It took just under a month.[22] The war would leave in its wake not only a vast surplus of supply aircraft, and thousands of experienced pilots – the Americans alone had trained 400,000 by 1944 – but also a greater familiarity with flight and its possibilities.[23] Most people still moved by sea, and rail, but many had moved through the air and there had been a profound shift in the public consciousness, and now there was clearly a rival. It was not cheap, it was not settled yet within the infrastructure of global communications, but it was there, nonetheless.

The context in which aviation grew so rapidly after the war was also a political one. As well as national independence movements and newly independent states, the end of the conflict brought about what has been characterised as a 'second colonial occupation' of much of Britain's colonial empire, and those of other colonial powers as well.[24] Trends already in development at the end of the 1930s, stymied by the war, now shaped the economic development and colonial welfare programmes of colonial administrations. This acknowledged the power of nationalism, and the limited power of the colonial state to contain it through force, and sought partly to undermine it by raising living standards, but also by entrenching British interests in new developing states and economies – as the Colonial Office put it in 1948, they had a 'mutual interest ... in one another's prosperity', which also served as an insurance against political decolonisation, for an economic presence would remain. This modern incarnation of colonial power deployed technicians and scientists, agronomists and engineers, state-of-the-art technology and modern ideas and practices. Aviation was a vital tool in the new practice of empire. It was needed to move people, mail and goods. It brought with it radio. As well as a tool of development, it

was also always a tool for surveillance, control and violence. It was far
cheaper to build an aviation infrastructure than ports or railroads, and
could be done much more swiftly and run much more economically.
Aviation had already become familiar as a facet of imperial modernity
in the interwar period: air forces policed colonial subjects (as the
euphemism had it), and state-supported airlines such as Britain's
Imperial Airways made movement swifter across the far-flung networks
of the maritime empires.[25]

In only its second post-surrender issue, Hong Kong's *China Mail*
had carried an excited front-page story: 'HK–Sydney Daily Air Service!'
A Royal Navy Dakota had flown in on 11 September 1945. The navy
had 'pioneered several Pacific air routes', it ran, gaining invaluable
experience 'for peacetime air routes'.[26] Heads were still light in these
early days of liberation, but the prospect was not a new one. As early
as 1933 John Swire & Sons had discussed the possibility of securing
the agency for Imperial Airways – the British government's 'chosen
instrument' for empire aviation – if and when it began a service to East
Asia. Before Imperial set up its own agency in Hong Kong in 1936,
Butterfield & Swire had secured the agency there and retained it in
Shanghai thereafter. On 24 March 1936, the first Imperial Airways
service, a de Havilland Express mail plane, had coasted into the airfield
at Kai Tak, escorted on its final approach by nine Royal Air Force
aircraft, where it was received by His Excellency the Governor and with
editorial pride: distance had been annihilated, and 'to be but ten days
from the hub of the Empire restores the feeling … that Hongkong is
part of the Empire and not a no-man's land'.[27] The war brought an end
to this phase of Hong Kong's involvement in international air routes,
but not before Jock Swire himself boarded an Imperial Airways flight
at Kai Tak in May 1939 when he headed home after his duty visit 'out
East' that year. It was, he wrote, a 'truly wonderful journey'.[28] The
close of Imperial's Hong Kong office in 1941 prompted a detailed and
compelling proposal from Walter Lock, then Hong Kong Taipan, for a
Swire venture into aviation that would include the purchase of aircraft.
Perhaps a 'wildcat' scheme, he ventured, diffidently.[29]

Or perhaps not. Jock Swire had pondered such a move himself in
early 1939. The dockyard would need an 'aeronautical wing' to protect
itself 'against the future', he thought. Aviation was, however, notably
absent from the discussions about the company's post-war strategy in

the wartime correspondence between the directors, but they had, Jock later wrote, 'for a long time been determined that CNCo should by some means or other, if only for the protection of its own position, get into air'. In this he was in step with the directors of many other shipping interests at this time. And as Jock Swire landed back in Hong Kong in 1946 he was still thinking about it. Chance threw Jock on board a flight out east that carried a mission sent to explore a potential new airport site at Hong Kong, among them a senior manager from BOAC (as Imperial Airways was now renamed). Hong Kong, he told Swire, would most likely be 'the air focal point for the Far East' for that company in future. Jock wrote to Lord Knollys, chairman of BOAC, offering the firm's services informally, pointing out, of course, that CNCo provided 'valuable experience' on which BOAC could draw, and a network of branches. This did not make much headway, but they already had in mind a different potential proposition as Jock left England. The early stage of the war had brought CNCo into contact with the New Guinea-based Australian trading firm Colyer Watson. After a visit to wartime England, its chairman, Rupert Colyer, sent Warren Swire gossip, food parcels, and on 25 July 1945 a proposal that Butterfield & Swire should talk to 'two very good friends of mine', whose ideas and organisation might well mesh with the firm. This was Australian National Airways (ANA), a private venture run by Ivan Holyman and Ian Grabowsky. Grabowsky was a veteran of the development of air services in New Guinea; Holyman, whose family background lay in shipping – shipping interests that had established ANA in 1936 – had led the company since its inception, and its precursor, Holyman's Airways, since 1932.[30]

Once in Hong Kong events moved fast, and Jock Swire opened discussions with ANA that led to Butterfield & Swire formally securing the agency for its services from Australia to Hong Kong in June 1946. The only matter of detail that proved problematic was that ANA did not in fact yet run services any further north than Manila. This was thought a temporary hitch that could be smoothed out, but despite intense lobbying in Australia, Hong Kong and in London, the government in Canberra declined to offer it the route, reserving it instead for Qantas, as the state overseas airline. ANA had been the target of a sustained attack from the government in Canberra, which it had defeated in the courts in order to secure its own continued existence in the face of nationalisation, and from London, through the imperial government's

support for BOAC as state airline. 'There is a lot of politics in this air
business', Warren Swire had written after news of the ANA agreement
had first reached London, and there was so very much more of it to
come. Dirty politics, too, it was feared: Holyman believed that telegrams
not exchanged in cipher would swiftly find their way to the Australian
government. ANA's attempts to secure the China–Australia route were
also unsuccessful. This stalemate then turned the attention of Swires,
ANA and others, to more parochial opportunities, specifically to those
that might be offered to a Hong Kong-based airline. There was in fact
one to hand in the shape of a small 'tramp' outfit that had secured
formal registration in Hong Kong in September 1946.[31]

So the story of what became Cathay Pacific (CPA) certainly sits in
these earlier discussions and the network of clubbable contacts that
John Swire & Sons had always worked within, but it also begins with
a cargo of toothbrushes, combs, lipstick and second-hand clothing.
One legacy of the Hump enterprise was a small cargo company, set up
by two former Hump pilots, using a surplus C47 aircraft, in civilian
life a Douglas DC-3 airliner, known to the British as a Dakota. Roy
Farrell, a 45-year-old Texan, brought the plane with this motley load
into Shanghai for the first time on 9 January 1946, then started to
shuttle to and from Sydney via Hong Kong and Manila, drawing into
partnership a friend from the days of Hump traffic, an Australian pilot
named Sydney de Kantzow. Like Farrell, de Kantzow had also flown
commercially before the war. Consummate publicists, news stories about
the new firm found their way regularly into the press across Asia, helped
by advertisements for goods shipped into Hong Kong on the firm's fleet:
'Sydney Rock Oysters By Air', radios, Australian children's books in time
for Christmas and 'chic Australian swimwear', 'brought to you from
Australia's Sunny Beaches' in time for the summer by the Roy Farrell
Import-Export Company. Silk flew the other way, the first consignment
received in Australia for five years, it was claimed, and so did 'hand-
carved and hand-painted' 'luxury clogs', soon to be seen in Sydney night
clubs. 'Air Traders Discover China's Great Market' screamed one article
heading. And they claimed to have established the 'first International
Airmerchandising Service in the World'. 'It costs LESS today to send it
by CPA; 'Wing your way by CPA', barked the advertisements.[32]

Once it had restructured itself to create a majority British share
ownership, Cathay Pacific Airways was permitted to secure formal

registration in September 1946 and an expanding portfolio of routes out of Hong Kong. These included what it claimed was 'The FIRST Direct Air Service between Hong Kong and Australia', a flying boat service to Macao that was largely servicing a traffic in gold that was smuggled into China, Hong Kong to Manila services, and Hong Kong–Bangkok–Singapore, as well as a subsidiary that flew flights within civil war-torn Burma. CPA had a cowboy feel to it, and for all the alternately fairground barking and silkily smooth presentation of its services in the press, it has been the subject in retrospect of some of the mythmaking and romance that saturates the figure of the pilot and the history of flight more widely. In this story there are heroes and pioneers, poets and philosophers, doomed youth and aces – the few – and always a fair slathering of machismo, perhaps the many.³³ As a company CPA certainly flew by the seat of its pants. Crews accrued hours far beyond those that even then were considered suitable (for they were paid by the hour over a basic salary, and there was no limit to the hours), and it kept no proper accounts and little by way of statistics. Fittingly, its first public relations officer turned out to be a serial confidence trickster who was later fished out of Sydney harbour and jailed. It was 'a pirate outfit run on a shoe-string by a number of Australian adventurers' was one report. 'Australian' was possibly the most damning of the charges in the eyes of some of the Britons who looked askance at it.³⁴ Then a complaint to the Ministry of Aviation from the Singapore-based overseas manager of Horlicks about his 'nightmare' journey from Rangoon to Singapore made its way across ministries in Whitehall, over to the Hong Kong government and back, CPA's own rebuttal heading out to meet it. The aircraft was 'unfit for passenger service,' he claimed, conditions on board 'a disgrace to British Aviation', sanitary arrangements 'equivalent to a third rate latrine', and the pilots had flown dangerously long hours.³⁵ The complainant has 'perhaps had very little opportunity of travelling in Asiatic countries,' responded Hong Kong's director of civil aviation, Albert Moss, drily. Moss was by all accounts indulgent of the firm; and his alleged official partiality for CPA sparked BOAC's chairman to talk to and then write to the Permanent Under-Secretary of State at the Colonial Office, complaining about this hostility to its ventures in the colony. BOAC was, after all, 'the Government's chosen instrument', he noted. This was a 'monstrous' charge, responded Hong Kong's governor in turn, who expressed full confidence in Moss, but BOAC runs things 'extravagantly' and I do not want them 'controlling any local concern'.³⁶

This upstart airline attracted the attention of Butterfield & Swire's Hong Kong managers, who in January 1947 alerted ANA to CPA's new Sydney services and its ambitions to run a Hong Kong–London route. The 'neighbours' – as Jardines were now routinely labelled in correspondence – had pulled a surprise on them by securing a strong partnership with BOAC. (By this point, although the respective companies' directors largely remained on friendly terms, all the commercial amity and solidarity of the dark days of 1942 had long vanished.) Across 1947, Swire managers and directors struggled to make sense of the rapidly evolving world of aviation in Asia. John Masson and colleagues discussed their frustrations in Hong Kong in May that year. Should we stick to ANA, they asked, despite the lack of progress with securing routes, 'or should we start going down the scale? CPA?'. Should we form a local company ourselves, as Walter Lock had proposed back in 1941? 'Stick to ANA' was the conclusion. They liked Grabowsky and Holyman – the latter 'quite the most outstanding man we have yet met,' thought Jock Swire – and their operation was a strong one. They had vision and spirit. Then the neighbours pulled another surprise, and news broke in August 1947 that back in March, in collaboration with BOAC, they had established Hongkong Airways, a local company of their own, or so it seemed (and this claim was contested, for what was 'local' about BOAC which until the winter of 1948 owned most of the company?). What now forced a resolution, however, was CPA's own need to alter its ownership structure and regularise its British status 'as expeditiously as possible'.[37] The politics of national ownership had intervened, and remaining American ownership of some 35 per cent of the firm was now an impediment to its existence and registration in Hong Kong, let alone its future development.

Roy Farrell sold out, which eased things. After December 1947, initial discussions between de Kantzow and Grabowsky, who had arrived in Hong Kong after an unsuccessful visit to China to try to secure a concession for an Australia–China route, evolved into a set of negotiations about forming a 'genuine local company' involving Butterfield & Swire, as well as, until almost the last minute, Skyways, a privately owned British airline with international ambitions.[38] Finally, on 6 June 1948, Butterfield & Swire sent out a circular announcing the takeover of CPA, and its new role as managing agents of the firm; branches across China announced their role as its general agents and sought agency agreements with China's own state airline, aiming to feed traffic towards CPA, ANA and, initially, Skyways. In fact, two companies had been created: a new Cathay Pacific Airways, in which CNCo took 35 per cent, and John Swire & Sons 10 per cent of the shares, ANA 35 per cent, and de Kantzow and existing shareholders the remainder. De Kantzow was the manager, and Butterfield & Swire Hong Kong appointed one of its staff managing director. In addition, the CPA maintenance operation at Kai Tak was absorbed into a new Pacific Air Maintenance & Supply Company (PAMAS, as it became), a subsidiary 80 per cent owned by CPA and 20 per cent by Taikoo Dockyard and Engineering, which was to manage it. This seemed a natural extension of Taikoo Dockyard expertise, and it was noted that former Taikoo Dockyard staff had already found work as aircraft mechanics. It was a development that Jock Swire initially felt much more comfortable with.[39] 'Air', as the business was designated in company documents, involved bigger politics, and rather bigger egos, than John Swire & Sons was used to. Prime ministers intervened to protect national interests; state airlines drew on their masters to secure routes and monopolies. And de Kantzow's 'drive and dash' needed somehow to be 'grafted' on to Butterfield & Swire experience, and, of course, John Swire & Sons had no experience of the aviation business. But now its new operation was soon made clear to all, for one of de Kantzow's first suggestions was that the company install a neon sign on the Praya hong, 'sufficiently large to shine across the harbour'.[40]

So 'CATHAY PACIFIC AIRWAYS' shone out across the water, a calculated risk for Butterfield & Swire, for there was debate about keeping the name due to the potential 'bad odour' that might envelope it generally because of the more free-wheeling facets of its operations. In the end it was decided that for travellers, Horlicks' executives aside, it was known 'only as an ordinary airline'.[41] But Cathay Pacific's new era began with a criminal tragedy, partly a legacy of the less legal side of the Farrell/de Kantzow enterprise, but also a reflection of the endemic disorder and desperation that grew out of China's economic collapse and the hyperinflation that was settling in. On 16 July 1948 the evening return flight of Cathay's Catalina seaplane from Macao failed to arrive in Hong Kong. What looked like an accident that had consumed the lives of 22 of the 23 people on board turned out to have been a botched hijacking, and a grim landmark in the history of civil aviation, for it was the first such incident on a commercial aircraft. The only survivor was a member of the gang which, having purchased European clothing so as to blend in, had attempted to seize control of the aircraft, fly it to a secure location and rob its passengers or hold the wealthy to ransom. As the incident took place in Chinese airspace, with a British-registered aircraft, and the one potential defendant in custody in Macao, an effective prosecution seemed impossible. The man was never tried for the crime. So Cathay Pacific was in the news for all the wrong reasons, but at least it was not the airline's fault.[42]

This disaster was the least of the problems the new model airline faced, for even as it moved in an accountant, and started to try to get a grip on the figures and statistics, it was clear that there was little point in having an airline if it did not have routes, and CPA had been hemmed into its place in two ways. Firstly, it had been pushed out of its Hong Kong–Sydney run early in 1947. The Australian government withdrew its permission for the service, which formally had only been temporary, to support its own carrier's traffic to Singapore and then to London, and after a long delay granted CPA the right to a monthly unscheduled flight that was not permitted to carry passengers back to Hong Kong. The post-war period was one in which shipping interests like Swires, and, for example, Cunard White Star, realised that the growth of aviation needed consideration and a response, but it was at the same time a moment when political currents militated against the easy entry of private enterprise into a business that was seen as needing a state monopolistic response.[43] Secondly, in the autumn of 1947, Hongkong Airways – as BOAC's subsidiary – was granted the routes from Hong Kong to Macao, Shanghai and Guangzhou by the colony's government. Cathay Pacific and other airlines in Hong Kong had been permitted to continue their services to other destinations, including its Australia run, but not on any permanent basis.[44] Now it had no route south.

The politics were convoluted. The Hong Kong governor lobbied the Colonial Office on the basis that the hiatus in services to Sydney meant that demand could not be met (for passage space on shipping remained tight): it could not move its own policemen and their families when it wanted to send them on leave. On a visit to London Australian prime minister Chifley met the British Colonial Secretary, Arthur Creech-Jones, to press the case against Hong Kong allowing CPA to fly south. Well, responded Creech-Jones, 'the prosperity of

Hong Kong had been built up on private enterprise', and he could not therefore tell the colonial government that a private company could not be allowed to operate to Australia.⁴⁵ Colonial Office officials thought Australian demands impertinent, their tone 'particularly high-handed and unacceptable', and that they were 'simply holding a pistol at our heads, which seems to me', one wrote, 'a very improper thing for a Dominion to do to the mother country'. BOAC sat in strength in British Ministry of Civil Aviation meetings that made decisions about imperial 'trunk' routes, and through this presence Hong Kong Airways was able to take 'secure advantageous treatment for themselves vis a vis Cathay Pacific', who were not.⁴⁶ The chorus of pious self-interest was deafening. The assumption of control by Butterfield & Swire clearly enhanced the confidence the colonial government had already demonstrated in the firm – for while it was 'far from immaculate', it was contracted to fly the mail from Hong Kong to Singapore, for example – and this was reinforced in London: 'there is no doubt that the character of Cathay Pacific Airways has been changed completely by the recent reorganisation and that it is becoming a reputable company under the management and control of an old-established Hong Kong business firm'. And even if it wanted to continue the gold trade to Macao – which obviously supported smuggling into China – this was not illegal, and even if officials did not like it, or any trade which was not illegal but which disgusted them, there was no reason to obstruct it.⁴⁷

When taken over, CPA was flying twice weekly to Manila, monthly to Australia, twice weekly to Singapore via Bangkok, weekly to Calcutta and was still operating its Macao and Burma operations. On 28 June 1948 the firm formally applied for designation as the Hong Kong government's recognised airline on an extensive set of new routes, and outlined its intention to apply for permission to fly services to China as well. This hung fire until Lord Douglas, Marshall of the Royal Air Force and a director of BOAC, arrived in Hong Kong in January 1949, partly with the aim, he told the press, of discussing with the governor the issue of 'splitting the air routes'.⁴⁸ His guidance was quite clear: Hongkong Airways and CPA should come to an agreement themselves, which he for a start would then support. The firms started talking swiftly after this in the Jardines board room in Hong Kong, and then formal negotiations began in London which reached a conclusion on 11 May when BOAC, Jardine Matheson, and John Swire & Sons, agreed what was termed a north/south division of routes. As Jardines/BOAC were already in possession, they focused on preserving their hold on traffic north; for Butterfield & Swire the south was 'absolutely vital', for without it CNCo's Straits business would be overflown. The Ministry of Civil Aviation and Governor Alexander Grantham in Hong Kong quickly signalled their approval.

So lines were drawn on the map, the only overlap being the Hong Kong–Manila route where both retained equal rights, and BOAC's 'trunk' services. In retrospect, and retrospect would clearly be the only perspective, this proved to be a spectacular own goal for Jardines and BOAC: on 16 May, three days after the agreement was approved by the Ministry of Aviation, a Hongkong Airways plane made the firm's last ever landing in Shanghai; thereafter all services were suspended. Up to five planes a day had been setting north to bring out refugees as Communist forces advanced on the city.[49] The lull in services became permanent. The airline continued flights to Guangzhou and Kunming, but these ended as the Communists moved to occupy the rest of the country. The 'present disturbance' of air services in China became a prolonged hiatus that became a cessation. There were to be no flights to China from Hong Kong. So that, in fact, was that. All Hongkong Airways retained an exclusive right to was the Hong Kong/Tokyo route.

Success could not be built on luck. It would take some time for Cathay Pacific to begin to show any profit. And rapidly the clash between de Kantzow's 'buccaneering' style and the management culture at Butterfield & Swire turned into a problem. Admiration turned to anxiety, and worse: 'it terrifies me,' reported John Masson. It went beyond personalities. To the steady mercantile eyes of men like Eric Price, acting Hong Kong Taipan, it seemed to be embedded in the culture of the world of aviation, and that included ANA. Nothing in their careers with B&S had prepared men like these for working with their new associates. Price had joined in 1925 and had done his time: assistant on CNCo business, sugar travelling in north China and Manchuria, CNCo chartering at Shanghai, agent at Chongqing, Xiamen, Kobe, chief at Bombay and now the plum post after 20 years of steady work. 'These air people are rather extraordinary,' he exclaimed, at what seemed the sudden transfer of Grabowsky out of Hong Kong, where he held ANA's seat on the CPA board, to Ceylon where the company was making a further investment into a regional airline. And

the following month, 'I continually find myself horrified,' he wrote,
unable to let go of the thought, 'by the gay "Well, why not? Let's try it"
attitude one encounters around a table when people like de Kantzow,
Roy Farrell, Grab[owsky] are at it.'[50]

By the summer of 1951 all could sit around that table a little less
anxiously. De Kantzow had resigned and·sold out, taking his creative
talents, eye-watering expense account habits and 'outrageous business
proposals' back to Australia.[51] This left the problem of what to do with
the air-conditioned 'box' in which he had worked at the Butterfield &
Swire headquarters, for de Kantzow was not, in both the ways it might
be read, a man who was prepared to sweat out his days in the hong.
CPA's losses were being partially offset by 'considerable profits' that the
Burma venture delivered, but these would be cut off in July 1950 when
the government there looked set to nationalise civil aviation and CPA
withdrew. It was not until 1951/2 that a small surplus was made. But
slowly thereafter the business grew, investing in new aircraft, and by
1954 passenger numbers had doubled on those at takeover, and cargo
tonnage had tripled. The relationship with ANA remained vital. The
Australians provided expertise, training and staff, mentoring the new
firm. But at the same time Holyman's company was losing its battles in
Australia to the state-owned domestic carriers.

The fastest scheduled flight from London to Hong Kong in the winter
of 1950/51 cost £193, one way, and took just under 48 hours, while a
more leisurely journey with two overnight stops and time for a spot of
sightseeing, took three and a half days.[52] Some with a choice preferred
less hurry as they travelled, or thought they did. On his directorate visit
east in the winter of 1951/2, John Scott sailed on P&O's liner *Canton*,
a 'beastly, hot, dirty, noisy' ship, carrying no fewer than 130 children in
first class: 'I shall stick to flying in future,' he wrote.[53] Most people had
no choice, and so still travelled by sea, which was significantly cheaper,
even in first class. As well as attempting to defend itself by getting into
aviation, CNCo needed to open new routes, or refresh old ones. CNCo
had from the start identified re-establishing its routes to the Straits as 'a
first priority' – assuming in this that the Shantou and Xiamen emigrant
trade could be restarted – and the Australian trade as 'Priority 2'. By
1947 it was also looking to establish itself on routes to Japan from
Shanghai and Tianjin. The move into the Dutch East Indies traffic
was one such initiative, but the more substantial one was that priority

no. 2: Australia. The vehicle for this was the Australian Oriental Line, a
service with old partners Yuills, somewhat moribund as a business, but
tenacious when it came to the deal that they struck with Jock Swire in
1946 and which was elaborated thereafter. The old CNCo services from
China to Australia had ended in 1912. Immigration restrictions, and
the rapid decline in the market for green teas, had crippled the original
trade. A revived service focused on the trade north to Manila in frozen
meat – the American occupation of the Philippines and technological
innovation had provided a dual opportunity – but in 1912 the
remaining CNCo steamers on this route were sold to Yuills. In spring
1939, there was much chat about starting again as the Japanese invasion
had so crippled CNCo's business activity. There was 'a new world to
conquer', thought one manager, but Jock Swire was dubious, for the
China contribution to the trade would be 'infinitesimal', and China
was the company's speciality.[54] Only with the onset of the European
war had a connection resumed, with the assigning of the *Yunnan* to
pick up the export trade in copra that had previously been the business
of German interests.

For CNCo the need for a southern policy was now existential. It
had the ships, despite its losses, and had invested £2 million in new
tonnage, with five ships in construction, and they needed business.
This new trade first used the *Yochow* and *Yunnan*, once they had
been released from the Ministry of War Transport, and then the new
builds, culminating in the large liners *Taiyuan* and *Changsha*, delivered
from Scotts, bigger and better furnished than ever had been CNCo
custom, among the additions air-conditioning and dedicated tourist-
class accommodation.[55] Ships needed cargo and passengers, and they
needed crews. Restoring an effective marine staff proved difficult, for
good men had been leaving CNCo before the climacteric of 1941/2.
The 'seniors are very loyal,' reported John Masson in January 1947, 'but
the new recruits … have no traditional company loyalty.' Conditions in
Shanghai 'disgusted' them; Hong Kong was too expensive; promotion
prospects – the old complaint – looked poor, and terms of service
contrasted badly with those in other companies managed by Butterfield
& Swire: dockyard employees, for example, had free housing. Men
wanted leave, and they wanted to be with families.[56]

And what of the man who had once routinely pointed out that these
were his ships? While images of the founder were reinstalled in branch

offices, the last man living who had actually taken a photograph of the Senior, his son Warren Swire, was still involved in discussions about company policy and operations. But this was by now a problem. He had bypassed Jock Swire and John Scott entirely when he railroaded through the Swire & Maclaine deal in their absence in April 1946. 'We just can't agree and what happens next I don't know,' Jock confided to his diary on receiving the news. What happened next was that Warren was ousted as chairman in November that year, resigning, as he put it, 'in response to the urgent representations of the other directors', and was replaced by Jock, and thereafter Warren Swire played no determining role in the 'Brave New World', as he sarcastically called it, although his neat pencilled comments continued to pepper the letters in the files, and he could remain 'very obstructive', as he was over the CPA deal in 1948. In a note on directorial responsibilities drawn up in October 1946 he is almost entirely missing: this assigns TSR, insurance, and Swire & Maclaine primarily to John Swire Scott, shipping and shipbuilding to Sir John Masson (who had been knighted for his wartime work), with all staff, most properties, the paint company and air to Jock Swire. Only in 'politics' and the China Association did Warren Swire retain a formal presence. For the Scotts and Jock, recovery was predicated on a 'virile machine', and that involved, they all agreed, forcing the chairman of nearly 20 years' standing to step down.[57]

In later life, Jock would write that Warren had a 'mad streak'. He was characterised by all who knew him as difficult, and in individual appreciations, even when positive in many ways (which all in their various ways were), he was described as obstinate, bigoted and ruthless. He was clearly a man who struck fear into his subordinates, and wore down his partners (Colin Scott decamped to Scotland), and the tone and content of his private wartime letters, and much in his behaviour towards Jock Swire, signal that these were the manifestations of a far deeper problem, and one that grew worse in the 1940s. Failing health certainly did not help, but it provides no explanation. Warren Swire died in November 1949 of a heart attack, CNCo putting its ships into mourning in the aftermath, but he had attempted to pursue a vendetta against his nephew even from beyond the grave, his only weapon his will, more obvious eccentricities in which attracted bemused attention from the press.[58] The challenges facing John Swire & Sons as the war had drawn to a close were fantastically and bewilderingly diverse and they were dishearteningly steep, but we should also note that one of those challenges was its chairman, Warren Swire. The firm survived after 1945 partly through his forced removal from its direction, and through the new direction, priorities and tone that were set by Jock Swire, with the support of his colleagues, and with the very strong support, in the shape of generous credits, from the Hongkong & Shanghai Bank's chief manager in Hong Kong, Sir Arthur Morse.[59] This is a story of capital, technological innovation, international politics and economics, but it is also always a story, too, about people, and the far-reaching impact that an individual could have.

It is also a story of place. One feature of the history of British presence in China across the 1930s and 1940s was a steady drift of its centre of gravity to Hong Kong or, from a wider historical perspective, back to Hong Kong. As the Nationalists consolidated their authority and started drafting and implementing legislation and myriad forms of registration across all sectors, British firms had slowly started to shift formal registration to Hong Kong. The invasion in 1937 prompted an increase in the scale of this strategic rethinking by British interests: Butterfield & Swire's Orient Paint & Varnish Company (OPCo) was just one of those firms: incorporated in Shanghai in 1936, its registration was transferred to Hong Kong in 1947.[60] It also sparked an exodus of British residents as well, for many of those who fled the fighting did not return. The world war and the difficulties of the peace further accelerated these trends. Many stayed on, their experience and expertise of limited use away from the Bunds at Shanghai, Tianjin or Wuhan, however different these now looked, but for a growing number Hong Kong was a good alternative, and then it would become the only option. John Masson remarked in early 1947 on the 'Invasion of Hong Kong' by British Shanghai firms: Mardens, Moller, and Ellis Hayim were shifting operations into the colony.[61] Many more would follow, and not the British ones alone.

When Masson had visited Tianjin in spring 1947, he also noted that Communist guerrillas were active around the city, effectively blockading its communications with its hinterland, and that the city was under curfew. Its position was buffeted to an extent by the American military presence, but this was not permanent. A later note he sent home on the 'General Political Situation' was downbeat. 'Corruption', 'inefficiency' and 'conceit' – for which read nationalist self-confidence – were gnawing away at Guomindang rule. But like very many foreign observers, Masson also thought that the Communists, even if they triumphed, would inevitably oversee much by way of continuity from the current regime. How could they manage large and complex industrial and commercial cities? They had no experience, and they would need to retain experienced civil servants and men of commerce. Any victory would be a rerun of '1927', that last handover – setting aside the Japanese interregnum – still crisply fresh in many British minds. The idea that the Chinese Communist Party was in essence an agrarian socialist movement was pervasive and led to a woeful underestimation of their ambitions wholly to reform society.[62]

On his second post-war visit to China in early 1948 Jock Swire thought it astonishing that 'any nation could go as rapidly downhill in two years as these people had'. Tianjin was 'dying on its feet' but even though godowns were healthily full at Wuhan, and 'the coolies are singing', the hollowing out of the Chinese state by the long war, the widespread demoralisation of China's peoples by continuing economic crisis, the vicious reaction of Guomindang security agencies towards popular protest and the growing strength and opposition of the Communist Party's insurgency were pushing the country to the edge.[63] US president Truman's administration engaged in a series of mediation efforts, but peace deals when brokered soon fell apart. It also supplied significant amounts of aid and military assistance to the Nationalist government as the Cold War grew frostier. But it seemed that that simply whetted their appetite for more, to no tangible effect. When John Scott secured an interview with Song Ziwen in December 1948 he found him playing this card: 'the world must support the K.M.T. [Guomindang] as a barrier against communism,' Song barked, 'international war against communism was unavoidable, and China was in the front line'. Fine words. A month later, in Shanghai, the chief of protocol for Minister for Foreign Affairs Wu Tiecheng called on Scott to ask if he might, as a favour, arrange shipment of 120 packages of 'the Minister's personal luggage to Hong Kong'. So while the Guomindang's rhetoric was all fight; its actions were, instead, increasingly all flight.[64] And if you page through contemporary records and news reports, you will invariably spot, in among the upheavals of 1948 and 1949, references to Butterfield & Swire and its companies, for despite the difficulties they laboured under, operations were kept in train. Two such, however, point to the dramatic direction in which events were starting to turn. In November 1948, Nationalist army deserters piled on to the *Hanyang* at embattled Tianjin, defying efforts to remove them, and were shipped south. And when *Tsinan* returned to Hong Kong on 29 November 1948 from shipping rice to famished Shanghai, it brought back 350 refugees, described as such.[65] People were on the move: cities were falling to the Communists, whose momentum was accelerating and to whose victory some now looked, simply because it might bring some stability and peace: China had been at war most of the time since 1937.

On 1 October 1949 Mao Zedong proclaimed the establishment of the People's Republic of China (PRC). The stop-start conflict had rapidly swung in favour of the Communists in 1948/9. They had seized control of Manchuria, then captured Tianjin in January 1949 and Shanghai by the end of May. A confidential circular to Butterfield & Swire staff – that was only to be read in the office and was not circulated – outlined a strategy of constructive engagement with Communist-held areas. Trade with the West was 'the only means of economic survival' for China, it claimed; keeping communications open would help encourage party factions that wished to engage and benefit from foreign expertise and assistance.[66] As the noose tightened, defeat turned to rout and foreign interests found themselves behind the lines as the fighting moved on. After Tianjin fell Butterfield & Swire attempted to reopen services as soon as it could. The disorder seemed to offer an opportunity for a neutral third party to service a divided country, for none expected the coming collapse. An early report from the city, three weeks after its capture, was guardedly optimistic. Practical difficulties aside, things gave 'the appearance of normality', old regime officials had been ordered to stay at their posts and the behaviour of the Communists had been 'exemplary' as regards discipline. A portent of things to come might have been spotted in the 'feeling of utter hopelessness' engendered by attempts to communicate with the Foreign Affairs Bureau of the new regime. But that was perhaps just a detail and temporary and for some there was much to be hopeful about for, despite inflation and anxiety, north China was now at peace, 'and we feel that the Chinese merchant will find a way' to get things moving again properly.[67] But the Communists would not recognise the British as a neutral party, and in July 1949 the Guomindang, having been pushed out of the north and east, their capital captured and relocated first to Guangzhou and then to Taipei, ordered an embargo of Communist-held territory. In early August foreign shipping at Tanggu was seized by the Nationalist navy. This would be enforced well into the 1950s as the new regime entrenched itself on the Chinese mainland.

It was not simply a paper blockade. Blue Funnel's SS *Anchises* was bombed as it entered the Huangpu in June 1949, with one serious injury. The following day it was strafed. CNCo's *Anhui* hit a Nationalist mine as it entered Shantou's harbour in June 1950. Nationalist aircraft bombed and strafed it during subsequent salvage operations. The absence of casualties was simply a matter of chance. Foreign-flagged ships running the blockade were still being attacked in 1954/5, although in general they were simply ordered to turn back to Hong Kong, at gunpoint. Butterfield & Swire would be caught up in this continuing low-intensity phase of the civil war in other ways. The *Hupeh* was boarded by heavily armed pirates outside the Yangzi estuary in October 1951, the assailants being allowed to leave unharmed when a Royal New Zealand Navy vessel came to its rescue. They were in all likelihood Nationalist guerrillas, but the distinction was at many points quite unclear.[68] Also unclear was the actual guilt of two of the ship's stewards, who were arrested in Tianjin in November 1953 and charged with being members of a Nationalist secret service sabotage team. Well, British diplomats thought, how else might Nationalist agents get into north China, except via the blockade runners. Captain William Hargrave disagreed. A near-25-year veteran of the fleet, he thought the men were simply smuggling for profit, as crews always had, and six more of the men had resigned as soon as the ship got back to Hong Kong. The point was academic. One of the men was executed, the other jailed, along with other accomplices of this 'Chiang Bandit Group'.[69] On 23 July 1954 a Cathay Pacific Skymaster en route back to Hong Kong from Singapore was shot down by Communist air force jets in international airspace near the island of Hainan. With steady nerves and a great deal of skill, the pilot managed to ditch his burning aircraft, which was followed most of the way down by the fighters, which continued to fire at it. Prompt action by the US air force delivered eight survivors to Kai Tak, but 10 people died. The government in Beijing did provide a formal apology, explained that the attackers thought it was a Nationalist plane on its way to raid Hainan and provided a quarter of a million pounds by way of compensation. That did not bring anybody back.[70]

The British government had formally recognised the new regime on 6 January 1950.[71] But, bewilderingly, this elicited no response whatsoever from the new capital at Beijing. Instead, the authorities refused to recognise the status of British or other NATO-bloc diplomats. The situation was further complicated by the entry of Chinese 'volunteers' into the Korean War in late 1950 and at times a much wider conflict appeared to threaten as that conflict continued into 1953. British officials pondered, for example, what to do with Chinese seamen on British ships in the event of strife. Since 1948 they had also been fighting a mostly Chinese Communist insurgency in Malaya. And there was extreme anxiety over the security of Hong Kong. Companies like John Swire & Sons certainly wondered about the wisdom of heavy investment in the colony when a violent takeover seemed possible, although this threat would pass as the new regime seemed content to leave forcing the issue to another time.[72] But the potential of events in the colony to spark a response across the border has been a feature of this history. That continued to be the case. In January 1948 Butterfield & Swire's Guangzhou office had been burned out during a riot in protest at Hong Kong police attempts to evict squatters from the Kowloon Walled City.[73] The civil war itself washed people into the colony. Between 1945 and 1951, when border controls were imposed, 1.4 million refugees found shelter in the colony, and just over 400,000 more came in the following 10 years. These included many entrepreneurs whose impact on Hong Kong's economy would be significant. They brought with them skills, capital, and in some cases, their assets, not excepting ships.[74] Hong Kong now set out on its road to becoming a Cold War enclave, and a manufacturing marvel.

Formal diplomatic relations between Britain and the People's Republic of China would not be established until 1972, and it was only from 1954 onwards that the British envoy in Beijing was recognised in any way. Meanwhile, as it consolidated its hold on the mainland, conquering the south and south-west, and dislodging Nationalist forces from Hainan island, and then launching a bloody 'campaign to suppress counter-revolutionaries' in March 1950 during which more than 700,000 people were killed (far more than was required in the quotas set by the government), the new state appeared not to initiate any specific policy towards the foreign business establishment in China.[75] There was one exception to this: it required them to keep functioning, and this was increasingly to prove no easy matter.

Like other foreign-owned firms, the Swire company interests were effectively held hostage in China until they were finally closed down. At first, the directors and managers had assumed that Communist victory would lead to a resumption of commercial life, and that that might continue to evolve as its interests did so. In June 1949, Butterfield & Swire had even mulled over seeing if they could find a way for Cathay Pacific to provide a service from Hong Kong to Shanghai.[76] Although obstacles began to be put in the way of their operating competitively or effectively, and so receiving income, they were required to continue to keep staff employed, and to keep their installations in good working order. New taxes and levies were imposed. Eventually, official permission was needed even to sell anything surplus to requirements, including in one request, 16 desks and tables, three ceiling fans and eight old typewriters (for there was less and less to type up). The response to this trivial list was so delayed that even the British ambassador was called on to help them secure an answer, any answer.[77] Ready money grew short. And so opened the 'China drain', into which by early 1954 Butterfield & Swire was throwing £10,000 a month remitted into China from Hong Kong. To keep the money flowing, foreign staff were prevented from leaving China, some for years after they had formally applied for exit visas. Individuals were held responsible for their firms, and this would also include being held personally to account for administrative or technical errors. This period of 'hostage capitalism', as it has been termed, would last in the case of Butterfield & Swire for five years, and the departure from China took place as other major enterprises also extricated themselves. By 1957 only Shell and the Hongkong & Shanghai Bank remained, last remnants of the 114-year British presence in Shanghai.[78]

Reflecting on the firm's experience during these years, John March, who negotiated the final exit, identified three phases in the ways their operations were handled after the coming to power of the Communists.[79] First there was a period of consolidation, then from late 1952 a period of control, and then from autumn 1953 onwards a period of 'impatience'. In the first, labour was encouraged to confront management, which was forced to recognise and deal with it, and at the same time obstacles were introduced to prevent companies retrenching in any way. Increased staff costs needed to be met, somehow. The post-war economic crisis had underpinned seemingly incessant labour conflict in Shanghai, the Swire enterprises experiencing their share of that. The blockade, augmented by Nationalist air raids, further damaged the economy. Now organised labour bargained from a position of very great political strength. You have no right, Butterfield & Swire told the city Labour Bureau in Shanghai in 1950, to set levels of pay in a 'private enterprise'. Oh yes it did, replied the Labour Bureau, ordering Taikoo to meet the demands made to it for increases by the Seamen's Union.[80] In the second period, party cadres began to wield greater power both within firms and from without, reining in the exuberance of labour and moving to restrict the options open to managers. In the third, the pressure grew so intense that Butterfield & Swire moved to wind up its China operations completely. Many of these strategies were deployed against Chinese companies as well, and foreign enterprises were to an extent buffered from the full force of what began to be unleashed against private enterprise. This realisation did not make it any easier for them. There was little outright requisitioning (although all the hulks, those survivors in some cases of the days of sail, were taken over, some 'unused' land was taken over at Tianjin, and CNCo godowns and properties were seized at Guangzhou in February 1953).[81] One factor which shaped this process overall, and which underpinned Chinese policy, was that in some instances there was initially no alternative cadre of staff or any agency that could take over these complex established interests. But once something had been readied, the pace of change quickened rapidly. Throughout this period there was a steady policy of what staff described as harassment. In late 1953, for example, accusations were made that some of the firm's activities in Shanghai in 1951/2 had been illegal. (Cross-financing 'general B.& S. interests' with the proceeds of Swire & Maclaine sales was the point of vulnerability.)[82] A team of investigators then descended on the offices, 'rummaging for weeks through files, removing sheaves of correspondence, and muttering about the penalties that should be awarded those who sabotaged the country's economy'.

Some branches remained self-financing, drawing an income from rentals, but when the authorities decided to move their costs steadily mounted: tenants would be ordered not to pay, or applications for approval of rental agreement renewals went undecided. After Shanghai closed its insurance business in December 1952, it took 18 months and round after wearying round of negotiation with the unions, to pay off 16 now idle employees. When a manager secured his exit visa and left, the firm found itself required to employ his otherwise redundant personal servants. Contractors' staff were ordered to be brought on to the company's own books. It took a year and a half to pay off four lunchroom stewards who had no lunchroom to service, and two chauffeurs who had no cars to drive. Three hundred and fifty seamen, paid off at Wuhan in 1939 after it fell to the Japanese, lodged claims for post-1949 retiring grants. Those staff who did actually have something still to do stuck strictly to their precise responsibilities and refused to take on any others. No ships docked at Holt's Wharf in Shanghai for three years after May 1949, yet the firm was required to continue to employ and pay 439 staff. It cost the company £100,000 a year. Applications to shut down the Orient Paint & Varnish Company in September 1951 and April and then June 1952 were simply ignored. The last request also covered Holt's Wharf and the Shanghai operations of Swire & Maclaine and TSR. In November 1952 a further request to close down Holt's Wharf finally secured a response. Clearly the local authorities were now ready, and a successor Wharf Company had been organised. On 2 February 1953 the company was closed and its assets transferred. At the same time 'more than normal indoctrination' of staff at the paint factory was assumed to be a prelude to an opening of negotiations there as well. On 29 July 1953, after some difficult negotiation during which, at a late stage, the company's sales representatives were ordered by the Chinese authorities to instruct customers not to buy their company's products and not to pay debts to it, the Orient Paint & Varnish Company's plant and all assets and staff were transferred to a Chinese enterprise.[83]

If the impact on the business of Butterfield & Swire and its companies was significant, the effect of the stresses of this period on its staff was wearing. Disputes might see them locked in their offices well into the night. Their interlocutors often followed them to their homes and continued disputes there. The police arbitrarily summoned them for questioning. An example of the ease with which minor matters could be magnified out of any seeming proportion was the detention in a police cell for more than three weeks in September 1950 of Shantou agent Martin Speyer. This partly stemmed from the aftermath of Nationalist attacks on SS *Anhui*. The skeleton crew kept on board during salvaging operations fled the ship on a lifeboat when it was attacked, and the salvage tug fled back to Hong Kong. The crew made landfall, their lifeboat being wrecked in the process, and made their way to Shantou. Speyer was ordered by the Navigation Bureau to produce the boat, which seemed to him as pointless an operation as it was a difficult one, and also to explain why it had another vessel's name on it. As this became an object of controversy in itself, so did the unauthorised departure of the tug, and the arrival of the SS *Hanyang* in port carrying its standard complement of seven armed piracy guards, who were registered as such with the Hong Kong police force. The men were promptly arrested, their presence on board deemed an unlawful entry into China, their arms illegal and their relationship to the colonial police force an affront to China's sovereignty. On the afternoon of 2 September Speyer was arrested and held in the Public Security Bureau station at Shantou, questioned over several days about these charges and detained until the end of the month while the case was referred to the provincial government for consultation. Speyer had promptly, and sensibly, as the easiest way to resolve matters, signed a 'confession' and apology – some points, such as the status of the guards, having been clarified sufficiently.[84]

It might have been worse. Speyer, born in Shanghai in 1914, and the son of a piece-goods trader, spent the time reading, and studying Chinese, was permitted to see his sub-manager Maurice Ching, and to conduct company business this way, and have meals sent in from his home. He suffered, he reported, 'no particular hardship'. His attitude, the Hong Kong Taipan thought, was 'extremely charitable'. Speyer would in later life rise to senior positions in the firm in Australia, and was never known to be a patient man: his charity was a function of the fact that he knew his letters were likely to be intercepted.[85] The piracy guards had a tougher time. They were put through a 'course of education', they stated in their own 'letter of confession', and 'we now fully realise our fault in having been instigated by the Imperialists to break the shipping regulations'. Speyer was fined 300 million yuan (then roughly £3,000), and left China six months later. Xiamen manager R. D. Morrell left in March 1951. The entire region was still a civil war front line, with Nationalist-held Jinmen island (Quemoy) barely a mile offshore.[86] For the previous 12 months, after being arrested and detained overnight for unwittingly wandering into a prohibited area, Morrell had not dared venture out of the office or his home on Gulangyu island. The entire experience felt like being incarcerated and left him unsettled.[87] At Tianjin in January 1954, after being pelted with obscenities and threatened with an occupation of the firm's offices, Sidney Smith was knocked down and left unconscious during an altercation outside the People's Court where dependants of former CNCo seamen were pursuing claims against the company.[88]

Looked at another way, Speyer, Morrell and Sidney Smith had had it easy, and they will have been well aware of this. Chinese staff were under much more intense pressure. Yao Kang had joined the company in Shanghai in April 1948, after graduating from what became Peking University. Trained in Hong Kong and then in London – where he was the Hong Kong office's representative at Warren Swire's funeral – Yao was appointed to the Shanghai office in early 1951. From the moment of his arrival in China he was regarded with suspicion, required to provide an account of his life for the authorities and once at work was spied upon routinely, his wastepaper basket rifled through at the end of each day, his house searched and his daily activities subject to surveillance. The house was at least a large one, much grander than a man of Yao's junior status would normally secure. This was a company tactic, scattering its staff across its by then quite extended estate to keep squatters at bay. Yao's status as a returnee, who worked for a foreign firm, and who had graduated from a foreign-run university, made him triply suspect, even before his family background and networks were brought into the equation. The house also proved a liability: much of it was closed off, but when investigators rifled through it they found evidence that it had formerly housed a senior wartime collaborator. That taint attached itself to Yao.[89] His wife swiftly sought permission to return to Hong Kong.

Yao's work largely involved deflecting as far as possible charges laid against the firm by the tax authorities and the police – for now the expediency of receiving sterling payments overseas became a liability, for it was charged as being designed to allow the firm to evade taxes. The worst period was that of the movement attacking corruption, tax evasion and other economic crimes generally known as the Five Antis campaign – *wufan yundong*.[90] This also served to terrorise the urban middle classes. One of the company's senior managers was 'severely questioned and forced to confess' to the firm's use of Japanese raw materials taken over at the end of the war, as well as currency 'crimes'. Another was 'severely questioned on two occasions for a number of hours', and was now 'on the verge of suicide'. To make matters even worse, 'one of his very close friends murdered his four children and his wife and then committed suicide'. There were large numbers of self-killings in Shanghai. This note, forwarded to the Foreign Office, records without much remark that a man had just jumped from a neighbouring building, falling to his death close to Butterfield & Swire's front door.[91] Despite these peaks of crisis and the fear they instilled, the agility, persistence and realism of men like Yao, Shantou China manager Maurice Ching, and Shanghai sub-manager Ma Zung Yee, would prove critical to the firm extricating itself from China.

Getting out of Shanghai was discussed as early as March 1952: conditions there were 'becoming utterly intolerable' as the Five Antis campaign unfolded, but it was still thought that other branches might hold on. Consideration of the problem was hampered by some practical difficulties. One of these was communicating with the staff in China. Hong Kong and Shanghai could talk by telephone, but all knew that this was not secure, and any move would need to be prepared discreetly in advance. In letters and telegrams names were replaced by a rough code. The second problem was more challenging: the difficulty of actually finding somebody to talk to. Former Shanghai manager Bill Rae-Smith found it 'not possible to see anybody higher than the office boy', John Scott reported in March 1953, or if they did manage this, they found it impossible to get a decision.[92] But in the autumn of 1953, a memorandum from Shanghai manager Deryk de Sausmarez Carey reached Hong Kong 'by a safe and circuitous route'. Carey assessed the situation to date, and recommended a closedown, or, as he put it clearly and bluntly, 'a policy of scuttle'. 'I'm aware,' he wrote, 'that empires were not built on defeatism but there is no room for adventure under communism.' And, this 20-year veteran of Butterfield & Swire operations across a number of branches pointed out, this was also a matter of nationalism. In fact, Carey argued,

> rampant Chinese nationalism. And this upsurge is not new. It represents the arrival at maturity of the movement that has been stirring all this century, but this time it has a dedicated leadership and a sense of purpose.[93]

So in early May 1954 Jock Swire, visiting Hong Kong, recorded a terse note in his diary: 'Decided to get out of China lock stock and barrel if possible.'[94] It took some time to arrange an entry visa, but on 20 July

1954 John March arrived in Shanghai as its new manager with a very clear remit: he was to shut everything down. After just under 90 years of operating in China, John Swire & Sons had concluded that nothing was to be gained by staying on any longer. The firm needed to find a way to liquidate its assets and service its liabilities. March was set the objective of securing an all for all agreement.

On 2 September discussion began with a negotiator named Ho arranged by the Shanghai city government's Foreign Affairs Bureau, a man who had negotiated the surrender of Holt's Wharf in 1952. The key points of principle were quickly agreed. All the associated companies were to be treated as a single entity, and the 11 negotiating sessions thereafter, which lasted until 15 December when the deal was signed, and which included a significant hiatus when the Chinese refused all contact, largely revolved around valuation and a number of minor claims. The company had to make one final remittance, but then was relieved of this drain on its finances. As John Scott put it in a note to the British Foreign Office in October 1954, 'as the assets were worth anything from £2/3,000,000, while the liabilities total well below £200,000, it would seem not difficult to arrange a settlement on the basis of handing over the one for the other'. So, ultimately, it would prove. The China Ocean Shipping Agency (COSA) received everything from across the firm's China estate, that is across the 18 cities in which Butterfield & Swire operated, 'to hold unto them for ever'. When John March finally left only seven foreign staff remained, all of them locally engaged men and not career employees. Most branches were formally taken over by the end of January 1955, letter after letter arriving in Hong Kong confirming that the firm's official seals and name chops had been destroyed, and the last handover in Shanghai took place on 1 June 1955. The acting manager handed over all remaining files, and the office furniture. Some photographs of former managers, directors and compradors had been shipped to Hong Kong together with old sporting trophies. At the end of June the company's SWIRE telegraph address expired. All gone.[95]

Detailed transcripts survive of the weary rounds of negotiation as every minor detail of the company's activity was picked over. It could get tense.

Comrade Ho: Once again I have to complain about your attitude. I do not like it.

Mr March: Don't try to be tough with me. This is a normal discussion
   and there is no need to get excited.
Comrade Ho: Lately, every time we have a meeting you lose your
   temper. If you wish to behave properly, we will continue; if not,
   I will close all negotiations.
Mr March: Mr Ho, please do not threaten me; I do not like it.
   ...
Mr March: How many times do you expect me to explain to you?
   I have given you all the facts at least twice already.
Comrade Ho: Do not lose your temper. Your attitude is bad.

This late-stage exchange concerned two pontoons at Shantou, sunk
by the Japanese during the war, and the question of liability for their
removal. The two men sparred their way towards an agreement on this
question and others, but it was exhausting.[96] For Ma Zung Yee who
translated, it carried also the possibility of being seen as pro-Taikoo,
pro-British, and indeed pro-imperialist. This was not a good position
to be in. One mild consolation, John March noted, the firm having
moved into the Jardine Matheson building, now vacated by its former
owners who had themselves closed down and left, was the thought
that they had outlasted the Princely Hong in China, for its staff never
tired of reminding the Swire staff that their company was historically
a late arrival.

Minor but troublesome claims had continued to be made as the
negotiations unfolded, the rocky history of the previous decade of the
Sino-Japanese and the world war and their derangements catching up
with Butterfield & Swire. As the agreement was signed these still included
the widow of an engineer on the SS *Kweiyang*, who had committed
suicide in Bombay in August 1943: she claimed that it was murder
and demanded a compassionate grant. Two of the *Anhui*'s wartime crew
asked for 'wages, severance and danger money'. The 'alleged mother'
('identity not proven') of an engineer on SS *Chenchow* who had served
before the war claimed his retiring grant. The wife of another former
engineer, who had served on the *Wanhsien*, made the same claim. But
as he was now living in Taiwan, it was easy to suggest that he deal with
this himself, and with the Hong Kong office. Two men arrested in 1952
demanded retiring pay.[97] The single most awkward problem, however,
was provided by dependants of crewmen who died during the war on the

Shuntien, Pakhoi, Hoihow and *Sinkiang.* These pursued claims against the Tianjin branch for compensation for their deaths, as well as retiring grants and compensation for loss of personal effects. A man described as a 'vengeful B. & S. pre-war employee', who had not been re-engaged after 1945, led the charge (and knocked Sidney Smith down). It was not until July 1955 that the case was deemed resolved, and Smith was permitted to leave China, with the branch deemed officially closed.[98]

A continuing worry was the fate of the 'loyal and trusted senior staff', or 'agents of capital' in Communist eyes. All were paid off at the point of withdrawal, at their request, there being no future for them in the successor company. Ma Zung Yee, a native of Nanjing, who had joined the firm in its insurance office in Shanghai in 1922, was a key figure in the negotiations as translator and adviser. Ma's background as someone who had worked his way up from the bottom gave him some status with the Chinese negotiators, although his role as director of the International Settlement's rice rationing system during the Japanese occupation of Shanghai, and his secondment on the same work for Song Ziwen's administration in Guangzhou in 1948, would have been black marks on his record. In fact, John March had been ordered to hand over staff files for senior Chinese managers at short notice, and while he had filleted as much as he dared from them, those and all other records of the firm's operations were transferred to COSA.[99] But no hurried editing would have helped. These men, who had held senior positions in a foreign-owned company, who had, as many had, studied or travelled abroad, who spoke foreign languages, and had contact with foreigners, or who even simply lived the cosmopolitan lifestyle that characterised internationalised Shanghai, were all under threat. British diplomats thought that the concerns Butterfield & Swire raised about the danger their employees were now facing were overdramatic and that even the men themselves were overdoing things: 'we also have to remember,' wrote the consul-general at Shanghai, 'that the Chinese are great actors.' Events would prove the diplomats completely wrong.[100]

Some of the senior staff certainly managed to leave China. Yao Kang arrived in Hong Kong in spring 1953. H.T. Lee, son of the former comprador in Shantou, retired from Tianjin in 1955, rejoined in Hong Kong in 1961. Yang Xiaonan had arrived in Hong Kong, 'bewildered' to find himself out, in March 1957, left the firm and went to live in Canada.[101] Maurice Ching was paid off at Shantou in February 1955, lived frugally, under surveillance and short, he noted, of tennis balls, managing to leave in March 1957 and rejoining the firm in Hong Kong. Ma Zung Yee had rejoined Butterfield & Swire in Hong Kong by May 1957. These were exceptions, and there were simply not any other jobs for all those who left China. It was less senior men, middle-ranking managers mainly, who provided the remaining targets for the new order within the former companies. The former Ningbo agent could only find work as a labourer. The Shanghai cube plant's supervisor was set to digging ditches, overseen in his work by the yard sweeper; department heads were reassigned to routine tasks.

If the experience of the paint plant is a guide, and there is no reason to doubt that it was not, then on the day of the handover a 'work group' of cadres would have entered each of the company's installations and called a meeting of older workers and of department heads. At Orient Paint the objective was to stress the need for stability, to maintain production, and for unity, and its manager, Yao Jialing (who had run the plant since the last British manager had left), was deemed important to its productivity. 'The factory is now already ours' this group was told. A 'welcome meeting' was held the following day for all employees, with celebratory and exhortatory speeches. Daily political meetings were held after work every day, sometimes long into the evening. Before too long Yao Jialing was subjected to criticism as an imperialist 'running dog'; his was a 'grave case of pro-foreign worship, especially pro-British'.[102] He had been offered a job in Hong Kong by Swires, but was not permitted to leave. Charles Yao, as he was known within the firm, was 40 years old when OPCo was surrendered. A Roman Catholic, he was one of the very first class to graduate from the American Jesuit order's Gonzaga College in Shanghai in 1935, and had then joined the firm as a chemist. On each and every count, this was a politically damning CV.[103] Many staff like him were deemed 'contaminated', had to attend political lectures and study meetings, and work on self-criticisms and histories, as Yao Kang had on his arrival. John March noted that the official working day at Butterfield & Swire was immediately extended after the handover, and that salaries, which were high, comparatively, would probably be reduced to the same level as government officials. Conversely, it is clear that working conditions for employees at OPCo did improve, as they did for industrial workers across Shanghai in the 1950s during a honeymoon period that came to an end with a wave of strikes in 1957.[104] The revolution had its losers and victims, as revolutions do, and it is always easy to focus on those, but it had its winners, too, and we should acknowledge that there was widespread and genuine support for the new dispensation.

But we need now, however, to leave the Swire interests in the People's Republic of China, the workers at OPCo getting used to having lunch in their new canteen, ceiling fans cooling the air, for what was now to unfold there lies largely outside this story, and it lay wholly outside the ability of John Swire & Sons to affect or influence. Reports emerged that five months after COSA moved its staff into the Butterfield & Swire offices and merged the two groups, all the former Taikoo men were ordered, as one put it, 'to strengthen their political study and to wash up the brain'; that is to reform their thinking. This was not a quick process, and the 'recalcitrant' 10 per cent deemed not to be making sufficient progress had 'a pretty bad time' in late 1956. Brains 'washed', staff found themselves transferred to Dalian, Beijing or Chongqing. The company did not wholly sever its China ties, for it continued to run the services north from Hong Kong to Shanghai and Tianjin, and COSA served as its agent. After he left Maurice Ching would make regular visits to Guangzhou, Shanghai and Beijing to meet COSA officials and discuss Blue Funnel and CNCo matters. Chinese seamen on CNCo vessels whose families lived in China had to have allotments paid to their dependants. Directors and managers remained active in the limited engagement of British firms and interest groups with China, joining delegations, making individual visits, sometimes meeting former employees. 'Good wishes to J. K.', said 'an old boy', discreetly, serving tea to Adrian Swire in COSA's Shanghai office in 1957, one of 50 COSA staff there who had once served Taikoo (Jock's younger son, Adrian, had joined the firm in 1956).[105] But China's dark course for the two decades after 1954 was now largely not a direct or vital factor in the company's operations, except as it remained a critical factor in Hong Kong, especially in the early and later 1960s.

Sentiment aside, this radical break with the past in China might arguably be viewed as one of the best things that could have happened to John Swire & Sons at this point in its history. It made everything much, much simpler. In the aftermath of the Second World War, the firm had resumed control (mostly) of a heterogenous if not dizzyingly diverse set of properties, relationships and operations in China, each port with its own history of entrenched interests and practices, much of the estate degraded, ageing, impaired or not yet restored to its full control. Disentangling all this, and trying to reconstruct a set of operations that were politically feasible in the hyper-nationalistic new political era, and that made sense in a global economy that was substantially reordered, was a huge challenge. The past made concrete in the company's assets across China hampered its ability wholly to respond effectively to the new political and economic world that opened up after 1945. A Guomindang victory in the civil war would not have provided any respite from the political challenges it had faced since the new Anglo-Chinese treaty was signed in 1943. A clean slate would have been easier to work from. On 15 December 1954 a large part of this congeries of problems was simply cut away from the firm. It was costly, and it caused much anguish, and there were long-serving staff with whom ties were sundered, but it allowed John Swire & Sons to pursue new ventures. It could now in many ways simply turn its back on China and look outwards from Hong Kong, and, unencumbered by that treaty port past, reach out into the rest of Asia and the Pacific more widely and more deeply than it had yet ever managed to do.

13

Making Asia

The Second World War, revolutions, the descent of the Iron Curtain and the retreat from empires all changed the map of East and Southeast Asia. This was more than cold warrior metaphor. Fresh real borders appeared; old ones dissolved. Lines needed redrawing: so cartographers were kept fully employed, and printers, too. Surveyors stalked borderlands marking out with their feet and instruments routes for new boundaries. Builders threw up border posts and fences; roads were blocked off; towns and villages cut in half. Signwriters were kept busy as street names were changed in liberated cities. Old statues and monuments were removed, new heroes and martyrs rose up instead. Empire seemed overthrown for good, wiped out with the old borders and carried off with the crumbling busts of kings, queens, governors and generals, but what took its place, for all the optimism of independence, proved fragile. There were unexpected changes in political direction, sharp reversals in policies and startling denouements. Instability in the short -term, or the long term, undermined confidence, and encouraged caution.

By 1955 the map of the operations of John Swire & Sons had been dramatically redrawn as well. Much of its long past in China was only noticeable in the names of the ships of the CNCo fleet, or in the yarns the older staff could tell, if only younger post-war recruits would listen. The past often lives on this way, overlaid with the present, fainter and fainter as time clouds over it. Changes in political power have always altered maps, but even when barriers were thrown up, tangible connections often remain. People or goods continue to flow along established routes, or find new destinations, or simply snake their way to where they have always gone. New restrictions also provided opportunities, for covert as well as for legal trades. New technology always played a defining role: Alfred Holt's compound engine or the aircraft that crested the Hump have been two examples in this story; and as we have seen, too, entrepreneurs have looked to develop routes, to find employment for their ships, or aircraft, sometimes looking for a share of a growing trade, sometimes seeking to kindle one, banking on a hunch, sound intelligence, a promise.

The history of post-war East and Southeast Asia was marked by two significant and interconnected factors: its rehabilitation and economic development, and this shaping and reshaping of the region we know today as 'Southeast Asia' – an idea of a place that largely did not exist before the Second World War – and the sundering of China's open borders with Korea and Japan, with Taiwan, and with routes to the south. Leaders and elites in such newly independent states as Indonesia were committed to creating their own networks and connections free from the old colonial powers and the new global hegemons, through the 1947 Asian Relations Conference in New Delhi, and the 1955 Bandung Conference of Asian and African nations, for example. The Western Cold War powers were equally as committed to welding the region into an anti-Communist bloc, establishing in 1954 the Southeast Asia Treaty Organisation (SEATO) in a bid to 'contain', as they put it, the 'spread' of communism in Asia. Ethnic nationalisms also militated against the Bandung spirit, notably those which generated immense hostility against Chinese diaspora communities across the region, and practical restrictions against free movement. Hong Kong served as a site of Chinese refuge, and transit, both for hundreds and thousands of people fleeing China, and for those seeking respite from the difficulties and dangers of life in Southeast Asia.[1] Against this backdrop, we can explore the role of Butterfield & Swire in Japan's recovery and development, in the story of Hong Kong, now perched perilously on the edge of a hostile state and brimful of people, and we can chart the growth of Cathay Pacific and the ways in which it served to integrate this new region, bringing into contact the polyglot, multicultural worlds of the cities among which it flew.

Cathay Pacific's brochures, passenger magazines and staff newsletters show us how this knitting together of Asia was undertaken, represented, encouraged and reported. Route maps had always promised opportunity, the pamphlet unfolded reveals a set of possibilities, ease and convenience, tempting the reader to turn traveller, as the finger traces a line: Tokyo, Taipei, Hong Kong, thence to Manila; or Calcutta to Singapore, now Bangkok. Newspapers in Hong Kong printed daily flight schedules, and lists of passengers arriving and departing, too. Why, they asked, is your name not here also? Now marketing also offered speed, and the story of air travel in this period is one of speedier and speedier and more and more frequent services, to increasing numbers of destinations. The original Cathay Pacific Dakotas carried up to 28 passengers, flew at 167 mph, and took 14 hours to fly to Singapore from Hong Kong via Bangkok. The DC-4 acquired in 1949 carried 48 and cruised a little more swiftly. The DC-6 bought in 1954 housed 64 travellers and flew at 313 mph. Although it travelled a little more slowly, the DC-6B brought into service the same year carried 72 passengers. The purchase of two Lockheed Electras in 1959 brought into the fleet planes that could carry 78 people at a cruising speed of 406 mph. When it began operating these turbo-prop aircraft, Cathay Pacific's passenger and freight traffic started rapidly to increase. In 1962 it added its first jet, a Convair 880-22M, capable of carrying 104 travellers at a steady 560 mph. Now, the flight from Hong Kong to Bangkok took two hours and 25 minutes. Speed brought fresh food as air cargo – fresher in the case of the Sydney rock oysters that reappeared on Hong Kong hotel and restaurant menus in late 1959, courtesy of a relaunched service to Australia. Speed meant faster flights for passengers, but it also meant more frequent flights for CPA and greater use of the aircraft. A plane sitting on the ground was an asset not earning its keep. In 1949 the airline was getting 32 hours of flying a week from its DC-4, and aimed to get this to 48. In 1951 it was getting 66 hours weekly from the Dakotas. By 1954 it could report 80 hours of use a week from the DC-4 which, it was thought, could not be 'surpassed anywhere in the world'.[2] These changes reflected the wider development of commercial aviation, which needed new airports, the extension of existing ones – Kai Tak, in 1958 – new systems for handling cargo, and this press of people. There was more work, too, for the Hong Kong Aircraft Engineering Company (HAECo), into which joint venture with Jardine Matheson, Butterfield & Swire's PAMAS was folded in 1950.

These purchases needed capital, more than John Swire & Sons had spent on such assets before.[3] A restructuring and new share issue in 1954 brought more cash into Cathay Pacific from John Swire & Sons,

China Navigation Company, and a new partner, the shipping line P&O, which took a large share in the firm, ANA's own diminishing. Even so, the Hongkong & Shanghai Bank – which continued to support the company – financed the two Electras with a loan – they cost £1 million each – and was also required to fund the jets, one at a time: for the Convairs cost £2 million apiece.[4] While the airline now proved steadily profitable, it had recurring problems stemming from the political volatility of 1950s Asia: destinations might be withdrawn, or suspended as a result of conflict. Insurgencies, emergencies, confrontations and civil strife pepper the record. Well, runs one report from the agent in Haiphong in March 1954, yes, the Viet Minh are deploying anti-aircraft equipment, but it is 'rudimentary'. We parked, a pilot reported that same week, next to the French fighter aircraft, so the guards watched their plane overnight as well.[5] More routine were the exchange controls that caused significant problems with the repatriation of revenue from Rangoon, Vientiane, Saigon, Calcutta, and especially Manila. Funds were blocked either by regulations, which aimed to support national industrial development, or by simple lack of foreign exchange. In Manila the firm had to buy gold to get its funds out, losing heavily on exchange as it did so. It was certainly worth considering, as indeed the company did, and more than once, whether it would be better to liquidate CPA altogether, and leave with some profit. It seemed too fragile a trade, prospects uncertain, the corporate effort too great for the return, and trying on managerial patience and on the nerves.[6]

Then in 1957, on top of all this, Hongkong Airways, mothballed in 1951 when it lost its China access and sold its aircraft, chartering Northwest Airlines to run its Japan route, was brought back to life by Jardines with support from BOAC. With two new turbo-prop Vickers Viscounts the firm started serving its northern routes itself, but two years later surrendered, and was absorbed, together with those destinations into CPA. This marked the end of a conflict that had continued, despite the agreement of May 1949, and in contravention of it. BOAC had continued to operate the Singapore/Hong Kong route, seeing it as a 'trunk' line. It was, the company's chairman pointed out in October 1951, the same distance as from London to Moscow. Regional airlines like CPA should focus instead on regional traffic. Ostensibly, this seemed a reasonable position, but BOAC then also offered 'excursion' fares that significantly undercut CPA prices on the route.[7] A compromise had been found in October 1951, brokered by the Colonial Office and Ministry of Civil Aviation, but subsequent attempts to reach agreement on some amalgamation of the three firm's interests in a single regional carrier, also including Malayan Airways, were stymied.[8] The aggressive re-entry of BOAC in 1957 set the dispute in motion again. But the revived service did not pay. BOAC 'have lost £167,000 themselves and cost us a million in revenue', noted Jock Swire in October 1958 after talking with BOAC board member, Lord Rennell of Rodd, who had arrived in Hong Kong (by CPA from Singapore) to discuss a solution. And do you appreciate the difference, Hong Kong's governor, Robert Black, asked Rennell, 'between HK Airways and what HK regarded as Hong Kong's Air Line'?[9] On this point BOAC finally saw the light, and Rennell had agreed in principle to a merger, with Hong Kong Airways becoming a wholly owned subsidiary of a restructured Cathay Pacific, and BOAC and Jardine Matheson securing a seat each on the new board. Hong Kong Airways lost another £135,000 in 1959 before it was brought into CPA, and it was shortly thereafter retired as a name.[10] The Viscounts were sold, and CPA's Electras began to operate the routes to Japan. This would transform the business of the firm. It was all very well having traffic rights and aircraft, and the clearly now partisan support of the colonial administration, which had lost patience back in 1954 with the 'complete contempt' shown by BOAC for government directives, but all the lines needed passengers.[11] So who flew, and why, and where to?

It might be useful to start with the original assumptions that the Swire directors and managers worked with as they sought routes. As Cathay Pacific and Hong Kong Airways negotiated their division of the outward routes in February 1949, the character of the trade for each was sketched. Hong Kong/Shanghai was 'Coastal Interport Passage and Freight', Hong Kong/Japan was 'Normal Inter-territory Trading and tourists in summer'. Hong Kong/Manila 'Normal Inter-territory and Immigrant'. But as Eric Price noted in August 1949, for example, while 'the lower class Chinese are not travelling by air to the South in large numbers', Butterfield & Swire had placed their bet on the belief 'that we shall be able to educate them to do so'. (Smugglers, he noted, needed no lessons: they were buying single tickets to Manila, then carrying contraband to Xiamen by sea.) 'Education' needed brokers, and staff who could teach.[12] Chinese ground staff helped passengers with documentation as they prepared to navigate terminals, and board, and on arrival pass through customs and immigration checks, a strange experience to many at first, and in strange languages. Habitual travellers already familiar with CNCo's services transferred their business to the company's airline.[13] But even so, this was a limited traffic. People did not travel unless they needed to, or they wanted to, or until they could. None of this came naturally, and marketing became vital. Changes in currency control and travel and visa regimes – such as the lifting of government restrictions on personal travel from Japan on 1 April 1964, or Hong Kong's own ending of a requirement for visas for short-term visitors from the US and 16 European countries in 1966 – and the growing and affluent economies of the United States and Australia, provided traffic for airlines.

The raw numbers show a pattern of reasonably steady growth. Cathay Pacific carried 9,345 passengers in 1949 – the first year for which such statistics become reliable – and 10 years later it carried 68,929. Throughout the 1960s, after the arrival of the Electras and the acquisition and extension of the Japan route, Cathay secured a steady quarter share of steadily rising civil passenger traffic in and out of Hong Kong. By 1967, when 325,000 out of 1,300,000 Hong Kong passengers flew Cathay Pacific, the share was closer to 30 per cent on average, and in 1969 it flew 504,369 people on what was then exclusively a fleet of six Convairs. By the mid-1970s the share of total traffic stayed at a steady 40 per cent.[14]

These figures tell one story, and in 1967 a survey showed a quarter share of Cathay Pacific's passengers were North Americans, 18 per cent were Chinese, 16 per cent Japanese and 9 per cent came from the Straits.[15] But who actually travelled? Well, most visibly, for the firm: the gallery includes the president of Peru, the vice-president of Bolivia, (then) former vice-president Richard Nixon, Aneurin Bevan, Tennessee Williams, the author Han Suyin, Charlie Chaplin (in 1961), local film mogul Run Run Shaw (with Malaysian film star Saloma), prime ministers current (Malaysia, Singapore) and former (Japan), Miss China 1961, Miss Hong Kong 1959, queens (Nepal), princesses (Thailand), a crown prince (Sikkim), the Boston Symphony Orchestra, the Vienna Boys' Choir, The Beatles (in 1965), a Rockefeller, a travelling circus (Sheum's, though the elephants, tigers and leopards travelled by sea), a 'travelling champion walking postman' (a Hong Kong athlete, Lee Chi-shing), and a 'champion walking Punjabi policeman', foreign ministers and now obscure statesmen, several of Hong Kong's governors (and one of Trinidad's, and of British North Borneo's), a Max Factor ambassador beautician, the Emperor Haile Selassie of Ethiopia, ex-Emperor Bao Dai of Vietnam, Ava Gardner, Jane Russell, Dame Sybil Thorndike, Henry Luce, the Chief Scout, the Deputy Chief Girl Guide, Cantonese opera singers, Hong Kong cinema stars, ships crews, golfers, Midwest American tour groups, 'hundreds of Rotarians and their wives', the president of Rotary International himself, bishops (Anglican), goodwill missions from cities like Phoenix, Arizona, and from Japanese NGOs.[16] The airways knitting Asia together were busy. The company supplied copy and notes to its agents across its network, circulating a newsletter, encouraging them to push stories into the local press, and keep it alerted to news of any 'personality' (the term then used) who might be settling into a Cathay Pacific journey, scheduled or chartered. Photographs of arriving and departing passengers were a feature in the Hong Kong press. Much of this was incidental, of course, the convenience of scheduling and seat availability, but there was also much that came about by design: Asians and visitors to Asia travelled around in greater and greater numbers, and more and more frequently, and with more and more publicity, because governments wanted them to.

Why was this? We might preface an explanation with an Olympic episode, and in particular the long journey to London in 1948 of a team that represented a country that did not yet quite formally exist: Korea. It would soon afterwards be the site of a devasting conflict that hardened Cold War battle lines, pitting US and British troops against China's, one side effect of which was the revival of the Japanese economy, and another was a profound knock to confidence in Hong Kong's position. Bill Rae-Smith, a 10-year veteran of Butterfield & Swire shipping operations, had been seconded to the Ministry of War Transport in Pusan, Korea, in November 1947. This he combined with scouting for business for the firm. In May 1948 discussion began about chartering a flight from Korea to Hong Kong, and then on to London, to carry some 67 Olympic athletes and officials to the Fourteenth Olympiad. Plans changed, and it proved cheaper for the team to set off by sea to Japan, crossing the country by rail to board another vessel at Yokohama. Arriving at Hong Kong via Shanghai on 2 July 1948, they flew on to raise the Korean flag at the Olympic Centre in Uxbridge, west London, on 9 July, having paraded it in Seoul Stadium before they left.[17] It was actually the first to be raised, and also quite possibly the first time the Korean flag as a legitimate state emblem had been raised in Britain, if not one of the first occasions it was raised anywhere officially outside the Korean peninsula since the end of colonial rule. The participation by the Koreans, at a moment of great tension back home, was an important episode on the journey to nationhood of a country that had emerged from Japanese control. The team secured two bronze medals, but more importantly their long trek was a stage in the establishment of Korea as a nation in its own right, as its flag flew in London and the anthem was played there, too (nearly, for there was a problem over finding the music for it, but it was at least attempted). The importance of sport in nation-making, in international politics and in the symbolic realm of international relations cannot be underestimated. By the time the team flew back, the last of them leaving Hong Kong on 30 August, the new Republic of Korea – governing the formerly US-administered south of the country – was two weeks old. Butterfield & Swire earned a healthy commission on the business.[18]

This had not been Cathay Pacific business. But putting on an extra charter from Manila to and from Sydney in December 1948 to carry Philippine Boy Scouts to take part in the third Pan-Pacific Scout Jamboree in Melbourne certainly was. One hiccup aside (for the youngsters were not seasoned travellers, and a flight had to be delayed as a result), they garnered more attention than their numbers might warrant – there were 21 of them, among 11,000 participants – not least as they included teenaged former anti-Japanese guerrillas. CNCo took a Hong Kong contingent to the next, carrying the materials for an arch, with attendant dragons, to mark the entrance to their campsite. It carried Hong Kong delegates to the World Scout Jamboree in Britain in 1957, and Australian Scouts and Guides who attended the 1959 Manila World Jamboree and Nippon Jamboree in Tokyo (and a kilted Irish Scout leader for a one-day Hong Kong shopping trip from Manila).[19] If the Olympic movement was steadily evolving still into the global event that it would become, an important national showcase for its hosts, the notion that there was a 'Pan-Pacific' community, whether of Boy Scouts or political or economic interests was an even fresher concept. The war, and before that the series of conferences held in the 1920s and 1930s by bodies such as the policy and international affairs think-tank the Institute of Pacific Relations and the Pan-Pacific Women's Association,

Jock Swire on patrol, Deep Water Bay,
Hong Kong, winter 1914–15

Butterfield & Swire offices, Shanghai
bund, 1911–12

Keeping an eye on the staff: John Samuel
Swire looks over the Butterfield & Swire
Shanghai Private Office, 1912

Glimpses of sugar travelling life: photographs from Gordon Campbell's China memoir

Pekin cart

Cattle truck

Ice sled

Ready for anything:
Gordon Campbell, 1929

Taipan and principal: N.S. Brown and G. Warren Swire, Shanghai, 1934

Family business: Shanghai comprador Chun Shut Kai and his father and predecessor Chun Koo Leong, *c.*1915

Butterfield & Swire office staff, Andong, 1934

Melée at the terminal: while a Sikh watchman keeps order, porters and rickshaw pullers wait for passengers, Hong Kong, 1920s

Thrills on the Yangzi: CNCo cruising advertisement, c.1935

Thrills on the Yangzi: negotiating the rapids, 1937

The Pirated Tungchow Returns to Shanghai

TUNGCHOW PIRACY EXHIBITS
The electric torch, picked up by children on the Tungchow, bears the imprint "Made in Hongkong."

"N.-C. Herald" Photo.

BANK NOTES ON TUNGCHOW
It is understood that the banknotes carried by the Tungchow were in process of delivery from London to Tientsin by Messrs. de la Rue and Co., Ltd., the printers. For rapidity of carriage they were transhipped at Shanghai for consignment on the Tungchow. The pirates are believed to have taken 250,000 one yuan notes which are unsigned and unissued. They are consequently of no value to the pirates but appropriate arrangements have been made for the apprehension of anyone attempting to put the notes into circulation.

Wei Fong Photos.

WHEN THE PIRATED SHIP RETURNED TO SHANGHAI
Having on board more than 70 children and teachers from the Chefoo Schools, the ss. Tungchow, pirated on January 29, returned to Shanghai on Thursday morning. Mr. and Mrs. L. J. Hughes' three sons are seen holding pieces of a pirate's mauve jacket. Master Owen, between his brothers, David and Evan, actually was fired at by the pirate whose garment they are holding. On the right, Ethel and John Quimby appear quite happy, in spite of the fact that John lost his school cap on the vessel.

AS THE SS. TUNGCHOW LEFT THE PORT
The above photograph was taken on the morning of February 5 as the ss. Tungchow left the French Bund with over seventy children bound for the C.I.M. Schools in Chefoo after their holidays.

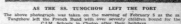

A MOMENT'S RELAXATION FROM PIRATES   Photo Wei Fong.
Fond parents and friends are as highly elated as are the rescued children that the rabbits escaped and will continue as greatly valued companions in the exciting episode of the Tungchow piracy.

Photo Krainukov.

REJOICING PARENTS GREET TUNGCHOW CHILDREN
Of the many parents and relatives of children on the Tungchow, few seemed happier than Mrs. and Mr. L. J. Hughes as they greeted their progeny.

A school trip to remember: the *Tungchow* piracy, 1935

SUGAR east of Suez!

SOMETHING NEW!

TAIKOO—a special household sugar, refined, packed and sold by a British Company in a British colony.

Can now be had throughout India, Burma, China, Malaya and elsewhere in the East.

TAIKOO—packed in cartons and tins of convenient size, designed specially for Eastern climates and conditions.

HALF CUBES
1 lb. Cartons and 4 lb. Tins.
DIAMOND CRYSTALS
("Coffee" Sugar)
1 lb. Rolls.
GRANULATED
1 lb. Rolls, 18 lb. and 40 lb. tins.
CASTER AND ICING
1 lb., 2 lb. and 4 lb. tins.
Also Taikoo Golden Syrup in 1 and 2 lb. tins.

TAIKOO
sugar●

Butterfield & Swire, General Agents, Taikoo Sugar Refining Co., Ltd., Hong Kong

British sugar east of Suez, advertising Taikoo Sugar in *Punch* magazine, 1932

Chinese sugar cubes, detail from a Taikoo Sugar calendar, 1910

女祕書……

每當工作繁忙
的時候喝一杯
用太古糖來調
味的飲品提神
醒腦工作效率
倍增.

各大商店
士多均售

一磅,兩磅及五磅防濕包庄

太古車糖

由一八八四年起在香港煉製

Just my cup of tea: and Hong Kong made since 1884. Newspaper advertisement, 1960

Part of the Chinese landscape: Taikoo Sugar dealer's sign in a Yichang street, 1929

Billiter blitzed. Remains of the Book Office, May 1941

Kiangsu captives: dockyard staff and others marking the Emperor's birthday, at Gulangyu, Xiamen, in 1942

Business as usual under the rising sun: launch of a ship at Taikoo Dockyard during the Japanese occupation

Bombing the Taikoo Dockyard, 1945

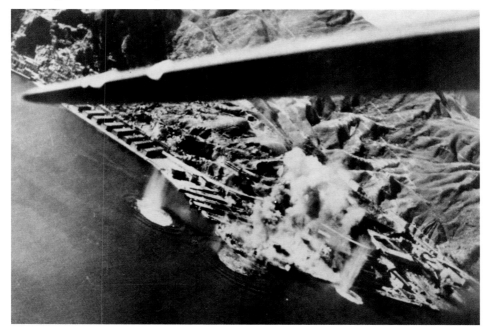

'It's even better than I thought': Taikoo Dockyard in September 1945 from Korn Hill

Moving people: the pilgrim trade, SS *Anshun* at Singapore, 1967

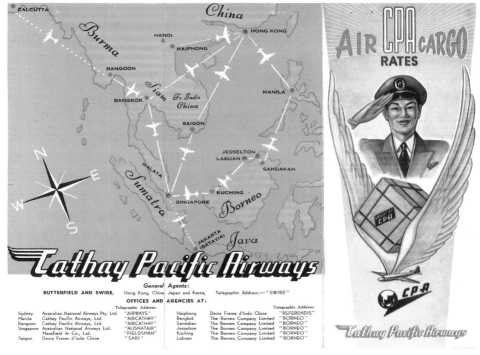

Making Asia: Cathay Pacific route map, 1950

Old and new: Cathay Pacific Convair overflies the Taikoo Dockyard, 1968

New sign on an old Hong, Butterfield & Swire offices, Hong Kong *c.*1960

Fatshan in the movies: Orson Welles at his worst in *Ferry to Hong Kong* (1959)

Tourist economy: Hong Kong Tourist Association advertisement, 1961

Solidarity: yearbook of the Taikoo Dockyard Chinese Workers' Union, 1959

太塢工人

太古船塢華員職工會

太古船塢華員職工會十一週年紀念特刊

宣教部編印

會址：西灣河民興街二十二號二樓　　電話：七一一九二二

出版一九五七年五月一日出版

福利部辦事處：西大街六一六九號三樓

★非賣品★

The bloody and tearful story of the Taikoo Dockyard (1967)

33. 對於這次慘劇的原因，太古方不敢吭聲。其實是因爲"太古富"只有五噸拖力，拖曳"好運"號負荷重，而且鋼纜已殘舊發霉，資方却加更換，所以造成這次一死六傷的慘劇。

34. 當時水手鄉就，兩腿重傷殘廢，船長梁滿和機房二手何生重傷胸部，其他的人都受傷。梁根慘死後，他的遺孤繼續在太塢受剝削，最近還被開除，這伙英國財狠多麼狠毒啊！

Zombie jamboree: Bahamas Airways advertisement for the ill-fated New York service, 2 October 1970

Bahamas style: flight attendant, with pith helmet

Flamingo pink jet at Nassau airport

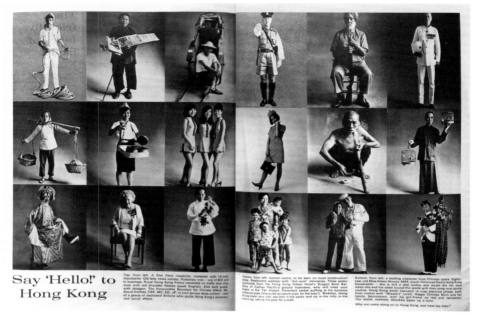

Making Hong Kong: Cathay Pacific inflight magazine spread, 1969

Connectivity: celebrating the Hong Kong-London route, August 1980

Old and new: Taikoo Shing, Dockyard and Floating Dock, *c.*1972

Celebrating a century in Hong Kong: Taipan John Browne, John A. Swire, and Jock Swire, City Hall, January 1967

Ship owners, Adrian Swire and Y.K. Pao in conversation, 1968

had brought into being the idea that there was such an entity.[20] And like 'Southeast Asia' its reality was given concrete form through sports, cultural exchanges, jamborees, tournaments and competitions.

US Cold War cultural diplomacy funded educational exchange schemes and scholarships. Visits by performers were supported by a 'Cultural Presentations Program' (also known as the President's International Program for Cultural Exchange) that despatched classical musicians and variety stars from North America to East Asia.[21] Asian states ran their own initiatives, such as the South-East Asia Cultural Festival organised by Singapore's Ministry of Culture in 1963. Billed as the first such event, it proved to be the only one, for the continuing brittle politics of the region stymied as many such initiatives as it prompted. In this case the break-up of the federation with Malaysia truncated future plans.[22] And while those involved in these still sometimes travelled by sea, more and more often they came to travel by air, and, as half of Hong Kong's contribution did in 1963, they travelled by CPA: 'Invasion of Glamour: Planeloads of Actresses for Festival' yelled one excited headline in Singapore.[23] There were ostensibly commercial ventures, too, as markets reshaped by the constraints of Cold War borders were bolstered by regional events. A peripatetic South East Asian Film Festival (the 'South East' soon dropped) was held for the first time in Tokyo in 1954. The aim was marketing and publicity, and in this it proved very successful, especially for Hong Kong's Shaw Brothers, but the venture was also secretly sponsored in its first few years by the Asia Foundation, itself covertly funded by the CIA.[24]

'Planeloads of Actresses' aside, Cold War networking attracted most attention when it involved sport, especially through prestige international tournaments. The resumption of a pre-war series of 'Far Eastern Championship Games' as the 'Asian Games' at New Delhi in 1951 was one notable post-war landmark.[25] The Indian organisers presented the games as a symbol of post-war, and indeed post-colonial, 'Asian Rebirth'. But the second tournament, held in Manila in May 1954, was used by the hosts to project themselves unambiguously as part of the 'free world'. The Games included only fellow non-Communist states; and the city was the publishing centre of the United States Information Agency, which ensured that film, pamphlets and other material about the events was generated and widely circulated. The rhetoric of international friendship expressed through sport masked a sustained anti-Communist agenda.

A contrasting, anti-imperialist agenda, could be set out, too: Indonesia's 1962 hosting of the Asian Games took place with facilities built with Soviet aid and expertise, and proved controversial when the Republic of China and Israeli teams failed to receive invitations because of objections from Beijing and from Indonesia's Arab state allies. Jakarta's new stadium, big international hotel and roads, and its inauguration of television broadcasting all point also to the function of such games for these new nations. They were grand prestige symbols of modernist development strategies. In 1958 the Japanese had made the third Asian Games a dry run for their bid to host the Olympics in 1964 – the International Olympics Committee held its first-ever meeting in Asia in Tokyo during the games – and as part of its efforts to rehabilitate its image in Asia, and internationally. The reporting, broadcasting and recording of these events was a key objective: these were spectacles, meant to be seen from a distance in print, on screen, and in the mind's eye – and many were meant to change minds, too.

The Hong Kong, Burmese, Malayan and Thai teams flew CPA to Manila in 1954. Cathay carried India, Burma, Malaya, Sarawak, British North Borneo, Singapore and Hong Kong to the 1962 games in Jakarta. Reaping some of the benefits of Perth's hosting of the 1962 British Empire Games (later renamed the Commonwealth Games) was much on Jock Swire's mind in 1961.[26] Association football's Asian Cup was first held in Hong Kong in 1956 (South Korea the victors, Hong Kong in third place); the Junior Asian Cup was first held in Kuala Lumpur in 1959, the local press carrying a photograph of Hong Kong's team about to board their Cathay Pacific flight.[27] Teams were flown out to 'interport' cricket matches, the Asian Table Tennis Championships (first held in Singapore in 1952), annual football tournaments, inter-city cups, or friendly tours around Southeast Asian states. Increasingly, 'Hong Kong's Air Line' carried Hong Kong's teams. What had been a strategic political position in route disputes with BOAC and in discussions with governors became a vital part of Cathay Pacific's branding and its identity. Its own history as a local start-up, as Hong Kong's airline, a makeshift new venture for a battered city, and one that grew as the city grew, also became an important asset, told in advertising supplements marking its anniversaries, or the arrival of new aircraft, as well as in a brochure marking its coming of age in 1967. Cathay Pacific was at the heart of this web of intra-Asia connections.

Of course, celebrities made good copy, and team photographs on the tarmac in front of the plane with the company's name in full view and each player clutching his present of a CPA bag (logo facing the camera) were easy fodder for publicity, but such passengers did not buy many tickets. Business travellers and officials shuttling about the region bought more, but tourists would fill more and more seats on more and more flights if they could be persuaded to travel. Tourism did not grow naturally either. While there had been a spike in the 1930s – as shipping lines introduced cruises as a strategy to use tonnage during the prolonged slump (even CNCo had stepped into this, marketing its Yangzi services for tourism) – overseas pleasure travel was an elite, not a mass, activity, certainly for visitors to Asia. Pan American Airways had pioneered services across the Pacific via Hawaii but this was a select service. After the war middle-income Americans began to travel, and the figure of the American tourist rapidly became a staple feature in popular culture in post-war Europe. This was entirely by design, for it was an integral part, first, of the Marshall Plan for post-war recovery, and then of Cold War strategy.[28] Tourism was seen by post-war US policy-makers as a cheap way of delivering US dollars to overseas economies, of exporting American culture – 'the American way of life' – and of building Cold War Western-bloc solidarity. Asia was no different, and promoting Hong Kong and Taiwan as the 'real China', and bastions of its true culture, also served, it was hoped, to undermine the legitimacy of the Communist regime. The British colony was rebranded as 'a capsule of China' by one influential travel writer.[29] The Korean War and Taiwan Straits crises in 1954/5, and 1958 – when Communist forces contested Guomindang control of offshore islands – and, for example, the shooting down of CPA's DC-4 in 1954, certainly fostered a lingering perception of the region as an unstable war zone, which dampened tourism in the early and mid-1950s. But US government investment in promoting tourism initiatives underpinned the steady rise in numbers heading across the Pacific by the end of the decade and in the early 1960s.

In 1947 only 200,000 US citizens held passports; in 1953 one million travelled overseas; six years later nine million did, one and a half million beyond Mexico or Canada. In 1961 half a million alone travelled to Asia. In 1966 143,000 visited Hong Kong.[30] Dedicated holiday magazines and news weeklies highlighted the ease of travel, the slow and steady fall in prices, the 'Oriental' 'mysteries' to be found and experienced, purchased or eaten. American writers like James Michener, first incidentally and then instrumentally, boosted interest and business. *Tales of the South Pacific*, Michener's Pulitzer prize-winning 1947 wartime romance, spawned a hit musical in 1949 and film in 1958 whose complex story was swamped by its sumptuous colour photography. And the Broadway musical's star, Mary Martin, remarked the co-founder of the influential trade body, the Pacific Area – later Asia – Travel Association (PATA) helped this shift: 'because of her the beauty and romance of the Pacific Ocean countries are a much more real and desirable thing for millions of Americans.' Michener turned out travel pieces that further boosted the Pacific as a place to visit. 'General reading' would be reported by visitors as the key source of information about Hong Kong, and 'general reading' in American magazines and in American bookstores more and more featured Asia.[31] A self-described 'child of aviation', Michener later wrote in his foreword to PATA's official history that it was air travel that made real the possibility that Americans might see Asia for themselves. Michener himself worked at one time or another with four of the largest US airlines, and Australia's airlines sponsored trips for Australian travel writers. Their popular works intersected with more overt marketing campaigns to foster the idea of a stopping off in Asia on the long haul to Europe – often at no extra cost to the passengers – and while they were in Hong Kong, one survey found, they shopped and they dined, then shopped and dined again, pumping cash into its economy.[32]

American demand had come first from military personnel in the Philippines, who headed north to Hong Kong for its 'climate, scenery, shopping, and entertainment'. The colony would later become a major R&R hub for United States forces in Vietnam, but the pattern had been established earlier, and was enhanced by the impact of films like *Soldier of Fortune* (1955), *Love Is a Many-Splendored Thing* (1955), based on Han Suyin's novel *A Many-Splendoured Thing*, or *Ferry to Hong Kong* (1958) all filmed on location with cheaper new colour technology, and most importantly the 1960 movie *The World of Suzie Wong* and its seductive fantasy of Hong Kong's nightlife. More innocent visitors, perhaps, were to be found in the tour groups from North America that swung around 'the Orient', 45 per cent of them arriving in Hong Kong from Japan.[33] Travellers answering the 'Call of the Pacific' had increased threefold in just five years, ran a March 1958 report. 'The Lure of Hong

Kong' proved increasingly irresistible, and increasingly easy to surrender to. And free-port Hong Kong was an 'Oriental bargain basement for American shoppers', one Phoenix, Arizona, newspaper reported that autumn: 'German and Japanese cameras, French perfume, Swiss watches, Swedish glass.' The making in 48 hours of a suit (or cocktail dress) was a recurring feature, even the butt of enduring jokes (for the 'Hong Kong suit' lasted, humourists claimed, just about as long as it had taken to be made). Still, six out of 10 American visitors had a suit or dress made. By 1959 CPA was appointing its own representatives in the US to encourage visitors.³⁴ In 1957 the colonial government had established a Hong Kong Tourist Association (HKTA) to encourage and facilitate an industry 'of prime importance for the Colony'. To popularise the city as a destination, the association set about producing brochures, posters, and films, and material for the NBC radio network in the US, including interviews with the governor, 'rickshaw coolies and bar girls', and about the Hong Kong experience, while working to improve the tourist experience.³⁵ Publicity ventures also included sponsoring a Hong Kong-built luxury junk, the *Ding Hao*, that displayed Hong Kong crafts and fashions and was part of Montreal's Expo '67, and a first prize-winning parade float in Pasadena's annual Tournament of Roses (in the form of a dragon, while 'Chinese maidens added decoration').³⁶ Between 1958 and 1961 numbers of incoming visitors to Hong Kong – primarily tourists – doubled; the total had doubled again by 1966, and tripled again by 1975. The aim of fostering the idea of a 'real China' was partly undermined by the Hong Kong shopping and dining experience – American visitors devoted 60 per cent of their time, and Australians 70 per cent of theirs to these activities alone – but the effect on the economy of the region was profound.

The working committee set up in Hong Kong to explore the potential of tourist promotion for the colony included among its number Butterfield & Swire Taipan Bill Knowles representing Cathay Pacific, who became the new association's first chairman. Born in India, the son of an accountant, Knowles was a 'shy craggy man', and a very talented mathematician, who had spent 10 pre-war years in China with the firm, mostly in shipping work at Shanghai, along the Yangzi and at Tianjin, and including a stint at Hong Kong. Returning to the company after war service in India, his shipping experience had been transferred to Cathay Pacific in 1950, and in 1957 he became Hong Kong Taipan.³⁷

Perhaps more than any other figure, Knowles represented how absolutely embedded in Hong Kong the Swire interests now were. He was also sometime chairman of the Hongkong & Shanghai Bank, the Chamber of Commerce, treasurer and later vice-chancellor of the University of Hong Kong, served on the colony's Legislative Council, and as founder chairman of the Tourist Association. Taikoo, remarked more than one governor, was important to Hong Kong's confidence, stability and prosperity.[38] And Hong Kong's growth was vital to Taikoo's businesses. Bill Knowles worked to market Hong Kong, but as Chamber of Commerce chairman with a seat on the Legislative Council, he also worked to market its industries.[39] The overlapping of tourist promotion and Cathay Pacific marketing was only to be expected. 'Discover a new World! Discover the Orient' encouraged the firm's adverts; for 'Nobody knows the Orient like Cathay Pacific'. CPA offices in Japan and in San Francisco organised HKTA promotional talks and film shows for travel agents (two of the 12 countries in which the firm represented the association). In 1961/2 Knowles was president of PATA, which held its 1962 annual meeting in Hong Kong, the conference dinner taking place in the Butterfield & Swire hong.[40]

The Electras began a revived Cathay Pacific Sydney service in July 1959, Bill Knowles travelling on the first flight, along with the Hong Kong Tourist Association's director.[41] This venture was immediately threatened by Qantas, which responded by running more flights per week, and then in November 1961 introduced a Boeing 707 jet, which killed it off. Cathay had countered the original threat by positioning its own service, first branded as the 'Cathay Pacific Jet Express' as the 'Cathay Oriental Jet Flight'. On the new service 'Exotic dishes to tempt the palate' were served by its 'charming hostesses', chopsticks made available for Chinese food, as were Japanese happi jackets. The passenger experience was overseen by 'slender Chinese girls, colourful in cheongsams – their national costume – and petite, demure Japanese girls, in their traditional kimonos'. A woman in a cheongsam beckoned to readers from Australian pages. Passengers were promised 'Oriental Charm and courtesy' as soon as they stepped on board.[42] The slogans that had first graced newspaper advertisements were quite different. They urged travellers to 'Be Specific ... fly Cathay Pacific', and reminded them that this was 'A British Airline with British Pilots', and suggested that 'All the Orient is your Orbit'. Japan Air Lines had adopted a similar strategy when it launched its Pacific services in 1954, and Taiwan-based Civil Air Transport (CAT) did so with its 'Mandarin Flight' in 1958 (and 'Mandarin Jet', from October 1961).[43] Steadily the flight itself had become an experience, or, rather, its staff had.

Its female staff, that is. In general, the airline industry's history of its use of female cabin staff to sell its services was consistently and unabashedly sexist. Cathay Pacific's deployment of female Asian cabin staff in its marketing and publicity was striking in the way it merged this industry-wide sexism with an objectifying 'orientalism' and 'exoticism'. Its cabin crews were 'inherently blessed with Oriental grace and tact', claimed a 1962 company advertisement, and 'passengers write lyrical letters about them'. Some of this blended with the way Hong Kong in general was sold as a tourist experience, and with trends in advertising more widely, but much of it was specific to the airline industry. Well into the 1970s, these trained professional crew members, the first large cohort of female workers in any of the Swire companies working with customers directly, were the focus for marketing stunts and advertising copy that traded on notions of glamour, 'Oriental' beauty, and 'demure', self-effacing subservience.[44] Cabin staff were encouraged to participate in beauty contests and fashion shows. A 'Cathay Beauty' rolled around San Francisco in a rickshaw in 1964 as part of a Hong Kong promotion, and a 'stunning collection of Oriental Exotica' on display there in November that year included, 'for example', a press report noted, two Cathay Pacific staff. They were deployed as hostesses at trade conventions – receiving guests at PATA's 1962 dinner at the 'head of a line of oriental beauties' – and, bikini-clad, were later used in television advertising.[45] 'The latest Cathay Pacific look', in 1969 was announced not just as a change in aircraft livery, but in a redesigned – above the knee – 'firecracker red' dress and jacket uniform.[46]

The destinations were being sold as well, of course, and this was not simply 'occidental' travel to the 'orient'. Asia travelled: tour groups were organised from Singapore to Japan for the Cherry Blossom season. Expatriates in Borneo were encouraged to take leave in Hong Kong or Japan. 'It's better fun to fly' called out a paid-for article in a Singapore paper in 1958, and 'CPA gets there faster and cheaper and attends to everything – from hotels to shopping and sightseeing trips'.[47] Successive Cathay Pacific newsletters introduced to passengers and potential travellers what to do and see and what to buy in Singapore,

Bangkok, Manila, Tokyo and Rangoon, and how to bargain, when not to and where to stay when there. If the pilots and maintenance engineers remained, as the advertising continued to stress, 'British' (or, in time Australian), this regional network required a much more diverse workforce in the airports and in the air, and a polyglot one, too. In the air as well, new destinations meant new recruitment of staff who could assist. The opening of routes to Japan, and then in 1964 the lifting on private travel restrictions by the Japanese government, created a need for a swift increase in numbers of Japanese cabin attendants. Japanese visitors to Hong Kong alone nearly tripled in number between 1963 and 1967. In 1964 they made up nearly 40 per cent of the total of travellers from overseas arriving in the colony.[48] The Japanese came to Hong Kong on average for three and a half days. Faster and faster air travel reshaped conceptions of distance, and so of time, and what might be achieved within it. Jock Swire's own trips from Britain out to Hong Kong on business provide some flavour of the new norms that air travel created. In 1940 Warren Swire had talked of a directorial visit as lasting 'the usual eight months'. By 1960 the tour could last as little as a month. Rapid advances in telecommunications also changed how the firm worked, but the world reordered and recalibrated by flight, in which process Cathay Pacific played a substantial role in Asia, was important, too.

Cathay Pacific Airways grew, then, as tourists came into the region, and as Asia started to move. Asians flew in greater and greater numbers and with greater and greater frequency, and Asians played or toured across what became increasingly conceived of as a coherent region, a place, not simply a geographical term, a 'way of life' (with diverse Asian particularities) walled off in the north from a hostile state. It also grew because Asia's economies grew, and as Japan's and Hong Kong's grew.

Japan would surprise John Swire & Sons. Before the war, the Butterfield & Swire offices in Yokohama and Kobe, organised in 1928 as Butterfield & Swire (Japan) Ltd, were largely restricted to the Blue Funnel and some insurance agencies. But the reconfiguration of operations led to a great increase in activity after 1945. Blue Funnel sailings were resumed, CNCo began sailing from Tianjin and Shanghai, and then started experimenting with its own ocean routes. From 1956 its ships started carrying wool to Japan from Australia, and then in the early 1960s meat imports also began to take off. There were opportunities for Swire & Maclaine, which established a branch, and once the Cathay Pacific routes were set up, business grew very swiftly indeed (in 1963 alone, receipts from CPA commissions doubled). The airline made the inaugural international flight into Osaka Airport in April 1960 and was met with a 'tumultuous reception'.[49] The 1964 Olympics, one manager later recalled, 'was responsible for Tokyo making a huge leap forward'.[50]

Japan's post-war beginnings were not auspicious. Managers and visiting directors complained about the squeezing out of British interests by the ebulliently confident US occupation establishment. This was literal: the Yokohama office (which had survived the 1922 earthquake) had been requisitioned by the Americans as a mess, and the army colonel who occupied 'the nicest house in Yokohama' extended his posting by a year because it was so pleasant. This was the company manager's house. So shocked was John Scott in 1948 by the condition of Japanese staff – a few 'old retainers' from pre-war days, and some wholly inexperienced but willing youngsters – that he authorised the issue of a free tin of meat a day to each one, free season tickets for travel, delivery from Hong Kong of new clothing for sale on easy and generous terms to them and cheap loans for housebuilding.[51] The economy was largely stagnant, though, and prospects for growth uncertain. But then came a 'gift from the gods', as then Prime Minister Yoshida put it: then came the Korean War.

Misery on the peninsula meant massive US orders for supplies and material from Japan. Dollars poured in, stimulating production across all sectors, and supporting that meant new machinery and supplies from overseas. As the China position had declined, Japan had already become a site of opportunity in Swire eyes. It was 'the one place where we are really doing something for Blue Funnel', Scott noted in early 1949. They had found new partners (Nippon Express) and opened new offices in Osaka. The country was, declared Jock Swire in 1951, 'probably the better new base for the future than Australia'.[52] In fact it seemed that the Pacific war and then the occupation had a similar revivifying effect as, in time, the China closure would have. Jock remarked in 1951 that it had forced the company 'to escape from our self-made cage'. The closed complacent world of pleasant old Yokohama, where W. J. Robinson had collected his antiquities and helped manage the old foreign cemetery, was redolent of the treaty port era, long after the Japanese had secured treaty revision. Now that was gone, and old partners faded away. The opportunities provided by Korea helped a new cadre of talented staff show their worth, including John Browne, who would go on to manage Hong Kong, and Michael Fiennes, who would become a director in 1956. By 1959 the company employed nine Britons and 176 Japanese staff in Tokyo and Yokohama, Kobe and Osaka. Japanese university graduates started to apply to join the firm, which largely serviced CNCo and Cathay Pacific, but which also now held a portfolio of other shipping agencies alongside Blue Funnel and its insurance business. In 1951 a Japan manager was appointed with responsibility for activities in the country as a whole. Bill Rae-Smith would hold this post from 1955 until 1972 with a brief interlude when he directed CPA from Hong Kong. This long tenure broke with a now firm practice of appointing managers for only relatively short periods which had been instituted after 1918. It reflected a view that success in Japan needed a different approach – and not just for the manager – and that staff ought also to learn Japanese.[53] In the longer term, success in Japan proved to be success for Japanese business, not foreign interests, and progress for Swire would start to stall in the later 1960s, but it proved a vital field and training ground as the firm reconfigured its operations after 1950, not least in shipping.

Hong Kong remained the company's shipping centre, its harbour busier than ever before. Beyond the tourist marketing, the cheap goods and tasty dishes, how did Hong Kong fare? And how did the Swire interests fare in Hong Kong? Put simply, the colony had been on a roller-coaster ride since 1945, waves of refugees arriving from China and at times overwhelming its existing infrastructure, not least because of a steadily held official view that they would return once conditions there settled down. These were sojourners, not migrants, certainly not – officially – 'refugees' (for the word was not in the official lexicon); they were deemed instead to be moving across the border on the basis of familial or other similar links, kith and kin as the British would put it, and the challenge was their assimilation in a crowded enclave: they formed 'the problem of people'.[54] But Mao's China did not settle down, so sojourns became migration: these arrivals needed settling. Most dramatically, the 1958 campaign to rapidly industrialise China known as the 'Great Leap Forward' led swiftly towards an apocalyptic famine that drove yet more refugees across the border. In the next four years at least 142,000 people arrived; 85,000 in 1962 alone. Refugees formed an estimated one-third of the population by 1961. The government's Resettlement Department was 'in daily contact with over one million two hundred thousand people', in 1963, it reported: 555,000 squatters, the same number in 'resettlement' housing, and 100,000 transitioning between the two.[55] Fearful of the political consequences that might flow from squatter settlement, it had begun a housing programme in 1952. Hong Kong was full, yet still people always came, and while they moved back and forth, and restrictions were introduced in 1962, the drift into the colony continued.

And what was there for them to do to earn a living? The Communist victory in 1949 had impaired existing trade links, but then a US-led United Nations embargo of the PRC instituted during the Korean War threatened the very basis of the colony's entrepôt economy. People proved a resource, however, as well as a problem; constraint encouraged innovation and adaptation; and into this mix came the influx from Shanghai of refugee businessmen, their skills, and their capital. (And equipment: Taikoo Sugar Refinery godowns received 'large quantities of refugee cargo' from Shanghai in 1949.) The contribution of the Shanghai element can be overstated, but it was certainly substantial.[56] In 1947, Hong Kong had no spinning mills: by 1953 it had 13, and in 1964 it had 40. The labour force in registered manufacturing establishments tripled between 1955 and 1965. Hong Kong industrialised, growing far beyond the long-established manufacturing base in which Taikoo firms featured prominently. Textiles and then plastics led the way. This was no easy transition, and the colony would face opposition from competitors and governments overseas, but there had been a fundamental shift in the nature of Hong Kong's economy. Most of the colony's exports by 1965 were its own manufactures.[57] Hong Kong grew, steadily, rapidly, and in unexpected ways.

John Swire & Sons continued to play its part in the manufacturing sector, and, as we shall see, Swire & Maclaine would play a role in this, too, but the core contribution lay in reviving its sugar refining and shipbuilding interests after the war. In time, however, the core focus of each evolved and their prominence within the colony diminished as the new industries and new industrialists and Chinese business elites grew in stature and confidence. The refinery had just started getting back to profitability after the difficulties of the late 1920s and 1930s when the colony fell to the Japanese: all things being equal, it had been on course for a substantial profit in 1941. In August 1945, while the buildings were largely intact, the equipment had been dismantled and then looted. It was deemed 'irrecoverable'. Some of the foreign staff were taken on by the dockyard, nearly half were retired, and only one foreman and a small Chinese maintenance team remained until 1948. The company covered expenses and made a useful profit from sales of water from its reservoirs, selling off scrap metal and renting out its empty godowns. A new awareness started to be shown in the asset of potentially greatest value that the company held, and which it was, literally, sitting on: that is, its land. But in 1948 orders were placed for new equipment: the plan was to rebuild a smaller plant, focusing only on high-grade refined sugar. The original firm, its articles and structure of ownership all a relic of John Samuel Swire's bid in 1881 to better Jardine Matheson, was voluntarily liquidated in 1949, and its assets transferred to a new company, to be managed in Hong Kong by a board of directors that included two figures from outside Butterfield & Swire. By then the Quarry Bay installation had been rehabilitated, a sales department reinstituted and production in train again by June 1950, and ahead of that sugar-cubing machinery had been set in motion once more.[58]

'Now back in the shops again' cooed advertisements in the Singapore press, 'One lump or two?' 'Back in the shops', they announced in Hong Kong, 'and back in my kitchen too'. 'Excellent idea for food parcels' urged another piece of copy, and 'Everybody will be glad you sent Taikoo Sugar' ran another, as Singapore Britons sent gifts back to a still-rationed Britain. Some people took their own. When the captain of Thailand's first international rugby team arrived in Britain, by air, in January 1952, he was photographed on arrival clutching a large bag of Taikoo sugar. Reproduced in the *China Mail* in Hong Kong the image neatly captures a convergence of several developments in which the Swire interests were active. Taikoo sugar usually did not travel quite that far, but it travelled, CNCo carried Taikoo bags and cubes out along its network to the Straits, Brunei, Borneo and Cambodia, and then further on it went, to Aden, Kenya, Iraq, India and Sri Lanka. 'Remember', urged a 1959 pamphlet for retailers in Singapore, 'October is Taikoo Month, Sell Taikoo on Purity Quality Economy, Are you pushing Taikoo Too?'[59]

But despite doing 'extraordinarily well', the directors thought, in getting back towards pre-war production levels in a vastly reduced overseas market, TSR would again face strong challenges. Securing supplies of raw sugar was one. Taiwan was an obvious source. But why should we sell our sugar 'for worthless sterling' objected K. Y. Yin, director of the refugee Nationalist state's Central Trust, when John Scott went to discuss 'sugar chasing' there in February 1952. Well, mused Scott, men like Yin 'had no love for the British' since the UK's recognition of the Communist regime, but political economy was working against Taikoo when it came to the island's sugar crop, not political sentiment.[60] The Taiwanese instead sent their sugar to Japan. But the most devastating threat was finally realised in 1964 when Malaysia's first sugar refinery was opened at Perai by the Malayan Sugar Manufacturing company. As well as hitting the market to which TSR had been exporting some two-thirds of its output from Hong Kong, and which was vital for its entire model of operation, this also hit CNCo, which had by then an important steady trade north from New Zealand of raw sugar for the company. The end had long been in sight. In 1956 there had been discussion about abandoning Hong Kong refining, and offering 'a package deal' to the Malaysian government 'to set up a Sugar Refining Industry for them'. As well as securing an entrée into Malaysia for Butterfield & Swire, there was that sweet premium to be realised on land at Quarry Bay. The belief that British interests could not only weather the transition of colonies to statehood largely untouched, and even enhance their position as partners in new independence development strategies, was widespread, but the optimism of the late imperial and post-imperial moment did not last, and such plans were repeatedly thwarted.

In this case, others took the initiative: Perai was a joint venture between a new company established by a Malaysia-born Chinese entrepreneur, Robert Kuok, together with the Malaysian federal land agency, and Japanese enterprises, and ahead of its opening the Malaysian government introduced import quotas to protect its new industry. Kuok had once held the Taikoo agency for Johor Bahru, fetching 80 tons a month from Guthrie's in Singapore, and making 'very, very good money' until abruptly cut off. He already had little taste for dealing with the British, and he had friends and connections, determination and anger, and post-colonial history on his side. International politics, and the protectionist development strategy of a newly independent state and the connections and deal-making of emerging figures like Kuok, forced John Swire & Sons to reshape its operations. Such tariff preference strategies were quite familiar within the world of British power, and when they could, British interests like the Swire companies made full use of them and secured preferential positions. They pondered a bid for sole supplier status for Malaya's sugar ration in 1948, for example, as they worked on restarting production. Having secured a guaranteed order from the Ministry of Food both for that market, and Hong Kong's, they had, Jock Swire reported, gained some protection as they restarted 'before we have to meet the full hazards of competition'.[61] But now they found quotas and monopolies being used against them, as Britain's formal power waned. The impact was immediate: exports of refined sugar from Hong Kong fell by two-thirds in the first year of the new Malaysian operation.[62] Kuok's business undid TSR. Enough proved enough: in 1973 the firm ceased refining altogether, but still continued to cube and pack refined sugar, and the brand remained a fixture in shops and stores. The company warehouses at Quarry Bay had continued to be let out for storage, providing a steady income, and when, for example, in 1960, the firm redeveloped its raw sugar godowns, the new buildings were designed to house four floors of commercial storage space above one floor for company use. The business transacted on the site was already in transition. So ended one phase in a long-standing venture. Its original strategic objectives, to tempt East Asians, Chinese in particular, to foreswear their unrefined sugars for Taikoo's refined whites had largely been accomplished, as tastes and consumption patterns had changed dramatically. But others now crowded out TSR. Still, as Jock Swire noted in his diary, while the rebuilt plant was itself now entirely surplus to requirements, 'they are sitting on a gold mine' at Quarry Bay.[63]

A similar 'package deal' was suggested to Butterfield & Swire in 1958 by an American marine surveyor in Hong Kong, Julius M. Pomerantz, 'a strange man,' wrote John Scott, 'who enjoys no very good reputation'. Pomerantz had his eye on the Taikoo Dockyard, and on matchmaking it with the port of Vitória in Brazil. He had a contract to supply 'and install a complete shipbuilding industry', with all labour and equipment. Surely Taikoo Dockyard, with its experienced staff and Butterfield & Swire, with its wider resources, ought to consider such an attractive opportunity, far from an unsettled Asia and 'the uncertainty of the future of Hong Kong'.[64] Although partly fantastic speculation, this was also an idea firmly in the long history of shipping Chinese expertise and labour overseas, within which the Swire interests had long been associated. But the proposal was declined: Taikoo Dockyard had had a happier rebirth after 1945, had launched its first post-war ocean-going vessel for a firm outside the company family in 1953, and in 1958 its order books were full.

Taikoo itself was obviously a fixed asset. While its expertise might be loaned or transferred – might you help us at Manila, came a request in 1951; might we do something in Australia, the directors wondered in 1952 – the yard itself was well and truly entrenched.[65] But the Brazilian idea was not entirely a novel one. It is quite unlikely that Pomerantz had got wind of high-level discussion within John Swire & Sons, but doing something about this vulnerable site had been a continuing topic of discussion for nearly a decade. The original British-registered company had been liquidated in 1940 and re-established in Hong Kong, in a more favourable tax environment, for wartime Britain's, Warren Swire had declared, was 'confiscatory'.[66] But in the aftermath of the Communist victory in China, and the onset of the Korean War, this pragmatic decision began to look like a mistake. Hong Kong was now a vulnerable front-line territory, effectively defenceless – as the collapse in December 1941 had shown – and potentially harbouring a strong fifth column bolstered by incomers from the north. We have, 'via Dockyard, too big a stake in politically insecure Hong Kong,' wrote John Masson in late 1949, 'and we should like to get some of it out'.[67] The dockyard's profitability also complicated matters, as this contributed to the building up of strong reserves.

'Nationalistic tendencies' across Asia were of concern, but the 'danger of control by Communist China' was the biggest threat. In 1939, London later estimated, the Swire companies had £4 million of assets in China. They had lost it all, and had in addition, by August 1954, remitted £861,000 to the hostage companies. As well as the immediate threat to Hong Kong, there was a long-term anxiety about '1998' – as it was then put – and the end of the New Territories lease. Taikoo Dockyard's status as a local company with a local board, made it vulnerable to a loss of control under any new regime, without compensation. The plan that evolved and which was first detailed in 1954, was to unlock and withdraw the reserves through a share issue in Hong Kong. The capital would be reinvested in a British-based company – Scotts Shipbuilding – and would also help finance development of the Australian activities of John Swire & Sons. John Scott was also a director at Scotts, that long-standing intertwining of families and firms still tangible, and

Taikoo Dockyard had already acquired one-third of Scotts as a 'lock-up investment' in 1953, safe, it was thought, from Asia's politics. In 1958 John Swire & Sons definitely moved towards floating 30 per cent of Taikoo Dockyard on the Hong Kong stock exchange. The Taiwan Straits crises in 1954, and especially in 1958, further alarmed the company, and Hong Kong's security was yet again questioned.[68]

Jock Swire arrived in Hong Kong in October 1958 to smooth the way with the Hongkong & Shanghai Bank chief manager, Michael Turner, and governor Sir Alexander Grantham (in that order). There 'would be little use in attempting any camouflage', Swire reported Turner advising, 'whatever [you] say, the public will think the purpose is to get money out of the Colony', which, Jock added privately, 'is in fact true'. Grantham was 'not entirely happy', for it potentially compromised 'the stability and confidence structure of Hong Kong'. 'I don't think he likes it one bit,' recorded Jock in his diary. But such initial fears, and Turner's about whether Hong Kong's still fledgling stock market could absorb the sale, were reconsidered. In fact, inviting local interests into the ownership of Taikoo Dockyard and Engineering served a useful additional purpose, for it could, of course, also be understood too as a sign of the firm's confidence in Hong Kong's future, even though it was a pragmatic dilution in the overall financial commitment there of John Swire & Sons. The share offer was 100 per cent oversubscribed.[69] At this time also the firm sold its offices in Hong Kong, moving into leased accommodation in a new block, Union House, in mid-June 1960. Bill Knowles lowered the house flag from the flagstaff on the roof on 11 June, and the new owners would demolish the 1897 building, now some distance from the harbourside. The old hong had grown crowded and dilapidated. While the brothel that had been installed in part of it by the Japanese had promptly been removed, even with a new floor and installation of air-conditioners in 1954, it had grown unfit for purpose. A sale had been on the cards since 1952, with discussions on a scheme that would entail leaseback from a publicly floated land investment company that would buy it, or even perhaps buy all Butterfield & Swire properties, and reinvestment in property in safer Sydney. Fear of 'catastrophe' in Hong Kong and loss of capital was the prime factor here as well, as they had been in the appointment of J. A. Blackwood as Taipan in October 1951, for he was considered a safe pair of hands in the event of a Chinese takeover. He had, after all, been through one such already as Shanghai manager. In August 1963 a new wholly owned office block, Swire House, was completed in Sydney.[70]

The Dockyard's rehabilitation became an iconic tale, central to the rebirth of Hong Kong's economy after 1945. And while Bill Knowles as Chamber of Commerce chairman would stress the need to market Hong Kong's industries in markets overseas, in his guise as Taipan, with his predecessors and successors, he helped oversee one part of that same effort. 'While I was gazing … almost in despair, at the scene of desolation and ruin,' recalled C. C. Roberts in 1950 of his first sight of the yard after venturing out of Stanley camp, 'I was astonished to hear my companion exclaiming to himself "It's even better than I thought!"' This was the manager, John Finnie, and he was in fact right. Unknown to them, as the two men looked on the debris and rubble-strewn sight, the one with dismay, the other with hope, a new cassion – a lock gate – was already on its way out and had reached Colombo. Plant, tools and steel to the value of £100,000 were in transit. Post-raid photographs taken by the US air force had reached Billiter Square, so the extent of the bomb damage was clear, and rehabilitation planning, which had commenced in 1943, could be advanced. London requested the Foreign Office work to transfer the dockyard staff who had been interned in Shanghai back to Hong Kong where they were wanted 'at once'. In Stanley itself, the interned dockyard architects and draughtsmen had been drawing up plans (there being little else to do). The first of the slipways was cleared by January 1946, the navy undertaking some 'ticklish' work to remove some large unexploded bombs, and shortly afterwards the dry dock was ready, receiving its first ship on 8 February. In September 1950 a new SS *Anshun*, its predecessor having been sunk in 1942 in New Guinea, was the first new ship launched. Lady Morse, whose husband, the Hongkong & Shanghai Bank's manager, Sir Arthur, had overseen a very large overdraft facility for the company, cracked a bottle of champagne and sent the 7,000-tonner down the slipway. By 1952 the dockyard was 'full of work for sometime ahead', subject, of course, to the political instability of the times.[71]

The rebuilt yard worried London in other ways as well. Finnie, another in the long line of Greenockians to work at Quarry Bay, ran it largely as his own domain (and organised it in his head), and was not what the directors and Taipans thought a commercially minded character, nor a modern manager, but he had got it going again. While

at first the dockyard staff improvised as they reconstructed and did
so with anything that they could salvage, in time the new buildings
that were erected seemed 'extravagant'. Finnie, reasonably, aimed to
modernise the 40-year-old installation, as well as rehabilitate. Even after
severe pruning of the £1.5 million reconstruction programme, Finnie
seemed to have got his way. The new offices were 'No doubt extremely
efficient but [it] reeks of megalomania', thought Jock Swire in 1951.
And securing sufficient quantities of steel would prove a continual
headache. Directors on tour lobbied in Japan and Australia, looking
to guarantee supplies. The dockyard would mark its resurrection and
fiftieth anniversary in 1954 with a lavishly illustrated volume – the
business undertaken during the Japanese-run hiatus excluded – and
launching a new *Chungking* for CNCo, the fourth of that name,
and the 35th ship delivered to the company.[72] On average 700 ships
a year were being repaired by the firm. The *Taikoo*, a powerful new
steam tug, an anachronism designed in Stanley camp where time rather
did stand still for those interned, was launched in 1950, operating the
salvage arm of the business. Typhoons were a good source of work, and
the ill wind that caused some damage to the dockyard's installations
provided a harvest of casualties in the harbour.[73] Repairs and coal to
diesel conversions increasingly became the dockyard's core business.

The dockyard was its work, and it was its workers. The labour force
at Quarry Bay was one of the largest in the colony. Figures varied as
business varied, but a 1954 note suggests an average of 4,500 workers,
with 350 clerical staff and 93 Britons; this might fluctuate as high as
5,700 men, women and adolescent apprentices. The structure of labour
employment remained complex. As well as a core staff paid monthly by
the dockyard, including the apprentices, or on a daily rate, there were
pieceworkers supplied by various contractors, who made up to a fifth of
the total complement generally employed. Jock Swire had commented
in 1946 that the war had seen many men work elsewhere, who on their
return had 'higher standards', by which he meant higher expectations.
Aviation repair shops at Kai Tak, as we have seen, were providing new
outlets for trained Chinese mechanics. Chinese office staff could only
be retained with substantial increases in salary and regrading, and for
the first time as well Chinese women were hired for white-collar work
(as they were in the hong offices).[74] Expectations, higher or otherwise,
and the colony's fragile economy, fuelled a first post-war strike in May

1946 involving 2,000 contract workers, another in November 1946; a month-long colony-wide mechanics' strike in August 1947 that secured a 50 per cent increase in pay – contract workers at Taikoo stayed out for another week; a successful petition for increases was made in 1956, and in 1959 there was a serious dispute about company housing. In 1947 the firm had appointed a Welfare and Labour Officer, who oversaw an expanded welfare programme. This was not entirely new. As well as housing provision in the 'Quarry Bay Village', which accommodated about a third of the workforce, Taikoo had established a free school in 1923 (which from 1924 onwards hosted classes for its apprentices), and ran a clinic for staff and their families. Now it opened a canteen at the yard, and a clinic there, set up two shops in the village to sell essentials 'at reasonable prices', and hosted a Rotary Club public clinic there for the neighbourhood, working with the local welfare association. Directors out east, and their wives, regularly appeared in the press opening a welfare centre (1951), a swimming pool (1954) (which sent Wan Shiu Ming to represent Hong Kong at the Melbourne Olympics in 1956), and a recreation ground (1961), visiting the school, and hosting events at which long-service presentations were made to staff. The firm set up a Taikoo Dockyard Chinese Welfare Society, supporting it with an annual grant.[75] This was better by far than welfare provision in much of the colony's industrial sector, but even so, in hard times, and with the hard struggle faced by many in overcrowded Hong Kong, they were never going to be enough, while as conditions did improve, so of course also did expectations.

The workforce, like Hong Kong's in general, was fractured in many ways, not least politically, with a notable divide between leftist and right-wing unions. The most vocal of the associations representing staff came to be the leftist Taikoo Dockyard Chinese Workers' Union, which had been established in 1946. The Hong Kong government's Labour Office and Hong Kong Police Special Branch reports shed light on the activity of an organisation in which Communist politics and labour activism were intertwined. In 1959 it had some 1,700 members – roughly half of the regular labour force – although barely half of those could afford to pay their dues. The union ran its own welfare centre, put on literacy classes for members' children, ran political classes for its members and set up a death gratuity scheme. It housed a Chinese National Products outlet at the centre – a mainland operated enterprise – and had its own

Cantonese Opera Troupe (the latter likely to have been an agit-prop initiative, as thousands of such troupes in the PRC were). Surviving union publications allot much more space to the achievements of the New China, than to its own work at Quarry Bay. On 1 October 1956, national day in the People's Republic, the union erected a huge mural on the side of its offices celebrating New China's achievements.[76] Ten days later, when 'rightist' – pro-Guomindang – groups in the colony celebrated the Republic of China's national day, bloody riots ensued that left nearly 60 people dead. This was not simply poster politics.

Affiliated with the Communist colony-wide Federation of Trade Unions the Taikoo Dockyard union was active in supporting its campaigns in Hong Kong, working against squatter clearances, for example, and it took part in drives to recruit skilled mechanics to move to China, notably in July 1958 when 400 men left to take part in the Great Leap Forward campaign. Many of them came back, smartly, disenchanted, and feeling deceived. The Labour Office ran a programme of visits to unions, and relayed their concerns to management. 'We have read of your visit with interest' was the bland response of manager R. D. Bell in August 1959 to one memo, 'and the Unions already have our considered opinion on these points'. The union's own presentation of the circumstances of dockyard staff life and work, and that of the firm's management, naturally often contradict each other, and the union certainly had a Communist Party affiliation, but they can also complement each other to form a picture of life for dockyard workers. While Labour Office staff and others were routinely sceptical about union statements about staff circumstances, or safety lapses, we might also reasonably be sceptical about some of the management responses. But as one official minuted in 1959, 'while not being philanthropists', they 'know how to run a good ship yard'. 'We rank them high on our "Good custom" list.'[77] Quite what anybody made of the persistence into the 1950s of the dockyard's employment of sedan chair carriers to ferry the managers to and from work is unclear.[78]

Several thousand dockyard employees and their dependants lived in the Quarry Bay company dwellings. Taikoo was its installations, but it was also the company village it had built at Shau Kei Wan east of the yard along the shore, a set of three-storey tenements, and the cook shops and food stalls that fed its labourers – and the moneylenders and pawnbrokers there as well – and the families, and former staff or the dependants of those who had died, who lived on in the staff houses. A dockyard worker might have three or four dependants, often more. Hong Kong's 'problem of people' also involved its high birth rate. Dockyard workers were, the union contended in 1957, having between them 440 children a year on average, new mouths to feed and bodies to house on wages that had been stagnant since 1947, when food was now over 25 per cent more expensive than it had been 10 years earlier.[79] And the school, which had begun with 170 children, was restarted in 1946 with 200, had nearly 600 in 1951, and over 700 by 1956.[80] The dockyard's owners, the union argued, 'have made profits by millions', the 'New Office building' that London thought extravagant was singled out as contrasting sharply with the 'iron facts' of hardship faced by staff. By 1960 three generations of some families had worked for Taikoo. Chan Sing-kwan's grandfather worked for 20 years under a carpenters' contractor, dying during the Japanese occupation; his father had worked for over 20 years for another contractor before his death in about 1950. Chan was a casual worker in the garage. Apprentice Cheung Tak-sing's father had also joined as an apprentice, aged 16, dying during the occupation. Lo Too, a joiner, joined in 1921 aged 13, retiring in 1971 after 50 years, both sons working for the yard. Head pieceworker Wong Hing retired in 1969 after 60 years, having joined at about the age of 16.[81] China's politics, and Hong Kong's, the colony's economy and the wider region's, all affected life and work at the dockyard.

The contradictions came into sharp relief with the building of new flats and demolition of old ones. These tenements were in a poor state even by the 1940s. We know that early on there had been subletting and subdivisions – a man might but rent a bunk bed, not even a cubicle, and 20 people might live on each floor – and there was an informal management of access to the housing over which the dockyard had no control. Demolition would solve one set of problems at a stroke, for only those clearly entitled to live there would be allowed back, and the quality of the flats would be markedly better (with an impact on staff morale). But while easing out squatters, this also left out in the cold retired or invalided staff who lived on in the blocks, and dependants of men who had died, who all felt they had a moral right to consideration. We also know that subletting the tenements formed a vital part of many household incomes.[82] The firm had secured an exemption from a 1947

Landlord and Tenants Ordinance that had imposed rent controls, so that the monthly rents in the reconstructed blocks were $25 a month, up from $5. The union organised protests, and opposed the change, and evictions, but in the firm extolled the improvements that the new housing represented, as did, it was claimed, the wives of protesting workers.[83] Company and union vied for the loyalty of the workforce. In this case Taikoo won, most staff accepted the rehousing, and those who were ineligible were compensated, or rehoused by the resettlement office. The episode provides us with a picture of breadline Hong Kong in Taikoo's shadow, with no glamour, no cheongsams, no actresses. There in the old village was a CNCo mariner's widow, living with her 'mentally-ill' son; fitter Kwok's widow and young son; retired contract carpenter Lai; casual painter Cheung, father of four, seven years in dockyard service; Wong, casual worker, her husband sometime casual worker painter; paint scraper Ng, disabled after a workplace accident, worsened by poor medical treatment, unable to work; widow Chan, a contract casual worker, late husband a casual painter, three dependants; deceased paint scraper Leung's wife, 'lives now by begging': he had died 22 years earlier. Most of those connected, however tenuously, to the firm, actually lived in private rentals, some afloat. Disaster stared dockyard casual worker Fung Kei three times in the face on Christmas Day 1967: the arrival of triplets threatened to throw into utter destitution a family with five children already, who lived on a sampan in a typhoon shelter.[84] This was another Hong Kong, most of Hong Kong, much of the time; even when secure in work, rarely a rice bowl or two away from an empty pot.

Hong Kong, of course, remained a British colony, and that needs to be remembered. It looked, sounded and felt like one. It was not so much a capsule of China, as tourist marketing had it, but as the decades passed, and as Britain surrendered its colonial possessions first one at a time, and then in a whirlwind of change, Hong Kong looked like a capsule in which could be found an outmoded British colonial past. Governors might arrive from a post in the Solomon Islands, for example, and depart to one in Singapore, arrayed in all the ostrich-feather plumage of Colonial Office formal dress. Name cards were left by new arrivals, as Edwardian social practices long abandoned in Britain lingered on in sweatier climes. And it was 'very much a place of racial divisions and social cliques,' commented a visitor in a 1952 Colonial Office publication, noting that the Peak, although now no

longer reserved exclusively by law for Europeans, still felt socially far
above even the British hoi polloi. There 'were very few genuine social
relationships with the Chinese at all,' recalled later chairman Adrian
Swire, who arrived in 1956 to start to learn the ropes. 'All the pre-war
colonial practices were aggressively still in place.' There was in the main
no informal interaction with Chinese peers. Distance was maintained
by lack of much real encouragement to learn Chinese, and a social code
in firms like Butterfield & Swire that tabooed male British staff having
(formal) relationships with Chinese women.[85] This was indeed a real
'self-made cage'. Social segregation was reinforced by political distance.
In wartime, officials and residents in London and in internment camps,
serving with BAAG or refugees in Macau, had reflected critically on the
disaster of 1941, and on what underpinned the collapse. Grand plans
for political reform were sketched out, but all were abandoned. Hong
Kong remained an official autocracy, lacking any popular legitimacy,
working with a handful of co-opted 'unofficial' representatives (the
very term indicating that the norm was otherwise) drawn in the main
from select British interests. Butterfield & Swire was now routinely
one of them. No one ever voted Bill Knowles, or J. A. Blackwood,
or other taipans, on to the Legislative Council (where as a result they
became 'the Hon'). The relationship between the big British hongs and
the colonial administration was close, too close felt some observers,
while for others the interests they represented were too important to the
economy to be held at arm's length. A useful myth (in British minds)
endured that Hong Kong's Chinese residents actually had no interest
in politics, and were content instead to leave it to others, if efficiently
done. And the British assured themselves that this was indeed being
done. It would soon become clear that this was not the case, notably
because corruption was ingrained at all levels in the colonial state, and
in all spheres of public and private life.[86]

New recruits to the firm, or new arrivals from other branches, recall
being struck by the pre-war atmosphere that enveloped official life and
British social life. Yao Kang arrived there from Shanghai, and thought
the prevailing norms distorted not only British behaviour, but the
attitudes of Hong Kong-raised Chinese who he felt routinely deferred
to the British without need. This overlapped with questions of status
and hierarchy, and even when, as a management trainee, he was entitled
to use bathroom facilities reserved for senior staff, he found Britons of

equal status would object, as colonial Hong Kong had trained them
to. The encounters were jarring for British employees for it was still
unusual for a man like Yao to share that status. The corporate hierarchy
largely remained a hierarchy of race. Colonial society was shaped by
the formal and informal policing of difference. 'It was so nice to go to
Japan,' recalled Adrian Swire, 'because it was a "proper" country and
you did not have that divide.'[87] The atmosphere in the firm's office
was drawn from pre-war air well into the 1960s. 'It was quite a shock
to the system', a new secretarial arrival in the Private Office in 1964
remembered in later life, meeting a rigidly formal layout of desks,
and office dress codes wholly unsuited to the climate, let alone the
times outside.[88] In this regard the firm was on the cusp of definitive
change. The previous year it had appointed a University of California
graduate, Hong Kong-born Lydia Dunn, to a management trainee
role in Swire & Maclaine. Steadily, if slowly, it hired more Hong
Kong graduates who had long avoided the firm. 'Top-notch' Chinese
graduates assumed that their path to seniority in a foreign-owned firm
would be blocked, so chose instead to work for Chinese companies, or
entered the professions. 'We perhaps missed out on the real live wires,'
reflected Tom Lindsay, who had been centrally involved in personnel
matters, after his retirement in 1966.[89] And after the withdrawal from
China, the company had a surplus of mid-career staff, and had tried
to find billets for them in new departments like Swire & Maclaine, or
else it had shipped them into its Australian venture. But with its Asian
centre of gravity increasingly fixed in Hong Kong, even if that colony
was a steady source of anxiety, it needed Hong Kong people to run a
Hong Kong firm.

Yao Kang would later blame the culture of 'unequal treatment
left over by history' in the practices of the firm for some of its staff
problems. One we might note was the practice by which Chinese
executives, regardless of their actual role, represented or led the staff
as a body. A Taikoo Chinese Staff Association had been set up by a
group of employees in 1949 and was provided with accommodation by
the company in which it was hoped office staff might play mah-jong,
eat cheaply and indulge in hobbies. It was viewed at first with some
suspicion, for there was a 'political and Trade Union smell' about it,
ran one report (not helped by a statement of purpose that drew on the
language of the US Declaration of Independence), and some of those

involved were thought to be 'radicals', but the firm decided to work with 'and guide' the new association.[90] This was not a representative body, and tight government regulation of societies and organisations meant that it was registered as a 'benevolent society'. It was prohibited from engaging in any discussions on behalf of staff over pay or conditions. But as the only formally organised staff body, and with a board of elected representatives, it had in the mid- and late 1950s attempted to do just that. One of the Chinese staff leaders, Chester Yen, was credited with taming it. Yet this was a symptom of the colony's wider contradictions. Into the 1960s these executives were men who had joined before the war, some as compradors or as relatives of compradors, while others were veterans of the old Chinese House Staff recruitment initiative. They had formally taken retirement in China in 1954/5 in most cases, for as 'agents of capital' – as they were designated – they had no future in the bodies that took over the Butterfield & Swire companies. Most had then made their way out. 'Leader of one part of the staff', Tom Lindsay wrote of one in April 1966; 'leader of quite a section of the staff', of another; 'he represents one of the two major elements in Swatow life' of a third, who everyone else thought in fact a Communist, or sufficiently close enough to allow him to serve as a conduit for communications with leftist organs in Hong Kong.[91] These were men with skills and experience within the firm, but they did not always represent the new world in which the company worked. Cantonese executives with strong roots in local society were in a minority.

The sclerotic limitations of an unreformed colonial state were starkly demonstrated in May 1967, when Hong Kong exploded. What grew out of a labour dispute in a factory that made plastic flowers was not the first episode of serious civil disturbance in the colony – there had been riots over a proposed increase in Star Ferry fares the previous year, itself a signal of the fragility of individual livelihoods – but it became the most violent, and longest lasting, and it forced the Hong Kong administration, once the insurgency was suppressed (and it was dealt with, eventually, as such), to adopt a new range of policies that cautiously aimed to redraw relations with Hong Kong society, without instituting any political reform.[92] The insurgency was certainly sustained by local Communist cadres and leftist activists, who set up 'Fighting Groups' and 'Anti-Persecution Struggle Committees', turned their welfare centres and union offices into fortresses that they defended with violence and improvised but deadly weapons, and directed a campaign of initially peaceful protests, and then bomb attacks, in a crisis for the colony that would eventually leave 51 dead. The context was certainly shaped by developments within the Cultural Revolution in China, which had been launched by Mao Zedong in late spring 1966 to protect his dominant position in China's politics. Long concerned that his own fate, even in life, might be foretold in the fall from grace after his death of Joseph Stalin – who was denounced by Nikita Khrushchev in 1956 in a speech that split the Communist world – the Chinese Communist Party's Chairman led China's youth in a violent attack on his own party, and on all aspects of Chinese life, society and culture. As the campaign unfolded, many in Hong Kong's Communist circles began to feel that staying aloof from it because they were comfortably over the border looked like being a misplaced bet. So, when on 15 May the Ministry of Foreign Affairs in Beijing, which was itself in the throes of a takeover by Cultural Revolution leftists, issued a condemnation of a fracas that had involved police and strikers in Hong Kong nine days earlier, the left went into action. Even so, the confrontation that unfolded would not have gained the traction it did unless there were underlying social problems, and problems of governance. The vast majority of the Hong Kong population supported the government as it fought to restore order, and it would eventually do so, but Hong Kong's old corruption got its comeuppance all the same.

The year had actually begun pleasantly for John Swire & Sons, for it started with a series of events to mark the centenary of the firm's establishment in China. After the Hongkong & Shanghai Bank marked its own 100 years of business in 1965, discussion about the looming anniversary of John Samuel Swire's first journey to China had commenced. The decision was taken to adopt 1 January 1867 as the date of the foundation of Butterfield & Swire, and events were organised in Hong Kong, Taipei and later in the year in Japan. Medallions were issued to long-serving staff (bronze for the many, silver for the few and a gold one for the royal guest in Tokyo, Princess Chichibu), new scholarships were announced and gifts to the University of Hong Kong and the recently established Chinese University of Hong Kong. Fourteen hundred staff from the Swire and Swire-managed firms were entertained to an opera performance and cabaret at Hong Kong's City Hall (where an unexpected turn by an 'Australian go-go dancer, complete with ostrich feathers', who undertook a demure and uncompleted striptease, added a surreal note to events). More senior staff and the Britons had a reception at the Hong Kong Club. Much of the way colonial Hong Kong's brittle state hampered its smooth functioning can be seen in the small notes of difference and distinction, and simple points of confusion: while the gift to the Chinese University was to fund composition of a new Chinese-English dictionary, nobody realised that the dates in Chinese and in English on the medallions were different. Jock Swire toasted the future. His near 53 years of visiting the city was trumped by the fact that John Scott was able to note in Japan that his own father had arrived there in 1867. It was evident that the continuities were both corporate and, unusually, personal.

When some of the directors gathered in Hong Kong at New Year in 1967, a new generation was running John Swire & Sons. Jock's elder son, John A. Swire, had first arrived in Hong Kong on company business in October 1950. Over the next four years he worked there in a number of departments, as well as in Japan and Australia, returning to join the board in London in 1955. His brother Adrian had arrived in September 1956, starting off, like many new recruits, with 'ship jumping': meeting incoming vessels, and going on board to talk with the captain and crew. In 1961 he headed to London to join the board where he was schooled by John Masson in the business of managing the shipping interests before the latter's resignation in 1963. He had retained this core focus when, in June 1966, Jock Swire stepped down as chairman, and John Scott, after 42 years on the board, as deputy, being succeeded by John Swire and Adrian respectively. John Scott's nephews James Hinton Scott and Edward Rankin Scott had also joined the company, and James joined the board on 1 January 1967. There were other multi-generational continuities within the firm, notably within the network of senior Chinese executives. Wong Pao Hsie, CNCo's Chinese manager, had joined in 1931, and his grandfather had from its very earliest days had a close association with CNCo as a shipping agent. Hua Tshai Lee's father was the former Shantou comprador. Maurice Ching was the son of the former comprador at Niuzhuang. Both worked within CNCo. In 1958, three years after the death of his father C.P. Wong, formally Swire & Maclaine manager, and informally the leader of the Chinese staff, his son Benjamin had joined the firm as well, and would in time join the board of directors in Hong Kong.

But if 1967 began well for the Swire companies, with celebration, speech and spectacle, by the late spring of the year Hong Kong itself was on fire. Socio-economic discontent, political activism, Cultural Revolution posturing and obtuse colonial governance produced a concatenation. The British publicly talked of it as 'the riots'; in private, and in official papers, it was a 'confrontation'. They had had some warning of the general drift towards a more volatile politics, for in December 1966 a foretaste of what was to come had played out on the streets and in the harbour of Macao, which had seen the colonial administration capitulate to Chinese demands. The Hong Kong government had watched this closely, its own Essential Services Committee – its emergencies unit – circulating a report on the episode which found its way to Swire House in London. And what might the company do in the event of serious civil disturbances, mused John Browne, who had succeeded Bill Knowles as Taipan in 1964.[93] Browne was also 'shadow Ministry of Transport representative', and – a lingering effect of the Korean War crisis, and a legal requirement between 1951 and 1961 – many of Butterfield & Swire's staff in Hong Kong served in the auxiliary air force, police or the Royal Hong Kong Defence Force (as the volunteers were now known). Many would find themselves kept busy out of office hours as the crisis in the colony rapidly unfolded across the spring and summer of 1967.

James Cassels had joined the dockyard in 1946. While he will have seen a lot in the course of his first 20 years in Hong Kong, he will probably not previously have found himself at the wrong end of a spear. Yet on the afternoon of 6 June 1967 Cassels, then general manager of the company, and his shipyard manager Tom Duncan were surrounded by an angry crowd of workers, many of them carrying spears improvised out of metal poles. With one of these, a welder forced the manager against a wall. The previous day the police had launched a colony-wide operation to clear away posters pasted up by leftist activists. The government had issued an emergency order to ban 'inflammatory' posters on 1 June. On the morning of 6 June 500 workers gathered and 'began to chant slogans, sing communist songs and hold aloft a banner with the words, "We sternly protest against the unwarranted dismissal of workers by the Company which colludes with the British-Hong Kong authorities".' The dockyard had started removing posters from its own launches and as tensions rose one Chinese foreman had to swim out into the harbour to a passing junk to escape the crowd. In the afternoon a smaller crowd surrounded Cassels and other staff. While Tang Tsuen, president of the leftist Taikoo Dockyard Chinese Workers' Union, demanded that they sign a document agreeing to union demands, another activist conducted 'the crowd in the singing of political songs and the chanting of political slogans'.[94]

The first sign of trouble at the dockyard had been a one-hour token strike on 23 May called to protest against 'British brutality' at the flower factory. Three thousand workers took part. One hundred and fifty TSR employees also held a similar protest three days later. But it was the poster ban that provided fuel for a storm of protests across public utilities, both the dockyards and the Star Ferry company. Governor David Trench's situation report on 8 June struck a note of concern about the 'increased bellicosity of some of the workers particularly those in Taikoo docks'. On the night of 7 June, after an emergency board meeting, the gates were locked and staff told not to return until called for. The company undertook a 'reorganisation', and 168 men were not recalled on 14 June when the dockyard reopened; they were also later evicted from company housing. Another 140 men joined a general strike on 24 June, and would also be prevented from returning. A month later, as the government response hardened, a combined police and military operation was launched against the barricaded offices of various leftist organisations. The Taikoo Dockyard Union's Welfare Department on Shaukiwan Road was one target, and the TSR Workers Union's Welfare Centre another. Molotov cocktails, improvised bombs, spears and knives were found at Shaukiwan Road. At least two of the union's officials arrested in that swoop were later served with detention orders, and held for six months without trial. Tang Tsuen, also seized that day, and who was also a member of the standing committee of the colony-wide 'All Circles Struggle Committee' which co-ordinated the insurgency, was sentenced to six years in jail for his part in the affair on 6 June, as was the man who conducted the chorus.[95] In all around 43 men were arrested, most being held until late the following year.

At TSR a first small token strike on 19 May was followed by the pasting up all over the yard and on its delivery vans of 'inflammatory posters'. Deliveries stopped. During a second short stoppage involving most of the workforce a week later 'new posters appeared daily', the offices of the chief engineer and works manager not excepted. Attempts to negotiate proved fruitless. Over a third of the workforce joined the general strike. All were immediately dismissed, and most were invited to apply for reinstatement and explain why they should be. This option was not offered to the 'hard core of militants'. Those were paid off and given notice to leave their company housing.[96]

Leftist propaganda during the months of unrest included a cartoon strip, 'The bloody and tearful story of the Taikoo Dockyard Workers', which ran weekly in the Communist newspaper *Wen Wei Po*, and was published as a booklet. This portrayed brutal British foremen disciplining apprentices with kicks; showed victims of unsafe working conditions, suffocating, trapped and killed by fire, falling to their deaths or, starving and ill, throwing themselves to their deaths. When not emaciated, the workers are models of heroic proletarian strength, and anger. Several of the strips narrated actual events, and individual calamities, at least one of which had the coroner demanding the company be prosecuted. This was classic agit-prop material of its era: 'Now is the time for us to settle our account once and for all with the British Imperialists!', it concludes. 'We must fight against them until they are utterly finished'![97] The dockyard responded with publicity that pointed to the welfare and training activities of the firm. But the potency of the leftist charges against the dockyard, while indicative of the wider social and economic problems that fuelled the unrest in Hong Kong, and the crisis of legitimacy of an unreformed colonial regime, also drew on real causes of concern for the workforce.

Post-strike analysis by the firm, and external consultants, was damning.[98] There was too much reliance on expatriate supervisory staff, a dearth of adequate means for staff to discuss grievances, an 'inequitable wage structure' and no progress had been made on implementing a January 1967 commitment in principle to implement an increase that would 'give all workers a realistic living wage without it being necessary for them to work overtime to achieve this'. That proposal had been accompanied by a plan to advance more Chinese staff – 'of known integrity' – into supervisory roles, but that, too, was not being carried out with any sense of urgency. Tellingly, the company's 'Senior Chinese Staff Service Conditions' booklet was printed entirely in English. By October a $40 a month wage increase had been agreed, which meant a 22 per cent increase for the lowest paid, significant moves had been made to accelerate the replacement of expatriate staff with Chinese, a programme to move pieceworkers on to a time-employed basis had accelerated and apprentice training was to be overhauled. In the autumn of 1967, Taikoo started to establish a set of Inter-Liaison Shop Committees, with staff representatives. As Cassels noted, these rapidly 'aired a lot of problems which would not rapidly have come to our attention'.[99] These were all Taikoo Dockyard problems, but they were also all symptomatic of the state of colonial Hong Kong.

The British clampdown, together with the hostility towards the riots of by far the greatest part of the Hong Kong public, and the exhaustion in time of the wider base of support for the activists (for strike funds were quickly used up), took steam out of the insurgency in the autumn. By January 1968 it was all but over, except for those in prison or detained without trial, and bitter traces of that experience lingered long in Hong Kong society. The police registration of the Taikoo Dockyard Chinese Workers' Union was suspended in 1967. Dismissed workers at both the Dockyard and TSR petitioned for reinstatement in July 1968. 'We must point out,' wrote the TSR union, 'that the strike was entirely forced on us by the Hong Kong British Authorities. Our strike was not directed at the factory.'[100] Labour activism would resurface at the dockyard in 1972, and a leftist political organisation would be reconstructed. The government launched a series of administrative reforms, embarked on significant infrastructure projects and ran campaigns aimed at bridging the gap between the colonial state and Hong Kong society. There was no return to frustrations on the scale that had fuelled the upsurge in 1967.

We need to recall the wider context, too. This was the year of The Beatles' *Sgt. Pepper* album and the 'Summer of Love', a moment across the industrialised West of a loosening of social, legal and cultural restraints, associated in Britain with the important reformist legislation that was emblematic of what has been termed a 'liberal hour' in British politics, building on the abolition of the death penalty, and landmark Race Relations act with the decriminalisation of adult male homosexuality, and legalisation of abortion. The year was at the same time one of political crisis: the Six-Day War in the Middle East, riots in American cities, and the US intervention in Vietnam moving towards its peak in 1968. Facing a sustained insurgency in Aden, the British ignominiously withdrew after a 130-year colonial occupation. The unravelling of the British empire was marked by two further landmark decisions: the June 1967

Defence White Paper, which outlined a withdrawal of British forces
from bases 'East of Suez', and in November, after years of expensive but
fruitless resistance, the devaluation of sterling. The impact of this last
decision on Hong Kong, which was the second largest holder of sterling
overseas in October 1967, and which received inadequate warning and
little consideration of how it would be affected, was profound. The
colony's establishment including its administration felt cut loose by
the imperial centre, and relations with policy-makers and officials in
London were to remain brittle long afterwards.

The anniversary year had proved a complicated one for John Swire
& Sons. History worked for and also against the company. Hong
Kong trade associations and the Tourist Association too bounced back
with a business as usual campaign, but the experience was profoundly
unsettling. Its minutes record that the TSR board's decision in November
to return 80 per cent of its capital to stockholders 'was not prompted
by the situation in Hong Kong', but of course it was.[101] In total, well
over 40 per cent of the investments of John Swire & Sons in 1966 were
in Hong Kong, and well over 70 per cent of its profits were drawn from
the colony. And yet, in the midst of the heady days of the summer of
rage, despite the commitments that had been reaffirmed, and despite
Jock Swire's final ringing declaration at the Hong Kong Club of his
grandfather's core principles, that the firm should 'Never give in
to Blackmail', he would note in late August 1967 that these figures
meant 'Too much Hong Kong', and that this was 'our really serious
weakness'.[102] What then, might be done about this?

14

Making Hong Kong

Crisis in Hong Kong and generational change in London prompted a period of intense reflection within John Swire & Sons about the way it worked, about where it operated and about what its activities should actually involve. It also provoked Jock Swire to outline what he considered to be some core principles that lay at the heart of the company. But Jock, who more than any other single figure brought the company back into action after 1945 and nurtured its growth across the volatile post-war decades, would also come to find himself perplexed at the pace and scale of change that subsequently unfolded. Over the next decade the company was reimagined, core parts of it were renamed – old Butterfield was finally pensioned off – long-standing activities were scaled down and some brought to a close, and a new-looking business would emerge. Much of this stemmed from the self-reflection of directors and managers, but advice was also sought from management consultants, and implemented. This process of change was also shaped by, and shaped, the evolution of Hong Kong itself, both its urban environment and its changing political culture and economy, and especially its spectacular growth across the 1970s. John Samuel Swire, long ago, had routinely warned against locking up capital unprofitably into land and buildings. He wanted his money moving. Now the company would pour cash into property, and where it once employed thousands it would instead house tens of thousands. Some in the firm would rue the scale and some of the detail of these changes, but it made sound commercial sense. There were some problems on the way, but across a decade when, in Hong Kong, several long-established

British firms found themselves fatally compromised, and even Jardine Matheson found itself on the verge of collapse, the Swire Group proved an unusual survivor.

This began with some introspection. From the early 1960s, the company had been commissioning the pioneering firm of British management consultants Urwick Orr and Partners to examine its activities. Cathay Pacific, Swire & Maclaine, Taikoo Dockyard and the Butterfield & Swire Japan and Hong Kong companies, were among the operations analysed. In mid-June 1967 Urwick Orr were asked to look urgently at the organisation of activities in London 'for determining the policy and long range plans (including diversification) of the Swire Group as a whole'.[1] The report provides an unusually detailed snapshot of John Swire & Sons itself in the summer of 1967. The London firm was worth some £12.5 million (about £220 million in 2019), with well over 50 per cent of its assets held outside the companies it managed (and 20 per cent in the old, old network: in Scotts and Holts).[2] What was clear to the outside eye was that its operations had grown organically, if not in fact haphazardly, the choice rather influenced by the 'ability and flair' of those involved, but not as part of any systematic and agreed strategy. This was not entirely fair, at least over the longer term, for there had been a logic to, for example, setting up TSR once CNCo was firmly established, and the logic of building the dockyard was apparent long before John Samuel Swire's death, while many shipping interests had got into air as soon as they could. But to an outsider not steeped in company history, what could be seen in 1967 looked rather peculiar. There were 32 companies in the Swire Group, and it was hard to place Swire & Maclaine, Duro Paints or more recent developments, such as the acquisition in 1965 of soft-drink firm Hong Kong Bottlers (which held the Coca-Cola franchise) or Hotel Express or a refrigerated truck company in Australia. The key finding, though, was that not only was there a lack of a coherent agreed strategy, but that even the capacity to develop one was hindered by traditions of directorial practice, and by flows of information from 'the East' which looked overwhelming to an outsider. Mail from Asia arrived on Mondays, for example, was presented for all the directors to see, and was responded to, en masse, on 'mail day' – Friday – and this office-defining rhythm was counterpointed in Hong Kong with what one employee remembered as the 'weekly ceremony of the London mail' (all must be ready to go by 1.55 p.m.).³ Conversely, there were obstacles to locating key information in other areas. There was no financial director, for example, and no annual plans and budgets were set for any of the companies. The men on the spot had devolved to them significant responsibility and autonomy, which was, for jurisdictional reasons, as it needed to be, but much – too much – depended on personal relationships and trust. There were 'no formally defined procedures for the direction of subsidiary and associated companies'.

Well, 'the mutual confidence & respect which has made this possible has been our greatest strength,' minuted Jock Swire in response to the last point as he read the report with evident and clearly increasing exasperation, pencil in hand, nib sharpened. But was 'mutual confidence and respect' all that was needed to meet the significant challenges the company faced? You need to diversify, the report argued, and for that you need a strategy, and to co-ordinate development and implementation of that you need to appoint someone to a strategic development role, and you need to create a development budget. In addition, appoint a group finance director, and introduce some improved systems which enable the directors better to direct, and not, as was the case, focus too much on managing existing activities and their problems. In addition, for all the trust and devolution to managers overseas, and although the pattern was slowly changing, London was wholly in control, and London's tax situation was an important factor, shaped also by worries about the policies of Harold Wilson's Labour government. John Swire & Sons acted as proprietor: its decisions were final. Some of the Urwick Orr report, thought Jock, was 'mumbo jumbo' ('what does this mean,' he scribbled next to definitions of 'Objective' and 'Policy'), some was sensible and overdue. But, he responded

> Our management has been the envy of the world. Change with the times ... by all means but don't depart lightly from the fundamental principles that have been the secret of this success. Eg. A) An intimate knowledge & control of House staff & managers of other interests by Chairman & whole Board b) Final control of House Finance by family directors. C) Keep firm's cash conservatively liquid to help subsidiaries in trouble. D) Don't invest heavily in anything you don't manage, except for exceptional reasons eg OSSCo.

But Jock was not now chairman, and in a year would step down from the board altogether. However, he had over four decades of experience. The consultant was a 28 year old, not long out of university. Here he was telling Jock, C. C. Roberts – sometime Hong Kong Taipan, veteran of Stanley camp, out in China long before Urwick Orr's man was born – and Michael Fiennes – out to China in 1935, 20 years in Asia and Ministry of War Transport service to boot – how they should be running a company. But he was right; in fact both he and Jock were. Intertwining these methods and philosophies would prove critical to what became a second post-war rebirth of John Swire & Sons.

The consultants also restated what everybody also knew, and had been discussing for nearly 20 years already. Too much depended on Hong Kong, and Hong Kong looked too vulnerable. Across the autumn and into the early months of 1968, directors developed a diversification plan, and scouted around hungrily for information about opportunities. In January 1968 Adrian Swire travelled to Japan for the launch of a new bulk carrier, SS *Eredine*, then moved on for strategic discussions in Hong Kong and in Kuala Lumpur. On his return London set out its thoughts on the company's development policy. There was to be no new investment in Hong Kong, barring logical developments of existing activities. Japan was the highest priority for growth in shipping and aviation activity, and perhaps in property. Australia, which was proving under-profitable, was to join it as a new 'base area' for development. The company aimed to sell minority stakes in various companies to British-based interests it could trust, and use the funds for new investment. Half was to go to the two new base areas, and half to other territories (although this plan would be refined, and Australia and Japan were directed to finance development out of their own revenue or local loans). Please send us current trade directories, ran a January letter to Hong Kong, for Korea, Taiwan, the Philippines, Borneo & Brunei, Malaysia, Thailand and Indonesia, and our Singapore one is also eight years out of date. Here is a report on Cambodia (no, we shall not invest, stay clear). We need to know a lot more about Singapore, and Taiwan. What might be done in British Columbia? What might be done in the Seychelles or Caribbean? Wherever we go, we must not make new 'ad hoc' investments. We have never been good at 'merchanting', but should we look again? Well, whatever we do we need to prioritise opportunities that allow us to use our own management and management skills, and bear in mind 'the future deployment of our present staff in the event of possible political upheavals eg the sudden demise of Hong Kong'.[4]

'Hong Kong are raring to go,' reported Adrian Swire of the managers there in 1968, and had money in hand. Everybody was impressed by Japan. Jock Swire also attended the *Eredine* launch, noting in his dairy:

> The dynamism and spirit of this country is simply terrific. Everyone working with a will and apparently out to do his d—est to put his country on top of the world. They are miles ahead of us in roads and railways and will soon beat us in everything. They seem to have an incredible knack of getting their priorities right and once they have decided on a line go straight at it and finish the job regardless of everything. I have the most profound admiration for them and we simply must strengthen and broaden our base here as an eventual replacement for HK.[5]

Eredine was part of a new move for the group. It was built in Japan for John Swire & Sons, chartering through Y. K. Pao's World Wide Shipping to the Japanese shipper Shinwa Kaiun and manned and managed by CNCo. It represented a new venture in two ways, firstly in a collaboration with Y. K. Pao and Chinese shipping interests in Hong Kong, and secondly with long-term chartering. The ship was the first of several that would be ordered and operated in this way between Australian and Asian ports (a condition for Swire entering the business), and would prove a profitable response to additional challenges of a shipping slump in the late 1960s, and for CNCo an additional problem of the suspension of its monthly services to China because of the chaos of the Cultural Revolution.[6] China remained the troubling backdrop to these moves. The disorder there saw Butterfield & Swire in Hong Kong, as agents for Blue Funnel, trying to make sense in February and March 1968 of the detention at Shanghai for five weeks of the line's *Demodocus* after it had initially left the port with a routine cargo. Maurice Ching was despatched to Guangzhou, to try to settle matters, but neither that visit, nor contacts with New China News Agency in Hong Kong, the semi-official representative office of the Chinese government, brought good news, or any firm news at all. It would later emerge that the second officer, Peter Crouch, had taken notes on naval shipping in Shanghai, a breach of harbour regulations that would see him jailed for three years after a public trial in front of thousands, which all foreign ship captains in port were ordered to attend.[7] Blue Funnel ended its twice-monthly China service in 1969 for good even though 'some easement in Chinese attitudes to foreigners' had been noted: 'factory visits' were arranged in Qingdao, for example, 'for ships' people including the Master's wife'.[8] Other Britons found themselves in detention, and several other mariners – the only regular foreign visitors – ran afoul of the times. In August 1967, in a move prompted by the British clampdown in Hong Kong, Red Guards in Beijing stormed and set fire to the offices of the British Mission (it did not have embassy status), manhandling and abusing its staff. All this reinforced the need to look elsewhere.

Where Hong Kong raringly went first was the Caribbean and specifically the Bahamas. It all seemed familiar enough. After all, it was a British colony and so naturally a statue of Queen Victoria, unveiled on Empire Day in 1905, graced the waterfront of the capital, Nassau, and Saturdays saw a ritual changing of the guard outside Government House with the band playing the 'Eton Boating Song' and 'Daisy, Daisy'.[9] But while this seemed a good idea at the time, it was to prove a flamingo-pink fiasco. Discussion had begun in late March 1968 with BOAC, eager to divest itself of the regional airlines that had once been a central part of its strategy (and which had caused so much controversy in Hong Kong). Bahamas Airways Limited (BAL) had long drained BOAC of money, and was offered to John Swire & Sons for a nominal payment. For its part, the Bahamas government was keen to see Bahamas Airways focus more on supporting the social and economic development of the islands. BOAC, its prime minister Lynden Pindling felt, was only interested in its long-haul routes.[10] This opportunity caught Cathay Pacific's management at the height of their confidence, given growth over the previous decade, and the directors in London in the midst of diversification. It might offer sanctuary for staff – and capital – 'if anything happened to Hong Kong', and to Cathay Pacific, and would thereby also be 'important for morale'. They had looked at Fiji Airways ('too tightly held to leave room for us'), explored Air Jamaica, which was 'open to offers', but failed a closer inspection, and then BOAC's representative on the Cathay Pacific board brought them Bahamas Airways to consider. Blue Funnel and P&O joined John Swire & Sons in taking an 85 per cent share of the airline from 1 October, with BOAC retaining a minority stake.[11] CPA's commercial director, Duncan Bluck, moved to Nassau to take over as chairman, and other experienced CPA staff joined him as operations, engineering and administration managers. Plans emerged to re-equip the airline with BAC One-Eleven jets, and to expand its schedule beyond its main service to Miami. This was a large operation, with 80 pilots, and 800 staff in total, although to aviation officials in London it also looked 'extremely rickety'.[12] But it was the single biggest private-sector employer in the islands, and when it took on new aircraft it at a stroke became its biggest importer. 'Everything's *new* but the name at Bahamas Airways,' announced the advertisements in the Florida press, offering, *con brio*, 'the fun way' to fly to the islands, a striking new flamingo-styled livery (pink-tailed jets), free on-board cocktails ('Flamingo Slings') served by freshly restyled 'pretty Bahamian girls' dressed in an incongruous combination of mini skirt and pith helmet – a style that did not catch on more widely – offering on-board 'Flamingo Bingo' with 'winners on every flight'.[13]

'I trust all goes well in this case,' minuted one diplomat, 'though I am not so foolish as to suppose there may not be difficulties.' Officials also noted, confidentially, that the promoter of another airline had been 'advised' that if he wished his proposal to 'prosper', then he needed to hire a particular local firm.[14] Conceivably, more than politesse and cash might be needed (another local operator funnelled 1 per cent of earnings direct to the government). But CPA had just begun its 1968/9 operations with four of its most profitable months ever recorded, and BOAC had by any standards badly mismanaged Bahamas Airways and the opportunities it presented.[15] The islands were in the throes of a boom. Tourism had increased by 50 per cent from 1964 to 1967, and most came and went by air, and many travelled around by plane, or took day trips across to Miami to break up their stay. The son of a Shanghai department store manager, Duncan Bluck had been born in the city the week Chiang Kai-shek's forces had captured it during the Nationalist Revolution. He had joined the company in 1948 after wartime naval service – 'Britain was a pretty drab place with rationing etc. so the Far East seemed a sensible place to go', he later recalled – and after working for the firm in Japan began a long association with CPA. Viewed with suspicion by older colleagues, for aviation still seemed a brash sector and memories of the Australians were vivid – 'we shall have to keep a very close hand on Duncan', Jock was told in November 1968, 'or he may get megalomania like all air operators'; Bill Knowles thought he had needed 'the edges knocked off him in another field' – Bluck's achievements over the next two years were, in many ways, considerable. The airline was overhauled and reimagined with some accompanying panache, and four jets arrived.

An extensive public relations campaign in the islands stressed BAL's local identity – 'I fly our own airline' ran the headlines – and, fulfilling a commitment it gave to Pindling's government, the company recruited new staff, including pilots, and sent them overseas for training. This was all part of its '30 million dollar investment in the Bahamas'.[16] It had failed to get recognition as 'the national carrier', and while it had work as 'a national carrier' (the distinction recurs in documents), it acted as if it had gained that status, and was led to believe that it had sufficient guarantees in place with which to do so, including first option on all routes. The casinos remained a draw, filling the night-time flights to and from Miami. A big push was at the same time made to market the Bahamas themselves further overseas. The country was 'the envy of the Caribbean', ran an eight-page supplement placed in *The Times* in December 1968 (with an article on the airline, and its new advertisement) and copy that highlighted the islands' prosperity and stability, and the 'in-flow of tourist dollars'. 'Paradise!' claimed one advertisement; 'Are you big enough for the Bahamas' ran the Tourist Office's.[17] But then on 10 October 1970 the jets departed for good. The previous day the latest of a series of advertisements was published in New York, heralding the launch on 12 November of a new daily service from the city to Nassau. 'Why just fly?' ran the copy, when you could experience 'red hot calypso' on board – 'the first thing you hear on our flight is "back to back, belly to belly"', the chorus of 'One of the wildest' – and, of course, 'champagne for everybody', 'lobster or steak', 'lavish service', and 'surprise extras'.[18] The surprise extra turned out to be Duncan Bluck's announcement at six the previous evening that BAL was being put into liquidation. The One-Elevens – all leased – took off to Montreal (although rumour had it, to Hong Kong), out of the reach of an angry Bahamas government. As they taxied to the end of the runway the prime minister himself rang to see if they could be stopped, but was given a 'nearly true' answer, and they took off. The flights involved some improvisation, with Adrian Swire and Bluck making verbal promises that John Swire & Sons would pay for the fuel, for Bahamas Airways had not one cent available.[19]

Lynden Pindling addressed his nation by radio on 11 October. It was a 'momentous weekend in the history of our country,' he announced – and it put 1.5 per cent of the workforce out of employment at a stroke – and the wider problem was actually the persistence of colonialism. 'It was part of the Bahamas,' he said of the airline, 'but we found in the final analysis we were not part of it.'[20] So much for those 'our airline' advertisements. This was clever rhetoric from the leader of the first majority-rule administration the country had elected, and it aimed to deflect public dismay and anger away from problems closer to home than London. Put another way, 'It was a Zombie Jamboree took place in a New York cemetery'. Perhaps the New York copyeditor knew much more than was being let on, for the 'back to back, belly to belly' advertising strapline opened the chorus of Harry Belafonte's 1969 calypso hit which began with those words. And 'I don't give a damn, I done dead already' continued the chorus. 'Cumulative losses over the years have been considerable', remarked one airline industry report in the immediate aftermath – something in the range of £829,000 in the four years prior to the takeover, it was estimated.[21] The problems the new operators faced included a reliance on what proved to be a quite unstable US tourist trade (which declined sharply in 1970), unequal competition from the US airline Pan Am, and from charter flights, and a Bahamas administration that contrived to issue traffic rights on that plum new 'Royal Flamingo' route to New York to Bahamas World Transport (later Airways), an airline that did not yet have any aircraft, or much else besides that was tangible (although soon it had office space above a fried-chicken restaurant). It was owned by a Bahamian-born New York businessman, sometime dental apprentice, butler, doorman, a 'lifelong friend' and political ally of the prime minister, a 'very persuasive person' who became a key 'consultant' for mafia interests, as well as fraudster Robert Vesco, and was later revealed – by his son, before a US Senate Subcommittee hearing – to be at the heart of a complex web of violent drug-trade corruption.[22]

Pindling himself had quietly directed that traffic rights be issued to Bahamas World in June, and that made sense, for the company had been incorporated into the offices of local law firm Pindling & Nottage: that is, his own. Done dead already, really, all the makings of a zombie airline: but London had sent in a CPA finance director, more cash (Cathay's profits in 1968/9 will cover the loss, thought Jock), fought discontent among some of the pilots (and there were reports of some minor sabotage by staff), was building new offices at the airport, had just leased premises in New York, and it had negotiated fruitlessly with the colony's government from July onwards for a resolution. While it was not 'the' national carrier, a 25 per cent share of Bahamas Airways Holdings had been reserved for sale to the Bahamas public, with the firm offering to place this in trust with the government, but Pindling's administration had proved reluctant to accept the offer. The islands' governor, Ralph Grey, thought Swires had secured little more than 'rather vague goodwill' when it took on the airline. When it came to crisis point in the summer of 1970, Pindling's government took six weeks to respond to the company's proposals that it take a majority share of the carrier, then asked for 90 days more to consider things – for nobody had troubled to read the documentation already provided – and it refused to accept any share of what would be further substantial losses that would be involved, which it claimed amounted to over Bahamas $31 million. Bluck publicly countered the government's presentation of the figures and story in general, swiftly and effectively, and details of the Bahamas World deal – and Pindling's own role in the company itself – were swiftly the subject of public controversy.[23]

The lackadaisical pace of deliberation in the summer was too much for London, but it was always a trickier story underneath, and it was hardly as if corruption could have come as a surprise, even if aviation officials in London had kept their confidential notes to themselves.[24] Widely circulated exposés in February 1967 in *Life* and the *Saturday Evening Post* – with photographs of beautiful beaches – detailed the New York mafia role in Bahamas corruption. A Royal Commission had promptly been set up and delivered a damning and detailed report at the end of the year. It would become clear that the election that had brought Pindling to power in January 1967 had inconvenienced and displaced one corrupted elite, but it had certainly not ended corruption. All of this was reported far beyond Nassau.[25] Jock Swire visited the islands twice. For him this was a (corporate) 'gamble with life and death'. The 'original object was to find a new world in which to build a new Taikoo & for that a big gamble was justified', but the danger, as money drained away (and as experienced staff were deployed away from Asia to try to stem the flow), was that 'if it fails it may well bust Taikoo'. By the autumn of 1970 the directors in London seemed to be all-consumed with trying to resolve the situation (Hong Kong, it was noted, had only had three letters in five months). Well they might. Adrian Swire later described it as the one post-war initiative that proved a 'threat to the fabric of the firm'.[26]

We might see the episode as Pindling and his government tried to spin it: the colonial power had tried to retain its economic ascendancy as the islands headed towards independence, and his government had not only worked to ensure investment in Bahamians within the Bahamas Airways – and this had not only been made manifest in the public relations campaigns of the new Swire-owned firm – but also to stimulate an indigenous alternative in Bahamas World Transport. Having a national carrier had also become part of the accepted repertoire of national symbols, and of its independent status, identity and dignity. Having gained self-rule in 1965, the Commonwealth of the Bahamas was working towards the independence it would gain in July 1973. That repertoire encompassed, too, the sort of rabble-rousing speech given at the ruling party's annual convention later that month by a former Bahamas Airways employee – shortly thereafter an airline promotor himself – who lambasted the 'tremendously powerful and wealthy British organisation' that 'wanted to embarrass the ... government because it was a black government ... We will not be patsies for any fast talking blackmailing bunch of profiteers.'[27] This was routine nationalist rhetoric, and Pindling's presentation of the situation an unexceptional and familiar nationalist economic development tactic. Across the twentieth century it had increasingly been a challenge for John Swire & Sons, whether in Nationalist-era China or independent Malaysia. But we might more confidently view the Bahamas episode as one in which nationalist crony capitalism and corruption defeated the company. Many Bahamians thought so, too. As things started to unravel at the start of 1970 Michael Fiennes dropped a note to the Ministry of Aviation to report that the directors had been offered another airline, somewhere in the region (probably, it would turn out, the Dominican Republic), but Fiennes was not interested in finding out: 'I have turned it down,' he noted.[28]

'We are not good at being ruthless with unprofitable businesses', London had remarked in one of the strategy discussions back in early 1968.[29] While in taking on Bahamas Airways it had contravened one of the guidelines then set down, that the firm was not in the business of 'putting other people's headaches to right' and taking on unsuccessful companies, now the directors showed themselves capable of doing just that. Folding the company meant a very heavy loss, but it was, Adrian Swire later claimed, the single best decision he ever made for John Swire & Sons. Bluck returned to Hong Kong, and became managing director at Cathay Pacific. 'One of the best investments Swires made', later chairman Edward Scott would joke of the Bahamas Airways episode, for it 'checked the arrogance, fuelled by success, of the top management of Cathay Pacific of the time from over-expanding, and believing that we uniquely had mastered how to run a profitable regional airline'.[30] More broadly, it clearly helped London in its continuing search for a new direction, most strikingly in that, in tandem with other developments, it largely reinforced its focus back on the area it knew best, Asia-Pacific.

CNCo was still knitting together the Asia-Pacific operations of the John Swire & Sons companies, and while it faced one revolution in China, it faced, alongside the entire global shipping industry, a quite different revolution that originated in the United States: containerisation. 'Unit' transportation systems were not new, and there had long been experiments with systems that allowed easy transfer of cargo units from one mode of transport to another (intermodality). 'Questions for early decision', runs a 1958 John Swire & Sons board report, include 'how best to develop what is known as the "piggy-back" system.'[31] The Cold War incubated the container. The reach of the US military presence and its massive supply contracts encouraged the development of what became the globally standard form of shipping container, which gained traction more rapidly and extensively than any previous innovation in shipping practices. The military presence in Western Europe, and then in Vietnam, in particular, and the contracts to supply it secured by the American shipping firm Sea-Land led to a reshaping of harbour installations, road networks, design and rapid building of new ships, and the nature of the industry globally. New firms were formed as the established shipping giants combined to counter the threat, sometimes building on conference links, to pool resources and make the substantial investments in new ships that were needed. Impetus was also given by the fact that the fleets rebuilt immediately after the war were coming to the end of their working lives and needed replacing. And as global trade had grown in the post-war era, congested ports and high labour costs in a labour-intensive business had become frustrating. These recur in

John Swire & Sons reports as problems that sharply increased costs and impaired service. This combination of factors saw rapid take-up of the new system: in the spring of 1966 there were three lines offering container services; by June 1967, 60 did so. It was a 'hurricane from America' announced *The Economist*, and all the language about it was dramatic.[32] And there was also panic: Blue Funnel, for instance, were 'running scared' about the issue in early 1966, thought Butterfield & Swire Hong Kong, and they were right to be. 'It was a shock to the system,' recalled Adrian Swire, 'requiring much radical rethinking.'[33]

The immediate impact on John Swire & Sons operations was to come through the formation by Holts and three partners of Overseas Containers Ltd (OCL) in August 1965, a company sketched out, legend had it, on a 'soaked napkin' in a London club (or the back of the menu), and the new company's order for six new vessels, the first of which would sail in 1969.[34] Containerisation of the Asia-Pacific operations of the OCL combine was completed by the end of 1973. The 58,000 ton *Tokyo Bay*, the 'world's largest and fastest' ship, was the first OCL arrival in Hong Kong from Southampton, docking on 5 September 1972 at the brand-new, though mostly unfinished, terminal, having sailed from another, navigating past – just – the half-sunk wreck of the former RMS *Queen Elizabeth* in Hong Kong's harbour as it did so. It was greeted by OCL's chairman, a just-laid asphalt surface that had not yet fully dried, and 600 filled containers with their 'perfectly protected' cargoes waiting to head to Europe.[35] The berth, one of four at the new container port, was built by a new combine, Modern Terminals Limited, managed by Swires, and co-owned with a number of partners including OCL, and the Hongkong & Shanghai Bank. Containerisation saw substantial savings in time, labour costs and insurance rates, and fewer ships (and those with smaller crews) would be needed to run a lower number of services carrying the same freight, and spending less time in port, incurring lower charges. Transport chains would be transformed to accommodate the box, and in time new global chains of production would develop as well. This new system's complex logistics accelerated the use of computers in shipping management as well, and needed to: container traffic at Modern Terminals grew 20 per cent a year as the installation was completed.[36] The revolution toppled once-dominant global shipping centres – such as the Port of London – with significant social and economic costs. While the container 'perfectly protected' cargoes, it left urban wastelands in its wake. It hit Liverpool, once the British heart and home of this story, not least of all, the British port city left high and dry in its wake, technological change reinforcing the self-inflicted harm of the city's continued reliance on empire trading connections, that left it ill-equipped for the turbulent new economy of the post-colonial world.[37]

CNCo itself gained a role in the 'container revolution' (as the Swire board records it) when it was taken over by Blue Funnel and John Swire & Sons as equal co-owners, a process completed by May 1967. This was a pragmatic, defensive measure, part of a suite of developments undertaken by each company to improve its performance and options.[38] There were other developments as well, such as the astonishing growth of Asian shipping combines, such as Y. K. Pao's Worldwide. 'I sat next to Y. K. Pao on the flight to Tokyo last week,' reported Adrian Swire in March 1971, 'he is currently building 55 ships in Japan and will soon be operating 8 million tons of shipping.'[39] Pao's rise was funded by an unprecedented alliance with the Hongkong & Shanghai Bank – which provided the finance – novel because it broke with old-established, if not racist, practice at the bank which had not previously involved providing such funding for Chinese-owned operations like this, or, in fact, any operations to this extent. It proved immensely profitable for all concerned.[40] This forced the firm to think about change. The management consultants came nosing around, too, Urwick Orr being commissioned in 1969/70 to undertake a Work Study programme that led to reductions in crew numbers ('though with compensating higher pay') and development of more flexible crewing practices. Crew certification would start to be transferred from Britain to Hong Kong. The shipping container had its rivals, and there were other 'unitisation' systems still in development. As the fracas at the Taikoo Dockyard unfolded in early June 1967 with improvised spears and Maoist chants, a former Norwegian ship, the *Bahia*, was being converted in the yard, with a new side-loading capacity being installed to allow for 'palletisation'. Inspired by innovations instituted in the Olsen Line, the *Papuan Chief*, as the ship would be christened, would transform the operations of CNCo's New Guinea Australia Line.

This, too, was part of the drive to diversify, and to grow the Australia operations where CNCo was seen as crucial to the firm's reputation and profile. As with containerisation, side-loading operations would require construction of new quayside facilities and retraining of staff, but it was much cheaper, for existing ships could be converted, and several more vessels were purchased and worked on at Quarry Bay to add to this 'Chief' class. It was also more appropriate given existing trade and facilities. By 1969 the line had switched wholly to sideport operations, and the *Shansi* and *Soochow*, the final two purpose-built China coasters, both 1947 vintage – now an era away – were sold off. Palletisation would prove a successful move at this point for CNCo, but it was the box that would change the world, not the pallet.[41] In August 1968 CNCo entered the container world more directly through the creation of the Australia Japan Container Line (AJCL), initially a joint venture between OCL – not Blue Funnel – and John Swire & Sons on the one hand, and the Australia West Pacific Line on the other. It was a 'perch' for CNCo (in the words of Blue Funnel chairman, Sir John Nicholson), but would become a profitable one in time. AJCL started a service in early 1969, and placed orders for two new vessels from Japanese yards, *Ariake* and *Arafura*, as well as chartered vessels, including CNCo's latest iteration of the *Nanchang*.[42] Unlike the OCL business with Australia, AJCL and the Europe-Asia traffic was profitable almost straight away. OCL retained Butterfield & Swire as its agents in Hong Kong – which was not at all assumed to be a given – and Japan, where they already gained container experience from another agency. Swires had lobbied the Hong Kong government to investigate setting up a container terminal, and also asked the Foreign Office about how best to keep China abreast of developments, and how to keep the British in Chinese minds as potential suppliers of expertise and equipment. The firm earned well from Australia Japan Container Line operations, and agency earnings from OCL and AJCL were considerable, especially for the Japan branch, a largely overlooked field of group operations (even in fact within the company, where it often seemed an outlier).[43]

There were other lines of development. In 1961 there had been detailed discussions about a merger of CNCo with the Jardine Matheson Indo-China SNCo, but it became clear that the problems of such a union would far outweigh any benefits that might be gained, and the plan was dropped.[44] A fitfully profitable venture launched in 1953 had become known in the firm as the 'Pilgrim Trade'. Blue Funnel had long carried Malay pilgrims on the Hajj – and the British role in general in the administration and organisation of the pilgrimage had been extensive – but CNCo moved to provide the service instead, using capacity initially built for the China–Straits emigrant trade that was now closed off to it.[45] It also potentially offered a useful entry into Malaysia, building up goodwill – if handled well – with emerging powerholders as independence became a reality, for this government charter led to high-level discussions with ministers, who also attended launches and departures. There were two voyages each year for two ships, carrying roughly 5,000 pilgrims, generally men and women of quite moderate means, and always more of them westwards than eastwards, for the rigours of the Hajj took an annual toll of the elderly, including in 1967 a 103 year old shortly after his return – but that same year baby Mohamed Ali, born on the *Anshun* as it sailed home, was granted free passage on the vessel for life.[46] Additional business was picked up in the 1955/6 seasons carrying Syrian pilgrims from the Jordanian port of Aqaba, and in 1957 from Latakia in the Mediterranean, and in the 1958 season pilgrims from Pakistan. *Anking* and *Anshun* carried a different faith community at times between 1959 and 1963, accepting charters to transport Russian 'Old Believers' who had left or been expelled from Manchuria, from Hong Kong to Australia.[47]

The *Anking* certainly looked clean, peaceful and uncrowded in a 1957 photo-essay published in London, but Michael Fiennes reported conditions on board as 'really bad' (ventilation was a problem), although these ships had been built for the Straits migrant trade, and were better suited than the Blue Funnel liners (and faster, making Jeddah in 12 days). The *Kuala Lumpur*, introduced in 1961 after being converted at Quarry Bay (one of its 'largest ever jobs'), offered 'cool comfort' for 200 first class, and 1,800 tourist class pilgrims, with air-conditioned accommodation – and on-board mosque – and a swimming pool. A converted liner that had seen time as a troopship, its introduction went some way to dealing with criticisms of the service.[48] The trade was a complex operation, with the state Pilgrim Office placing medical officers on board, provision of seven different types of diet needed and a delicate politics that required negotiation with officials. Fiennes was greatly relieved in 1959 when the prime minister, Tunku Abdul Rahman, did not make a promised 'incognito' inspection of the *Anking*. Jock Swire saw the *Kuala Lumpur* depart from Port Swettenham (Port Klang) in 1967, a seemingly chaotic affair, crowds of well-wishers, loudspeakers blaring, a sultan arriving unannounced to see off his wife and her train.[49] The trade was sometimes quite usefully profitable, but provided little gain in political capital and it was dropped after 1970. Air travel was cheaper and quicker, but the Malaysians also created a new pilgrim organisation, the Tabung Haji, and the charters were taken by a new Great Malaysia Line. Here, too, Swires were outmanoeuvred by those with other connections: despite its name, Great Malaysia was set up and owned by a Hong Kong entrepreneur with strong connections to the ruling United Malays National Organisation, two of whose directors held substantial shares in the company. It would not prove a success. Reviving the CNCo role was later discussed, but nothing came of this.[50]

Passenger traffic in general fell away dramatically across the 1960s as travellers took to the air: CNCo's loss was, in the greater scheme, Cathay Pacific's gain. Some passenger firms reconfigured themselves as holiday providers, and a new age of cruising developed. CNCo also ventured into this, having packaged its Asia–Australia and Hong Kong–Taiwan services as leisure travel, and using *Kuala Lumpur* for Australian cruises outside the pilgrim season (when a Filipino band played tunes for its dancefloor). In 1971 Taikoo Dockyard refitted a dowdy nine-year-old Spanish-built vessel, renamed *Coral Princess*, hiring a British interior designer to oversee its transformation into a 'luxuriously appointed one-class ship', aimed at the Japanese market. There were even reading lamps, 'sensibly positioned': into the 1930s, CNCo ships had no reading lights fitted by the beds, for Warren Swire did not read in bed, and so his passengers would not either. The venture would last 20 years, taking groups on study tours including in 1973 to Shanghai and Tianjin, when the *Coral Princess* would be the first foreign cruise ship to visit Chinese ports since 1949. 'She is the most lovely cruise ship I have seen,' recorded Jock Swire, 'but it can't possibly pay us', and the returns proved uneven.[51]

With these various operations, John Swire & Sons' shipping business would provide some 47 per cent of group turnover in 1973, some 42 per cent of its profits, and form some 35–40 per cent of its assets. By then a quarter of its shipping capacity was in container vessels, half in the bulk carriers, and general cargo carriers including the pallet loaders, formed some 15 per cent. Strictly speaking, it made little business sense to have remained committed for so long so strongly to shipping, for the returns were uneven and often low. But the additional benefits to the group were large – the work it provided for Butterfield & Swire – and the credibility it helped Swires retain with partners such as Blue Funnel as other interests grew. It also delivered significant tax advantages in London, which were vital to the operation of John Swire & Sons.[52] As the group diversified, concerns began to develop about the overall shape of the Swire interests. Adrian Swire had, from 1972, started to 'get away' from a direct role with CNCo to focus on a wider portfolio as deputy chairman, and worried that key partners might now think the company 'nowadays so involved in property, company structure, airlines, Coca-Cola etc that we can no longer be serious about shipping', despite its fundamental importance to overall activity. He would also raise concerns about co-ordination across this varied group. Might not companies increasingly follow the logic of their own development, sometimes against the interests of others in the group? 'This is a new problem for us … and it is very fundamental … [and] bound to alter the nature of our business.'[53] If logic might suggest different policies within the same group, what, then, actually defined the common endeavour?

For a start, Swire Group was now the name, not just a descriptor. From 1 January 1974 there were 'Name changes with a world of meaning', as full-page newspaper advertisements proclaimed that day, with the formal creation of The Swire Group. Out for good went Butterfield, that curious hangover from the days of Yorkshire wool exports and the mill at Haworth, and in came John Swire & Sons (Hong Kong) Ltd, and John Swire & Sons (Japan) Ltd and 21 more Swire this or Swire that. Taikoo Dockyard had already become Taikoo Swire, and now became Swire Pacific. Only CNCo, Cathay Pacific and TSR retained their names. The new identity was splashed across the pages of the local press, and in London, too, in a concerted effort to raise the profile outside Hong Kong of the Swire operations. In, too, came a new group magazine, *Swire News*, to foster an identity across the diverse set of companies and operations that constituted the new group. But it would take more than names and snippets of news about Cathay's landmark carrying of over a million passengers within 12 months, or long-service reunions, or dockyard amalgamation, to achieve this. Even so, the recording of staff service, appointments and departures, marriages and more, with men and women from across the diverse operations of the group appearing for the first time in great numbers in a company publication, and named, receiving long service awards marks a profound change in the way the company presented itself. 'Pins Galore' ran one headline, and there are photographs of long-service pins (gold for 30 years, silver for 25, 10 and 20 marked in enamel) being awarded to paint company staff, cashiers, sugar packers and bottling plant employees. Some scoffed, but the contrast with the more exclusive approach adopted at the China centenary is marked.[54]

What reinventing the firm also took was 'House Staff'. What had developed since Jock Swire's revelation after his journey home in 1920 that the firm could offer good prospects to graduates (and good fun), and would gain from employing them, was a system of recruitment, training – largely in post, but not exclusively so – assessment and development that came to lie at the heart of the firm's understanding of what it actually provided. Certainly, it was a shipping firm, processed sugar, built ships, sold insurance, bottled soft-drinks, merchanted, and ran an airline, but what united all of these, primarily, was the business of management.[55] Aside from some specialists, it sought those managers from the universities of Oxford and Cambridge, broadening out its pool, slowly, after the 1960s. You were either Eton, or similar, but mostly Eton, and Oxford or Cambridge, had an 'Eastern connection' or were ex-services (preferably Guards), recalled Peter Roberts, who joined in 1964, most likely two of these. Roberts had the eastern connection – his father was C. C. Roberts and he had graduated from Oxford. Recruits were also, until 1970, male. Roberts had considered working for Shell, BP or Metal Box as well, but the Swire job was the best paid. Graham McCallum (Oxford, RAF), had been considering an opening in South America when the board steered him towards Swires. Michael Miles (army) decided on joining the company 'because the job was abroad'. Another man (army) had been aiming at the Colonial Office, accepted a job with Shell and was then pointed to Swires by the appointments board – 'a splendidly upper crust employment exchange'. Of Swires he recalled, 'I had no idea who they were or what they did', but they took him seriously, and off he was sent, carrying a suitcase of clothes for the next director heading east (or to be precise, the man's wife's).

So, eccentrically, began one career in Asia. Viewed from the other side of the appointment board's table, there was more science, or at least more carefully crafted art in the company's hiring. Before and after he became chairman, John Swire interviewed all candidates himself, looking for 'energy and a sense of humour', aimed to mix the cohorts that were sent: academic high-achiever, 'Foreign Office sort of people', someone from the north of England, or Scotland, someone risky, 'zany' even (one in three of whom proved a success, he ventured). From the mid-1960s onwards recruits started to be sent on short courses before heading to Asia: Urwick Orr's Management Course, or the Overseas Service Course at Farnham Castle in Surrey, for 800 years the home of bishops, and a quite unlikely setting for an intercultural awareness programme. Set up in 1953, largely by missionary groups, by 1971 this was training some 1,300 people a year, mainly going to work for the Overseas Development Agency, but 350 of them heading into commerce. The residential courses were region-specific, and the Hong Kong Chamber of Commerce advertised the 'Far East' programme, and former governor Robert Black served on the Board of Governors. Journalists, officials and historians gave talks, there were practical discussions about health, fitness and finance, what could be found easily in the shops, what could not be bought, films and tasters of local music and culture. 'Wives and fiancées' were also encouraged to attend.[56] The Appointments Committee at Oxford had evolved from being regarded before 1914 as a mechanism for channelling chaps into schoolmasters' jobs, through a period of steady growth between the wars when business vacancies became more and more prominent a feature of its work, and so, too, as a destination for graduates, to becoming an important vehicle for business recruitment after the Second World War. In 1967, the number of male graduates entering business was double what it had been in 1945. Representative figures for Cambridge suggest that just over 20 per cent of graduates headed into business between 1951 and 1955, and this will have continued to grow.[57] Where Swires had led the way, somewhat, after 1921, a business career was now much more a graduate norm.

Staff records are rich in the continuing assessment of men during their first probationary three-year period of service (during which they were not permitted to marry), and thereafter. There was a 'huge failure rate', recalled a later director, an impression borne out by the records: 'not management material', 'a whopping dud', 'seems to lack fire in his belly', 'unlikely to make the top grades', 'thoroughly decent second rater', 'you had come to the limit of your capabilities', one man was told, another was 'possibly rather more of an "outport" man than a "Head Office" man', which was not what he had been recruited for. Conversely, the academic high-achievers recruited in 1969/70 'had not settled in', having found 'that their first-class brains were not being adequately utilised'.[58] The mildly facetious comment pointed to a real problem. Men recruited in the 1940s and 1950s began with ship jumping, or – in one case – on the wharves in Sydney, which could be rough – and spoke warmly of the 'carefree and enjoyable life' they lived. They were also often fresh from National Service commissions, and in some ways junior life in the Swire world was not that much of a change, at least initially. But the graduates of the 1960s and 1970s, children of a less deferential culture and a richer economy, who had higher expectations and less patience, could and did look elsewhere for a better return on their talents, and a different style of management, when they found the work they were first set on too tedious and routine.

Reports could be quixotic: 'One wonders if his real interest in life is not the stage, rather than commerce', runs a report on another (but there is no later evidence that it did). 'I am sure he will go a long way if he can cure his present youthful tendency to radical extremes', commented another manager on one man, 'particularly in dress' (in which area 'zany' did not work); another's 'pompous Managing Director-like appearance, e.g. monocle, watch-chain, stiff-collar, did not go down well'. Neither the young fogey or 1970s à la mode – these reports almost overlap – worked well with colleagues and managers. As much as the firm let men go at the end of probation, recruits opted to leave, sometimes well ahead of time: this man wanted to get married, and had been refused permission; this one 'wants to live and work in the U.K.', 'does not wish to make a career in the Far East', 'Wishes to make his career in South Africa', 'Feels unsuited to commerce and life in the East'. At least one man left to start a PhD, another to join the Church (both succeeded in their respective fields). This one went on to work in the circus industry. Nassau proved amenable to one Cathay Pacific manager who decided to stay on after Bahamas Airways folded. Some were too ambitious – 'still sees himself as an embryo Chairman' – but for most of those sent back it was quite the opposite. Some reports indicate that intercultural training had not had much of an effect on their notions of the proper ordering of relations with Chinese or Japanese. But getting on well with Chinese is a recurring category comment. For others the cultural problem was expatriate life: 'hates Hong Kong … boring, superficial, and materialistic'; another found it 'much as he expected', he reported, 'materialistic and claustrophobic – but the Chinese are interesting'. Sport continued to play an important role – 'Plays rugger and is learning Cantonese. We think he will do well' (but he left after three years), 'ill-equipped for most sports'; declines even to use the firm's yacht – but mainly as a marker of the ability to mix with peers, and mixing was vital. The shy and bookish headed home.

One way or another, out of this mix of talents came the House Staff through which the firm was 'training bright young potential principals'.[59] Recruits studied colloquial Cantonese – with a substantial bonus for passing the second exam (equivalent to a month's salary) – rotated round different desks and were sent – often at quite short notice – to different branches. Until 1967, the pattern of leave remained the old one – six months every three years, allowing substantial opportunity for junior staff to be tried out in different roles, gaining experience and having their competence tested. Annual leave, introduced thereafter, made that more difficult. One future chairman began in sales in shipping agencies in Hong Kong, then was posted to Taiwan and Japan with other companies in the group, acted as a regional manager in Japan for Cathay Pacific, then with John Swire & Sons (Japan) and was then shipping director back in Hong Kong before becoming managing director of the Australian firm, shipping and then insurance director back in Hong Kong, then chairman and managing director of CNCo. Men on leave might be sent on Urwick Orr courses, or to the Oxford Business Summer School that was set up in 1953 and overseen by a joint business/academic committee and the Appointments Committee. In the 1970s there was an even greater focus on management training and recruits might also be sent to the business school at INSEAD. And 'it is not enough for us to have excellent career planning', Adrian Swire reported being told by one recent recruit in June 1975, 'without being seen to have it by involving the individual more': the ingrained, paternalistic approach ill suited the times, and ill matched the staff.[60] By the end of the decade, as he stepped down from his post as Hong Kong Taipan, John Bremridge argued that the system needed rethinking so that it avoided looking like 'the English mistake of preferring decent amateurs to professionals', and that selecting 'visible crown princes at 21' was now 'invidious'.[61] The response, in effect, was more substantive professionalisation.

We might see a statement of the rationale for this focus on generalist training and skills in a 1970 memorandum prepared for the London board by Michael Fiennes in the wake of the Bahamas Airways fiasco.

At this point, some on the board were deliberating whether the firm should reduce its exposure in Cathay Pacific, for the Nassau episode suggested that with aviation 'disaster comes with less warning and bites quicker than with other forms of transport'. In his case against any change, Fiennes also set out an argument for Butterfield & Swire to continue to manage the airline. And, after all, there was a logic that an airline might best be managed by aviation industry professionals, which would in addition be cheaper. Historically the justifications for group management were that:

a) You get a higher calibre of man in management ...
b) You can quickly transfer men from other departments in emergency or to cover leave ...
c) Sharing B&S logistical, accounts, etc support results in general savings ...
d) The discipline of existence within a conglomerate where feet are on the ground, rather than in the rarefied cloudland of the Air World, is good for staff ...
e) There is positive virtue in the exchange of ideas at the top of B&S and in the Managing Directors, or others at the top, having other responsibilities ...
f) Being with the B&S organisation leads to better acceptance and representation abroad, eg. In Japan, Australia, and U.K.

Fiennes thought a) remained 'still very true', as were d), e) and f). Much of this was about the virtues of a shared set of values and diverse experience across the group and a consistent focus on management development. Its consistently restated group 'philosophy' was that in the main its activities focused on 'managing and doing things', rather than evolving into an investment operation.[62] For this it needed its managers. This was what the Swire House Staff offered, and as the group expanded and its operations grew yet more complex, its selection and training became more systematic and professional.

But it also offered men, and it only offered men. Until Oxford graduate Catherine Hicks was appointed as an 'experiment' in September 1970, no woman had ever been recruited to the House Staff. The firm had continued its practice of recruiting women in Britain for secretarial positions, preferring to staff the confidential posts in the Private Office with women unconnected to the small world of expatriate Hong Kong. In their case, mixing might be problematic, and the stenographer suspected of having become too friendly out of hours with a business rival was moved into a different post. The history of British women's work overseas has been little studied, nursing and teaching aside, but while their voices can be hard to hear among the babble of sugar travellers and ship jumpers joshing with the wharfies in Sydney, a class of independently minded women also headed out to Asia for the company. Joan Weld arrived on the standard three-year initial contract in 1949 to work as Private Office stenographer in the dockyard. The daughter of a banker, she had secured her Royal Aero Club pilot's certificate 14 years earlier and made quite an impact in the colony on her 1947 350 CC Triumph, for she was, the police told her, Hong Kong's only female motorcyclist.[63] If, for other reasons, Weld was thought too indifferent to the job itself, another recruit was too involved. While she might not 'meet the requirements of one of the Private Secretaries in a general way,' wrote her manager, he regarded her 'more in the light of an assistant than secretary'. The simple fact was that the firm in Hong Kong largely restricted the talents and experience of female staff into such roles, and this was, by the end of the 1960s, as much out of date as it was untenable. Between 1960 and 1967 just over 14 per cent of female science graduates, and 4 per cent of female arts graduates at Oxford University, entered the business sector (broadly defined).[64] John Swire & Sons recruited none of them.

Catherine Hicks's appointment was 'a good experiment,' reported Jock a year later on meeting her in Hong Kong, but it was not immediately repeated. For one thing, it proved difficult to decide on how to fit her into the traditional House Staff training practices, for CNCo and the shipping world was thought too masculine an environment to plunge a 22-year-old female university graduate into, and it proved difficult to think how to house her: the junior mess where her male peers lived was ruled out. The firm's practices and thinking were man-shaped. Hicks worked in Cathay Pacific, and was housed separately. She was not the first female graduate to work for the firm in Hong Kong – that had been stenographer Mary Whimster in 1922 – and the first woman who was hired with the clear aim of providing her with management opportunity was Lydia Dunn, while women with degrees had been recruited in Japan as well, but Hicks was the first recruit to the House

Staff as then conceived. Dunn's background – her father had once been a business associate of the Soong family – was as of limited a relevance as family or business connection now was generally for the British recruits ('there was no automatic entry,' recalled the son of a director). Hicks had none, and knew nothing of the firm, although she had the historic routine connections that could be found in much of British society, coming as she did from a naval family: her father's career had included, as most did, a stint on the China Station, including visits to Weihaiwei. Such connections persisted, some fading gently, traces left in family photograph albums and stories, others more concrete in the Chinese galleries in museums, barracks-town streets named after China battles, in chinoiserie designs, in literature and in art.

But Lydia Dunn's was the type of new appointment that would shape the firm's future, and in the first instance started to make a success out of Swire & Maclaine. This had limped along in routinely unspectacular fashion, reports enlivened only by the odd mass resignation of British staff – an 'epidemic' of them in 1955/6, three more two years later – while 'a strong supporting cast of Eurasian, Chinese and Japanese Section Heads' held things together. The Britons were also expensive, and a decision was taken in principle in 1965 to 'bring along some of our young locals who are showing great promise'.[65] Dunn became head of the Export Section in Hong Kong in early 1967, replacing a British salesman who left to set up his own firm. What Dunn offered the company was her experience of the United States (she was assigned an American department store chain's large account) – 'I thought my gosh – why do they write like that' to Americans, she recalled noting – and her ability to mix with the Shanghai manufacturers who supplied the goods. She persuaded the latter to adapt their product design and range better to fit the US market (turning designer, it was reported), and she persuaded Swires to adapt their customer relations to a more informal American style.[66]

Hong Kong's image overseas more widely could be a handicap for exporters like Swire & Maclaine, for it was all sweatshops and low-quality goods, a picture encouraged by trades unions and manufacturing associations abroad facing very strong competition from the colony, but also by labour activists and more disinterested observers. While a robust social and industrial reform policy might have been the principled response, that was only fitfully to come, and countering both of these

images, and as one part of the colony's response to the damage done
to its trade by the confrontation, was part of the aim of a Festival of
Fashions held during 'Hong Kong Week' in the autumn of 1967.[67] This
was part of the wider move to project Hong Kong overseas as tourist
destination and manufacturing hub, and it became an annual Ready to
Wear Festival, in which Dunn's leading organisational role helped build
the public profile that, alongside her career within the firm – a director
of Swire & Maclaine in 1973, managing director in 1976, and director
of John Swire & Sons (Hong Kong) in 1978 – would take her on to the
Legislative Council in 1976. Some of the British men who left the House
Staff were moved out as they were 'blocking' the prospects of Chinese,
as one man was told, while another's departure was part-explained by
the fact that 'our Chinese graduates are developing', which, clearly, they
were. So much so, Bremridge argued in 1980, that 'totally different pay
structures' for Chinese and expatriate staff could not much longer be
justified.[68] Dunn aside, those Chinese staff who held senior positions
into and beyond the 1970s were largely those who had come out of the
unstructured hiring practices co-ordinated by Tom Lindsay, or from
familial connections. Yao Kang, who became a director in Hong Kong
in 1977, and came to run the insurance businesses, had joined at the
suggestion of David Au, and was the last of the old Chinese House
Staff-type appointments. Benjamin Wong's father, Charles Wong, had
been the senior Chinese figure in the Hong Kong firm at his death in
1955. The son joined in 1958, assuming that he would follow his father
into TSR, but worked largely on the shipping desk, including a long
stint in Australia, becoming a managing director of Swire Shipping
Agencies in 1978. Patrick Tsai, who would become a leading figure in
Cathay Pacific, had been brought into the company by Chester Yen in
1962 from CAT.

One prominent feature of the firm's new presentation of itself was
its active use of its own history. Retired staff drew up short accessible
accounts of the company's story, and that of CNCo, printed in the
Hong Kong press or the journals of partner firms. The centenary was
marked by the commissioning of a history from a University of Liverpool
historian – fittingly – which focused, rather drily for many tastes, on
John Samuel Swire and the management of the firm in London. 'This is
a disaster,' retorted Jock Swire on reading the first draft, and moreover
it did not go beyond the death of the Senior, who provided the focus

for the work. Much of the underlying analysis was provided by former CNCo manager Arthur Dean. The book was followed by a more anecdotal account drawing heavily on surviving China correspondence, prepared by a former naval officer and MI6 agent. This largely failed to get beyond the dates of his own naval experience in China, which concluded in 1928.[69] *Swire News* printed short accounts of piracies, sugar travelling and life in old China from company pensioners and their families. Michael Fiennes took charge of the records of the firm that had survived German bombs and office moves, and in 1975 the pre-Second World War archive was deposited at the School of Oriental & African Studies. An oral history programme was commissioned that between 1978 and 1982 secured interviews from former Butterfield & Swire and CNCo staff, extracts from which were published in book form. That was partly prompted by a 1972–74 British radio series, *Plain Tales from the Raj*, based on interviews with British men and women who had lived and worked in British India, and what would develop into a strong wave of 'Raj nostalgia' in Britain. The focus of the work on the Swire histories was nearly always on the receding era of treaty port China, that lost world, war-, pirate- and boycott-ridden, that nonetheless seemed from the vantage point of the troubled and frantic 1970s, attractive in its own eclectic way.[70]

To scholars what that history featured most strongly, and what the business of the firm continued to demonstrate, was the century-long history of the Swire–Blue Funnel–Scotts network. This had evolved – after 1971 the Holt family were no longer involved in senior management at Blue Funnel (formally, since 1967, the name 'Alfred Holt & Co.', had been retired) – and Scotts shipbuilding was in a weaker position, but that was true of British shipbuilding in general.[71] The intertwined marriage of families, capital and business had evolved into a networked alliance of corporate interests, elastically linked, sometimes more distant, sometimes – such as in the manoeuvres around OCL – much tighter. To this might be added the newer 'special relationship', still described as such in the mid-1970s, with the Hongkong & Shanghai Bank. John Swire & Sons in London was also reliant on a congeries of personal relationships centred on the city of London, especially in shipping – Adrian Swire became vice-president (1979) then president (1980) of the General Council of British Shipping. They networked, too, with ministers and civil servants. Business relationships were smoothed further by the fact that they and their peers had largely been at the same schools or at university together.[72] Important new ventures and relationships developed out of the contacts this network provided. In the smaller world of Hong Kong, the corporate archive and private papers show how networking took place in such informal venues as the Hong Kong Jockey Club, and in the weekly 'Tripe Hounds' lunch of business leaders, government officials and visiting worthies at the Hong Kong Club. 'I sat next to' and 'I saw' recur in notes about contacts and discussions pursued over these Thursday lunches, and gossip picked up there. The first-class cabins of flights in and out of the colony were also chance settings for discussions. As the Swire Group looked more and more a conglomerate, its business seemed even more to rely on such intimate ties and encounters.

And paradoxically also, despite the turn away from Hong Kong in 1968 and the moves to invest elsewhere, John Swire & Sons turned back and dug itself further into the colony. Hong Kong, reported Jock Swire in 1974, was 'dry land in a flooded world' – the world of the OPEC shock, and on that dry land the Swire Group built.[73] The rebranding in 1974 accompanied some significant changes in the nature of Hong Kong operations; most dramatically, the closure of the Taikoo Dockyard at Quarry Bay was set in motion. There had been no profit in ship making for 15 years, ran one report, and while Taikoo handled roughly a thousand ships a year (and Kowloon 600), the colony's director of marine mused in 1972 that even this large-scale ship repair industry would fade away in the long term. Shipbuilding operations ended at Taikoo in 1970.[74] Meanwhile, as there was plenty of repair work still to pick up, the time had come to take to its next stage the long-standing pooling arrangement with the Kowloon Docks. On 3 July 1972 the two companies announced their intention to merge their operations – retaining ownership of the properties – and from 1 January 1973 a new Hongkong United Dockyards (HUD) came into operation, leasing both sites, and a sizeable contingent of the Quarry Bay management staff were transferred across the harbour. This sparked an efflorescence in union activism among the 3,200-strong workforce, despite the Dockyard management by then being seen as adept at handling labour relations. An eight-day strike in September secured substantial concessions from the company.[75] The site was kept in operation until 1978 although parts of its historic estate were being redeveloped alongside the still working yard.[76] The old company itself became redundant: Taikoo Dockyard & Engineering held its final meeting on 27 April 1973, sold all its remaining industrial interests to a new arm of the group, Swire Industries, renamed itself Taikoo Swire, and increased the capital of the firm dramatically, setting itself up to rebuild Quarry Bay.

One part of the reason for the seemingly convoluted set of restructuring moves was fear. 'H.K. has gone mad,' reported Adrian Swire in 1972, 'and the unexpected can happen when megalomaniac paper-pushers are at large.' The problem was that the old ownership and management arrangements worked when partners could be trusted, and were robust. What if they proved vulnerable? What about OCL, which included at least one weak partner? And now there were new and aggressive interests in the colony. 'Let's just say,' one of them famously announced at a Hong Kong press conference in March 1972, that 'it's my kind of town.' This was Jim Slater, chief executive of asset-stripping investment bank Slater Walker. The firm had set up shop in Hong Kong in late 1970, but Slater's own arrival heralded a new phase in its local operations. 'Most people like making money and perhaps we can make it easier,' he announced. 'A Slater Walker presence in Hong Kong will help draw the attention of British stockbrokers and stimulate interest among institutional investors.' The Hong Kong stock markets – there were four – soared in value and intensity of business across 1972 and into 1973. The Hang Seng monthly average rose almost eight times in value from 1970 to the end of 1973.[77]

What was feared was a bid aimed at the landbank, directed through the publicly listed Dockyard or Butterfield & Swire Industries (BASIL) into which TSR, Swire & Maclaine, and Hong Kong Bottlers had been folded, and which had been floated in December 1969. Not only did the flotation mean that the company's books were now on display, it also showed that 'B&S control neither company' (only 36 per cent of the Dockyard, and 46 per cent of BASIL, if the Hongkong Bank was included). 'There are some unpredictable madmen about', agreed the bank's chairman, Guy Sayer. Slater Walker largely turned its attention to Singapore in late 1973, where its vehicle there became mired in a fraud scandal that reached back into Hong Kong, but the general threat remained.[78]

In addition, the market was under-regulated which, along with Hong Kong's low tax regime, was a large part of its attraction for operators like

Slater Walker. But while the uncertainty of the financial environment thereafter caused one set of problems, a new change was brought about by another, belated, post-1967 reform. The colony's endemic corruption, not restricted to the police force, but most striking there, had been one of the broader factors that had fuelled the rage of 1967 and the 1966 'Star Ferry' riots. There is some evidence, too, that in the aftermath of 1967 corruption actually increased in scale. After high-level police scandals in 1973, an Independent Commission Against Corruption (ICAC) was established to deal with the situation aggressively and, it turned out, comprehensively.[79] The police later went on strike in protest. To the consternation of the business world, ICAC started to pursue cases built out of what had until then seemed to be the routine culture of giving and accepting of individual personal commissions on commercial deals: 'rebates, discounts, or brokerages', or bribes in other, legal, words.[80] In March 1976 the trading firm Gilman & Co. admitted offences under the colony's Prevention of Bribery Ordinance. In addition, a Chinese salesman, and one of the firm's British managers, also faced charges. One of the recipients of the salesman's attention was a Cathay Pacific staffer, who was offered HK$1,500 to agree to the firm's purchase of a photocopier. Neither individuals, nor the firm, were immune. At issue, it was argued in response, was the entire routine culture of commercial life. 'The whole of Hong Kong operates on a Commission basis', the official inquiry into bribery had been told in 1973, 'there is a great deal of truth in this,' commented the report's author, 'and I have good reason to believe that the vast majority of business in Hong Kong would not have it otherwise.'[81] While the legislation itself was not new, few had ever distinguished between formal and secret commissions in practice, and fewer expected the activities of the ICAC to be extended into the commercial sector. There was a great deal of lobbying against this development, in which the Swire local managers in Hong Kong took part, but it rapidly became apparent that 'the die is cast', as Taipan John Bremridge put it: 'the climate of things, both in Hong Kong and in the world, is undoubtedly changing, and we must change with it.' Bremridge directed that all such practices should cease: 'our overall policy must be to act commercially within the law. There is no doubt now what the law is.'[82]

While this was unfolding, so was the Lockheed bribery scandal: the American aerospace firm was revealed to have strewn the world of politics and aviation management internationally with bribes and secret commissions in a campaign to sell its wide-bodied passenger jet, the TriStar, on which its corporate future depended. It had not hesitated to bribe then Japanese prime minister, Tanaka Kakuei, finance, defence and aviation ministers, and, for good measure, a Dutch prince. Lockheed's chief executive later wrote that he believed that an endorsement of his firm's services from Wakasa Tokuji, president of All Nippon Airways, which had contracted for the jets as well, was 'helpful in Cathay Pacific Airways' later decision to purchase TriStars. Wakasa had been well primed from the contents of the many bags of yen notes couriered in from a Hong Kong exchange bank for TriStar 'marketing'. So Lockheed certainly did not hesitate in November 1974 to pay US$80,000 – worth at least $400,000 in 2019 – to Cathay Pacific's high-flying former pilot Bernard Smith, now board member and operations director, for 'marketing services', that is, his assistance in promoting its wide-bodied TriStar to the Malaysian national carrier, after Cathay chose the plane as its first wide-bodied jet.[83] Joining Cathay Pacific in 1952, Smith had made his name as a senior manager in Nassau, and he was the face of the new aircraft for the company and the 'New Era in Asian Aviation' it heralded. On 2 September 1975 he piloted the first Super TriStar to be delivered, with Governor Murray MacLehose there to meet it at Kai Tak. Six months later, Smith resigned and scuttled rapidly out of the colony and into hiding as the news broke, his provident fund intact, but debited at his request the equivalent of the commission – thereby rendering it a proper payment from Lockheed to Cathay, and so releasing him from the threat of prosecution (as an ICAC officer contacted by telephone confirmed) – which the airline attempted to return to Lockheed. '$uperTri$tar' jeered the *Far Eastern Economic Review*, biting the corporate hand that fed it lucrative colour advertisements, most recently one of those featuring Smith extolling the virtues of 'the most intelligent aircraft I've ever flown'.[84] As news emerged that Smith had then written from overseas to his senior pilots and aircrew arguing that he had acted in Cathay's 'best interests', it shared the same page with information on the Gilman & Co. summons.[85]

But there were other sweeteners that came into the Lockheed story, and which would later resurface. Some observers at the time Cathay made the decision had been puzzled by it, for the rival MacDonnell Douglas DC-10 seemed better to fit the airline's stated requirements although ultimately it was more expensive. They put it down to government pressure, which was 'vigorously denied'. But John Swire had found himself offered a different type of inducement from senior British civil servants and government minister Michael Heseltine if the company opted for the TriStar, whose RB211 engines were made by Rolls-Royce, which had been taken into state ownership in 1970. This was a matter of foreign policy – specifically Anglo-American relations, which became fraught over the issue in 1970/71 – and a matter of national politics. 'The Minister made plain to him', noted a telegram to the Hong Kong governor, 'the inference that would be drawn if a British airline were to decide against TriStar in a close competition of this kind.' Heseltine observed that 'HMG had a great interest in CPA, not least in developing its routes through negotiations with other Governments'. Off the record, and out of hearing of his civil servants, Heseltine talked of 'negative payoff' if the airline bought the DC-10, which, on 29 January that year, the CPA board had decided 'unanimously' to do.[86]

As well as a resumption of the Hong Kong–Sydney route, it was already clear that CPA wished to gain rights to fly to London: and traffic rights remained in government hands as a matter of bilateral treaties. Cathay's most important considerations were that the DC-10 was capable of modification for longer routes, and that Lockheed's financial position looked precarious. Heseltine and his officials persuaded Swires to delay a month, harassing the firm in London, and in Hong Kong, with importunings – mostly more delicately flavoured once Heseltine was out of hearing – and at the same time urging Rolls-Royce and Lockheed to talk again with them. State support for the RB211 engine by then had amounted to £140 million, and Heseltine's successor in the Labour government elected in February reaffirmed his preference for a Lockheed decision. All were content, ultimately, when the board reversed its decision and ordered aircraft from Lockheed, which had by then delivered better terms. The decision could now truthfully be said to have been made on commercial grounds alone which, these having now changed, aligned happily with politics. 'These Americans are stickers,' reported Bluck of Lockheed's CEO, although the Rolls-Royce's sales pitch had been 'appalling'. The operations director had not needed persuading, for he had all along preferred the TriStar. 'We are dealing here,' noted George Rogers, Under-Secretary of State in the

Department of Trade & Industry, 'with two British companies (Cathay Pacific and Rolls-Royce) both of which are very heavily dependent upon the State'. Reflecting that this might seem an odd description of a private firm ('revolutionary', he wrote) Rogers clarified:

> Cathay's success depends – and will continue to depend – upon the skill and energy with which the representatives of the British Government pursue Cathay's interests no less than upon Cathay's own commercial acumen. Osaka, Perth and Sydney are only three of the current examples![87]

For British officials, further CPA TriStar purchases – and two more were acquired in 1975 – and its route negotiations clearly remained intertwined and interrelated issues.

British civil servants and politicians had tried not to get into a fight, as they put it, with the Hong Kong government during this episode. Since the handling of the announcement of the devaluation of sterling in November 1967, there had been a steadily growing alienation of British Hong Kong interests from London, for it was clearer and clearer in Hong Kong that they did not align, and that London would always prioritise its own over the colony's. This had made it all the more important that Hong Kong worked on reforming itself, where needed. The anti-corruption drive had certainly been about law, and about the legitimacy of the colonial state, but it was also about the wider ongoing issue of the colony's international image. Police strikes over an anti-corruption crackdown drive did not look good. In addition, the sweatshop charge still stuck, fuelled also by reports on child labour, the subject of press and broadcasting exposés in Britain in 1975/6. It was 'a smug, rich British rock', John le Carré has a character in his 1977 novel *The Honourable Schoolboy* say, 'run by a bunch of plum-throated traders'. His unflattering portrait of Hong Kong tells us much about how it was then seen overseas. There was much discussion about what might be done to try to salvage the colony's reputation. Putting on a 'Hong Kong Day' at the Sandown Races in the autumn of 1977, however, was not seen as the best response. 'A singularly unfortunate juncture to connect plump, cigar-smoking Hong Kong racegoers with child labour', thought Bremridge. 'Even the Romanovs would hardly have been so inept.'[88]

Conversely, Britain's reputation in Hong Kong declined as well. From the quality of British-made cars, to power station turbines, British manufacturing standards were felt to be declining; Chinese students increasingly went to universities in the United States, an ever important market for Hong Kong's goods, and Britain seemed to be looking more and more towards Europe, except when it wanted to protect jobs, at Rolls-Royce, for example, and through those, votes. Hong Kong pushed back, selecting a Japanese consortium to develop the Mass Transit Railway, for example, to the dismay and anger of officials in London.[89] If the Bolshevik firing squads were not quite being readied, the longer-term future of the colony – which from the mid-1970s was instead routinely termed 'territory' by the Hong Kong government – was increasingly a subject of some discussion. This involved, too, updating of 'emergency' plans in the event of a 'Mao takeover', the old subject of what to do if things went very badly wrong (and 'the Taipans were all in Tiger cages in Statue Square'). Jardine Matheson, Adrian Swire reported in 1975, 'have had for many years a mechanism whereby all their non-H.K. assets can be transferred into a Bermuda company at the drop of a hat'. The rapidly changing spread of the interests of both firms meant that the scale of external assets that might be under threat of expropriation if the Hong Kong companies were seized had grown more important than simple concerns about Hong Kong assets themselves.[90]

Image was another factor in the arrangement and rearrangement of Swire operations in Hong Kong in the mid-1970s. By the end of 1976 Swire Pacific had ingested Swire Industries, and so thereby its recently established arm Swire Properties, and secured controlling stakes in Cathay Pacific (buying out CNCo) and HAECo. The Group's historically looser set of alliances was transformed into a much tighter corporate structure, and that structure was more prominent. 'Esse Quam Videri' – To be, rather than to seem to be – the old company motto, now rather came into more use and provides one way of understanding the emerging philosophy and strategy: Swire Pacific was given substance. Efforts had focused on 'building up' – a common refrain – the reputation and standing of publicly quoted Swire Pacific, over John Swire & Sons (Hong Kong), which was wholly owned by London. Partly to support this, the firm had broken with past practice, and the Hong Kong Taipan and other senior staff began regularly to give interviews, the first press conference being held to mark the rebranding. There was a 'policy of inserting firecrackers into the revamped Swire Group', remarked one analyst in 1974. Other moves had been explored, notably in 1974 under the cover name 'Operation Happy Valley', the idea of a merger with Hutchison International, or with significant elements of it. The suggestion came from Hutchison, viewed widely as one of the four key British hongs, with its longer history in China than Swires, and there seemed some virtue in the proposal. The Hongkong & Shanghai Bank offered '100 per cent support', but that was before it got a full picture of Hutchison International's finances. Nobody trusted its chairman, Sir Douglas Clague, and there were concerns about corporate culture and practices. Quite rightly so, it transpired, and while insider trading was not then a crime, it was certainly unattractive and reinforced opposition to any merger of interests especially on the part of the Hong Kong managers. Hutchison had also overextended itself and, deemed by the government too big to be allowed to fail, was effectively taken over by the Hongkong Bank the following year.[91] In 1976 another opportunity seemed to be provided by the troubles of Wheelock Marden, another of the big four, but it was the 'enormous scale' of the cash inflow from Swire Properties that was to transform the capacity of the Group (becoming its 'money bags'). But what sort of a Group was it? What should the balance there be between 'the "Go-go" and the conservative', Adrian Swire had pondered in a 1972 note. Property development, he thought, 'should give us the right element of "go-go" in the eyes of the Hong Kong public'. History was an asset, but it could also be a dead weight around the corporate neck. Swire Pacific was 'the most paternalistic and the most Victorian of the major British companies in Hong Kong', reported *The Economist* in 1977, but it did so in the context of the announcement of the flotation of Swire Properties, and the transformation of the structure of the group.[92]

Perhaps building up Swire Pacific might lead to a future in which John Swire & Sons 'phase ourselves out of' Hong Kong, Adrian Swire ventured in January 1975. It might lead gradually to a diminution of London's holdings in the firm, and it would be vulnerable to being taken over.[93] But at the same time as John Swire & Sons was continuing to explore other areas – deciding in 1973, the year Britain joined the European Economic Community, to secure a significant continental European opportunity of some sort, weighing up the risks and opportunities of Manila and the imperatives of their 'Pacific Basin "spread of risks" argument', and acquiring interests in Malaysia and Mauritius through Blyth Green, and in India and East Africa through tea traders James Finlay, acquiring 30 per cent stakes in each in 1976, and moving to take full control of Scotts early the following year, they dug deep into Hong Kong.[94] John Samuel Swire had always warned against buying land, for him a largely sterile investment, and he wanted money to flow fast and bring swift returns. By 1941 the firm's operations were located on its vast estate across China and Hong Kong. Its developments had helped physically reshape parts of many of these cities. Most dramatically, at Quarry Bay the refinery and dockyard had involved building the company village, and attracted around it a bustling, bursting new suburb – private housing and shops straggled out along the tram line and later the bus route – and as the twentieth century progressed this was subsumed into urban Hong Kong. John Swire & Sons had lost the China estate by 1954, but it still retained this significant parcel of land in Hong Kong.

By 1970 the Dockyard Company was already working with the Jardine Matheson-controlled Hong Kong Land to redevelop the old Taikoo Club site, with its recreation ground on which Taikoo men, women and children had played and drilled. Rising in its place would come six 26-storey apartment blocks aimed at a middle-class market. The first response of the government's Director of Public Works and other officials to the proposals was shock, for there were also hazy statements about broader development at Quarry Bay and on the site of the old TSR staff housing and it was only in 1972 that they were given sight of plans drawn up in 1967. Hong Kong needed the housing, but this piecemeal development would mean little thought given to the infrastructure that would be needed for what was calculated as a very high-density new suburb of around thirty or forty thousand people, without schools, shops, enough public transport, water and sewage capacity. Earlier disposal of small plots meant that other private developments made this an even more awkward proposition. Two nearby privately owned streets were already 'hopelessly congested with hawkers [and] illegally parked cars'. Hong Kong managers 'frankly feel that they are getting out of their depth,' Adrian Swire reported in October 1971. Even when in July 1972 TSR and the Dockyard set up a new company, Swire Properties, bringing into the firm property consultants Berkeley Hambro to manage the operations, it still failed to mollify officials. By then the plans suggested developments that would bring 120,000 residents into Quarry Bay, and the former sites of the TSR reservoirs: 'such a population would mean that Hong Kong has a continuous built-over and densely populated belt stretching from Causeway Bay to Shaukiwan.' It would 'make a mockery' of existing urban development plans. Why not, the Secretary for Home Affairs suggested, plan a land swap, offer them one of the new town sites then planned. 'I recognise that this will not bring the same quick and rich returns but I believe that it would be in the best interests of Hong Kong.' Perhaps even 'more drastic action' might be needed 'to acquire the land' from the company.[95]

'This scheme horrifies me,' minuted the Commissioner for Transport. Nobody in government liked what they saw in the plans being developed. But the new developments went ahead, objections suitably answered. The plan was approved in early 1974, and in time a trading estate, a 61-block housing complex 'Taikoo Shing' – Taikoo City – with over 15,000 apartments and light industrial development was built, the largest private development Hong Kong had ever seen. Even so, Jock Swire did not like what he saw of Hong Kong or the district in 1973.

> We went out by Quarry Bay. Huge blocks of flats and offices all over West End of old Dockyard and the office is let out with the welfare centre and swimming pool. No club bowling green or CNCo. hostel. Most Dockyard work and offices have all moved over to Kowloon under Hong Kong United Dockyards ... It's money, money, money all the way and I don't like the new American-influenced atmosphere at all.[96] ... We visited ... Swire Properties' development at Quarry Bay. We were given a lecture with film and shown a complete mock-up of the proposed concrete mass housing 60,000 people. Where they are going to work now that every individual site is being turned into presumably better paying houses I don't know.[97]

The landbank delivered 'money, money money', as the Taikoo Shing flats rose up, their shadows falling across the still humming dockyard, unprecedented revenue, cash in-flow on an 'enormous scale' for the Swire Group, but this feeling that something had been lost was not simply the reaction of an 80 year old who had spent most of his working life directing the activities that had employed thousands at Quarry Bay, who could recall how news of its construction problems had soured the atmosphere of family holidays 75 years earlier, and who had overseen its reconstruction after 1945.[98] It echoes in its language and concerns the reflections of Michael Hope, one of those whose company was taken over, and gutted, by Slater Walker. The triumph of finance – 'the product we are going to make is MONEY,' announced Slater at the firm's first takeover board meeting – appalled many for whom manufacturing and invention, and the human relations at the heart of industrial relations, were the bedrock of British enterprise.[99] John Swire reflected 30 years later that he was

> not sure I was really in favour of the winding up of the dockyard and the sugar refinery and making it into real estate, although it did provide a big infusion of finance. I wouldn't have done that. It was the right thing to do for the business, but it meant losing contact with a lot of people.[100]

But it was probably the right thing to do for the people, as well, in time. Michael Hope had reflected that the actual impact on his staff had been cushioned by full employment and generous redundancy terms. His was partly a moral concern about the ethics of business. John Bremridge announced in 1975: 'We have made a lot of money out of a patch of dirt, and it is only right that some of that should be ploughed back into ensuring the jobs of the shipyard workers.'[101] What that meant in practice was funding a new site for HUD at Tsing Yi. Early Taikoo Shing sales brochures show the dockyard alongside, still in action, but after July 1980 business was wholly moved to the new site, the Kowloon docks land also being turned over to real estate. It was symbolic of a major change that the first vessel to be serviced at Tsing Yi had come from China. Across the arc of the 1970s China moved from the extremes of the Cultural Revolution – all but civil war in parts of the country, violent and unprovoked military confrontation with the USSR, stasis in the state, economic stagnation, Reds in command and the experts in improvised jails – towards a tentative reopening of contacts and trade. The resumption of contacts with the United States and the ending of the US trade embargo in 1971, and the Nixon visit to Beijing in 1972, signalled the start of a geopolitical shift. The death of Mao Zedong in 1976, the coup which thereafter removed from power afterwards his key allies – the 'Gang of Four' – and the coming into power within the party-state of Hua Guofeng and then Deng Xiaoping, set the scene for economic reforms that started to be initiated at the end of the decade. 'See that little man there?' Nikita Khrushchev recalled Mao Zedong once remarking to him as he pointed out Deng. 'He's highly intelligent and has a great future ahead of him.' Deng would bring China back out into the world.

Already by 1977 Swire Pacific was contemplating the need to appoint a political adviser, to assist with the emerging new environment in the north, and in April 1978 the firm discussed whether or not to set up an office in China. In 1973 and 1975 HAECo had secured two of the earliest contracts with the Chinese signed after the normalisation of relations with Britain in 1972, and aircraft started to fly south into Kai Tak to have their engines serviced.[102] In 1978 Jardine Matheson already had representatives based in Beijing, who would establish an office there in 1979, with one in Guangzhou following soon after. Swire Group interests in 'trading, insurance, shipping, dockyards, paint, and aircraft engineering' had already had dealings with the Chinese by then, although it was 'very difficult to make profits out of China'. Hong Kong urged caution, for now, and later saw in others 'unbridled euphoria' at China trade prospects.[103] What this 'reform and opening up' policy would mean in time, was that Hong Kong played a key role in the transformation of reform-era China after 1978, and that its own manufacturing sector would begin to decline. Where people were 'going to work' in Hong Kong-managed manufacturing would in future be over the border, as Hong Kong businesses took advantage of lower manufacturing costs. By 2000, a workforce an estimated five million strong worked for Hong Kong interests in Guangdong province, five times the size of the territory's own. What Hong Kong's own people would do instead would largely be shaped by the services it offered, its role as an entrepôt, and its continuing transformation into an international finance centre.

This new phase in its history and prime role in the Chinese economy reinforced for many a feeling that perhaps some arrangement might be made with China ahead of the end of the New Territories lease in 1997 that would preserve a British role, even a British administration, for really, they thought, and would say, had they not actually managed things rather well? But China's anti-imperialist nationalism, which the British largely underestimated or simply failed to understand, would make this impossible. The British, who ran a colony on Chinese soil, believed despite this self-evident truth, the colonial ground beneath their feet, that the treaty ports belonged in a closed box safely marked 'history' that might now be left to gather dust. They could not see themselves as the Chinese saw them, or as any rational observer did. Governor Sir Murray MacLehose was the first formally to be disabused of the notion that there was any possibility of negotiating an arrangement, when his attempt to raise the question of the lease with Deng Xiaoping met with a 'rebuff' – his word – in 1979. A course had been set, but for the best part of another five years British diplomats and politicians failed to realise that the future of the colony was to be directed by China, even at the possible cost to it of some or all the advantages it delivered.

By 1980 Hong Kong's services and manufacturing sectors were roughly equal in scale across an economy that doubled in size across the decade, services growing at some 17 per cent a year, much faster than in the 1960s, with manufacturing now growing more slowly – but growing nonetheless.[104] The ride was not always smooth, especially in 1974 and into 1975 when a recession bit deeply, but per capita GDP doubled between 1970 and 1980. Manufacturing wages alone doubled in the second half of the decade. 'The shortage of labour continues,' reported Bremridge in July 1978, 'and the general prosperity is evident.'[105] Under Governor MacLehose – a diplomat and not a career colonial office administrator, which made a significant difference to the tone and style he adopted, and the assumptions he brought with him – the administration introduced free compulsory primary and secondary education, a substantial increase in its social assistance programme, public housing schemes and the New Towns plan, and gave clearer official standing to Cantonese as an official language. MacLehose's hand was strengthened by the increased revenues economic growth delivered; it was also forced by the crisis of 1966/7 and the continued taint that was attached to Hong Kong manufacturing practices. The pace, scale and impact of many of these and other reforms can be over-exaggerated, but in the context of the style of colonial administration that had been in operation in the mid-1960s, this was quite radical. Across the 1970s, too, Hong Kong's society changed. Hong Kong's people were better educated, more skilled and they had more disposable income. Taikoo Shing apartments were aimed at younger married couples who set up home on their own, and not with their parents, as had been the custom. A different market was served by Swire Properties, which invested in US developments 'to satisfy the assumed aspirations' of Chinese shareholders and directors.[106] A stronger sense and articulation of a particular Hong Kong identity became more prevalent, too, fuelled by the film industry, television and Cantopop. It was also informed by increased tourist travel to China, where Hong Kong's differences could more keenly be felt. And Hong Kong's people also increasingly travelled much further afield, and often they travelled on Cathay Pacific.

There was another metal shipping container revolution unfolding in the 1960s and 1970s: the arrival of the Boeing 747 – the Jumbo jet – and of cheap mass air travel. Like the standardised container, the 747 was a by-product of US military needs, in this case a jet-transport aircraft project. Losing out to Lockheed in that competition, Boeing took its plans forward with Pan American Airways signed up as a launch customer in December 1968, and on 21 January 1970 the first Pan Am 747 left New York for London.[107] Bigger, noisier, more cost effective and profitable than its wide-bodied rivals, the 747 soon led – like the container revolution – to changes in the global infrastructure of air travel, in travelling habits and in the shipping of freight. Wary of its huge passenger capacity, Cathay Pacific took a little time to take the plunge. Hong Kong passengers flew in Boeing's 707s first, which entered service from 1971. Past, present and future could be found in the same landscape. As the first 707 took off on 24 August 1971 en route to Taipei and then Osaka, the old CNCo ferry *Fatshan*, long since sold off (and renamed), lay part-overturned in the harbour, a freshly made grave for scores of mariners, who had drowned when the ship was battered by Typhoon Rose a week earlier.

The Boeing 707s took 154 passengers; 286 could be accommodated in the wide-bodied TriStars; 404 people could fly on the 747s – powered by Rolls-Royce engines, as Cathay advertising in Britain was diligent in pointing out, a £70 million investment over five years in British manufacturing, it calculated in 1979 – that started to arrive in Hong Kong in 1979. The first aircraft had flown in on 30 July 1979, ritually met by Governor MacLehose, who might well have reflected, as the police brass band played in front of an aircraft hangar, on the repeated eccentricities, like this one, that decorated the role he was performing for Her Majesty's Government in Hong Kong.[108] However, he had formally arrived in the colony to assume his post on one of the Cathay 707s, landing from Tokyo on 19 November 1971, and then swapping his suit for gubernatorial garb, ostrich feathers now garlanding his jet-age arrival, crossing the harbour by launch to Queen's Pier, the traditional point of disembarkation for Hong Kong's governors.[109] MacLehose was one of 653,000 Cathay passengers in 1971. In 1972 827,000 flew the airline, a figure that had doubled by 1976, and which reached 2,880,000 by 1980. It ran a quarter of all flights in and out of the colony, and carried some 30 per cent of Hong Kong's tourists; and this growth rate was far in excess of the roughly 85 per cent increase in passenger traffic internationally in the same period.[110] The new 747s were scheduled first to fly south to Sydney and Melbourne, and on the very profitable route north to Tokyo. But Cathay's eye was set on another prize, too: London. In 1976 the TriStars began a service to Bahrein, and in December 1979 the company formally lodged an application in Hong Kong for the right to fly to London, which it secured, and in January 1980 to the Civil Aviation Authority (CAA) in London for the reciprocal rights, which it did not. This was a 'shameless abuse of imperial privilege,' thundered the *South China Morning Post* – without a trace of irony – for exclusive rights to join British Airways on the route were granted to British Caledonian, which looked like cosy protectionism through which 'London' denied reciprocal rights to Hong Kong that it would have had to grant an independent state. Trade bodies joined the chorus of outrage that was taken up in the Chinese press (although John Bremridge had thought that they had only a 50:50 chance of success). The Hong Kong government had supported its bid, and had put the airline 'under pressure' to consider opening the route as early as 1974, John Browne had then reported. Informal discussion with MacLehose focused on how and when his government's own support would be most usefully deployed.[111] 'Airline route planning was a commercial function,' Duncan Bluck had told the British Civil Aviation representative in Hong Kong in January 1975. Well, came a 'relaxed' retort, 'any CPA services to London ... inescapably involved many aspects of the governmental function'.[112]

Positive 'payoff', perhaps, and a return for that £70 million came on 17 June when Trade Minister John Nott overturned the ruling and allowed Cathay Pacific to run three flights a week, a concession extended also to British Caledonian and to a third competitor, Laker Airways.[113] 'Deep resentment' in Hong Kong, he noted in a briefing to Prime Minister Margaret Thatcher justifying his decision, arose not least as 'CPA is regarded very much as the local airline', and the CAA's decision had 'been alleged by critics to represent a colonialist approach'. His decision, he told the annual dinner of the Hong Kong Association in London, 'should result in bringing Hongkong and Britain closer together'.[114] A month later, serenaded as it left by the police band, and greeted on arrival by a Chinese dragon, Jock Swire and a Spitfire, Cathay's 747 disgorged 400 passengers, including Duncan Bluck, into the terminal at Gatwick Airport. Within a year, while through passenger traffic grew some 35 per cent, Cathay's share of the total rose from 23 to 40 per cent.[115] 'We know Asia Best' purred advertisements taken out in the British press the day after Nott's announcement: 'From Hong Kong to London' ran those in Hong Kong, harbour junk and the Houses of Parliament on facing pages, 'the way you want us to be'.

One of the tens of thousands of passengers who flew Cathay east in 1981 was Jock Swire, 88 years old, making the last of nearly two dozen trips since he joined a Blue Funneler in late February 1914, steaming out of Liverpool on its voyage east. He had changed then at Colombo to join a P&O liner, *Arcadia*, arriving in Hong Kong on 25 March, the day the colony's newspapers there reported the sighting of a large tiger on the Peak. In November 1981 six hours' flying took Jock to Bahrain, and seven more on to Hong Kong, landing there 'in thick fog', he reported. It was 115 years to the week since his grandfather John Samuel Swire had first arrived in the colony. The scale of change in Hong Kong now obscured Jock's view of its past, and hid the sites and scenes he had grown with over seven decades and which his grandfather had set in motion.

the office ... is now a complete maze and I can't recognize anything! I signed the Governor's book on the way in and spent the morning writing in the Director Out East's new room. Statue Square is quite unrecognizable; the Club and HK&S Bk. have been pulled down and the Club are in temporary accommodation next our office. The Office has been completely poshed up and modernized. Everyone has his own room. I am completely lost.

In two brief stays, sandwiched around a journey to Australia, Jock also took in lunch at the Tripe Hounds, a drive to the new combined dockyard at Tsing Yi – 'The whole thing is quite unbelievable' – an afternoon at Sha Tin Racecourse, which had opened three years earlier, lunching in the Hongkong Bank's box (its chairman's horse running third). Jock was driven around the old sites of the Swire enterprise, to Shau Kei Wan, through Quarry Bay, and 'a fascinating tour of Taikoo Shing which has to be seen to be believed. Quite amazing.' MacLehose arranged a helicopter tour of the harbour and New Territories.

Veteran staff came back from overseas to meet Jock, some of whom had first been selected for the 'east' by him through the board at Oxford, or through the Chinese House Staff initiative in the 1930s. Alongside the foundation stone he had laid at Taikoo School back in 1965 (and not much else by now physically survived), these people more than anything else provided continuity between the disorientation of contemporary Hong Kong and those decades of endeavour in China, Japan, Australia. CNCo and B&S veterans joined former Cathay pilots for lunches and dinners, presenting a bewildering array of faces and stories from the past. The descendants of compradors and shipbrokers hosted a Chinese banquet. Chester Yen, who had joined in Shanghai in 1933, flew in from retirement across the Pacific. Along to see Jock came Yangzi shipmasters, Stanley camp veterans, children of the Dockyard managers, and the Holyman family, a living history of this British-directed transnational venture. On 7 December 1981, Jock left Kai Tak 'by CPA 10.20 p.m. Bahrain 2.15 a.m.' and 'Landed Gatwick 7.45 in a snowstorm, deep snow everywhere.' Jock died two years later, and with him a last direct link to his grandfather, the Senior who, nearly 90 years earlier, attended his christening. Let me, then, conclude this stage of the Swire story of people, goods and connections between cities and across oceans – and of enterprise, endeavour, war, nationalism, the decline of empire, upheavals of two centuries, technological, social and cultural transformation – as we began, with an arrival, this arrival in deep December snow, of a vessel from Asia with its passengers, its news from China, ever-changing China, its story yet unfolding, and with it a cargo of history and memories.

15

Here

This has been the story of a company, and it has been the story of the relationship between two countries in the main, but not exclusively, and it has been a story of the shaping of the modern world. With John Swire & Sons and its history we have been able to thread a way through the course of the history of the past two centuries that perhaps shows parts of this in a different light to or at least a different angle from the way in which they are routinely seen. The view from the counting house, the board room, the hong, was different from that from the consulate, Government House or the ministry. Certainly, this has been a tale of the rise and demise, and capacities and constraints, of one form of British power in Asia – call it empire, for that is it was, the flag flying over foreign domains (or painted on the ship, the roof, the aircraft fuselage), and pressure and influence applied beyond those formal territories – and of its agents and subjects, collaborators and opponents, and of those who made use of its opportunities as those intersected with their own enterprise and ambition. That includes the partners, directors, agents and many of the employees of John Swire & Sons. It has been a story, too, of the adaptation of the Qing, its peoples, its economy and society, to the demands and importuning of the British men in a hurry who arrived in their cities and took to their rivers and coasts, but also of their successors in the decades of the Chinese republics who completed the task of restoring China's sovereignty. This has been a tale of the people of the Chinese diaspora, the 'Cantonese Pacific' as it has been termed, and the merchants from Xiangshan, the emigrants from Shantou, the seamen on ships far from home (and sometimes men far from their ships).[1] And it has been a story of the strange persistence yet contemporaneous withering of colonial power in Hong Kong, and that enclave's development. The rise of Asian nationalisms has shaped this tale, and so has decolonisation, and the strategies that British interests adopted in order to try to survive geopolitical change.

It has been the story of this company's people. We might remember the French Bund's odd couple, Zheng Guanying and Henry Bridges Endicott, conspiring to rule the Yangzi and the coast by fair means and foul; Dr Korn's scientific sugar refining; Katie Reece, pioneer typist, unsettling from Billiter Street the Taipan in Hong Kong; Walter Fisher protecting his staff at Tianjin from British soldiers; Jim Scott, against his grain, investing in a university; C. C. Roberts managing the firm interned in Hong Kong; the CNCo shipmasters guiding their refugee vessels out of the colony's harbour and into the winter war at sea; John Finnie's joy at the sight of the ruined Taikoo Dockyard; Syd de Kantzow, bowing out of Cathay Pacific early enough to bring relief to rattled Eric Price. It is not a history lacking in such stories, and more of those could have been told. These, though, are all tales of the firm, in their way, but so, too, are the other tales that have filled this volume: striking Taikoo Dockyard workers: the Ningbo cooks on the CNCo steamers; the anonymous composer of the verses on the *Shanghai*; the teaboys hated by passengers and ships' captains alike (who were themselves simply finding a living); the Sing-Song girls raising funds for the boycott in Guangzhou; the bright sparks from St John's University in Shanghai joining the Chinese House Staff, all of them own this story, too. This company's story lies in this congeries of experiences, this entangled history of men and women across cultures and nations, mostly here across the intertwined histories of the nineteenth- and twentieth-century British and Chinese worlds.

It has been unusual to be able to chart a path over an extended time and in detail through such developments of a single corporate entity that has retained, with justification, a single identity, and that entity rooted in a network of families, or networks of families.[2] We are more generally used to thinking in terms of the histories of states, of cities, institutions or commodities, or of ideas, episodes, phenomena or technologies. We have biographies or studies of families, and we do have some studies of multi-generational family firms. Certainly, this entity has evolved and the John Swire & Sons and its world of 1980 was far removed from the world of John Swire of Liverpool in 1816, bewilderingly so. Step back in your thoughts and in these pages to John Swire and his modest agency work, servicing two ships a year sailing to the Caribbean, and then page forward to the diverse range of activities and polyglot and polycultural companies his descendants came to manage so far away from Liverpool. The task has been to show how the one got to the other across five generations. And this gains interest when we consider that, with very few exceptions, most of its peers, associates and competitors, at any one point long ago ceased to be, even some of the most important in this story. Liverpool's world of business, the great China Merchant houses of the 1860s, most of the largest British firms even in post-war Hong Kong have all fallen away. But what do we gain from this, aside from a fuller knowledge of a corporate history, and more evidence of the unpredictable vagaries and varieties of human experience? That history is rich, and richer even than this book has managed to encompass – the archive is vast, the unarchived yet vaster – and there is always more that could be done.

The obvious question to be asked at the conclusion of this history is how, against all historical odds, has this particular company lasted so long? One answer is family, and after all John Swire & Sons remained in 1980, and remains in 2020, a privately owned company in which the majority shareholding remains with the Swire family. We might start with the ethos this engendered. John Samuel Swire was driven by many impulses, but his sense of family duty was certainly one of those. Jack Swire spent 40 years in a business he clearly did not love out of a strong sense of inescapable duty, partly to his father – and perhaps to prove to him, and to his memory, that he had worth – and partly to those the firm employed. Warren Swire was more jealous than any other character in this story of his ownership of the firm; they were 'his' ships, remember. Jock Swire's loyalty I think lay more towards the men he brought into the firm, his 'contemporaries at Univ.' and their successors. Both world wars scarred him, and both drove him. Rebuilding the Swire companies after 1945, and reorientating the firm after the China closure, or the Hong Kong scare of 1967, was very much aimed at fulfilling his side of a contract with the staff. On two occasions family presented existential challenges, at both the commencement and at the end of Warren Swire's working life. And the Mackintosh problem, which was for a time a thorny one, was also a problem of family. These men did not work alone, and drew heavily on the Scotts, whose holdings in the firm amounted to a third of it in 1914 and continue so to do. Jim Scott's sons were important principals in the company for most of it, Colin C. Scott from 1910 until his death in 1950 on a train taking him to a John Swire & Sons annual general meeting, and John Swire Scott from 1931 until he stepped down in 1966, most notably his support of Jock Swire in the 1940s in the conflict with Warren. In this he was perhaps also something in the manner of a substitute for Jock's younger brother Glen, lost at Ypres in the First World War.[3]

'Family' is not answer enough, and it does not stand without qualification. A family-owned company might well be able to take a longer-term view of investments than one publicly owned, but one model in the literature on business history has most family firms failing by the third generation or evolving into public companies. This assumes that after the founding and subsequent generations there is a decline in entrepreneurial interest and a disengagement from the source of family wealth. Jack Swire, Master of the Essex Hunt, horseman, country gentleman, might well have fitted that model. Certainly, family-owned companies that went public, one study of overseas trading firms like Swires has shown, largely failed to survive when more short-term shareholder demands were made of them.[4] The idea of inevitable failure has its critics, and John Swire & Sons is not unique in enduring long after its founder, but it is unusual and it took hard work. It took close supervision and hard words to break Warren Swire into the culture of the firm, and even if, ultimately, the result was patchy, Jack Swire's greatest contribution to it was probably the restraint he put on his brother's more brutal impulses. Jock Swire's apprenticeship was interrupted by the First World War, but subsequent family recruits to the firm spent some years gaining experience and training in Asia before joining the board, but also, as Jock Swire put it in 1920 of his plans for young John Scott in learning 'what Taikoo is and what it means'.[5] Different individual talents across the five generations followed here were crucial: John Samuel Swire's cold cheek, drive, and his strikingly scrupulous fairness; Warren Swire's singlemindedness, and his unexpected warm openness to Chinese nationalism; Jock Swire's talent for people: each of these different, each meeting their times. But still, the paternalism that characterised the management and culture of the firm was in the main literal. A family owned the firm; it owned its duty to its staff. This is not to say, as we have seen, that it did not run on reasonably logical and efficient corporate managerial lines, if often tardily, but as interests diversified in the 1960s, and especially in the 1970s, this became a much more robust set of structures and managerial practices deployed through an elite and trusted and increasingly more professionally trained House Staff. At the same time, the presentation of family, history and tradition became more important to its identity. Family, of course, also has a certain charisma and a wider cultural resonance, perhaps best reflected in the world of the Hong Kong fantasies of writer James Clavell in which the Struan and Gornt families, effectively Jardines and Swires, fight – literally – across generations. John Samuel Swire never wielded a knife except in the shape of a sugar refinery. His revenge on Jardines was to be sweet, not blood-sour.

A second key answer to the puzzle of endurance is empire; not the jingo, but the banal kind: the rational exploitation of opportunity provided by the exercise of colonial might. The political geography of British power provided the terrain in which the company worked. It found its niche within that, and it worked this ground thoroughly in association with its partners. We might note that in the Victorian era of British imperial expansion the firm largely kept its distance from the state. Liverpool men made their own way through this expanding landscape, in their minds and rhetoric at least. In the midday sun of British global power, John Swire & Sons and its agents called on the state to protect their rights, as the treaties had them, and sought justice (in their eyes) from the courts, but I cannot conclude that they were, philosophically, truly comfortable with or wedded to that infrastructure of power, although they sheltered within it. They did not believe that consuls or colonial administrative officers understood their world, and they assumed that enterprises of mutual advantage might be organised across cultures, borders and antipathies regardless (at times) of any evidence to the contrary. For their part, the agents of the state held 'trade' largely in low regard. They upheld British interests – that was their job – but often they clearly did not like them. The John Swire & Sons relationship with British state power in fact grew closest as empire came under attack and as it began to retract (a process paradoxically coincidental with the massive expansion of the British state itself), when the company sought to survive in a changing and increasingly hostile landscape, and conversely as the interventionist state was used to put pressure on a private company to help its masters achieve their political ends.[6]

John Swire & Sons also looked to alliances it might make with the opponents of, or successors to, colonial power, if they were minded so to make them, which in China after 1949, or Malaysia after 1957, for example, proved not to be the case, no matter how much political capital the company gained by transporting pilgrims or retaining shipping services to post-closure China. The firm was not wedded to empire, but still, it sought safety in the British Commonwealth, mused on Canada, and invested extensively and successfully in Australia and disastrously in the Bahamas. It was the quite unexpected persistence of Hong Kong, the British empire's last formal redoubt – its last of any substance, and what substance that became – that provides the key explanation for the puzzle of the firm's survival. It survived because Hong Kong survived. The greatest number of British overseas trading firms did not long survive decolonisation in the position they held at the transfer of power. Outright nationalisation, formal or informal 'localisation' policies, or taxation or restrictive regulations saw the end of most.[7] As we have seen, Hong Kong was time and time again thought too insecure a shelter, but it proved a place of safety nonetheless. And out of Hong Kong, in the main, all that diversification aside, John Swire & Sons drew the resource it needed to enter into and grow new areas such as aviation and move out of declining ones such as shipbuilding and repairing and sugar refining. In 1980 John Swire & Sons drew 44 per cent of its group profits from the colony, which accounted for only 9.5 per cent of its turnover, and the greater part of this came from property: 38.5 per cent.[8] The company was utterly bound to Hong Kong, as it was always bound to China.

It was a networked enterprise, and this provides a third explanation for its longevity. Among the notable features of this story are the networks that have characterised it, and through which capital, expertise and experience have been mobilised and deployed and redeployed. We might start with the Swire and Butterfield families – with Liverpool trading and Yorkshire exports working across the Atlantic world in the 1850s; then think of Swire, Butterfield, Heards and Moks and their interests in Hong Kong, Shanghai and Yokohama in the 1860s; or Swire, Fairrie, Martin, and sugar in the 1880s; Swire and Holts, Scotts, and Mansfields, and the world of the CNCo fleet and Blue

Funnels in Asia; or Swire and Zheng (and then Yang and Chun) on the Yangzi and the coast after 1873; or Swire, Scott, Zheng, Chun, Mok, and Yang in the Butterfield & Swire branch network, a shifting set of relationships, some falling, some rising, and linked into all of these were others. There was the Swatow network, and the relationships with the Shanghai banking elites in the 1930s and after. And we should not forget the later corporate partners in CPA or OCL. In some important instances the relationship was based on trust – Swire, Holt and Scott in particular, and with the Hongkong Bank after the Second World War – but not exclusively so. In many others it was contractually based and could be legally enforced. But even in those cases there is a very substantial evidence in the archive of extra-contractual exchange. Certainly, Zheng Guanying was jailed as a debtor for a year. But this was rather the exception. One former comprador down on his luck was housed and provided with a living income. His widow was looked after. Sons of others were brought into the firm. A 'compassionate list' was kept in the mid-1950s of former staff and associates that it would help leave revolutionary China if it could. Humane relationships and qualitatively rich connections – *guanxi* – were a feature of the way that the firm operated, and which might not be justifiable in any other form of firm. We might see this simply as Butterfield & Swire protecting its own reputation, and there was an element of that, but it clearly went further.

We might think this set of relationships better illustrated with diagrams, but we might best step back from this confusing set of lists, to think of these at root as a core British network based around Swire, Holt and Scott, and a network in China of Swire and its Cantonese partners. We might in fact start to think of a need to reconceive of much of this phase in Sino-British relations as Cantonese-British relations, of the prime functional relationship at the heart of the British and Chinese experience between (in this case) the 1860s and 1930s actually being this intertwining of British interests with Cantonese interests, even more specifically in the main, with interests from a small region within Guangdong province, from Xiangshan county (or Zhongshan, as it is known today), and its neighbours. At Wuhan, or at Tianjin, certainly at Shanghai, the merchants of Xiangshan worked with the agents of the Swire network, as they did, too, with other foreign firms. The state has not been absent from this story, and understanding it – the Qing, the

Chinese republics, the British state and its colonial satellites – is vital to fully understanding this history, but this has been a history in which the shape of the state has been far less important than the transnational alliances that have characterised the practices and structures of John Swire & Sons and its work. Until the 1960s, and unlike many other British firms (such as Jardine Matheson), John Swire & Sons did not draw in Chinese capital, at least not directly, but its entire structure of operations was based on an alliance of capital and interests, firmly separated (mostly), the comprador's business and the company's side by side (though on different floors, in different offices), mutually constitutive, wholly interdependent.

These networks were anchored in cities, of course. One of the most important resources the firm made use of over the course of its history was the city. Standing out among others are Liverpool, Melbourne, Shanghai and Hong Kong, and, of course, London, each in its own way and in the era when most important, London apart, a new city, makeshift, or rapidly reinventing itself as Hong Kong did after the 1940s. All were port cities, in-between places for the transit of goods, people, capital and ideas, in which developed new communities of traders, shippers, journalists, financiers, and all those servicing this business, in high and in low ways.[9] These cities were nodes in communications networks, as well as shipping and aviation hubs. Swire was clearly a restless enterprise, ever on the move from city to city and from opportunity to opportunity, even when some proved dismal, such as William Lang's rifles, or a coal concession in Guangdong. Setting aside the literal aspect of this – which is nonetheless important, the company's prime activity until the 1970s lying in shipping, and moving commodities, people, expertise, technology, at different speeds and adding value in different ways – this was a company always in flux, seeking new advantage through place, technology, alliance, or responding to the upheavals of war, revolution, nationalism and the wider course of the global economy. Despite its emphasis on continuity and history, or perhaps to mask this restlessness, the firm reinvented itself time and time again across the course of this history.

It continued to do so. In the 1980s China began a process of reinvention that is still unfolding in the second decade of the twenty-first century. John Swire & Sons returned to China, invested in manufacturing and property development in Guangzhou in 1979/80, flew a one-off charter to Guangzhou in late 1979, reopening air links between the two cities with a cargo of tennis players and fans travelling to an exhibition match, and commenced a regular Cathay Pacific service from Hong Kong to Shanghai in March 1980. In 1983 it opened an office in Beijing, and Yao Kang, who had once helped the firm navigate its way out of China, now, three decades later as the country slowly but steadily reversed course, helped it find its way back in. Ten years later it opened up once more in Shanghai. Increasingly the closed decades of the Mao years were understood as the historical exception, not an insular Chinese norm. The old Bunds and the old hong, the stages on which this history was set, actually mostly remained intact in the 1980s and 1990s, but the business of foreign enterprise in reform-era China was very different. History was hardly forgotten, not least as it was always prominent in Chinese debates, but it was a different firm that expanded back into China. It developed partnerships in the People's Republic in aviation, property, paint, soft drinks and sugar. The new China opportunities initially provided a wild ride for some, those in thrall to the old myths of the China market, but things have settled. The handover of Hong Kong from British rule in 1997 marked the opening of a new era there, one now established firmly on Chinese terms.

But this, together with all the related developments that ensued across the 1980s and after properly forms another story, or, rather, the same story continued, as indeed it does continue today, so I leave it there at the point a new phase in this history commenced.

16

Today

In 2020 Swire is a highly diversified global group with a turnover exceeding US$30 billion and with over 130,000 employees on four continents. It is much changed from the Liverpool born, one-man, trading business first recorded in trading reports in 1816 importing a hundred barrels of a tree bark used in the dyeing industry. The firm's interests can now be broadly gathered under five main descriptors of aviation, property, marine services, beverages & food chain, and trading and industrial. Many of its core businesses are still found within the Asia Pacific region, and retain the names that emerged during this history. And 2020 will mark the 150th anniversary of Swire opening its office in Hong Kong. Within Asia, Swire's activities largely come under the group's publicly quoted arm, Swire Pacific Limited.

Headquartered in Hong Kong, where its very first DC-3 is on display at the city's Science Museum, Cathay Pacific now flies a fleet of over 200 aircraft. The China Navigation Company, operating now from Singapore, owns over 50 vessels traversing the globe under the flag first raised in defiance of Russell & Co on the Yangzi in 1873. From its origins in the terraces built for the Sugar Refinery workforce, the property division has evolved to employ capital of over US$40 billion with residential, retail, office and hotel mixed-use developments throughout China and in the United States. Swire Beverages has a Coca-Cola franchise population of 668 million people in China and nearly 29 million in the US operating 24 bottling plants across both countries. Whilst no longer involved in sugar refining, Swire still packages and sells premium sugar products under the Taikoo Sugar brand throughout China, Singapore, the Middle East and Canada. Its sales force has an easier time than did some of the hardy young sugar travellers of the 1920s.

Elsewhere in the world, many businesses are held directly by the London-based parent company, John Swire & Sons Limited, in Australia, Papua New Guinea, East Africa, Sri Lanka, the Netherlands, the United States and United Kingdom. Key to Swire's development remains the ethos of investing for the long-term – a strategy that has carried the group through different periods of economic volatility and political turmoil. The Swire group is an anomaly: an organisation rooted in the past, but with its focus firmly on the future; a multinational with a family business as its parent company. Its history has been one of strength in diversity, and of tenacity through countless chapters of hardship.

Acknowledgements

This history began with an invitation. I am grateful to the directors of John Swire & Sons, who invited me to consider writing this book, who gave me a free hand to shape it as I thought most effective, and agreed without hesitation to respect my interpretation of the course of the firm's history. I wish to thank then Chairman, the late James Hughes-Hallett, his successor Barnaby Swire, Swire Pacific Chairman Merlin Swire and Sam Swire, for their enthusiastic endorsement of the project when its outline was presented to them. I regret very much that James, along with Sir John and Sir Adrian Swire, who likewise strongly supported this project, passed away before the manuscript was completed. When we met to talk about it, Sir Adrian's irrepressible enthusiasm for news of what I might have found in the archive, fair, foul or middling, was unfailingly heartening.

The project has been overseen at John Swire & Sons by Group Archivist Rob Jennings, who has been extremely patient and generous (and who has never before had to mind a writer). I could not have been better or more affably supported in the preparation of a book. I really am very grateful to him for his support and guidance. I would like to thank also Bonnie Sze and the Group Archives team in Hong Kong, Matthew Edmondson, and Angharad McCarrick; and in London Kathryn Boit and Julie Makinson at the School of Oriental and African Studies. I am especially grateful to Charlotte Bleasdale for her strong support of my various forays into the company's history over the past 30 years. As former Group Archivist, Charlotte knows a thing or two about this history. Dr Sabrina Fairchild and Dr Kaori Abe patiently secured a great deal of material from the archives for me, and I would not have been able to complete this in any reasonable time without their help. I am grateful also to Wai Li Chu and Joan Chan, Zhou Fen, Shawn Liu, Chris Wemyss, Vivian Kong, Thomas Larkin, Yuqun Gao, and Jiayi Tao who have all collected material from archives they were visiting. Thoughts and documents were also provided by John Carroll and John Wong, Tom Cohen, Vaudine England, Kees Metselaar, Paul C. Aranha, Elizabeth Ride, Vivienne Lo, Jeff Wasserstrom, Stephen Lloyd, and Jon Howlett. I would like to thank Jonathan and Karen Lovegrove-Fielden for allowing me to borrow the Mary Martin diaries, and I am grateful to Lynn James whose notes on the early history of the Swire family in Liverpool I draw on in Chapter 2. Drafts of part or the whole of the manuscript were read by Andrew Hillier, Tim Cole, Peter Kwok-Fai Law, Su Lin Lewis, James Thompson, Charlotte Bleasdale and Rob Jennings. I am grateful to them for their time and their thoughts and queries. I alone am responsible, of course, for the text you have in your hands. Sir Adrian Swire, Paul C. Aranha, James Hughes-Hallett and Catherine Boylan, all spared time in person or by email to answer questions from me for which I would like to thank them. The late David Miller oversaw the first phase of discussion about this commission, but my agent Bill Hamilton helped the book get underway and I am grateful to both for their support. Ian Hallsworth at Bloomsbury has been very patient, and I am grateful too to Allie Collins and Richard Collins, and to Cecilia Mackay for her work on the illustrations.

As I researched some of the episodes and personalities discussed here, I swopped queries and leads, as I have done for three decades now, with my doctoral mentor, collaborator and friend Gary Tiedemann, who knew a thing or two about the Meadows family, and about the Endicotts, and about many, many others. To the great sadness of those who knew him, Rolf Gerhard Tiedemann died unexpectedly as this volume went into production. Unobtrusive contributions from Gary, in matters of detail, of method, and in spirit, can be found throughout this book, as they could be found in all my work to date, and I would like to acknowledge my indebtedness to him here.

At the University of Bristol, I am particularly grateful to Mike Basker, and to Simon Potter for supporting me in finding time to work on the book, and to all my colleagues in the Department of History for making it such a stimulating and pleasant place in which to work. 'The Swire book' has been a prominent feature of family life for rather too long, and Kate, Lily and Arthur have been extraordinarily patient, as ever. Now it's done.

Archival Sources

Bank of England Archives
    Liverpool Branch: Letter Books
Cambridge University Library
    Jardine Matheson Archive
John Swire & Sons Ltd, London
    Archives of John Swire & Sons Ltd
John Swire & Sons (Hong Kong), Archive Services
    Butterfield & Swire (Hong Kong) Ltd
    Cathay Pacific Airways
    Taikoo Dockyard & Engineering Company
    Taikoo Sugar Refining Company
Harvard Business School, Baker Library Special Collections,
    Forbes Family Business Records, Francis Backwell Forbes Papers
    Heard Family Business Records, Augustine Heard & Company
    correspondence
    George U. Sands Business Records
Hong Kong Public Records Office
Liverpool Record Office,
    American Chamber of Commerce minute book, June 1801–December
    1841
    Holt Family Papers
        Alfred Holt papers
        Richard Durning Holt papers
Merseyside Maritime Museum, Maritime Archives and Library,
    Liverpool Ships' Registers
National Archives of Australia
    Department of Defence Co-ordination

Department of External Affairs [II], Central Office
Department of Immigration
National Archives of the United Kingdom
ADM: Records of the Admiralty
AIR: Records created or inherited by the Air Ministry, the Royal Air Force, and related bodies
BT: Records of the Board of Trade
CO: Records of the Colonial Office, Commonwealth Office and Foreign and Commonwealth Offices
FCO: Records of the Foreign and Commonwealth Office and predecessors
FO: Records created or inherited by the Foreign Office
HS: Records of Special Operations Executive
PREM: Records of the Prime Minister's Office
WO: Records created or inherited by the War Office
National Library of Wales, Aberystwyth
J. Glyn Davies Papers
National Maritime Museum, London
Captain T. T. Laurensen papers
Captain John Whittle papers
Queen's University Belfast, Special Collections and Archives
Papers of Sir Robert Hart
School of Oriental & African Studies, University of London, Archives & Special Collections Library
Archives of John Swire & Sons Ltd
PP MS 2: Papers of Sir Frederick Maze
PP MS 49: Scott Family papers
MS 380906: Correspondence of Charles Collingwood Roberts
Second Historical Archives of China, Nanjing
679 Chinese Maritime Customs Services Archives
Shanghai Academy of Social Sciences, Institute of Economics, Business History Resource Centre
Swire Group Extracted Records
Shanghai Municipal Archives
University of Liverpool, Special Collections and Archives, Rathbone Papers

Shanghai English-language newspapers have mostly been accessed through the Proquest 'China Coast Newspapers' archive. For the *North China Daily News* I have used the Shanghai Library's platform, for *Shenbao* searched Hytung's

'Hantang jindai baokan' and *Renmin ribao* has been sought from various sites. Hong Kong newspapers have been explored through the Hong Kong Library system's 'Old Hong Kong Newspapers' platform in its Multi-media Information System. The *South China Morning Post* has been accessed through Proquest, as have been the *Guardian*, the *Times of India*, and the *New York Times* and other US newspapers. The Singapore National Library Board's NewspapersSG resource has been used for Singapore and some Malaysian titles. British newspapers have been searched through: Times Digital Archives, British Newspaper Archive, and Nineteenth-Century British Newspapers. The National Library of Australia's Trove platform has been invaluable, as have been the genealogy websites Ancestry, FamilySearch, Findmypast, and Scotland's People, and the Carl Smith Collection, available digitally via the Hong Kong Public Records Office. The Hong Kong Memory website hosts a great deal of Taikoo Sugar Refinery material at www.hkmemory.hk, and the Industrial History of Hong Kong Group's website has been very useful: industrialhistoryhk.org. John Swire & Sons Ltd operates an online resource at www.wikiswire.com which holds a great deal of historical information about the firm's marine and aviation activities.

As well as these sources you can find a great deal of directly and contextually relevant visual material on my 'Historical Photographs of China' platform at hpcbristol.net, and I have also set up 'China Families' www.chinafamilies.net which brings together genealogical records relating to China.

END NOTES

The archive used most extensively below is that of John Swire & Sons Ltd, held in the Archives & Special Collections at the School of Oriental & African Studies, University of London. Files are catalogued with the prefix JSS.

Abbreviations used in the endnotes

HBS   Harvard Business School

HKPRO   Hong Kong Public Records Office

JS&SHK John Swire & Sons, Group Archives Service, Hong Kong

JS&SL   John Swire & Sons Limited, Archives

LRO   Liverpool Record Office

NAA   National Archives of Australia

NCDN   *North China Daily News*

NCH   *North China Herald*

NLW   National Library of Wales

NMM   National Maritime Museum

SASS   Shanghai Academy of Social Sciences

SCMP   *South China Morning Post*

SHAC   Second Historical Archives of China

SOAS   School of Oriental & African Studies, London

TNA   The National Archives, London

List of Illustrations & Photographic Credits

PLATES SECTION I

Page 1
The Customs House and Revenue Building, Liverpool. Lithograph by William Herdman and James
Marples, from *Modern Liverpool Illustrated*, 1864. *The Stapleton Collection/Bridgeman Images*
John Swire of Liverpool. Portrait miniature, mid-19th century (c.1830). *John Swire & Sons Ltd.*
Strand Street, Liverpool. Watercolour by William Herdman, 1857. *Liverpool Record Office, Herdman Collection*

Page 2
View of Bradford. Painting by William Cowen, 1849. Bradford Museums & Art Galleries. *Bridgeman Images*
The clipper ship *Evangeline*. Watercolour by an anonymous artist, 1853–68(?). *National Maritime Museum,
Greenwich*
New Orleans from the Lower Cotton Press. Lithograph by John William Hill, 1852. *The Historic New
Orleans Collection, 1947.20*

Page 3
Gold Diggings, Ararat, Australia. Painting by Edward Roper, 1855–1860. *Dixson Galleries, State Library of
New South Wales*
Hobsons Bay Railway Pier, Sandridge (now Station Pier, Port Melbourne). Photograph by Charles
Nettleton, c.1878. *National Gallery of Victoria, Melbourne. Purchased, 1992*

Page 4
John Samuel Swire. Portrait miniature, c.1854. *John Swire & Sons Ltd.*
Alfred Holt. Portrait by Robert Edward Morrison, c.1880–1903. *National Museums Liverpool*
Agamemnon. Photograph, 1865. *John Swire & Sons Ltd.*

Page 5
The Bund at Shanghai. Painting by Chinese school, 19th century. *John Swire & Sons Ltd.*
The Residence of Augustine Heard and Co., Hong Kong. Painting by an anonymous artist, c.1860.
Peabody Essex Museum, Salem. *Bridgeman Images*
The Bund at Hankow. Photograph by John Thomson, c.1870. *The Wellcome Collection*

Page 6
Crowds gather on the banks of the Yangzi. Photograph by John Thomson, c.1871. *The Wellcome Collection*
The north coast of Hong Kong island from West Point to Quarry Bay. Detail from a map surveyed by
Lieutenant Collinson of the Royal Engineers, c.1845. *National Library of Scotland*

Page 7
View of the harbour at Hong Kong. Photograph by R. H. Brown, 1880. The Royal Geographical Society.
Getty Images

Page 8
CNCo steamers *Glengyle* and *Ichang* at Shanghai. Photograph, 1874. *John Swire & Sons Ltd.*
The fours team, Shanghai Rowing Club regatta. Photograph, late 1870s or early 1880s. *John Swire & Sons Ltd.*
James Dodds and his family outside the Swire office at Yokohama, Japan. Photograph, 1878. *John Swire
& Sons Ltd.*

Page 9
View of the hulk *Cadiz* at Zhenjiang. Photograph, c.1880s. *Pump Park Vintage Photography/Alamy*
Construction of the Taikoo Sugar Refinery at Quarry Bay. Photograph, 1882. *John Swire & Sons Ltd.*

Page 10

John Samuel Swire. Photograph, 1886. *John Swire & Sons Ltd.*

James Henry Scott. Photograph, c.1894. *John Swire & Sons Ltd.*

Letter from John Samuel Swire to William Lang, 19 December 1879. *John Swire & Sons Ltd.*

Page 11

Butterfield & Swire's Shanghai shipping staff. Photograph, early 1880s. *John Swire & Sons Ltd.*

Robert McQueen and Henry Bridges Endicott, Shanghai. Photograph, c.1883. *Endicott Family Photographs, The Phillips Library, Peabody Essex Museum, Salem (PHA 199)*

The Taikoo Sugar Refinery. Photograph, 1890. *John Swire & Sons Ltd.*

Page 12

The launch of the Blue Funnel Line's *Menelaus*. Photograph, 1895. *John Swire & Sons Ltd.*

Workers in a trench during the construction of Taikoo Dockyard. Photograph, 1904. *John Swire & Sons Ltd.*

Page 13

John Samuel Swire. Photograph by G. Warren Swire, 1896. *John Swire & Sons Ltd.*

Page 14

Loading cargo at Jiujiang. Photograph by G. Warren Swire, c.1906–07. *John Swire & Sons Ltd.*

Deck passengers on the *Taming*. Photograph by G. Warren Swire, 1911. *John Swire & Sons Ltd and Historical Photographs of China, University of Bristol (www.hpcbristol.net)*

Page 15

View of shipping in a storm off the Praya at Hong Kong. Photograph by William Nicholson, 1906. *John Swire & Sons Ltd.*

Page 16

The launch of the SS *Tencho Maru* from Taikoo Dockyard. Photograph by G. Warren Swire, 1911. *John Swire & Sons Ltd and Historical Photographs of China, University of Bristol (www.hpcbristol.net)*

Butterfield & Swire clerks relaxing in the Praya building, Hong Kong. Photograph by William Armstrong, c.1897. *John Swire & Sons Ltd.*

PLATES SECTION 2

Page 1

Jock Swire on patrol, Deep Water Bay, Hong Kong. Photograph, 1914–15. *John Swire & Sons Ltd.*

Butterfield & Swire offices, Shanghai. Photograph, 1911–12. Photograph by G. Warren Swire, 1911. *John Swire & Sons Ltd and Historical Photographs of China, University of Bristol (www.hpcbristol.net)*

Interior of the Butterfield & Swire Private Office, Shanghai. Photograph by G. Warren Swire, 1912. *John Swire & Sons Ltd and Historical Photographs of China, University of Bristol (www.hpcbristol.net)*

Page 2

Four scenes of sugar travelling life. Photographs, 1929, from Gordon Campbell's memoir *Recollections of Some Aspects of Earning a Living in China Between the Wars,* 1968. © *Gordon Campbell*

Page 3

N.S. Brown and G. Warren Swire, Shanghai. Photograph, 1934. *John Swire & Sons Ltd.*

Shanghai comprador Chun Shut Kai and his father and predecessor Chun Koo Leong. Photograph, c.1915. *John Swire & Sons Ltd.*

Butterfield & Swire office staff, Andong. Photograph by G. Warren Swire, 1934. *John Swire & Sons Ltd and Historical Photographs of China, University of Bristol (www.hpcbristol.net)*

Page 4

Pier for steamship services, Sheung Wan, Hong Kong. Photograph, 1920s. *History of the Port of Hong Kong and Marine Department*

Advertisement for Yangzi cruises. Issued by CNCo, c.1935. *John Swire & Sons Ltd.*

The steamer *Shu-Tung* and the *Shu-Tung Flat* negotiating rapids on the Yangzi. Photograph by William Palmer, 1937. *C.A.L. Palmer FRCS and Historical Photographs of China, University of Bristol (www.hpcbristol.net)*

Page 5
The return to Shanghai of the pirated *Tungchow*. Report in the *North China Herald*, 13 February 1935. *SOAS Library, School of Oriental and African Studies, University of London*

Page 6
Advertisement for Taikoo Sugar for the British market, published in *Punch*, 19 October 1932. *Private collection*
Detail of an illustration from a calendar issued to promote Taikoo Sugar, 1910. *John Swire & Sons Ltd.*
Advertisement for Taikoo Sugar for the Hong Kong market, 1960. *Swire HK Archive Service*

Page 7
Taikoo sugar agent's shop sign in a street in Yichang. Photograph, 1929. *Peter Covey-Crump and Historical Photographs of China, University of Bristol (www.hpcbristol.net).*

Page 8
Remains of the Book Office, Swire offices, Billiter Street, London, after the Blitz. Photograph, 1941. *John Swire & Sons Ltd.*
Taikoo Dockyard staff interned at Gulangyu Island, Xiamen. Photograph, c. April 1942. *John Swire & Sons Ltd.*

Page 9
Launch of a ship at Taikoo Dockyard during the Japanese occupation. Photograph, c.1943. *John Swire & Sons Ltd.*
Aircraft from the USS *Hancock* attack Japanese ships and the Taikoo Dockyard. Photographed by the US Navy, 16 January 1945. *Getty Images*

Page 10
View of Taikoo Dockyard from Korn Hill. Photograph, September 1945. *John Swire & Sons Ltd.*
Pilgrims depart on the SS *Anshun* at Singapore, bound for Mecca, 1964. *Photonico/National Archives of Singapore, T2004 02289*

Page 11
CPA route map. From a cargo rates leaflet issued by Cathay Pacific Airways, 1950. *John Swire & Sons Ltd.*
A Cathay Pacific Airways Convair overflying the Taikoo Dockyard, 1968. *John Swire & Sons Ltd.*

Page 12
Butterfield & Swire offices, Hong Kong. Photograph, c.1960. *John Swire & Sons Ltd.*
Ferry to Hong Kong. Movie poster, 1959. *Everett Collection/Rex/Shutterstock*
Advertisement for tourism in Hong Kong for the American market. Issued by the Hong Kong Tourist Association, 1961. *Granger/Rex/Shutterstock*

Page 13
Cover of the yearbook of the Taikoo Dockyard Chinese Workers' Union, 1957. *Courtesy East Asia Library, Stanford University*
Illustrations from *The Bloody and Tearful Story of the Taikoo Dockyard Workers*, originally drawn for the Communist newspaper *Wen Wei Po*, 1967

Page 14
Advertisement for Bahamas Airways New York service, 1970. *John Swire & Sons Ltd.*
Bahamas Airways flight attendant. Photograph, 1969. *John Swire & Sons Ltd.*
Bahamas Airways jet at Nassau airport. Postcard, 1969. *Courtesy of Paul C. Aranha*

Page 15
Say 'Hello!' to Hong Kong. Feature published in the Cathay Pacific Airways inflight magazine, *Cathay News*, April–June 1969. *Swire HK Archive Service*
Advertisement for Cathay Pacific Airways' Hong Kong to London route, August 1980. *Private collection*

Page 16
Taikoo Shing, Dockyard and Floating Dock. Photograph, c.1972. *Swire HK Archive Service*
John Browne, John A. Swire, and Jock Swire, during the Swire centenary celebrations at City Hall, Hong Kong. Photograph, January 1967. *John Swire & Sons Ltd.*
Adrian Swire and Y.K. Pao in conversation. Photograph, 1968. *John Swire & Sons Ltd.*

Notes

CHAPTER 1 TAIKOO

1 Sheila Marriner and Francis E. Hyde, *The Senior John Samuel Swire 1825–98: Management in Far Eastern Shipping Trades* (Liverpool: Liverpool University Press, 1967); Charles Drage, *Taikoo* (London: Constable, 1970); Zhang Zhongli (chief ed.), *Taigu jituan zai jiu Zhongguo* (The Swire Group in Old China) (Shanghai: Shanghai renmin chubanshe, 1991). See also Gavin Young, *Beyond Lion Rock: The Story of Cathay Pacific Airways* (London: Hutchinson, 1988).

CHAPTER 2 LIVERPOOL'S WORLD

1 Shipping: *Liverpool Mercury*, 31 October, 7 November 1834. Dock: *Liverpool Mercury*, 5 September, 10 October 1834. *Georgiana*: *Tasmanian*, 1 February 1833; *The Colonist and Van Diemen's Land Commercial and Agricultural Advertiser*, 8 March 1833; *Singapore Chronicle and Commercial Register*, 7 November 1833; William Jardine to Thomas Weeding, 20, 23 April 1834, in Alain Le Pichon (ed.), *China Trade and Empire: Jardine, Matheson. & Co. and the Origins of British Rule in Hong Kong 1827–1843* (Oxford; New York: Oxford University Press, 2006), pp. 208–10.

2 *Liverpool Mercury*, 7 November 1834; first: 'Liverpool', *Illustrated London News*, 1 October 1842, p. 328.

3 'Petition of the Trustees of the Dock', *Liverpool Courier*, 18 March 1812, p. 3, quoted in Yukihisa Kumagai, *Breaking into the Monopoly: Provincial Merchants and Manufacturers' Campaigns for Access to the Asian Market, 1790–1833* (Leiden: Brill, 2012), p. 122. See also 'Meeting at the Town Hall on the East India Trade', *Liverpool Mercury*, 20 March 1812.

4 *Morning Post*, 5 January 1835, 6 August 1836; Ruth D'Arcy Thompson, *D'Arcy Wentworth Thompson: The Scholar Naturalist, 1860–1941* (London, 1958), p. 3 (the scientist was Thompson's grandson).

5 John Skelton Thompson, Batavia, to Jardine Matheson & Co., Canton, 13 May 1833: Cambridge University Library, Jardine Matheson Archive [hereafter JMA], MS JM/B6/6; Benjamin Mountford, *Britain, China and Colonial Australia* (Oxford: Oxford University Press, 2016), p. 16; *Liverpool Mercury*, 7 November 1834.

6 On the EIC see, most recently, Nick Robins, *The Corporation that Changed the World: How the East India Company Shaped the Modern Multinational* (2nd edn, London: Pluto Press, 2012).

7 Kumagai, *Breaking into the Monopoly*, p. 135; Anthony Webster, 'Liverpool and the Asian Trade, 1800–50: Some insights into a provincial British commercial network', in Sheryllynne Haggerty, Anthony Webster and Nicholas J. White (eds), *The Empire in One City? Liverpool's Inconvenient Imperial Past* (Manchester, 2008), pp. 38–41; Anthony Webster, *The Twilight of the East India Company: The Evolution of Anglo-Asian Commerce and Politics 1790–1860* (Woodbridge: Boydell Press, 2009).

8 Kumagai, *Breaking into the Monopoly; Proceedings of the Public Meeting on the India and China Trade, held in the Sessions Room, Liverpool, on the 29th January 1829* (Liverpool: Committee of the Liverpool East India Association, 1829), p. iii.

9 The words of John Gladstone, then still a significant slave owner: *Proceedings of the Public Meeting on the India and China Trade*, p. 10.

10 At Liverpool the *Euphrates* was launched on 22 May 1834, and the *Symmetry* sailed to Asia the same day: Christina Baird, *Liverpool China Traders* (Bern: Peter Lang, 2007), p. 38.

11 *Canton Register*, 29 April 1834, p. 65; William Jardine to Thomas Weeding, 20 April 1834, in Le Pichon, *China Trade and Empire*, p. 209; *Canton Register*, 9 June 1835, p. 90; *Liverpool Mercury*, 7 November 1834, p. 368. On the Canton press see Song-Chuan Chen, *Merchants of War and Peace: British Knowledge of China in the Making of the Opium War* (Hong Kong: Hong Kong University Press, 2017).

12 [Robert Southey], *Letters from England by Don Manuel Alvarez Espriella*, Volume 2 (2nd edn: London, 1808), p. 122. For a case study of such a 'transition' see Martin Lynn, 'Trade and Politics in 19th-Century Liverpool: The Tobin and Horsfall Families and Liverpool's African trade', *Transactions of the Historic Society of Lancashire and Cheshire*, 142 (1993), pp. 99–120.

13 Memorial, The Committee of the London East India and China Association to Viscount Palmerston, 2 November 1839, in *Memorials addressed to her Majesty's Government by British Merchants interested in the trade with China* (London: T. R. Harrison, 1840), p. 12.

14 See Robert Bickers, *The Scramble for China: Foreign Devils in the Qing Empire, 1832–1914* (London: Allen Lane, 2011), pp. 29–31. In fact it was not always originally so punctilious, and Warren Hastings, then governor-general, had despatched two ships on an unsuccessful smuggling foray in 1781: Robins, *The Corporation that Changed the World*, pp. 153–4.

15 As well as Chen, *Merchants of War and Peace*, see Kaori Abe, *Chinese Middlemen in Hong Kong's Colonial Economy* (London: Routledge, 2017), chapter 1; Fa-ti Fan, *British Naturalists in Qing China: Science, Empire, and Cultural Encounter* (Cambridge, MA: Harvard University Press, 2004); Emile de Bruijn, *Chinese Wallpaper in Britain and Ireland* (London: Philip Wilson, 2017).

16 Le Pichon, *China Trade and Empire*, p. 209; for a comprehensive study see John M. Carroll, *Canton Days: British Life and Death in China* (Lanham: Rowman & Littlefield, 2020).

17 *Canton Register*, 29 April 1834, p. 65; 5 March 1835, pp. 70–71; Le Pichon, *China Trade and Empire*, p. 208.

18 Bickers, *Scramble for China*, pp. 45–8.

19 Southey, *Letters from England*, p. 115–22, part cited in P. J. Waller, *Democracy and Sectarianism: A Political and Social History of Liverpool 1868–1939* (Liverpool, 1981), p. 1; Merton M. Sealts, Jr (ed.), The Journals and *Miscellaneous Notebooks of Ralph Waldo Emerson*, Volume X, *1847–1848* (Cambridge, MA, 1973), p. 178.

20 *Liverpool Mercury*, 26 April 1816, p. 343.

21 Trevor Hodgson and David Gulliver, *The History of Cononley: An Airedale village* (Cononley: Kiln Hill, 2000), pp. 35–43.

22 *Liverpool Mercury*, 1816–34, *passim*; Sheila Marriner and Francis E. Hyde, *The Senior John Samuel Swire 1825–98: Management in Far Eastern Shipping Trades* (Liverpool: Liverpool University Press, 1967), pp. 11–12.

23 *Gore's Liverpool General Advertiser*, 1822–47 *passim*. There are gaps in the record for 1816–21, 1824–5 and 1842. On Burrow and Nottage and their West Indies trade see: Rob David, and Michael Winstanley with Margaret Bainbridge, *The West Indies and the Arctic in the Age of Sail: The Voyages of Abram (1806–62)* (Lancaster: Centre for North-West Regional Studies, 2013).

24 *Liverpool Mercury*, 11 September 1840 (infirmary); 23 December 1825 (Miramichi fire relief); W. O. Henderson, 'The American Chamber of Commerce for the Port of Liverpool, 1801–1908', *Transactions of the Historic Society of Lancashire & Cheshire* 85 (1935), pp. 1–61; petition: American Chamber of Commerce minute book, June 1801–December 1841 (March 1834): Liverpool Record Office, 380 AME/1.

25 Merseyside Maritime Museum, Maritime Archives and Library [hereafter MMM], Liverpool Ship Registers, 157/1840: *Christiana*; *Liverpool Mail*, 6 April 1841, p. 4.

26 Will of John Swire, Merchant of Liverpool, Lancashire: The National Archives [hereafter TNA], PROB 11/2065/237. Decline: Mary Martin diary, 20 July 1854; firm: *Gore's Liverpool General Advertiser*, 24 June 1847.

27 John Samuel Swire to Mary Warren, 24 July 1881, JS&SL.

28 'Old Liverpool Streets: Hope Street [1843]', *Liverpool Citizen*, 11 September 1889, p. 12: Liverpool Record Office, 050 CIT.

29 Tristram Hunt, *The Frock-Coated Communist: The Life and Times of the Original Champagne Socialist* (London: Allen Lane, 2009), pp. 208–10. An 1870 auction notice shows that Swire had ridden regularly with the Cheshire in the previous winter: *Liverpool Mail*, 14 May 1870, p. 14; *The Australasian*, 3 September 1870, p. 17.

30 James Picton, *Memorials of Liverpool*, Volume 1 (1875), quoted in Francis E. Hyde, *Liverpool and the Mersey: An Economic History of a Port 1700–1970* (Newton Abbot: David & Charles, 1971), pp. 79–83.

31 Graeme J. Milne, *Trade and Traders in Mid-Victorian Liverpool: Mercantile Business and the Making of a World Port* (Liverpool: Liverpool University Press, 2000), p. 33.

32 *Kilvert's Diary 1870–1879: Selections from the Diary of The Rev. Francis Kilvert* Chosen, edited & introduced by William Plomer (London: Jonathan Cape, 1938), pp. 181–3. Kilvert's visit took place from 19 to 21 June 1872.

33 *Morning Chronicle*, 20 September 1854, p. 4; *Liverpool Mercury*, 22 September, p. 9.

34 For details of Tobin's deep involvement in slavery see his entry on the 'Legacies of British Slave Ownership' platform: https://www.ucl.ac.uk/lbs/person/view/42424 accessed 12 October 2017.

35 William Jardine to Sir John Tobin, 21 January 1837, in Le Pichon, *China Trade and Empire*, p. 295; *Morning Post*, 23 June 1836. I am grateful to Song-Chuan Chen for drawing my attention to this fact. Tobin had been a member of the East India Committee in 1812: *Liverpool Mercury*, 20 March 1812. Petition: Le Pichon, *China Trade and Empire*, pp. 566–7

36 *Liverpool Mercury*, 25 November 1842, 2 December 1842.

37 *The Era*, 26 January 1840, p. 219. On the *Nemesis* see Adrian G. Marshall, *Nemesis: The First Iron Warship and Her World* (Singapore: NUS Press, 2016).

38 Elizabeth Sinn, *Pacific Crossing: California Gold, Chinese Migration, and the Making of Hong Kong* (Hong Kong: Hong Kong University Press, 2013); beer: Thomas N. Layton, The *Voyage of the 'Frolic': New England Merchants and the Opium Trade* (Stanford: Stanford University Press, 1997).

39 Sinn, *Pacific Crossing*, p. 1.

40 J. S. Swire to Mary Warren, 15 November 1879, recalling that this occurred 'nearly thirty years ago': JS&SL.

41 *Gore's Liverpool General Advertiser*, 6 September 1849, p.2

42 This paragraph draws on Scott P. Marler, *The Merchants' Capital: New Orleans and the Political Economy of the Nineteenth-Century South* (Cambridge: Cambridge University Press, 2013).

43 James M. Phillippo, *The United States and Cuba* (London: Pewtress & Co., 1857), pp. 301–17, quotation from p. 305.

44 Mary Martin journal, *passim*.

45 The detail comes from: *Supreme Court. Richard S. Butterfield* [et al.] *against Alexander Dennistoun* [et al.] (New York: Wm C. Bryant and Co., 1859).

46 *Times-Picayune*, 11 October 1854, p. 2; MMM, Liverpool Ship Registers, 171/1853 *Evangeline*.

47 J. S. Swire to Lang, Scott & Mackintosh, 27 May 1881: JSS I 1/5, Papers of John Swire & Sons, Special Collections and Archives, School of Oriental and African Studies [hereafter file reference only].

48 Mary Martin journal, 6 March 1856; Marriner and Hyde, *The Senior*, p. 16.

49 *Liverpool Mercury*, 6, 9, 16, 27 April 1852.

50 Dickens, 'Off to the Diggings!', *Household Words*, 17 July 1852, p. 121, quoted in Geoffrey Serle, *The Golden Age: A History of the Colony of Victoria, 1851–1861* (Melbourne: Melbourne University Press, 1963), p. 38. Serle's book is a richly detailed account of course of events.

51 Mary Martin journal, 1854 *passim*.

52 Mountford, *Britain, China and Colonial Australia* p. 48; George Henry Wathen, *The Golden Colony, or Victoria in 1854* (London: Longman, Brown, Green, and Longmans, 1855), pp. 21, 31, 38; *Punch*, 1 May 1852, p. 185.

53 *Newcastle Journal*, 17 June 1854, pp. 4–5; *The Argus*, 22 December 1854, p. 4; *Sydney Morning Herald*, 11 December 1854, p. 4; *The Argus*, 23 December 1854, pp. 1, 8; Mary Martin journal, 24 July 1854, quoted in Charlotte Havilland and Maisie Shun Wah, *Swire: One Hundred and Fifty Years in Australia* (Sydney: John Swire & Sons Pty. Ltd., 2005), p. 13.

54 Havilland and Wah, *Swire*, pp. 11–13; *The Argus*, 8 January 1856; Chamber: 12 July 1855, p. 4; Jury: 12 August 1856, p. 6; Hunting: *The Australasian*, 24 August 1918, p. 15; *The Age*, 23 August 1879, p. 4; *The Age*, 28 September 1857, p. 5.

55 Swire re-encountered them in later life: J. S. Swire to Mary Warren, 21 August 1895: JS&SL.

56 Such as a clerk, David Ogilvy Palmer, son of a widowed neighbour, who arrived in late 1859, and would become principal of the Adelaide branch of Lorimer, Rome and Co.: *Evening Journal*, 9 December 1859, p. 3; 1851 Census; on O'Brien's responsibilities see the report on 'Learmonth and Others v Swire' in *The Age*, 22 June 1860, p. 6; William: Mary Martin journal, 4 September 1855, 9 October 1855.

57 J. S. Swire to Mary Warren, 24 July 1881: JS&SL.

58 *The Argus*, 8 December 1859, p. 4; 11 January 1859, p. 8.

59 SS *Australasian*: Capt. H. Parker and Frank C. Owen, *Mail and Passenger steamships of the Nineteenth Century* (Philadelphia: J. B. Lippincott, 1928), p. 24; *Morning Chronicle*, 6 August 1858, p. 4; *North Wales Chronicle*, 14 August 1858, p. 8; *Morning Advertiser*, 16 August 1858, p. 8; *Morning Journal*, 23 October 1858, p. 4.

60 *Liverpool Mail*, 4 September 1858, p. 2; Geoffrey Blainey, *The Tyranny of Distance: How Distance Shaped Australia's History* (Melbourne: Macmillan, 1968), pp. 206–11; Johnston & Paul v The Royal Mail Steam Packet Company, 21, 25 November 1867, *Law Journal Reports for the year 1868*:

Common Law and Equitable Jurisdiction ... (London: Edward Bret Ince, 1868), pp. 37–50.

61 Bank of England Archives, C129/17, Liverpool Branch: Letter Book, William Fletcher, Memorandum 10590, 29 August 1862; Bleasdale and Shun Wah, *Swire*, p. 15.

62 Dissolution: *The Argus*, 2 July 1861, p. 3; Lorimer was in Liverpool during the census of 7 April 1861: TNA, RG 9/2708; folio 73, p. 36; *The Argus*, 11 May 1858, p. 4; Marriner and Hyde, *The Senior*, p. 50; *The Age*, 8 July 1861, p. 3; on Lorimer see C. R. Badger, 'Sir James Lorimer (1831–1889)', in *Australian Dictionary of National Biography* online: http://adb.anu.edu. au/biography/lorimer-sir-james-4038;

63 Advertisement in *Liverpool Mail*, 5 May 1860, p. 2; Roy Anderson, *White Star* (Prescot: T. Stephenson & Sons, 1964), pp. 1–39.

64 Details of Swire Brothers agency work 1859–61 extracted from searches of the Australian press in the National Library of Australia's Trove platform: http://trove.nla.gov.au/newspaper/.

65 Davison, *Marvelous Melbourne*, p. 26.

66 Christopher Munn, *Anglo-China: Chinese People and British Rule in Hong Kong, 1841–1880* (Richmond: Curzon Press, 2001); John M. Carroll, *A Concise History of Hong Kong* (Lanham: Rowman & Littlefield, 2007); for a broad account of these Australian-China connections see: Mountford, *Britain, China and Colonial Australia*.

67 S. G. Checkland, 'An English merchant house in China after 1841', *Business History Review*, 27 (153), pp. 158–89, quotations from pp. 161, 189, 165.

68 *Liverpool Mercury*, 11 January 1866, p. 8; see also *Liverpool Daily Post*, 6 April 1866, p. 8.

69 See correspondence in Harvard Business School, Baker Library Special Collections, Heard Family Business Records, Augustine Heard & Company correspondence [hereafter Augustine Heard Archives], Carton LV-1, Folder 411865, Hong Kong from Butterfield Bros, Bradford; also, Augustine Heard Sr, London, to Butterfield Brothers, Bradford, 20 July 1864: JMA, MS JM/ B6/10.

70 Milne, *Trade and Traders in Mid-Victorian Liverpool*, pp. 149–51.

71 Prospectus: Bank of England Archives, C129/17, Liverpool Branch: Letter Book, William Fletcher, Memorandum 10953, 29 October 1863.

72 *Saturday Review*, 11 June 1864, p. 710. On the controversy see also *Liverpool Mercury*, 24 March 1864; *The Economist*, 26 March 1864, pp. 383–4, and also TNA, C 16/193/D34, 'Daunt v Australian and Eastern Navigation Company Ltd', 1864.

73 *The Australian and Eastern Navigation Company Limited, Statement of the Directors* (1864), in Swire MISC 88, ACC 2012/102: JS&S; Baines evidence: London Stock Exchange Commission, *Minutes of Evidence taken before the*

Commissioners together with appendix, index, and analysis (London: George
Edward Eyre and William Spottiswoode, 1878), pp. 229–34.

74 Market-rigging: David Kynaston, *The City of London*, Volume 1: *A World of
its Own, 1815–1890* (London: Chatto & Windus, 1994), pp. 223–24; more
widely on these new market institutions and the morality and behaviour
of participants see Paul Johnson, *Making the Market: Victorian Origins of
Corporate Capitalism* (Cambridge: Cambridge University Press, 2010).

75 Alfred Holt, 'Fragmentary Autobiography of Alfred Holt … written mainly
in January 1879' (Privately printed, 1911), pp. 46–7.

CHAPTER 3 ORIENTATION

1 T. R. Banister, 'A History of External Trade of China, 1834–1881', in
China. Maritime Customs, *Decennial reports on the trade … of the Ports
Open to foreign commerce, 1922–31* (Shanghai: Statistical Department of the
Inspectorate General of Customs, 1933), p. 58; Bickers, *Scramble for China*,
p. 175; Thomas Hanbury, 5 February 1865, in *Letters of Sir Thomas Hanbury*
(London: West, Newman & Co., 1913), p. 114.

2 William Frederick Mayers and N. B. Dennys, *The Treaty Ports of China and
Japan …* (London, Trübner and Co., 1867), p. 372.

3 Consul: *Commercial Reports from H.M. Consuls in China, Japan and Siam
1865* Cmd. 3707 1866 (London: 1866), pp. 54–5; *Shanghai Trade Report
for 1866*, p. 848. Fast living and clerks: Hanbury letters 3 August 1865,
15 December 1869, in *Letters of Sir Thomas Hanbury*, pp. 124, 205; stable:
Alexander Cock's, *North China Daily News* [*NCDN*], 3 January 1865, p. 94;
furniture: William Hargreaves, part of the wider Liverpool trading network:
North China Herald [*NCH*], 18 October 1870, pp. 295–9, 29 September
1871, pp. 740–43; Jardines: R. W. Little to Father and Mother, 10 January
1867, Little papers.

4 This and succeeding paragraphs draw on *NCDN*, 28 November,
30 November 1866, and *NCH*, 1 December, 8 December 1866.

5 Charles M. Dyce, *Personal Reminiscences of Thirty Years' Residence in the
Model Settlement Shanghai, 1870–1900* (London: Chapman & Hall, 1906),
pp. 21–2; *The China Sea Directory*, Volume 3 (London: Hydrographic
Office, 1874), pp. 340–64.

6 Russell & Co. to P. S. Forbes, 6 June 1866: Baker Library Special Collections,
Forbes Family Business Records [hereafter HBS, Forbes Papers], MSS 766,
Box 3, folder 15. The largest building, the 'Stone house', the Shanghai
partner's home, although decrepit, is today the oldest surviving building on
the Bund.

7 Dyce, *The Model Settlement*, pp. 41–9; E. S. Elliston, *Shantung Road Cemetery
Shanghai 1846–1868* (Shanghai, 1946). Theatre: R. W. Little to father and
mother, 20 February 1867, Little papers; *NCH*, 8 December 1866, p. 194.

8 *NCH*, 8 December 1866, pp. 195–6; Mayers and Dennys, *The Treaty ports of China and Japan*, p. 374.

9 *Commercial reports from Her Majesty's Consuls in China 1864* (London: Harrison and Sons, 1866); *Commercial Reports from H. M. Consuls in China, Japan and Siam 1865 Cmd. 3707 1866* (London: 1866).

10 W. H. Medhurst, *The Foreigner in Far Cathay* (London: Edward Stanford, 1872), pp. 19–20.

11 A. F. Heard to G. B. Dixwell, 28 December 1866: HBS, Heard papers, HL-28.

12 J. S. Swire, Memorandum, 13 July 1886: JSS I 1/7. It was advertised in London around mid-October: JSS I 7/1: London Cash Book, 1866–, entry for 15 October 1866: 'Butterfield & Swire Advertising William & Smith 15s'.

13 See the precis of 1865–7 correspondence on Butterfield Brothers and Butterfield & Swire's Yokohama business in: Augustine Heard Archives, Carton 30, Folder 211865, 'Copies of letters re: Butterfield Accounts'; and the file 'Correspondence with Butterfield & Swire and others', Correspondence of Augustine Heard & Co.': JM/D8:3; Liverpool Record Office, Holt family papers [hereafter LRO, Holt papers], 2/52, Alfred Holt Diary, 1 October 1866.

14 *NCH*, 29 September 1866, p. 154; McLean to Leonard, 4 August 1864, Transcript of David McLean, letter books, Volumes I–III, 1862–1873: SOAS, MS 380401, Box 3 Folder 11.

15 *London Gazette*, 4 April 1865, p. 1910; *Liverpool Commercial List* 1866 p.12; *NCH*, 15 December 1866, p. 199, 22 December 1866, p. 203; *NCDN*, 31 December 1866, p. 3; *Liverpool Daily Post*, 19 January 1867. On Smith see Orchard, *Liverpool's Legion of Honour*, pp. 644–5. To add to the joy, the receiving ship captain, William Roundy, was also stealing balls of opium from each chest, including those owned by the Hongkong & Shanghai Bank's agent: McLean letters 6 May and 12 June, Transcript of David McLean, letter books, Volumes I–III, 1862–1873: SOAS, MS 380401, Box 3 Folder 11.

16 'To M. Daley, Foochow', J. S. Swire to A. M. Daly, Fuzhou, 20 June 1867: HBS, Augustine Heard Archives, Carton LV-22, Folder 13, 1865–1870.

17 Albert F. Heard to G. B. Dixwell, 1 January 1867: Heard to A. M. Daly, 29 January 1867: HBS, Heard papers, 28-3; J. S. Swire to Lang, Scott & Mackintosh, 4 November 1881: JSS I 1/5. The issue of the Yokohama losses persisted until the collapse of Heards in 1876 and the winding up of the firm's business: J. S. Swire to R. Holt, 19 December 1874, J. S. Swire to A. Heard, 19 December 1874: JSS I 1/4; Memo on 'Heards Estate', 8 August 1881: JSS I 1/5.

18 R. I. Fearon to Albert F. Heard, 23 January 1873: HBS, Heard papers, HM 43-3.

19 *NCDN*, 3 January 1867, p. 1.

20 Holt, 'Fragmentary Autobiography, p. 48.

21 Thomson letters of 10 July 1866, 21 September 1866, quoted in Baird, *Liverpool China Traders*, p. 60; *Hongkong Daily Press*, 30 June 1866, p. 3;

NCDN 21 September 1866, p. 3; Kidd, quoted Baird, *Liverpool China Traders*, p. 66; Singapore: A. Jackson and C. E. Wurtzburg, *The History of Mansfield & Company*, Part 1, *1868–1924* (Singapore: n.l., 1952), p. 1.

22 *NCDN*, 20, 21, 24, 25 December 1866; LRO, Holt papers, 2/24, Instructions to Captain Middleton, 14 April 1864.

23 For example, Captain James Hardie, of the Shanghai Steam Navigation Company: the reference is in Butterfield & Swire Shanghai to John Swire & Sons, 15 February 1872: JSS I 2/15.

24 A. O. Gay, Yokohama, to Butterfield & Swire, Shanghai, 31 December 1866: JMA, D8/3.

25 Butterfield & Swire Shanghai to Augustine Heard & Co, Shanghai, 4 May 1867: JMA, DB/3.

26 J. S. Swire to William Lang, 20 September 1869: JSS I 1/1.

27 This section draws on the standard account: Yen-p'ing Hao, *The Comprador in Nineteenth-Century China: Bridge between East and West* (Cambridge, MA: Harvard East Asian series, Center for East Asian Studies, Harvard University, 1970).

28 John Wong, *Global Trade in the Nineteenth Century: The House of Houqua and the Canton System* (Cambridge: Cambridge University Press, 2016).

29 *NCDN*, 31 December 1866, p. 3.

30 On the evolution of the trading environment see: Eiichi Motono, *Conflict and Cooperation in Sino-British Business, 1860–1911: The Impact of the Pro-British Commercial Network in Shanghai* (London: Palgrave, 2000); on Zheng: Hao, *Comprador in Modern China*, p. 282, n. 78.

31 R. I. Fearon to Albert F. Heard, 20 February, 1868: HBS, Heard papers, HM 43-3. William Pethick, one of these later worked for several decades for Chinese statesman Li Hongzhang.

32 G. B. Dixwell to Augustine Heard (Hong Kong), 30 October 1868: JMA D8/3.

33 *Shenbao*, 9 May 1877; *NCH*, 22 January 1880, pp. 57–60. Hop Kee (or Hop-Kee) might refer to the name of Zhuo's own firm.

34 'Lauo Felecha': *NCH*, 15 July 1865, p. 109; 'Tai-Koo Yuen Hong': *NCDN*, 3 December 1866, p. 1. Writing over 40 years later, J. H. Scott attributed the choice of name to Thomas Taylor Meadows, then British consul at Niuzhuang, the only member of the consular service who had studied Chinese before taking the job, and an erudite, though difficult, man. It is not clear how this might have transpired, however: Scott, *A Short Account of the Firm of John Swire & Sons*, p. 3. A better candidate might be his merchant brother, John A. T. Meadows, then living in Tianjin, who had certainly in the past advertised himself as a translator: John A. T. Meadows, Circular, 24 June 1848: HBS, Augustine Heard & Company, China Records, Series II, A-18, Circulars Canton.

35 Cash Book, 10 October 1866–1867: JSS I 7/1.

36 John Hodgson, *Textile Manufacture, and other industries, in Keighley* (Keighley: A. Hey, 1879), pp. 104–6; Charlotte Brontë to Revd Patrick Brontë, 2 June 1852, in Margaret Smith (ed.), *The Letters of Charlotte Brontë: With a Selection of Letters by Family and Friends*, Volume 3: *1852–1855* (Oxford: Oxford University Press, 2004), pp. 50–51; *Bradford Observer*, 3 June 1852, p. 6; John Lock and Canon W. T. Dixon, *A Man of Sorrow: The Life, Letters and Times of the Rev. Patrick Brontë, 1777–1861* (London: Nelson, 1965), pp. 432–9; grasping: J. S. Swire to John Cunfliffe, 26 February 1877: JSS I 1/4.

37 G. B. Dixwell, Shanghai, to Augustine Heard Sr, Hong Kong, 13 March 1869: JMA, D8:3; *Bradford Observer*, 1 July 1869, p. 5; *Bradford Daily Telegraph*, 2 July 1869, p. 2; *Halifax Courier*, 3 July 1869, p. 5. In late 1868 Butterfield retired altogether from his business interests: *London and China Telegraph*, 4 January 1869, p. 6; see also *Leeds Mercury*, 16 January 1878, p. 7.

38 The firm's earliest surviving cash book, which commences from 10 October 1866, does suggest that Samuel Martin, William Swire's father-in-law, had substantial capital in the firm, for he withdraws from it as regularly as the Swire brothers: Cash Book 1866-7 *passim*: JSS I 7/1.

39 *London and China Telegraph*, 4 January 1869, p. 6. This partnership was dissolved in 1873, and on Holt's bankruptcy in 1876 John Swire & Sons became involved in a legal dispute that settled Redman's continued liability for bills due on goods consigned under a 31 December 1868 agreement: *The Weekly Reporter*, 2 September 1876, pp. 1069–73.

40 LRO, Holt papers, 2/52, Holt diary, 24 October 1867; for a fine exploration of this world see Emma Goldsmith, 'In Trade: Wealthy Business Families in Glasgow and Liverpool, 1870–1930' (Northwestern University: Unpublished PhD dissertation, 2017).

41 J. S. Swire to William Lang, 20 September 1869: JSS I 1/1. William Moir (1825–72) was married to Lang's eldest sister, Emma. Moir's nephew worked in Bombay-based mercantile partnership with one of Lang's brothers, two others of whom also worked in Bombay.

42 Milne, *Trade and Traders in Mid-Victorian Liverpool*, pp. 151–61.

43 G. B. Dixwell, Shanghai, to Augustine Heard Sr, Hong Kong, 7 July 1869: JMA, D8/3; J. S. Swire to J. H. Scott, W. Lang and E. Mackintosh, 4 July 1881: JSS I 1/5; rotten: C. W. Warren, Birley & Co. Hong Kong, to Rathbone, 13 July 1874, University of Liverpool, Special Collections and Archives, Rathbone Papers [hereafter RP] XXIV.3 (9) 104; Newby career: *NCDN*, 15 January 1906, p. 7.

44 Scott, *Short Account*, p. 10; *Hongkong Daily Press*, 6 April 1868; Michael Clark, 'Alexander Collie: The Ups and Downs of Trading with the Confederacy', *The Northern Mariner/Le marin du nord*, 19:2 (2009), pp. 125–48; Angus family: *Aberdeen Journal*, 13 November 1878, p. 5; *Aberdeen Weekly Journal*, 4 November 1895; *Daily Telegraph* (Sydney), 9 January 1917, p. 6.

45 Marriner and Hyde, *The Senior*, p. 43.

46 J. S. Swire to J. Keith Angus, 21 April 1876: JSS I 1/4.

47 *NCH*, 21 September 1867, p. 263; *NCH*, 13 September 1873, p. 209; *NCH*, 20 April 1872 p. 314; Butterfield & Swire Shanghai to John Swire & Sons, 15 February 1872; JSS I 2/15.

48 Kerrie L. Macpherson, *A Wilderness of Marshes: The Origins of Public Health in Shanghai, 1843–1893* (Hong Kong: Oxford University Press, 1987).

49 J. S. Swire to William Lang, 20 September 1869: JSS I 1/1.

50 R. W. Little to parents, 2 December 1862, Little letters; Sheila Marriner, *Rathbones of Liverpool, 1845–73* (Liverpool: Liverpool University Press, 1961), pp. 178–86.

51 Edward LeFevour, *Western Enterprise in late Ch'ing China: A Selective Survey of Jardine, Matheson & Company's operations, 1842–1895* (Cambridge, MA: East Asian Research Center, Harvard University, 1968), pp. 25–30; see also Stephen C. Lockwood, *Augustine Heard and Company, 1858–1862: American Merchants in China* (Cambridge, MA: East Asian Research Center, Harvard University, 1971), pp. 26–30.

52 Storage: Butterfield & Swire Shanghai to John Swire & Sons 21 March 1872: JSS I 2/15 SP; rates: 'Freight Tariff', 27 January 1883: JSS I 4/1/1; *NCDN*, 17 December, 31 December 1866.

53 *China Mail*, 24 June 1879, p. 3; on the place of opium in Chinese life see: Yangwen Zheng, *The Social Life of Opium in China* (Cambridge: Cambridge University Press, 2005).

54 Dennys and Mayers, *Treaty Ports of China and Japan*, p. 12. This section draws more widely from the description of Hong Kong provided in this guide.

55 Christopher Cowell, 'The Hong Kong Fever of 1843: Collective Trauma and the Reconfiguring of Colonial Space', *Modern Asian Studies* 47:2 (2013), pp. 329–64; Christopher Munn, *Anglo-China: Chinese People and British Rule in Hong Kong, 1841–1880* (London: Routledge, 2001), pp. 341–58.

56 The earliest notification can be found in: *Hongkong Daily Press*, 16 May 1870, p. 3; the first ship, the *Ajax*, arrived in late June: *Hongkong Daily Press*, 10 June 1870, p. 3.

57 In 1880, to Elizabeth Rose Hampson, daughter of Liverpool's Collector of Pilotage: *Hongkong Daily Press*, 27 December 1880.

58 J. S. Swire to Lang and Scott, 3 August 1877: JSS I 1/4.

CHAPTER 4 STRANGE REVOLUTION

1 This section draws extensively from Kwang-Ching Liu, *Anglo-American Steamship Rivalry in China, 1862–1874* (Cambridge, MA: Harvard University Press, 1962), and Anne Reinhardt, *Navigating Semi-Colonialism: Shipping, Sovereignty, and Nation-Building in China, 1860–1937* (Cambridge, MA: Harvard University Press, 2018).

2 Quoted in Liu, *Anglo-American Steamship Rivalry*, p. 14.

3 Robert B. Forbes, *Personal Reminiscences* (2nd edn, Boston: Little, Brown & Co., 1882), p. 367.

4 *The journey of Augustus Raymond Margary* ... (London: Macmillan, 1876), pp. 74, 88; R. W. Little letter, 2 May 1864, Little papers.

5 Quoted in Liu, *Anglo-American Steamship Rivalry in China*, p. 73.

6 *NCH*, 11 September 1868, p. 442; 19 September 1868, pp. 455–6.

7 J. S. Swire to Scott and Harrison, 29 September 1871; John Swire & Sons to Butterfield & Swire Shanghai, 22 March 1872: JSS I 1/2; HBS Forbes Papers, F. B. Forbes to E. S. Cunningham, 11 November 1872.

8 'What people are saying', *NCDN*, 16 January 1872, p. 47; *London and China Telegraph*, 22 January 1872, p. 62; University of Liverpool, Special Collections and Archives, Rathbone Papers, T. Guy Paget to Samuel Rathbone, 1 February 1872, RPXXIV.3.74; F. B. Forbes letters to: William Forbes, 25 January 1872; King, 14 February 1872; William Forbes, 18 April 1872; Cordier, 17 August 1872: HBS, Forbes Papers, N-5. Heards: G. B. Dixon to Albert F. Heard, 12 December 1871: HBS, Heard papers, GM 1-9.

9 *Daily Alta*, 2 May 1874, p. 1.

10 Arrival: *NCH*, 1 January 1874, p. 1; from Hankou: *NCH*, 22 January 1874, p. 57; to Hong Kong: *Hongkong Daily Press*, 27 January 1874, p. 3.

11 Survey from: 'China Navigation Company Review of Leases', 2 August 1873: JSS III, 8/2, PS.

12 Butterfield & Swire Shanghai to John Swire & Sons, 13 July 1872: JSS I 2/15.

13 Augustine Heard Jr, Hong Kong, to G. B. Dixwell, Shanghai, 5 March 1870: HBS, Heard papers, GL 4-3; Butterfield & Swire to John Swire & Sons, 13 July 1872: JSS I 2/15,SP.

14 U.S.N. Co. Statement of Accounts, *NCH*, 6 September 1873, p. 197; John Swire & Sons to Butterfield & Swire Shanghai, 13 January 1873: JSS I 1/2; dollar premium: Hao, *Commercial Revolution*, pp. 35–40.

15 Liu, *Anglo-American Steamship Rivalry in China*, p. 72.

16 Butterfield & Swire Shanghai to John Swire & Sons, 13 July 1872: JSS I 2/15; John Swire & Sons to Butterfield & Swire Shanghai, 13 January 1873: JSS I 1/2.

17 'Kiukiang Trade Report for the Year 1873', in *Reports on the Trade at the Treaty Ports of China for the Year 1873* (Shanghai: Imperial Maritime Customs Statistical Department, 1874), p. 29.

18 The conflict is covered in Liu, *Anglo-American Steamship Rivalry in China*, pp. 119–29; the course and tenor of the negotiations in Liverpool and in London is captured in correspondence copied to Lang in JSS I 1/2.

19 Report in *London and China Telegraph*, 21 July 1873, p. 475; *Shenbao*, 16 April 1873, p. 2.

20 Reinhardt, *Navigating Semi-Colonialism*, p. 34; 'Ningpo Trade Report for the Year 1873' in *Reports on the Trade at the Treaty Ports of China for the Year 1873*, p. 77.

21 CNCo Shareholders' Register No. 1: JSS III 17/1.

22 Bryna Goodman, *Native Place, City and Nation: Regional Networks and Identities in Shanghai, 1853–1937* (Berkeley: University of California Press, 1995); Kaori Abe, *Chinese Middlemen in Hong Kong's Colonial Economy, 1830–1890* (London: Routledge, 2017).

23 This draws on: Yen-Ping Hao, *The Comprador in Nineteenth-Century China: Bridge Between East and West* (Cambridge, MA: Council on East Asian Studies, Harvard University, 1970), pp. 196–7; Guo Wu, *Zheng Guanying: Merchant Reformer of Late Qing China and His Influence on Economics, Politics, and Society* (Amherst: Cambria Press, 2010), pp. 21–2; Goodman, *Native Place, City and Nation*, p. 60.

24 Existing accounts confuse Endicott with his namesake and uncle, who died at sea in 1832. His medical certificate of death, the US consulate register of American Citizens, and newspaper notices, give his age at death as 51, while James Bridges Endicott's will names him, and his brother and sister, in a separate category to his children with his English wife: NARA, RG59, Consular Letters, Shanghai, Volume 42, Despatch No. 45, 2 February 1895; Will: James B. Endicott, 15 June 1870: Massachusetts, Wills and Probate Records, 1635–1991, via Ancestry.com; NARA RG84, Consulate Files, Shanghai, Volume 0797, 'Register of American Citizens, 1880–1904.

25 Christopher Munn and Carl T. Smith, 'Ng Akew', in May Holdsworth and Christopher Munn (eds), *Hong Kong Dictionary of Biography* (Hong Kong: Hong Kong University Press, 2011), p. 33; Carl T. Smith, 'Abandoned into prosperity: Women on the Fringe of Expatriate Society', in Helen F. Siu, *Merchants' Daughters: Women, Commerce and Regional Culture in South China* (Hong Kong: Hong Kong University Press, 2010), pp. 136–9.

26 R. I. Fearon to Albert F. Heard, 16 January 1873: HBS, Heard papers, HM 43-3; Albert F. Heard to George B. Dixwell, 22 October 1868: HBS, Heard papers, GL 4-3; Butterfield & Swire Shanghai to John Swire & Sons, 6 February 1873: JSS I, 2/15. His Chinese name was Yan Erji 晏尔吉.

27 Liu, *Anglo-American Steamship Rivalry in China*, p. 131; Zhang Zhongli et al., *The Swire Group in Old China*, Appendix 1, pp. 298–300.

28 F. B. Forbes to W. S. Fitz, 10 April 1873: HBS, Forbes Papers, N-7.

29 *Commercial Reports from Her Majesty's Consuls in China, Japan, and Siam 1865* (London: Harrison, & Sons, 1866), p. 196; *Shenbao*, 8 April 1873. For more on these changes see Yen P'ing Hao, *The Commercial Revolution in Nineteenth-Century China: The Rise of Sino-Western Mercantile Capitalism* (Berkeley: University of California Press, 1986), pp. 199–202.

30 Zhang Zhongli et al. (eds), *The Swire Group in Old China*, pp. 214–16.

31 *China Mail*, 24 June 1879, p. 3, 25 June 1879, p. 3.

32 John Swire & Sons to Butterfield & Swire Shanghai, 15 November 1872; Butterfield & Swire Shanghai to John Swire & Sons, 9 January 1873, 6 November 1873, 18 December 1873: JSS I 2/15. Holt had found this, too. You might need to buy a separate cooking range for Chinese passengers, if you pick them up, he had told the captain on the *Agamemnon*'s first voyage, but 'as I believe rice and tea is their chief food' this should be inexpensive: Alfred Holt to Captain Middleton, SS *Agamemnon*, 14 April 1866: Holt papers, 2/24.

33 H. Kopsch 'Kiukiang Trade Report for the year 1873', in *Reports on Trade at the Treaty Ports in China for the year 1873* (Shanghai: Imperial Maritime Customs Statistical Department, 1874) p. 32; W. M. H., 'Reminiscences of the Opening of Shanghae to Foreign Trade', *Chinese and Japanese Repository*, 2, pp. 85–7.

34 Memorandum, 3 October 1874, JSS I 1/4.

35 Liu, *Anglo-American Steamship Rivalry in China*, pp. 131–5, 146–7; Marriner and Hyde, *The Senior*, pp. 62–4; competition: J. S. Swire letters in: J. S. Swire to Forbes, 24 April 1873, in John Swire & Sons to Butterfield & Swire, 25 April 1873; John Swire & Sons to P. S. Forbes, 19 June 1873, and 7 August 1873: JSS I 1/2.

36 Secrecy: F. B. Forbes to Edward Cunningham, 6 January 1875: HBS, Forbes papers, N-11.

37 J. S. Swire to Lang, 22 April 1884, J. S. Swire to Gamwell, 25 April and 25 May 1884, J. S. Swire to H. B. Endicott and J. L. Brown, 17 May 1884, all in JSS I 3/2.

38 Kwang-ching Liu, 'British-Chinese Steamship Rivalry in China, 1873–85', in C. D. Cowan (ed.), *The Economic Development of China and Japan* (London: Allen & Unwin, 1964), pp. 52–8; for China Merchants see: Albert Feuerwerker, *China's Early Industrialization: Sheng Hsuan-huai (1844–1916) and Mandarin Enterprise* (Cambridge, MA: Harvard University Press, 1958), especially pp. 96–188; J. S. Swire to W. Lang, 2 October 1874: JSS I 1/4; R. I. Fearon to Albert F. Heard 13 February 1873, 7 June 1873: HBS, Heard papers, HM 43-3

39 *Shenbao*, 18 July 1874, p. 2; 3 October 1874, pp. 3–4.

40 J. S. Swire to Scott, 27 November 1876, JSS I 1/4; LRO, Holt papers, 2/52, Holt diary, 15 September 1866.

41 Hyde, *Blue Funnel*, pp. 20–39; Falkus, *Blue Funnel Legend*, p. 103.

42 *Hongkong Daily Press*, 22 January 1867; *NCH*, 23 February 1867; *Daily Alta*, 21 March 1867, p. 1; J. S. Swire to Swire Brothers, New York, 23 June 1875; J. S. Swire to Lang, 19 November 1875: JSS I 1/4.

43 Detail from correspondence in: HBS, Heard Archive, folders SI-16, SI-17.

44 J. S. Swire to James Dodds, 16 September 1875, J. S. Swire to Lang and Scott, 28 January and 15 June 1876: JSS I 1/4; J. S. Swire to Lang 6 February 1879: JSS I 1/5. Dodds's lasting claim to fame would be his role as

a founding director of the Japan Brewery Company, which later became the Kirin Brewery Company.

45 J. S. Swire to James Lorimer. JSS I 1/4.

46 The cash books show items for 'John Swire & Sons London' cease to be recorded from 1 July 1870, and 'John Swire & Sons Liverpool' commence, the firm at that point having become London-based. The lease on the Billiter Street premises was renewed annually on 24 June. The first few appearances of the address linked to the firm are in advertisements for Blue Funnel sailings in August 1870: *Manchester Guardian*, 3 August 1870. From November no reference is made in sailing notices to the Liverpool house: *Lloyds' List*, 2 November 1870, p. 1.

47 J. S. Swire to J. P. O'Brien, 5 June 1875: JSS I 1/4.

48 This section draws from notebooks on staff appointments in JSS I 7/7/1, and biographical details from various genealogical platforms. The staff books record names, salaries and benefits (if any), in most cases have the date an appointment started, and some record departures, or transfers to China. Occasionally they record an address or prior employment. A separate folder contains copies of the contracts men signed who were heading to Asia. No personnel records, as such, survive.

49 This paragraph draws on Benjamin Guinness Orchard, *The Clerks of Liverpool* (Liverpool: J. Collinson, 1871), with details from pp. 4, 7.

50 Milne, *Trade and Traders*, p. 58.

51 Pledge: P. Phillips, 18 September 1876: JSS I 1/4; first class clerk: J. S. Swire to Salisbury, 18 September 1877: JSS I 1/5; Loan: J. S. Swire to Richard Pickup, 22 November 1879, 18 September 1880: JSS I 1/5; accountant: J. S. Swire to Thomas Ball, 15 September 1880: JSS I 1/5; separation: John Swire & Sons to Butterfield & Swire Shanghai, 15 March 1878: JSS I 1/5; Poor Young: J. S. Swire to Alfred Holt & Co, 17 September 1881: JSS I 1/5.

52 J. S. Swire to J.P. O'Brien, 20 May 1879: JSS I 1/4.

53 Orchard, *The Clerks of Liverpool*, p. 4.

54 J. S. Swire to Lang, Scott and Mackintosh, 3 August 1876, 21 August 1877, JSS I 1/4.

55 F. B. Forbes to William Howell Forbes, 2 January 1873, quoted in Liu, *Anglo-American Steamship Rivalry in China*, p. 121; Frederick Cornes to Winstanley, 29 August 1873, in Cornes Letter book, 13, in Peter Davies, *The Business, Life and Letters of Frederick Cornes: Aspects of the Evolution of Commerce in Modern Japan, 1861–1910* (London: Global Oriental, 2008); J. S. Swire to John Cunliffe, 26 February 1887, JSS I 1/4. McLean letter, 6 July 1870, Transcript of David McLean, letter books, Volumes I–III, 1862–1873, SOAS, MS 380401, Box 3 Folder 11; John Swire & Sons to Lang, 12 March 1877, JSS I 1/4. For the record, Butterfield died of typhoid in Haworth on 26 June 1869, fate dealing poetic justice to a robust opponent

of sanitary reform in the village. Swire seems to have attended the funeral, for on 30 June 1869, shortly after Butterfield's death the cash book records 'JSS ... Exp to Bradford RSB 60s': Cash Book No. 1, JSS I 7/4/1.

56 J. S. Swire to Alfred Holt, 10 April 1875 and draft letter, JSS I 1/4; *The Times*, 13 April 1875, p. 10; see also G. U. Sands to Sturgis, 18 December 1875: HBS, Sands papers, MSS:766, Volume 11.

57 G. U. Sands to R. Sturgis, 18 [illeg] 1875, in: HBS, Baker Library, MSS:766, George U. Sands Business Records, Vol. 8; 'Business competition', *Straits Times*, 7 August 1875, p. 1.

58 J. S. Swire to Scott, 24 June 1875, JSS I 1/4.

59 Hong: J. S. Swire to Scott, 2 October 1876; Horses: J. S. Swire to Lang, 22 May 1876; Harrison: J. S. Swire to Lang, Scott, Smith and Hall, 6 November 1875: JSS I 1/4; *Hongkong Daily Press*, 24 June 1875.

CHAPTER 5 SWEET SMELL OF HONG KONG

1 J. S. Swire to Lang, Scott & Mackintosh, 9 November 1881: JSS I 1/5.

2 *Hongkong Telegraph*, 31 March 1882; J. S. Swire to Alfred Holt, 5 December 1879: JSS I 1/5; J. S. Swire to Mary Warren, 24 July 1881: JS&SL.

3 Phobia: J. S. Swire to Gamwell, 4 March 1884, JSS1 3/2.

4 John Swire & Sons to H. I. Butterfield, 16 November 1874: JSS I 1/4.

5 Kwang-ching Liu, 'British-Chinese steamship rivalry', in Cowan (ed.) *The Economic Development of China and Japan*, pp. 58, 63–4.

6 *Hongkong Daily Press*, 21 July 1875, p. 3; John Swire & Sons to Chairman and Directors, Hongkong & Macao Steam Boat Company, 15 September 1875, in J. S. Swire to J. H. Scott, 15 September 1875: JSS I 1/4.

7 J. S. Swire to Alfred Holt, 9 January 1880: Holt papers; on the Boat Company and the rivalry see: H. W. Dick and S. A. Kentwell, *Beancaker to Boxboat Steamship Companies in Chinese Waters* (Melbourne: Nautical Association of Australia, 1988), pp. 145–62. An agreement reached in October 1879 saw Swires agree to accept a three-eighths share to the Boat Company's five-eighths.

8 Kwang-ching Liu, 'British-Chinese steamship rivalry', in Cowan (ed.), *Economic Development of China and Japan*, pp. 59–60.

9 *NCH*, 25 January 1877, p. 77.

10 *The Journey of Augustus Raymond Margary* ... (London: Macmillan, 1876), pp. 102–3, 108.

11 S. T. Wang, *The Margary Affair and the Chefoo Agreement* (London: Oxford University Press, 1940); Bickers, *Scramble for China*, pp. 252–5.

12 *NCH*, 18 January 1877, p. 49.

13 *Office Series, No. 4, Parts 1–2, Chinkiang: China Navigation Company's hulk "Cadiz"* (Shanghai: Statistical Dept. of the Inspectorate General, 1876–77). Some of this material was also published in *Correspondence relating to the*

       Hulk "Cadiz" at the port of Chinkiang, China (Shanghai: *North China Herald*, 1877). A pithy survey of the affair can be found Stanley Wright, *Hart and the Chinese Customs* (Belfast: Queen's University Press, 1950), pp. 434–4.

14   J. S. Swire to Earl of Derby, 12 July 1877: JSS I 1/4; Robert Hart to James Duncan Campbell, 8 February 1877, in John King Fairbank, Katherine Frost Bruner and Elizabeth MacLeod Matheson (eds), *The I.G. in Peking: Letters of Robert Hart Chinese Maritime Customs 1868–1907*, Volume 1 (Cambridge, MA: Belknap Press of Harvard University Press, 1975), pp. 237–8.

15   On the service see P. D. Coates, *The China Consuls: British Consular Officers, 1843–1943* (Hong Kong: Oxford University Press, 1988).

16   Butterfield & Swire Shanghai to Secretary of State, 31 January 1877, in Shanghai No. 7, 31 January 1877: TNA, FO 228/592; J. S. Swire to Earl of Derby, 12 July 1877: JSS I 1/4.

17   Others had not forgotten the 'easy life' on board this steamer which had once met the company's ships from Suez at Hong Kong, and which had brought many foreigners to Shanghai for the first time: *NCH*, 29 November 1889, p. 656.

18   See *NCH*, 17 October 1879, p. 388.

19   Shanghai No. 65, 12 July 1877, Shanghai Intelligence report, 15 January to 30 June 1877, including 'Steam Fleet of China Merchants Steam Navigation Company', Enclosure 3, 12 July 1877: TNA, FO 228/593.

20   Campbell to Hart, 9 March 1877, in Chen Xiafei and Han Rongfang (chief eds), *Archives of China's Imperial Maritime Customs: Confidential Correspondence between Robert Hart and James Duncan Campbell 1874–1907* (Beijing: Foreign Languages Press, 1990), Volume 1, pp. 260–61.

21   Hart to Campbell, 5 August 1877, Fairbank et al. (eds), *The I.G. in Peking*, p. 247. The impressions of Guo and his colleagues bear exploring: J. D. Frodsham (ed.), *The First Chinese Embassy to the West: The Journals of Kuo Sung-t'ao, Liu Hsi-hung and Chang Te-yi* (Oxford: Clarendon Press, 1974); Jenny Huangfu Day, *Qing Travellers to the Far West: Diplomacy and Information: Order in Late Imperial China* (Cambridge: Cambridge University Press, 2018).

22   Derby to John Swire & Sons, 14 February 1878: TNA, FO 17/801. This and file FO 17/800 contain the vast majority of papers on the affair.

23   J. S. Swire to Lang, 19 July 1877; John Swire & Sons to Butterfield & Swire Shanghai, 17 August 1877: JSS I 1/4.

24   Ciphers: undated document, pp. 212–13 in JSS I 1/4; Shanghai No. 12, 16 March 1878, Enclosure, Shanghai Intelligence Report, 1 November 1877 to 1 March 1878: TNA, FO 228/614.

25   J. S. Swire to Gamwell, 21 December 1877, 27 December 1877, and J. S. Swire to Tong King Sing, 16 May 1878: JSS I 2/2. Frederick Robison Gamwell (1835–1901) had joined the firm in 1875, having worked in

Shanghai from May 1857 until 1874, mostly in silk. In 1877 he became a partner in London, based there until his retirement in 1896.

26 J. S. Swire to Gamwell, 23 January 1878: JSS I 2/2.

27 Lang to J. S. Swire, 1 July 1879: JSS I 2/16.

28 Margery Masterson, 'Dueling, conflicting masculinities, and the Victorian Gentleman', *Journal of British Studies*, 56 (2017), pp. 605–28.

29 LeFevour, *Western Enterprise in Late Ch'ing China*, pp. 94–110; Hsien-Chun Wang, 'Merchants, Mandarins, and the Railway: Institutional Failure and the Wusong Railway, 1874–1877', *International Journal of Asian Studies*, 12:1 (2015), pp. 31–53.

30 J. S. Swire to James McGregor, 21 April 1880: JSS I 1/5. On Jardine shipping see Dick and Kentwell, *Beancaker to Boxboat*, pp. 1–60.

31 J. S. Swire to Scott, 14 March 1878, J. S. Swire to H. B. Endicott, 14 March 1878: JSS I 2/2. This excluded grains, which were being shipped to Yantai and Tianjin.

32 J. S. Swire to James McGregor, 21 April 1880, J. S. Swire to F. B. Johnson, 22 July 1880, and J. S. Swire to Lang, Scott and Mackintosh, 17 September 1880: JSS I 1/5. McGregor had married Endicott's widowed stepmother in 1875, a connection that had no bearing on these talks, but which provides an odd reminder of the relative smallness of this China coast world.

33 J. S. Swire to William Keswick, 19 January 1882: JMA, NS JM/B1/10; 'Old Pool Agreements', Yangzi: 27 May 1882; Tianjin: 20 December 1882: JMA, MA JM/F1/84; J. S. Swire to Lang, Scott & Mackintosh, 17 February 1882, quoted in *The Senior*, p. 78; J. S. Swire to Mackintosh, 22 January 1880: JSS I 1/5.

34 Sidney W. Mintz, *Sweetness and Power: The Place of Sugar in Modern History* (New York: Viking Penguin, 1985).

35 Carl T. Smith, *Chinese Christians: Elites, Middlemen, and the Church in Hong Kong* (Hong Kong: Hong Kong University Press, 1985), p. 50; *Hongkong Daily Press*, 17 July 1869, 28 January 1868.

36 'The sugar industry in Hongkong', *China Mail*, 26 November 1886; *Hongkong Telegraph*, 31 March 1882.

37 J. S. Swire to Mackintosh, 23 July 1879: JSS I 1/4; J. S. Swire to Lang, Scott and Mackintosh, 11 February 1881: JSS I 1/5.

38 J. S. Swire to Lang, Scott and Mackintosh, 11 February 1881: JSS I 1/5.

39 Geoffrey Jones, *Merchants to Multinationals: British Trading Companies in the Nineteenth and Twentieth Centuries* (Oxford: Oxford University Press, 2002), pp. 227–56; Gordon H. Boyce, *Co-operative Structures in Global Business: Communicating, Transferring Knowledge and Learning Across the Corporate Frontier* (London: Routledge, 2002), Chapter 3, 'The Holt–Swire–Scott connection, decision-support systems and staff development, 1860–1970', pp. 35–53.

40 J. S. Swire to H. I. Butterfield, 7 May 1875: JSS I 1/4. R. S. Butterfield's estate was still a subject of dispute.

41 The claim that significant amounts of Chinese capital were invested in the refinery has become entrenched in the literature, but is mistaken: Hao, *The Commercial Revolution in China*, p. 255, fn. 66.

42 J. S. Swire to A. J. Fairrie, 17 March 1880; J. S. Swire to Mackintosh, 9 April 1880: JSS I 1/5; *New York Times*, 22 June 1880, p. 8.

43 J. S. Swire to Lang, Scott and Mackintosh, 29 April 1881; John Swire & Sons to Blake, Barclay & Co, 8 July 1881: JSS I 1/5.

44 [Bruce Shepherd], *A Handbook to Hongkong* ... (Hong Kong: Kelly & Walsh, 1893), p. 111.

45 J. S. Swire to Gamwell, 4 March 1884: JSS I 3/2; *Hongkong Daily Press*, 19 March 1884.

46 This draws on, among other letters, Mackintosh to JSS, 3 July 1884, 14 August 1884, and 14 October 1884: JSS I 2/4.

47 *China Mail*, 26 January 1886, 28 January 1886, *Hongkong Daily Press*, 27 January 1886; J. S. Swire to Gamwell, 4 March 1884: JSS I 3/2.

48 Frank Dikötter, *Things Modern: Material Culture and Everyday Life in China* (London: Hurst, 2007); Karl Gerth, *China Made: Consumer Culture and the Creation of the Nation* (Cambridge, MA: Harvard University Press, 2003).

49 This paragraph draws on G. Roger Knight, *Commodities and Colonialism: The Story of Big Sugar in Colonial Indonesia, 1880–1942* (Leiden: Brill, 2013), pp. 19–23.

50 E. Mackintosh to J. S. Swire, 26 January 1886, 31 March 1885: JSS I 2/4.

51 Marriner and Hyde, *The Senior*, pp. 109–12.

52 Tai-Koo Sugar Refining Company, Ltd, Minute Book: JSSV 7/1; J. S. Swire to Gamwell, 4 March 1884: JSS I 3/2; *Hongkong Daily Press*, Supreme Court reports on 14, 20 and 25 July 1883.

53 Jung-fang Tsai, *Hong Kong in Chinese History: Community and Social Unrest in the British Colony, 1842–1913* (New York: Columbia University Press, 1993), pp. 124–46.

54 *Hongkong Daily Press*, 19 and 23 February 1886.

55 Mackintosh to J. S. Swire, 17 June 1885, 17 September 1885: JSS I 2/4.

56 For reports and comment see: *Serious disturbance at Canton: Houses on Shameen Burnt and Looted* (Hong Kong: China Mail, 1883).

57 Hart to Campbell, 6 January 1884, Fairbank et al. (eds), *I.G. in Peking*, Volume 1, p. 513.

58 Canton No. 30, 25 February 1884: TNA, FO 228/744.

59 J. S. Swire to Gamwell, 4 March 1884: JSS I 3/2; Consul Hance to Parkes, 'Separate and Confidential', 13 March 1884; Canton No. 29, 25 February 1884; Canton No. 39, 15 March 1884; Canton No. 40, 17 March 1884: TNA, FO 228/744. Diaz was removed from Canton for his own safety,

and eventually tried at Macao's Supreme Court in November 1884, when he received a three-month jail sentence, a term mitigated by his having been in custody since the incident, and as it was concluded that he had been attempting simply to enforce regulations: *Hongkong Daily Press*, 18 November 1884; *Boletim Da Provincia De Macau E Timo*, 13 December 1884, extract in Canton No. 138, 24 December 1884: TNA, FO 228/745.

60 Canton No. 74, 14 June 1884, Canton No. 79, 1 July 1884, and enclosure: TNA, FO 228/744.

61 Daniel H. Bays, 'The Nature of Provincial Political Authority in Late Ch'ing Times: Chang Chih-tung in Canton, 1884–1889', *Modern Asian Studies* 4:4 (1970), pp. 325–47; Mackintosh to J. S. Swire, 17 June 1885, 3 September 1885: JSS I 2/4; rifles: Mackintosh to J. S. Swire 4 November 1884, 3 February 1885: JSS I 2/4; Marshall J. Bastable, *Arms and the State: Sir William Armstrong and the Remaking of British Naval Power, 1854–1914* (London: Routledge, 2004), p. 118.

62 LeFevour, *Western Enterprise in Late Ch'ing China*, p. 69.

63 In 1880 he was expelled from his membership of the Hong Kong Club for libelling a fellow member: Vaudine England, *Kindred Spirits: A History of the Hong Kong Club* (Hong Kong: Hong Kong Club, 2016), p. 47; *China Mail*, 31 March 1880.

64 Mackintosh to J. S. Swire, 4 November 1884, 17 February 1885: JSS I 2/4; Frank H. H. King, *The History of the Hongkong and Shanghai Bank*, Volume I, p. 309;

65 Tate, *Transpacific Steam*, pp. 44–8; J. S. Swire to T. H. Ismay, 24 June 1881, and J. S. Swire to Lorimer, 26 August 1881: JSS I 1/5; Marriner and Hyde, *The Senior*, pp. 121–4.

66 Holt diary, 12 April 1878: LRO, Holt papers, 920 Hol 2/52; J. S. Swire to Gamwell, 23 January 1878: JSS I 2/2

67 Hyde, *Blue Funnel*, pp. 49–53; Falkus, *Blue Funnel Legend*, p. 40.

68 This section draws on Hyde, *Blue Funnel*, pp. 56–79; and Marriner and Hyde, *The Senior*, pp. 135–59; Hyde, *Far Eastern Trade*, pp. 26–41. More widely on this see B. M. Deakin and T. Seward, *Shipping Conferences: A Study of Their Origins, Development, and Economic Practices* (Cambridge: Cambridge University Press, 1973), and Daniel Marx Jr, *A Study of Industrial Self-regulation by Shipping Conferences* (Princeton: Princeton University Press, 1953).

69 J. S. Swire to Alfred Holt, 25 September 1879: LRO, Holt papers, HOL 92, Swire letters.

70 D. H. Cole, *Imperial Military Geography*, 6th edn (London: Sifton Praed & Co, 1930), p. 59; Marx, *International Shipping Cartels*, pp. 45–67; Gregg Huff and Gillian Huff, 'The Shipping Conference system, Empire and Local Protest in Singapore, 1910–11', *Journal of Imperial and Commonwealth History* 46:1 (2018), pp. 69–92.

71 John Samuel Swire, 188, quoted in Marriner and Hyde, *The Senior*, p. 181.

72 Hyde, *Far Eastern Trade*, p. 37.

73 For a survey and witheringly effective critique see Jim Tomlinson, 'Thrice Denied: "Declinism" as a Recurrent Theme in British history in the Long Twentieth Century', *Twentieth Century British History*, 20:2 (2009), pp. 227–51.

74 W. H. Swire to J. S. Swire, 3 August 1881, Letters to Mary Warren, 1873–1898: JS&SL.

75 John Swire & Sons to Novelli & Co., 14 October 1878: JSS I 1/4.

76 J. S. Swire to Mary Warren, 24 July 1881: JS&SL.

77 J. S. Swire to Gamwell, 4 March 1884, 25 April 1884: JSS I 3/2.

78 Holt diaries, 28 March 1873, 24–30 May 1875: LRO, Holt papers, HOL 920 2/52.

79 W. H. Swire left most of his capital in the partnership. Ill health had long plagued him, and he died of liver disease in July 1884.

80 J. S. Swire to Earl of Derby, 12 July 1877: JSS I 1/4.

CHAPTER 6 AT WORK

1 Swire had married Mary Warren, daughter of shipowner George Warren, in Liverpool on 18 October 1881. Warren ran a line of packet ships, journeying between the city and Boston. This was a connection that dated back to at least 1848, when Mary was born in Boston: Swire was her godfather.

2 Robert Hart diary, 10, 12, 14 April 1884, Hart papers, Ms 15.1.29, Queen's University Belfast, Special Collections and Archives; menus for dinners hosted by Robert Hart preserved in the scrapbooks of J. O. P. and Daisy Bland, courtesy of Tom Cohen.

3 J. O. P. Bland diary, 'Wednesday to Sunday 13th', 1884: Thomas Fisher Rare Books Library, University of Toronto, Papers of J. O. P. Bland, Box 29, Diary 1883–1885.

4 James Legge, 'The Colony of Hongkong', *The China Review* 1:3 (1874), pp. 163–76; *Shanghai Considered Socially: A Lecture by H. Lang* (Shanghai: American Presbyterian Mission Press, 1875); J. W. MacLellan, *The Story of Shanghai from the opening of the port to foreign trade* (Shanghai: North China Herald Office, 1889); *The Jubilee of Hongkong as a British Crown Colony …* (Hong Kong: Daily Press Office, 1891); *The Jubilee of Shanghai 1843–1893* (Shanghai: NCDN, 1893).

5 Shanghai Municipal Council, *Annual Report 1885* (Shanghai: Kelly & Walsh, 1886), pp. 20–21.

6 J. S. Swire to John Scott, 1 September 1880: JSS I 1/5; J. S. Swire to William Lang, 22 May 1876: JSS I 1/4.

7 *The Economist*, 17 January 1891, p. 99. The firm kept its name out of this and other advertisements, but this is a precise fit with just such an advertisement

identified as appearing in the magazine in a letter from Hong Kong: Edwin
Mackintosh to J. S. Swire, 15 April 1891: JSS I 2/6.

8   J. H. Scott to Edwin Mackintosh, 12 June 1891: JSS I 1/10. This most likely
    refers to the Eurasian family associated with Brown & Co, nutmeg and then
    coconut plantation owners.

9   H. M. Brown to John Swire & Sons, 2 March 1893, J. W. Cumming to
    J. H. Scott, 26 December 1895, both in: JSS II 7/1/1; Edwin Mackintosh
    to J. S. Swire, 15 April 1891: JSS I 2/6. Cumming did not turn out well.
    He was eventually 'given notice to leave', and moved from Hong Kong to
    California, where in 1916 he is recorded as a 'labourer'.

10 Charles M. Dyce, *Personal Reminiscences of Thirty Years' Residence in the
    Model Settlement Shanghai 1870–1900* (London: Chapman & Hall, 1906),
    pp. 3–5, P. G. Wodehouse, *Psmith in the City* [1910] (Harmondsworth:
    Penguin Books, 1970), p. 27.

11 John Swire & Sons to Stephen Forsyth, 9 December 1891, and John Swire
    & Sons to Mr Whitworth, 2 December 1893: JSS I 1/10.

12 Forsyth did not in fact stay until the end of his contract. In 1901 he was
    partner in a firm of maltsters in Sunderland, and by 1908 had taken Holy
    Orders: *Sunderland Daily Echo and Shipping Gazette*, 3 September 1900;
    Dundee Courier, 9 June 1924.

13 Matriculated 1881, aged 20.

14 J. S. Swire to Mackintosh, 20 May 1891: JSS I 1/10. Brown stayed 11 years
    with the firm, but died from cholera in Shantou in 1902.

15 J. S. Swire to Land & Scott, 3 August 1876: JSS I 1/4.

16 J. S. Swire to Gamwell, 12 April 1878: JSS I 2/2.

17 Robinson to Mackintosh, 30 March 1891: JSS I 2/6; servants: *China Mail*,
    13 March 1876.

18 This is also evident in the guide to 'subjects connected with the Far East'
    prepared by Consul Herbert Giles: *A Glossary of Reference* [1878] (2nd edn:
    Hong Kong: Lane Crawford, 1886). Places had their specificities, but it was
    really one 'place'.

19 E. Mackintosh to J. S. Swire, 6 August 1890, see also E. Mackintosh to J. S.
    Swire, 18 June 1890: both in JSS I 2/6. Biographical details in this paragraph
    drawn from the notes of Carl Smith held at the Hong Kong Public Record
    Office.

20 William Armstrong to J. H. Scott, 20 July 1900, JSS I 2/9.

21 J. S. Swire to Lang, 6 February 1879: JSS I 1/4.

22 J. H. Scott to John Swire & Sons, 25 December 1893: JSS I 2/7.

23 Knollys, *English Life in China*, p. 43; Dyce, *Personal Reminiscences*, pp. 199–202.

24 H. Lang, *Shanghai Considered Socially*, p. 55.

25 *Hongkong Telegraph*, 17 November 1891, 23 July 1892. The campaign seems
    to have been sparked by Mackintosh's leading role in the expulsion of Smith

from the Hong Kong Jockey Club in 1891 after the journalist was convicted and jailed for conspiracy.

26 J. S. Swire to William Lang, 6 February 1879: JSS I 1/4.

27 J. Keith Angus, 'A Paper Lighthouse', *The Merchistonian*, 9:4 (1882), pp. 189–93; 'Among the Hills near Shanghai', *The Merchistonian*, 11:4 (1884), pp. 230–34; J. H. Scott to Gamwell, 21 November 1877: JSS I 2/2.

28 *Western Daily Press*, 19 September 1889, p. 7.

29 'Death of an Old Resident', *Japan Weekly Chronicle*, 26 February 1931, p. 221.

30 J. S. Swire to Bois, 17 May 1892: JSS I 1/10.

31 J. S. Swire to Bois, 15 June 1892: JSS I 1/10; Dowler to Scott 30 October 1893, enclosure in Scott to Gamwell, 31 October 1893: JSS I 2/7. No prosecution was sought. Shepherd's wife arrived in Seattle in September 1893, where she would settle. She listed herself in local directories as a widow from at least 1903 onwards, but Shepherd's fate is unclear.

32 The San Francisco earthquake and fire also helpfully intervened, allowing him to 'lose' all papers and possessions: private information.

33 J. S. Swire to Lang, 20 December 1878, 6 February 1879: JSS I 1/4.

34 Herbert Smith to J. H. Scott, 21 December 1899: JSS I 2/9.

35 J. H. Scott to J. S. Swire, 3 January 1893, and A. J. Franks to Scott, 18 December 1892: JSS I 2/7.

36 Lang, *Shanghai Considered Socially*, pp. 54, 56.

37 See correspondence in Probate file for John Shadgett: TNA, FO 917/291; Danby: *South China Morning Post* (*SCMP*), 28 January 1950, p. 6.

38 Lang to John Swire & Sons, 14 December 1878: JSS I 2/16.

39 Shepherd had married in Yokohama in 1891.

40 Butterfield & Swire Staff book, Volume 153: JS&SL; Butterfield & Swire Hong Kong to John Swire & Sons, 9 September 1905: JSS II 7/4/10. Census and other records suggest that Knox seems also to have lied about his age, shaving off eight of his thirty-four years on joining.

41 The note on this man reads: 'Married Yes. Unhappy', Staff Notebook No. 1, entry No. 74. When the man died in 1903 he left nothing for his wife, who the census records in 1901 as 'separated', and a meagre five shillings a week for his three 'reputed children'.

42 Frederick Baptiste Aubert: TNA, FO 917/674.

43 J. S. Swire to Edwin Mackintosh, 2 July 1891: JSS I 1/10. Her first husband, Temple Wilcox, died in Yokohama in 1877, where the couple had been living for the best part of a decade already.

44 Kevin C. Murphy, *The American Merchant Experience in Nineteenth-Century Japan* (London: Routledge, 2004), p. 34. On Yokohama's social world see also: J. E. Hoare, *Japan's Treaty Ports and Foreign Settlements: The Uninvited Guests 1858–1899* (Folkestone: Japan Library, 1994), pp. 18–51.

45 Herbert Smith to J. H. Scott, 21 December 1899: JSS I 2/9.

46 J. H. Scott to J. S. Swire 17 May 1872: JSS I 2/16.

47 William Lang to JSS, 9 January 1878, J. S. Swire to J. H. Scott, 11 February 1878: JSS I 2/2; William Lang to JSS, 28 March 1878: JSS I 2/16; C. Hall to E. Satow, 19 February 1898, in Ian Ruxton (ed.), *The Correspondence of Sir Ernest Satow, British Minister in Japan, 1895–1900*, Volume 4, p. 347.

48 'Report on the riots at Chinkiang' in Chinkiang No. 3, 14 February 1889: TNA, FO 228/876; *NCH*, 8 February 1889, pp. 142–4, 5 April 1889, p. 394; 18 May 1889, p. 602; 1 June 1889, p. 673; Hart to Campbell, 10 February 1889, in Fairbank et al. (eds), *The I.G. in Peking*, p. 736. Claim: in Chinkiang No. 11, 16 May 1889: TNA, FO 228/876.

49 *The Anti-Foreign Riots in China in 1891* (Shanghai: *North China Herald*, 1892), pp. 10–21; Bickers, *Scramble for China*, pp. 305–6.

50 Henling Thomas Wade, *With Boat and Gun in the Yangtze Valley* (Shanghai, 1910), pp. 28, 180–82.

51 This paragraph draws on correspondence in JSS II 1/3, 1894–97, and JSS II 1/6.

52 *In the Far East: Letters from Geraldine Guinness in China. Edited by her sister* (London: Morgan & Scott, 1889), pp. 33–4.

53 Drawn from letters in JSS II 1/2.

54 Circular in Butterfield & Swire Hong Kong to John Swire & Sons London, 3 March 1899: JSS I 2/9.

55 J. S. Swire to Scott, 7 February 1878: JSS I 2/2; J. S. Swire to Lang, 6 February 1879, 30 January 1880: JSS I 1/5.

56 Knollys, *English Life in China*, pp. 151, 155; J. S. Swire to Butterfield & Swire Shanghai, 26 January 1876: JSS I 1/4. J. S. Swire to F. B. Johnson, 27 December 1877: JSS I 2/2.

57 Marriner and Hyde, *The Senior*, pp. 44–5.

58 J. S. Swire to Lang, 24 August 1877: JSS I 2/4; Box 1086; J. S. Swire to Gamwell, 6 December 1877, 28 January 1878: JSS I 2/2.

59 J. S. Swire to Lang & Scott, 21 August 1877: JSS I 1/4.

60 *NCH*, 1 November 1875, p. 466.

61 J. S. Swire to F. Gamwell, 4 March 1884: JSS I 2/2.

62 *China Mail*, 2 April 1891.

63 Thomas Grimshaw, reminiscing in 1929 at the end of his 39 years of service: *SCMP*, 18 April 1929, p. 7, and John Blake, after 25 years: *SCMP*, 2 May 1908, p. 2.

64 *Hongkong Daily Press*, 6 February 1886, 4 January 1887; Mackintosh to Swire, 31 March 1885: JSS I 2/4; Mackintosh to Swire, 18 June 1890: JSS I 2/7.

65 The course of the crisis can be followed in letters from Mackintosh in Hong Kong to London in July to October 1886: JSS I 2/4; *SCMP*, 18 April 1929, p. 7.

66 Edwin Mackintosh to J. H. Scott, 10 February 1892: JSS I 2/6.

67 George Fitzpatrick to Edwin Mackintosh, 25 October 1891: JSS I 2/6. This seems to have been successful: Crombie remained with the refinery for another two years.

68　Korn: Herbert Smith to J. H. Scott, 2 May 1900, D. R. Law to J. H. Scott, 9 September 1900, Butterfield & Swire Hong Kong to John Swire & Sons, 19 October 1900; Obrembski: 16 September 1899, both in JSS I 2/9. Obrembski had joined the firm in 1888, and remained with the refinery until 1931, dying in the colony in 1933: *Hongkong Telegraph*, 26 April 1933, p. 11.

69　Butterfield & Swire property and staff register, 1872–1901: JSS II 2/5/2; Helbling to Scott, 15 March 1889: JSS II 1/1/2/1; Baker to Bois, 14 March 1898: JSS II 1/1/2.

70　Jennifer Field Lang, 'Taikoo Sugar Refinery and company town: Progressive design by a pioneering commercial enterprise' (University of Hong Kong, PhD thesis, 2018), pp. 84–93.

71　*Hongkong Telegraph*, 27 September 1897; *China Mail*, 27 September 1897, *Hongkong Daily Press*, 28 September 1897; Beaconsfield: J. H. Scott to Mackintosh, 8 August 1893: JSS I 2/7; *China Mail*, 5 December 1898. Its typhoon-proofing was demonstrated to spectacular, if grim, effect during the devasting typhoon of 18 September 1906 when a clerk, William Nicholson, took a series of astonishing photographs from its secure walls of the harbour water boiling with fury: *SCMP*, 25 September 1906, p. 2, 27 February 1924, p. 10.

72　*Hongkong Telegraph*, 15 October 1889; Mackintosh memorandum, 16 October 1889: JSS I 2/6; will: HKRS-144-4-761, Ng a Heap, alias Ng Yung, deceased; bond: details from Carl Smith research notes, cards relating to Mok Wai (died 1892). On the Moks see the entries on Mok Man Cheung (Anthony Sweeten and Christopher Munn) and Mok Sze-yeung et al (Christine Loh) in May Holdsworth and Christopher Munn (eds), *Dictionary of Hong Kong Biography* (Hong Kong: Hong Kong University Press, 2012), pp. 323–6.

73　Zheng Zhizhang, 'Tianjin Taigu yanghang yu maiban Zheng Zhiyi' (1965) (Butterfield & Swire in Tianjin and Comprador Zheng Zhiyi), *Tianjin wenshi ziliao xuanji*, No. 9 (Tianjin: Tianjin renmin chubanshe, 1980), pp. 107–24.

74　On the Chun and Wong families see the biographical sketches in Arnold Wright (ed.), *Twentieth-Century Impressions of Hongkong, Shanghai, and other Treaty Ports of China* ... (London: Lloyd's Greater Britain Publishing Company, 1908), pp. 548–55.

75　J. S. Swire to William Lang 22 April 1884, J. S. Swire to Frederick Gamwell, 25 April 1884: JSS I 3/2; *Shenbao*, 25 September 1884, p. 4.

76　Edwin Mackintosh to JSS, 10 February 1885, 16 February 1886: JSS I 2/6; Mackintosh to John Swire & Sons and to Butterfield & Swire Shanghai, 24 October 1892: JSS I 1/10.

77　Mackintosh to Swire, 22 March 1892: JSS I 2/6; J. S. Swire to Butterfield & Swire China and Japan, 29 April 1892, and J. H. Scott to Bois, 29 April 1892: JSS I 1/10.

78 As well as the *North China Herald*, the series ran in the *China Mail* and *Hongkong Telegraph* in 1888/9, and was printed in book form in 1890, and remained in print well into the 1930s: see Charles W. Hayford, 'Chinese and American Characteristics: Arthur H. Smith and His China Book', in Suzanne Wilson Barnett and John King Fairbank, eds, *Christianity in China: Early Christianity in China: Early Protestant Missionary Writings* (Cambridge, MA: Harvard University Press, 1985), pp. 153–74. Quotation from the chapter on 'The Absence of Sincerity', in *Chinese Characteristics*, 5th edn, revised (Edinburgh and London: Oliphant Anderson and Ferrier, 1900), p. 281.

79 Bois to J. S. Swire, 25 March 1892: JSS I 2/18.

80 Bois to J. S. Swire, 25 March 1892: JSS I 2/18.

81 Quoted in Chen Lilian, 'Maiban shengya dui Zheng Guanying de yingxiang' (Zheng Guanying's comprador career and its influence on him) in Chinese University of Hong Kong Art Gallery, and Chinese University of Hong Kong Department of History (eds), *Maiban yu jindai Zhongguo* (Compradors and modern China) (Hong Kong: Sanlian shudian, 2009), pp. 233–54, quotation at p. 237. I am grateful to Dr Kaori Abe for directing me to this reference.

CHAPTER 7 SHIPPING PEOPLE

1 *SCMP*, 24 January 1910, p. 6; *NCH*, 4 February 1910, p. 274.

2 'Cost of working the Foochow ss and Swatow ss in China', March 1875, JSS IV 1/7.

3 Reinhardt, *Navigating Semi-Colonialism*, pp. 141–4; F. H. Davies to Gwen Davies, 14 December 1905, in J. Glyn Davies Papers, National Library of Wales, Fonds GB 0210 JGLIES [hereafter NLW, Davies letters].

4 *NCH*, 13 April 1876, p. 534. Filomena V. Aguiar Jr, 'Manilamen and seafaring: Engaging the maritime world beyond the Spanish realm', *Journal of Global History*, 7:3 (2012), pp. 364–88.

5 No lives were lost, which was largely down to Whittle's command of events in the aftermath of the accident, but all aboard lost everything. The official enquiry exonerated him: *Times of India*, 27 July 1880, p. 4, 30 July 1880 p. 3; *Shipping & Mercantile Gazette*, 18 November 1880, p. 8.

6 Details on *Tamsui* from JSS IV 2/49. Whittle: *NCH*, 16 May 1884, p. 544, 22 April 1911, p. 207; Logbook, *Changchow*, National Maritime Museum, Captain John Whittle papers [hereafter NMM], WHT/7. Mack: *NCH*, 15 October 1885, p. 430; *SCMP*, 28 April 1920, p. 8. Whittle prospered in Shanghai. At his death in 1913 he owned 70 Chinese-style houses, and two foreign ones, which together with his portfolio of shares in foreign companies in Shanghai meant his estate in China was valued at nearly £18,000: TNA, FO 917/1622, John Whittle.

7 J. S. Swire to Butterfield & Swire Shanghai, 3 November 1871: JSS I 1/2; John Swire & Sons to Butterfield & Swire Shanghai, 13 January 1873: JSS I 1/2; *NCH*, 28 September 1867, p. 275; J. S. Swire to William Imrie & Co., 9 November 1881: JSS I 1/5.

8 Data compiled from available copies of the *Desk Hong List*, 1883–1900. A record of ships registered at Shanghai and their officers and engineers was published in this from 1883 onwards. There are no systematic company records of nineteenth-century marine staff.

9 Richard Lewis, *Sampans and Saffron Cake: From the Diaries of Fritz Lewis in China and Cornwall 1872–1950* (Leominster: Kenwater Books, 2012); F. H. Davies letter to Glyn, 4 February 1904: NLW, Davies letters.

10 *Hongkong Telegraph*, 30 October 1891; James Tippin, 'Life Record', private collection. Tippin was originally known as Jones. One son would go on to work for Butterfield & Swire.

11 J. S. Swire to Alfred Charlton, 10 October 1892: JSS I 1/10. Blue Funnel's management placed a high premium on the ability and autonomy of its masters, which encouraged this approach to relations with agents: Falkus, *Blue Funnel Legend*, p. 69.

12 For a discussion see: Eric W. Sager, *Seafaring Labour: The Merchant Marine of Atlantic Canada, 1820–1914* (Montreal: McGill-Queen's University Press, 1989), pp. 81–8, quotation from p. 90.

13 *NCH*, 14 November 183, p. 895; the details are extracted from Whittle's logbook: NMM WHT/7. This and its companions are rough working logs, which also include aides-memoires, lists of route marks, timings, capacity and consumption. A picul was 133 1/3lbs.

14 Charlotte Havilland, *The China Navigation Company: A Pictorial History 1872–2012* (Hong Kong: Swire, 2012), p. 79; *Auckland Star*, 15 September 1884; *New Zealand Herald*, 18 September 1884. Blue Funnel: Falkus, *Blue Funnel Legend*, pp. 37–9.

15 *NCH*, 24 April 1885, p. 467, 14 August 1885, p. 191; Bleasdale and Shun Wah, Swire, pp. 26–7; *Sydney Morning Herald*, 20 August 1883, p. 6; *Tasmanian*, 1 September 1883, p. 1019; *China Mail*, 21 September 1883; *Report of the Royal Commission on Alleged Chinese Gambling and Immorality and Charges of Bribery Against Members of the Police Force, Appointed August 20, 1891, Presented to Parliament by Command* (Sydney: Charles Potter, 1892), pp. 14, 480; Elizabeth Sinn, *Pacific Crossing: Californian Gold, Chinese Migration, and the Making of Hong Kong* (Hong Kong: Hong Kong University Press, 2013), chapter 5, 'Returning Bones', pp. 265–94; Christian Henriot, *Scythe and the City: A Social history of Death in Shanghai* (Stanford: Stanford University Press, 2016), pp. 76–9; rates: freight tariffs in JSS I 4/1/1.

16 *NCH*, 9 September 1876, pp. 257–9, 27 June 1898, pp. 113–15. This was not the fleet's commodore, Captain James Hardie.

17 Frank H. Davies to Gwen Davies, 5 April 1905; 12 May 1905, NLW, Davies letters.

18 Sydney S. Kemp, *A Concise History of the Mercantile Marine Officers' Association and Club* (Shanghai: [Mercantile Marine Officers' Association] 1936), quotation from p. 153.

19 Butterfield & Swire Shanghai to T. Russell, Manager, Marine Engineers' Institute, 6 June 1885: JSS I 2/17.

20 *NCH*, 24 October 1879, p. 410.

21 Graeme J. Milne, *People, Place and Power on the Nineteenth-Century Waterfront: Sailortown* (London: Palgrave Macmillan, 2016), p. 13.

22 See doctor's notes dated 9 July 1875, JSS IV 2/4a; *NCH*, 21 November 1890, p. 641.

23 *NCH*, 24 May 1873, pp. 458–60; Stephen Davies, *Strong to Save: Maritime Mission in Hong Kong from Whampoa Reach to the Mariners' Club* (Hong Kong: City University of Hong Kong Press, 2017).

24 *NCH*, 1 July 1879, pp. 19–20.

25 Frank H. Davies letters: 23 December 1904, 8 August 1907, 4 December 1905: NLW, Davies letters.

26 *NCH*, 21 August 1903, pp. 371–2, 375, and 28 August 1903, p. 452.

27 *NCH*, 24 October 1884, p. 439; *Hongkong Telegraph*, 7 September 1892, p. 3; *NCH*, 1 April 1910, pp. 44–5, 8 April 1910, pp. 98–100; David Martin, probate, TNA: FO917/1265.

28 Davies to Glyn, 3 December 1908: NLW, Davies letters. He did marry, in 1919 in London, the Hong Kong-born daughter of an auctioneer, but he never worked ashore.

29 J. S. Swire to Frederick Gamwell, 11 February 1878: JSS I 2/2; William Lang to JSS, 24 June 1881: JSS I 2/16.

30 Louis Ha, 'The Sunday Rest issue in Nineteenth Century Hong Kong', in Lee Pui-tak (ed.), *Colonial Hong Kong and Modern China* (Hong Kong: Hong Kong University Press, 2005), pp. 57–68; *Report of the Committee of the Hongkong General Chamber of Commerce for the year Ending 31st December 1890* (Hongkong: Noronha, 1891), pp. 27, 49–57; Davies to Gwen, 5 April 1905: NLW, Davies letters.

31 *NCH*, 4 January 1877, p. 12.

32 *NCH*, 23 March 1888, pp. 341–2.

33 *Hongkong Daily Press*, 27 October 1891; *Hongkong Telegraph*, 30 January 1891.

34 Reinhardt, *Navigating Semi-Colonialism*, pp. 152–4.

35 Warrick to Butterfield & Swire, Shanghai, 15 May 1874: JSS I 2/15. Tickets might also be forged: a Chinese shopkeeper was jailed in Shanghai in 1880 for issuing counterfeit tickets for CNCo steamers, in collusion, it was assumed, with staff of the firm: *NCH*, 18 September 1880, p. 275.

36 *Shanghai: Shenbao*, 14 October 1878, 18 October 1878; *Kweiyang: Shenbao*, 19 February 1897; *Hangchow: Shenbao*, 16 July 1899, 30 June 1899; W. Fisher to John Bois, 12 September 1894: JSS II 1/3/3/2; Wright, *Twentieth-Century Impressions*, p. 550.

37 William Spencer Percival, *The Land of the Dragon: My Boating and Shooting Excursions to the Gorges of the Upper Yangtze* (London: Hurst & Blackett, 1889), pp. 32–3.

38 *In the Far East: letters from Geraldine Guinness in China, edited by her sister* (London: Morgan & Scott, 1889), pp. 30–35; James Dow, 'Journal of a Voyage to China, etc.', 23 July 1851 (private collection).

39 *China Mail*, 5 July 1888, p. 3; M. Horace Hayes, *Among Men and Horses* (London: T. Fisher Unwin, 1894), pp. 172, 150.

40 *Glengyle: NCH*, 25 November 1875, pp. 531–4; *Pakhoi*: J. S. Swire to William Imrie & Co., Box 1087; correspondence in JSS IV 1/6, Box A17; *NCH*, 29 November 1881, pp. 587–8; *Wuhu*: 21 February 1883, pp. 211–15; *Foochow: NCH*: 31 August 1883, p. 267; *Tientsin: China Mail*, 2 September 1897; *Swatow: NCH*, 2 March 1888, p. 255, 9 March 1888, pp. 268, 286.

41 *Shanghai: NCH*, 2 January 1891, pp. 14–15, 9 January 1891, pp. 43–45, 11 September 1891, p. 342; *Ichang*: 27 November 1891, pp. 752–3; *Yunnan: NCH*, 8 January 1892, pp. 20, 23–4, 15 January 1892, pp. 56–7.

42 *NCH*, 3 August 1889, p. 135; John Swire & Sons to Bois and Mackintosh, 24 September 1889, J. S. Swire to Mackintosh, 3 October 1889, J. S. Swire to Mackintosh, 16 January 1890: JSS I 1/9; Bois to J. S. Swire, 19 August 1889: JSS I 2/18.

43 John Whittle to John Swire & Sons, 22 January 1890: JSS I 2/18.

44 Robert Bickers, 'Infrastructural Globalization: Lighting the China Coast, 1860s–1930s', *The Historical Journal* 56:2 (2013), pp. 431–58; J. S. Swire to Frederick Gamwell, 29 May 1878: JSS I 2/2.

45 J. S. Swire to Edwin Mackintosh, 4 January 1892, J. S. Swire to Edwin Mackintosh and J. C. Bois, 29 January 1892: JSS I 1/10.

46 J. S. Swire to Mackintosh and Bois, 18 December 1891: JSS I 1/10.

47 Bois to J. S. Swire 16 May 1890: JSS I 2/18.

48 *Hongkong Daily Press*, 24 October 1891, *Hongkong Telegraph*, 24–30 October 1891, *passim*

49 *The Chinese Confessions of Charles Welsh Mason* (London: Grant Richards, 1924), pp. 206–22. In fact, it was a Jardines steamer and hulk: *NCH*, 9 October 1891, pp. 503–7. For more on this see Catherine Ladds, 'Charles Mason, the "king of China": British imperial adventuring in the late nineteenth century', *Historical Research*, 90 (2017), pp. 567–90. See also Alan R. Sweeten, 'The Mason gunrunning case and the 1891 Yangtze Valley antimissionary disturbances: a diplomatic link', *Bulletin of the Institute of Modern History, Academia Sinica*, iv (1974), pp. 843–80.

50 Swatow No. 3, 31 January 1884: TNA, FO 228/763; *NCH*, 24 August 1883, p. 220; *Maryborough Chronicle*, 24 September 1883, p. 2: *Sydney Morning Herald*, 19 April 1884, p. 12.

51 Falkus, *Blue Funnel Legend*, pp. 37–9; Mackintosh to J. S. Swire, Lang, Scott & Gamwell, 4 May 1883, and Mackintosh to J. S. Swire, 19 July 1883: JSS I 2/3a.

52 James Francis Warren, *Rickshaw Coolie: A People's History of Singapore* (Singapore: National University of Singapore Press, 2003 [1986]), pp. 14–20; A. V. T. Dean, 'Notes on the history of the China Navigation Co. Ltd.', Section III, 1900–1918': JS&SL; A. D. Blue, 'Chinese emigration and the deck passenger trade', *Journal of the Hong Kong Branch of the Royal Asiatic Society*, 10 (1970), pp. 88–9.

53 John Swire & Sons to Butterfield & Swire Hong Kong, 29 October 1875, and John Swire & Sons to Lorimer, Marwood & Rome, 29 October 1875, both in: JSS I 1/4; Marriner and Hyde, *The Senior*, p. 123.

54 *Morning Bulletin*, 31 October 1884, p. 5, 1 November 1884, p. 3; *North Australian*, 28 November 1884, p. 3; *Sydney Morning Herald*, 15 November 1884, p. 10.

55 On the 1888 crisis see Benjamin Mountford, *Britain, China, and Colonial Australia* (Oxford: Oxford University Press, 2016), pp. 116–42, Swire is quoted on p. 142. On the *Changsha*: (Sydney) *Daily Telegraph*, 30 May 1888, p. 5, *Sydney Morning Herald*, 12 June 1888, p. 8, and 7 August 1888, p. 4, *China Mail*, 6 July 1888, *Hongkong Telegraph*, 6 July 1888. The police were called by telegraph: by 1891 the firm had two telephones.

56 J. S. Swire to Edwin Mackintosh and John Bois, 3 August 1892: JSS I 1/10. Profits: Marriner and Hyde, *The Senior*, pp. 82–97.

57 H. B. Endicott to J. H. Scott, 6 October 1893: JSS I 2/7; Bois to Scott, 11 May 1893, enclosed in J. S. Swire to William Keswick, 27 June 1893: JSS I 1/11.

58 Mackintosh to J. S. Swire, 18 June 1890: JSS I 2/6.

59 J. H. Scott to J. S. Swire, 4 January 1889, and various letters in this volume: JSS I 2/4; death: *Celestial Empire*, 11 January 1895, pp. 29, 45.

60 Shanghai No. 45, 2 February 1895, in Shanghai Consulate Despatches, Volume 42, NARA, RG 59. Endicott had secured a new US passport in 1891 stating that he was born in Macao, that his domicile was Boston, and that his father was a native citizen of the United States: Ancestry.com. *U.S. Passport Applications, 1795–1925* [database on-line].

61 Falkus, *Blue Funnel Legend*, pp. 114; *The Times*, 14 November 1892, p. 7.

62 'Sole policy advocated by J.S.S. for the O.S.S.', June 1882: JSS XI 1/1. On the company's fortunes see Falkus, *Blue Funnel Legend*, pp. 103–16; see also Marriner and Hyde, *The Senior*, pp. 116–21.

63 See 'Richard D. Holt: Diary of a voyage to the East', comments on the coolie trade: 23 January 1892, 14 March 1892: LRO, 920 DUR 14/40. For a discussion of this trip see Goldsmith, 'In trade', pp. 52–65.

64 Jack Swire letters from Japan, June–September 1886: JS&SL.

65 Jack Swire to Mary Swire, 1 July 1905, Jack Swire Letter Book: JSS I 1/9/1.

66 J. S. Swire letters to Mary Warren, 25, 27 July, 1 August 1890, 24 October 1894: JS&SL.

67 *NCH*, 10 July 1898, p. 34; *Hongkong Telegraph*, 4 July 1898.

68 The tour can be followed in letters from Scott between 25 September 1888 and 10 May 1889: JSS I 2/18.

69 *Dundee Advertiser*, 28 July 1891, p. 4; *Dundee Courier*, 20 August 1891; *Shipping Gazette and Lloyd's List*, 31 July 1889; India: *Japan Weekly Mail*, 7 March 1891, p. 272, 15 August 1891, p. 198; *Japan Weekly Mail*, 23 May 1891, pp. 607–8, and 13 June 1891, p. 689.

70 *Shanghai: NCH*, 11 September 1891, p. 342; Vardin: J. S. Swire to Mackintosh and Bois, 29 January 1892; Mitchell: J. S. Swire to Mackintosh and Bois, 11 December 1891: JSS I 1/10; *Hongkong Telegraph*, 7 July 1892, *Hongkong Daily Press*, 13 September 1892; J. S. Swire to Crompton, 24 February 1892: JSS I 1/10; *Tungchow*: NMM, WHT/07; *Dardanus*: *Hongkong Telegraph*, 25 September 1891; Japan: J. S. Swire to Mary Swire, 17 August 1891: JS&SL.

71 *Japan Weekly Mail*, 18 April 1891, p. 452, 25 April 1891, p. 475; *Boston Post*, 18 August 1891, p. 6.

72 Halved: *Spectator*, 9 May 1891, p. 3 (the claim was contested, but the journey was still now swifter: *NCH*, 26 June 1891, p. 791–2); *Punch*, 15 August 1891, p. 78. They did not yet take them to China or Japan, although Cook's had just the previous year tried to open an office in the latter country, according to a letter from Cook's son John M. Cook – written on board CNCo's SS *Chingtu* as he journeyed from Hong Kong to Australia – published in *The Times*, 4 January 1894, p. 10.

73 For the conference system as British imperial asset see: Gregg Huff and Gillian Huff, 'The Shipping Conference system, Empire and Local Protest in Singapore, 1910–11', *Journal of Imperial and Commonwealth History*, 46:1 (2018), pp. 69–92.

CHAPTER 8 NEW ERAS

1 Mackintosh to Alfred Holt, 2 December 1898, John Swire & Sons to Albert Crompton, 5 December 1898, John Swire & Sons to Bois & Poate, 9 December 1898: JSS I 1/13.

2 J. S. Swire to Mary Swire, 9 May 1898, c. 16 July 1898: JS&SL.

3 This section draws on correspondence in 'Letters on the death of John Samuel Swire': JSS I 9/2.

4 J. S. Swire to Mary Swire, 30 May 1894: JS&SL.

5 J. S. Swire to Mary Warren, c. 4/5 April 1881: JS&SL. Gamwell retired and left the partnership in February 1896.

6 *Liverpool Journal of Commerce*, 6 December 1898; *China Mail*, 3 December 1898.

7 *The Field*, 10 December 1898, p. 941; *Leighton Buzzard Observer*, 6 December 1898; *NCH*, 5 December 1898, p. 1036.

8 *Leighton Buzzard Observer*, 2 December 1894, 13 December 1898.

9 Kang: Shanghai No. 59, 27 September 1898: TNA, FO 671/240. This section draws on Bickers, *Scramble for China*, pp. 324–36.

10 Fisher to Wright, 10 October 1899: JSS II 1/3/3. On the Boxers see: Joseph W. Esherick, *The Origins of the Boxer Uprising* (Berkeley: University of California Press, 1987), and Paul A. Cohen, *History in Three Keys: The Boxers as Event, Experience, and Myth* (New York: Columbia University Press, 1997).

11 *NCH*, 9 May 1898, p. 795; Fisher to Wright, 3 July 1900: JSS II 1/3/3; *Western Daily Press*, 25 July 1882, p. 8.

12 The best narrative of the Boxer uprising and war is provided by Cohen, *History in Three Keys*, pp. 14–56. On Tianjin see: '[William McLeish], *Tientsin Besieged and After the Siege ... A Daily Record of the correspondent of the "North-China Daily News"*' (Shanghai: North China Herald Office, 1900). Fisher's letters to Shanghai are in JSS II 1/3/3.

13 Quotations from Fisher to Wright, 24 June 1900; Detring: Fisher to Wright, 9 March 1895: both in JSS II 1/3/3.

14 Customs Commissioner: Second Historical Archives of China, Nanjing, Customs Service Archive [hereafter SHAC], 679(2), 1938, Tientsin Despatch 2380, 20 August 1900.

15 Quotations from Fisher letters to Shanghai: No fear: 5 June 1900; naivety: 15 June 1900; done up: 3 July 1900; pandemonium and villains: 25 June 100; staff: 15 July 1900; Indians: 20 July 1900: all in JSS II 1/3/3. Bar: *Tientsin Besieged*, p. 12.

16 *Shengking*: *NCH*, 18 July 1900, p. 141; details from Fisher letters, 1900, and quotations from: rice: 28 August 1900; Americans: 16 September 1900; Yik Kee: 21 August 1900, and Dowler to Fisher, 25 August 1900: JSS II 1/3/3. Zheng Yizhi, known as Yik Kee, was one of Zheng Guanying's younger brothers: Kang Jin-A, 'Cantonese Networks in East Asia and the Chinese firm Tongshuntai in Korea', *Asian Research Trends*, New Series, 12 (2017), pp. 73–4.

17 Weatherston to Wright, 23 June 1900; Garrick to Wright, 23 and 27 August 1900; Baker to Wright, 31 July 1900: JSS II 1/2/1.

18 Fisher to Butterfield & Swire Shanghai, 12 June 1901, and Fisher to Wright, 12 June 1901: JSS II 1/3/3; T. J. Fisher to A. V. T. Dean, 1 September 1953: JSS II 1/3/3.

19 TVC: *Peking & Tientsin Times*, 20, 29 January, 19 February, 5 March 1898, 20 January, 9 February 1899; HVC: *Hongkong Weekly Press*, 15 July 1901, pp. 48–9; 'Report of the Hongkong Volunteer Corps ... 1899–1900', *Hongkong Government Gazette*, 9 June 1900, pp. 931–44; Patrick Hase, *The*

Six-Day War of 1898: Hong Kong in the Age of Imperialism (Hong Kong: Hong Kong University Press, 2008).

20 Coronation: *Hongkong Telegraph*, 14, 22, 23 May 1902, 30 July, 27 August 1902; *China Mail*, 8 July 1902; *Hongkong Weekly Press*, 14 July 1902, p. 30, 28 July 1902, p. 72, 6 October 1902, pp. 252–3; orders: *Hongkong Telegraph*, 5 October 1905; invasion: *SCMP*, 10 February 1905, p. 5; Range and gun: *Hongkong Daily Press*, 18 December 1907; *SCMP*, 27 June 1904, p. 2.

21 Hoskins: *SCMP*, 17 November 1908, p. 11: she was also quite handy, it seems, with a revolver; John Swire & Sons to W. G. Feast, 2 January 1899; John Swire & Sons to W. W. Feast, 2 January 1899: JSS I 1/13.

22 Lena Wänggren, *Gender, Technology and the New Woman* (Edinburgh: Edinburgh University Press, 2017), p. 36; Gregory Anderson, *The White-blouse Revolution: Female Office Workers Since 1870* (Manchester: Manchester University Press, 1988).

23 Smith to J. H. Scott, 27 January 1900: JSS I 2/9; J. H. Scott to Smith, 1 March 1900: JSS I 1/13. Reece: Black staff notebook, entry 14: JSS I 7/7/1; London Staff Ledger: JSS I 5/1.

24 Anderson, *Victorian Clerks*, p. 57; Gillian Sutherland, *In Search of the New Woman: Middle-Class Women and Work in Britain 1870–1914* (Cambridge: Cambridge University Press, 2015), p. 99.

25 Anderson, *Victorian Clerks*, pp. 52–60. Details on female employees from Butterfield & Swire Staff Record Book 154: JS&SL.

26 *SCMP*, 23 January 1908, p. 2, 20 February 1908, p. 2, 5 October 1910, p. 10.

27 Mackintosh to Swire, 14 October 1884: JSS I 2/4.

28 Fisher to Wright, 30 November 1899: JSS II 1/3/3.

29 *SCMP*, 28 March 1917, p. 10; *Hongkong Telegraph*, 3 October 1908.

30 J. S. Swire to Lang, Scott and Mackintosh, 11 February 1881, and 30 November 1881: JSS I 1/5.

31 Albert Edwin Griffin, 'Taikoo Dockyard, Hong Kong', *Minutes of the Proceedings of the Institution of Chartered Engineers*, Volume 183 (1911), pp. 252–62; D. R. Law to J. H. Scott, 29 July 1908: JSS I 2/10.

32 E. R. Belilios to Mackintosh, 30 May 1899, and to Poate, 3 June 1899: JSS I 2/9. Calcutta-born Emanuel Raphael Belilios was an influential figure in the colony. A prominent landowner (he owned Beaconsfield), and philanthropist, he was keen to co-develop a dockyard with B&S (he has 'been bothering us freely'), and seems also to have approached Jardines about his plans through Sir Thomas Jackson, Chairman of the Hongkong & Shanghai Bank: Herbert Smith to J. H. Scott, 21 December 1899, J. J. Keswick to Jackson, 1 March 1900: JSS I 2/9.

33 Danby: Law to Scott, 20 October 1900: JSS I 2/9 (Danby's son worked for Butterfield & Swire); Macdonald: John Swire & Sons to Poate, 30 November 1900, 21 February 1901, 12 July 1901: JSS I 1/13. One senior

consultant engineer was Arthur Paul Dashwood, who later married the writer E. M. Delafield: we might rue the fact that his connection with Taikoo was over by then.

34 Butterfield & Swire, Hong Kong to John Swire & Sons, 17 July 1907: JSS I 2/10; Undated cutting, probably March 1900, attached to J. J. Keswick to Jackson, 1 March 1900: JSS I 2/9. Corruption allegations – pistol-packing Miss Hoskins's father was quietly investigated – seem not to have been proved: D. R. Law to J. H. Scott, 11 March 1904, 21 August 1905, and Law to John Swire & Sons, 18 April 1904: JSS I 2/10.

35 *China Mail*, 2 January 1908; James Henry Scott, *A Short Account of the firm of John Swire & Sons* (Letchworth: Privately Printed, 1914).

36 *Directory and Chronicle for China, Japan, Corea ... 1905* (Hong Kong: *Hongkong Daily Press*, 1905) p. 420; *Greenock Telegraph and Clyde Side Shipping Gazette*, 16 January 1909, p. 3.

37 *Hongkong Government Gazette*, 22 August 1891, p. 757, 28 September 1901, p. 1694; 10 May 1905, p. 234.

38 *SCMP*, 4 September 1909, p. 3.

39 'Notes from the South' in *NCH*, 15 May 1900, p. 870, and 19 September 1900, p. 600.

40 Riot: *Hongkong Weekly Press*, 29 December 1902, p. 494; 23 February 1903, pp. 142–3, 28 February 1903, p. 160; Hynes: *SCMP*, 19 October 1904, p. 5, 20 October 1904, p. 2; Roi: *SCMP*, 19 April 1906, p. 2. On the 1902 riot see also Sheilah E. Hamilton, *Watching Over Hong Kong: Private Policing, 1841–1941* (Hong Kong: Hong Kong University Press, 2008), pp. 103–4.

41 For a survey see Thomas R. Metcalf, *Imperial Connections: India in the Indian Ocean Arena, 1860–1920* (Cambridge: Cambridge University Press, 2007).

42 The travails of the dockyard in 1909–12 can be followed through the Hong Kong correspondence in JSS I 2/11.

43 C. C. Scott to J. H. Scott, 22 December 1910: JSS I 2/10; Austin Coates, *Whampoa: Ships on the Shore* (Hong Kong: Hongkong and Whampoa Dock Company, 1980), pp. 173–81, 187–91; Marriner and Hyde, *The Senior*, p. 202.

44 See, for example, reports on conflict between Hakka 'clans' and 'different classes of Chinese', *Hongkong Telegraph*, 5 November 1906, 5 February 1909. Equipped: Butterfield & Swire Hong Kong to John Swire & Sons London, 26 April 1912: JSS I 2/11.

45 Butterfield & Swire Hong Kong to Woo Tong Sam, 11 June 1909: JSS I 2/10.

46 Captain C. V. Lloyd, *From Hongkong to Canton by the Pearl River* (Hongkong: Daily Press Office, 1902), pp. v, 2, 5.

47 Transcript of evidence, 'Rex v. C. de Noronha', enclosure No. 3 in Canton No. 71, 9 December 1908: TNA, FO 228/2255.

48 Reports on the incident: *SCMP*, 2, 4, 7 December 1908, p. 7, *Hongkong Daily Press*, 3, 4, 7 December 1908; letter: *Hongkong Telegraph*, 3 December 1903. For accounts of the controversy see Edward J. M. Rhoads, *China's Republican Revolution: The Case of Kwangtung, 1895–1913* (Cambridge, MA: Harvard University Press, 1975), pp. 141–3, and Bernard Mellor, *Lugard in Hong Kong: Empires, Education and a Governor at Work, 1907–1912* (Hong Kong: Hong Kong University Press, 1992), pp. 79–126.

49 Lloyd, *From Hongkong to Canton*, p. ix; Ants: poem by Loong Chow Ng of Fatshan: Enclosure No. 4, in Canton No. 72, 11 December 1908: TNA, FO 228/2255.

50 Canton No. 72, 11 December 1908: TNA, FO 228/2255.

51 See Peter Zarrow, 'Felling a dynasty, founding a republic', in Jeffrey N. Wasserstrom (ed.), *The Oxford Illustrated History of Modern China* (Oxford: Oxford University Press, 2016), pp. 90–117.

52 See Guanhua Wang, *In Search of Justice: The 1905–1906 Chinese anti-American Boycott* (Cambridge, MA: Harvard University Press, 2001); Rhoads, *China's Republican Revolution*, pp. 122–52.

53 D. R. Law to Lugard, 23 June 1909, Box 1170; Butterfield & Swire Hong Kong to H. H. Fox (Acting Consul-General Canton), 12 August 1909, Enclosure in Canton No. 91, 14 August 1909: TNA, FO 228/2255.

54 *Hongkong Weekly Press*, 21 August 1909, p. 163; British official fury and Law's responses can be found in: TNA, FO 228/2255 and in relevant correspondence in JSS I 2/10; G. E. Morrison to Valentine Chirol, 12 September 1909, Hui-min Lo (ed.), *The Correspondence of G. E. Morrison*, Volume 2, *1912–1920* (Cambridge: Cambridge University Press, 1978), pp. 523–4.

55 *Hongkong Weekly Press*, 16 August 1909, pp. 131–2, 147–8. The link between the donation and the *Fatshan* problem has been readily assumed, but it is not clear that it was anything but a useful coincidence, not least as the initiative stood at a very great remove from the demands of the boycott activists. While it was prominently noted in some of the public notices from Chinese officials, it does not feature as a factor in its resolution in correspondence within the firm, nor with British officials. On the perceived link see: Alfred H. Y. Lin, 'The Founding of the University of Hong Kong: British imperial ideas and Chinese practical common sense', in Chan Lau Kit-ching and Peter Cunich (eds), *An Impossible Dream: Hong Kong University from Foundation to Re-establishment, 1910–1950* (Hong Kong: Hong Kong University Press, 2002), pp. 11–13; and Bernard Mellor, *Lugard in Hong Kong: Empires, Education and a Governor at Work, 1907–1912* (Hong Kong: Hong Kong University Press, 1992), *passim*.

56 China Association General Committee Minutes, 4 May 1909: SOAS, China Association papers, CHAS/MCP/4; D. R. Law to J. H. Scott, 18 June 1909: JSS I 2/10.

57 *Hongkong Telegraph*, 2 December 1909.

58 The recruitment scheme in South China is the subject of chapter 2 of Peter Richardson, *Chinese Mine Labour in the Transvaal* (London: Macmillan, 1982), pp. 78–103, quotation from p. 93, table: A2, p. 192. Scepticism: Butterfield & Swire, Hong Kong, to Alfred Holt & Co., 3 July 1903: JSS I 2/10.

59 D. R. Law to J. H. Scott, 24 December 1904: JSS I 2/10.

60 D. R. Law to J. H. Scott, 24 April 1900, and enclosure, Butterfield & Swire Hong Kong to Alfred Holt & Co., 23 April 1909: JSS I 2/10; Falkus, *Blue Funnel Legend*, pp. 49–50.

61 This section draws on Butterfield & Swire Staff Books 1153, and 1154: JS&SL.

62 W. Poate to John Swire & Sons, 28 February 1902, and to J. H. Scott, 1 October 1902; H. W. Robertson to John Swire & Sons, 28 August 1905: all JSS I 2/10.

63 Lord Charles Beresford, *The Break-up of China: with an account of its present commerce ...* (London: Harper, 1899), p. 457.

64 John Swire & Sons to Butterfield & Swire Hong Kong and Shanghai, 21 April 1904, 5 May 1904: JSS II 7/4/1.

65 *Liverpool Echo*, 28 June 1916, p. 5.

CHAPTER 9   NEW CHINA

1 *Hongkong Daily Press*, 21 January 1914.

2 J. H. Scott to F. W. Butterfield, 29 May 1911: JSS I 1/15; Marriner and Hyde, *The Senior*, pp. 198–201.

3 *China Mail*, 9 July 1914; John Swire & Sons to H. W. Robertson, 3 June 1912; John Swire & Sons to H. W. Robertson, 3 and 17 June 1906: JSS I 1/15.

4 Henrietta Harrison, *The Making of the Republican Citizen: Political Ceremonies and Symbols in China 1911–1929* (Oxford: Oxford University Press, 2000).

5 Quoted in Jack Swire to E. F. Mackay, 10 November 1911: JSS I 1/15.

6 A pithy and insightful maritime history of the conflict can be found in Michael Miller, *Europe and the Maritime World: A Twentieth Century History* (Cambridge: Cambridge University Press, 2012), pp. 213–44. More detailed surveys of the British experience can be found in the volumes of the official histories: Sir Archibald Hurd, *The Merchant Navy* (3 volumes, London: John Murray, 1921–9); C. Ernest Fayle, *Seaborne Trade* (3 volumes, London: John Murray, 1920–24); as well as J. A. Salter, *Allied Shipping Control: An Experiment in International Administration* (Oxford: Clarendon Press, 1921).

7 Miller, *Europe and the Maritime World*, p. 223; Salter, *Allied Shipping Control*, pp. 73–5. Much of the disdain in London correspondence can be attributed to Warren Swire.

8 E. F. Mackay to John Swire & Sons, 30 October 1914; John Swire & Sons to Butterfield & Swire Hong Kong, 30 October 1914: JSS I 4/4/1; Lothar Deeg, *Kunst and Albers Vladivostok: The History of a German Trading Company in the Russian Far East 1864–1924* (Vladivostok: Far Eastern Federal University Press, 2012), pp. 283–98. One of those who served as assistant and interpreter in Vladivostok was George Faitzer, who in 1918 resigned to work as staff photographer for the American Red Cross in the city. Faitzer's later photographic portrait work in the United States can be found in various museum and archive collections, including the Library of Congress.

9 G. K. Nuttall to John Swire & Sons, 1 October 1914: JSS I 4/4/1.

10 Jack Swire to Mary Swire, 27 June 1905: JSS I 1/9/1. As of 31 December 1914 1,666 shares were each held by Jack and Warren Swire. Jim Scott's son Colin C. Scott held 418, and Jack, Colin and John Leslie Hunter, as executors of Jim Scott's estate, held 1,250: enclosure to John Swire & Sons to Butterfield & Swire, Shanghai, 9 April 1915: JSS I 4/4/2.

11 Jack Swire to Mary Swire, 27 June 1905; Jack Swire to Warren Swire, 11 December 1911: both in JSS I 1/9/1.

12 Jack Swire to Mary Swire, 29 June 1905: JSS I 1/9/1; Warren's entry into the partnership was not made public until that year: *SCMP*, 29 July 1905, p. 1.

13 Detailed records of the dispute seem not to survive, but in the calendar of charges prepared by the company's lawyers for November 1908 to August 1909 Mackintosh's letter is recorded as being received on 15 April 1909: JSS I 8/8; Scott: Butterfield & Swire Staff Record Book 154: JS&SL.

14 Jack Swire to William Swire, 4 December 1906; university: quoted in Charles Drage, *Taikoo* (London: Constable, 1970), p. 114; Jack Swire to J. H. Scott, 5 and 19 February 1909: JSS I 1/9/1; the course of the dispute can be followed in the detailed calendars of charges in JSS I 8/8; 'manipulation' and audit: report, probably by Dowler, in JSS I 8/8/2; perplexity: J. Ashton Cross 'Opinion', 22 December 1908, enclosed in Jack Swire to J. H. Scott, 8 January 1909, JSS I 3/1. The dispute got quite tense. Jack Mackintosh left Oxford in 1909 without taking a degree, and later that year undertook that rite of passage, a journey around the globe. When he and his sister, arriving in Hong Kong, asked to visit the dockyard and refinery, London, on legal advice, directed that Hong Kong was to 'receive civilly no more … do not give any information': see D. R. Law to John Swire & Sons, 11 December 1909: JSS I 2/10.

15 Jack Swire to J. H. Scott, 4 September 1911: JSS I 1/9/1.

16 John Swire & Sons pulled out of the Liverpool Porter Store when Lorimers went bankrupt. John Samuel Swire handed over his interests to Percy O'Brien, and the firm thereafter long remained in business: Marriner and Hyde, *The Senior*, p. 56.

17 Jack Swire to Warren Swire, 1 June 1904: JSS I 1/9/1.

18 Jack Swire to W. Rolles Biddle, 15 December 1902: JSS I 1/9/1.

19 John Swire & Sons London to Butterfield & Swire Shanghai and Hong Kong, 14 May 1917: JSS I 4/4/3.

20 F. H. Davies letter, 5 August 1914, NLW.

21 A. V. T. Dean, 'Notes on C. N. Co. History Section III: 1900–1918': JSS/11/2/8, JS&SL; tax: John Swire & Sons to E. F. Mackay and G. T. Edkins, 22 December 1916: JSS I 4/4/2; profiteering: W. C. Anderson quoted in: Paul Ward, *Red Flag and Union Jack: Englishness, Patriotism, and the British Left, 1881–1924* (Woodbridge: Boydell & Brewer, 1998), p. 135; shipowners: Margaret Morris, 'In search of the profiteer', in Chris Wrigley and John Shepherd (eds), *On the Move: Essays in Labour and Transport History Presented to Philip Bagwell* (London: A. & C. Black, 1991), p. 188. Requisition: Salter, *Allied Shipping Control*, pp. 70–75; prioritisation: Fayle, *Seaborne Trade*, iii, pp. 120–23. It was in fact the tenant farmer who profited most spectacularly overall, and whose sons were far less likely to fight: Adrian Gregory, *The Last Great War: British Society and the First World War* (Cambridge: Cambridge University Press, 2008), pp. 117–22, 137–42.

22 Blue Funnel: Falkus, *Blue Funnel Legend*, pp. 155–70; John Swire & Sons to Butterfield & Swire, 11 May 1917 (coast requisitions), Butterfield & Swire Hong Kong to John Swire & Sons, 5 June 1917 (lean time), John Swire & Sons to Butterfield & Swire, 1 February 1918 (Warren Swire); jailing: Butterfield & Swire Hong Kong to John Swire & Sons, 14 March 1917, all: JSS I 4/4/3; *SCMP*, 15 March 1917, p. 3.

23 Butterfield & Swire Hong Kong to John Swire & Sons London, 21 November 1916: JSS I 4/4/2; Butterfield & Swire Hong Kong to John Swire & Sons London, 17 October 1918: JSS I 4/4/3; Evans died there: *SCMP*, 8 April 1918, p. 2. One account of a Blue Funnel transport can be found in Daryl Klein, *With the Chinks!* (London: John Lane The Bodley Head, 1919). On the shipping of the Labour Corps recruits see Xu Guoqi, *Strangers on the Western Front: Chinese Workers and the Great War* (Cambridge, MA: Harvard University Press, 2014), pp. 52–3. In 1920 the Vladivostok branch was involved in organising Blue Funnel's carriage of Czech Legion troops across the Pacific, part of the Allied evacuation of some 60,000 former prisoners-of-war who had fought their way across Russia through the civil war: see Butterfield & Swire Hong Kong to John Swire & Sons, 10 July 1920, enclosure R. D. Holt to W. T. Payne, 7 May 1920: JSS I 4/4/4.

24 *SCMP*, 28 May 1915, p. 7; *Shanghai Times*, 6 June 1916, p. 8; 'Arthur B.-W.' [Brooke-Webb], 'With H.M.S. *Triumph* at Tsingtau', *Blackwood's Magazine* (May 1916), pp. 577–94. Brooke-Webb worked for the Huangpu Conservancy Board before joining up. James returned to the China Navigation fleet after the sinking, retiring after 30 years of service in 1936.

Blackie did not return after demoblisation. Langton Jones stayed in the Royal Navy, saw action at Jutland, was later a China Station gunboat commander and in 1929 became Inspector of Lighthouses in Bermuda: *SCMP*, 23 May 1936, p. 9; *The Times*, 2 September 1929, p. 17.

25 Bell: Jack Swire to E. F. Mackay, 13 November 1914: JSS I 4/4/1; Bell, John Alexander: TNA, WO 364/211; Jack Swire to Colin Scott, 23 August 1914, and Jack Swire to E. F. Mackay, 27 November 1914: JSS I 1/9/1.

26 J. K. Swire to Emily Swire, 13 August 1914, 17 November 1914, J. K. Swire to Jack Swire, 7 December 1914: J. K. Swire Letters, 1914: JS&SL.

27 On this see: Robert Bickers, *Getting Stuck in for Shanghai, or, Putting the Kibosh on the Kaiser from the Bund* (Sydney: Penguin China, 2014), and Sara Shipway, 'The Limits of Informal Empire: Britain's economic war in Shanghai, 1914–1919' (Unpublished PhD thesis, University of Bristol, 2018).

28 Jack Swire to E. F. McKay, 13 November 1914: Jack Swire Letters, 1914: JS&SL; Jack Swire to Colin Scott, 28 August 1914: JSS I 4/4/1.

29 Information collated from Butterfield & Swire Staff Record Books 153, and 154: JS&SL, and London Staff Ledger, 1904–1933: JSS I 5/1.

30 *Szechuen*: see *The Register of the Hongkong Memorial Commemorating the Chinese of the Merchant Navy and others in British Service who died in the Great War and whose graves are not known* (London: Imperial War Graves Commission, 1931), pp. 22–3, and 'Torpedoing of SS "Szechuen". Court of Enquiry', TNA, ADM 137/3583; *Kalgan: North China Herald*, 16 March 1918, p. 622, 'Loss of s.s. KALGAN', TNA, ADM 137/3580; *Yochow: Shanghai Times*, 23 March 1918, p. 7; *Anhui: North China Herald*, 31 August 1918, p. 523, and 'Loss of S.S. Anhui', TNA, ADM 137/3587. In total at least 945 Chinese seamen died on British naval and merchant marine vessels in 1914–18. Four days after Captain R. H. Lloyd was lost with SS *Kalgan* his wife gave birth to a child in a Shanghai hospital: *NCH*, 30 March 1918, p. 797.

31 *SCMP*, 29 August 1934, p. 9.

32 Joseland: *NCH*, 29 January 1916, pp. 257–8, 5 February 1916, pp. 318–19; *SCMP*, 2 October 1917, p. 3; Richardson: TNA, WO 339/49497.

33 *SCMP*, 25 March 1923, p. 10.

34 He was it seems very lucky not to have been court-martialled. For a taste of his war see his letters from the Middle East to John Swire and Colin Scott in JSS I 3/5.

35 *NCH*, 12 June 1915, pp. 799–802, 26 June 1915, pp. 953–4. This man's later army record suggests that the plea for mitigation was entirely misplaced. He was 'a stinker', a 'cool customer who has never been released from arrest without prejudice' are but two comments in a file detailing his unimpressive service as a lieutenant in the Machine Gun Corps in 1917–18: see file TNA, WO 359/92005. The army was unaware of his Shanghai escapade.

36 John Swire & Sons to G. T. Edkins and E. F. Mackay, 1 October 1915: JSS I 4/4/2.

37 Butterfield & Swire Hong Kong to John Swire & Sons, 4 November 1915: JSS II 7/4/22.

38 *SCMP*: 11 July 1918, pp. 6, 10; 20 July 1918, p. 11; 27 July 1918, pp. 10–11; appeal: *SCMP*, 26 July 1918, pp. 10–11. One of the three was excused on a second appeal: *SCMP*, 13 August 1918, p. 10.

39 'Hongkong Letter', *NCH*, 17 August 1918, p. 393; May: G. R. Sayer, *Hong Kong 1862–1919* (Hong Kong: Hong Kong University Press, 1975), p. 123.

40 Kemp, *Concise History*, p. 80.

41 F. H. Davies to Glyn Davies, 3 December 1908, NLW, Davies letters.

42 Davies: John Swire & Sons to Butterfield & Swire Shanghai and Hong Kong, 14 July 1911: JSS I 1/15; Frank H. Davies to mother, 21 February 1913: NLW, Davies Letters; Hong Kong University: 'J.H.F' in *SCMP*, 7 December 1912, p. 7.

43 Resignations: Jack Swire to E. F. Mackay, 29 January 1912; Scandinavians: John Swire & Sons to E. F. Mackay, 2 August 1912: both JSS I 1/9/1; and Frank H. Davies to Glyn Davies, 17 December 1915, NLW; John Swire & Sons to G. T. Edkins, 25 July 1913: JSS I 1/9/1. The dispute in 1911–13 can be followed in: JSS I 1/15.

44 *SCMP*, 16 December 1913, p. 3.

45 Davies letter, 21 February 1913: NLW, Davies letters; the course of the strike and the steady capitulation of the Swire management to the demands can be seen in John Swire & Sons to Butterfield & Swire Shanghai, 12 May and 19 May 1916: JSS I 1/15; *Shanghai Times*, 24 April 1916, p. 7.

46 Frank H. Davies letters, 3 April and 14 April 1916: NLW, Davies letters. Davies stayed in China until he was evacuated, in poor health, in 1937. In his 35 years there he worked for all three of the big lines, and for a number of smaller companies.

47 'Manifest', *NCH*, 22 June 1912, p. 858; Book-keeper, 'A Clerks' Protection Society', *NCH*, 30 December 911, p. 879.

48 Walter Fisher to A. Wright, 14 September 1900: JSS II 1/3/3.

49 As well as other sources noted below, this section draws in particular on S. Sugiyama, 'Marketing and Competition in China, 1895–1932: The Taikoo Sugar Refinery', in Linda Grover and Sinya Sugiyama (eds), *Commercial Networks in East Asia* (London: Routledge, 2001), pp. 140–58.

50 D. R. Law to John Swire & Sons, 26 January 1904: JSS I 2/10; the financial loss in Yokohama was substantial, but much more keenly felt was the potential reputational damage of publicity about such a childishly simple deceit: John Swire & Sons to Butterfield & Swire Hong Kong, 18 May, 12 July 1900: JSS I 1/13; Butterfield & Swire Hong Kong to John Swire & Sons, 17 August 1900: JSS I 2/9; John Swire & Sons to Butterfield &

Swire Hong Kong, 12 July 1918: JSS I 4/4/3. Instructions from 'Up-country Selling Organisation', 30 June 1929, in JSS V 6/3.

51 J. C. Fraser, 'Hupeh and Hunan per Luhan railway', 23 January 1905, Shanghai Academy of Social Sciences, Institute of Economics, Resource Centre for China Business History: Butterfield & Swire Archive Extracts [hereafter SASS], 02-008 (Lu-Han was the original name of what was later renamed the Jing-Han line); a contemporary account of this railway's development, and views of its potential, can be found Percy Horace Kent, *Railway Enterprise in China: An Account of its Origin and Development* (London: Edward Arnold, 1907), pp. 96–108.

52 Butterfield & Swire Newchwang to Butterfield & Swire Hong Kong, 4 June 1908: SASS 01-008.

53 'Up-country Selling Organisation', 30 June 1929: JSS V 6/3; Butterfield & Swire Newchwang to Butterfield & Swire Hong Kong, 4 June 1908: SASS 01-008.

54 J. H. Scott to H. W. Robertson, 2 December 1910, John Swire & Sons to Butterfield & Swire Hong Kong, 3 July 1914: JSS I 1/15 SP.

55 Details drawn from Butterfield & Swire staff books Nos 154, 155 and Butterfield & Swire Staff Register No. 4, 1924: JS&SL.

56 Butterfield & Swire Shanghai to John Swire & Sons 1 February 1918: JSS I 4/4/3. Robinson resigned to go to war, he was 'not worth holding to his contract', thought the firm. He was killed in East Africa in 1915: Butterfield & Swire Staff Book No. 155, JS&SL.

57 Gordon Campbell, 'Recollections of some aspects of earning a living in China between the wars', Private collection.

58 For reference see John Crompton's: *The Hunting Wasp* (London: Collins, 1948), p. 80, 109–12; *The Snake* (London: Faber & Faber, 1963), p. 27; *The Spider* (London: Collins, 1950), p. 230; *Ways of the Ant* (London: Collins, 1954), p. 214. Lamburn – his full name was John Battersby Crompton Lamburn – also published a number of novels. His extensive notes and diaries were destroyed in a fire in the 1930s.

59 A. V. T. Dean, 'Around China with the Sugar men', *Swire News* (December 1975), p. 7; *NCH*, 14 June 1924, p. 408. See also the extracts from interviews with former Swire staff undertaken by Christopher Cook and published as *The Lion and the Dragon: British Voices from the China Coast* (London: Elm Tree Books, 1985), pp. 35–48. John Barton left the company two years later, and took up managing a durian plantation in British Malaya instead. Some might have preferred bandits.

60 On BAT and Standard Oil see Sherman Cochran, *Encountering Chinese Networks: Western, Japanese, and Chinese Corporations in China, 1880–1937* (Berkeley: University of California Press, 2000), pp. 12–69.

61 Butterfield & Swire Shanghai to John Swire & Sons 1 February 1918: JSS I 4/4/3.

62 Sample 'Preliminary Report' form, in 'Up-country Selling Organisation', 30 June 1929: JSS V 6/3.

63 Copies of a selection of documents from the records of the Shanghai Butterfield & Swire office were made by historians from the Shanghai Academy of Social Sciences in the 1980s, and these are now held at the Academy's Centre for Business History Materials in its Institute of Economics. They were used in the preparation of a Chinese study edited by Zhang Zhongli, Chen Zengnian and Yao Xinrong, *Taigu jituan zai jiu Zhongguo* (The Swire Group in Old China) (Shanghai: Shanghai renmin chubanshe, 1991). The originals were then in the Shanghai Harbour Bureau Archives, but their current whereabouts is unclear. Danby: 'Motion at Special Meeting of the Chinkiang Municipal Council held on 1st May 1906', enclosed in Danby and Lewis H. Tamplin to B. G. Tours, 1 May 1906: SASS, 02-003; J. H. Scott to William Keswick, 8 July 1904: SASS, 02-007; Reinhardt, *Navigating Semi-Colonialism*, p. 119.

64 C. F. Remer, *Foreign Investments in China* (New York: Macmillan, 1933), pp. 423, 425, 469.

65 Reinhardt, *Navigating Semi-Colonialism*, pp. 115–25.

66 Warren Swire letters to Edith Warren, 20 December 1919–2 May 1920: JS&SL; Falkus, *Blue Funnel Legend*, pp. 185–6.

67 Revised terms and conditions: John Swire & Sons to Butterfield & Swire, 23 October 1920: JSS I 4/4/4. There was a caveat regarding salaries for women: 'refer to us if likely by comparison to raise any question of the sufficiency of the home agreement men's scale'.

68 Warren Swire to Edith Warren, 26 February 1924: JS&SL.

69 Almost 2,000 of Swire's photographs can be found on the 'Historical Photographs of China' platform: https://www.hpcbristol.net.

CHAPTER 10 BUILDING BRIDGES

1 On the National Products movement this chapter draws on Karl Gerth, *China Made: Consumer Culture and the Creation of the Nation* (Cambridge, MA: Harvard University Asia Center, 2003); a classic case study is Sherman Cochran, *Big Business in China: Sino-Foreign Rivalry in the Cigarette Industry, 1890–1930* (Cambridge, MA: Harvard University Press, 1980); more generally in this chapter I draw on my books *Britain in China: Community, Culture, and Colonialism, 1900–49* (Manchester: Manchester University Press, 1999), and *Out of China*.

2 See the essays in Sherman Cochran (ed.), *Inventing Nanjing Road: Commercial Culture in Shanghai, 1900–1945* (Ithaca: Cornell East Asia Program, 1999).

3 Dikötter, *Things Modern*, pp. 177–82. The companies concerned were Standard Oil of New York, and Asiatic Petroleum Company: on SOCONY see Sherman Cochran, *Encountering Chinese Networks: Western, Japanese, and Chinese Corporations in China, 1880–1937* (Berkeley: University of California

Press, 2000), pp. 12–43; Frans-Paul van der Putten, *Corporate Behaviour and Political Risk: Dutch Companies in China 1903–1941* (Leiden: Research School of Asian, African and Amerindian Studies, Leiden University, 2001), pp. 64–150.

4   See Virgil Kit-yiu Ho, *Understanding Canton: Rethinking Popular Culture in Republican Period* (Oxford: Oxford University Press, 2005), especially chapter 2, 'The Limits of Hatred: Popular Cantonese Attitudes Towards the West in the 1920s and the Early 1930s', pp. 49–94; novel: Mao Dun, *Midnight* [Ziye] (1933); poem: Xu Zhimo's, 'Leaving Cambridge' [1928].

5   Robert Bickers, 'British Concessions and Chinese Cities, 1910s–1930s', in Billy K. L. So and Madeleine Zelin (eds), *New Narratives of Urban Space in Republican Chinese Cities: Emerging Social, Legal and Governance Orders* (Leiden: Brill, 2013), pp. 157–96. The following section draws on voluminous documentation in files of Peking Legation correspondence in 'Dossier 108E Concessions and Settlements Amoy', Volumes 1 and 2: TNA, FO 228/3181 and FO 228/3182.

6   See Guanhua Wang, *In Search of Justice: The 1905–1906 Chinese Anti-American Boycott* (Cambridge, MA: Harvard University Asia Center, 2001); C. F. Remer, *A Study of Chinese Boycotts with Special Reference to Their Economic Effectiveness* (Baltimore: Johns Hopkins Press, 1933).

7   Livelihood: John Swire & Sons to Butterfield & Swire Shanghai, 17 November 1921, in Butterfield & Swire Shanghai to Consul Fraser, 27 December 1921, enclosed in Fraser to Alston, 26 February 1922: TNA, FO 228/3182; used: John Swire & Sons to Foreign Office, 2 February 1922, enclosed in Foreign Office to Alston, 16 February 1922: TNA, FO 228/3182.

8   Quotation from *Fujian ribao* 10 June 1921, enclosed in Amoy No. 32, 17 June 1921: TNA, FO 228/3181.

9   Mackay to John Swire & Sons, 24 March 1922: JSS I 4/4/5.

10 This section draws on: Ming Chan, 'Labor and Empire: The Chinese Labor Movement in the Canton Delta, 1895–1927 (Stanford University: Unpublished PhD thesis, 1975), pp. 268–307; Chan Lau Kit-ching, *China, Britain and Hong Kong, 1895–1945* (Hong Kong: Chinese University Press, 1990), pp. 169–76; John M. Carroll, *Edge of Empires: Chinese Elites and British Colonials in Hong Kong* (Cambridge, MA: Harvard University Press, 2005), pp. 131–59.

11 *SCMP*, 12 July 1913, p. 10.

12 *SCMP*, 4 March 1922, p. 14.

13 *SCMP*, 25 February 1922, p. 3, 22 March 1922, p. 8; Butterfield & Swire Hong Kong to John Swire & Sons, 10 March 1922: JSS I 4/4/5.

14 A list with details is in *SCMP*, 10 March 1922, p. 7: 120,000 men and women, equivalent to a fifth of the entire Chinese population of the colony, was estimated to be on strike.

15 *SCMP*, 4 March 1922, p. 7.

16 *SCMP*, 7 March 1922.

17 Strike post-mortems can be found in Butterfield & Swire Hong Kong to John Swire & Sons, 10 March 1922, John Swire & Sons to G. T. Edkins, 27 April 1922 and Butterfield & Swire Hong Kong to John Swire & Sons, 30 May 1922: JSS I 4/4/5.

18 Shanghai strike: see Shanghai Municipal Police, Special Branch, file IO 4652, 'Shanghai Seamen's Union, 1922–24': NARA, RG 263; Alan Hilton-Johnson, 'Confidential Report', 26 March 1922, enclosed in Butterfield & Swire Shanghai to John Swire & Sons, 5 May 1922: JSS I 4/4/5.

19 Arthur Ransome, *The Chinese Puzzle* (London: George Allen & Unwin, 1927), p. 30.

20 *SCMP*, 13 June 1925, p. 11; *Shenbao*, 16 June 1925, p. 5; *China Press*, 2 August 1925, p. 3; H. Owen Chapman, *The Chinese Revolution 1926-27: A Record of the Period under Communist Control as Seen from the Nationalist Capital, Hankow* (London: Constable, 1928), pp. 14–15; see also Peking No. 446, 5 July 1925, and enclosures, F3915/134/10: TNA, FO 371/10946.

21 *NCH*, 18 September 1926, pp. 529–37; Peter Gaffney Clark, 'Britain and the Chinese Revolution, 1925–1927' (University of California, Berkeley: Unpublished PhD thesis, 1973), pp. 234–76; John Masson to T. H. R. Shaw, 12 September 1926: JSS III 15/2/2. This file contains a great deal of material on the incident.

22 'Copy of Captain Bates' Report on S.S. "Wantung"': JSS III 15/2/2. Inflammatory press reports had it that he had been shot in the water. Warren Swire to Sir Miles Lampson, 18 January 1927: JSS I 4/3/4; *NCH*, 9 October 1926, p. 65. Missionaries downriver reported that his body had been found and buried: A. P. Blunt to Masson, 16 September 1926: JSS III 15/2/2.

23 TSR Minute Book, 45th Ordinary General Meeting, 31 May 1926: JSS V 7/1.

24 Reproduced in Robert Bickers, 'Changing British attitudes to China and the Chinese, 1928–1931 (University of London: Unpublished PhD thesis, 1992), p. 181.

25 *China Navigation Company: A History*, p. 141.

26 G. M. Young to John Swire & Sons, 25 March 1927: JSS I 4/4/7.

27 Lamburn's book, *Squeeze: A Tale of China* (London: John Murray, 1935), published after he had left the company (and under the surname Lambourne), is explicitly set in a firm that is set apart from Butterfield & Swire, mentioned as a different, much bigger firm, than his main character's employer, 'John Deepcar (Hong Kong) Ltd', but it is quite clearly based on his former employers.

28 John Swire & Sons to G. M. Young and T. H. R. Shaw, 23 October 1925: JSS I 4/4/6.

29 Donald W. Klein and Anne B. Clark, *Biographical Dictionary of Chinese Communism, 1921–1965* (Cambridge, MA: Harvard University Press, 1971), Volume 2, pp. 654–5.

30 See J. W. Robertson, 'Refinery Labour', March 1927, in G. M. Young to John Swire & Sons, 25 March 1927; on the Dockyard see G. M. Young to John Swire & Sons 14 January 1927, both in: JSS I 4/4/7. On labour organisation in China in the republican era see: Jean Chesneaux, *The Chinese Labor Movement*; Gail Hershatter, *The Workers of Tianjin, 1900–1949* (Stanford: Stanford University Press, 1986); Emily Honig, *Sisters and Strangers: Women in the Shanghai Cotton Mills, 1919–1949* (Stanford: Stanford University Press, 1986).

31 CNCo: John Swire & Sons to Butterfield & Swire Hong Kong and Shanghai, 31 October 1927: JSS I 4/4/6; *SCMP*, 12 July 1913, p. 10.

32 Roberts report, 'Chinese Staff'; wedding: to be accurate, they bowed to the bride and groom: Tom Lindsay 'No Mountains: Life and Work in Taikoo (Butterfield & Swire) from March 1933 to February 1949' (Unpublished MSS), Chapter 9: JS&SL. On gangsters and Shanghai dockers see Elizabeth J. Perry, *Shanghai on Strike: The Politics of Chinese Labor* (Stanford: Stanford University Press, 1993), pp. 53–4; S. A. Smith, *Like Cattle and Horses: Nationalism and Labor in Shanghai, 1895–1927* (Durham, NC: Duke University Press, 2002), pp. 175–6. On the Green Gang see Brian G. Martin, *The Shanghai Green Gang: Politics and Organised Crime, 1919–1937* (Berkeley: University of California Press, 1996).

33 Chihyun Chang, *Government, Imperialism and Nationalism in China: The Maritime Customs Service and its Chinese Staff* (London: Routledge, 2013), pp. 41–61.

34 W. E. Kirby, Secretary, China Coast Officers' Guild, 'C.N.Co', 5 October 1926, enclosed in Butterfield & Swire Shanghai to John Swire & Sons, 11 March 1927: JSS I 4/4/7.

35 John Swire & Sons to Butterfield & Swire Hong Kong, 18 June 1926; T. H. R. Shaw, Shanghai, to John Swire & Sons, 6 January 1927, both in JSS I 4/4/7.

36 See especially the correspondence back and forth to China in JSS I 4/4/6 and JSS I 4/4/7.

37 John Swire & Sons to Butterfield & Swire Shanghai, 23 September 1927, refers to a pamphlet on 'Works Committees' and clippings from the *Railway Review* and *The Times* on railway company staff relations innovations: JSS I 4/4/7.

38 System: C. C. Roberts, 'Chinese Staff', April 1934: JSS II 7/1/4/1 [hereafter Roberts' Report]; the elder Chun died aged 89 in late August 1919: *NCH*, 6 September 1919, p. 615; *Shenbao*, 22 September 1919, p. 11; Mok funeral: *SCMP*, 10 September 1917, p. 2; palace and swindle: Mok Ying

Kwai, 'Yingshang Taigu Yanghang zai Huanan de yewu huodong yu Mo shi jiazu' (The British firm Butterfield & Swire's commercial activities in South China and the Mok family) [1965] *Wenshi ziliao xuanji*, No. 114 (1988), pp. 127–75 [quotation from p. 160]; audit: N. S. Brown to John Swire & Sons, 27 June 1928: JSS V 1/3; Howard Cox, Huang Biao and Stuart Metcalfe, 'Compradors, Firm Architecture and the "Reinvention" of British Trading Companies', *Business History*, 45:2 (2003), pp. 22–3.

39 Butterfield & Swire Shanghai to Butterfield & Swire Hankow, 21 March 1927, Chun Shut Kai to Butterfield & Swire Shanghai 8 and 9 November 1927, 9 December 1927, and Butterfield & Swire Shanghai to Butterfield & Swire Hankow, 30 September 1927, all in: JSS I 4/4/7; bankruptcy: *Shenbao*, 27 May 1932. Given a second chance, Wei later absconded, leaving his affairs in 'a perfectly shocking state' and indebted to a significant degree: N. S. Brown to J. K. Swire, 13 and 24 June 1930, J. K. Swire to H. W. Robertson, 29 May 1930: JSS I 3/6.

40 Butterfield & Swire Shanghai to Butterfield & Swire Hong Kong, 20 December 1927, John Swire & Sons to Butterfield & Swire Hong Kong, 18 June 1926, 17 June 1927: JSS I 4/4/7. Yang's father was the disgraced first CNCo shipping comprador, Yang Guixuan, who had died of tuberculosis before he could be tried for fraud in early 1885: T. J. Lindsay, 'Biographies', c. 1966: JS&SL.

41 Roberts' Report; Roberts, staff record, Butterfield & Swire Staff Register (4): JS&SL. Roberts rated 'A. 1' in an early assessment with great potential, would later become a director of the firm in London (1952–8).

42 The Swire Archives at John Swire & Sons, London, holds two sources for information about GFA: [David Bentley-Taylor], 'George Findlay Andrew', an undated MSS memoir by a nephew, and T. J. Lindsay's unpublished memoir. Contact with Swire staff probably first came about through Andrew's pioneering discovery of a Neolithic burial site in Gansu. Shanghai Taipan N. S. Brown built up an extensive and important collection of Yangshao pottery through Andrew, sold at Sotheby's in 1948: Freer-Sackler Museum, collector biography, 'George Findlay Andrew 1887–1971 Missionary and Collector', https://www.freersackler.si.edu/wp-content/uploads/2017/09// Andrew-George-Findlay.pdf.

43 Warren Swire to J. S. Scott, 3 January 1935: JSS I 3/9.

44 Tom Lindsay, 'No Mountains: Life in China and work in Taikoo (Butterfield & Swire) from March 1933 to February 1949', unpublished memoir: JS&SL. This two-volume unpublished memoir provides a detailed and candid history of the Department of Chinese Affairs from its inception.

45 'Further thoughts', undated, c. January 1920, J. K. Swire diary: JS&SL; 'New Scheme for Ex-Officers', *The Times*, 23 February 1920, p. 14; 'Unemployed Officers', *The Times*, 19 August 1920, p. 12.

46 J. K. Swire interview with Christopher Cook, 5 February 1979: JS&SL; Timothy Weston, *From Appointments to Careers: A History of the Oxford University Careers Service 1892–1992* (Oxford: Oxford University Careers Service, 1994), pp. 89–90.

47 London Staff Ledger: JSS I 5/1.

48 Lindsay, 'No Mountains'. For his career see also Lindsay staff record, Butterfield & Swire Staff Register (4): JS&SL.

49 John Swire & Sons to Butterfield & Swire Shanghai and Hong Kong, 20 December 1923: JSS II 7/4/32; Mary Whimster, a graduate of St Andrew's University, was one of these, first heading to Shanghai in 1922 as a 28-year-old, and working with the company there and then in Hong Kong until 1935, when the fall in exchange led her to leave. She had 'all along kept my standard to that of second rate boarding-house accommodation and I do not think this could be considered too high': Warren Swire to John S. Scott, 3 April 1936: JSS I 3/9.

50 J. S. Scott to John Swire & Sons, 7 May 1936: JSS I 3/9. Whimster's career can be traced through Staff Letter Books 7, 8, 9 and 12, and her resignation in No. 48: all in JSS II 7/4/48.

51 John Swire & Sons to Butterfield & Swire, 20 January 1927; and the replies in letters to John Swire & Sons from Butterfield & Swire Hong Kong, 26 February 1927, and Shanghai, 27 March 1927: JSS II 2/6. British American Tobacco had established a unit to make films at which its products could be marketed and sold, but while the company found it also useful as a diplomatic tool, it proved too expensive and was shut down: Harold Cox, *The Global Cigarette: Origins and Evolution of British American Tobacco, 1880–1945* (Oxford: Oxford University Press, 2000), p. 162; Yingjin Zhang, *Chinese National Cinema* (London: Routledge, 204), pp. 72–3.

52 G. W. Swire to Edith Warren, 9 February 1929: JS&SL; C. C. Scott to G. W. Swire, 16 October 1931: JSS I 3/7. On Whyte see my *Britain in China*, p. 38.

53 This section draws on the reports at the annual meetings of TSR shareholders in: JSS V 7/1, especially 1929–32 (in a sign of the legacy of the original financing of the plant, one of those attending in 1929 was Antonia Marian Gamwell, one of the daughters of former partner Frederick Gamwell); staff: 'Refinery Staff', Box 178: JS&SL.

54 This also raised questions about housing them suitably – not as European staff might be housed, but also not on the same lines as the Chinese hands – as well as teaching them to consider themselves different in status to the mass of refinery Chinese staff.

55 Plant: H. W. Robertson to C. C. Scott, 16 March 1928: JSS I 3/6; advertisements: *Shenbao*, 15 January 1929, p. 16; *SCMP*, 19 April 1929, p. 7; details of the winding up of CSR can be found in: *SCMP*, 19 May 1928, p. 16, 15 May 1929, p. 16 and 22 May 1933, p. 18.

56 Talati: *SCMP*, 17 May 1933, p. 12, and Wright, ed., *Twentieth-Century Impressions of Hongkong, Shanghai, and Other Treaty Ports of China*, p. 226; Damri: J. K. Swire to John Swire & Sons, 2 February 1935: JSS I 3/9.

57 Advertisements in *Times of India*: 27 October 1932, p. 14; 5 January 1934, p. 14; 27 November 1937, p. 13; brief: Butterfield & Swire Hong Kong to Stronach & Co., Bombay, 9 May 1930: JSS V 1/5/2.

58 Chinese characters: G. E. Mitchell (Bombay) to Butterfield & Swire, Hong Kong, 14 December 1929: JSS V 1/5/1; Laughing Buddha & blue: Butterfield & Swire Hong Kong to John Swire & Sons, 14 January 1930: JSS V 1/5/1; brand: G. E. Mitchell (Bombay) to John Swire and Sons, 31 March 1932, JSS V 1/5a; A. R. H. Philips, TSR, to John Swire & Sons, 3 March 1933: JSS V 1/8/2; *Punch*, 19 October 1932, p. iv.

59 Böcking, *No Great Wall*, pp. 159–88.

60 Emily M. Hill, *Smokeless Sugar: The Death of a Provincial Bureaucrat and the Construction of China's National Economy* (Vancouver: University of British Columbia Press, 2010), pp. 148–78; Colin C. Scott to J. S. Scott, 16 December 1932; refinery: John Swire & Sons to J. S. Scott, 17 February 1933, both: JSS I 3/9; smuggling: Philip Thai, *China's War on Smuggling: Law, Economic Life, and the Making of the Modern State, 1842–1965* (New York: Columbia University Press, 2018).

61 J. K. Swire to John Swire & Sons, 8 March 1935, and 'Notes on Conversation with Mr. T.V. Soong', and 'Minute of Meeting and chat with T.V. Soong', 9 May 1935: JSS I 3/9.

CHAPTER 11 CATASTROPHE

1 *SCMP*, 30 November 1920, p. 1; *China Press*, 26 January 1938, p. 1; *Nanjing Despatch*, No. 4216, 5 March 1938: SHAC, 679(1), 14875; Consul, Nanjing, to Embassy, 25 November 1937, TNA, FO 676/346.

2 Butterfield & Swire offices Hankow and Shanghai, telephone conference, 18 November 1937, Butterfield & Swire Shanghai to John Swire & Sons, 5 and 19 November 1937: JSS III 2/21; Graham Torrible, *Yangtze Reminiscences* (Hong Kong: John Swire & Sons, Ltd, 1990), pp. 60–61; Suping Lu (ed.), *Terror in Minnie Vautrin's Nanjing: Diaries and correspondence, 1937–38* (Urbana: University of Illinois Press, 2006), pp. 56–64.

3 For the best recent history of the conflict see Rana Mitter, *China's War with Japan: The Struggle for Survival* (London: Allen Lane, 2013).

4 Mitter, *China's War with Japan*, pp. 119–40.

5 Lloyd E. Eastman, 'Facets of an Ambivalent Relationship: Smuggling, Puppets, and Atrocities During the War, 1937–1945,' in Akira Iriye (ed.), *The Chinese and the Japanese: Essays in Political and Cultural Interactions* (Princeton: Princeton University Press, 1980), pp. 275–303.

6 Paul van de Meerrsche, *A Life to Treasure: The Authorised Biography of Han Lih-wu* (London: Sherwood Press, 1987), p. 28.

7 *Daily Telegraph*, 21 December 1937, p. 7; 'Skipper of B. & S. Coaster Whangpu tells of rescue', *China Press*, 26 January 1938, p. 1.

8 Its weak grasp on the history of British actions in China, which was wholly representative of British understandings of that story, was reinforced by its statement that this had taken place during the 1900 Boxer uprising: *Manchester Guardian*, 20 April 1938, p. 8.

9 This section draws on McKenzie's report, 'Nanking Evacuation December 1937', 17 December 1937: JSS III 2/21.

10 'Australian's story of attack', *The Herald*, 14 December 1937, p. 24.

11 See Japanese explanations in memorandum enclosed in Sir R. Craigie (Tokyo) to Foreign Office, No. 50, 2 February 1938: TNA, FO 371/22049.

12 Butterfield & Swire offices Hankow and Hong Kong, telephone conference, 6 December 1937: JSS III 2/21.

13 Lindsay, 'No Mountains', pp. 230–31.

14 See Bickers, *Out of China*, p. 199.

15 Antony Best, '"That loyal British subject?": Arthur Edwardes and Anglo-Japanese relations, 1932–41', in J. E. Hoare (ed.), *Britain and Japan: Biographical Portraits*, Volume III (London: Japan Library, 1999), pp. 227–39.

16 NARA, RG263, SMP D4454, 'Translation of documents seized on February 1 1933, From the offices of the Central Headquarters of the Chinese Communist Youth League …', Exhibit 15, 'Minutes of the Presidium Meeting on February 1, 1933'; on Zhu see Smith, *Like Cattle, Like Horses*, pp. 100, 139–40, and 'Zhu Baoting xiao zhuan' (Short biography of Zhu Baoting', in *Shanghai haiyuan gongren yundong shi* (History of the Shanghai seamen's labour movement) (Beijing: Zhonggong dangshi chubanshe, 1991), pp. 311–17.

17 J. Swire, 18 July 1927 in: John Swire & Sons Minute Book No 2: JSS I 12/1.

18 *Chelmsford Chronicle*, 28 January 1910, p. 7; *Essex Chronicle*, 26 May 1933, p. 7, 2 June 1933, p. 2; *NCH*, 31 May 1933, p. 335; Adrian Swire, 'John Swire 1861–1933', unpublished note: JS&SL.

19 Ramon H. Myers, 'The World Depression and the Chinese Economy 1930–6', in Ian Brown (ed), *The Economies of Africa and Asia in the Inter-War Depression* (London: Routledge, 1989), pp. 257–78; this and the following paragraph draw on Ronald Hope, *A New History of British Shipping* (London: John Murray 1990), pp. 357–81; and Miller, *Europe and the Maritime World*, pp. 245–75.

20 Profits: John Swire & Sons to Butterfield & Swire Shanghai, 11 December 1931: JSS III 2/12; glasses: John Swire & Sons to Butterfield & Swire Shanghai, 21 August 1931: JSS III 1/11; correspondence: John Swire & Sons

to Butterfield & Swire Hong Kong, 31 October 1931: JSS III 2/10; Falkus, *Blue Funnel Legend*, pp. 207–10.

21 M. W. Scott letters, 6 May 1934, SOAS Special Collections, Scott papers, PPMS 49, Box 1 Folder 5; Lindsay, 'No mountains', pp. 233–5.

22 Figures from: CNCo to Sedgwick Collins & Co, undated, referring to October 1930 (foreign staff), JSS III 3/1; John Swire & Sons to Butterfield & Swire Shanghai, 27 February 1931, JSS III 2/11, and CNCo Minute Book No. 2: JSS III 17/3.

23 *SCMP*, 17 March 1933, pp. 19, 21.

24 CNCo, Minute Book No. 2: JSS III 17/3. Generally on this topic see Anne Reinhardt, '"Decolonisation" on the Periphery: Liu Xiang and Shipping Rights Recovery at Chongqing, 1926–38', *Journal of Imperial and Commonwealth History*, 36:2 (2008), pp. 259–74.

25 In 1879 a Chinese passenger, Cheong Wan, who had booked a first-class ticket, failed in his suit for damages against the *Ichang's* master, Captain Martin, after Martin refused to allow him to dine at table: 'No Chinese allowed' had been the response: *China Mail*, 12 June 1879. Martin supplied the catering, and had the right, the judge ruled, to refuse. See also Reinhardt, *Navigating Semi-Colonialism*, pp. 253–94.

26 Cabin names: John Swire & Sons to Butterfield & Swire Shanghai, 15 May 1931: JSS III 2/8; compradors: Butterfield & Swire Shanghai to John Swire & Sons, 26 December 1930: JSS III 1/9; passengers: Butterfield & Swire Shanghai to John Swire & Sons, 11 January 1929, and enclosure: JSS III 2/8; control: John Swire & Sons to Butterfield & Swire Shanghai and Hong Kong, 17 March 1933: JSS III 2/17.

27 Butterfield & Swire Shanghai to John Swire & Sons, 23 October 1936: JSS XII 1/3.

28 Teaboy practices are outlined in SMP Special Branch file D5293, report dated 8 August 1933; 'How Tea Boys harm Shipping firms', *NCH*, 21 October 1936, p. 120; robbery: 'Notes on Canton Seamen's Union Agitation', 1 July 1933: JSS XII 1/3; *Hanyang*: Butterfield & Swire Shanghai to John Swire & Sons, 27 November 1931: JSS III 1/11. This section draws on the discussion on the teaboy crisis in Reinhardt, *Navigating Semi-Colonialism*, pp. 263–78.

29 In his frank account of shipping work just after the war, one senior Chinese employee remembered that ship compradors took 40 per cent of any excess over recorded fares; captains, chief officers and chief engineers secured a cut of the remainder according to their degree of overall responsibility on board: Transcript of Interview with Dawson Kwauk, 15 September 1992, pp. 10–13: JS&SL.

30 Hankow Semi-official letter, 20 August 1934: SHAC, 679 (1), 32145; Butterfield & Swire Shanghai to John Swire & Sons, 5 June 1931: JSS III 1/10; *Tuckwo*: G. Clarke to General Manager, Indo-China SNCo,

11 August 1931, in SHAC, 679(1) 27977; Swire: CNCo, Minute Book No. 2: JSS III 17/3; masters and mates: see, for example, John Swire & Sons to Butterfield & Swire Shanghai and Hong Kong, 27 November 1931: JSS III 1/11.

31   *China Press*, 22 January 1933, p. 9; handling: 'Notes on Canton Seamen's Union Agitation', 1 July 1933: JSS XII 1/3; on the teaboys see also Peter Kwok Fai Law's doctoral work in progress: 'Maritime Teaboys and the making of Chinese working class culture in China, 1927–1950'.

32   Martin, *Shanghai Green Gang*, pp. 129–31.

33   *China Press*, 10 August 1933, p. A; *SCMP*, 28 November 1933, p. 19.

34   *Daily Telegraph*, 9 September 1933, p. 9; Clifford Johnson, *Pirate Junk: Five Months Captivity with Manchurian Bandits* (London: Jonathan Cape, 1934); J. V. Davidson-Houston, *The Piracy of the Nanchang* (London: Cassell, 1961), pp. 82–3.

35   Letter from the captives, 12 July 1933, enclosed in Peking No. 1061, 4 August 1933: TNA, FO 371/17132.

36   *Chelmsford Chronicle*, 26 May 1933, p. 7.

37   This was Arnolis Hayman, eventually held for 14 months. R. A. Bosshardt, seized with him, endured an even longer captivity: Anne-Marie Brady (ed.), *A Foreign Missionary on the Long March: The Unpublished Memoirs of Arnolis Hayman of the China Inland Mission* (Honolulu: University of Hawai'i Press, 2011).

38   C. C. Scott to G. W. Swire, 10 February 1935: JSS I 3/9. Dr W. S. Sinton, *Memoirs of an Ex Sailor* (Bristol, privately published, 2008), pp. 12–17; *NCH*, 6 February 1935, pp. 206, 212, 13 February 1935, pp. 251–4, 273; treat: J. O. P. Bland, 'The Genial Chinese Pirate', *Saturday Review*, 16 March 1935, p. 333.

39   C. C. Scott to John Swire & Sons, 15 February 1935: JSS I 3/9.

40   A rich source about the seizure is provided in statements and reports in Shanghai No. 70, 14 February 1935 and enclosures: TNA, FO 371/19316.

41   *NCH*, 13 February 1935, p. 273.

42   This discussion draws from the appeal court judgements: *China Navigation Company, Limited V. Attorney-General* [1930. C. 2497.]

43   Butterfield & Swire Shanghai to John Swire & Sons, 2 May 1930: JSS III, 2/9; Butterfield & Swire Shanghai to John Swire & Sons, 27 February 1931: JSS III, 1/10; Butterfield & Swire Hong Kong to John Swire & Sons, 22 August 1930: JSS III 1/9; Butterfield & Swire Hong Kong to John Swire & Sons, 26 April 1929: JSS III 1/7; Butterfield & Swire Shanghai to John Swire & Sons, 4 January 1929: JSS III, 2/8; 'Guards turn pirates', *Shipping & Engineering*, 24 April 1925, extract in: NMM, T. T. Laurenson Papers: MS 87/085, U1414, folder A4.

44   China Navigation Company, Limited V. Attorney-General [1930. C. 2497.], p. 211.

45 This survey largely draws on reports in CNCo Minute Book 2: JSS III 17/3.

46 A. V. T. Dean, 'The blockade of the Yangtsze and the last days of C.N.Co. river navigation', Misc Acc 2013/07: JS&SL.

47 *SCMP*, 26 September 1939, p. 15.

48 Antony Best, *Britain, Japan and Pearl Harbor: Avoiding War in East Asia, 1936–41* (London: Routledge, 1995), pp. 111–31.

49 G. W. Swire to Wingfield Digby, 20 July 1940, 'Letters to Edith Warren': JS&SL. This paragraph draws on various of these letters from July to December 1940.

50 Richard Overy, *The Bombing war: Europe 1939–1945* (London: Allen Lane, 2013), pp. 91–4.

51 *The Times*, 12 December 1940; *NCH*, 18 December 1940; *SCMP*, 12 December 1940. On the urban secret service war see: Frederic Wakeman Jr, *The Shanghai Badlands: Wartime Terrorism and Urban Crime, 1937–1941* (Cambridge: Cambridge University Press, 1996).

52 Quentin Reynolds, *Only the Stars are Neutral* (New York: Blue Ribbon Books, 1943), pp. 27–41, quotation from p. 35; Terence H. O'Brien, *Civil Defence* (London: HMSO, 1955), pp. 419–20; J. K. Swire letters, 11 and 13 May 1941: JS&SL.

53 John Swire & Sons to Butterfield & Swire Shanghai and Hong Kong, 16 May 1941; 'Records to be replaced', c. May 1941; Butterfield & Swire Hong Kong to John Swire & Sons, 3 October 1941: JSS I 2/29; Lindsay, 'No Mountains', p. 240.

54 Gordon Campbell, 'Recollections of some aspects of earning a living in China', pp. 16–18.

55 Transcript of Interview with Dawson Kwauk, p. 10: JS&S.

56 J. B. Woolley, Royal Naval Offices, Shanghai, to Butterfield & Swire, 6 August 1941: SASS 03-008; *The Royal Navy and the Mediterranean*, Volume II, *November 1940–December 1941* (London: Routledge, 2002) [London: Historical Section, Admiralty, 1957], p. 214; Liu: casualty card in 'Lists of Merchant Seamen Deaths. National Maritime Museum, Greenwich', via Ancestry.co.uk.

57 CNCo Minute Book 2, p. 363: JSS III 17/3.

58 Details from: Refinery Staff Book, Box 178; Dockyard Staff book, Box 175: JS&SL. These records include details of the fate of employees who had been killed. For accounts of the fall of Hong Kong and the occupation see: Chi Man Kwong and Yiu Lun Tsoi, *Eastern Fortress: A Military History of Hong Kong, 1840–1970* (Hong Kong: Hong Kong University Press, 2014), pp. 161–224; Philip Snow, *The Fall of Hong Kong: Britain, China and the Japanese Occupation* (New Haven: Yale University Press, 2003).

59 The letter survives in Japanese archives, and is reproduced in: Brian Coak, 'The Boys in Blue: Escape from Shanghai 43', https://gwulo.com/sites/gwulo/files/misc/Brian-Coak-on-Jack-Conder-Part2.pdf (accessed 2

February 2019). Conder made his way to safety, and by September 1944 was working again for Butterfield & Swire in Bombay.

60 C. C. Roberts to A. V. T. Dean, 6 July 1942: C. C. Roberts papers: SOAS MS 380906.

61 A. V. T. Dean to G. W. Swire, 27 June 1942; A. V. T. Dean to John Swire & Sons, 27 March 1942; Butterfield & Swire India, to John Swire & Sons, 19 January 1945, all in: JSS I 5/1a.

62 E. McLaren to C. C. Roberts, 25 September 1942: SOAS MS 380906; J. K. Swire to John Masson, 14 July 1942: JS&SL.

63 E. McLaren to A. V. T. Dean, 3 August 1942: JSS I 5/1a.

64 Lindsay, 'No Mountains', pp. 245–51; A. V. T. Dean, 'Recollections of Two World Wars', and A. V. T. Dean, 'Report of Arrest and Imprisonment in Gendarmerie Prison in Shanghai (Bridge House)', 28 August 1945: JS&SL; A. V. T. Dean to John Swire & Sons, 29 September 1945: JSS I 5/1a.

65 Kwauk's family were leading figures in the Swatow business community in Shanghai, and patrons of CNCo. After 1949, Kwauk would become head of the Swire operations in Taiwan.

66 These details come from various BAAG reports, courtesy of Elizabeth Ride: Kukong Intelligence Report No. 2, 8 June 1942: Australian War Memorial, PR 82/068 11/10; J. D. Clague, 'Report on conditions in Occupied Hongkong', 1 March 1945: TNA, WO 208/7147. See also documents and extracts in 'Taikoo Dockyard during the Occupation 1942-1945', on the Industrial History of Hong Kong Group website: https://industrialhistoryhk.org/taikoo-dockyard-occupation-1942-1945/ (accessed 16 January 2019).

67 'Japan News No. 136', NHK 'War Testimonials Archives', URL: https://www2.nhk.or.jp/archives/shogenarchives/jpnews/movie.cgi?das_id=D0001300521_00000&seg_number=004, accessed January 2019; J. K. Swire and J. S. Scott to John Swire & Sons, 16 May 1946: JSS I 3/15.

68 Edwin Ride, *BAAG: Hong Kong Resistance 1942–1945* (Hong Kong: Oxford University Press, 1981), pp. 205–7.

69 'Employment available in Southern Regions', *Hongkong News*, 20 April 1944, p. 2; Charles Cruikshank, *SOE in the Far East* (Oxford: Oxford University Press, 1983), pp. 154–6; Loss of life: 'Dockyard', 28 August 1945, enclosed in Butterfield & Swire Hong Kong to John Swire & Sons, 31 August 1945: JSS I 5/1a; Kweilin Intelligence Summary No. 66, 15 September 1944; Kweilin Intelligence Report No. 80, 5 January 1945, courtesy of Elizabeth Ride; Steven K. Bailey, *Bold Venture: The American Bombing of Japanese-Occupied Hong Kong, 1942–1945* (Lincoln NE: Potomac Books, 2019).

70 Jack Robinson to John Masson, 20 October 1943: JSS I 5/1a.

71 N. P. Fox, 'Report on Conditions in Hong Kong during and after the Outbreak of Hostilities on 8th December 1941'; 'Refinery', 31 August 1945, enclosed in Butterfield & Swire Hong Kong to John Swire & Sons, 31 August 1945: both in JSS I 5/1a.

72 Stanley Salt, 'Sinking of the *S.S. Sinkiang*', in Joyce Hibbert (ed.), *Fragments of War: Stories from Survivors of World War II* (Toronto: Dundurn Press, 1985), pp. 32–43; *Hoihow* and *Kaying*: see their entries on WikiSwire: https://wikiswire.com/wiki/Category:Ships.

73 Hope, *New History of British Shipping*, p. 383; Benton and Gomez, *Chinese in Britain*, pp. 76–80.

74 A. V. T. Dean to John Swire & Sons, 27 March 1942, and 5 February 1942: JSS I 5/1a (for the capture of the ship see 'The reminiscences of Andrew Watson', on 'Chekiang 1', WikiSwire, URL: https://wikiswire.com/wiki/Chekiang_I (accessed 1 February 2019)); Tony Fletcher, 'Fremantle 1939 to 1945: Extraordinary Events at the Port', *Fremantle Studies* 1 (1999), pp. 25–9; 'Chinese seamen help army', *Canberra Times*, 6 September 1943, p. 3. See National Archives of Australia file, NAA: A433, 1949/2/9033, 'Chinese Labour Battalion in WA, 1942–1947'; Drew Cottle, 'Forgotten foreign militants: The Chinese Seamen's Union in Australia, 1942–1946', paper presented at the 2001 Australian Society for Labour History conference: https://labourhistorycanberra.org/2014/10/2001-conference-forgotten-foreign-militants-the-chinese-seamens-union-in-australia-1942-46/.

75 *Liverpool Echo*, 11 April 1942, p. 3; Tony Lane, *The Merchant Seamen's War* (Manchester: Manchester University Press, 1990), pp. 78; Meredith Oyen, 'Fighting for Equality: Chinese Seamen in the Battle of the Atlantic, 1939–1945', *Diplomatic History*, 38:3 (2014), pp. 526–48.

76 Kenneth H. C. Lo, *Forgotten Wave: Stories and Sketches from the Chinese Seamen during the Second World War* (Padiham: Padiham Advertiser Ltd, 1947); see also his *The Feast of My Life* (London: Doubleday, 1993), pp. 127–41. Lo became rather better known in later life as a chef and writer.

77 J. S. Scott to J. R. Masson, undated, c. August 1943: JS&SL. On the role of British shipping experts in the war see Miller, *Europe and the Maritime World*, pp. 283–6.

78 J. S. Scott to G. W. Swire, 19 January 1943; G. W. Swire to John Masson, 21 April 1943, G. W. Swire to Colin Scott and John Scott, 13 August 1943: JSS I 3/13.

79 This paragraph draws on transcripts of various letters to John Masson from Jock and Warren Swire, and John Swire Scott, 1942–5: Masson Letters: JS&SL.

80 J. K. Swire to J. S. Scott, 30 July 1942, and *passim* thereafter; John Keswick to John Masson 8 July 1943, in Masson to G. W. Swire, 14 July 1943: JSSI 3/13. On Keswick's war see Richard J. Aldrich, *Intelligence and the War Against Japan: Britain, America and the Politics of Secret Service* (Cambridge: Cambridge University Press, 2000), pp. 281–3.

81 J. R. Masson to G. W. Swire, 29 March 1944: JSS I 3/13; G. W. Swire to J. R. Masson, 21 April 1944, Masson Letters: JS&SL.

82 J. S. Scott to G. W. Swire, 11 March 1944 and related correspondence: JS&SL; John Swire & Sons to Butterfield & Swire Shanghai and Hong

Kong, 27 October 1936, and Butterfield & Swire Shanghai, 3 October 1936: JSS I 2/30/5.

83 'Has intelligence', ran the 'Staff First Impression Report' on one man in 1934, but 'gives the impression of being slow in picking up things' (Staff Letters No. 38: JSS II 7/4/46). Sir Edmund Leach, thus damned, later became a Professor of Social Anthropology at Cambridge University and Provost of King's College; but his three years in China from 1933 to 1936 had at least given him his first exposure to cultures outside his own.

84 C. C. Roberts to John Swire & Sons, 30 August 1945, JSS I 5/1c; see also Butterfield & Hong Kong to John Swire & Sons, 31 August 1945, and enclosure 'Report on Taikoo Sugar Refinery, and Report on Taikoo Dockyard': JSS I 5/1a.

85 R. M. Chaloner to John Swire & Sons, 8 September 1945: A. V. T. Dean to John Swire & Sons, 29 September 1945; 'Record of Post-war recovery of Holt's wharf property from the Japanese', 10 September 1945, in R. M. Chaloner to John Swire & Sons, 15 September 1945: JSS I 5/1c.

86 A. V. T. Dean (Beijing) to John Swire & Sons, c. 12 September 1945; R. J. Tippin to A. V. T. Dean, Memorandum, 30 May 1942: JSS I 5/1c; Lindsay, 'No Mountains', p. 277.

87 *SCMP*, 5 September 1945, p. 2, 26 September 1945, p. 2; C. C. Roberts to John Swire & Sons, 30 August 1945: JSS I 5/1c.

CHAPTER 12 FLIGHT

1 Chris Bayly and Tim Harper, *Forgotten Wars: Freedom and Revolution in Southeast Asia* (London: Allen Lane, 2007).

2 *SCMP*, 12 September 1945, p. 2.

3 'Tug 5', 19 December 1947: SASS 04-001.

4 Lists of CNCo returnees to Hong Kong on the *Cheshire* are in National Archives of Australia [hereafter NAA]: A433, 1949/2/9033; 'Chinese seamen', *SCMP*, 22 December 1945, p. 9; Minute dated 28 July 1949, in file on 'Repatriation of Chinese: Special Arrangements re departure': NAA, A445 236/2/43.

5 J. K. Swire to John Swire & Sons, 8 February 1946, 18 February 1946: JSS I 3/15. He would later bump into the US air force intelligence officer who had been responsible, and who was 'extremely proud' of his handiwork: Jock arranged for him to have a look around: J. K. Swire to John Swire & Sons, 9 February 1948: JSS I 3/19.

6 J. S. Scott and J. K. Swire to John Swire & Sons, 22 March 1946: JSS I 3/15.

7 J. S. Scott and J. K. Swire to John Masson and G. W. Swire, 31 March 1946: JSS I 3/15.

8 J. K. Swire diary, 15 March 1946: JS&SL.

9   J. K. Swire to Sir Ronald Garrett [date], enclosed in DNOE to John Swire
    & Sons, 19 April 1946: JSS I 3/15.

10 Rana Mitter, 'Imperialism, Transnationalism, and the Reconstruction of
    Post-war China: UNRRA in China, 1944–71', *Past & Present*, 218 (2013),
    pp. 51–69; *UNRRA in China, 1945–1947* (Washington DC: UNRRA,
    1948).

11 R. Frost, Ministry of War Transport, Shanghai, to O. S. Lieu, CNRRA,
    27 November 1945, enclosed in J. A. Blackwood, FESA, to L. K. Little,
    Inspector-General, Chinese Maritime Customs, 19 January 1946, in:
    SHAC, 679(1), 31727; Zhang Zhongli et al. (eds), *Swire Group in Old
    China*, pp. 253–62.

12 See the discussion on shipping and sovereignty in Zhang, *Swire Group in Old
    China*, and Butterfield & Swire Shanghai to John Swire & Sons, 17 July 1946,
    and letter: *NCDN*, 21 July 1946; Shenbao, 21 October 1947, all in: SASS
    04-002; CNRRA: Sherman Cochran and Andrew Hsieh, *The Lius of Shanghai*
    (Cambridge, MA: Harvard University Press, 2013), pp. 264–6; Wuhan: John
    Masson to John Swire & Sons, 21 March 1945: JSS I 3/15.

13 'CNCo Future Policy: Notes of Discussions with J. A. Blackwood
    on 11.4.46': SASS 04-002; John Masson to John Swire & Sons, 14
    February, 18 April 1947: JSS I 3/15.

14 Acting Commissioner of Customs, Shanghai, to Butterfield & Swire Shanghai,
    9 January 1949: SASS, 04-006; *American Aid-Food for China: A Photographic
    Report* (Shanghai: Economic Cooperation Administration Mission to China,
    1949), p. 25; *SCMP*, 14, 18 November 1945, both p. 16.

15 Agenda, Hong Kong, March 1948: JSS I 3/19. It was thought that these would
    never need to be paid. Chinese Maritime Customs records include diagrams of
    the hides discovered in the *Fatshan* in July 1947 in which significant quantities
    of contraband were found: Commissioner, Canton Customs, 'Smuggling
    report for July 1947', 1 August 1947: SHAC, 679(1), 28210.

16 John Masson to John Swire & Sons, 14 February 1947: JSS I 3/15; J. C.
    Hutchinson to Butterfield & Swire Shanghai, 18 September 1946: SASS
    04-003.

17 Butterfield & Swire Shanghai to J. C. L. Hutchinson, British Consulate-
    General, Shanghai, 24 December 1947: SASS 04-005. This file documents
    the discussions about policy and establishment of the new firm.

18 J. K. Swire and J. S. Scott to G. W. Swire and John Masson, 31 July 1946,
    and John Masson to John Swire & Sons, 14 February 1947, 21 March 1947:
    JSS I 3/15; Butterfield & Swire Hankow to Butterfield & Swire Shanghai, 4
    February 1947: SASS 04-003; J. K. Swire to John Swire & Sons, 30 March
    1948: JSS I 3/19; Chihyun Chang (ed.), *The Chinese Journals of L. K. Little,
    1943–54: An Eyewitness Account of War and Revolution*, Volume II (London:
    2017), p. 19; J. K. Swire to John Swire & Sons, 5 April 1946: JSS I 3/15.

19 Cinderella: J. K. Swire diary, 7 April 1939; J. K. Swire to John Swire & Sons, 1 March 1946: JSS I 3/15; Alexander Claver and G. Roger Knight, 'A European role in intra-Asian commercial development: The Maclaine Watson network and the Java sugar trade c. 1840–1942', *Business History*, 60:2 (2008), pp. 202–30; Miller, *Europe and the Maritime World*, pp. 190–93.

20 'Swire & Maclaine', undated, c. 1946–7: SASS, 4-004; J. K. Swire diary, 13 April 1946: JS&SL.

21 John D. Plating, *The Hump: America's Strategy for Keeping China in World War II* (College Station, TX: Texas A&M University Press, 2011).

22 'Notes on a journey from England to Calcutta – February 1942', J. R. Masson: JSS I 3/13.

23 Familiarity with its dangers, too: a rising star within the firm, Walter Lock was one of those killed with Polish army commander-in-chief Władysław Sikorski, when their plane crashed shortly after taking off at Gibraltar, on 4 July 1943. Pilots: Alan P. Dobson, *A History of International Civil Aviation: From its Origins Through Transformative Evolution* (London: Routledge, 2017), p. 38.

24 John Darwin, *The Empire Project: The Rise and Fall of the British World-System, 1830–1970* (Cambridge: Cambridge University Press, 2009), pp. 558–60.

25 Colonial Office, *The Colonial Territories (1948–1949)* Cmd. 7715 (London: HMSO, 1949), p. 2; Gordon Pirie, *Air Empire: British Imperial Civil Aviation 1919–39* (Manchester: Manchester University Press, 2009); David E. Omissi, *Air Power and Colonial Control: The Royal Air Force 1919–1939* (Manchester: Manchester University Press, 1990).

26 *China Mail*, 12 January 1945, p. 1.

27 *China Mail*, 24 March 1936, p. 1; *SCMP*, 25 March 1936, p. 12.

28 J. K. Swire diary, 22 May 1939: JS&SL.

29 *SCMP*, 19 March 1941, p. 15; Young, *Beyond Lion Rock*, pp. 100–101.

30 J. K. Swire diary, 23 February 1939: JS&SL; J. K. Swire to Butterfield & Swire Hong Kong, 9 January 1948: JSS I 3/19; R. A. Colyer to G. W. Swire, 25 July 1945, 13 August 1945: JSS XIII 1/1; Peter Yule, *The Forgotten Giant of Australian Aviation: Australian National Airways* (Flemington: Hyland House, 2001), pp. 10–25.

31 J. K. Swire to John Swire & Sons, 8 February 1946, J. K. Swire to Lord Knollys, 7 March 1946, F. Kowarziak to Butterfield & Swire Hong Kong, 12 June 1946, all in: JSS I 3/15; John Swire & Sons [G. W. Swire] to R. A. Colyer, 14 June 1946: JSS XIII 1/1; for a general history of Cathay Pacific, from which this and following section draws, see Gavin Young, *Beyond Lion Rock: The Story of Cathay Pacific Airways* (London: Hutchinson, 1988).

32 Cuttings, 1946–47, from the Australian press in Chic Eather Scrapbook No 1: CPA Archives, JS&SHK, and advertisements in the *SCMP*, 1946–47, *passim*.

33 On this subject see, for example, Gordon Pirie, *Cultures and Caricatures of British Imperial Aviation: Passengers, Pilots, Publicity* (Manchester: Manchester University Press, 2012), and Peter Fritzsche, *A Nation of Fliers: German Aviation and the Popular Imagination* (Cambridge, MA: Harvard University Press, 1992). We might think of Lindberg, Amy Johnson, Antoine de Saint-Exupéry, Richard Bach, Richard Hillary, Baron von Richthofen …

34 'Pilots' pay', enclosure in Butterfield & Swire Hong Kong to John Swire & Sons, 28 January 1949: JSS XIII 1/5/1; Charles (Chic) Eather, *Syd's Pirates* (Sydney: Durnmount, 1986), pp. 56–7; 'Extraordinary career of William T. Dobson', *Daily Mercury* (Melbourne), 25 August 1949, p. 1; Note on J. S. Scott meeting with McLellan, Mansfields, Singapore, 30 March 1949, in Butterfield & Swire Hong Kong to John Swire & Sons, 8 April 1949: JSS XIII 1/5/1.

35 E. Dudley Bateman to Ministry of Aviation, 30 April 1948, and A. J. R. Moss minute to Colonial Secretary, 14 July 1948: HKPRO, HKRS-163-1-147.

36 Harold Hartley to Sir Thomas Lloyd, 2 June 1948, and Sir Alexander Grantham to Lloyd, 26 June 1948, in: TNA, CO 937/69/4. On BOAC see the official history: Robin Higham, *Speedbird: The Complete History of B.O.A.C.* (London: I. B. Tauris, 2013).

37 Holyman: J. K. Swire diary, 9 June 1948: JS&SL; surprise: Butterfield & Swire Hong Kong to John Swire & Sons, 29 August 1947; local: Butterfield & Swire Hong Kong to John Swire & Sons, 30 October 1947: JSS XIII 1/2; CPA ownership: Sydney de Kantzow to W. J. Brigg, Colonial Office, 19 August 1947: HKPRO, HKRS-163-1-147.

38 Butterfield & Swire Hong Kong to John Swire & Sons, 19 December 1947, enclosing M. H. Curtis, 'Plans to Form Genuine Local Company': JSS XIII 1/2. This note contains a detailed history of the course of the discussions.

39 Agencies: see correspondence in: SASS, 04-103; 'Preliminary notes on Air Services Operating from Hong Kong', 8 August 1947, in Butterfield & Swire, Hong Kong, to John Swire & Sons, 15 August 1947: JSS XIII 1/2; J. K. Swire diary, 29 May 1948: JS&SL.

40 CPA Board Minutes, 23 September 1948: CPA 1/1/1, JS&SHK. It can be seen in 1950s photographs of the building, running across the whole of the frontage across above the second floor. 'Butterfield & Swire' ran across the top.

41 Butterfield & Swire Hong Kong to John Swire & Sons, 12 March 1948: JSS XIII 1/2.

42 Eather, *Syd's Pirates*, pp. 91–113.

43 Gordon Boyce, 'Transferring capabilities across sectoral frontiers: Shipowners entering the airline business, 1920–1970', *International Journal of Maritime History*, 13:1 (2001), pp. 1–8.

44 Butterfield & Swire Hong Kong to John Swire & Sons, 19 December 1947, enclosing M. H. Curtis, 'Plans to Form Genuine Local Company': JSS XIII 1/2.

45 Mark Young, Governor, to A. Creech Jones, 18 April 1947: HKPRO, HKRS-163-1-147; W. J. Bigg, Minute on discussion, 14 March 1948: TNA, CO 937/69/4.

46 Pistol: J. B. Johnston, minute, 19 July 1948: TNA, CO 937/69/5; J. B. Johnston, minute, 13 March 1948: TNA, CO 937/69/4; BOAC: J. B. Johnston, minute, 16 December 1948: TNA, CO 937/69/5.

47 J. B. Johnston, minute, 13 March 1948: TNA, CO 937/69/4; W. J. Bigg, CO, to L. J. Dunnett, Ministry of Civil Aviation, 27 September 1948, and 19 June 1948: TNA, CO 937/69/5.

48 C. C. Roberts and S. H. de Kantzow to Director of Civil Aviation, Hong Kong, 28 June 1948, both JSS XIII 1/2; *SCMP*, 12 January 1949, p. 6; Butterfield & Swire Hong Kong to John Swire & Sons, 14 January 1949: JSS XIII 1/2.

49 Records of the Hong Kong discussions in January and early February 1949 can be found in: JSS XIII 1/2; the course of the negotiations in London, the agreement, and approvals are documented in the Colonial Office file 'Civil Aviation Hong Kong: Local Air Services': TNA, CO 937/69/6; vital: 'J.S.S.'s notes on Scott/Price/Landale conversation of 3.2.49', enclosed in Butterfield & Swire Hong Kong to John Swire & Sons, 11 February 1949: JSS XIII 1/5/1; Suspension: M. Wylie to G. M. Chivers, 19 May 1949: TNA, CO 937/69/6.

50 J. R. Masson to John Swire & Sons, 14 February 1949: JSS I 3/20; E. G. Price to J. S. Scott, 4 January 1949: JSS XIII 1/5/1; E. G. Price to J. K. Swire, 25 February 1949: JSS XIII 1/2.

51 C. C. Roberts to J. K. Swire, 23 December 1949: JSS XIII 1/6/2.

52 *SCMP*, 30 October 1950, p. 10.

53 J. S. Scott to J. K. Swire, 1 January 1952, and J. S. Scott to J. R. Masson, 4 January 1952: JSS I 3/21.

54 J. K. Swire diary, 20 February, 3 April 1939: JS&SL.

55 Martin Speyer, *In Coral Seas: The History of the New Guinea Australia Line* (Nautical Association of Australia in association with John Swire & Sons: Caulfield South, 2004), pp. 2–4; Bleasdale & Shun Wah, *Swire*, pp. 30–34; 'New motor vessel Changsha', *Daily Commercial News and Shipping List*, 20 July 1949, p. 1.

56 John Masson to John Swire & Sons, 31 January 1947: JSS I 3/15.

57 J. K. Swire diary, 13 April 1946: JS&SL; Assignment of directorial responsibilities, 18 October 1946, and note by G. W. Swire on these, 22 October 1946; J. K. Swire diary, 25 May 1948. This paragraph also draws on notes on G. W. Swire by J. K. Swire, 1950, and a file of letters compiled by M. Y. Fiennes in 1983, 'G. W. Swire 1883–1949'. All documents are in the Swire Archives, John Swire & Sons, London. Resignation: G. W. Swire to John Swire & Sons, 29 December 1946: John Swire & Sons Minute Book No. 2: JSS I 12/2.

58 'Gift to Eton from Merchant: State Aid Banned', *Daily Telegraph*, 8 February 1950, p. 1; '"Nonsensical fuss": Father about will', *Chelmsford Chronicle*, 10 February 1950, p. 1; *SCMP*, 22 February 1950, p. 10.

59 See, for example, 'Conversation with Sir Arthur Morse on 27.2.50', enclosed in J. R. Masson to John Swire & Sons, 28 February 1950: JSS I 3/20.

60 Catherine R. Schenk, *Hong Kong as an International Finance Centre: Emergence and development, 1945–65* (London: Routledge, 2001), pp. 19–20; on the broader pattern see: Robert Bickers, 'The Colony's shifting position in the British Informal Empire in China', in Judith M. Brown and Rosemary Foot, *Hong Kong's Transitions, 1842–1997* (London: Macmillan, 1997), pp. 33–61.

61 John Masson to John Swire & Sons, 14 February 1947: JSS I 3/15; Siu-lun Wong, *Emigrant Entrepreneurs, Shanghai Industrialists in Hongkong* (Hong Kong: Oxford University Press, 1988).

62 Kenneth E. Shewmaker, 'The "Agrarian Reformer" Myth', *China Quarterly*, No. 34 (1968), pp. 66–81.

63 J. K. Swire to John Swire & Sons, 9 January and 30 March 1948: JSS I 3/19.

64 J. S. Scott to John Swire & Sons, 13 December 1948, and J. S. Scott to Sir Ralph Stevenson, 19 January 1949: JSS I 3/18.

65 Butterfield & Swire Hong Kong to Butterfield & Swire Tianjin, 12 November 1948: SASS 04-013; *SCMP*, 30 November 1948. p. 2.

66 John Masson to John Swire & Sons, 18 November 1947: JSS I 3/15; Memo: Butterfield & Swire Shanghai, 29 July 1948: SASS 04-006.

67 'Notes on the present situation in Tientsin', W. B. Rae-Smith, February 1949: SASS 04-013.

68 Bruce A. Elleman, 'The Nationalists' Blockade of the PRC, 1949–58', in Bruce A. Elleman and S. C. M. Paine, *Naval Blockades and Seapower: Strategies and Counter-Strategies, 1805–2005* (London: Routledge, 2007), pp. 133–44; *SCMP*, 22 and 23 June 1949, p. 1; *SCMP*, 29 October 1951, p. 1.

69 See documents in file on 'Subversive activities of Kuo Min Tang organisation': TNA, FO 371/110196, and *Renmin ribao*, 3 January 1954, p. 3, and 1 July 1955, p. 3.

70 Young, *Beyond Lion Rock*, pp. 133–42.

71 David C. Wolf, '"To Secure a Convenience": Britain Recognizes China – 1950', *Journal of Contemporary History*, 18:2 (1983), pp. 299–326.

72 J. R. Masson to J. K. Swire, 2 December 1949: JSS I 3/20.

73 Bickers, *Out of China*, pp. 245–7; Butterfield & Swire Hong Kong to Alfred Holt & Co., 22 January 1948: SASS 04-013.

74 Wong, *Emigrant Entrepreneurs*.

75 Yang Kuisong, 'Reconsidering the Campaign to Suppress Counterrevolutionaries', *China Quarterly*, No. 193 (2008), pp. 102–21; see David Clayton, *Imperialism Revisited: Political and Economic Relations Between Britain and China, 1950–54* (Basingstoke: Macmillan, 1997).

76 Butterfield & Swire Hong Kong to John Swire & Sons, 10 June 1949: JSS XIII 1/5/1.

77 Deryk de Sausmarez Carey, Butterfield & Swire Shanghai, to Alan Veitch, HBM Consulate-General, Shanghai, 10 June 1949: JSS XIII 1/5/1.

78 On this process see Thomas N. Thompson, 'China's Nationalization of Foreign Firms: The Politics of Hostage Capitalism, 1949–57' (Baltimore, MD: School of Law, University of Maryland Occasional Papers, no. 6, 1979); and Jonathan J. Howlett, 'Accelerated Transition: British Enterprises in Shanghai and the Transition to Socialism', *European Journal of East Asian Studies*, 13:2 (2014), pp. 163–87; Frank H. H. King, *The Hongkong Bank in the Period of Development and Nationalism, 1941–1984: From Regional Bank to Multinational Group* (Cambridge: Cambridge University Press, 1991), pp. 404–11, 612–13.

79 Unless otherwise noted, this section draws on John March's memorandum, enclosed in Butterfield & Swire Hong Kong to John Swire & Sons, 30 December 1955: China Closure CL-6, JS&SL.

80 *NCDN*, 14 January 1951, p. 2.

81 *Renmin ribao*, 27 February 1953; for more detail on Guangzhou see 'China Withdrawal – 1953', in CL-3, JS&SL.

82 See: Butterfield & Swire Hong Kong to John Swire & Sons, 7 March 1952, enclosing untitled memorandum, 29 February 1952: TNA, FO 371/99283.

83 Paint company: Jonathan J. Howlett, '"The British boss is gone and will never return": Communist takeovers of British companies in Shanghai (1949–1954)', *Modern Asian Studies*, 47:6 (2013), pp. 1941–76.

84 'Report by M. N. Speyer ...', enclosed in Butterfield & Swire Hong Kong to John Swire & Sons, 30 October 1950: TNA, FO 371/83512. This file contains several reports on the case which are drawn on here, including the confessions, all dated 6 October 1950. The answer to the puzzle of the lifeboat's name, which did not satisfy the authorities, was that the *Hanyang* had taken the passengers off the stricken *Anhui* and left a replacement lifeboat of its own for the skeleton salvage crew on board.

85 'Very hot tempered,' reported Jock Swire in 1952: J. K. Swire diary, 27 December 1952: JS&SL.

86 Michael Szonyi, *Cold War Island: Quemoy on the Front Line* (Cambridge: Cambridge University Press, 2008).

87 'Report on Amoy by Mr. R. D. Morrell 17.4.51', in Staff Officer (Intelligence, Hong Kong) to Director of Naval Intelligence: TNA, FO 371/92197.

88 Butterfield & Swire Tianjin to People's Court, 29 January 1954: in TNA, FO 676/497.

89 This section draws on the memoir 'Yao Kang and the Swire Group': JS&SL; housing: Butterfield & Swire Shanghai to Sir John Masson, 22 January 1950: JSS I 3/20.

90 See John Gardner, 'The Wu-Fan Campaign in Shanghai: A Study in the Consolidation of Urban Control', in A. Doak Barnett (ed.), *Chinese*

Communist Politics in Action (Seattle: University of Washington Press, 1969), pp. 477–539.

91 Both these men would survive and would in fact go on safely to leave China: Butterfield & Swire Hong Kong to John Swire & Sons, 7 March 1952, enclosing untitled memorandum, 29 February 1952: TNA, FO 371/99283. On the experiences more widely of 'capitalists' in Shanghai see: Christopher Russell Leighton, 'Capitalists, Cadres and Culture in 1950s China', unpublished PhD thesis, Harvard University, 2010'.

92 J. S. Scott to Butterfield & Swire Hong Kong, 7 March 1953: JSS I 3/21.

93 Memorandum dated 23 September 1953, enclosed in Butterfield & Swire Hong Kong to John Swire & Sons, 20 November 1953: JSS I 3/21.

94 J. K. Swire diary, 3 May 1954: JS&SL.

95 J. S. Scott to C. T. Crowe, 15 October 1954: TNA, FO 676/497; the agreement can be found as an enclosure in Shanghai Consulate-General to British embassy, Beijing, 17 February 1955: TNA, FO 676/524. This transfer included all 'title deeds, files, charts' etc. Minutes of the meetings can be found in 'China Withdrawal – 1954': CL-3, JS&SL; files: Gould to Butterfield & Swire Hong Kong, 3 June 1955, in 'China Closure Shanghai 1952–1955': JS&SHK.

96 'Closure of Taikoo Interests in China', Record of Tenth Meeting …', 10 December 1954, 'China Withdrawal – 1954': CL-3, JS&SL.

97 'List of liabilities in Shanghai', 21 October 1954: CL-3, JS&SL.

98 Sidney Smith to Humphrey Trevelyan, 29 January 1954: TNA, FO 676/497.

99 The subsequent use of these records can be gauged from the fact that a stamp reading 'Card already made' can be seen next to names of Chinese individuals mentioned in Butterfield & Swire Shanghai branch records held in archives today in China.

100 F. F. Garner to W. I. Combs, 5 May 1955, enclosure in Humphrey Trevelyan, Beijing, to C. T. Crowe, Foreign Office, 18 May 1955: TNA, FO 676/525.

101 Butterfield & Swire Hong Kong to John Swire & Sons, 8 March 1957, in 'China 1957–1960', and file: 'Staff: Maurice Ching, 1947–Dec. 1961': JS&SHK.

102 John March, 'Closure of Taikoo Interests in China', 12 May 1955: CL-3, JS&SL; OPCo takeover: Howlett, '"The British boss is gone and will never return" pp. 1941–76, quotations from p. 1974.

103 Butterfield & Swire, Chinese Staff Book, Box 180: JS&SL; *NCH*, 26 June 1935, p. 526.

104 Elizabeth J. Perry, 'Shanghai's Strike Wave of 1957', *China Quarterly*, No. 137 (1994), pp. 1–27.

105 Yang Bew Tuan to T. J. Lindsay, 23 July 1956, Butterfield & Swire Hong Kong to John Swire & Sons, 10 August, 2 and 23 November 1956, all in 'China General 1955–1956': JS&SHK; A. C. Swire letters from Hong Kong and Japan, JS&SL.

CHAPTER 13 MAKING ASIA

1   The complex story of Chinese migration, mobility, and flight, during the Cold War is the subject of Laura Maduro, *Elusive Refuge: Chinese Migrants in the Cold War* (Cambridge, MA: Harvard University Press, 2016).

2   M. S. Cumming, 'Notes for Sir John Masson ...', 15 December 1949, and W. G. C. Knowles, 'Flying Staff', 20 March 1952, 'CPA Correspondence 1947–55': CPA CPA/CE/6/1, JS&SHK; 'Cathay Pacific', *Flight*, 22 January 1954, pp. 88–9; CPA Minutes of the Fifth Ordinary General Meeting', 1954: CPA/1/1/2, JS&SHK.

3   This paragraph draws on Minutes of CPA's Annual Meetings, 1954–62: CPA 1/1/2, JS&SHK.

4   J. K. Swire diary, 5 September 1961: JS&SL.

5   Denis-Freres d'Indochine, Haiphong, to Cathay Pacific Airways, 11 March 1954; Capt. Charles E. Eather to Operations Manager, Cathay Pacific Airways, 18 March 1954: 'CPA Correspondence 1947–55': CPA CPA/CE/6/1, JS&SHK. In between these reports, the Viet-Minh had launched the attack on Dien Bien Phu, defeat in which would lead the French to withdraw from Indo-China.

6   W. G. C. Knowles to J. K. Swire, 5 June 1953, 'CPA Correspondence 1947–55': CPA CPA/CE/6/1, JS&SHK; J. K. Swire to John Swire & Sons, 10 May 1954: JSS I 3/22.

7   'Notes of a meeting held on 8th October 1951 in the Colonial Office to consider Hong Kong Civil Aviation Problems', enclosure in J. K. Swire to C. C. Roberts 9 October 1951, 'CPA Correspondence 1947–55': CPA CPA/CE/6/1, JS&SHK.

8   See correspondence on BOAC's withdrawal from further discussions with John Swire & Sons in late April 1954: JSS I 3/22g KongHon.

9   J. K. Swire diary, 29 October 1958: JS&SL.

10 *SCMP*, 11 August 1960, p. 22.

11 J. K. Swire to John Swire & Sons, 28 April 1954, referring to comments made by Hong Kong's then governor, Alexander Grantham: JSS I 3/22.

12 'Cathay Pacific Airways/Hong Kong Airways: Notes of a Meeting held at Hong Kong ... 7th February 1949': TNA, CO93/69/6; Butterfield & Swire Hong Kong to J. K. Swire, 8 July 1949: JSS XIII 1/5/1.

13 Young, *Beyond Lion Rock*, pp. 144–5.

14 *Hong Kong Statistics 1947–1967* (Hong Kong: Census & Statistics Department, 1969), p. 122; *Hong Kong Annual Digest of Statistics 1978* (Hong Kong: Census and Statistics Department, 1978), p. 113; *Hong Kong Annual Digest of Statistics 1980* (Hong Kong: Census and Statistics Department, 1980), p. 135; Young, *Beyond Lion Rock*, Appendix III, pp. 234–36. The figures are not precisely comparable, for the Cathay Pacific totals include passengers not departing or arriving at Hong Kong, but by far the greatest part by far of them did so.

15 *SCMP*, 24 September 1967, p. XII (this is an eight-page anniversary advertisement).

16 *SCMP*, 9 April 1962, p. III; 24 September 1967, pp. IV–V; *Cathay Pacific Airways Newsletter*, 1958–61, *passim*: CPA/7/4/1/1, JS&SHK; circus: *RIL Post*, 6:14 (December 1959), p. 163. The pages of the *SCMP* are peppered with photographs and brief notes of celebrity arrivals and departures.

17 Butterfield & Swire Hong Kong to John Swire & Sons, 16 January 1948, 5 March 1948, 13 May 1948, 27 August 1948, and *passim*, May–August 1948: JSS XIII 1/2; *SCMP*, 3 and 7 July 1948; *Uxbridge Advertiser & Gazette*, 16 July 1948, p. 8; Brian Bridges, *The Two Koreas and the Politics of Global Sport* (Leiden: Global Oriental, 2012), pp. 48–9.

18 Brian Bridges, 'London Revisited: South Korea at the Olympics of 1948 and 2012', *International Journal of the History of Sport* 30:15 (2013), pp. 1823–33; *Pacific Stars and Stripes*, 3 August 1948, p. 2; 'XIV Olympiad: The Glory of Sport' (London: Dir Castleton Knight, 1948); *Daily Mail*, 2 September 1948, p. 3.

19 'General manager's report on activities of CPA, Limited, for the month of January 1949', enclosed in W. D. Doyle, Manager, to J. K. Swire, 4 March 1949: JSS XIII 1/2; *Hobart Mercury*, 5 January 1949, p. 1; *The Herald* (Melbourne) 29 December 1948, p. 5; *SCMP*, 29 January 1953, p. 5; *SCMP*, 4 September 1957, p. 8, 24 July 1959, p. 9, 20 August 1959, p. 7.

20 Tomoko Akami, *Internationalizing the Pacific: The United States, Japan and the Institute of Pacific Relations in War and Peace, 1919–1945* (London: Routledge, 2002); Fiona Paisley, *Glamour in the Pacific: Cultural Internationalism and Race Politics in the Women's Pan-Pacific* (Honolulu: University of Hawai'i Press, 2009).

21 Daniel Aaron Rubin, 'Suitcase Diplomacy: The Role of Travel in Sino-American Relations, 1949–1968' (Unpublished PhD thesis, University of Maryland, 2010), pp. 85–114. The corollary of this state facilitation of outward-bound travel, was the restrictions the US government placed on leftists and others, whose networking it opposed.

22 Jennifer Lindsay, 'Festival Politics: Singapore's 1963 South-East Asia Cultural Festival', in Tony Day, Maya H. T. Liem (eds), *Cultures at War: The Cold War and Cultural Expression in Southeast Asia* (Ithaca: Cornell University Press, 2010), pp. 227–45.

23 *SCMP*, 6 August 1963, p. 7; *Straits Times*, 7 August 1963, p. 10.

24 Sangjoon Lee, 'The Asia Foundation's Motion-Picture Project and the Cultural Cold War in Asia', *Film History*, 29:2 (2017), pp. 108–37; Poshek Fu, 'The Shaw Brothers Diasporic Cinema', in Poshek Fu (ed.), *China Forever: The Shaw Brothers and Diasporic Cinema* (Urbana: University of Illinois Press, 2008), pp. 10–12.

25 This paragraph draws on Stefan Huebner, *Pan-Asian Sports and the Emergence of Modern Asia, 1913–1974* (Singapore: National University of Singapore Press, 2016).

26 J. K. Swire diary, 1 November 1961: JS&SL.

27 *SCMP*, 17 April 1959, p. 4. The victors, South Korea, knocked Hong Kong out in the quarter final.

28 See Rubin, 'Suitcase Diplomacy', and Christina Klein, *Cold War Orientalism: Asia in the Middlebrow Imagination, 1945–1961* (Berkeley: University of California Press, 2003), pp. 41–60.

29 Quoted in Klein, *Cold War Orientalism*, p. 105. Real China: Rubin, 'Suitcase Diplomacy', p. 90; this was also a strategy used by the Nationalists: see Tehyun Ma, 'Total mobilization: Party, state and citizen on Taiwan under Chinese Nationalist rule, 1944–55' (Unpublished PhD thesis, University of Bristol, 2010).

30 Klein, *Cold War Orientalism*, p. 104; Robert C. Hazell, *The Tourist Industry in Hong Kong, 1966* (Hong Kong: Hong Kong Tourist Association, 1966), p. 5.

31 Mary Martin: Chuck Y. Gee and Matt Lurie, *The Story of the Pacific Asia Travel Association* (San Francisco: Pacific Asia Travel Association, 1993), p. 2. Michener: Klein, *Cold War Orientalism*, pp. 100–142.

32 Gee and Lurie, *The Story of the Pacific Asia Travel Association*, pp. X–XI; Agnieszka Sobocinska, 'Visiting the Neighbours: The Political Meanings of Australian Travel to Cold War Asia', *Australian Historical Studies*, 44:3 (2013), pp. 382–404.

33 *SCMP*, 24 September 1967, p. XII; 'Cathay Pacific', *Flight*, 22 January 1954, pp. 88–9; Chi-Kwan Mark, 'Hong Kong as an International Tourism Space: The Politics of American Tourists in the 1960s', in Priscilla Roberts and John M. Carroll (eds), *Hong Kong in the Cold War* (Hong Kong: Hong Kong University Press, 2017), pp. 160–82; Hazell, *Tourist Industry in Hong Kong, passim*. CNCo's *Fatshan*, sold in 1951 running on the Hong Kong to Macau route for its news owners, makes an appearance in *Love Is a Many Splendored Thing* (and later did so more centrally in (and as the) *Ferry to Hong Kong*), as does the mansion that was financed by comprador Mok's sugar-bag fraud: by the 1950s it was the home of the Foreign Correspondents' Club, used extensively in the film as the hospital.

34 *Independent Press Telegram*, 18 May 1958, p. 8; *Arizona Republic*, 21 September 1958, p. 7; *Honolulu Advertiser*, 24 July 1958, p. 14; Hazell, *Tourist Industry in Hong Kong*, p. 60; CPA Minutes of the Tenth Ordinary General Meeting', 1959: CPA/1/1/2, JS&SHK.

35 *Hong Kong Annual Report 1957* (Hong Kong: At the Government Press, 1958), pp. 222–3; *SCMP*, 11 March 1973, p. 15.

36 *New York Times*, 15 January 1967, p. B13; *SCMP*, 30 October 1967, p. 39; *Star News* (Pasadena), 2 January 1967, p. 1. The junk was later bought by

the British actor Oliver Reed. This did not secure a long-term future for the boat.

37 Knowles: information from Staff Book No. 4, and A. C. Swire interview (2007), p. 6: JS&SL.

38 See, for example, Governor Robert Black's comments reported in J. K. Swire to John Swire & Sons, 31 October 1958: JSS I 3/25.

39 *SCMP*, 20 March 1962, pp. 10, 15.

40 Adverts: *Sydney Morning Herald*, 29 November 1960, p. 7; *The Age*, 14 December 1960, p. 7; *The Age*, 16 May 1961, p. 12; *SCMP*, 7 May 1965, p. 12; *Cathay Newsletter*, 19 October 1970, p. 4; PATA: *SCMP*, 23 January 1962, p. 7.

41 *SCMP*, 24 July 1957, p. 7.

42 *Cathay Pacific Airways Newsletter*, December 1959; *The Age*, 9 September 1960, p. 7, 30 October 1960, p. 19.

43 Yoshiko Nakano, '"Wings of the New Japan": Kamikaze, Kimonos and airline Branding in Post-war Japan', *Verge: Studies in Global Asia* 4:1 (2018), pp. 160–86; *SCMP*, 16 October 1958, p. 12, 25 October 1961, p. 14.

44 For publicity about training see: *SCMP*, 23 July 1959, p. 13. Staff turnover was high, for its experienced cabin staff were much in demand by other airlines, as traffic in the region expanded: Lindsay, 'Like a Phoenix', p. 38. Pictures of young women also continued to illustrate Taikoo Sugar's calendars, and these had evolved to mimic portraits of film stars. See the selection on the 'Hong Kong Memory' platform, url: www.hkmemory.hk/collections/swire/Swire_promotion/Swire_PP_Advertisements/.

45 *SCMP*, 9 April 1962, p. I; *San Francisco Chronicle*, 4 October 1964, p. 30, and 17 November 1964, p. 10; *SCMP*, 23 January 1962, p. 7; 'Oh those scenic beauties', *Cathay Newsletter*, November 1977, pp. 4–5. The seventeen-day CPA cabin staff strike in 1993 brought much of this out into open debate: Stephen Linstead, 'Averting the Gaze: Gender and Power on the Perfumed Picket Line', *Gender Work and Organization* 2:4 (2007), pp. 192–206. On the history of cabin staff see: Kathleen M. Barry, *Femininity in Flight: A History of Flight Attendants* (Durham, NC: Duke University Press, 2007).

46 *Cathay Newsletter*, 24 March 1969, pp. 1–4. There is some evidence that consistent and continual presentation of female cabin staff in this way was taken literally by some travellers: Lindsay, 'Like a Phoenix', p. 38.

47 *Singapore Free Press*, 28 February 1958, p. 13.

48 *Hong Kong Statistics 1947–1967*, p. 199.

49 *Japan Times*, 2, 3 April, p. 6; *SCMP*, 8 April 1960, p. 12.

50 Michael Miles interview, 23 September 2008: JS&SL.

51 J. S. Scott to John Swire & Sons, 3 December 1948: JSS I 3/19.

52 'Where,' he continued, 'nobody works.' Disquiet at the power of organised Labour in Australia was a recurring theme in company correspondence: J. K. Swire to John Swire & Sons, 19 April 1951: JSS I 3/20. J. S. Scott to John

Swire & Sons, 1 January 1949: JSS I 3/19. On the occupation in general see John Dower, *Embracing Defeat: Japan in the Aftermath of World War II* (London: Allen Lane, 1999), and on the economy and boom see pp. 525–46 (Yoshida is quoted on p. 541).

53 J. S. Scott to John Swire & Sons, 28 February 1952: JSS I 3/21; J. S. Scott to John Swire & Sons, 20 November 1959: JSS I 3/26; P. F. McCabe to W. B. Rae-Smith, 21 March 1964: JSS II 9/2/1.

54 Agnes Ku, 'Immigration Policies, Discourses, and the Politics of Local Belonging in Hong Kong (1950–1980)', *Modern China* 30:3 (2004), pp. 336–8; Chi-kwan Mark, 'The "Problem of People": British Colonials, Cold War Powers, and the Chinese Refugees in Hong Kong, 1949–62', *Modern Asian Studies*, 41:6 (2007), pp. 1145–81.

55 Maduro, *Elusive refuge*, p. 1; Alan Smart, *The Shek Kip Mei Myth: Squatters, Fires and Colonial Rule in Hong Kong, 1950–1963* (Hong Kong: Hong Kong University Press, 2006), pp. 169 (quotation), p.174. For the colony's history in this period I have drawn on John M. Carroll, *A Concise History of Hong Kong* (Lanham: Rowman & Littlefield, 2007), pp. 140–79.

56 Wong, *Emigrant Entrepreneurs*; Minute of Ordinary General Meeting, 20 May 1949, Taikoo Sugar Refining Company Minute Book: JSS V 7/1.

57 Catherine R. Schenk, *Hong Kong as an International Finance Centre: Emergence and Development 1945–1965* (London: Routledge, 2001), pp. 3–8.

58 This paragraph draws on meeting reports from 1941 to 1951 in the Taikoo Sugar Refining Company Minute Book: JSS V 7/1; *China Mail*, 13 January 1950.

59 *Singapore Free Press*, 6 February 1952, p. 5; *SCMP*, 14 March 1950, p. 6; *Straits Times*, 18 October 1952, p. 3; *China Mail*, 19 September 1952, p. 4 (reproduced from the *Daily Express*). The Thais also took a thousand eggs. 'History of Taikoo Sugar Refinery', a rich online gallery of TSR advertisements, posters and packaging, as well as photographs of the plant, can be found on the 'Hong Kong Memory' platform. URL: https://www.hkmemory.hk/collections/swire/about/index.html.

60 J. S. Scott to John Swire & Sons, 7 February 1952: JSS I 3/21.

61 Nicholas J. White, *British Business in Post-Colonial Malaysia, 1957–70: Neo-colonialism or Disengagement?* (London: Routledge, 2004), p. 78; on Kuok (sometimes 'Kwok'), see Robert Kuok, with Andrew Tanzer, *Robert Kuok A Memoir* (Singapore: Landmark Books, 2017); Annabelle R. Gambe, *Overseas Chinese Entrepreneurship and Capitalist Development in Southeast Asia* (Münster: LIT Verlag, 2000), pp. 93–5; Joe Studwell, *Asian Godfathers: Money and Power in Hong Kong and South-East Asia* (London: Profile Books, 2007), *passim*; J. S. Scott to A. F. Taylor, 28 December 1948: JSS I 3/19; Minute of meeting on 27 October 1950, Taikoo Sugar Refining Company, Minute Book No. 2: JSS V 7/2.

62 *Hong Kong Statistics 1947–1967*, p. 95.

63 *Kuok Memoir*, pp. 119–37; J. S. Scott to John Swire & Sons, 23 November
    1956 and enclosure, J. S. Scott to C. C. Roberts, 23 November 1956: JSS I
    3/25. 'Sugar refinery' supplement, *Straits Times*, 12 December 1964; model:
    C. C. Roberts to J. S. Scott, 16 June 1955: JSS I 3/22; *SCMP*, 12 June 1964,
    p. 20; *SCMP*, 8 February 1973, p. 4; J. K. Swire diary, 29 September 1960,
    13 November 1973: JS&S.

64 J. S. Scott to John Swire & Sons, 16 November 1956, and enclosures: JSS I
    3/25.

65 Manila: J. K. Swire diary, 15 May 1951; Australia: J. R. Masson to J. S.
    Scott, 5 October 1952: JSS I 3/21.

66 Taikoo Dockyard & Engineering Company Minutes, 21 October 1942: JSS
    VI 7/1.

67 J. R. Masson to J. K. Swire, 2 December 1949: JSS I 3/20. This note
    accompanies a formal record of a discussion with the equally worried
    chairman of pool partners Hong Kong and Whampoa Dockyard.

68 C. C. Roberts to J. R. Masson, 11 January 1955 and enclosure, Price
    Waterhouse & Co. to Secretary, H.M. Treasury, 14 August 1954. This was
    too incendiary a document to hold in Hong Kong, and Roberts was sending
    it back for that reason. See also Roberts to Masson, 3 December 1954, both
    in JSS I 3/22. In retrospect, the investment by Taikoo Dockyard in CPA also
    served this strategy. On the investment in Scotts see: Lewis Johnman and
    Hugh Murphy, *Scott Lithgow: Dejá Vu All Over Again! The Rise and Fall of a
    Shipbuilding Company* (St John's: International Maritime Economic History
    Association 2005), pp. 89–92. The scheme proposed in August 1954 was for
    the Dockyard's investment in Scotts to be bought out by John Swire & Sons.

69 Discussions on the state and fate of the building can be found in J. S. Scott
    to John Swire & Sons, 15, 18, 26 February, and 7 and 14 March 1952: JSS
    I 3/21, and M. Fiennes to J. S. Scott, 19 December 1958, and to John Swire
    & Sons, 20 March 1959: JSS I 3/25. Lindsay, 'Like a Phoenix', pp. 4–5; J. K.
    Swire to John Swire & Sons, 24 and 31 October 1958: JSS I 3/25; *SCMP*, 10
    January 1959, p. 1; 1 April 1959, pp. 14–15; 11 May 1959, p. 14.

70 *SCMP*, 8 January 1960, p. 9, and 12 June 1960, p. 3; Adrian Swire, 'Senior
    Staff 1945–1950', 1 March 2016, Swire House; *SCMP*, 24 August 1963, p. 12.

71 *SCMP*, 13 September 1950, p. 13 (the view itself can be seen in a photograph
    taken on 30 August 1945, in *Fifty Years of Shipbuilding*, p. 18); J. K. Swire,
    note, 1982, on his 1946 diaries; G. E. Mitchell to Sir Allan Mossop, 30
    August 1945: TNA, FO 371/46242; J. S. Scott to J. K. Swire and J. R.
    Masson, 21 January 1952: JSS I 3/21.

72 J. R. Masson to John Swire & Sons, 9 May 1947, and enclosed 'Dockyard
    notes': JSS I 3/15; J. K. Swire diary, 18, 21 February, 1946, 25 January 1951;
    J. S. Scott to John Swire & Sons, 3 December 1948, J. S. Scott to J. K. Swire,
    28 December 1948: JSS I 3/19; *Fifty Years of Shipbuilding and Repairing in*

the *Far East* (Hong Kong: Taikoo Dockyard & Engineering Company of Hong Kong Ltd, 1954); *SCMP*, 8 December 1954, p. 13.

73 Captain William Worrall with Kevin Sinclair, *No Cure No Pay* (Hong Kong: *SCMP*, 1981), pp. 136–40; *SCMP*, 26 May 1965, p. 19. A former Blue Funnel and then CNCo mariner, Worrall captained the *Taikoo* for two decades, claiming to have received his appointment while in Stanley.

74 'Memorandum of information regarding the working for the year 1946 ...', 24 February 1948, Taikoo Dockyard & Engineering Company, Minute Book: JSS VI 7/1. This note in fact surveys developments down to late 1947.

75 Strikes: *SCMP*, 1 November 1946, p. 3, 21 August 1947, p. 1, 12 September 1947, p. 1; welfare: 'Memorandum of information regarding the working for the year 1946 ...', 24 February 1948, Taikoo Dockyard & Engineering Company, Minute Book: JSS VI 7/1; *SCMP*, 16 January 1948, p. 3, 17 November 1952, p. 8.

76 *Taiwu gongren* (Taikoo Dockyard Workers) (1957), p. 9.

77 This and the preceding paragraph draws on material in Labour Office file on 'Taikoo Dockyard Chinese Workers Union 2.7.1959–10.6.1975' including Minute of C.L.I., 5 November 1959, and 'Taikoo Dockyard Chinese Workers' Union', 8 December 1959 (possibly a Special Branch report): HKPRO, HKRS1161-1-10; copies of its yearbook, *Taiwu gongren* (Taikoo Dockyard Workers) survive for 1949, 1954 and 1957.

78 J. R. Masson, 'Dockyard Notes', 9 May 1947: JSS I 3/15; A. C. Swire interview, 20 July 2002: JS&SL.

79 'Taikoo Dockyard Workers' Committee for Improvement in Living Conditions and Treatment' to R. D. Bell, Manager, Taikoo Dockyard, 1 June 1956, in file 'Industrial Relations – Taikoo Dockyard – General Correspondence': HKPRO, HKRS940-1-2; *Hong Kong Statistics 1947–1967*, p. 144.

80 *The Taikoo Chinese School* (Hong Kong, 1966).

81 Details in report attached to Li Ki, Chairman, Taikoo Dockyard Chinese Workers' Union, to Commissioner of Labour, 19 November 1960, in file 'Industrial Relations – Taikoo Dockyard – General Correspondence': HKRS940-1-2; *SCMP*, 6 October 1971, p. 25, 3 January 1970, p. 6.

82 See profiles from a 1939 government report on Labour and Labour Conditions in Hong Kong reproduced in David Faure, 'The Common People in Hong Kong History: Their Livelihood and aspirations until the 1930s', in Lee Pui-tak (ed.), *Colonial Hong Kong and Modern China: Interaction and Reintegration* (Hong Kong: Hong Kong University Press, 2005), pp. 32–4.

83 *China Mail*, 4 May 1960, p. 1; *SCMP*, 29 October 1960, p. 8; Lindsay, 'Like a phoenix', p. 74; see also various documents in file 'Industrial Relations – Taikoo Dockyard – General Correspondence': HKPRO, HKRS940-1-2.

84 Details in T. J. Bartlett, Welfare Office, Taikoo Dockyard, to Commissioner of Labour, 15 December 1960, and Li Ki, Chairman, Taikoo Dockyard Chinese Workers Union to Commissioner of Labour, 19 November 1960:

HKPRO, HKRS940-1-2; *SCMP*, 27, 28 December 1967, p. 1. They were resettled, and Fung was given a job with the Resettlement Department: *SCMP*, 20 January 1068, p. 5.

85 Harold Ingrams, *Hong Kong* (London: HMSO, 1952), p. 114; 'Interview with Sir Adrian Swire, 6 February 2007: JS&SL.

86 See a discussion in Leo Goodstadt, *Uneasy Partners: The Conflict Between Public Interest and Private Profit in Hong Kong* (Hong Kong: Hong Kong University Press, 2009), pp. 31–48, 139–58.

87 'Yao Kang and the Swire Group'; 'Interview with Sir Adrian Swire, 6 February 2007: JS&SL.

88 Interview with Jenny Grant, 13 April 2013: JS&SL.

89 Lindsay, 'Like a Phoenix', pp. 34, 40.

90 Various Chinese Staff members to Manager, Butterfield & Swire, 3 March 1949; note by 'G. C.', July 1949; note on 'B. & S. Chinese Staff Association', 27 May 1950, in file 'B. & S. Chinese Staff Association': JS&SHK.

91 Yao Kang and the Swire Group': JS&SL; Lindsay, 'Like a Phoenix', p. 20; Lindsay notes on senior staff, April 1966: JS&SL.

92 This section draws in particular on the essays in Robert Bickers and Ray Yep (eds), *May Days in Hong Kong: Riot and Emergency in 1967* (Hong Kong: Hong Kong University Press, 2009).

93 John Browne to John Swire & Sons, 6 February 1967, and Browne to Adrian Swire, 6 February 1967, and enclosure, J. L. Hillard, 'Analysis and study of Macao riots with comments on suggested implications and lessons': JSS I 4/4/19.

94 *SCMP*, 12 September 1967, p. 6. The document was then reproduced on the front pages of the pro-Communist press: *Ta Kung Pao*, 7 June 1967, p. 1.

95 Hong Kong No. 799 to CO, 8 June 1967: TNA, FCO 21/192; *SCMP*, 7 June 1967, p. 1; John Cooper, *Colony in Conflict* (Hong Kong: Swindon Book Company, 1970), pp. 37–8, 133–4, 144; *SCMP*, 17 July 1967, pp. 1, 6. 'Confrontation Detainees', 20 June 1968, enclosed in Hong Kong Dept, CO, to Mr Boyd, 11 September 1968: TNA, FCO 21/194. Tang died in jail two years later of hepatitis: *SCMP*, 30 December 1969, p. 6, 4 January 1970, p. 3; see also Luk Tak Shing's contribution to '1967: Witnesses remember', in Bickers and Yep, *May Days in Hong Kong*, pp. 170–72. Luk was an apprentice, and unionist, and was jailed for two years after his arrest on 14 July.

96 'Memorandum to the Board', 3 July 1967, in TSR Minute Book: TSS/1/15, JS&SHK.

97 The strip was also republished in the English edition of *Ta Kung Pao* in 1969, and the company collated and translated these: JS&SHK. Inquest: *SCMP*, 14 April 1960, p. 1.

98 This paragraph draws on material from: 'Taikoo Dockyard Minute Book, June–October 1967, May 1967–January 1968', TKDY/1/1/1; and 'Memoranda to the Board, July 1967', TKDY/1/2/24: JS&SHK.

99 J. Cassels to M. S. Cumming, 2 January 1968, 'Master File, Chairman to Director': TKDY/1/3/9, JS&SHK.

100 'Report on visit by Tallymen Delegation, 7th June 1968'; TSR Chinese Workers' Union to David Edgar, 4 July 1968: 'News translations (2/2) 1968–1970', JS&SHK.

101 Minutes, 3 November 1967, TSR Minute Book: TSS/1/15, JS&SHK

102 Urwick, Orr and Partners, 'John Swire & Sons Headquarters Survey', 14 August 1967, p. 4: JSS I 10/14.

CHAPTER 14 MAKING HONG KONG

1 This section draws on J. K. Swire's copy of Urwick, Orr & Partners Ltd, 'John Swire & Sons Headquarters Survey', 14 August 1967: JSS I 10/14. For a history of the firm see *The Urwick Orr Partnership, 1934–1984* (Maidenhead: The Lyndal Urwick Society, 2007).

2 There was £1.5 million in Blue Funnel; £750,000 in the Scotts Shipbuilding 'lock-up'; £2 million in property (outside Hong Kong) and £2.5 million in 'General Investments'.

3 Interview with Jenny Grant, 13 April 2013: JS&SL.

4 John Swire & Sons to Butterfield & Swire Hong Kong, 9 February and 21 March 1968, see also A. C. Swire 'J.S.&S. Ltd. Diversification', 5 February 1968: JSS II 2/35. The Australian story is told in Bleasdale and Shun Wah, *Swire: One Hundred and Fifty Years*.

5 J. K. Swire diary, 19 January 1968: JS&SL.

6 *CNCo: A Pictorial History*, pp. 127–9.

7 F. Muller, Captain, *SS Peter Rickmers*, to Mr Rickmers, 16 April 1968, in: TNA, FCO 21/159. The charge against Crouch was that he had done this at the request of British naval intelligence, a charge also laid against a second British officer later in the summer. This was possibly true, although Crouch, in later admitting it, said he had done it in this instance on his own initiative: *SCMP*, 26 October 1970, p. 1. More widely on this era in Britain–China relations and the Cultural Revolution see Bickers, *Out of China*, pp. 343–7.

8 R. B. Thomas to James Murray (FCO), 2 April 1969: TNA, FCO 21/512.

9 *The Times*, 16 October 1970, p. 6.

10 'Note of a Meeting between Mr J. P. W. Mallalieu, Minister of State, Board of Trade and Mr L. O. Pindling, Premier and Minister for Tourism and Development of the Bahamas', 31 May 1968: TNA, BT 45/1351.

11 Higham, *Speedbird*, pp. 186–7; BOAC retained 15 per cent of the holding company, Bahamas Airways Holdings with a new Swire Air Holdings taking the rest (shares in this were held by John Swire & Sons (51 per cent), P&O (33 per cent) and Blue Funnel (16 per cent). The board's perspective – and comments quoted here – can be found in 'John Swire & Sons Record

of Events', JSS I 14/1. For a history of BAL see Paul C. Aranha, *Bahamas Airways: The Rise and Demise of a British International Air Carrier* (Corydon: Heartland, 2018), and his *The Island Airman and his Bahama Islands home* (Nassau: Media Enterprises, 2006).

12 R. K. Saker, memorandum, 18 July 1968: TNA, FCO 14/417.

13 *SCMP*, 14 September 1968, p. 1; *Palm Beach Post*, 20 November 1968, p. 11. The episode is not mentioned in Gavin Young's history of Cathay Pacific, *Beyond Lion Rock*.

14 R. K. Saker minute, 25 September 1968; 'Recent Cases of Difficulty with Bahamas', undated memorandum (c. May 1968): TNA, FCO 14/417.

15 R. J. Martin, 'Caribbean Withdrawal', *Flight International*, 16 January 1969, pp. 846–7.

16 Examples reproduced in Aranha, *Bahamas Airways*, pp. 245–9.

17 'The Bahamas: A Special Report', *The Times*, 7 December 1964, pp. i–viii.

18 *Newsday*, 9 October 1970, p. 20.

19 'John Swire & Sons Record of Events', JSS I 14/1. Aranha, *Bahamas Airways*, p. 259. Aranha piloted one of the planes, and I am grateful to him for sharing his collection of newspaper cuttings with me.

20 Pindling: *The Times*, 16 October 1970, p. 6.

21 *Flight International*, 16 May 1968, p. 541, 9 July 1970, p. 40, 15 October 1970, p. 583, 22 October 1970, pp. 617–18.

22 Michael Craton and Gail Saunders, *A History of the Bahamian People: From the Ending of Slavery to the Twenty-First Century* (Atlanta: University of Georgia Press, 2000), pp. 356–7; *Washington Post*, 19 March 1973, pp. A1, A18; *Wall Street Journal*, 6 August 1984, p. 21; *Courier-Post*, 10 February 1985, pp. 1a, 7a; United States Senate Committee on Foreign Relations Subcommittee on Terrorism, Narcotics and International Operations, *Drugs, Law Enforcement and Foreign Policy: Volume 1 The Bahamas* (Washington DC, United States Senate, 1989), pp. 21–42.

23 *The Tribune* (Nassau), 10 October 1970, pp. 1, 3, and: issues of 13, 15, 16, October 1970, all p. 1.

24 There is extensive documentation on the financial situation and contacts with government, in 'Bahamas Airways Limited Government Correspondence': JSS I 4/2/5.

25 'Las Vegas East', *Wall Street Journal*, 5 October 1966, p. 1; 'Bahamas: Trouble in Paradise', *The Economist*, 15 October 1966, pp. 98–9; Richard Oulahan and William Lambert, 'The Scandal in the Bahamas', *Life*, 3 February 1967, pp. 58–74; William Davidson, 'The Mafia: Shadow of Evil on the Island in the Sun', *Saturday Evening Post*, 26 February 1967, pp. 28–38; *Bahama Islands: report of the Commission of Inquiry into the Operation of the Business of Casinos in Freeport and in Nassau* (London: HMSO, 1967); Avril Mollison, 'The "Coney Island" of the Caribbean', *The Listener*, 1 June 1967, p. 716.

26 J. K. Swire diaries, 27 February, 11 March 1970, 29 October 1970: JS&SL; A. C. Swire, 'Mistakes & Regrets', July 2002: JS&SL.

27 Dierikx, *Clipping the Clouds*, pp. 47, 64–5; *The Tribune*, 21 October 1970.

28 M. Y. Fiennes to Gerry Lanchin, 8 January 1970, enclosing Wallace G. Rouse to John Swire & Sons, 30 December 1969: TNA, BT 245/1351.

29 John Swire & Sons to Butterfield & Swire Hong Kong, 21 March 1968: JSS II 2/35.

30 A. C. Swire, notes on 'London Role post-1945', and 'Swire Group: Mistakes and Missed Opportunities, 1950–2000': JS&SL.

31 'John Swire & Sons Record of Events': JSS I 14/1, f.45. This is a discussion on consolidating the purchase of the refrigerated transport company that became known as FrigMobile.

32 Marc Levinson, *The Box: How the Shipping Container Made the World Smaller and the World Economy Bigger* (paperback edn, Princeton: Princeton University Press, 2008), p. 166; *The Economist*, 15 January 1966, pp. 219–20. This is a comprehensive account of this revolution; see also: Frank Broeze, *The Globalization of the Oceans: Containerisation from the 1950s to the Present* (St John's: International Maritime Economic History Society, 2002), and Miller, *Europe and the Maritime World*.

33 'Swire/OCL – A Memoir by Sir Adrian Swire', in Alan Bott (ed.), *British Box Business: A History of OCL (Overseas Containers Limited)* (London: SCARA, 2009), p. 96.

34 *SCMP*, 21 August 1978, p. 44; Bott (ed.), *British Box Business*, pp. 16, 203; see also Miller, *Europe and the Maritime World*, pp. 340–41. On OCL and Blue Funnel see Falkus, *Blue Funnel Legend*, pp. 356–70.

35 *SCMP*, 15 August 1972, p. 48, 5 September 1972, p. 29, 6 September 1972, p. 29; Kevin Sinclair, *The Quay Factor: Modern Terminals Limited and the port of Hong Kong* (Hong Kong: Modern Terminals Limited, 1992), pp. 4–10.

36 Sinclair, *Quay Factor*, p. 77.

37 Nicholas J. White, 'Liverpool Shipping and the End of Empire: the Ocean Group in East and Southeast Asia, c. 1945–73, in Sheryllyne Haggerty, Anthony Webster, Nicholas J. White (eds), *The Empire in One City? Liverpool's Inconvenient Imperial Past* (Manchester, Manchester University Press, 2008), pp. 165–84.

38 Blue Funnel had gone public in 1965: Falkus, *Blue Funnel Legend*, pp. 333–44.

39 A. C. Swire to H. J. C. Browne, 1 March 1971: JSS I 3/28.

40 King, *The Hongkong Bank in the Period of Development and Nationalism, 1941–1984*, pp. 720–22; Studwell, *Asian Godfathers*, pp. 98–9; see also Robin Hutcheon, *First Sea Lord: the Life and Work of Sir Y. K. Pao* (Hong Kong: Chinese University Press, 1994).

41 Speyer, *In Coral Seas*, pp. 34–50.

42 Nicholson: 'Swire/OCL – A Memoir by Sir Adrian Swire', in Bott (ed.), *British Box Business*, p. 96 (and pp. 92–4 on AJCL); *China Navigation*

Company: A Pictorial History, pp. 94–5; Chih-lung Lin, 'Containerization in Australia: The formation of the Australia-Japan Line', *International Journal of Maritime History*, 27:1 (2015), pp. 118–29; Broeze, *Globalization of the Oceans*, p. 50.

43 Agency: H. J. C. Browne to John Swire & Sons, 5 April 1966: JSS I 4/4/19; Terminal: John Browne to John Swire & Sons, 5 April 1966: JSS I 4/4/19; A. C. Swire to A. G. S. McCallum, 5 December 1975: JSS I 3/28; China: David Laughton, Peking, to E. J. Sharland, FCO, 30 May 1969: TNA, FCO 21/512 (this records a discussion with Hong Kong Taipan John Browne).

44 John Browne to W. G. C. Knowles, 10 September 1962: JSS I 4/4/19.

45 On the British role in general see: John Slight, *The British Empire and the Hajj, 1865–1956* (Cambridge, MA: Harvard University Press, 2015), and Michael Miller, 'Pilgrims' Progress: The Business of the Hajj', *Past & Present*, No. 191 (2006), pp. 189–226; on Malaysia see: Mary Byrne McDonnell, 'The conduct of Hajj from Malaysia and its socio-economic impact on Malay society: a descriptive and analytical study, 1860–1981' (Unpublished PhD thesis, Columbia University, 1986), especially pp. 419–29 on the shipboard experience during the years of CNCo charters; and Eric Tagliacozzo, *The Longest Journey: Southeast Asians and the Pilgrimage to Mecca* (New York: Oxford University Press, 2013).

46 *Straits Times*, 15 April 1967, p. 14, 30 April 1967, p. 5.

47 *SCMP*, 19 November 1962, p. 8, 21 January 1963, p. 5; see also the gallery of photographs at: International Organization for Migration, 'Resettlement of Russian Old Believers', https://www.iom.int/photo-stories/resettlement-russian-old-believers (accessed 1 May 2019). In 1960 Butterfield & Swire had also arranged charters of CNCo and Blue Funnel ships to repatriate to Hainan, Guangzhou and Fujian some of the 100,000 Chinese who fled Indonesia that year in the face of hostile government policies, and violent attacks.

48 'Muslims Voyage on a Pilgrim Ship', *The Sphere*, 7 December 1957, p. 374; *SCMP*, 5 February 1961, p. 27; *Straits Times*, 25 July 1960, p. 2; *China Navigation Company: A Pictorial History*, pp. 84–5.

49 M. Y. Fiennes to John Swire & Sons, 10 March 1959, 'Pilgrim Trade' and 'Talk with Ghazali Ben Shafie and Hadji Ali Rouse', both 5 March 1953: JSS I 3/25 (the Hajji was Pilgrim Commissioner); J. S. Scott to John Swire & Sons, 27 February 1960: JSS I 3/26; J. K. Swire diary, 18 January 1967: JS&SL.

50 Tagliacozzo, *The Longest Journey*, pp. 213–15; *Straits Times*, 27 May 1971, p. 5; 'Moslem Captain of a Modern Haj ship', *SCMP*, 31 July 1972, p. 5; 'The World of Eddy Wong', *The Economist*, 16 April 1977, p. 117; A. C. Swire to C. G. N. Ryder, 5 September 1972: JSS I 3/28.

51 *The China Navigation Company*, pp. 79–81; Miller, *Europe and the Maritime World*, pp. 322–32; *SCMP*, 6 June 1971, p. 24, 31 August 1973, p. 1; J. K. Swire diaries, 17 November 1973: JS&SL.

52 A. C. Swire, 'China Navigation Company', 14 April 2002: JS&SL.

53 A. C. Swire, 'Swire Group Shipping', 1 February 1974, Memorandum prepared for Woodstock Conference, enclosed in A. C. Swire to J. A. Swire, 1 February 1974; A. C. Swire to J. A. Swire, 11 February 1972 and 27 June 1972; A. C. Swire to J. A. Swire, 6 December 1974, 'Hong Kong Visit': JSS I 3/28.

54 'The house magazine is certainly replete with photographs of "taipan" John Bremridge handing out silver watches to ancient employees': 'The Iron Rice Bowl', *The Economist*, 2 April 1977, p. 133.

55 J. K. Swire diary, 1919–20, 'Further thoughts': JS&SL.

56 M. L. Cahill, 'Overseas Development Administration. Preparation for service overseas: the British Government's role', in *La formation des coopérants* (The training of aid workers) (Nice: Institut d'études et de recherches interethniques et interculturelles, 1973), pp. 150–53; Hong Kong General Chamber of Commerce Bulletin 66:15 (1966), p. 5; Michael Thornton, 'Preparing for life Overseas', *Overseas Challenge*, No. 8 (1967), pp. 9–11.

57 Daniel I. Greenstein, 'The Junior Members, 1900–1990: A Profile', in Brian Harrison (ed.), *The History of the University of Oxford*, Volume VIII, *The Twentieth Century* (Oxford: The Clarendon Press, 1994), pp. 67–74; Christopher N. L. Brooke, *A History of the University of Cambridge*, Volume 4, *1870–1990* (Cambridge: Cambridge University Press, 1993), pp. 314–15.

58 'Minutes of a meeting of the Directors', John Swire & Sons, 30 June 1970: JSS I 11/1.

59 H. J. C. Browne to John Swire & Sons, 19 September 1972: JSS I 3/28.

60 *The Times*, 17 August 1954, p. 2 (the Oxford programme was one of the precursors of the university's Centre for Management Studies); from 1983, training expanded to include an annual Senior Management Programme at INSEAD tailored for the company: *Swire News*, 15:3 (1988), 'Staff Events, p. 2. A. C. Swire to J. A. Swire, 5 June 1975: JSS I 3/28.

61 J. H. Bremridge to J. A. Swire, 24 November 1980: JSS I 4/4/20.

62 M. Y. Fiennes, 'C.P.A.: An appreciation based on Adrian [Swire]'s note of 29.10.1970', John Swire & Sons Board Papers, 1970–71: JSS I 11/1; D. G. Thomson, 'Group Investment Philosophy', 25 June 1974: JSS I 11/2.

63 'Great Britain, Royal Aero Club Aviators' Certificates, 1910–1950', via Ancestry.com; Joan Weld, 'Missee Catchee New Part', *The Motor Cycle*, 12 April 1951, pp. 256–7: 'taxi drivers were so dumbfounded … they actually gave way to me'; Weld moved to Texas in 1951, leaving the bike behind: *SCMP*, 2 December 1950, p. 11.

64 Greenstein, 'The Junior Members, 1900–1990: A Profile', in Harrison (ed.), *The History of the University of Oxford Vol. VIII*, pp. 73–7.

65 'John Swire & Sons Record of Events', JSS I 14/1; Swire & Maclaine Ltd, Annual General Meeting, 18 June 1966: JSS X 2/1.

66 *SCMP*, 17 February 1966, p. 4. This paragraph draws on 'Interview with Baroness Dunn, 16 March 2006': JS&S.

67 The political failures around factory reform are discussed in David Clayton, 'The riots and labour laws: The struggle for an eight-hour day for women factory workers, 1962–1971', in Bickers and Yep (eds), *May Days in Hong Kong*, pp. 127–44, and a broader response in his 'Constructing Colonial Capitalism: The Public Relations Campaigns of Hong Kong Business Groups, 1959–1966', in David Thackeray, Andrew Thompson and Richard Toye (eds)', *Imagining Britain's Economic Future, c. 1800–1975: Trade, Consumerism, and Global Markets* (London: Palgrave Macmillan, 2018), pp. 231–52; 'Women behind the Festival of Fashions', *SCMP*, 7 September 1967, p. 4.

68 J. H. Bremridge to A. C. Swire, 24 November 1980: JSS I 4/4/20.

69 Sheila Marriner and Francis E. Hyde, *The Senior: John Samuel Swire 1825–98: Management in Far Eastern Shipping Trades* (Liverpool: Liverpool University Press, 1967); Charles Drage, *Taikoo* (London: Constable, 1970); Christopher Cook, *The Lion and The Dragon: British Voices from the China Coast* (London: Elm Tree Books, 1985); 'Note by J. K. S. on 1st draft', c. Dec 1965, in JSS/11/2/8: JS&SL. In the 1980s, historians in Shanghai, drawing on the records surrendered at the time of the closure, prepared a more critical account of its commercial operations in China: Zhang Zhongli (chief ed.), *Taigu jituan zai jiu Zhongguo* (The Swire Group in Old China) (Shanghai: Shanghai renmin chubanshe, 1991).

70 J. A. Swire to A. V. T. Dean, 24 October 1975, in JSS/11/2/8: JS&SL.

71 'Old China Hands across the Sea', *The Economist*, 17 June 1967, p. 1275.

72 *The Economist*, 13 August 1972, p. 92.

73 J. K. Swire diary, 16 November 1974: JS&SL.

74 Director of Marine, Memorandum, 21 November 1972: HKPRO, HKRS-394-24-19; *SCMP*, 15 October 1970, p. 23.

75 Employees were offered the option of taking redundancy and their accrued benefits. Some 75 per cent of them did, immediately in most cases then securing employment direct with the new United Dockyards. Some 800 older workers and 1,600 contractors' staff remained at Quarry Bay: see reports in: HKPRO, HKRS-90-1-2.

76 Coates, *Whampoa*, pp. 250–54.

77 A. C. Swire to W. Rae-Smith, 10 February 1972: JSS I 3/28; *SCMP*, 17 March 1972, p. 33; Goodstadt, *People, Politics, and Panics*, p. 173.

78 A. C. Swire to J. A. Swire, 9 November 1972: JSS I 4/4/19; *SCMP*, 20 November 1973, p. 25.

79 This section draws on H. J. Lethbridge, *Hard Graft in Hong Kong: Scandal, Corruption, the ICAC* (Hong Kong: Oxford University Press, 1985); Melanie Manion, *Corruption by Design: Building Clean Government in Mainland China and Hong Kong* (Cambridge, MA: Harvard University Press, 2009), especially pp. 27–83.

80 J. H. Bremridge to A. C. Swire, 9 March 1976: JSS I 4/4/20.

81 *Second Report of the Commission of Inquiry under Sir Alastair Blair-Kerr* (Hong Kong: Government Printers, 1973), p. 23.
82 Lethbridge, *Hard Graft in Hong Kong*, pp. 159–93; J. H. Bremridge to J. A. Swire, 16 March 1976, 8 April 1976, 8 May 1976, and J. H. Bremridge to D. R. Y. Bluck, R. S. Sheldon, D. A. Gledhill, 8 April 1976: JSS I 4/4/20.
83 The phrase recurs in *Lockheed documents: Multinational Corporations and US Foreign Policy, Part 14. United States Congress, Committee on Foreign Relations, Subcommittee on Multinational Corporations* (Washington, DC: U.S. Government Printing Office, 1976). On Smith see pp. 356–8. Carl A. Kotchian, 'Lockheed Sales Mission: 70 days in Tokyo', unpublished typescript, c. 1976, pp. 110–12 (via Hathi Trust Digital Library).
84 *Far Eastern Economic Review*, 16 January 1976, facing p. 13, 20 February 1976, pp. 10–11.
85 The money went to charity. Smith's mistress was also provided for, but not his – estranged – wife: *SCMP*, 13 March 1976, p. 1, 29 April 1977, p. 8, 25 May 1977, p. 8; letter: *SCMP*, 13 March 1976, p. 1, 14 March 1976, p. 10.
86 Jack Spackman, 'TriStar choice: it's a British connection', *China Mail*, 19 March 1974; *SCMP*, 26 March 1974, cuttings in CPA 7/2/10/5; 'Why Cathay Pacific chose to buy Lockheeds', *TTG Asia*, 31 May 1974, cutting in CPA 7/2/10/4, both: JS&SHK; A. J. Lawe to G. T. Rogers, 31 January 1974, A. O. Saunders to Governor, 31 January 1974, Heseltine: G. T. Rogers, 'Note for the record: Cathay Pacific's Choice of wide-bodied aircraft', 29 March 1974: TNA, BT 245/1723. See also: Raj Roy, 'The politics of planes and engines: Anglo-American relations during the Rolls-Royce-Lockheed Crisis, 1970–1971', in Matthias Schulz (ed.), *The Strained Alliance: US–European Relations from Nixon to Carter* (Cambridge: Cambridge University Press, 2009), pp. 169–93.
87 Bluck: Aston to DTI, 14 March 1974; Smith: 'Memorandum of Discussion: Cathay Pacific Airways: Choice of Wide-Bodied Aircraft', 14 March 1974: TNA, BT 245/1723; G. T. Rogers to G. Mc. Wilson, 26 February 1974: TNA, BT 245/1723. The wider politics of state involvement is discussed in Keith Hayward, *Government and British Civil Aerospace: A Case Study in Post-war Technology Policy* (Manchester: Manchester University Press, 1983).
88 John le Carré, *The Honourable Schoolboy* (London: Hodder & Stoughton, 1977), p. 6; J. H. Bremridge to J. A. Swire, 18 January 1977: JSS I 4/4/20.
89 Chris Wemyss, 'Building "Hong Kong's Underground": Investigating Britain's Management of Empire in the 1970s', unpublished paper, 2018.
90 A. C. Swire to J. A. Swire, 6 June 1975: JSS I 3/28; A. C. Swire 'Emergency Provision', 4 September 1975: JSS I 11/2. The Jardine Matheson plan, which was being updated and rethought in 1975, was reportedly rooted in its own strategic response to the 1967 shock, with a decision to move towards 50 per cent of its assets and earnings coming from outside Hong Kong: *SCMP*, 23 March 1994, p. 40.

91 *SCMP*, 29 December 1973, p. 23, 9 April 1974, p. 21; King, *The Hongkong Bank in the Period of Development and Nationalism, 1941–1984*, pp. 708–11. In 1979 the group, now Hutchison Whampoa (having merged with its asset rich subsidiary, the Hong Kong & Whampoa Dock Company), was sold by the Bank to Li Ka-shing. 'Happy Valley' can be followed through correspondence between May and November 1974, in: JSS I 4/4/20, and a board paper prepared by Adrian Swire, 29 May 1974: JSS I 11/2.

92 J. H. Bremridge to J. A. Swire, 'Wheelocks on the Brink', 28 October 1976: JSS I 11/2; money bags: J. H. Bremridge to John D. Spink, 11 November 1980: JSS I 4/4/20; image: A. C. Swire to John Swire & Sons, 4 February 1972: JSS I 3/28; 'The Iron Rice Bowl', *The Economist*, 2 April 1977, pp. 133–34.

93 A. C. Swire to J. A. Swire, 10 January 1975: JSS I 11/2.

94 A. C. Swire, 'Europe', 4 September 1975: JSS I 11/2; A. C. Swire, 'Philippines', Note to J. H. Bremridge, 14 March 1975: JSS I 3/29. Scotts of Greenock became a holding company for investment into two Scottish shipbuilding yards, and North Sea oil-related ventures. The majority-owned shipbuilding operations of the company – as Scott Lithgow – was nationalised later in 1977, sparking a long and ultimately futile legal battle for satisfactory compensation after the firm was reprivatised in 1984.

95 *SCMP*, 18 December 1971, p. 31; J. Robson to H. J. C. Browne, 9 July 1971: HKPRO, HKRS-394-24-19; A. C. Swire, 'Hongkong', 20 October 1971: JSS I 3/28; D. C. C. Luddington to Colonial Secretary, 27 October 1972, HKRS-394-24-19, HKPRO, and more widely in this file.

96 J. K. Swire diary, 11 November 1973: JS&SL.

97 J. K. Swire diary, 21 November 1973: JS&SL.

98 J. H. Scott, Board memorandum, 12 November 1975: JSS I 11/2; *Swire News*, 9:1 (1982), p. 3.

99 Michael Hope, 'On Being taken over by Slater Walker', *Journal of Industrial Economics* 24:1 (1976), pp. 163–79.

100 J. A. S. interview, 4 August 2005: JS&SL.

101 *SCMP*, 7 November 1975, p. 25.

102 *Swire News*, 1:2 (1974), p. 2, 2:1 (1974), p. 2; *SCMP*, 1 January 1974, p. 1; 21 May 1974, p. 4.

103 J. H. Bremridge to J. A. Swire, 13 April 1978, 2 and 9 March 1979: JSS I 4/4/20.

104 This paragraph draws on Goodstadt, *Profits, Politics and Panics*, *passim*, and Carroll, *Concise History of Hong Kong*, pp. 160–72.

105 J. H. Bremridge to J. A. Swire, 14 July 1978: JSS I 4/4/20.

106 J. D. Spink, 'B.H.I., Notes for Meeting 5 p.m. Wednesday 12th November 1975', board papers: JSS I 11/2.

107 Laurence S. Kuter, *The Great Gamble: The Boeing 747* (University: University of Alabama Press, 1973); Dierikx, *Clipping the Clouds*, pp. 76–8.

108 CPA, 'Hong Kong London Route Application' (1979): CPA 2013/11/25, JS&SHK; *SCMP*, 1 August 1979, p. 1.

109 *SCMP*, 20 November 1971, p. 7.
110 Dierikx, *Clipping the Clouds*, p. 146.
111 John Bremridge to A. C. Swire, 10 August 1979: JSS I 4/4/20; J. Sumner, 'Cathay Pacific: Future Plans', 6 December 1974: TNA, BT 245/1723.
112 Graeme Wilton to Guy Rogers, 9 January 1975: TNA, BT 245/1723.
113 The Hong Kong licensing authorities rejected the Laker Airways application. All the lines appealed the restrictive detail of the new concessions, Cathay securing the right to run a daily service from July 1981. Laker Airways went into liquidation in February 1982, without having established any Hong Kong service.
114 John Nott to Margaret Thatcher, 12 June 1980: TNA, PREM 19/1414; *SCMP*, 18 June 1980, p. 1.
115 R. S. T. to John Browne, 15 December 1981, JSS XIII 2/12/2.

CHAPTER 15 HERE

1 Henry Yu, 'The Intermittent Rhythms of the Cantonese Pacific', in Donna R. Gabaccia and Dirk Hoerder, *Connecting Seas and Connected Ocean Rims: Indian, Atlantic, and Pacific Oceans and China Seas Migrations from the 1830s to the 1930s* (Leiden: Brill, 2011), pp. 393–414.
2 Unusual, but hardly unique, of course, and my footnotes have, for example, drawn on corporate histories that match or almost match, or surpass, the two centuries of the Swire story. In the main, these have largely had a narrower focus than I have adopted with this book.
3 Nephews of both these men joined the firm: after joining in 1960 Edward Scott ran the Australia operations from 1976 until he took the post of chairman of John Swire & Sons in 1998 which he held until his death in 2002; his older cousin James Hinton Scott joined in 1960 and was a director from 1967 to 1987.
4 Jones, *Merchants to Multinationals*, pp. 341–2.
5 'I would start John with a Cook's tour of the East,' mused Jock Swire in 1930, 'accompanied by one of us to teach him in the course of the voyage what Taikoo is and means, this at the age of 21': J. K. Swire diary, 26 March 1920, Swire Archives.
6 David Edgerton, *The Rise and Fall of the British Nation: A Twentieth-Century History* (London: Allen Lane, 2018).
7 Jones, *Merchants to Multinationals*, pp. 126–38.
8 John Swire & Sons Ltd, Annual Report and Accounts 1980.
9 Elizabeth Sinn, 'Hong Kong as an in-Between place in the Chinese diaspora, 1849–1939', in Gabaccia and Hoerder, *Connecting Seas and Connected Ocean Rims*, pp. 225–47.

Index